European Prudential Banking Regulation and Supervision

The financial market events in 2007–9 have spurred renewed interest and controversy in debates regarding financial regulation and supervision. This book takes stock of the developments in EU legislation, case-law and institutional structures with regards to banking regulation and supervision, which preceded and followed the recent financial crisis. It does not merely provide an update, but anchors these developments in the broader EU law context, challenging past paradigms and anticipating possible developments. The author provides a systematic analysis of the interactions between the content of prudential rules and the mechanisms behind their production and application.

European Prudential Banking Regulation and Supervision includes discussions of the European banking market structure and of regulatory theory that both aim to circumscribe prudential concerns. It scrutinises the content of prudential norms, proposes a qualification of these norms and an assessment of their interaction with other types of norms (corporate, auditing and accounting, consumer protection, competition rules). It also features an analysis of the underpinning institutional set-up and its envisaged reforms, focusing on the typical EU concerns related to checks and balances. Finally, the book attempts to revive the debate on supervisory liability, in light of the developments discussed.

This book will be of great value to all those interested in financial stability matters (practitioners, policy-makers, students, academics), as well as to EU law scholars.

Larisa Dragomir completed her PhD at the EUI and Master of Arts at the College of Europe. She is an expert in EU banking law and supervisory issues. She has worked with the European Savings Banks Group (Brussels) and the European Central Bank (Frankfurt).

Routledge research in finance and banking law

Forthcoming titles in this series include:

International Secured Transactions Law
Facilitation of credit and international conventions and instruments
Orkun Akseli

The Legal and Regulatory Aspects of Islamic Banking
A comparative look at the United Kingdom and Malaysia
Abdul Karim Aldohni

European Prudential Banking Regulation and Supervision

The legal dimension

Larisa Dragomir

Routledge
Taylor & Francis Group
LONDON AND NEW YORK

First published 2010
by Routledge
2 Park Square, Milton Park, Abingdon, Oxon OX14 4RN

Simultaneously published in the USA and Canada
by Routledge
270 Madison Avenue, New York, NY 10016

Routledge is an imprint of the Taylor & Francis Group, an informa business

Typeset in Baskerville by
Wearset Ltd, Boldon, Tyne and Wear
Printed and bound in Great Britain by
CPI Antony Rowe, Chippenham, Wiltshire

British Library Cataloguing in Publication Data
A catalogue record for this book is available from the British Library

Library of Congress Cataloging in Publication Data
Dragomir, Larisa.
European prudential banking regulation and supervision : the legal dimension / Larisa Dragomir.
p. cm.
Includes bibliographical references and index.
1. Banking law–European Union countries. I. Title.
KJE2188.D73 2010
346.24'082–dc22 2009038570

ISBN13: 978-0-415-49656-8 (hbk)
ISBN13: 978-0-203-85641-3 (ebk)

To my parents

Quidquid agis, prudenter agas, et respice finem

Contents

Abbreviations

AMA	Advanced Measurement Approach
APFSE	Advisory Panel of Financial Services Experts
BAC	Banking Advisory Committee
BCBS	Basel Committee on Banking Supervision (or Basel Committee)
BIS	Bank of International Settlements
BSC	Banking Supervision Committee of the ESCB
CAD	Capital Adequacy Directive
CBD	Codified Banking Directive
CEBS	Committee of European Banking Supervisors
CEIOPS	Committee of European Insurance and Occupational Pensions Supervisors
CEIS	Centre for International Studies in Economic Growth
CEPS	Centre for European Policy Studies
CERF	Cambridge Endowment for Research in Finance
CESR	Committee of European Securities Regulators
CIUs	Collective investment undertakings
COREPER	Committee of Permanent Representatives
CRD	Capital Requirements Directive
DGS	Deposit Guarantee Schemes
EAD	Exposure at default
EBA	European Banking Authority
EBC	European Banking Committee
EC	European Community
ECB	European Central Bank
ECJ	European Court of Justice
Ecofin	Economic and Financial Affairs Council
ECON	Committee on Economic and Monetary Affairs
ECR	European Court Reports
ECU	European Currency Unit
EEA	European Economic Area
EEC	European Economic Community
EFC	Economic and Financial Committee

EFR	European Financial Services Roundtable
EFTA	European Free Trade Area
EIB	European Investment Bank
ELEC	European League for Economic Cooperation
EMAC	Committee on Economic and Monetary Affairs
EMU	Economic and Monetary Union
EP	European Parliament
ESA	European Supervisory Authority
ESC	European Securities Committee
ESCB	European System of Central Banks
ESFR	European System of Financial Regulators
ESFS	European System of Financial Supervisors
ESRB/ESRC	European Systemic Risk Board/Council
ESRC	Economic and Social Research Council
EU	European Union
FBD	First Banking Directive
FESCO	Forum of European Securities Commissions
FSA	Financial Services Authority
FSAP	Financial Services Action Plan
FSB	Financial Stability Board
FSC	Financial Services Committee
FSF	Financial Stability Forum
FSPG	Financial Services Policy Group
G10	Group of Ten
G20	Group of Twenty
GATS	General Agreement on Trade in Services
GdC	Groupe de Contact
ICAAP	Internal adequacy assessment process
IIMG	Inter-Institutional Monitoring Group
IMF	International Monetary Fund
IOSCO	International Organisation of Securities Commissions
IRB	Internal ratings-based (approach)
ISD	Investment Services Directive
JURI	Committee on Legal Affairs
LGD	Loss given default
LOLR	Lender of last resort
M&A	Mergers and acquisitions
MiFID	Directive 2004/39/EC on financial instruments markets
MoU	Memorandum of Understanding
NBER	National Bureau of Economic Research
NCB	National Central Bank
OECD	Organisation for Economic Cooperation and Development
OJ	Official Journal
OLAF	European Anti-Fraud Office
OTD	Originate-to-distribute

PD	Probability of default
RAS	Risk assessment system
SA	Standardised Approach
SBD	Second Banking Directive
SEA	Single European Act
SREP	Supervisory review and evaluation process
TFEU	Treaty on the Functioning of the European Union
UCITS	Undertakings for collective investment in transferable securities
UN	United Nations
VaR	Value at risk
WTO	World Trade Organisation

Table of cases

European Case Law

National Case Law

Austria

France

Germany

Italy

Netherlands

United Kingdom

United States

Preface

This book is a study of the European normative and institutional framework for prudential banking regulation and supervision. It is based on the research I undertook in 2000–5 at the European University Institute in Florence (Italy) in obtaining my doctoral degree. When I first approached the topic the European Union had just codified most of its disparate pieces of legislation into a single directive. I considered then that the creation of a consolidated banking code provided a good opportunity for assessing the stage of integration of the EU banking market and a good basis for analysing the interactions between regulation and supervision and between the European and the national levels, as well as the nature and legal effects of prudential standards. Soon after I engaged on this path of analysis, developments in the field precipitated and the static approach had to be abandoned in favour of an evolutionary perspective that attempted to keep abreast of the remarkable multi-faceted transformations affecting prudential issues.

There is hardly any prudential aspect that has been left unchanged in the past decade. Two main factors drove the comprehensive changes in the EU's regulatory and supervisory framework at the junction of the millennia. These are the outstanding evolution of the financial industry worldwide, with its peaks and lows, and the renewed acceleration of the integration process in the European Union following the introduction of the single currency. They are reflected in the current fine-tuned prudential rules enshrined in the Capital Requirements Directive and the Basel II Accord and the streamlined decision-making process provided by the four-level Lamfalussy framework. This book anchors these developments into the broader EU law paradigm and attempts to identify their specificities. It provides a systematic analysis of the interactions between the content of prudential rules and the procedural and institutional mechanisms underpinning their production and application. The dynamic aspects are emphasised and examined by challenging past paradigms and anticipating possible future developments.

The 2007–9 financial crisis unveiled important failures in the current EU regulatory and supervisory framework. Financial stability was profoundly shaken and policy-makers, as well as other stakeholders are now determined to repair the whole prudential system. They propose to fill in gaps in regulation and to reshuffle the distribution of competences for supervision with the aim of preventing any such dramatic and wide-ranging events from occurring in the future. These recent developments place our evolutionary analysis very much into real events. What seemed, only a few years ago, merely a theoretical discourse – especially as regards the EU supervisory architecture – now constitutes a tangible challenge, on top of the agendas of EU policy-makers. This book attempts to facilitate understanding of the complex multiple layers underpinning prudential supervision and to point to the legal effects attached to specific developments.

This book contains my personal views, and all mistakes are ultimately mine. When undertaking this research I have benefited enormously from the support of many people, and I am thankful to all of them. Especially, I would like to express my warmest gratitude to Professor Jean-Victor Louis for introducing me to this topic and for his always enlightening and very useful remarks on my writings. I am immensely appreciative of Professor Louis' invaluable advice on this manuscript and for his having kindly agreed to write the foreword to this book. I am particularly thankful also to Professor Rosa Maria Lastra, both for her useful comments and for her belief in my research and her encouragement to publish it. I would equally like to thank Professor Fabrizio Cafaggi and Dr Mauro Grande for their valuable comments and encouragements on earlier drafts. I have benefited enormously from the fruitful discussions I had in the stimulating professional environments of the European University Institute, the European Central Bank, Columbia University and New York University, as well as from access to their rich libraries and resource centres. I am grateful especially to Professor Valentin Constantin, Professor Christian Joerges, Professor Jacques Ziller, Dr Chiara Zilioli, Christian Kroppenstedt, Luc Roeges, Giacomo Caviglia, Pedro Teixera, Professor Geoffrey Miller and Professor Petros Mavroidis, for thought-provoking exchanges of views. The European Savings Banks Group provided me with valuable opportunities to be in direct touch with policy-makers and the banking industry during exciting times of reform and I am most grateful for that. I am also thankful to the two anonymous reviewers of an earlier version of the manuscript, whose useful suggestions I tried to incorporate into the final version. Last but not least, I would like to express my sincerest appreciation to the editorial and publishing team at Routledge, particularly to Ms Khanam Virjee, Ms Jessica Moody and Ms Liz Jones.

I owe a debt of gratitude to my dearest friend, Floarea Vîrban, who patiently scrutinised the manuscript and made most valuable comments. I am thankful to Thomas Fetzer for his useful suggestions on parts of this book and to Barbara Gabor, Isabela Atanasiu, Gerhard Salzer and Luca Di Preso for having consistently encouraged my efforts.

My heartfelt thanks go to my family for their untiring support and unlimited belief in me. They are so special. This book is dedicated to my parents, Elena and Toma Dragomir.

Foreword

The author asked me to write a foreword to her book, which, as a matter of fact, does not need any introduction. The reader will observe by himself the merits of this well-thought-out-work, which, as Larisa Dragomir recalls in her preface, was first a PhD thesis.

It is a difficult field of research for somebody with a background as a lawyer because the subject is by nature multidisciplinary, and the author has managed to penetrate its different aspects, helped not only by extensive readings of economic and legal literature but also by her practical experiences at the European Central Bank and, more recently, at the European Savings Banks Group.

The word 'European' in the title is important. It is a significant page of the process of European integration on which the book focuses. It is obviously a matter in flux, not only because banking regulation is part of the building of the single market and has followed the various stages of both it and, more generally, the European construction, but also because the banking industry worldwide has evolved. It is trivial to observe that banks are part of a global system. It is obviously true for cross-border banks but local banks are also influenced by what happens on the international scene, where they are more spectators than actors.

The reaction to the present crisis has been marked by the interplay between international and European actors. It was the G7 which as early as October 2007 asked for a thorough analysis of the situation and an agenda for solving the crisis to the then Financial Stability Forum (FSF). The EU elaborated its action plan at the same date and its progress depended considerably of the work done in parallel by the Standards Setting Bodies (SSBs), in particular the Basel Committee on Banking Supervision (BCBS) and the International Accounting Standards Board (IASB). A number of the same experts who are sitting in the so-called level 3 Lamfalussy Committees are present in most of the SSBs.

If the link between what happens at the global level and the EU level is a necessity, it doesn't mean that regulation has to proceed from the global to the regional to the national levels, or that it should always be so. Not only is the EU able to adapt standards – as, for example, those coming from the Basel Committee – to the specificities of the Union, as recalled by Larisa Dragomir, but it can also take the lead and inspire solutions which could be adopted afterwards, for example by the G20 or by an international SSB. This was the case for the EU-proposed rules on credit-rating agencies (CRA), which are more preceptive than the Code of Conduct adopted by the International Organisation of Securities Commission (IOSCO).

The role of experts is of utmost importance in a matter which has so many technical aspects with important political implications. This raises in a specific context the classical question of the relations of experts and policy-makers. The author refers to an 'epistemic community'. Commissioner McCreevy less emphatically once evoked the 'tourist-committees', alluding to the dispersion of their workplaces and their consequent nomadism. The author rightly observes that the EU does not have the position it should have in these bodies, and evokes its presumed role of coordinator. In most of them, the Commission has the status, formal or informal, of an observer. The task of the EU executive is made difficult because most of these committees, especially when composed of central bankers, are jealous of their independence. The role of the Commission is important because often, as for the Capital Requirements Directive (CRD), amendments to EU legislation result from the recommendations of these bodies. The Commission, as a guardian of the general interest, must also reflect the standpoint of those Member States which are not members of these bodies. The author rightly mentions that the representation and role of the EU in such bodies should be rethought.

Larisa Dragomir qualifies the Larosière report and the first steps made by both the Commission and the Council before the 2009 summer recess, as audacious, and she adopts an optimistic view on the prospective result of the current repair exercise on which – as the devil is in the detail – it is difficult to adopt a definitive judgement.

The readjustment now in progress – the author speaks about a 'reshuffling' – is a serious challenge for the 'better regulation' paradigm. Self-regulation that was presented as an alternative to legislation has proved not to be sufficient in the financial sector and the Larosière report has remarkably demonstrated that in order to fight the renewal of the crisis, action was needed at the level of the EU and its Member States in order to fight the causes of the turmoil. The question is now to draw the right balance between the need for central rules, a 'single rulebook', and the necessity to leave room for innovation, on condition, of course, that it is transparent and controlled by supervisory authorities. The author evokes the 'light touch' of the regulator, meaning that at the end of the day it is the bank itself which has to exercise due diligence. No rule can exempt the bank's managers from the need to appreciate the risk. The legislation cannot dispense with common sense. Somebody evoked the 'dangerous dogs' regulation: you still need to act with caution with the dogs that are not on the list.

A balance has also to be respected as far as the rhythm of the legislative process is concerned. 'Better regulation' implies impact assessment and consultation of stakeholders. It needs time to respect stages of the co-decision procedure. So neither precipitation nor procrastination is good, and if the Commission was right in proposing an acceleration of the process, this acceleration should not be at the cost of neglecting a thorough reflection on the proposed text and on its implications. Maximum clarity is needed on the legal basis of the actions, on the status of the organs and on the chains of responsibility. The author rightly insists on the question of liability in the exercise of prudential micro- as well as macro-supervision. In this context, I would quote the words of Baroness Cohen of Pimlico when, as chairman of the committee, she thanked an eminent lawyer at the end of his hearing by the European Union Committee of the House of Lords entitled 'The future of EU financial regulation and supervision' on 5 March 2009. She said:

> it has been particularly useful, if I may say so, to have a lawyer to talk to us, because in designing new systems, we very often forget what there is in place, what is possible, and what is just not going to be possible to design and you have very usefully reminded us.

So Larisa Dragomir also reminds the reader.

Crises are said to be an opportunity. This has unfortunately not always proved to be true. It was not so for the monetary union in the oil and financial crises of the 1970s, and protectionist as well as nationalist reflexes could also be observed this time. I was among those who would have favoured a more ambitious solution than the one the Larosière Group proposed and that the chairman of the Group himself called a moderate one, but I recognise that if European Supervisory Authorities, well coordinated among themselves, can have (compulsory) powers – as conceived of by the report – on mediation, collection of information and uniform interpretation of the rules, as well as the power of licensing and supervising some EU-wide institutions like CRAs and post-trading infrastructures (quoted from Mr de Larosière's hearing by the House of Lords committee), a big step will have been made which could lead to a true European System of Financial Supervisors. The concept of the European Systemic Risk Board must be better defined before an appreciation can be made.

I am convinced that this book will render great services to the reader, whether a professional or an academic, and I hope that Larisa Dragomir will continue to produce books like this one.

Jean-Victor Louis
Professor Emeritus, Université Libre de Bruxelles (ULB)

Introduction

During the past decade, prudential banking regulation and supervision have been constantly in the spotlight, as they have been affected by fundamental and far-reaching changes. These developments reflect the spectacular evolution of financial markets and financial actors, which has reached unprecedented peaks and lows during this period. They also mirror the endeavours of policy-makers to keep abreast of such evolutions and to adjust the regulatory and institutional frameworks accordingly. In Europe, this has coincided with a new stage in the development of the European Union, which implied substantial transformations (enlargement, European Monetary Union) and the hereto linked efforts for adjusting the European governance structure in the quest of legitimacy and accountability. The financial crisis unveiled many of the shortcomings of this recent framework and introduced efforts for its repair. It has brought renewed focus on both prudential regulatory aspects and banking supervision and predicts vigorous changes.

This book discusses these developments and analyses the legal frameworks for banking regulation and supervision in the EU, by looking at their past, present and future. It compares the current framework with its predecessor and the proposed amendments in response to the crisis. Thereby, it tries to identify the changes in the underlying regulatory approach.

The 'European' dimension lies at the core of this research. Our main ambition is to set the remarkable changes in the area of banking regulation and supervision, already undertaken or envisaged at the time of writing, within the context of EU law. We aim to examine EU financial law developments with a view to understanding their impact on national prudential frameworks and, ultimately, on the concrete application of prudential standards. We focus particularly on the limits and potentialities entailed by the broader EU legal system, as well as on the possible frictions between prudential concerns and the typical EU checks and balances mechanisms. We endeavour to identify the scope of the 'European' dimension encompassed in both the normative and the institutional frameworks, and to understand the consequences attached to the different degrees of centralisation of the regulatory and supervisory functions.

This book will focus on prudential aspects, which have to a large extent constituted the object of European policy-making. In our understanding, prudential issues encompass all those preventive measures intended to ensure the soundness and safety of individual institutions (micro-prudential aspects) and of the system as a whole (macro-prudential aspects) so as to preclude the emergence of individual or systemic banking crises. Hence, our analysis is limited to the so-called *ex ante* measures and does not extend to *ex post* interventions (e.g. crisis management and resolution, lender of last resort, safety networks). Yet we are aware that such a division is open to being considered artificial given that, in practice, the demarcation line is blurred and actors entrusted with prudential competences will always be closely involved in any action which is required in a crisis situation. Furthermore, *ex post* measures, although sometimes functioning in a framework dominated by 'contextual ambiguity', operate within a pre-established structure that might be characterised as 'prudential'. Still, although admittedly controversial, the delimitation was necessary to keep the research within manageable dimensions. Therefore, *ex post* measures, which are currently underdeveloped at EU level, will be only marginally considered in this book, mainly in connection with the calls for supervisory reform.

The topic is further circumscribed by the choice of the banking sector. Some justification is needed, given the context of the proliferation of financial conglomerate structures and the blurring frontiers among the various financial sectors. Such developments triggered an intertwining between financial institutions and markets that previously belonged to clearly distinguishable branches and led to the common use of sophisticated financial instruments. Also, reforms affecting the banking sector are undertaken at European level under the general heading of financial services regulation or financial supervision. Nevertheless, at least for prudential purposes, we consider that the sectoral perspective is still useful, especially because of the distinctive features that the banking sector has preserved. The legal delimitation of the banking industry is justified by its position in the economic gear and in the payments system, as well as by its specific risk profile. This explains why the banking sector has been traditionally underpinned by a separate regulatory framework at European level.

Last but not least, our topic considers the prudential aspects of both regulation and supervision of the banking industry. For the purposes of the present research, regulation is broadly understood as the ensemble of norms setting standards of behaviour, incentives for prudent action and procedures for the interaction between the authorities and the regulated entities. Supervision refers to the complementary process of implementing rules, especially by monitoring behaviour of individual actors and taking corrective action with a view to ensuring compliance (micro-prudential supervision). Supervision also refers to the broader survey of developments in the financial markets, macro-prudential analysis and the issuance of warnings in relation to identified emerging risks, as well as the policy follow-up (macro-prudential supervision). The distinction between regulation and supervision, which could be described simply in terms of rule-making/standard-setting and enforcement, is not so straightforward, given the complex nature inherent in prudential issues. Thus, as will be shown, the nature of banking supervision has been constantly evolving and currently entails an ever more important component of standard-setting. Also, prudential regulation is now to a large extent risk-sensitive and process-oriented, which makes it ever more interwoven with the supervisory process. One might be inclined to use the unitary concept of a prudential regulatory regime encompassing the set of processes by which norms are established and the behaviour of those regulated is monitored and fed back into the regime, as well as the enforcement mechanisms capable of constraining behaviour within the defined limits. However, we have chosen to use the dual terminology of regulation and supervision because of its relevance within the European context, where regulation is largely centralised at EU level, whereas supervision pertains mainly to the remit of the Member States and some centralisation is envisaged only in response to the crisis. Yet we will also frequently refer to the 'prudential framework' or the 'regulatory regime' to underline the intrinsic link between prudential regulation and supervision.

Our incentive to elaborate on this topic came from a series of extensive changes that have occurred in the past years and which, in our view, have significantly reshaped the European prudential framework. These changes affect both normative and institutional aspects and could be classified into three broad categories. The first relates to the general endeavours of EU policy-makers to fuel integration in still-fragmented financial markets, as reflected in the Financial Services Action Plan (FSAP), the post-FSAP strategy and the Lamfalussy framework. The second category pertains to the efforts undertaken to improve the substantive prudential framework so as to respond to the real challenges posed by a dynamic banking industry developing under the drive of globalisation, financial innovation and technological development. This refers especially to the capital requirements framework inspired by the Basel II Accord. Third, there is the regulatory and supervisory repair envisaged as a reaction to the crisis, which seeks to address gaps and inadequacies in banking regulation and supervision. It tackles further prudential aspects (e.g. resecuritisation, liquidity, the originate-to-distribute model, remuneration, dynamic provisioning and other countercyclical measures, leverage) and, most importantly, the EU supervisory architecture.

Faced with such recent or envisaged changes, we have formulated our research question in an open way: how do the reforms impinge on the European prudential framework? This implies an inquiry into various aspects. Do these reforms change the traditional paradigm depicting the

European framework in terms of minimum harmonisation, mutual recognition and home-country control? What are the character, nature and policy objectives of the new normative framework? Do the institutional changes constitute a mere adaptation to market realities in the new millennium, or were they conceived from the start as an intermediary stage in the pursuit of further radical institutional reforms? What will be the impact of the regulatory and supervisory repair measures envisaged in response to the shortcomings revealed by the crisis? How do all normative and institutional changes influence eventual liability claims based on EU law?

When analysing these issues we do not pretend to build a meta-theoretical framework, a new paradigm that would explain all aspects of the new prudential regime. Such an approach would be overambitious, considering not only our bounded capacity biased by a legal background but also the impossibility of embarking on such a task in the midst of substantial reviews. Our ambition is more limited. It is confined to presenting some of the legal consequences that emerge when contextualising prudential norms and institutions, and some possible ways forward.

The methodology employed seeks to compare the current framework to the old one, so as to underline the changes and the consequences triggered. Also, we seek to determine the extent to which proposals for reform currently discussed by EU policy-makers address identified shortcomings. Thereby, we make as much use as possible, against the background of an EU law approach, of traditional legal analysis consisting of 'the normal lawyerly process of distinguishing, defining, analogizing' (Cordero 1990: 56). Also, we attempt to locate the EU prudential framework in the broader international context, and constantly correlate the normative and institutional facets. We also have recourse to some interdisciplinary instruments developed in the 'law and economics' literature, in order to shed some light on the rationale and policy objectives underpinning the new regulatory framework.

In terms of sources, our analysis is based on the study of legislation, legislative proposals, case-law and other official documents, as well as on legal, economic and political literature. The text reflects, as much as possible, the state of play as it stands at the beginning of August 2009.

The book is structured in four broad parts, each divided into various chapters. The first part sets out the general context of banking, the second concentrates on normative aspects and the third provides an institutional analysis, while the fourth deals with supervisory liability. Although they look at the new European framework from different perspectives, the parts have to be understood as being interconnected.

Part I (Chapters 1–2) describes the broader context underpinning European regulatory reform. Chapter 1 analyses current banking realities in the EU from the perspective of structural market developments (consolidation, conglomeration, concentration, diversification) responding to the influence of powerful forces such as globalisation, technological development and financial innovation. It also highlights the specific developments related to the financial crisis that erupted in 2007. Against this background, we inquire whether banks have managed to preserve their specificity, when compared to other financial intermediaries. Moreover, we try to identify the degree of integration in the banking sector and the stage of construction of the European banking market.

Chapter 2 sets out to explain why prudential banking regulation is needed and what its objectives are. For this purpose, we make use of elements of regulatory theory and identify the relevant market failures and the possible policy responses. Also, we distinguish between different categories of banking regulation, in terms of their objectives and their effects, and establish their complementarity with respect to market discipline.

Part II (Chapters 3–6) aims to examine the substantial aspects of prudential regulation and supervision in the EU by reference to legal norms. It does so by using an evolutionary perspective, and by considering that the legislation and strategies underpinning European banking are an intrinsic part of the wider processes directed at achieving the single market. Such a perspective should, nevertheless, not obscure the internal dimension of prudential rules, which stimulates regulatory adjustments so as to reflect the financial markets' own dynamics and the need to address new risks. Two aspects have to be considered jointly when assessing the intensity of European intervention: the choice of regulatory strategies, and the substance of prudential rules.

Chapter 3 aims to delineate the body of prudential norms as enshrined in the various legislative acts and policy documents adopted at European level. We will first identify the integration pattern that, over 20 years, has accompanied the enactment of prudential legislation. By analysing the most important aspects of the European directives and referring to the context in which they were adopted, we will attempt to grasp the dynamics of the regulatory strategy and understand the underlying impetus.

The various layers of prudential rules are considered in Chapter 4. Of crucial importance here is the interaction between the European and the international levels, given the fact that soft-law measures adopted in the Basel Committee on Banking Supervision (BCBS) consistently shape the content of EU prudential norms. Further layers can be identified within the EU framework itself, particularly as it appears from the four-level Lamfalussy process. Our inquiry looks at the circumstances and consequences of the interactions implied by a multi-layered prudential framework. This chapter also briefly outlines the interaction between prudential regulation and corporate law; accounting rules; the framework for audit; consumer protection law and competition law.

Chapter 5 analyses much of the content of the Capital Requirements Directive (CRD). By implementing the three-pillar structure as devised in the Basel II Accord (minimum capital requirements, supervisory review and market discipline), the new normative framework constitutes a substantial change with respect to the previous one (the Codified Banking Directive). We analyse the character and specificities of the new prudential approach and identify the substantial and procedural novelties brought about. The crisis has revealed some gaps and shortcomings in the CRD that already constitute the object of regulatory proposals for amending the current rules. It is questioned whether these forthcoming changes continue in the direction of maximum harmonisation, without challenging the very foundation of the regulatory regime.

Chapter 6 provides a critical analysis of the two regulatory principles that have been traditionally used for depicting banking regulation in Europe: minimum harmonisation and home-country control. We inquire whether, in the light of the new normative framework and the Lamfalussy procedure, European prudential regulation acquires an extensive character that indicates more of a move towards maximum harmonisation. Also, we critically analyse the home-country control principle in terms of its exclusive capacity to define the attribution of competences and the way prudential supervision operates. We then address the 'general good' clause, considering whether it needs to be seen as an impediment to market integration or as an instrument for correcting shortcomings related to home-country control and for rebalancing the powers of home and host countries. The home-country control principle is also assessed in relation to the equally important principles of cooperation and coordination, which were reinforced through the mandatory establishment of colleges of supervisors and the incentives for joint decision-making on supervisory issues affecting cross-border institutions.

Building on the normative analysis, Part III (Chapters 7–10) explores the various institutional aspects of the European prudential framework as they currently stand and as they may eventually evolve. This is important because the institutional structure has a direct impact on the way in which regulation is designed and supervision is conducted. The institutional framework is also largely illustrative of the horizontal and vertical distribution of competences and, ultimately, of the intensity of the European dimension.

Chapter 7 examines the general aspects related to European institutional design, such as the background that led to recent reforms, the philosophy underpinning the Lamfalussy framework, and the constant concern for preserving the institutional balance. It also points to the two open questions justifying policy-makers' reluctance to address the supervisory issue at EU level – namely, the equivocal relationship between integration and financial stability and the controversial aspect of burden-sharing in case of failures.

Chapter 8 focuses on the European institutional framework which is applicable to prudential banking regulation. It analyses the intensive interaction between the Commission, the Council and the European Parliament and the plethora of committees surrounding them. We assess the institutional balance in the context of the four-level Lamfalussy procedure. Specific attention is given to the European Banking Committee (EBC), which supports an institutionalised comitology procedure, and the Committee of European Banking Supervisors (CEBS), which has to bring about supervisory convergence and ensure uniform implementation of European rules. Chapter 9 also highlights the regulatory role of the European Central Bank stemming from its advisory functions, its participation in the various regulatory fora and, eventually, from the enabling clause in article 105(6) EC Treaty.

In Chapter 9 it is observed that unlike the regulatory framework, which is largely centralised at EU level, supervision has remained mainly decentralised at national level. However, we go beyond this simplistic representation and discuss whether the changes stemming from the CRD and the Lamfalussy process bring about an increased European influence on the way supervision is actually conducted at national level. In this context, we analyse the impact on the national institutional frameworks of the CRD, with its focus on supervisory review and the process-oriented approach to supervision, of the establishment of supra-national cooperative fora and of the increased contribution of national central banks to the supervisory process. We also look at the specific functions assumed by an ever more active meta-level of supervision, which consists of cooperative frameworks at EU level. Important players at the meta-level are CEBS, the Groupe de Contact and the Banking Supervision Committee. Furthermore we analyse the scope and effects of instruments employed for cooperation at the meta-level: memoranda of understanding, leadership in supervisory coordination, colleges of supervisors and delegation.

Chapter 10 analyses possible future developments of the EU institutional framework. Reforming the institutional set-up for supervision in the EU is a complex task that needs to be approached from the perspective of legal constraints related to the principles of conferral, subsidiarity and proportionality, and to the limits of delegation (*Meroni, Romano* case-law). Also, supervisory reform needs to take a holistic view, where competences for supervision are considered together with those for crisis management and burden-sharing in case of crisis resolution. In this context, Chapter 11 looks at the various institutional scenarios that may be envisaged for the future: decentralisation, centralisation, EBC, enhanced cooperation. Lastly, it discusses the proposals made in the Commission's Communication of 27 May 2009 on a new EU financial supervision architecture.

Based on the findings in the previous chapters, Part IV (Chapters 11–13) aims to examine the way in which increased Europeanisation of prudential regulation and supervision may impinge upon the issue of supervisory liability. In other words, the question is to what extent EU law may provide the legal basis and the criteria against which supervisory actions at national level should be checked and supervisory liability relied upon for legal remedy purposes.

Chapter 11 highlights various aspects in the evolution of EU prudential rules, which may justify the adoption of a common approach to supervisory liability (e.g. increased juridification and formalisation; emphasis on enforcement; the refined distribution of supervisory tasks; the proposed reform of the EU supervisory architecture). We endeavour to circumscribe the concept of supervisory liability by reference to the concrete duties of supervisors, the specific interests at stake and other instances resulting in depositor compensation.

Chapter 12 aims to identify the conditions under which a claim for supervisory liability could be based on EU law. The general paradigm is that of Member State liability for breach of EU law with its three conditions: the European norm infringed should be intended to confer rights to individuals, the breach should be sufficiently serious and there should be a direct causal link between the breach and the damage suffered by the individual. We provide a critical account of the judgment of the European Court of Justice (ECJ) in the *Peter Paul* case, criticising the contextual motive analysis employed by the Court. Thereby we speculate about the likelihood of the Court's dictum being upheld if the ECJ were to be again confronted with the same issue.

Chapter 13 is dedicated to testing the conditions of supervisory liability identified against the background of the new normative framework provided in the CRD. The analysis of specific provisions inquires whether the CRD may be held to confer rights upon depositors. At the same time, given the delicate policy and economic implications of supervisory liability, we discuss whether the other two conditions for Member State liability (seriousness of breach and causality) would be sufficient for containing liability claims and protecting supervisory authorities from undue pressures. Lastly, in light of forthcoming reforms of EU financial supervision, we make some tentative suggestions about the liability regime that could apply to the various players.

The book ends with some remarks which highlight an ever more prominent European dimension of the prudential regime and a refined approach towards prudential policy. Europeanisation of both the regulatory and the supervisory frameworks needs to be considered in conjunction with the internal evolution of prudential strategies reflecting the financial realities. The developments discussed are likely to trigger consequences for supervisory liability, which may find support in EU prudential norms.

Part I

European banking at the beginning of the third millennium

1 Banking and market structures

Attempting to set the scene by describing banking realities in the middle of a financial crisis is an exercise that needs to be viewed with lenience and under the benefit of doubt. Banking is by its very nature a dynamic activity, constantly adapting to evolving demands and easily outgrowing the regulatory framework. Moreover, financial crises, especially if they have the amplitude of the one starting in August 2007 and still ongoing at the time of writing, are very likely to shake markets hard and reshuffle their structures considerably. Recently observed trends and patterns characterising banking at the turn of the millennium are now likely to change substantially.

Nevertheless, we deem such an exercise to be necessary for understanding the underpinnings of current legal changes with respect to substantive and institutional aspects, particularly in a field where legal research is ancillary. Banking is definitely one of those fields where institutional design and substantial choices require complex interdisciplinary analysis (finance, economics, political science, law). Although these disciplines often make use of almost hermetic codes, methods and arguments, the complex realities of banking force those who deal with them to transcend their professional paradigms and attain a deeper and at the same time broader insight into the nature of the banking business. The discussion about prudential regulation and supervision of banking will therefore be preceded by a simple layperson's presentation of the functions and peculiarities of banking, in the context of the morphology of financial systems.

In this chapter we will point to recent changes in financial markets, their causes and possible consequences. The behaviour of banks and the outcomes of common macro-economic trends as reflected in bank strategies and structural changes in the banking market will be synthesised. Against this background and with the help of some elements of financial intermediation theory, banks can still be considered special. Last, we will highlight the specificity of the EU internal market and its regulatory framework, as important driver shaping the European banking environment.

1 Structural developments

It is beyond doubt that financial markets have undergone a remarkable evolution since the 1990s. The consequences of the latest developments are reflected in the crisis that started in August 2007 in the financial sector and spread into real economies worldwide.

Extensive research has highlighted the structural changes occurring in financial markets and the driving forces behind such developments. The acknowledgement of various trends is essential in gaining an in-depth understanding of the policy issues raised in connection with financial markets. Market developments reflect the characteristics and strategies of the financial industry – understood broadly as a mixture of financial instruments, markets and intermediaries operating in the economy – and implicitly shape regulation. Also, they influence the level of risk appetite in the financial industry, and have repercussions on financial stability.

It is not our ambition to provide an accurate analysis of the changing financial landscape – this task has already been undertaken and continues to be pursued in the light of the crisis by many well-read economists and market analysts.[1] We will give a general overview of the main aspects to facilitate a better understanding of the regulatory developments in the area of banking. In the following subsections, we will briefly indicate the underlying forces influencing the dynamics of financial markets. Further, we will concisely present the different trends characterising evolutions in Europe. In doing this, we will point out some consequences that can be attached to these structural developments and the accompanying policy concerns.

1.1 The underlying forces of change and related bank strategies

Three phenomena have largely determined the evolution of financial markets in the past decades: globalisation, technological development and financial innovation. Conversely, the development of financial markets favoured globalisation, gave an impulse to technological development and stimulated further innovation; hence, these processes are largely interdependent and evolutionary. Although the consequences brought about by these three forces are closely intermingled, we will try to highlight the specific manifestations of each one. By doing this, we will confine ourselves to mentioning them as factors that objectively impinge upon the morphology of financial markets, and refrain from making value judgements as to their suitability or adequacy, which would go beyond the aims of this study.

1 To cite just a few: Gardener and Versluijs 2001; Goddard, Molyneux, and Wilson 2001; Demirgüç-Kunt and Levine 2001; Shull and Hanweck 2001; IMF *Global Financial Stability Reports*. Particularly pertinent works, published since the beginning of the financial crisis, include: Alexander *et al.* 2007; Brunnermeier *et al.* 2009; Turner Review 2009; Commission 2009c (de Larosière report).

Globalisation

Globalisation, a disputed concept, has been defined as 'a set of economic, social, technological, political and cultural structures and processes arising from the changing character of the production, consumption and trade of goods and assets that comprise the base of the international political economy' (Bende-Nabende 2002: 7). Its core effects consist of 'shrinking space, shrinking time and disappearing borders' (United Nations 1999: 31) as a result of greater connectivity. Based on international interdependence and internationalisation, it is said that globalisation is capable of bringing about 'the progressive integration of the world economies' (World Bank 2000: 2).

It has been observed that one of the most important characteristics of economic globalisation is 'the transition from a "high-volume" into a "high-value" economy or rather from "labour-intensive" to "capital-intensive" production' (Bende-Nabende 2002: 8). This is consistent with the acknowledgement of a substantial growth of international financial flows since the 1980s.[2] Indeed, one of the striking dimensions of economic globalisation is the unprecedented integration of financial markets and the related mobility of financial capital.

Genuine globalisation of financial markets is not merely the result of action by financial intermediaries; it requires political willingness and combined efforts at the international level. The opening up of markets, the free convertibility of currencies and the free flow of payments and capital have necessitated the introduction of less discriminatory legislation and the gradual loosening of foreign exchange controls – the so-called processes of liberalisation and deregulation.[3] The first steps in this direction were made in the framework of the Organisation for Economic Cooperation and Development (OECD).[4] They were followed by measures fostering prudential rules and supervision counterbalancing liberalisation and deregulation, elaborated under the guidance of the Basel Committee on Banking Supervision. More recently, worldwide free movement of capital has received new support from the General Agreement on Tariffs and Services, concluded in the framework of the World Trade Organisation (WTO) on 12 December 1997.[5] Lastly, probably the most effective mechanisms promoting globalisation were the regional integration processes (of which the most refined is

2 Evidence of the link between globalisation and the increased cross-border flows of capital is provided, among others, by Kose *et al.* 2009.

3 For the history and development of the efforts undertaken at the international level, as well as for specific references and sources, see Metzger 1995: 49–151; Fischer 2006: 4–11.

4 In 1961 the OECD adopted the Code of Liberalisation of Current Invisible Operations and the Code of Liberalisation of Capital Movement, which were updated and strengthened in 1989. See OECD 1990.

5 WTO, the Uruguay Round Agreements, Annex 1B – General Agreement on Trade in Services.

the EU's internal market) and bilateral arrangements (e.g. agreements on bilateral administrative cooperation, double taxation treaties and free trade agreements).

For banking,[6] globalisation had major geographical implications, as financial intermediation became ever more disconnected from the location of the financial institution or the market. This implied that participants in the markets gained access to global financing opportunities, in a context of global allocation of funds and savings. Also, globalisation triggered increased internationalisation of shareholder structures, with ever larger proportions of shares of major banks being owned by foreigners. Thus, banking globalisation does not merely imply a growth of cross-border financial transactions and capital flows characterising the internationalisation process of banking, but has evolved into consolidating an ever rising presence of foreign institutions in local markets worldwide.[7] Hence the growing integration and interdependence of financial markets globally, with its related advantages (more choices and efficiency) and disadvantages (more systemic risks).

Liberalisation and deregulation not only allowed market participants to develop their activities across geographical borders, but also boosted their ability to seek new business in much wider fields of activity. The consequence was the emergence of large and complex financial institutions with sizeable market positions, eager to benefit from the potential advantages of economies of scale and economies of scope. This process is termed as consolidation and is closely linked to the conglomeration process that promotes the combination into a single financial institution of activities that have been traditionally performed by firms acting exclusively in one of the distinct financial sectors of banking, securities and insurance. Globalisation has blurred the demarcation between the various traditional financial sectors.

On the structural level, globalisation has brought about several changes in financial markets. On the one hand, there was growing competition, which provided more choices but also resulted in more rivalry for higher yields that ultimately impacted on the quality of lending standards. On the other hand, the consolidation and conglomeration processes have triggered concentration tendencies resulting in the emergence of large intermediaries. Size has become particularly important and pushed for mergers and acquisitions at both, national and supranational levels. The search for economies of scale and economies of scope gave many financial intermediaries the incentive to adopt the *Allfinanz* strategy[8] and to use extensive

6 For detailed insights into the globalisation of banking, see for instance Llewellyn 2006: 32–64; Goldberg 2009: 171–97.

7 On the difference between globalised and international banking, see McCauley *et al.* 2002: 41–51.

8 For a detailed overview, see Börner 2000.

branch and subsidiary networks to provide banking, insurance and investment services. Consolidation and conglomeration have initially taken place mainly at national level, contributing to the creation of the so-called national champions. However, in the past decade cross-border deals, consisting of mergers, acquisitions and alliances have intensified. While the main positive effect of mergers seems to be the improvement of operational efficiency (X-efficiencies) through cost reductions (Molyneux and Altunbas 1997; Vander Vennet 1998), surveys and academic studies have not found conclusive evidence of overall economies of scale (Mayes *et al.* 2001: 53). On the contrary, there is evidence of some diseconomies of scale arising for large banks in several European countries, as well as of diseconomies of scope for bank-insurance companies (EP 1999b: 10). Another strategy observed in almost all sectors is the development of so-called 'niche' markets. Niche players concentrate on their core business; this specialisation pursues not only the survival but also a sustainable and profitable development of small production entities (Pastre 2001).

The financial crisis that erupted in August 2007 unveils some of the dark side of global interconnectedness, mainly linked to unfettered greed, irresponsibility and weak surveillance and intervention mechanisms. Given its amplitude and dramatic effects on economies worldwide, the crisis questions the viability of the globalisation process as such. National rescue or stimulus packages, which have been adopted in response to the crisis, risk favouring local protectionism and are likely to step away from globalised finance. Yet important forces have been mobilised[9] to strive for worldwide concerted action that would globally address the consequences of the crisis and rebuild confidence around the world. The outcome of such efforts is far from clear and the future of globalisation is highly uncertain. Yet it seems pretty sure that globalisation, if it proceeds at all, will not advance at the same pace and probably also not under the same conditions as before August 2007.

Technological development

The second force considered decisive for the transformation of the financial industry is the extraordinary progress in information technology. It has been observed that technology, once merely a tool, has now become an enabler, which adds value and directly affects risk (Gros and Lannoo 2000).

The introduction and application of new technologies impinge on the way in which products are conceived and presented, as well as the way they are distributed. Thus, in recent years cash dispensers, telephone banking,

9 Such efforts include the unprecedented concerted lead taken by the G20 countries in addressing the crisis through internationally agreed policy responses, the decision to extend the membership of international regulatory bodies, such as the Basel Committee of Banking Supervision and the Financial Stability Forum, and the strengthening of the IMF.

direct marketing, intelligent cards and electronic banking have become part of day-to-day life. The arrival of the 'cyber wallet' (Shaw 2001) reflects changes in purchasing habits and the shifts in consumers' perception of financial products and services.

Technological development has also improved the availability of data on the situation of financial markets all over the world. Greater access to information allows customers to compare more easily products and services offered by different providers, especially with regard to standard financial products. Also, more information about markets opens up new business opportunities. This is especially true in the virtual world, where entry barriers are significantly lower. Yet the market share held by purely electronic banks appears to be still very small because of the distrust associated with the lack of physical presence and the high costs of marketing new brand names (Schilder 2001). Rather, e-banking constitutes an additional service offered by commercial banks.

In addition, information technologies enable customer information to be handled in a more consistent, systematic and strategic way. This determined the emergence and strengthening of the position of information-producing agencies, like rating agencies, which made inroads into what once constituted the comparative advantage of banks with regard to information about their clients. Also, faster data-processing techniques have contributed to making markets more liquid and more efficient. New distribution channels for traditional financial products enable a quicker and better service.

As regards costs, empirical studies show that technological change has generally reduced banks' costs, with the large banks benefiting more than their smaller competitors (Altunbas and Molyneux 2001). However, the impact of technical progress on bank costs seems also to have generally declined over time. Besides, the relentless growth and transformation of technologies requires constantly new investments from financial intermediaries. In this context, two kinds of organisational restructuring as a means for reducing costs have been used: outsourcing of activities and downsizing. Outsourcing mostly concerns those processes or products which are new-technology intensive and which require important investments. Banks subcontract them in order to benefit from the economies of scale obtained by specialised suppliers. Downsizing is a restructuring strategy using technology as a labour substitute, and often entails job reduction.[10] At the same time, reductions in human capital in the case of banks are usually balanced against the competitive advantages of relationship banking, stemming from the long-term contact between bank and customer.

10 Banking operations that entail significant innovation are custody of security portfolios, cash-management systems, home-banking operations, and complex software to grant and monitor loans; Altunbas and Molyneux 2001: 51.

Technological development is very likely to continue shaping banking activities. There is increased awareness that technology comes with associated risks that were only partly recognised in advance by policy-makers (for instance, through the imposition of capital requirements to cover operational risks). New, direct or indirect risks are starting to be recognised while the crisis unfolds[11] and new ways of addressing them will need to be devised.

Financial innovation

Intimately linked to globalisation and technological development, financial innovation substantially contributed to the change in banks' business models during the past years. The process of financial innovation entails the emergence of new products, services, institutions and new distribution channels that provide certain advantages over traditional financial products. Financial innovation is particularly reflected in three developments:[12] securitisation – the shift away from the dominance of non-marketable instruments (bank loans, deposits) to marketable securities; institutionalisation of investment through the increased use of collective investment vehicles (such as mutual funds, hedge funds, insurance companies, pension funds, money market funds, special purpose investment vehicles); and the emergence of complex financial instruments designed to unbundle, trade and transfer risks (e.g. credit derivatives). These all represented the successful ingredients for significant growth and dominance of the structured finance market at the beginning of the millennium. The rapid growth of this market was mostly welcomed as a tool for diversifying risk. Financial innovation underpinning the impressive development of structured finance was stimulated by a series of benign macro-economic conditions warranting an environment with low interest rates and ample liquidity, characterised by an exuberant willingness to invest in new products that were offering higher yields than the traditional products.[13] However, in the light of the crisis such credit risk-transfer mechanisms are now largely challenged. It is currently questioned whether they actually contributed to risk concentration instead of diversification, and whether they merely encouraged the redistribution of risks to those seeking higher yields without considering their effective risk-absorption capacities (Alexander *et al.* 2007: 8–28).

The immediate consequence of such processes is a remarkable sophistication and complexity, but also opacity, of contemporary finance (Tett 2009). The understanding of the new products – e.g. ABCPs, CDOs of

11 For instance, the run on Northern Rock in the summer of 2007 was accelerated by the panic resulting from customers' inability to access their online accounts on the bank's website. Interconnections in the wholesale liquidity markets are all supported by sophisticated technological platforms that allow for rapid contagion channels.

12 See Padoa-Schioppa 2002a: 3–7.

13 See ECB 2008c; Alexander *et al.* 2007: 20–7.

ABS, CDOs-squared, CMBS, RMBS[14] – and especially of their underlying risks became largely impenetrable for most bank managers and regulators, whose overview capacity was outgrown by developments. Furthermore, innovation was mainly based on statistical and mathematical models which, given the short existence of the new instruments, were not backed by reliable historical data. Moreover, they were built on assumptions that systematically underscored extreme scenarios.

At structural level, the described developments led to a gradual shift to market-based financial models and inter-bank borrowing, at the expense of traditional bank-based financial systems,[15] and to the resulting erosion of the conventional role of banks. New strategies reflect the efforts of financial intermediaries to adapt their functions to a radically different setting. In order to retain their competitive advantage and foster their position, banks have adjusted their business strategies by increasingly subscribing to the so-called 'originate and distribute' model. This model allows banks to take their originated loans off-balance, and to repackage and securitise them with a view of selling them or using them as collateral for raising short-term liquidity. This created an incentive structure that is now largely believed to have weakened firms' risk-management systems and substantially contributed to the financial crisis (ECB 2008c).

The 'originate and distribute' business model is currently subject to thorough scrutiny by policy-makers and constitutes the object of several new regulatory proposals. A halt has definitely been put to its proliferation for the time being. In parallel, more general questions arise about the future of financial innovation, which is likely to be much more closely monitored in the near future (Bernanke 2009). Finding the right balance so as to ensure that such closer control, and eventually regulation, does not stifle innovation altogether will be an important challenge for policy-makers.

1.2 The crisis and its aftermath

It is not our intention to provide an analysis of the financial crisis, which is still unfolding at the time of writing, or to give an outlook on the possible evolution of banking markets in the coming years. Many well-qualified experts are now digging into the causes of the crisis, analysing immediate action and looking for ways to prevent failures on such a scale from occurring in the future.[16] Our much more modest aim is to simply give a glimpse of the dynamics of events.

14 ABCP – asset-backed commercial paper; CDO of ABS – collateralised debt obligation with a pool of collateral consisting of asset-backed securities; CDOs-squared – re-securitised collateralised debt obligations; CMBS – commercial mortgage-backed security; RMBS – residential mortgage-based security.

15 For detailed discussions of market-based versus bank-based models, see Canals 1997.

16 For a detailed analysis of the crisis and its impact on market structures, see IMF 2009; Posner 2009.

Since mid-2007 we have been going through what has been described as 'the most severe financial crisis since the nineteen thirties, with repercussions on the "real" economy which, in terms of output and employment losses, are more severe than anything we have witnessed since the end of the war' (Lamfalussy 2009). This has been the outcome of the complex interaction of several general and specific factors that mutually reinforced each other.[17] The developments in the banking markets already described paralleled benign macro-economic conditions characterised by ample liquidity, low interest rates, low inflation and rapid credit expansion. The interlacement of these realities resulted in the unprecedented rise of asset prices, and increased leverage. It contributed to the build-up of global imbalances entailing, for developed economies, massive capital inflows from major developing countries. These developments, combined with risk-management failures related to proper risk assessment, the role played by credit rating agencies, the absence of appropriate corporate governance checks and balances, and regulatory and supervisory loopholes, led to an explosive cocktail.

The trigger came from the rising defaults in the US subprime loans market, and affected quickly inter-bank funding, drying up segments such as the residential mortgage-based securities (RMBSs) market in summer–autumn 2007. At that time the German IKB bank was rescued, BNP Paribas was freezing its funds and the retail run on Northern Rock occurred. Problems continued to spread, and by mid-2008 banks' trading books had registered severe mark-to-market losses; ever larger financial market segments, especially the commercial paper market, were under pressure, raising alarming liquidity concerns. In mid-March 2008 the US Federal Reserve organised the rescue of Bear Stearns. Yet losses continued to grow and funding problems became acute. The final blow to the confidence in financial markets came from the bankruptcy, in September 2008, of Lehman Brothers. This was followed by a waterfall of events, among which the most significant were the bail-out of AIG; the takeover of Bear Stearns by JP Morgan Chase and of Merrill Lynch by Bank of America; the failures of Washington Mutual, Bradford and Bingley, the Icelandic banks, Fortis and Dexia; the rescues of the German Hypo Real Estate and US Wachovia; and the transformation of surviving US investment banks Goldman Sachs and Morgan Stanley into commercial bank holding companies. Since October 2008 governments have intervened massively through recapitalisation, funding guarantees and central bank liquidity provision in order to prevent further bank failures. By the end of 2008, it was clear that the crisis had spread into the real economy worldwide, tightening credit conditions. This built up a vicious circle where reduced lending capabilities contributed to further worsening of the situation in the financial markets.

17 Clear descriptions of the causes of the crisis can be found in the de Larosière report (Commission 2009d: L 6–12); Turner Review 2009: 11–50.

In mid-2009, despite some optimism linked to several improved indicators, the situation in financial markets was still gloomy (*The Economist* 2009a: 15–16). Further losses were expected from other financial market segments, such as credit card and derivatives business. The confidence in the markets was still very low, inter-bank funding was still expensive; uncertainty about the counterparties was still high and further reinforced by continued disclosures of losses; many banks were downsizing and the number of branches was reduced. The persisting ambiguous inter-linkages in financial markets construed through sophisticated multi-layered products maintained fears as to the ultimate size of the current crisis. Banks tended to focus on de-leveraging and became much more risk-averse than in the previous year, thereby causing the credit squeeze.

A series of targeted policy actions has been undertaken to address the immediate concerns, and plans are currently being drawn to create the basis of a safer framework in the future. Government interventions for rescuing individual institutions have occurred on a massive scale, although the forms and details of the measures vary widely, ranging from complete bail-outs to various forms of recapitalisation, different guarantees, orchestration of takeovers or mergers, specific funding lines, etc. Furthermore, national packages have been prepared to address financing problems in the real economy. All these measures, although absolutely crucial for restoring markets, entail a high risk of potential distortions of competition. There is not only the risk of breaches to general State aid rules, but also the risk that bail-outs in one country might force further bail-outs in other countries, i.e. the so-called 'competitive bail-outs' (European Shadow Financial Regulatory Committee 2009: 2). Furthermore competitive distortions are also likely between various categories of financial market participants. National rescue or stimulus packages are prone to favour big banks or banks that incurred large losses, thereby risking putting small and more prudent banks at disadvantage.

In parallel, broader regulatory and supervisory reforms were launched to address the perceived shortcomings of the current framework. An unprecedented willingness to address common concerns at global level is demonstrated by discussions unfolding under the auspices of the Group of 20, the Financial Stability Forum and the Basel Committee on Banking Supervision. A range of regulatory proposals has been issued at international, regional and national levels. Regulation is the favoured instrument of politicians and is heavily employed. Regulating under uncertainty and ambiguity, as new pieces of information relevant for understanding what went wrong are constantly coming to the surface, is a challenging task. Furthermore, specific care will need to be given to managing all initiatives and understanding interactions. Also, the capacity of systems, markets and ultimately regulated entities to internalise new proposals and adjust their activities is limited and would need more consideration in the course of events triggered by the overall regulatory euphoria.

The structure of financial markets is adjusting. Short- and long-term strategies and policies are closely interwoven. An important – although temporary – element to consider is the presence of the State: many banks have come under complete or partial government control and are likely to remain so for some time. Explicit government involvement creates immediate distortions, as well as long-term implications for banking. Once the crisis is superseded, re-privatisation will be imminent and may impact on the structure of the market. Equally, current exit and survival strategies affect the geopolitics of financial markets. It is likely that the trend will be away from investment banking and towards retail activities. The effects of massive reorientation to retail business should be carefully considered by policy-makers. Grasping the emerging characteristics of financial markets will be crucial for understanding future risks to the system.

Herding behaviour, also referred to as strategic behaviour and indicating that market participants tend to act in light of and on the basis of expected behaviour of the other market participants, was one of the catalysts for the current crisis (Persaud 2000). Also encouraged by regulation, it has led to increased homogenisation of financial markets and financial actors. This has been indicated as posing significant risks to the stability and liquidity of markets. To avoid this it is considered fundamental to promote 'a wide range of participants with heterogeneous objectives and methods and with confident expectations that markets will be relatively stable' (Alexander *et al.* 2007: 3). It is particularly important that current adjustments and the restructuring of financial markets adopt a pluralistic approach in order to avoid extensive homogenisation and excessive herding.

Banking crises have always triggered regulatory reforms, which, because of the high costs involved, are hard to promote as preventive measures but easier to justify once losses imputable to regulatory failures become concrete. The current crisis, with its amplitude, high impact on the real economy and trillions of ascertained losses, has now created a momentum that may allow for substantial changes in banking regulation and supervision. Many changes are already in the pipeline. How substantial overall reforms will prove to be remains to be seen.

1.3 The European banking sector

Having highlighted the general trends sustaining the dynamics of financial markets, we proceed by examining how they are reflected in the European banking sector and what the specificities of the latter are. When doing so we should keep in mind an additional dimension of European financial markets, namely the process of integration. Thus, market developments in the EU are usually also considered from the perspective of their contribution to the achievement of a European single market and their integration potential. Finally, an important aspect of the European banking morphology is related to the 2004 and 2007 enlargements of the European Union, which brought into the single market twelve national banking systems largely dominated by foreign banks.

Despite the increasing use of investment funds, pension funds and insurance products as savings vehicles, the European financial system continues to be bank-dominated, while capital markets remain relatively small when compared to the US market-based system.[18] In the EU not only do banks compete with an ever larger array of non-bank institutional investors, but also different types of banks co-exist having different market shares. While their precise definitions differ slightly from one country to another, the typical legal forms of credit institutions in the EU are commercial private-stock companies, savings banks, cooperative or mutually owned banks, public banks and different specialised lending institutions, such as mortgage banks, agricultural lending banks, postal savings banks, etc. The variety of banking firms in Europe is the outcome of historical developments in the various Member States, reflecting public policies directed at ensuring universal access to savings instruments and the provision of credit to targeted segments of the economy. Also, it reflects waves of restructuring following the nationalisation and subsequent privatisation of different banking sectors.

With regard to the developments occurring in the European banking sector, we will shortly describe the long-term trends as identified and highlighted by the ECB in its regularly updated study on EU banking structures (ECB 2008b). The ECB observed a continuity of the main structural trends. Thus the consolidation trend,[19] although it appears to have slowed down moderately during past years, continued to characterise the European banking market – primarily visible in the continuously declining number of credit institutions and the growth of total assets. Yet behind the aggregate numbers there are large differences between Member States, both in terms of their numerical evolution and in terms of asset growth. At the same time, according to the ECB no clear trend could be identified from the number of mergers and acquisitions (M&A), except for a significant increase since 2005 of M&A by EU banks in third countries as compared to domestic M&A transactions. Despite falling cross-sector consolidation (conglomeration) between banks and insurance companies, relative to the peaks reached in 2000–1, conglomeration continues to be considered an important feature of the European banking sector.

18 Belaisch *et al.* 2001. Such a label typically results from the comparison of data on financial assets controlled by banking systems, bank loans to euro-area residents and equity and bond market capitalisation. The bank-based character of the European banking system was also confirmed more recently: Annett *et al.* 2005. The latter study explains the smaller size of European capital markets by reference to the long absence of a single currency and the existence of a variety of legal and regulatory hurdles in the EU.

19 Consolidation was already being highlighted as a long-term trend in 2001; see ECB 2002: 139.

Regarding the banking market structures,[20] differences between countries persist. The degree of concentration[21] may be relatively low, as in the case of Germany, Spain, Italy and the United Kingdom where there is significant fragmentation, or high, as in the case of most of the new and the smaller Member States (excepting Austria and Luxembourg, which have strong savings and cooperative banking sectors). Also, the ECB found evidence of cost-cutting and downsizing in some countries.

A key dimension of the European banking market regards internationalisation, which appears to be a growing trend. Despite the fact that the EU banking market is dominated overall by domestic institutions, evidence gathered by the ECB is indicative of the emergence of some regional banking clusters and an increasing market share of foreign branches and subsidiaries (ECB 2005c: 12). This trend is particularly reinforced by the evolution of the banking sectors in the new Member States, where foreign ownership of banks, according to 2008 data, amounts on aggregate to 70 per cent as compared to about 28 per cent in the EU15 (ECB 2008b: 11). Foreign banks in the new Member States operate mainly as subsidiaries and have predominantly an EU parent. The growing internationalisation trend is also apparent in the increased number of notifications for cross-border provision of financial services (predominantly in the new Member States), the rising cross-border holdings of inter-bank loans and securities. However, the fact that cross-border loans to the private sector remain low reflects the continuing importance of relationship banking and of the proximity of banks to their clients.

It has been argued that integration is progressing, albeit at a different pace, depending on the specificity of the markets of the various financial products.[22] Thus, empirical evidence suggests that in the past decade integration has advanced especially in wholesale money markets (i.e. those activities where the counterpart of a bank is another bank) and in capital markets (i.e. where the counterpart of a financial institution is the market itself) (Padoa-Schioppa 2004b; Commission 2009a: 17). Conversely, with regard to traditional banking activities in the retail area, where the counterparts of banks are households or small firms, geographical segmentation remained strong and the pace of integration was much slower.[23] The 2008 European Financial Integration Report

20 ECB 2008b: 14. Generally, it is held that EU banking markets tend to be characterised by monopolistic competition.

21 Concentration is measured by the share of the five largest institutions in total banking assets.

22 The European Commission issues a yearly European Financial Integration Report (EFIR) which gives an overview of the state of integration in the EU, recent trends and the impact of integration in the financial sector.

23 Owing to the importance of proximity in this area, integration follows the pace of cross-border consolidation reflecting especially the local establishment of foreign institutions; see Padoa-Schioppa 2004b.

signalled that integration is currently perceived as an ongoing process, particularly in the equity and retail markets, whereas integration has slowed down in some segments of the wholesale markets because of the crisis.[24] Integration of financial markets in the new Member States is still lagging behind, with the foreign subsidiaries being the main drivers and the perspective of adopting the euro considered as an accelerating factor (Commission 2009a: 19).

Concerning the banks' intermediation strategies, an important development in the EU is the increasing integration and centralisation of risk-management functions, moving away from the traditional country model towards a business line model (Schoenmaker and Oosterloo 2006: 9). This strategy allows for the development of the firm-wide assessment of risk, by way of transfer of risk-management functions from the separate entities of a financial group to the group level. As a consequence, divergences arise between the legal structure and the organisational structure of the group. This poses particular challenges for the supervisory authorities, whose mandate is generally linked to the legal structure of an entity.

Furthermore, the European banking sector was affected by the substantial changes in the funding strategies – as determined by both structural and cyclical economic developments.[25] Thus, EU credit institutions have diversified their funding beyond the loan–deposit ratio to other on- and off-balance types of funding. Also, in view of the higher competition in attracting savings, banks tended to offer ever higher interest rates and to introduce more sophisticated deposit products. Furthermore, there was increased recourse by banks to risk-transfer instruments. At the same time, banks' participation in securities markets through the issuance of their own debt securities gained importance, especially for large banks' funding strategies.

It follows that, faced with new challenges stemming from the benign macro-economic environment, banks have demonstrated daringly adaptive responses. Thus, EU banks' strategies mirroring international trends such as consolidation, conglomeration, internationalisation and diversification of activities and funding sources witnessed banks' endeavour to benefit from all the opportunities offered by new information technologies, globalisation and financial innovation.

These strategies are affected by the financial crisis. Banking intermediation, which was still growing in the EU in 2007, especially through sustained credit expansion, might go through adverse developments because

24 A deterioration as a consequence of the financial crisis is indicated, especially for the unsecured inter-bank segment, government bonds; see Commission 2009a: 17.

25 According to the ECB, structural trends consist of the increase in private pensions savings schemes, the changing composition of households and firms' financial wealth, changes in preferences, and shifts in EU banks' funding strategies. Cyclical trends refer to the low interest rate environment and to the changing risk/return trade-offs.

of the tightened credit market conditions. It is predicted that internationalisation strategies, especially of banks that focused on wholesale funding and investment banking, will be less prominent, though the decrease of some banks' equity prices might provide valuable M&A opportunities (ECB 2008b: 17). An important reaction to the financial crisis, as recently observed by the ECB, is the search for more stable funding sources, especially deposits. This results in a reorientation towards retail business, ever more competitive retail market conditions and possible changes to the market shares of those banks that were already relying on retail deposits (ECB 2009).

It is important to note that these broad common developments are not uniform and the structure of the European banking system remains diversified and intricate. The banking sectors in the various Member States continue to be characterised by very diverging structures. Also, integration proceeds at different speeds, depending on the specific financial product market considered.

2 Banks are still special

In globalised and ever more interwoven financial sectors, it appears legitimate to inquire into the role reserved for banks. Traditionally, banks were considered special and therefore required specific treatment when compared to other financial intermediaries. In light of the previously mentioned market developments, it is posited that banks preserve their specificity. In the following analysis, we will attempt to outline the main features of such specificity. For this purpose we will provide some preliminary notions on the relevant arguments developed in general financial intermediation theory and then highlight banks' main features as they appear in economic theory.

2.1 Insights from financial intermediation theory

Financial intermediation theories assume that an efficient financial system has to carry out five primary tasks: enabling and guaranteeing the operation of the payments system; facilitating the allocation and transfer of resources over time between sectors or geographical areas; offering a system of guarantees that reduces the uncertainty regarding the true value of money; making possible the issue of financial products (debt or capital) in order to invest into real investment projects; providing information on the price of financial assets (Canals 1997: 28).

In this context, the essential function of any financial intermediary is to transform one financial asset, under certain conditions, into another financial asset. The study of financial intermediation is usually undertaken from two different perspectives: institutional and functional. The institutional approach (Llewellyn 1986) consists of a detailed analysis of the institutions acting in financial markets and it focuses on their ability to adapt to changes in the relevant sector and markets. The functional approach (Canals 1997: 28) emphasises the functions that society expects from the financial system and financial intermediaries, and it looks at the activities undertaken by financial intermediaries from the point of view of their ability to respond to the assigned functions.

Our review of the banking market and the ongoing trends has highlighted that as the various financial sectors became increasingly intertwined, banks' diversification and re-definition of business activities was accompanied by the emergence of new types of firms undertaking traditional retail banking business. Banks and banking are changing: banks tend to be financial services firms, whereas other financial institutions are increasingly offering retail banking services and there are ever more alternative financial products that meet the demands of traditional bank products (Llewellyn 1999a: 9). A 'shadow banking system' has emerged, consisting of all those entities that were performing banking-like activities by offering close substitutes to banking products, without being subject to prudential regulation and control as banks. It has signalled the limits of an exclusively institutional approach to banking and underlined the merits of combining both institutional and functional perspectives.

Therefore, it appears that, from a functional perspective, demand for traditional retail banking activities will continue to rise, and there are plenty of financial institutions offering them. Inversely, banks, although still concentrating on their core competences, tend to extend their business into other financial sectors. Our interest is to determine whether banks, given their traditional key position in the economy, succeed in adapting to the new developments without altering their specificity. In other words, the question is whether banks maintain competitive advantages in providing banking activities, so that they continue to deserve special treatment. In the following subsection, we will underline the features that make banks 'special' compared to other financial institutions and will present the arguments favouring the 'specificity' of banks in the current context.

2.2 Banks in economic theory

Explanations for 'why banks are special' usually emanate from economic theory, which developed two streams of literature on the banking firm.[26] The 'old theories' (Gurley and Shaw 1960) merely assume the existence of banks in the economy and apply standard micro-economic theory to explain the transformation and consolidation of risks, as well as the broker function performed by banks. Since the 1980s the 'new theories' have presented a different view (Benston and Smith 1976: 215–31;

26 For a review of the literature, see Baltensperger 1980; Williamson 1987: 11.

Diamond 1984: 393–414), taking as a starting point the market imperfections (e.g. asymmetric information, transaction costs) and describing how these cause banks to exist and what economic functions result from that. All these complementary theories try to explain the very existence of banks, their role in the economy and the distinctive features of banking.

It is in the light of these theories that the common view of banks as special financial institutions has emerged, due above all to their particular way of undertaking financial intermediation. This is known as 'traditional banking' and implies accepting deposits with one set of characteristics and creating or holding assets with a different set of features (Llewellyn 1999a: 23). The general view in economic literature[27] is that banks are special because of their role as central players providing and re-distributing liquidity. Therefore, it is held that 'the banking industry is the key transmission channel for monetary policy; banks are the key operators in the payment system and they constitute the counterpart for the central bank operations' (Padoa-Schioppa 2004a: 46). Furthermore, banks are considered special because of information advantages, delegated monitoring, control theory, the insurance role of banks and regulatory subsidies (Llewellyn 1999a: 16–20). These elements have fostered and consolidated the strategic position of banks in the economy and ascribed them a specific public interest.

In the previous sections we have highlighted banks' capacity to develop strategies that allow them to withstand market pressures, which may be more or less transitory. This is indicative of the fact that banks retain powerful core competences that can be exploited in manifold ways, so as to continue to ensure their competitive advantages and to justify their characterisation as 'special', and hence the claim for special treatment. We will now briefly indicate three interconnected features of banks that make up for their specificity.

Banks are opaque

One core competence of banks is linked to the information base resulting from managing customers' bank accounts (Plihon 2000: 21). Banks enjoy a competitive advantage as regards the collection, treatment and conservation of information about the financing needs of economic agents, the quality of their projects and their reputation. The existence of banks and their market value is largely based on the exploitation of such private information, which is not easily transferred to open markets. Through their proximity to the customers and the long-term relationships, banks have access to valuable information unavailable to the markets, which they guard closely through bank secrecy rules (Plihon 2000: 21). Furthermore,

27 There are also different opinions developed by Burstein 1988: 63–84.

banks' opaqueness stems from the fact that it is problematic for outsiders to judge the banks' risks resulting from their loans, trading activities, fixed assets and leverage because they are either difficult to measure or they are easy to change.

Technological developments, the emergence of rating agencies and disclosure laws have definitely contributed to increasing the availability and access to information in financial markets. Nevertheless, the double-edged opaqueness of banks allowing them, on the one hand, to reinforce customer confidence and, on the other, to elude their own assessment by third parties, continues to preserve information advantages and makes banks 'special'.

Banks act as performers of deposit-taking and lending

It is frequently held that changes brought by technological and financial innovation enable other financial intermediaries to mimic traditional banking products and thus to erode the special position of banks. Nevertheless, banks will continue to be special as long as they are the only liquidity providers acting on the basis of the joint supply of deposits and loans and capable of transforming short-term liabilities into long-term assets (Padoa-Schioppa 2004a: 13).

The standard definition of a bank is that of a 'financial intermediary that participates in the payment system and finances entities in financial deficit (typically the public sector, non-financial firms and some households) using the funds of entities in financial surplus (typically households)' (Dewatripont and Tirole 1994: 13). The distinctive feature of banks stems primarily from their role in transforming liquid short-term liabilities (deposits that can be easily withdrawn) into illiquid long-term assets (commercial loans for which traditionally there is no market for illiquid assets).

This paradigm was thought to change with the development of ever-complex financial instruments that allowed the repackaging of loans into marketable instruments and the emergence of risk-transfer instruments and markets. Thus, banks became able to completely transfer the credit risk off-balance to other banks or other financial institutions such as insurance companies, investment funds or special investment vehicles. Yet the crisis has shown that risk-transfer instruments were not necessarily dispersing risks, but were largely concentrating it in new forms. The specificity of the banks' 'originate and distribute' model forced them to bring back on-balance many of the exposures for which risk had been considered as transferred, or to sustain them with expensive credit lines.

Furthermore, it appears that banks react to the new financial environment by reinforcing their traditional banking business, while banks' funding still relies consistently on the loan–deposit ratio (ECB 2009). Banks' combined provision of deposit-taking and lending activities gives rise to synergies and economies of scope that allow banks to preserve competitive advantages, especially regarding the information business and relationship banking.[28] Consequently, it is held that

> bank lending is fundamentally different in nature, and is inextricably tied up with banks' deposit-taking activities. If one insists on assigning activities to functional buckets, it may make more sense to stick both commitment-based lending and deposit-taking into a single bucket, and label the function 'liquidity provision'. According to this definition, banks are not so obviously spanned by other types of intermediaries, and may legitimately deserve to be thought of as a special type of financial institution.
>
> (Kashyap *et al.* 1999: 39)

Banks incur special risks

Banks are special because the risks they incur are different from those of other financial intermediaries. This special risk profile of banks is related to the specific character of deposits, to the vulnerability of banks caused by greater exposure to contagion channels and, last but not least, to the increased propensity of banks to take up higher risks because of the implicit subsidies offered by protective regulation. The expansion of banks into securities and insurance business does not mitigate traditional risks, but increases their complexity by rendering the differentiation between credit and market risks ever more indistinct, thus making risk management more intricate and harder to monitor.

Unlike the securities business, where in case of a run (i.e. rush to sell) tradable assets can be downsized in parallel with investors' withdrawals, the massive withdrawal of deposits is more likely to cause the illiquidity and subsequent insolvency of banks. Thus, the risk of failure in banking is associated with the fixed-value deposits, which need to be met by selling illiquid loans. Selling illiquid loans below their book value has the potential of transforming illiquidity into insolvency.[29]

One of the most typical features of banks' risk profile is their exposure to contagion risk. Contagion, which is at the core of the concept of

28 Kashyap *et al.* (1999) observed that

> there will naturally be synergies between the two activities, to the extent that both require banks to hold a large volume of liquid assets (cash and securities) on their balance sheets: if deposit withdrawals and commitment takedowns are imperfectly correlated, the two activities can share any dead-weight costs of holding the liquid assets.

29 While 'illiquidity' refers to banks' difficulty in readily converting assets into cash, 'insolvency' refers to banks' inability to meet financial obligations on an ongoing basis. Illiquidity and insolvency are closely linked: the former may cause the latter, for instance as a consequence of sales of assets below their quoted price in the rushed quest for liquidity.

systemic risk, refers to the possibility that failure of a bank spreads to other banks in the system.[30] It is held that contagion may occur either through the real (also called exposure) channel or through the information channel (Schoenmaker and Oosterloo 2005: 7). The real channel, also referred to as the 'domino effect', results from the explicit financial linkages between banks – stemming from real exposures in the interbank markets, overnight market and/or in payment systems. The information channel is caused by imperfect information about the type of failure or perceived threat of failure of one bank, which may easily induce customers to withdraw deposits from other banks.[31] The intrinsic opaqueness of banks and the limited disclosure to the public play an important role in spreading the failure of one bank to other banks in the system.

Last but not least, banks have incentives to take on higher risk exposures. This reflects moral hazard problems and is closely associated with access to central bank liquidity and the existence of public safety-net arrangements for banks. Lender-of-last-resort facilities and deposit insurance are forms of protective regulation available only or under less restrictive conditions to banks. Such regulatory subsidies make them special when compared to other financial intermediaries.

2.3 The definition of banks in European law

Let us now see whether the European legal norms reflect the specificity of banks as discussed in economic theory. In EU law, banks are termed 'credit institutions'. Their definition can be found in article 4 point 1 of Directive 2006/48/EC (referred to here as the Capital Requirements Directive, CRD[32]): a credit institution is '(a) an undertaking whose business is to receive deposits or other repayable funds from the public and to grant credits for its own account; or (b) an electronic money institution within the meaning of Directive 2000/46/EC'.

The definition appeared, in the same wording, in one of the first Community pieces of legislation regulating the banking business – the First Banking Directive – and all successive pieces of legislation. This points to

30 A second aspect of systemic risk refers to the risk of contagion in the whole financial system, and from the financial system to the real economy, so as to prevent the system from carrying out its core economic functions of channelling payments and allocating funds from savings to investment; see Padoa-Schioppa 2002a: 10.

31 Diamond and Dybvig 1983; Baltensperger and Dermine 1987; Postlewaite and Vives 1987; Bhattacharya and Jacklin 1988; Chari and Jagannathan 1988 cited by Goodhart 1998a: 12.

32 The denomination 'Capital Requirements Directive' commonly refers to both the Directive 2006/48/EC and Directive 2006/49/EC on the capital adequacy of investment firms and credit institutions (recast). In this book we will use CRD to indicate the former directive, while we will refer to the latter as 'recast CAD' (Capital Adequacy Directive).

its general acceptance, despite the still divergent national definitions.[33] Combined with the list of activities subject to mutual recognition detailed in Annex I[34] to the CRD, the definition actually imposes the universal banking model[35] in all Member States. This combination of a single definition with a list of permitted activities reflects the complex nature of banks. As observed, 'although banks are identifiable as a well-defined type of firm, banking is at the same time a multi-product industry: various banking products are exchanged in different markets, which are of different size and geographical coverage' (Padoa-Schioppa 2000: 48).

It is important to emphasise the two cumulative elements required by the definition: to receive deposits and to grant credits. Here, legal norms are mirroring economic theory. A financial institution allowed to undertake only one of those activities cannot be qualified as a credit institution. Nevertheless, in order to respond to this definition, it is enough that an undertaking has the statutory possibility of exercising the two types of activity, although in fact it exercises only one of them (Clarotti 1982: 68). Also, the requirement that received funds should be *repayable* clearly excludes insurance firms from the scope of the directive on credit institutions (Dassesse and Isaacs 1985: 74). Furthermore, note that the definition does not relate to the nature of the entity, but rather to the nature of the business transacted. Moreover, the term 'undertaking' may include in principle any form of business enterprise (Usher 2000: 116).

The importance of the definition of the credit institution also stems from its value as a benchmark: the fact that other financial institutions are defined in a negative way as undertakings 'other than a credit institution,

33 As pointed out in Pecchioli 1987: 59, countries like Greece, Spain and Portugal have tight restrictions on the range of financial activities open to banks, while countries like France, Belgium and Germany allow larger definitions of banks.

34 Annex I lists, apart from deposit-taking and lending financial leasing, money transmission services; issuing and administering means of payment (e.g. credit cards, travellers' cheques and bankers' drafts); guarantees and commitments; trading for own account and for account of customers in money market instruments (cheques, bills, certificates of deposit, etc.), foreign exchange, financial futures and options, exchange and interest-rate instruments or transferable securities; participation in securities issues and the provision of services related to such issues; advice to undertaking on capital structure, industrial strategy and related questions and advice, as well as services related to mergers and the purchase of undertakings; money broking; portfolio management and advice; safekeeping and administration of securities; credit reference services; safe custody services. This list can be amended through the comitology.

35 According to Dale 1992: 138, universal banking describes a 'banking tradition found in continental Europe in which banks engage in a full range of securities activities, usually through the bank entity itself rather than through separately incorporated subsidiaries'. It is also associated with close linkages between banking and industry which may be formalised by banks acquiring equity holdings in their client companies and seeking representation on those companies' boards of directors. More recently, account being taken of the growth of *bancassurance*, the definition of universal banking was expanded to contain also the insurance business; see European Commission (1997b).

the principal activity of which is to acquire holdings or to carry on one or more of the activities listed in points 2 to 12 of Annex 1' (article 4 point 5 CRD). Furthermore, according to article 5 CRD, Member States are required to 'prohibit persons or undertakings that are not credit institutions from carrying on the business of taking deposits or other repayable funds from the public'.

It follows that European legislation reflects the specificity of banks, and ascribes them a different treatment as that conferred to other financial institutions. At the same time the broad definition of a credit institution in EU legislation is indicative of the universal banking model, largely spread in Europe, and leaves space for accommodating different national particularities.

European legislation takes a combined functional and institutional approach, with the latter aspect being more pronounced when one looks at the detailed requirements for the registration and supervision of individual institutions. On the one hand, the EU law definition of credit institutions allows great flexibility, covering financial players having different forms and permitting financial intermediaries that de facto do not accept deposits and other repayable funds to actually take advantage of the specific treatment reserved to banks. On the other hand, the exclusive focus on acceptance of deposits and repayable funds from the public in the definition may be considered precarious in the absence of a common understanding of the characteristics of 'deposits' and 'repayable funds', and the lack of a common definition of 'public'. This allowed non-banks to develop a range of financial products that were close substitutes to deposits and to attract major funds from individual investors. It has allowed the shadow banking system to flourish largely unregulated and compete directly with banks in their traditional market segments, with the implicit risks as revealed by the ongoing crisis.

Legislation should be able to differentiate precisely between the different financial intermediaries in the market and assign to each an appropriate regulatory framework. This cannot be done by relying exclusively on the current definition of a credit institution, which needs to be broadly formulated to encompass the peculiarities of Member States' banking systems. To avoid opportunism in the choice of form and preclude emulation intended for eluding the regulatory framework, it is necessary that either 'shadow banking' should be better identified or the meaning of 'deposit taking and acceptance of repayable funds from the public' should be better specified.

3 Is there a single European banking market?

We have seen that despite common trends banking structures and developments in the EU Member States differ widely. It is thus legitimate to ask ourselves whether we can speak about a single integrated European banking market. There are important factors in the EU that can keep the variety of specific national banking landscapes under the same roof. Therefore, the question here is whether they have established a foundation that is sufficiently solid and consistent to promote the evolution of national banking realities into an integrated market. Such a foundation would allow us to think in terms of a single European banking market, irrespective of concrete current figures measuring integration versus fragmentation.

Here, we are taking for granted the advantages linked to the integration of the European banking and financial markets: it would bring banks the liquidity benefits of deeper and wider markets and lower costs when operating in several countries, a more efficient allocation of financial resources and risk-sharing and better choices for consumers. It is worth remembering that an integrated market entails greater contagion potential and interdependencies that might foster systemic risks.

In our view, there are two factors indicative of a strong European dimension of banking markets: the European regulatory framework and the euro. We shall first broadly indicate the evolution of the European regulatory framework, which will be subject to a detailed analysis in the subsequent parts of this book. Then we will consider, in general terms, the role of the euro in the integration of the banking system.

3.1 The European regulatory framework

Part of the single market, the European banking market was conceived as being built on the basic principles of the Rome Treaty – particularly the freedom of establishment, the freedom to provide services, and the free movement of capital. The project for European banking integration was initially based on the ideas of regulatory convergence with regard to the taking up and pursuit of banking activities and homogenisation of instruments of supervision. The rationale came from the necessity of creating a 'level playing-field' for securing a fair and symmetric distribution of the costs and benefits of deregulation for the participating national systems.

Community legislative efforts for the completion of a common banking market were initiated in the early 1970s and made it clear from the outset that the opening up of domestic banking markets had to be accompanied by prudential regulation ensuring that all Member States would be able to face risks incurred in the banking business.

By virtue of the full harmonisation philosophy, initial Community efforts concentrated especially on the adoption of substantive rules of prudential supervision. However, the divergent interests of governments regarding their banking systems, as well as different national traditions in this field, called a halt to ambitious projects and blocked the process of positive integration. The solution to the deadlock resulted in the context of the new impetus for the achievement of the common market coming from the 1985 White Paper and the development of the *Cassis de Dijon* doctrine:[36] mutual recognition and minimum harmonisation in essential matters. Thus, integration was fuelled by a second wave of Community legislation consecrating the new regulatory philosophy based on a European passport for banks.

This negative integration strategy relied first on the harmonisation of essential key standards for prudential supervision (capital requirements, solvency ratios, fitness and properness of management, disclosure of information, control of large exposures). Second, it was based on the mutual recognition of domestic banking supervision under both aspects: the legal framework and the effective exercise of supervision. Third, the obvious corollary in the area of prudential supervision is the home-country control principle, allocating, as a rule, the responsibility for the prudential control and supervision of credit institutions to the regulatory authorities that issued the authorisation.

The balancing of positive and negative integration strategies and particularly the principle of home-country control were successful in opening up banking markets in the EU. It was thought that the elimination of regulatory disparities would create the necessary and sufficient conditions for obtaining convergence in both financial structures and financial performances. Expectations referred to improvements in the efficiency of the financial services industry, the demolition of oligopolistic rents, convergence in managerial models, prices and product strategies, and the opportunities of banks to grow and to make profits. There was hope for trade-offs between efficiency and stability for all European banking markets (Montanaro *et al.* 2001). These prospects proved too optimistic, however, being partly based on weak foundations.

Mutual recognition and minimum harmonisation emphasise the differing views among national regulators. Competing regulatory regimes, on the one hand, have a tremendous integrative potential through reverse discrimination, but, on the other hand, leave room for oscillation between stringency and laxity and constitute incentives for 'supervisory shopping'.[37] The question arises of the suitable degree of regulatory competition in a context where the implementation of European directives perpetrated national differences. Also, uniform regulations applied to systems with substantial differences may be to the disadvantage of the weaker systems and may cause instability.

The home-country control principle was also seriously criticised (Paroush 1988; Baltensperger and Dermine 1990). With the extension of

36 The seminal case 120/78 *Rewe-Zentral AG* v. *Bundesmonolpolverwaltung fur Branntwein* (1979) ECR 649 launched the principle of mutual recognition; see Craig and de Búrca 1999a: 604–9.

37 For an accurate analysis of the effects of regulatory competition in the banking industry, see Reig 1997.

pan-European banking activities, national supervisors lost the competitive advantage related to the assessment of risks at national level. Systemic risk and the imperative of supervisory cooperation raised doubts about the functioning of the principle and its relevance in a more integrated European financial market.

Recognising that the EU's financial markets still remained segmented and acknowledging that the introduction of the euro was a unique opportunity to equip the EU with a modern financial regulatory apparatus, in the late 1990s EU policy-makers gave a new impetus to the efforts for establishing a single financial services market. This implied the completion of legislation with the measures envisaged under the Financial Services Action Plan (FSAP), and the parallel adaptation of the regulatory apparatus to render it more efficient and responsive (the Lamfalussy framework).

With the FSAP measures entering into force and a specific regulatory decision-making procedure in place, at the beginning of the millennium further guidance on stimulating the integration of financial markets in Europe was given through the post-FSAP strategy, which put emphasis on the implementation of the FSAP measures.[38]

The eruption of the banking crisis in August 2007 submitted the EU regulatory framework for financial services to a tough test. Specific failures, attributable to loopholes or inadequate regulation, surfaced, questioning its adequacy. Faced with these challenges, EU regulators reacted at an unprecedented speed, justified by the willingness to address shortcomings at EU level, but also stimulated by the 2009 European Parliament elections and the appointment of a new Commission. A range of legislative proposals was worked out and expeditively turned into law (e.g. amendments to the CRD and the DGS directive, regulation of credit-rating agencies, rules for hedge funds and private equity, rules on remuneration policies, amendments to accounting rules; Commission 2009d). This demonstrates that a framework is in place that is solid enough to allow for rapid regulatory adjustments, something which is particularly important for the feasibility of banking regulation in the EU. Yet the viability of the whole EU banking framework would require more than quick *ex post* regulatory adaptations. The shortcomings in regulation actually mirror the inadequate arrangements for real-time monitoring of market developments and for ensuring prompt adjustments and intervention before the situation becomes too critical. Speeding up regulation does not compensate for missing or inappropriate arrangements as regards oversight, control, timely adjustment, intervention and management of the application of banking regulation.

38 The Commission's strategy is enshrined in the White Paper on Financial Services Policy 2005–10, published on 5 December 2005, built on a consultative Green Paper that was published on 3 May 2005.

It is undeniable that at EU level there are powerful tools which promote the cross-border provision of banking activities, especially through a common regulatory framework. There was sustained political willingness in the EU to combine imperative regulatory needs determined by market developments with a strengthened commitment to achieving full integration between the Member States' financial markets. However, the measures adopted until the 1990s did not succeed in accomplishing the single European banking market. The measures implemented since the 1990s to address remaining fragmentation (FSAP and post-FSAP strategies) have definitely contributed to further dismantling barriers and achieving more integration in the banking markets. Yet they also have triggered greater risks because of increased interdependence and homogeneous developments. The existing framework could not prevent the financial collapse, nor were there arrangements in place to address appropriately common prudential concerns and crisis management at EU level.

This leads us to maintain that, from a regulatory perspective, we face a single European banking market 'under construction'. Albeit in an advanced phase, the framework that should sustain this single banking market is still lacking important pieces. Because of the crisis, there is now increased political willingness to consider filling in such gaps at EU level and intensive debates are being held throughout Europe. We will discuss these aspects in detail in later chapters. What we have pursued with this short account of the EU regulatory framework is to ascertain the commitment to the single European banking market objective, as well as the existence of a robust regulatory foundation on which it can build to attain the desired results.

3.2 The impact of the euro on banking

A bulk of new academic literature recognises the impact of currency unification on market integration (Rose 2000). Expectations were high and started to materialise, thus demonstrating that the single currency constitutes a powerful catalyst in contributing to further integration in financial markets.

It is beyond doubt that the single currency had the capacity to overcome some of the barriers that kept both the banking market segmented and cross-border penetration small. It was observed that Economic and Monetary Union (EMU) eliminates two sources of segmentation: exchange rate risk and the advantages enjoyed by the local banks because of their greater familiarity with domestic monetary policy (Vives 1991: 6). In addition, Vives considers that the euro makes pricing more transparent and reduces transaction costs. The consequences have been an increase of competition in the banking market, the deepening and expansion of the financial markets and an accelerated restructuring of the banking sector. However, overall segmentation could not be eliminated, but only reduced, because of barriers in retail banking (e.g. bank–client relationships), differences in preferences and culture between the Member States. Another effect brought about by the euro is that it has fostered the internationalisation of banking activities, and contributed in particular to the rapid integration of the wholesale and capital markets, as well as large-value payment systems (Duisenberg 2000; Bini Smaghi and Gros 2000).

The euro has also had an important impact on financial stability. A positive aspect is that wider euro-area money markets can more easily absorb liquidity shortages than before, as banks can borrow more readily from foreign institutions. The other side of the coin, however, consists of the facilitation of a spilling over into other euro-area countries of potential financial instabilities. Both aspects have been obvious in the current crisis. Generally, the EMU has been perceived as highly beneficial in the light of the crisis. The euro has been a powerful shield against currency speculations and the intervention of the ECB through the injection of liquidity in the markets was salutary, not only for EMU members.

Overall, it seems that the existence of a single currency and of a single central bank emphasises the capacity of the European financial sector to become more integrated. However, refusal of some Member States to adopt the euro, as well as the entry of the new Member States to the EU, of which only a few became ready to join the EMU,[39] could mitigate excessive enthusiasm about the integrative force of the euro. Yet preparation for adopting the euro in most of the new Member States is a powerful force driving towards integration of their banking markets into a single European financial market.

In conclusion, the question posed in the title of this section may be answered in the positive, with the addition of a qualifying remark: there is a single European banking market under construction. The construction of a common banking market aims at achieving integration, but also sustainable stability of financial markets. The crisis has revealed inadequacies and gaps in the existing EU regulatory framework and stimulated political willingness to repair it and to promote further integration. The advent of the euro has had an important contribution in re-shaping markets and opening up further integration perspectives. Such developments highlight that it is a crucial momentum that should not be missed if decision-makers are genuinely interested in promoting the benefits of a single, integrated and especially stable banking market.

39 The following new Member States have adopted the euro: Slovenia in 2007, Cyprus and Malta in 2008, and Slovakia in 2009.

2 Insights from regulatory theory

'Banking regulation' is, without doubt, part of the standard rhetoric of the literature on economics. Nevertheless, there is no consensus about its exact meaning, contents or even necessity. Hence, there is a certain discomfort for lawyers when operating with the various dimensions of banking regulation, and there are difficulties in differentiating prudential regulation from other types of banking regulation.

Although we do not aim to set this essentially political–economic concept as a univocal category for legal professionals, we hope to identify its underpinnings so as to ensure its consistent reception in the legal discourse related to prudential aspects. In doing so, we will make use of instruments provided by general regulatory theory, which appears to us as being the most appropriate for explaining developments in banking regulation. Our regulatory theory account is simple and descriptive, as our aim here is merely to introduce the reader to the underlying complexity of prudential banking regulation. However, a deeper analysis would be required to anchor prudential issues more firmly into a coherent regulatory theory.

We will start by reviewing the economic rationale behind public intervention in the banking market, and then proceed by identifying the corresponding policy reactions. Subsequently, we will identify the different typologies of regulation and their characteristics. Lastly, we will briefly explain the role of markets in the heavily regulated banking environment.

1 The rationale for banking regulation in economic theory

The examination of economic theory may constitute a helpful background for understanding the necessity of banking legislation. In the following pages, we will systemise, in a critical account, the arguments invoked in the literature for justifying regulation, underlying the aspects most pertinent for identifying prudential issues.

Traditionally, neo-classic economic theory explained regulation (as a form of State intervention) by observing that the assumptions of welfare economics about the market system[1] are not verified in the real world, and thus provide scope for 'market failures'. While the unregulated marketplace was considered the norm (the free market presumption), any government intervention had to be justified in terms of public objectives to demonstrate added value. There is a certain difficulty in differentiating between rationale and objectives of regulation and an imperative to corroborate economic and political theories for justifying its existence. When analysing the rationale for banking regulation we will refer to those economic factors that trigger a demand for regulation, while keeping in mind that objectives of regulation refer to the outcome that this form of public intervention aims to achieve.

We take up the distinction between economic and social regulation, as developed by regulation theorists (Majone 1996: 47). Although this typology is constructed in a very broad manner, it is suitable for understanding the reasons behind bank regulation and its evolution. Generally, *economic regulation* is used as a tool for restraining market power; thus, it is usually concerned with prices, profits, entry requirements and natural monopoly situations in certain industries. *Social regulation* typically deals with safety, as well as consumer protection issues, and takes the form of standards enforceable by government agencies.

1.1 The rationale for the economic regulation of banks

With respect to banking, economic regulation comprises those norms setting limits on prices charged by the banking industry (interest rates charged on loans or paid on deposits, fees applied for financial services), limiting the fields of activities or the branching locations, as well as setting entry requirements. The reasons behind such regulation may be synthesised into three categories: preventing banks from obtaining excessive economic power, suppressing competition, and concerns about the control over the money supply.

The fear of economically strong banks was one of the main concerns of US banking regulators and was translated into branching and activity restrictions. These regulatory limits were largely waived as a result of the deregulation that has occurred in the US since the 1980s, although some

1 Anthony Ogus analyses five assumptions of the market system: *individualism*, which maintains that social welfare can be understood as the aggregate of all individual welfare; *utility-maximising behaviour*, which assumes that individuals behave rationally so as to maximise their utility; *information*, which supposes that all market participants dispose of the information necessary for making utility-maximising choices; *the absence of externalities*, which assumes that allocative efficiency will only result if decision-making in the production process takes account of external costs and benefits; and *competitive markets*, which maintains that the existence of competition is crucial for the allocation of resources in a market system. Market failures arise because of the lack of fulfilment of these assumptions, notably adequate information, competition and the absence of externalities (Ogus 1994: 23).

restrictions were preserved (White 2002). On the contrary, economic bank regulation has been rather exceptional in Europe, where financial activities are dominated by the universal banking model and where banking regulators strongly encouraged branching in the quest to establish a single banking market.

Economic banking regulation in Europe was traditionally justified on the basis of the money supply and competition arguments (Wörner 2000). Thus, it was assumed that the efficiency of monetary policy measures is dependent upon the behaviour of banks. Competition in the banking market was seen as encouraging banks to maximise their profits by extending the amount of credits awarded and thereby threatening the stability of the currency through uncontrolled expansion of money supply. Further, it was argued that competition considerations might induce banks to delay the implementation of monetary policy measures. On the basis of these two arguments, it was held that properly designed limitations of competition, interest rate arrangements and credit ceilings could secure that money creation and interest rates develop in line with the objectives of the monetary authority (Wörner 2000: 64). Under this perspective, monetary policy is at the same time an objective to be protected by restricting competition between banks and the very rationale for regulation, given its potential to distort competition.

These arguments have been strongly criticised and considered superseded (Benston 2000). It was demonstrated that the money creation capacity of credit institutions can be controlled through the available amount of central bank money (Becker 1980: 248) and without needing to restrict competition for this purpose. Furthermore, competition restrictions can be counterproductive for the efficient implementation of monetary policy measures, while a functional competitive banking market has its merits (Becker 1980: 254).

Another aspect of economic regulation deserves to be mentioned: the so-called must-serve obligations. These refer to those regulations requiring that banks provide services to specific industry sectors and/or specific geographic areas and/or specific categories of end-users. The issue, which is also termed 'general access to banks', focuses on the problems related to the risk of financial exclusion. As it may entail regulatory intervention that interferes with entrepreneurial freedom by imposing the performance of specific activities in the public interest, the issue is at the crossroads of economic and social regulation. It is still to be ascertained whether such situations would constitute a rationale for banking regulation, whether such societal outcomes would be imposed on banks or rather on specific societal-oriented or non-profit entities, and to what extent they would overburden the system.[2]

2 This issue was developed in the United States, where must-serve obligations have been a reality. In Europe, they emerged only recently; see Commission 2008a.

Although it has been harshly criticised, it would be hazardous to conclude that there is no rationale at all for justifying economic regulation in the banking sector. We cannot do this here, especially because of the vague terms we have used to define economic regulation, which impede the accurate designation of a particular banking rule as pure economic regulation. Moreover, it is a reality that for several policy reasons banking regulation still contains norms aimed at restricting the exercise of market power in many instances. Also, the 2007–9 crisis brings the case for economic regulation of banks into the spotlight. This was the issue of 'too-big-to-fail' that justified public rescues of banks, because their systemic importance can ultimately be seen in terms of excessive power resulting from the unfettered expansion of the scope and scale of financial intermediaries' activities. Similarly, excessively intensive competition in financial markets may be perceived as an important driver in the race to the bottom as regards underwriting and credit standards. Also, the heavy presence of the State nowadays in the banking markets has triggered and will further push for policy measures that fall under the category of economic regulation. State control of large parts of the banking industry is often accompanied by imposed lending targets, limits on remuneration and constraints on the development of global strategies, to which important distortions of competition may be attached. Furthermore, the link between the loose monetary policy and banks' securitisation strategies against the background of favourable macro-economic conditions has to be thoroughly analysed. All these arguments prove that the debate on the rationale of economic regulation has been opened again and awaits new arguments.

1.2 The rationale for the social regulation of banks

'Social regulation', also called health–safety–environment (HSE) regulation, typically refers to issues that concern the protection of consumers, understood in its broadest sense. Social regulation targeting banking is designated as 'safety-and-soundness' regulation and especially includes: capital requirements; several kinds of limitations on banks' exposures; requirements on standardised information to be provided by banks; and rules concerning the corporate governance structure of banks. In a nutshell, all those rules are considered which aim to ensure that banks behave in such a way as supports the stability of the banking system and the confidence of its users.

The economics literature is largely divided as regards the economic rationale behind safety-and-soundness regulation of banks.[3] The variety of justifications identified may be broadly subsumed into two categories corresponding to the two motives justifying social regulation in general: the concern with

3 For two opposing approaches, see Llewellyn 1999b and Benston 1998, 2000.

informational deficiencies (information asymmetries) and the concern with negative externalities (spill-over effects). Within these two broad justifications for banking regulation, we can discern several dimensions.

Information asymmetries

Asymmetric information is a paradigm inherent to financial transactions in general. It stems from the time sequencing structure of financial contracts, which are based on an initial transfer of money from a lender to a borrower and the subsequent repayment. Several transformations in the borrower's position might occur in this time interval, so that repayment could be endangered. Informational deficiencies between the borrower and the lender adversely affect the latter's ability to assess the prospects of repayment. These informational deficiencies are termed 'asymmetric' because one party to the transaction has at its disposal information which it can use unilaterally to its own advantage. There are two types of information asymmetries: hidden information and hidden action (Wörner 2000: 67).

Hidden information relates to difficulties in ascertaining objectively the quality of products or services purchased. With respect to banking, this type of informational asymmetry directly affects the assessment of an essential qualitative characteristic of deposits: their security. The security of deposits is dependent upon the bank's ability to repay the liabilities it has taken (the bank's creditworthiness). The evaluation of a bank's creditworthiness relies on extensive information concerning the business policy of the bank, its capital, and the type and extent of risks taken. It involves sophisticated processes of interpreting not only the balance sheet, but also the worthiness over time of every single credit arrangement incurred by the bank and the real value of its portfolio of assets.

There is already a striking information asymmetry in favour of a credit institution at the time of the conclusion of a deposit contract. The bank best knows its own risk characteristics and the prospects for repayment of its customers (deposit holders). Prices (interest rates) do not have the ability to reflect the risk position of a bank; on the contrary, they may have perverse effects. Especially under high competitive pressure, the bank will be willing to risk by attracting more deposits through the offer of high interest rates. Adverse selection[4] may occur because depositors will choose higher interest rates without considering the solidity of the offering institution. Instead, the less risky banks will find it difficult to get an adequate price for their services.

4 'Adverse selection' refers to a market failure that reflects the likelihood of making the wrong choice of bad business opportunities, while ignoring good ones, especially because of information asymmetries. The problematic is also known as 'lemon market effects', as it was developed by reference to the automobile market in the US, where bad cars are known as lemons; see Akerlof 1970.

The hidden information paradigm reflects banks' role as 'information specialists' (White 2002: 143), while depositors are characterised by 'bounded rationality'.[5] Depositors are usually unlikely to be able to assess the riskiness of their bank (from the perspective of both its current risk profile and its risk appetite), to monitor its activity and to consequently protect themselves adequately. Correcting this market imperfection would require not only a high degree of information disclosure but especially an effective understanding of it. Such information can be obtained and interpreted only with high costs (Dermine 1996: 345). The depositor values these costs with respect to the costs likely to be incurred for the miscalculation of the risks implied by the loss of his or her deposit.

The second form of information asymmetries is termed *hidden action* (Wörner 2000: 68). It refers to the possibility of at least one of the parties to a transaction more or less perceptibly altering certain product characteristics or its own behaviour, during the contractual relationship, in its own favour and to the detriment of the other party. Especially in the case of long-term contracts characterised by time sequencing, each party can behave opportunistically so as to maximise its own interests and adjust its strategy, thereby rendering the other party more vulnerable.

Banks are particularly prone to this opportunistic behaviour because of the limited liability of their shareholders (Stiglitz 1972: 458) and the moral hazard[6] linked to it. Thus, in case of the failure of a risky business policy, the bank will participate in the losses just within the limits of its own capital – whereas losses that go beyond this threshold have to be borne by its creditors, including the depositors, who enjoy only limited protection through deposit guarantee schemes. On the contrary, if such a risky policy proves to be successful, banks will profit fully. As the bank's own capital is low with respect to the potential gains, it will be economically rational for the bank to enter into risky business. Moreover, poorly capitalised banks or those threatened by insolvency might try to stabilise their situation through such risky policies, at the expense of depositors and other creditors.

Creditors of the bank, especially small depositors, will most probably not be able to identify the deterioration of the quality of their investment after contracting. Distinguishing between risky and secure banks will become very difficult as banks are inclined to engage in ever more sophisticated risky policies, often behind attractive marketing strategies. This inevitably leads to a sub-optimal allocation of financial resources (Baltensperger 1988: 56).

5 The concept of bounded rationality refers to the limited capacity of individuals (depositors) to receive, store and process information; see Simon 1997.

6 The concept of moral hazard generally refers to the risk that a party to a transaction has not entered into a contract in good faith, has provided misleading information about its assets, liabilities or credit capacity, or has an incentive to take unusual risks in a desperate attempt to earn a profit before the contract settles; see Gastineau and Kritzman 1999.

Another form of information asymmetry is referred to in the economics literature as 'gridlock'. This occurs when banks, although conscious of their rational long-term interest not to behave against their clients' interests, still adopt risky strategies because of short-term advantages and because of the expectation that competitors will behave hazardously (Llewellyn 1999b: 27). This situation underlines information deficiencies between banks or between banks and other financial intermediaries, and may induce herd-like behaviour, also for competitive reasons. The moral hazard is provoked either by the bad behaviour observed in other competitors or by missing guarantees that the others will behave well. Herding induces homogeneous behaviour detrimental to due diligence requiring accurate risk assessments by each market participant. There is a case for regulation to break the gridlock by coercing all participants to behave within certain reasonable standards.

Last but not least, information asymmetries are linked to the complex products created and transacted by banks in the past decade. Structured finance is inherently hard to disentangle, as it involves the pooling of assets, their repackaging and slicing into tranches with various characteristics, destined for investors with different degrees of risk aversion. By their very structure these products are opaque, as information on the assets at the bottom of the pool, as well as on the underlying dynamics of the structured finance product, depends on the originator.

Market failures caused by asymmetric information have long been considered 'the primary and historical rationale for bank supervision' (Gardener 1986: 36). Information asymmetry takes a plurality of forms in the context of banking. As we have seen, information asymmetries preclude depositors from assessing the creditworthiness of a bank and implicitly the security of their deposits, both at the time of contracting and during the contractual relationship. This we consider to be the most important rationale, justifying public intervention aimed at addressing market failures of an informational nature. There is some information asymmetry also on the side of the bank with regard to the creditworthiness of loan takers, albeit less severe given banks' competitive advantages with regard to information. Yet, in the quest for higher yields and more clients, banks may have incentives to lower screening of their counterparties. Furthermore, information asymmetries relate to the behaviour of the other participants in the inter-bank market and in the payments system, as well as to the specificities of structured finance, and may induce herding behaviour.

All these are market failures that call for correction through some form of public intervention capable of enhancing the information available, preventing or limiting abuses and stimulating the alignment of incentives between the various participants in the banking market. Preserving confidence in financial markets is at the core of public intervention to correct information deficiencies (Llewellyn 1999c). Prudential standards are needed to give depositors some objective assurance about the quality of market participants and of products offered. As revealed by the crisis, public intervention is also needed for restoring confidence between financial intermediaries themselves. This requires substantial targeted interventions, such as explicit and implicit guarantees of soundness, and arrangements warranting firm supervisory action.

Negative externalities

The second category of market imperfections requiring banking regulation consists of negative externalities due to spill-over effects, which adversely affect third parties. Banks' behaviour does not only impact on those with whom they deal directly, but may have a bearing on third parties. This usually involves social costs that are not always reflected in the prices of bank products, so that market participants may have incentives to behave in a way leading to a misallocation of resources. The current crisis plainly illustrates these negative externalities: the banking crisis spread into the whole financial sector and from there into the real economy, which then suffered intensively because of the credit squeeze. Moreover, governments have committed large parts of taxpayers' money to save banks and restore confidence in financial markets.

The most prominent negative externalities occurring in the banking business are discussed in the literature under the heading of systemic risk or contagion risk. Contagion may arise in two ways: through real exposure or through information channels. There is no univocal understanding of systemic risk; economists use this concept for the description of various phenomena, ranging from 'crises related to the payment systems, to bank runs and banking panics, to spill-over effects between financial markets, up to a very broadly understood notion of financially-driven macroeconomic crises' (Summer 2002: 8). Indeed, banks are particularly prone to panics, contagion and systemic crises because of real financial linkages, because of the nature of bank contracts (transforming short-term liabilities into long-term assets), because of the likelihood of panic spreading and because of the impact of safety-net arrangements.

Informational contagion relates traditionally to the fact that banks are potentially subject to runs, reflecting depositors' reaction to negative news about the creditworthiness of their bank. Because of information asymmetries resulting in quality uncertainties, depositors will lose confidence in the repayment ability of their bank and rush to withdraw their deposits. As depositors know that latecomers may not be paid in full, they will all immediately withdraw their money to minimise losses, triggering the rapid exhaustion of the liquidity reserves of the bank. This phenomenon is called 'self-fulfilling prophecy', as the mechanism is such that, regardless of its correctness, information may cause a bank run just because it entails the mere supposition that other depositors will withdraw their funds (Herring and Litan 1995: 150). This may even cause a solvent bank to become insolvent, because it will be forced urgently to dispose of its assets that are likely to be sold below their real value (Llewellyn 1999c: 4). However, if the massive withdrawal is confined to one or few banks, it is expected that there will be enough liquidity in the inter-bank market to cover needs of solvent banks. Many economists argue that there is little evidence that bank runs cause solvent banks to become insolvent (Kaufman 1994; Benston 1998). The crisis also did not provide much evidence of the link between runs and insolvency. For instance, in the case of Northern Rock, it is held that insolvency was linked to its business and funding structure, whereas the massive withdrawals by retail depositors were merely a reaction to signals received from better-informed wholesale depositors (O'Connor and Santos-Arteaga 2008: 359).

The hypothesis of chain reactions resulting in massive withdrawals is mitigated by the existence of deposit guarantee schemes. These are designed particularly to reassure depositors who cannot distinguish whether a bank's problems originate from internal bank-specific reasons or from problems within the entire banking system. The increase of coverage, the shortening of the pay-out period and the smoothening of procedures, as currently planned in the EU, are aimed at preventing panic situations.

Real contagion mechanisms in the banking system stem from the extensive interconnectedness among banks, owing to mutual risk exposures coming either from complex corporative structures or from linkages in the inter-bank market or payment systems. For instance, the short-term character of money market transactions, corroborated with the large amounts involved, might cause the insolvency of a debtor bank to trigger the inability of the creditor bank to fulfil its own liabilities (Rochet and Tirole 1996). Normally, isolated bank insolvencies should not destabilise the whole banking system, thanks to the limits and permanent surveillance imposed by netting agreements and real-time gross settlement systems.[7]

The contagion risk increases when a group of banks suddenly become insolvent (Wörner 2000: 73). There is not necessarily a need for general runs on the banking system to provoke its collapse. Close inter-linkages stemming from the wholesale markets' and banks' homogeneous funding strategies, and from deep connections intrinsic to the very nature of a wide range of financial products transacted by banks (securitised products, derivatives, etc.) and the general herding environment can be important catalysts of contagion in the system.

An important dimension of systemic concerns relates to the pivotal role that banks play in the economy and in the money circuit. It concerns the fact that disruptions in the banking system will most probably have a bearing on other non-bank financial institutions, as well as on the whole economy. The failure of a bank may impact directly on its corporate

7 During the current crisis the financial infrastructure as a whole was submitted to a tough test. Fortunately, payment systems, clearing and settlement systems as well as organised exchanges were sufficiently resilient to withstand the shocks.

clients. As is apparent from the credit squeeze in 2008–9, banking crises inevitably affect the money supply, thereby triggering negative effects on demand and production in the whole economy.

Last but not least, negative externalities are implied by moral hazard linked to the safety-net arrangements. The latter are often praised for their capacity to prevent bank runs and contagion (Benston and Smith 1976; Kaufman 1994; and see also McCoy 2008). However, they also entail severe moral hazard problems, which often question the very necessity for such arrangements. Irrespective of discussions about the benefits and disadvantages implied, safety-nets have become 'a fact of economic life' (Benston 2000: 196) – and their role in preventing panic among retail costumers of banks is crucial during a crisis. Yet their effective use implies enormous costs that most often involve public money. Consequently, there is a role for banking regulation to counter the moral hazard by removing the possibility of exploiting it excessively.

The two typical forms of safety-net arrangements are government-provided deposit insurance and the lender of last resort (LOLR). Deposit insurance has the purpose of covering depositors' losses in the case of a bank failure, thus removing the rationality of immediate massive withdrawals and halting panic reactions. This triggers a moral hazard for depositors, who are likely to be less concerned with the solvency of their bank as long as they are sure of the repayment. They will simply look for banks offering high interest rates. The most serious moral hazard exists on the part of banks, as safety-nets are likely to multiply the risk appetite already stimulated by limited liability. The explicit protection of all or part of the deposits through legislation is likely to create perverse incentives for banks to take on added risks, as possible losses are largely guaranteed through deposit insurance. Furthermore, the risk-stimulus coming from deposit insurance is likely to proliferate even more in an environment characterised by globalisation and financial innovation, as banks enter new, riskier segments of the financial markets (Litan 1985: 21; Hoenig 1998: 791; McCoy 2008: 425).

Similar perverse incentives for taking excessive risks are also linked to the LOLR. LOLR refers to extraordinary loans offered to institutions in financial difficulty and to the injection of system-wide liquidity by the central bank to restore financial stability. LOLR-related moral hazard implications are reinforced by the constructive ambiguity inherent to the LOLR function (i.e. the uncertainty attached to its use). This form of moral hazard especially affects banks' incentives to properly select and monitor borrowers (Freixas *et al.* 2003).

Before the crisis, systemic issues were often underestimated. However, the probability of risk always has to be weighed against the seriousness of eventual risks occurring (Llewellyn 1999c). As proved by the 2007–9 crisis, once the systemic breakdown occurs, it involves particularly high costs that do not allow for neglecting spill-over effects – although their likelihood may be perceived as relatively reduced.

2 Policy objectives of banking regulation

So far, we have identified several instances of market failure, which on the basis of economic theory would call for correction by way of public intervention. This section examines how these shortcomings are addressed by the State, and whether and to what extent government intervention may correct them. When doing this we will focus on regulation as the most common form of public policy response, yet it should be considered that State intervention can take also other forms of intervention, as occurred during 2007–9 (e.g. recapitalisation, nationalisation, provision of explicit or implicit guarantees, liquidity injection, etc.).

Traditionally, regulatory theory attempts to explain the role of regulation are divided into two broad categories, one emphasising the public interest dimension, the other highlighting the importance of private interests in the regulatory process. More recent hybrid approaches focus on the dynamic aspects of markets. We will shortly review these theories by selecting in simple terms those aspects that we perceive as relevant for explaining public intervention vis-à-vis the economic rationales indicated in the previous section. These theories should be seen not as competing but as complementary approaches explaining the complexity of strategies underpinning State intervention.

2.1 The public interest approach

The conventional view of regulation, rooted in the welfare economics of A. Pigou (1932) and. P. Samuelson (1947), is that of a response to the deficiencies of an unfettered market (Ogus 1994: 28–54). Focusing on the interests of consumers, regulation is considered to be supplied in response to the public's demand for relief from inequitable or inefficient market practices (Gardener 1986: 30). The central element of the public interest approach is the concept of 'public good', from which the public as a whole or some group within it should benefit.[8] The core objective of regulatory measures is to protect consumers against market failures, notably monopoly, imperfect information and externalities. Consequently, regulation is viewed mainly as a remedy.

Under the public interest approach, banking regulation exists for the exclusive benefit of depositors and investors, actual and potential. State intervention is demanded to protect depositors' and investors' assets and to

8 Ogus describes public goods as having two characteristics: consumption by one person does not leave less for others to consume, and it is impossible or too costly for the supplier to exclude those who do not pay for the benefit (Ogus 1994: 33). Other theoretical accounts emphasise the non-exclusivity (i.e. excluding someone from consumption does not bring benefits) and non-rivalry (consumers' behaviour does not influence others' capacity to consume). It is held that State intervention is warranted because of 'free rider' concerns as regards insufficient provision by the market; see Musgrave 1959.

reduce their exposure to the risk of bank failure and insolvency. Security – understood as safety and stability – of the banking system represents a public good.[9]

Moreover, under the public interest approach information is also considered a public good and transparency a policy objective to be pursued in the interest of all stakeholders. Information is an important tool for establishing depositors' and investors' confidence, which is a key aspect of banking stability. As discussed, information deficiencies in the banking business call for corrective measures and guarantees for reliable information. Regulation combined with supervision may respond to such public demand.

In this context, the public interest hypothesis traditionally seemed to fit well with the rationale for economic and social regulation of banking. However, strong criticism emerged, considering this approach to be inconsistent and irreconcilable with reality. Theories on regulatory failure indicate that regulation, focusing exclusively on alleged public interest goals, does not always succeed in correcting market failures or does so in an inefficient way, by making other sectors worse off or by entailing excessive administrative costs (Ogus 1994: 55–7). Sometimes State intervention in the public interest may create a supplementary rationale for regulation, as in the case of moral hazard determined by safety-net arrangements. Moreover, there are no clear criteria for translating the defined public interest goals into the adequate regulatory action. Last, but not least, regulation is not always meant to promote strict public interest; in several cases it reflects the interests of individual actors involved in the specific sector.

This criticism does not mean that the public interest approach should be abandoned altogether as being unable to explain banking regulation. On the contrary, it seems to be still very attractive in many regards and ultimately it is still used to justify some forms of intervention, like safety-nets and the LOLR function. If it is not expected to exhaust explanations for banking regulation, it may be seen as a good starting point, as ultimately State intervention entails a market corrective dimension in the interest of the public at large.

2.2 The self-interest theory of regulation

As a response to the intense criticism of the public interest approach of regulation, a new ideology evolved, focusing on the pursuit of private interests. The new trend has also been labelled the 'capture hypothesis', because it generically maintains that the failure of regulation to attain purported public interest goals 'could most plausibly be explained by assuming that they had been subverted (captured) by pressure, influence and

9 This idea has been further developed to claim the existence of an alleged right to security of systems, which would correspond to a new type of subjective rights; see Frison-Roche 2000.

"bribery" to protect the interests of those who were the subjects of the regulation' (Ogus 1994: 57). There are several versions of the capture theory, of which two variants that developed into self-contained theories seem to have a bearing on banking regulation: the public choice theory and the economic theory of regulation.

Based on welfare economics, the public choice theory starts from the idea that what is good for society is the aggregate of individual preferences (Ogus 1994: 55–75). Thus, market failures can be corrected only by collective choice. Legislation is seen as a response to the demand of private interests, expressed in voting and other procedures employed by institutions for collective choice. Under public choice theory, it is assumed that, similar to market behaviour, voting behaviour reflects individual preferences taken by rational utility maximisers. Although votes do not show the intensity of preferences, the study of voting practices, as well as of organisations influencing policy-making (bureaucracies, interest groups), is held to be important for predicting the amount and nature of regulation supplied for private interests.

On the basis of the public choice theory and using conventional tools of economic analysis, the economic theory of regulation, elaborated by Stigler and further developed by Posner and Peltzman, concentrates on explaining 'who will receive the benefits and burdens of regulation, what form regulation will take, and the effects of regulation upon the allocation of resources' (Stigler 1978: 3). It relies on two assumptions. First, demanders of regulation are usually small groups (especially large producers), which, through the homogeneity of interests and relatively low organisation costs, seek to increase their wealth, sometimes to the detriment of others (rent-seeking). Second, suppliers of regulation are politicians in quest of political support, who ultimately impose or reduce regulation only when this action gives them more net votes than do alternative choices. Hence, it is held that 'as a rule, regulation is acquired by the industry and is designed and operated primarily for its benefit' (Stigler 1978: 3).

Under this theory, it is held that vote-maximising politicians tend to favour minorities and distribute costs more or less perceptibly to the whole electorate, although the social costs might outweigh the benefits of the favoured group. In banking, it is more likely that a group of banks will influence the outcome of regulation than the larger mass of small depositors. Also, within a pluralistic banking market interests are not necessarily aligned and different groups will tend to impose their views on the whole market (national options and discretions in EU legislation reflect this situation). Another illustration of the capture theory in banking is the case of crisis management and resolution through public bail-outs and liquidity injections, at the expense of taxpayers.

Another dimension of the private interest approach to regulation concerns the self-interests of bureaucrats, whether identified with budget maximisation or bureau-shaping, which are also considered to play a role in determining the form and content of banking regulation (Breton and Wintrobe 1982; Jackson 1982). The innovative character of banking activities constitutes an incentive for bureaucrats to extend their activities. Thus, bureaucrats are most likely to bring about a greater volume of regulation than that justified on the grounds of public interest.

The criticism of the self-interest theories centres on the narrow interpretation of private interests, which are identified with material gains or other wealth-maximising means (Ogus 1994: 73–5). Private interests, however, cannot be reduced to rational egotism (Rubin 1991: 17); they are often motivated by broader desires or needs (like altruism or ideology). At the same time, there is no conclusive evidence of straightforward correlation between financial benefits of individuals and their voting behaviour. Further, this approach is criticised for ignoring the fact that certain interests, such as consumer protection, may also profit the regulated industry. Also, it is unable to explain deregulation.

The synthetic overview of the private interest theories serves to provide a broader picture of the various issues behind regulation and the forces influencing those responsible for creating regulation. Actors involved in shaping policy will not always altruistically look for the maximisation of general welfare, and often are only concerned with their own objectives. If policy responses neglect this aspect, market failures may remain uncorrected or may even be aggravated.

2.3 Incentive–conflict theories of regulation

In response to criticism concerning the altruistic public interest theory, as well as the private benefits theory of regulation, economists have developed an alternative based on incentive–conflict explanations that looks for mechanisms to reconcile conflict between the private and societal goals (Kane 1997: 51). This theory takes a starting point from Hayek's observation that the advantages of a decentralised market economy lie particularly in its dynamic abilities to create market endogenous norms and institutions responding to new realities (Hayek 1952). It recognises the capacity of private parties to organise themselves in order to provide efficient regulatory discipline. It is assumed that 'rational self-interested people involved in co-operative endeavours always have incentives to reduce or control conflicts of interest so as to reduce the losses resulting from them' (Jensen 1994: 45). According to this theory, the role of a trustworthy outsider regulator is to mediate transactions entailing divergent interests and to improve the fairness, efficiency and enforceability of contracts.

There are two essential concepts in incentive–conflict theory: regulatory competition and principal–agent relationship. Regulatory competition reflects the idea that the incentive conflict needs to be solved by a mix of private and government regulation.[10] Under the incentive–conflict analysis, financial regulators are viewed as 'self-interested agents that compete atomistically to serve multiple principals: society and private sectoral interests whose goals diverge in part from societal goals' (Kane 1997: 51). This theory focuses on appropriate accountability mechanisms for agents towards all principals.

Briefly, the incentive–conflict theory emphasises the powerful role of market mechanisms in achieving regulatory objectives (e.g. correcting market failures). Government regulation is primarily directed at efficiently reconciling conflicts between the regulated and society (taxpayers) and ensuring fairness, efficiency and enforceability in transactions. The trustworthiness of regulators has to be strengthened by regulating the regulators through aligning public and private regulatory incentives. Emphasis is put on transparency and accountability, as regulators are supposed to make the right trade-off between industry's specific goals and societal goals.

This theory gives us an additional perspective on the regulatory problematic that does not necessarily have the ambition of rejecting other theories. With regard to banking, it can support the role of market discipline, as well as spread awareness about the regulators' incentives behind the policy goals they chose to pursue. Thus, in combination with the public interest and private interest theories, it may provide a conclusive explanation of policy objectives behind banking regulation.

These three theories do not exhaust the bulk of policy arguments brought forth in elucidating government intervention. However, they do offer three complementary perspectives and underline the complexity of the regulatory process. It is important for us to always bear in mind, when discussing a certain aspect of banking regulation, that there are public as well as private interests and mechanisms involved, which have to be reconciled. The 'proper' legal framework has to accommodate and guide the pursuit of self-interest by all parties (including regulators) so that it can be consistent with the public good.

Our analysis of prudential regulation will implicitly consider the various aspects highlighted when discussing the economic rationale and policy justifications of banking regulation. The assessment of the substantive and institutional issues related to European prudential supervision will entail the identification of the various stakeholders; their interests and the way they are represented in the institutional framework; the precise objectives; the added value of regulation; the various incentive structures; and the sanctions attached.

10 Thus, for instance, the competition between information produced by private rating agencies or accounting and auditing firms, on the one hand, and regulatory disclosure requirements, on the other hand, would be seen as beneficial for society as it will produce more reliable information about individual banks and the banking system in general.

We may draw out some immediate observations from this introductory account. Economic analysis demonstrates that banks are powerful actors in the economy that may put third parties at risk, either because of an abuse of their power position, or by taking advantage of information asymmetries, or because of negative externalities arising in an increasingly interconnected financial system. Public interest theories suggest that the public goods to be protected by banking regulation so as to correct the mentioned market failures are consumer protection and financial stability. The self-interest approach to regulation warns that banking regulators faced with conflicting goals are inclined to deviate from the exclusive pursuit of public goals and may follow their own interests (e.g. facilitating their control function, increasing their budgetary resources, bureau-shaping). Besides, regulators are also prone to be captured by groups with strongly delineated private interests. At the same time, incentive–conflict theories of regulation maintain that the regulatory creation of incentives capable of inducing all market participants to internalise the public goals, together with the attribution of a controlling role to the public regulator, is likely to be more successful. This implies that once its rationale is firmly ascertained, banking regulation requires a two-stage analysis: from the perspective of its general objectives, and from the point of view of its capacity to steer concrete behaviour in view of attaining those objectives.

3 Typology of banking regulation

As observed, banking regulation may be approached from the perspective of the protected objectives and from the point of view of its effects on market participants. Each approach allows the identification of several types of banking regulation.

3.1 Categories of banking regulation by objective

The two generic public objectives, the protection of consumers and the stability of the banking system, are inherent in all banking regulation. Nevertheless, according to the intensity with which each of these objectives is pursued by a concrete regulatory measure, we may distinguish between various categories of regulation: conduct of business regulation, prudential regulation and protective regulation. In this context we use regulation in its broadest sense, so that it is not confined to formal rules but encompasses all forms of legal control which are primarily enforced by a public institution. Regulation thus implies the processes of rule setting, monitoring and enforcement and their manifold modalities.

Consumer protection is central to *conduct of business regulation*, which sets rules that constrain banks to appropriate behaviour and business practices with their customers. This type of regulation includes requirements on mandatory disclosures, conditions for ensuring the honesty and integrity of firms and their employees, rules defining fair business practices and preventing fraudulent dealings, standards for marketing financial products, guidelines for the objectivity of advice, etc. (Llewellyn 1999c: 11). Public conduct of business regulation particularly characterises the investment sector, whereas in the banking sector the corresponding standards are mainly set via industry self-regulation.

Prudential regulation is intended to assure soundness and safety in the banking market by pursuing both objectives: financial stability and consumer protection (referred to as depositor protection). It is concerned with preventive aspects aimed at ensuring financial health and forestalling failures in banking markets. It has two dimensions: at the micro-level, it addresses the solvency and reliability of individual banks, and at the macro-level, it is concerned with the stability of the whole banking system. The case for micro-prudential regulation is made especially by information asymmetries between banks and their customers and by the propensity of banks to behave hazardously because of safety-net arrangements. Thus, guarantees have to be established for keeping risk-taking within reasonable levels and maintaining consumer confidence. The macro- (or systemic) dimension of prudential bank regulation responds to concerns raised by spill-over aspects and information deficiencies regarding the whole financial system. No clear line can be drawn between these two strongly interrelated dimensions; however, their distinct relevance is particularly apparent with regard to the organisation of supervision.

There is also a third category of bank regulation dealing with the resolution of bank failures, which has been termed *protective regulation* (Cranston 1997: 84). It sets the framework for intervention and rescue policies and provides more or less explicit resolution methods, especially once a crisis is imminent. The instruments provided by such regulation range from reorganisation to liquidation and public bail-outs. Safety-net arrangements (LOLR facilities and deposit insurance) are also included in the category of protective banking regulation. Such usually extremely costly *ex post* intervention is justified by the need to contain the proportions of a crisis and prevent it from spreading to the financial system or even to the economy as a whole.

All these general categories contribute to safeguarding the two public values, and are thereby closely linked to each other. Some rules may be included in more than one category. It is prudential regulation in the broad sense[11] and its various dimensions that will be handled in detail in this book. While focusing on prudential rules, our analysis will sometimes inevitably slip into aspects related to the other two categories.

11 'Prudential regulation' is broadly used when referring to the rules proposing substantive standards, monitoring and enforcement. In the narrow sense 'prudential regulation' refers only to substantive rules, whereas 'supervision' is generally applied to designate the effective monitoring and enforcement of prudential standards.

The concept of 'prudential' is highly equivocal and does not enjoy a common understanding either in the literature or in practice.[12] Legislation avoids defining it and confines itself to listing non-exhaustive and amendable lists of prudential elements relevant for individual pieces of law.[13] The specialist literature has not produced a mainstream understanding of 'prudential', but proposes different scopes for the concept according to the focus of the analysis. Variations specifically concern the inclusion/exclusion into the concept of the systemic/macro-dimension of the conduct-of-business aspects and/or of aspects related to safety-nets, crisis management and resolution. Uncertainties about the meaning of the concept are linked to its dynamic nature and illustrative of the necessity to adjust the scope and content of prudential measures and procedures to financial market developments.

When initiating our research we have opted to distinguish between prudential, conduct-of-business and protective rules for rather pragmatic reasons related to the need to delimitate more specifically the topic of the research. Our choice was determined by the rather neutral *ex ante/ex post* criterion of whether the primary objective of specific measures is to prevent a certain situation or to provide for remedies. This does not exclude the possibility that the same measure pursues further subordinate or ancillary objectives. Thus, we considered prudential measures to be characterised by the immediate and primary goal of safeguarding the 'soundness and safety' of individual institutions and of the system as a whole, *ex ante*, in order to prevent failures or crises from occurring. On the contrary, we consider that the primary focus of public intervention in relation to safety-nets and crisis management is chiefly on remedies to be applied *ex post*, once breaches or failures have occurred. In the case of protective regulation there is also an important subordinate *ex ante* dimension emphasising the need to establish in advance a clear framework for intervention, which should not be neglected. We could also qualify conduct-of-business regulation as *ex post* if we consider that, in banking, rules of conduct have traditionally constituted and, to a large extent, still constitute the remit of industry self-regulation, whereas public regulation focuses mainly on ensuring proper enforcement and remedies. Yet we admit that our distinction is somewhat artificial. The crisis has revealed deep interconnections between prudential supervision, safety-net and crisis management arrangements. For the same pragmatic reasons we will continue to include the latter aspects under the umbrella of a distinct category (protective regulation) and refer to them only marginally in this book, without, however, intending to minimise their relevance.

12 For a detailed and critical review of the concept of 'prudential', see Andenas and Hadjiemmanuil 1997: 403; Panourgias 2006: 9–17.

13 See, for instance, article 2(a) of the Annex on Financial Services to GATS; and Chapter 2, 'Technical instruments of prudential supervision', of the CRD.

3.2 Types of regulation by effect

Regulatory literature identifies various categories of regulation, according to their impact on shaping behaviour. This typology is useful for understanding that policy issues may be addressed in different ways and objectives pursued through the combination of various types of regulation. Subsuming a specific rule to a certain regulatory mode helps in identifying its addressees, the nature of the effects it hopes to obtain and the proper way of implementation and control. We see the following types of regulation as being relevant for banking: prescriptive regulation, contract regulation and incentive-based regulation.

Prescriptive banking regulation

Banking regulation, and most especially prudential regulation, tends to be particularly rules-based and prescriptive. This seems to be a common characteristic of financial regulation in general, because it is traditionally perceived in terms of command and control. A prescriptive approach focuses on specific steps required for the accomplishment of a determinate regulatory objective, whereby detailed rules precisely dictate what the regulated firm has to do and how it should do it. Prescriptive rules are the outcomes of the interaction between, on the one hand, the interests of regulators, who look for standards they may easily monitor and enforce, and, on the other hand, the interests of the regulated entities that seek standards they can easily comply with (Llewellyn 2001: 12, referring to Wallman 1999). Precision and detail in requirements on the part of the regulator correspond to the need for certainty and firm guidance on the part of the regulated.

There are several problems implied in a highly prescriptive approach to regulation, which are related to the fact that detailed rules address economic realities in a very fragmented way (Llewellyn 2001: 12–13). Prescriptive rules focus excessively on micro-aspects to the detriment of the macro-dimension. Prescriptive rules emphasise rather the different phases of a process, while the final general outcome risks being neglected. Operating by the letter of norms risks putting their spirit completely in the shadow. Moreover, no matter how detailed they are, rules can never encompass all facets and cannot catch all dynamic aspects of the market. Excessively prescriptive rules may easily be qualified as inflexible. They may concentrate on outdated situations, like the case of balance-sheet rules that reflect the position of a bank at a certain moment, which may change substantially over a short period of time. Rigid rules cannot grasp complex risks and do not respond to innovation. Furthermore, attempting to regulate all relevant aspects will result in rules being added over time, while few will be withdrawn. Over-regulation will be perceived as redundant and will fall into disrepute.

Additional criticism denounces the fact that an inflexible rules-based approach impedes banks from choosing their own least-cost way for meeting regulatory objectives. There is also scope for potential moral hazard, as long as banks may believe that if something is not yet regulated there is no regulatory dimension at all. In an ever dynamic financial environment where banks are confronted with deregulation and innovation, prescriptive regulation is likely to have stifling effects, as well as to be overtaken by reality.

Although specific and detailed rules have their advantages, especially with respect to legal certainty, they risk making abstraction of market situations. For prudential regulation this may equal regulatory failure. This is not to say that the prescriptive approach to regulation should be discarded altogether. On the contrary, we see the rules-based approach as the only way of setting meaningful thresholds and parameters, which are key to prudential issues. Some of the above-mentioned shortcomings can be addressed by establishing a procedural framework permitting quick and appropriate adjustments to regulation. To ensure, however, an overall picture, the prescriptive rules have to be combined with a different approach that allows comprehending and responding to developments that fall outside the pre-established categories. This could be a more principles-based or light-touch approach.

Contract regulation or incentive-based regulation

Contract regulation and incentive-based regulation represent alternatives to a rigid rules-based approach. The underlying idea is that a workable regulatory regime has to be anticipatory and capable of acknowledging and reacting flexibly to changes. This requirement implies to a certain extent a case-by-case approach, which would be impossible without cooperation of the regulated entities. This opens the door to some involvement of the regulated in the regulatory process and can shift certain aspects from the exclusive realm of public regulation to co-regulation.

Both types are centred on the idea of some agreement between the regulator and the regulated entity. The contractual approach emphasises procedural aspects related to enforcement, whereas the incentive-based approach focuses on more substantial aspects linked to the alignment of the interests of both regulators and regulated entities.

Economic contract theory was originally developed for industrial organisations and utilities regulation and only subsequently applied to financial regulation.[14] It is built on the principal–agent model with asymmetric information. Its main idea is that a contract determines the actions to be

14 Its basic ideas can be found in Williamson 1975, 1985 and Laffont and Tirole 1991 and were extended to financial regulation by Bhattacharya and Thakor 1993 and Llewellyn 1999b, 2001.

taken by each party consenting to it, and possibly the measures to be imposed on the parties who fail to undertake the agreed actions.

To put it simply, this approach perceives regulation as a sort of contract concluded between the regulator and the bank. It has as a prerequisite the obligation of the regulator to establish a clear set of objectives and general principles, while leaving up to the banks the concrete modes of compliance with the regulatory objectives. It is in the interest of banks to choose their own procedure for satisfying the regulator's general requirements. They may reduce compliance costs by adopting their own least-costly strategy. Furthermore, banks are more familiar than regulators with their own particular circumstances and structures and know better how to address them.

The bank may consequently choose its own models and procedures and submit them for approval to the regulator. Once the regulator has agreed with the bank on the modalities of satisfying the regulatory objectives and principles, the contract may be considered as being concluded. Such a contract requires the bank to deliver on the agreed conditions, under the threat of sanctions in the case of inadequate or non-performance (Llewellyn 2001: 31). The bank has to inform the regulator about the expected losses for a certain time interval and provide for capital to cover it. If real losses are above the indicated level, there is a contract infringement and the bank will be subject to penalties. The regulator also has the power to terminate the contract and oblige the bank to accept a standard contract. Alternative 'default' conditions established by the regulator have to be always available, as they are inherent to the contract regulation paradigm.

In prudential regulation, the most obvious example is the case of internal risk-measurement and management systems, as well as the supervisory review process devised under the Basel II framework. Moves in this direction took place even before the adoption of Basel II, as identified in the so-called pre-commitment approach (Llewellyn 2001: 31–2, referring to Kupiec and O'Brien 1997).

As regards incentive-based regulation, the essential concept in balancing external and internal regulatory modes is that of incentive structures. Because it will be always rational for market participants to behave in the pursuit of their own self-interests, regulators have to accommodate these private interests with the interests of society. In doing this they should create mechanisms that involve all market participants by making them responsible for their actions. Regulatory incentives are based on anticipation of the likely responses and steer behaviour towards public goals. As pointed out, the idea behind legal norms as incentives is that of basing rules on a clear and explicit division of responsibilities, and also establishing overt standards and exercisable sanctions (Mayes *et al.* 2001: 67). It is especially the supervisory review process of the Basel II framework that reflects the use of an incentives-based approach.

While incentive structures have to address and reconcile all market participants, the emphasis is on aligning the interests of bank management, bank owners and supervisors (Llewellyn 2001: 16). For these three categories the incentive structures have to be aligned along three dimensions: objectives (public versus private), the time-span (long-term versus short-term) and corporate governance arrangements (managers versus shareholders). Additionally, account has to be taken of all other market participants who have to be responsive to the regulatory framework: depositors, creditors, competitors, taxpayers, employees, analysts, auditors, etc. (Goodhart 1998a: 44).

Contract regulation and incentive-based regulation can be seen as useful complements to prescriptive regulation, especially as they allow for more proximity of regulators to market realities. They may be seen as a catalyst allowing for targeted and proportionate application of prescriptive rules. They provide a framework for interaction which could eventually also channel supervisory input determined by macro-developments to individual entities. Furthermore, this approach indicates the close interaction between prudential norms and other categories of norms such as corporate governance rules and company law. The key to effective prudential regulation is establishing a balanced interplay between prescriptive and lenient rules and precisely identifying the areas where a firm approach is needed and those where flexibility would guarantee better results for everyone.

4 The case for market discipline

Because of the mentioned market imperfections that constitute the very rationale for public intervention, there is no case for a complete reliance on free market forces, so a laissez-faire banking regime may be excluded from the outset. However, market discipline is not an alternative to regulation and supervision; on the contrary, market discipline is complementary to the regulatory regime and could be also reinforced by the latter. Market discipline could help mitigate negative effects of regulation, such as moral hazard linked to protective regulation. Consequently, there is a case for regulation to stimulate market forces to play an active role in controlling risk-taking.

Yet market discipline is effective as long as the market is heterogeneous and encompasses sufficiently diversified interests that motivate actors to be vigilant about new developments. However, if herding occurs, discouraging actors from watchfully seeking information on their own in favour of following majority action, market discipline is compromised, as was the case during the crisis. This is an aspect that should be properly considered if banking regulators are to encourage market discipline.

There are two ways, in particular, of combining regulation with market discipline: by stimulating market pressures and by giving value to market endogenous mechanisms such as rating agencies.

4.1 Stimulating market pressure

Banking regulation may encourage the market to play a positive role. By means of regulatory incentives banks can be exposed to market pressures, which may improve effectiveness of public regulation. Pressures coming from equity markets, debt markets, markets for different financial products, labour markets and the market for corporate control potentially have a disciplining effect on the actions of banks. For market discipline to work effectively, emphasis has to be put on accurate information disclosure and transparency. Rightly constructed disclosure requirements on banks' capital and some structural, ownership and management-related information should enable the control of peers in the market.

Regulatory theory suggests that the role of market discipline should be strengthened within the regulatory regime. This is also the approach taken by the Basel Committee, which has incorporated market discipline as the third pillar of the Basel II framework.

4.2 Market endogenous mechanisms – rating agencies

There are some market endogenous mechanisms capable of contributing to the correction of information asymmetries in banking. The typical market institutions that have an information-creative, respectively transaction cost lowering role are rating agencies.

The activity of rating agencies consists of checking and reporting regularly on the financial standing of single debtors and applying standardised stamps of quality to their creditworthiness. The mere existence of rating agencies is justified by the profit possibilities resulting from cost advantages in producing information. Specialisation and economies of scale may result from the public good dimension of information, which implies that there is no rivalry for its consumption and it is not devalued by multiple use. The demand for ratings comes principally from banks. Although depositors are in principle also interested in having rating agencies screening the financial situation of a credit institution, they tend to speculate by observing the attitudes of other depositors (e.g. increase in deposits or massive withdrawals at a single bank), information coming from supervisory authorities or information released by banks themselves – banks with an above-average solvency will be always eager to disclose their financial standing (Wörner 2000: 84).

For banks, rating agencies are important especially because they allow them to efficiently signal their creditworthiness, which entails easier and lower refinancing costs. The creation of rating agencies upon the unilateral demand of banks was criticised for possible conflicts of interest linked to ratings financed unilaterally by banks. Two counterarguments have been invoked. First, rating agencies are dependent upon their reputation, which takes time to be established, and they are concerned with the provision of qualitative information. Faulty information would be very risky. Second, banks have to be observed in their double function: they are interested not only in disclosing information through rating agencies, but also in acquiring information in their capacity as creditors.

Further criticism points to the unreliability of the information delivered by rating agencies. Because financial claims and liabilities fall due frequently, banks can substantially alter their financial standing within short periods of time. Not only can this very quickly outdate the information provided by ratings, but banks can also improve their risk position and rating score just prior to the examination date – this process is called 'window dressing' (Goodhart 1996: 626). Further, rating agencies can capture only information that is obviously relevant for the creditworthiness of banks. They ignore information that is without immediate relevance for a bank's solvency, such as broader developments in financial markets. Therefore, information provided by rating agencies can be qualified as being incomplete.

To conclude, rating agencies have the potential of reducing some information asymmetries, particularly to the advantage of financial intermediaries and supervisors, and therefore have gradually emerged as an endogenous market mechanism. Nevertheless, they do not have the potential to substitute altogether public regulation addressing the relevant market failures. Their role is complementary and may reinforce the effectiveness of public policy measures. Given the inherent limits of ratings, regulation should also prevent excessive reliance on them.

Part II

The normative analysis of prudential issues

3 An evolutionary perspective on prudential rules

In this chapter we review the EU legislation containing prudential norms for banking activities. We use an evolutionary perspective so as to emphasise the dynamics underlying the creation and implementation of prudential rules. We attempt to identify the extent to which prudential legislative developments reflect general European integration regulatory strategies, and whether they display specific features. Also, we will follow the evolutions in the character of European norms. In our view, prudential rules have changed over time, from broadly specified policy guidelines, aiming to create a minimal degree of convergence between disparate national realities and striving for the creation of a single banking market, to a very detailed and extensive set of principles, rules and standards, albeit still incomplete, which addresses substantial issues relevant for an integrated market. We inquire as to whether we can identify a coherent and substantive body of prudential norms at the core of European banking law, capable of setting out clear and precise benchmarks for the national legal systems. We undertake a joint reading of the relevant pieces of legislation and attempt to draw out the interactions between the principles and norms therein contained.

1 The European corpus of prudential norms

It is through efforts to consolidate legislation during the past ten years that it has become much easier to identify a compact body of prudential norms regulating European banking. Before that, the labyrinth of norms adopted at various times and levels seemed *a priori* deprived of a coherent logic. Indeed, it emerged gradually through a step-by-step approach, conditional upon political consensus in a very sensitive area.

When tracing European prudential developments, one inevitably has to go back to the EC Treaty articles that laid the foundation of the common market. This marks the starting point of any inquiry and constitutes its guiding principle. European banking regulation followed the pattern of the construction and deepening of the European integrated market. In addition, the dynamics of European prudential regulation have to keep pace with the rapidly evolving financial markets.

Our analysis will accord due account to the context in which prudential rules have been adopted. By taking an evolutionary perspective, we attempt to circumscribe the concept of prudential rules in accordance with its objectives, thereby avoiding a restrictive understanding. Prudential regulation should be understood broadly, so as to encompass all rules that were adopted in support of prudential policies; irrespective of whether they are technical norms, procedures, conflict-of-law-rules, incentive-based norms or framework principles.

But the normative prudential framework is characterised by continuous transformation, albeit at an unsteady pace. It has evolved towards an ever more coherent system that intervenes increasingly in Member States' regulatory regimes. However, by revealing many of the missing pieces in the puzzle, the crisis that erupted in August 2007 brought evidence that the prudential legislative framework has not yet been fully accomplished and needs further construction.

2 Early prudential concerns

The understanding of early prudential concerns takes us back to the roots of market integration[1] and the early steps towards creating a common banking market, based on the free movement of capital and services and the freedom of establishment. During the second half of the 1960s, when the European Community already boasted the customs union and a common agricultural policy, progress with regard to the free movement of services was only minimal. The awareness of developments in the various financial sectors, and the political willingness to promote cooperation in international trade, determined the Commission to entrust an expert group with the task of investigating problems posed by the liberalisation of capital movements and the consequences of integrating capital markets in Europe.

The committee chaired by Professor Claudio Segré examined all segments of capital markets – including the different banking regulations of the (at that time) six Member States. The report issued in 1966 underlined the importance of an integrated European capital market as a tool to finance economic growth and to foster implementation of Community policies in other areas. The Segré report identified as major obstacles likely to affect the movement of capital 'the rules under which they operate and the supervisory controls to which they are subject' (Commission 1966: 32).

1 One of the central objectives of the Rome Treaty establishing a European Economic Community was the creation of a common market for economic activities (art. 2 EEC Treaty) by means of 'the abolition, as between Member States, of obstacles to the free movement of goods, persons, services and capital' (art. 3(i) EEC Treaty) and 'the approximation of the laws of Member States to the extent required for the functioning of the common market' (art. 3(h) EEC Treaty).

On the basis of the report, the Commission prepared a first working document in 1969, aimed mainly at abolishing discrimination resulting from non-harmonised banking regulation and supervision. Divergences between the Member States, stemming from different ways of conceiving the organisation of the banking business, forced the Commission to prepare a series of successive documents – until in June 1972 it finally submitted the first draft directive. The proposal was an ambitious document amounting to a genuine banking law that collided with some Member States' legislation.[2] In an epoch when the Treaty imposed unanimity for the adoption of such secondary legislation and when banking was perceived to be a very sensitive area, where Member States traditionally had manifested strong interests, such initial ample project was doomed to fail. The Commission was forced to withdraw the initial draft, realising that coordination would require time and progressive steps. A new directive, with a much less ambitious reach, was proposed in December 1974 and was finally adopted in December 1977. Eleven years of arduous efforts finally resulted in the conclusion of the first step in the direction of genuine harmonisation in the field of banking: the First Banking Directive (FBD) (Directive 77/780/EEC).

It became apparent that further steps for creating a common market in financial services could no longer aspire towards an overall encompassing coordination strategy, as had been the case of the customs union. Interpreting the Treaty requirement for coordination of laws in the sense of achieving an extensive harmonisation of Member States' legislative and regulatory systems was not possible with regard to fields where traditionally organisation and practices were varying. Unanimity imposed long delays and forced compromises; consequently, a unique coordination project in banking regulation of encompassing scope had to be abandoned.

Prudential concerns were from the outset at the heart of the efforts aimed at creating a common banking market. The Segré report had already signalled that national divergent rules on the operation and control of credit institutions constituted a serious barrier in attempting to open up markets. National rules were backed by longstanding traditions and differentiated approaches to the way of conceiving banking. Moreover, until the early 1970s the governments of many Member States used the banking industry in order to implement broader macro-economic policies and jealously tried to safeguard such influence. However, given the competitive pressures in ever more liberalised global financial markets, Member States were constrained to change their approach. Thus, initial

2 Among the most fervent critics of the proposed banking directive were Italy and, to a certain extent, France, but the decisive stroke came from the UK, newly acceded to the Community, which formally opposed the mere idea of controlling banking activities (Sousi-Roubi 1995: 62).

European legislative efforts in this field were mirroring emerging willingness to allow for greater market integration – with the minimum sacrifice of national interests.

3 The First Banking Directive

Adopted on 12 December 1977 on the basis of article 57(2) of the EEC Treaty (now 47(2) EC Treaty) by unanimous approval of the Member States, the First Banking Directive (FBD) was the unworthy epigone of the earlier proposal and the proof of the change in the Commission's approach favouring consecutive measures (recital 7 FBD). The FBD was simply the 'initial stage' that only imposed 'certain minimum requirements' with a view to eventually introducing uniform authorisation requirements, and the principle of home-country control with regard to supervision (recital 12 FBD).

Undoubtedly, the FBD was one of the foundation blocks of the common market for banking services, aiming especially to open up national markets and to allow free competition in banking. The removal of entry barriers and obstructive divergent national norms was to be achieved through the adoption of a common, albeit broad, definition of a credit institution and various authorisation requirements. The introduction of the principle that credit institutions were to obtain authorisation before commencing their activities and the obligation of competent authorities to notify the Commission of the list of authorised credit institutions, although defined in broad terms by the directive, were considered to be radical steps towards the formalisation of national regulatory regimes through European legislation.[3] As for the conditions for authorisation, the directive did not provide specific details but confined itself to prescribing firm principles requiring the existence of separate and adequate own funds;[4] the four-eyes principle with regard to the banks' directors;[5] the requirement of a clear business programme and a comprehensive organisational structure; and the interdiction for national authorities to apply the criterion of economic needs of the market when considering an application for authorisation (article 3 paragraphs 3–4 FBD).

The step-by-step approach was also acknowledged by the European Court of Justice (ECJ) in two cases where the Commission had successfully obtained declarations against Belgium and Italy for breaching their obligations related to the timely implementation of the FBD. The Court held:

3 The requirement of preliminary authorisation already existed in some of the Member States, but for others – such as the UK – this was completely revolutionary.

4 In France, for instance, it was possible (until the adoption of the directive) to also undertake banking activities under the form of the *entreprise individuelle*.

5 Art. 3 second paragraph FBD required that there be at least two persons that effectively direct the business, of sufficiently good repute and with sufficient experience to perform such duties.

> Council Directive 77/780 constitutes the first step in the harmonisation of banking structures and the supervision thereof. The purpose of such harmonisation is to permit the gradual attainment of freedom of establishment for credit institutions and the liberalisation of banking services. In that respect the Directive introduces certain minimum conditions for the authorisation of credit institutions, which all Member States must observe. In order to facilitate the taking up and pursuit of business as a credit institution the Directive aims in particular to reduce the discretion enjoyed by certain supervisory authorities in authorising credit institutions.
>
> (Case 300/81 *Commission* v. *Italy* [1983] ECR 449: 455; Case 301/81, *Commission* v. *Belgium* [1983] ECR 467: 476)

Authorisation requirements, as elaborated in the FBD, served more as a tool for market construction and less for mitigating prudential concerns. The directive barely touched on prudential rules, which were understood in the 1970s as those rules permitting the assessment of the financial situation of an institution in terms of ratios applied to several items in the balance sheet. Nevertheless, the FBD outlined ambitiously successive steps to be undertaken, which would place the emphasis on such prudential concerns: the establishment of appropriate structural ratios (recital 16 FBD), further coordination measures concerning banks' solvency and liquidity, as well as the objective of consistent overall supervision of cross-border institutions by the Member States' authorities where it had its head office. In this sense, national competent authorities and the newly established Banking Advisory Committee were explicitly entrusted with a forward-looking preparatory mission (article 6 FBD).

The vague wording reflected the reluctance of the Member States in giving up their prudential competences and their concern to guard cautiously against predetermining the content of forthcoming measures.[6] The directive was harshly criticised for using empty notions, such as 'adequate minimum standards' or 'sufficiently good repute or lack of sufficient experience', which, although given a key role, were not defined. The vagueness of the provisions was attributed not to the eventual technical inability of the European institutions, but exclusively to the lack of political will on the part of Member States to renounce national provisions in favour of harmonised ones (Cordero 1990: 9). It should, however, be recalled that in the 1970s the European Community included Member States with longstanding regulatory traditions in banking (e.g. Germany), but also countries who almost

6 For instance, while the final Commission draft of the directive specified four ratios (deposits, total assets and non-liquid assets as own funds and liquid assets as current liabilities), agreement on this aspect could not be reached and Member States were allowed wider discretion in establishing the common instruments for observing and comparing the different systems; Dassesse and Isaacs 1985: 82.

completely lacked formal, public-law requirements for the taking-up and pursuit of banking activities and relied substantially on discretionary supervision (e.g. the case of the UK). Very divergent realities called on moderate measures, taken through successive steps at a time when European activism was seen as an unexpected intruder into the sensitive banking sector.

The FBD was an essential step in the history of European banking and it remains as a point of reference. This not only constituted the first step, accomplished after significant conflict, but it also had the remarkable merit of allowing for further development and pointed to the first programme for the future integration of banking markets (Schwark 1981: 13). It has never been repealed, but only amended and subsequently incorporated into the Codified Banking Directive (CBD; Directive 200/12/EC), which became the Capital Requirements Directive (CRD; Directive 2006/48/EC).

An important aspect related to the FBD concerns its legal basis: article 57(2) EEC Treaty (later article 47(2) EC Treaty and now article 53 TFEU), a legal provision which supports the freedom of establishment and the free movement of services,[7] and is complementary to article 54 EEC Treaty (later article 44 EC Treaty and now article 50 TFEU). While the latter focused on the elimination of unjustified obstacles to the freedom of establishment, article 57(2) allowed for the introduction within the legislation of Member States of provisions aimed at facilitating the effective exercise of these Treaty freedoms. As observed by the ECJ, article 57 (now 53 TFEU) is directed towards the reconciliation of the Treaty freedoms with 'the application of national professional rules justified by the general good, in particular rules relating to organisation, qualifications, professional ethics, supervision and liability, provided that such application is effected without discrimination'.[8] Such reconciliation may be achieved by means of the coordination directives provided for in paragraph 2, which represent the tool for harmonising national regulations on the taking up and pursuit of activities as self-employed persons.

Moreover, coordination directives can be used not only to remove extensive obstacles (Truchot 2000: 423) but, as constantly maintained by the Court,[9] they may favour the effective exercise of the freedom of establishment and the freedom to provide services. As such, the coordination directives serve to establish and insert essential principles for a sector, common to all the Member States. Although adopted in an unfavourable, almost hostile environment, the FBD managed to introduce several principles that forced Member States to radically change their banking legislations. This is remarkable, especially as at the time the FBD was adopted the Single

7 By virtue of art. 55 (ex art. 66) of the EC Treaty, the provisions in art. 47 are applicable not only to the freedom of establishment, but also to the free movement of services.

8 Case 71/76, *Jean Thieffry* v. *Conseil de l'ordre des avocats à la cour de Paris* [1977] ECR 765, para. 12.

9 Case 2/74, *Reyners* [1974] ECR 631; Cases 110–11/78 *Van Wesemael* [1979] ECR 35.

European Act (SEA) had not yet inserted article 8A (subsequently renumbered 7A and later 14) into the EC Treaty (now article 26 TFEU), which introduced the internal market objective in the European legal order and explicitly referred to article 47(2) as a tool for market integration.

The procedure used in adopting coordination directives is the common legislative procedure foreseen in article 251 EC Treaty (ex article 189b, now article 294 TFEU) applicable to secondary Community law, whereas the voting rules were specified in the second sentence of the second paragraph of article 47 EC Treaty (ex article 57). This requested unanimity whenever the implementation of a coordination directive involved, in at least one Member State, the amendment of the existing principles laid down by the national law regulating conditions of access in that sector. This was the case with the FBD, which was decided by unanimous action. Such voting requirements changed after the adoption of the SEA.

To conclude, with regard to prudential rules, the FBD contained only a few provisions, which served the purpose of creating the premise for a common banking market and were only marginally concerned with safety-and-soundness aspects. Nevertheless, the directive paved the way for subsequent measures, and constituted a firm commitment to future harmonisation of rules addressing solvency and liquidity requirements. It also anticipated the home-country control as a cornerstone principle in banking supervision. Article 47(2) remained the legal basis for all future European banking legislation that took the form of coordination directives.

4 Post-FBD regulatory measures

Until the conceptual change in market construction strategies brought about by the 1985 White Paper, the 'small steps' policy produced first measures setting the ground for further coordination.

In June 1983, the Council adopted by unanimity, and on the basis of the same article 57(2) of the EEC Treaty (later 47(2) EC Treaty now 53 TFEU), the first directive on consolidated supervision (Directive 83/350/EEC), which was a firm step on the road to home-country control.[10] The adoption of European rules on consolidated supervision was fuelled by various events, which disclosed the fragility inherent in ever more liberalised banking markets. In particular, behind the preparatory works on the directive and its rapid approval (less than two years after the submission of the draft directive by the Commission), there were the difficulties encountered by West German supervisory authorities, unable to monitor the

10 The directive recalled that the eventual aim, to be achieved through successive steps, would be to provide for overall supervision of credit institutions operating in several Member States by the competent authorities of the country where they have the head office, in consultation, where appropriate, with the authorities of the other Member State concerned.

activities of the subsidiaries of German banks set up in Luxembourg, and the crash of Banco Ambrosiano, which shed light on huge gaps in the supervision of banks at international level (Dassesse and Isaacs 1985: 94). Probably the most stimulating factor was the adoption in May 1983, by the Basel Committee of Banking Supervision, of the Principles for the supervision of banks' foreign establishments – the so-called Basel Concordat, which explicitly provided for the principle of consolidated supervision.[11]

The 1983 directive on consolidated supervision continued the minimalist approach, allowing Member States to introduce more stringent rules and not precluding, pending further harmonisation, the supervision on an individual basis by the authorities of the host State. The central issue of the form and extent of supervision on a consolidated basis was concentrated in a sole article, which focused on the situations subject to the consolidated supervision, whereas the details, methods and procedures for its application were left to the discretion of national competent authorities. Despite its vague, barely harmonising content, the directive is important as it succeeded in introducing in all Member States the mandatory requirements that national authorities supervise on a consolidated basis (which was not done by all of them at that time) and cooperate with each other in so doing. It also had the merit of obliging national competent authorities to provide each other with the necessary information. The paternalistic approach of Member States towards their national banking systems was still dominant at that time and could be mitigated mainly because of an emerging awareness of difficulties related to cross-border institutions. The directive was later repealed by the second directive on consolidated supervision (Council Directive 92/30/EEC).

Another important step consisted of the adoption of the directive on the annual accounts and consolidated accounts of banks and other financial institutions (Council Directive 86/635/EEC). Accounting rules were clearly differentiated from prudential rules; nevertheless, the inextricable link between the two categories was acknowledged. Obviously prudential supervision could not be coordinated without comparable predetermined items on the balance sheet of banks. The directive was adopted on the basis of article 54(3) (g) EEC Treaty (later article 44(2) (g) EC Treaty, now article 50(2) TFEU), concerning the coordination of national legislations on companies. It requires all credit institutions within the EU to keep similarly structured balance sheets and to use the same nomenclature and terminology for the various items (including off-balance-sheet items) and provides essential assessment rules, rules concerning the consolidated accounts and the publicity of annual accounts.

11 According to the Basel Concordat, the principle of consolidated supervision requires that parent banks and parent supervisory authorities monitor the risk exposure – including a perspective of concentrations of risks and of the quality of assets – of the banks and the banking groups for which they are responsible, as well as the adequacy of their capital, on the basis of the totality of their business wherever conducted.

5 The 1985 White Paper approach

European decision-makers chose to stimulate the slow recovery of Europe after the recession in the late 1970s by reinforcing European integration. Conventional wisdom was that Europe was held back by the fragmentation of national economies and the disparities between the legislations of Member States, despite the elimination of tariff barriers. In this context, the Commission engaged in the preparation of an ambitious programme that would reactivate the process of European integration and address the identified shortcomings. The White Paper on the Internal Market (Commission 1985) was drafted in early 1985, under the coordination of Commissioner Lord Cockfield, and endorsed by the Council on 28 June 1985 at the Milan summit.

The White Paper launched as a key concept the idea of the 'internal market', which was characterised by the following essential feature: the merger of the markets of Member States into a single enlarged market that would be dynamic and expanding, as well as flexible enough to channel human, material and financial resources in an optimal way. The viability of the project was ascribed to four methodological elements: the setting out of a clear programme of measures for achieving the internal market; the establishment of a strict timetable with mobilising effects in view of the general 1992 deadline for completion of the internal market; an underlying 'philosophical framework' proposing a new regulatory strategy; and the emphasis on the removal of barriers (Avgerinos 2003: 34). The almost 300 measures proposed by the internal market programme addressed a panoply of sectors ranging from financial services, public procurement and taxation to free movement of persons, free movement of capital and monetary policy. Paragraph 104 of the White Paper contains the specific concerns which the Commission had with regard to the banking sector: the coordination of standards and principles of financial stability and management, accounting, market access and banking reorganisation in times of crisis.

The Member States' commitment to the underlying ideas of the White Paper, to the envisaged measures and to the 1992 deadline was irreversibly expressed through the SEA, which was signed in February 1986 and entered into force on 1 July 1987. The SEA brought about the first important revision of the Treaties since their adoption.[12] The catalyst behind the revival of the Community momentum was the centrality of the 'internal market project', constitutionalised by the introduction of a new article 8a (later article 14) EC Treaty (now article 26 TFEU).

12 The SEA contributed to improving the decision-making process through the introduction of the cooperation procedure, an enhanced consultative role for the Parliament, the formal inclusion of the comitology procedure and more extensive use of the qualified majority voting.

This new phase of European integration provided the tools for unblocking a stagnation that could only disadvantage intermediaries acting in ever more dynamic and globalised financial markets. The alternative regulatory approach proposed was based on the three principles of minimum harmonisation, mutual recognition and home-country control, conceived to stimulate progress in the integration of markets, with due observance of national public policy interests and divergent local practices. The three modules of the internal market approach mark the change from the initial integration strategy, based on extensive all-encompassing harmonisation of national legislation, to a more flexible approach, relying largely on regulatory competition. Community legislation provided the framework by establishing minimum guarantees to ensure some measure of equivalence between the different national legal regimes (Chalmers and Szyszczak 1998: 35).

The principles are interdependent. Minimum harmonisation provides that only essential legislative measures, indispensable for the liberalisation of Member States' markets (i.e. removal of barriers) and the creation of a unified market with a certain level of standards of protection, be adopted at European level. The principle of mutual recognition, based on reciprocal trust and commitment between Member States and national authorities brought about through minimum harmonisation acknowledges the equivalence of corresponding measures taken in other Member States. Home-country control flows as a natural corollary from the other two principles and constitutes a sort of conflict-of-laws rule that determines the national regulatory framework applicable to a particular case. Hence, it is the responsibility of the competent authorities of the home Member State to regulate and supervise the institutions they have authorised, wherever these conduct business by taking advantage of the freedom of establishment and the free movement of services. Nevertheless, the White Paper itself mitigates the scope of the principle by providing a safeguard clause that permits host countries to intervene to the extent necessary for protecting the public interest. This new regulatory strategy pursued a ruthless pragmatic approach to market construction. Compared to the full harmonisation project it was considered 'an inferior integration mechanism, made necessary only by Council obstructionism in the Commission's pursuit of common rules' (Steil 1998: 3).

Although they have dominated the way financial regulation has been conceived at European level for more than a decade, it is important to note that the three principles did not receive a legal basis in the Treaty, nor were they derived from basic Treaty provisions. Also, even if their origin can be traced back to the famous 1979 *Cassis de Dijon* judgment of the ECJ,[13] the Court never raised them to the level of legal rules or principles of Community law. They may only be identified in secondary Community legislation as tools for achieving progressive harmonisation in several complex domains. They do not have the authority to subordinate systematically subsequent rules

13 Case 120/78 *Rewe-Zentral AG* v. *Bundesmonopolverwaltung fur Branntwein* [1979] ECR 649.

adopted within those complex areas, nor can such intention be inferred from the White Paper.

The ECJ toned down the role of the three principles after the 1992 deadline, when the quest for new regulatory strategies addressing shortcomings of the internal market programme had already started. In the *Deposit guarantee* case,[14] the Court declared that the so-called export prohibition[15] in article 4(1) of the directive on deposit guarantee schemes (DGS; Directive 94/19/EC) was an exception to the minimum harmonisation and mutual recognition that the directive was generally seeking to achieve. However, the ECJ also underlined that compliance with the two principles was by no means peremptory, and emphasised that harmonisation in complex fields where divergent national rules exist can be achieved only progressively.[16] Furthermore, the Court refused to grant an influential role to the principle of home-country control. It found:

> first, that it has not been proved that the Community legislature laid down the principle of home State supervision in the sphere of banking law with the intention of systematically subordinating all other rules in that sphere to that principle. Second, since it is not a principle laid down by the Treaty, the Community legislator could depart from it, provided that it did not infringe the legitimate expectations of the persons concerned. Since it had not yet acted in regard to the guarantee of deposits, no such legitimate expectations could exist.
>
> (ECJ Case C-233/94, para. 64)

Without ignoring the guiding role of the minimum harmonisation, home-country control and mutual recognition principles for the financial services sector, it has to be highlighted that they have been defined and illustrated only by secondary law. Consequently, although they might be ascribed a 'regulatory' role, they do not amount to supreme and *de jure* legitimate principles and recourse to them must be subjected to jurisdictional review. The ECJ's findings concerning the inapplicability of the principle of home-country control in a systematic way as the de facto principal rule to which all other norms in the banking sector are subjected reflect 'the constitutional legal position of EU primary law and the relevant subordinating role of black-letter law' (Avgerinos 2003: 62).

What matters from an evolutionary perspective is to acknowledge that applying the three modules of the new integration paradigm (i.e.

14 Case C-233/94 *Federal Republic of Germany* v. *European Parliament and Council of the European Union* [1997] ECR I-2405.

15 The export prohibition required that the cover provided by the home Member State for depositors, at branches set up by credit institutions in Member States other than those in which they are authorised, may not exceed the cover offered by the corresponding guarantee scheme of the host Member State.

16 Case C-233/94, para. 43 refers to Case C-193/94 *Skanavi and Chryssanthakopoulos* [1996] ECR I-929, para. 27.

minimum harmonisation, mutual recognition and home-country control) resulted in the adoption of a series of directives that contributed substantially to the construction of a common banking market and of which the hard core is constituted by prudential rules. Without diminishing the merits of the White Paper strategy in fuelling legislative activism in the banking field, we have to acknowledge the influence of the parallel evolution of international financial regulation, where since the adoption of the Basel Concordat consistent debates had taken place and various prudential principles had been endorsed as non-binding rules. Also, the White Paper strategy should not preclude an objective and neutral approach to the analysis of more recent prudential provisions, which do not necessarily fit into the pattern traced in the mid-1980s and open the door for a critical assessment of the three principles. As reflected in the DGS judgment, a contextual interpretation of the principles is the most appropriate, backed by the awareness that they are not timelessly true.

6 The Second Banking Directive

The key legislative act in creating a common banking market with unrestricted access of credit institutions to the territory of all Member States was the Second Banking Directive (SBD; Directive 89/646/EEC). As a corollary to the SEA and the 1985 White Paper, it proclaims itself 'the essential instrument for the achievement of the internal market' for banking (recital 5 SBD). By applying the triptych of principles designed for the Internal Market Strategy, the SBD creates the conditions for the use of the so-called European passport, which allows credit institutions duly authorised in a Member State to carry out within the whole Community the activities for which they were authorised.

The SBD was not a stand-alone piece of legislation, but the engine of an emerging vast prudential framework. The preamble explicitly stated that the SBD could only be implemented simultaneously with specific additional technical Community legislation on own funds and solvency ratios and should be interpreted in conjunction with the whole body of Community legislation already enacted in this field (the FBD, the directive on consolidated supervision, the directive on annual accounts and consolidated accounts, the two Commission recommendations on large exposures of credit institutions – Recommendation 87/62/EEC – and on the introduction of deposit guarantee schemes – Recommendation 87/63/EEC). Also, the SBD constitutes the anchor of further measures for regulating the banking sector, specifically further harmonisation of rules on the reorganisation and winding-up of credit institutions and arrangements necessary for the supervision of liquidity, market, interest rate and foreign-exchange risks.

The SBD contained minimal harmonised rules setting the conditions for the access and exercise of the banking business in the EU. It allowed home Member States to establish stricter rules with regard to most of the authorisation conditions. The principal goal of the SBD was to spur banking market integration; common authorisation requirements and prudential harmonisation were considered the main instruments to achieve this.

Building upon the principles laid down in the FBD, the SBD specified the conditions for authorisation, such as the amount of the initial capital, its structure, governance aspects related to management and shareholders.[17] At first sight, it appears that the prevailing policy objective for setting common essential authorisation requirements was to constrain national markets to open up and to create a level playing-field. Such minimum harmonisation was aimed at fostering reciprocal trust between competent authorities so as to facilitate effective mutual recognition of authorisations. The emphasis on the objective of opening up national markets might also be inferred from the central role that article 6, consecrating the 'European banking passport', occupies within the title on the harmonisation of authorisation requirements.[18] However, prudential concerns are inherent to the authorisation requirements, as results especially from supervisors' possibility to refuse granting an authorisation because of dissatisfaction with the shareholder structure, as well as from the requirements related to qualifying holdings. These requirements reflect preoccupation for financial solidity and shareholders' ability to supply the required own funds, as well as interest in identifying inter-linkages in ever more complex financial corporate structures.[19]

The prudential character of the SBD is more apparent in the requirements it establishes for the pursuit of banking activities. This results from provisions such as article 13(2) SBD, which introduced a generic but crucial requirement for sound administrative and accounting procedures and adequate internal control mechanisms. Similarly, prudential concerns are reflected in the requirement of prolonging the authorisation conditions during the pursuit of the business of credit institutions.

The most important contribution of the SBD lies in the explicit consecration of the home-country control principle as a cornerstone of the common banking market. The principle had already been announced in

17 Without entering into technical details, it suffices to mention here that, as a general rule, the minimum initial capital was set at 5 million ECU, required at the time of the authorisation. Also, the SBD provided for the control by the competent authorities over the identities of the shareholders and managers, whether direct or indirect, natural or legal persons having qualifying holdings and over the amount of those holdings and for the assessment of their suitability – art. 5 SBD.

18 The aforementioned article firmly imposed that 'host Member States may no longer require authorisation as provided for in art. 4 of Directive 77/780/EEC, or endowment capital for branches of credit institutions authorised in other Member States'.

19 Such concerns were confirmed later by the collapse of the Bank for Credit and Commerce International (BCCI) during the summer of 1992, which made clear that knowledge of the structure of the shareholders and holdings was not enough in the context of ever more complex financial intermediaries. As a consequence, the so-called post-BCCI directive (Directive 95/26/EC) required that the competent authorities also be properly informed of the group structure to which the credit institution applying for authorisation may belong.

the FBD and was also pushed forward by international fora: the Basel Committee had established in 1975 that the supervision of the solvency of foreign branches of domestic institutions should be the responsibility of the 'parent' authority and reaffirmed such a principle in the 1983 Concordat. The principle, as enshrined in the SBD, covering both authorisation and supervision by the Home Member State, was limited in scope, as it applied only to cross-border branching and provision of services. From the beginning, subsidiaries were not covered – an aspect which was carried on in successive developments of EU prudential regulation. The SBD constituted the skeleton for the later Consolidated Banking Directive.

7 The complementary body of technical prudential rules

The SBD essentially represented a framework directive setting the principles that underpin the minimum harmonisation strategy. It explicitly highlighted that such principles could be materialised only in the context of the simultaneous implementation of technical measures related to own funds and solvency ratios.

Thus, minimum harmonisation increasingly was equated with the adoption of prudential regulation prescribing Community-wide parameters for ensuring the sound and safe management of credit institutions. Such regulation had to pay due account to the very different institutional set-ups and powers of the competent authorities, and the wide variety of their regulatory and supervisory practices. The set of common core prudential parameters aimed at establishing a common ground, allowed for comparisons across supervisory systems and enforced mutual trust. Such rules were minimal in the sense that they harmonised only the essential aspects, while the national regulatory authorities could exercise discretion as to details or non-essential aspects, provided that the effectiveness of harmonised standards was not undermined.

The fact that, in accordance with the minimum harmonisation philosophy of the White Paper, Member States were allowed to adopt stricter and additional rules has to be interpreted with caution in the context of technical prudential measures agreed at Community level. Such common basic standards were not merely the lowest common denominator, from which it could be easily departed to adopt higher standards. They were not just defined in broad terms, but consisted of detailed descriptions of the various items and limits to be taken into consideration. Member States' discretion was often limited to the choice between defined categories without giving the possibility of adopting stricter rules.

Several separate legislative acts containing prescriptive detailed rules were adopted to give substance to the SBD. They were integral parts of the broader regulatory framework applicable to banking activities and formed from the outset a unitary and inseparable body of complementary norms. This led to the subsequent inclusion of most of those directives into the

Codified Banking Directive (CBD), now replaced by the Capital Requirements Directive (CRD).

It is interesting to note that some of these directives have been preceded by recommendations issued by the Commission. These recommendations sought to bring about convergence between largely disparate national legislations, at a time when article 57(2) EEC Treaty imposed hardly achievable unanimity for adopting binding legal acts. From this respect the SEA was completely revolutionary, as it introduced qualified majority voting in the fields pertaining to the establishment of the common market and thus substantially facilitated the adoption of Community measures in the financial sector. Moreover, the SEA changed article 145 (later article 202) of the EC Treaty in order to give a legal basis to the already de facto applied comitology procedure. By virtue of the comitology procedure, the Council could delegate to the Commission powers for the implementation of rules, which allowed the Commission itself to adopt implementing measures.

Hereinafter, we will sketch the object of prudential supervision as it is envisaged in the package of directives adopted in pursuance of the common banking market objective. We will not enter into technical details, and warn the reader that the simplistic description conceals a wide complexity of intricate and very technical provisions which are not easily accessible to laypeople. Such description at this point only aims to provide a better understanding of the nature of prudential rules and to introduce the fundamental concepts and instruments of prudential supervision, which are at the core of all subsequent legislation.

7.1 Own funds

The Own Funds Directive 89/299/EEC adopted shortly before but in view of the SBD reflects international efforts undertaken with a view to the approximation of existing national rules on the adequacy of banks' capital. Although regulation adopted at the international level does not have the legal force of secondary Community law, from the point of view of their substance the provisions are comparable.[20]

Own funds were not defined in an abstract manner in the directive, but by reference to specific items subsumed to two broad categories: the basic equity or the so-called core capital (tier 1) and the additional items of supplementary capital (tier 2). The core capital includes mainly paid-up share capital and published reserves.[21] The tier 2 capital consists of revaluation reserves, undisclosed reserves, certain hybrid debt capital instruments and subordinated term debt instruments. The calculation of the own funds of a

20 An accurate comparative analysis of the definition of own funds as provided by the regulations of the Basle Committee and the European directive can be found in Häuser 1995.

21 See also Directive 91/633/EEC.

credit institution implies the aggregation of the various items, subject to certain limits and deductions. Thus, the overall amount of supplementary capital is subject to a double restriction: it cannot go beyond the amount of core capital and the maximum threshold of 50 per cent of the own funds. Supplementary limits apply to the individual items of tier 2 capital (e.g. hybrid instruments, subordinated debt).

Own funds are key indicators to a majority of prudential concerns. Their first description in the Own Funds Directive has been perpetrated with only slight changes during the years, as apparent from articles 57–63 of the CRD. Yet the diverging understanding of the various capital items in the Member States because of different company law and corporate arrangements ultimately results in a very different composition of own funds. Also, financial innovation has prompted new forms of capital, with specific hybrid features, that do not obviously fit into these categories and blur the distinction between tier 1 and tier 2 capital. This is perceived as problematic, especially from the perspective of ensuring the quality of core capital and the effectiveness of the limits imposed to tier 2 capital. The ultimate declared goal of achieving a common definition of own funds (article 62 CRD) seems, however, a very difficult endeavour, as national legal specificities and developments are powerful counterforces.

7.2 Solvency ratio

The Solvency Ratio Directive 89/647/EEC introduced the solvency ratio and the risk-weighted approach, the other two central terms of reference for the assessment of the financial strength of a credit institution that have been developed gradually. The solvency ratio has been set from the beginning at 8 per cent and expresses own funds (the numerator) as a proportion of total assets and off-balance-sheet items, risk-adjusted in accordance with precise rules (the denominator).

Initially, prudential rules were centred almost exclusively on credit risks, although regulators acknowledged that recognition and measurement of interest rate, foreign exchange and other market risks were equally important. Thus, when adopted in 1989, the solvency ratio entailed risk-weighting of assets and off-balance sheet items merely in accordance with the degree of credit risk[22] and it was only gradually that it extended to other types of risk (predominantly market risks[23]).

22 'Credit risk' or 'counterparty risk' refers to the failure of the client of a bank: that is, the impossibility of the debtor to reimburse the bank in accordance with his contractual commitments. For such a risk to be evaluated it is essential to take account of the nature of the counterparty, and the existence of guarantees which will reduce or eliminate losses in case of a default of a debtor (Augustin 1995: 141).

23 Market risks are those related to market operations, especially to the fluctuation of certain elements of these operations, e.g. variations of the interest rates and foreign exchange rates.

The origin of the solvency ratio has to be traced back to the observation coefficients mandated by the FBD and established gradually by the Banking Advisory Committee since 1979, with the assistance of the informally established Group de Contact.[24] Although the work on a European solvency ratio started immediately after the adoption of the FBD, the decisive impulse came from the agreement reached within the Basel Committee on July 1988 with regard to the so-called Cooke ratio. Peter Cooke, the president of the Basel Committee, was also a member of the Banking Advisory Committee and ensured parallelism and consistency between the international and European norms.

The formula of the solvency ratio and the 8 per cent minimum target continue to constitute the basis for determining capital adequacy for credit risk. The numerator remained largely unchanged, reflecting the developments regarding own funds. On the contrary, much of the evolution of prudential regulation focuses on the denominator, its scope as well the determination of the most appropriate risk-weights. The Solvency Ratio Directive established the basis of a risk-based supervisory approach in the European Community, which has grown ever more prominent over time and is starting to be questioned only in the light of the crisis.

7.3 Large exposures

Another pivotal instrument adopted in the aftermath of the SBD was the Large Exposures Directive 92/121/EEC, dealing with the diversification of risks, which is one of the oldest prudential concerns related to banking. The directive was preceded by a Commission Recommendation 87/62/EEC adopted in December 1986 that served as a transitional tool aiming at gradually accustoming Member States to the concept of large exposures and the restrictions it entails. As the Recommendation had not been fully internalised by Member States, at the end of 1992 the time was ripe to pass a legally binding act under the auspices of the SBD framework. It was not just a change in the nature of the legal instrument incorporating the large exposures regime, but an evolution of such regulation towards stricter rules.

The 1992 directive defined large exposures in relatively broad terms. It referred to all exposures to the same client, arising either from assets or from off-balance-sheet items, which added together define the total exposure to the client. It also used the concept of a group of connected clients, which is considered as a single exposure in case there is a relationship of

24 The method used was an experimental one, which was justified, on the one hand, by substantial concerns related to the analysis and comparison of the various national coefficients and calculation methods and their relevance at Community level and, on the other hand, by the awareness that fierce imposition of common normative coefficients might have a destabilising effect within the banking system.

control or an economic interdependency. Initially, the large exposures regime adopted a mere quantitative approach from the perspective of the creditor's exposure, irrespective of the quality of the debtor. Thus, no weightings were applied to exposures; only partial deductions of guarantees such as mortgages and securities were authorised. Subsequently, the introduction of weightings with regard to exposures to regional and local authorities and to other credit institutions contributed to refining the conditions attached to large exposures and reflected the transition to more risk-based regulation (Augustin 1995: 145).

An exposure of a credit institution to a client or a group of connected clients is considered a large exposure when its value is equal to or exceeds 10 per cent of its own funds. The directive introduced a back-stop regime limiting the total exposure on a client or a group of connected clients, except for specific cases, to 25 per cent of the own funds of the credit institution. The large exposures regime has been adjusted to new market developments in 2009 in the framework of the first review of the CRD review – CRD 2. In response to the crisis that unravelled high inter-bank exposures, the large exposures regime applicable to inter-bank lending was tightened.

7.4 Consolidated supervision

Consolidated supervision is an essential tool for supervisors with regard to banking business undertaken within a national territory or cross-border through subsidiaries and affiliates or within holding groups.[25] Consolidated supervision was already provided for in the 1983 directive. Its scope and methods had become outdated in the light of the various prudential ratios and limits and the harmonisation achieved at European level with regard to annual and consolidated bank accounts, as well as in view of international regulatory developments.[26] The second directive on consolidated supervision 92/30/EEC introduced adjustments in consideration of the new regulatory environment.

The objective of the second Consolidated Supervision Directive was to reinforce prudential supervision by improving the quality of the assessment of risks incurred. Despite some hints as to the control of conglomerate

25 'Consolidated supervision' has been defined as

> a comprehensive approach to banking supervision, which seeks to evaluate the strength of an entire group, taking into account all the risks which may affect a bank, regardless of whether these risks are carried in the books of the bank or related entities.
>
> (MacDonald 1988: 5)

26 The terms of the 1983 Basel Concordat containing the Principles of the supervision of banks' foreign establishment have been specified by a Supplement to the Concordat issued on April 1990 on information flows between banking supervisory authorities.

structures, the scope of application of the directive was confined to credit institutions belonging to a pure banking group or a group dominated by a credit institution, leaving outside banks belonging to non-financial holding companies.

As for the scope of consolidation for supervisory purposes, the directive provided for 'full consolidation', but allowed also instances of 'proportional consolidation',[27] as well as situations[28] when the national supervisory authorities could determine themselves whether and how to carry out consolidation. Furthermore, the directive allowed Member States to choose, when a group is supervised on a consolidated basis, not to apply the rules on capital adequacy and large exposures on an individual basis to the parent undertaking or subsidiaries, under the condition of ensuring satisfactory allocation of capital within the group. Also, the directive listed a series of exemptions that allow Member States to waive consolidated supervision requirements in certain circumstances. The provisions on consolidated supervision have remained substantially unchanged and are now included in the CRD.

7.5 Capital adequacy

All the directives mentioned so far were merged in 2000 into what has become known as the Codified Banking Directive 2000/12/EC (CBD). The codification aimed at creating a single text characterised, as stated in the preamble to the CBD, by 'rationality and clarity', which would facilitate the reading and eliminate overlapping parts. The codification exercise of the scattered banking norms in EU law has been described as a first attempt at producing a systematic body of rules to be followed by further legislative interventions (Alpa 2004: 523, referring to Dalhuisen 2001: 3). Nevertheless, an important legislative instrument indispensable for the prudential supervision of credit institutions was left out of the systematisation: the Capital Adequacy Directive 93/6/EEC (CAD), whose application to credit institutions was controversial from the very beginning. The 2006 recast of the CBD was paralleled by the recast of the CAD, yet, again, the opportunity was not seized to merge the two documents. The outcome of the recast is referred to as the Capital Requirements Directive (CRD) which is often used to indicate both directives. However, we will use 'CRD' to refer exclusively to the recast of the Codified Banking Directive (Directive 2006/48/EC), whereas 'recast CAD' will be used to designate references to the amended capital adequacy rules (Directive 2006/49/EC).

27 'Proportional consolidation' refers to the case of participations and to cases when the parent company's liability is limited to the extent of its shareholding, where this is less than 100 per cent.

28 For example, where one financial institution exercises significant influence over another one, or two or more institutions have the same management, but there is no cross-shareholding amounting to participation.

Negotiated concomitantly with the Investment Services Directive (ISD) which established, pursuant to the model set by the SBD, a European passport in investment services for specialised investment firms,[29] CAD was initially conceived for applying only to investment firms, with a view to submitting them to a regulatory capital regime similar to that established for banks by the Solvency Ratio Directive and Own Funds Directive. Nevertheless, because of conflicts during the negotiations between Germany, keen on protecting its universal bank tradition, and the market-finance-prone UK, concerned with safeguarding the competitive position of its investment firms, but also because of increased competition between banks and investment firms in the context of the global financial markets, it was decided that CAD would apply on a functional basis to cover specific risks incurred by both types of institutions. Consequently, CAD deals with market risks associated to banks' activities, which had not been taken into account up till then.[30] It requires banks to establish, apart from the banking book, a 'trading book' destined for registering the investment business operations. Capital requirements, risk-weightings and large exposures associated with the various items in the trading books of credit institutions are regulated by the CAD.

CAD's autonomous status can be attributed to the functional approach adopted which, for the first time at European level, regulates both banks and investment firms, traditionally subject to different regulatory regimes. The functional approach has merits in terms of creating competitive equality between banking and investment institutions. It was criticised for constituting a compromise solution diluting the solvency protection afforded to banks, or a way to spill over moral hazard problems associated to banks into the investment business (Dale 1995: 59). Also, this approach has shortcomings in terms of blurring the frontier between credit and market risks as a consequence of financial innovation and has often led to arbitrary assignments of exposures between the banking book and the trading book.

7.6 Investment services

Last but not least, the SBD framework was completed with an important prudential provision enshrined in the Investment Services Directive 93/22/EEC (ISD). It concerns article 10 of the ISD, which, in accordance with article 2 first paragraph of the same directive, applied not only to

29 Investment firms are defined as those undertaking broking, dealing, underwriting and investment management as specified in the annex to the directive, whereas credit institutions are allowed by the SBD to engage in securities business. Consequently the ISD applies also to credit institutions providing investment services.

30 Some of the risks that were previously considered as credit risks have been reassessed under CAD as market risks – e.g. the risk on the issuer of a security owned by a credit institution (Augustin 1995: 143).

investment firms but also to credit institutions whose authorisation covers one or more investment services. Article 10 ISD assigned to the home Member States the task of drawing up 'prudential rules' that would impose special organisational duties on investment firms and credit institutions, both at the management level and also at the subordinated operating structures. From 30 April 2007 the ISD was definitively replaced by the Directive on Markets in Financial Instruments 2004/39/EC (MiFID), which explicitly provides in article 1(2) that a vast range of specifically indicated provisions, many of which have a prudential character, apply to credit institutions that undertake investment services.[31] These provisions apply in conjunction with the provisions in the prudential banking directives and constitute a helpful tool for determining the content of the generic norms contained therein, e.g. such as those requiring generically adequate procedures and internal control mechanisms.

8 Financial markets regulation – the Financial Services Action Plan (FSAP)

In the late 1990s the continued efforts to give effect to the Treaty freedoms of establishment and cross-border provision of services, accompanied by insistence on the creation of equal competitive conditions for all participants in a market characterised by blurring frontiers between the traditional financial sectors, brought about accrued focus on financial markets. The objective of creating a single banking market was incorporated into the broader ambition of achieving an integrated market in financial services. An ever more vast body of norms developing common principles for financial markets has emerged over time, which was rather subsequent to (purporting to catch up with) market developments – than aiming to promote market integration.[32]

At the same time, prudential concerns have been inevitably influenced by the increasing links between banking and securities activities, which triggered new implications for the risk profile of individual financial

31 The MiFID provisions applying to credit institutions concern: organisational requirements; operating conditions and rights of credit institutions; the designation of competent authorities; cooperation between authorities in the same Member State; powers to be made available to competent authorities; administrative sanctions; the right to appeal; extra-judicial mechanisms for investors' complaints; cooperation in supervisory activities; on-the-spot verification/investigations; powers of host Member States; precautionary measures.

32 It was held that

> the degree of harmonisation of national financial laws and the means that the European policy institutions use are not developed to a similar degree to the degree of financial market consolidation. It seems that market harmonisation (negative integration) is more developed than market regulation (positive integration).
>
> (Galanopoulou 2003: 295)

institutions and the financial system as a whole. Overall, financial stability was increasingly regarded as a common concern for all financial sectors, and cross-sectoral issues prompted enhanced cooperation between the different authorities concerned. Yet the sectoral approach retained its relevance and remained predominant with regard to prudential regulation and supervision. This was mainly justified by the access to the public safety-net.

In the mid-1990s, the Single Market Programme was assessed in terms of the degree of integration of the European financial services market, as reflected in the cross-border and cross-sectoral expansion of financial intermediaries and markets. The results were considered disappointing, as the financial markets of the Member States remained segmented, to a large extent depriving market participants of direct access to cross-border financial services. European financial regulation was criticised as an 'embryonic' regime that did not work, because it allowed for obstructive host Member State control and a series of exemptions and derogations to the harmonised rules, and often resulted in inconsistent and delayed implementation (Moloney 2003). Moreover, it was considered poorly suited to cope with rapid technological developments and structural changes in market activity – the traditional tools employed by financial market participants for circumventing compulsory norms.

Confronted with the changing financial landscape and recognising the inadequacy of the European regulatory framework, the Member States invited the Commission at the Cardiff European Council of June 1998 to draft a framework for action to improve the single market in financial services. In the autumn the Commission issued the Communication entitled 'Financial Services: Building a Framework for Action', which identified various imperative actions to be taken at European level in order to create a single financial market that would also take full advantage of the benefits of the single currency.[33]

At the Vienna European Council in December 1998 the Financial Services Policy Group (FSPG) was set up, composed of representatives of the Ecofin and of the ECB, under the chairmanship of the Commission in order to assist the latter in its task of selecting priorities for action. The work of the FSPG, as well as the broad consultation undertaken earlier for the Framework for Action and the Resolution of the European Parliament (EP 1999a) constituted the basis of the new Communication of the Commission: the Financial Services Action Plan (FSAP; Commission 1999).

33 Five directions where action was crucial were highlighted: (a) endowing the EU with a legislative apparatus capable of responding to new regulatory challenges; (b) eliminating any remaining capital market fragmentation so as to reduce the cost of capital raised on EU markets; (c) allowing users and suppliers of financial services to exploit freely the commercial opportunities offered by a single financial market, while benefiting from a high level of consumer protection; (d) encouraging closer coordination of supervisory authorities; (e) developing an integrated EU infrastructure to underpin retail and wholesale financial transactions.

The Commission's Action Plan was endorsed by European policy-makers[34] thus signalling a firm political willingness to improve the regulatory framework for the European financial market.[35]

The ambitious FSAP legislative agenda also had to be backed by some reforms aimed at refining and accelerating the processes for the adoption and implementation of norms. Consequently, in parallel with the planning of the FSAP the so-called Lamfalussy framework was created, which entails a four-level approach for approving and implementing European financial legislation. This framework not only facilitated and accelerated the legislative phase, but also set up a mechanism for further specifying the adopted FSAP measures and monitoring their application and enforcement.

The FSAP was an extensive reform programme composed of a set of 42 measures envisaged for adoption at EU level within a precise timetable by the end of 2005. A priority level[36] was ascribed to each measure, which was further subsumed into one of the three strategic objectives that lay at the core of the FSAP: the achievement of a single EU wholesale market, of open and secure retail markets and the assurance of sound supervisory structures. The Commission constantly monitored progress on the FSAP and issued reports bi-annually.

The FSAP not only proclaimed sound supervision as one of its three strategic objectives, but constantly also referred to prudential concerns while describing the measures to be taken within the other two strategic objectives: wholesale markets and retail markets. Consistently praising the merits of the supervisory and regulatory framework in place, the Commission appeared to justify the need for change only by the emergence of new challenges in the market. Thus, while avoiding an open assessment of the effectiveness of the 1985 White Paper Strategy, the Commission highlighted the heightened tempo of consolidation in the industry, the intensification of links between financial markets because of the euro, and the environment characterised by strong and immediate transmission effects between EU banking and securities markets as the decisive argument for acknowledging that the status quo was not tenable for the longer term (Commission 1999: 13). Without referring to the principle of minimum

34 The FSAP was approved at the Economic and Finance Council on 25 May 1999 and submitted to the Cologne European Council. Subsequent European Councils, e.g. the Lisbon European Council in March 2000, the Stockholm European Council in March 2001 and the Brussels European Council in March 2003, called for full implementation of the Action Plan by 2005, giving continuous impetus for the adoption of the envisaged measures.

35 For a detailed review of the literature on FSAP, see Balling 2004: 256–86.

36 Priority 1 was ascribed to areas where immediate action was needed at Community level; priority 2 corresponded to areas where already existing legislation required amendments; priority 3 was attributed to measures in areas where a clear and general consensus existed but new work had to be done with a view to finalising a coherent policy.

harmonisation, the Commission emphasised the need to strive for the highest standards of prudential regulation and the necessity to keep them up to date with market developments. Acknowledging that prudential legislation at European level was increasingly transposing the work of international standard-setting bodies (Basel Committee, IOSCO), the FSAP highlighted the need for the EU to assume a key role in ensuring that its voice is clearly heard in international financial regulatory fora.

The ten measures envisaged by the FSAP under its objective of achieving a reliable regulatory and supervisory framework were aimed at: eliminating any lacunae in the EU prudential framework arising from new forms of financial business or globalisation; setting rigorous and appropriate standards so that the EU banking sector can successfully manage intensification of competitive pressures; contributing to the development of EU supervisory structures, which can sustain stability and confidence in times of changing market structures and globalisation; developing a regulatory and supervisory approach which will serve as the basis for successful enlargement; and enabling the EU to assume a key role in setting high global standards for regulation and supervision (Commission 1999: 28). The overall main message of the FSAP was to push for a more risk-based approach to banking regulation.

Among the FSAP measures of particular relevance to prudential supervision were the adoption of Directive 2002/87/EC on the supplementary supervision of credit institutions, insurance undertakings and investment firms in a financial conglomerate, Directive 2002/47/EC on financial collateral arrangements, the Electronic Money Directive 2000/46/EC, Directive 2001/24/EC on the reorganisation and winding up of credit institutions, and Directive 2004/39/EC on markets in financial instruments. The most important prudential measures – the revised capital requirements for banks and investment firms – were the last FSAP measures to be adopted, in June 2006. They will be closely analysed in the following chapters.

Initially, banking legislation constituted the lever for change, which owing to the prevailing universal bank model triggered the opening up of fragmented financial markets in general and provided the model for the first Investment Services Directive. We observe that the situation changed in the 1990s. The new driving force stemmed from securities markets, and legislative innovations spilled over from the investment business to the banking sector. This further incited the blurring of frontiers between banking and investment.

9 The post-FSAP strategy – the 2005 White Paper on Financial Services Policy

Like the 1985 White Paper, the Financial Services Action Plan had the potential to stimulate progress towards the creation of an integrated market, in a period when the achievements and the shortcomings of the previous strategies became ever more pronounced. It had the capacity to reassemble, under a comprehensive programme, existing efforts to improve European financial markets legislation and new regulatory proposals. Four major driving forces characterising the late 1990s and the first years of the third millennium were behind this: the single market, the single currency, enlargement and the impact of globalisation and new technologies. The adoption of the FSAP was merely the first move that unleashed an entire regulatory mechanism underpinning the adoption, implementation and enforcement of financial rules in the EU. Thus, the FSAP should be seen in its dynamic dimension, which emphasises the need for systematic monitoring and adaptation to developments in the market.

Following such a dynamic approach and concerned with engaging in further discussions on the implementation and optimisation of the FSAP, the Council has reconfigured the Financial Services Policy Group into a new Financial Services Committee (FSC) endowed with similar tasks of providing political oversight and advice to the Ecofin Council and the Commission on issues related to the regulatory framework for financial markets (Council 2002a, 2002b). The FSC presented to the June 2004 Ecofin Council its Final Report on the overall progress of financial integration and the key areas where further financial integration could deliver more benefits.[37] Enthusiasm for the nearly completed FSAP was moderate and a cautious tone indicated that the substantial achievements and the real impact might be assessed only against timely and consistent implementation and enforcement. At the same time, the Commission drew attention to the fact that financial integration is an ongoing process and emphasised the importance of streamlined regulatory and supervisory structures as a key factor for good implementation.

The idea of a post-FSAP strategy emerged as a recurrent topic in the discourses of policy-makers (Padoa-Schioppa 2004b), highlighting the necessity to go beyond the legislative phase and concentrate on effective implementation and enforcement. Several measures paved the way: the Commission Communication on the better application and enforcement of Community law of 11 December 2002, the Internal Market Strategy (2003–6) and the novel and alternative mechanism for solving individual cases of misapplication of Community law (SOLVIT). In addition, post-FSAP action was needed to address further challenges in European markets so as to optimise the FSAP. In this context, remaining instances of

37 On the same occasion the Commission presented its 'financial integration monitor' report, alongside four expert group reports on banking, insurance, securities and assets management. The four reports were published on 6 May 2004 and launched a wide-ranging consultation in order to map out the state of integration and seek support for further actions.

market fragmentation and important financial scandals (e.g. the collapse of Enron in 2001, Cirio in 2002 and Parmalat in 2003) caused by improper corporate behaviour, lack of transparency, accounting manipulation and fraud, called for further legislative action at the European level so as to restore public confidence in financial markets. As observed in the June 2003 Progress Report on the FSAP, the Commission had already proceeded to the 'amplification of the original FSAP ambitions' by taking an integrated approach to such new challenges and promoting a coordinated package of measures and actions on financial reporting, corporate governance, auditing and international issues.[38] Although the overall intention was to keep post-FSAP legislative initiatives to a minimum, targeted legislative action in response to specific market failures or regulatory gaps was not *a priori* ruled out. To counterbalance the call for further action at European level and the implicit growing influence of the EU, a better regulation strategy was put in place (Commission 2001a, 2002b).

The post-FSAP strategy has been explicitly laid down in the Commission's White Paper on Financial Services Policy 2005–10 Commission 2005c); it was elaborated on the basis of the consultative Green Paper (Commission 2005a) and the feedback received. Under the *leitmotiv* of 'dynamic consolidation' the Commission envisaged action until the end of 2010 with a view to achieve the following policy objectives: consolidating progress towards integration; completing unfinished business by rigorously applying the better regulation agenda; enhancing supervisory cooperation and convergence; and removing the remaining economically significant barriers. Furthermore, the Commission's policy document stressed the need to enhance the external dimension, so that the EU acquires a leading role in standard setting at a global level.

The 2005 White Paper contained the explicit commitment to focus on the implementation and enforcement of the rules adopted pursuant to the FSAP and less on the creation of new rules. Legislative efforts were limited to two instances: eliminating current inconsistencies and legal ambiguities and completing the legal framework with regard to unfinished business. The adoption process for new rules had to follow a more open, transparent and participatory policy approach based on consultation and impact assessment.

The 2005 White Paper gave specific weight to the need for proper regulatory and supervisory structures. In this context, the Commission made a commitment to keep faith with the four-level Lamfalussy regulatory process and to develop it further.[39] With regard to supervisory arrangements the

38 A separate Action Plan of Company Law and Corporate Governance and a more far-reaching review of EU rules on statutory audit constitute first initiatives in this direction.

39 The key regulatory policy issues identified were: the comitology reform; improving accountability and transparency, especially vis-à-vis the Parliament and Council; developing cross-sectoral regulatory cooperation; ensuring that all four levels respect the better regulatory approach; working towards global convergence of standards.

Commission, for the first time, recognised the need for change – albeit with caution. It advocates 'an evolutionary approach, responding to demonstrated problems, striking the right balance between more efficient and consolidated supervisory arrangements and ensuring financial stability all over the EU'.[40] The reasons for the preferred bottom-up cooperative approach to supervision are linked to the 'difficult issues of political and financial accountability', as well as to the need to allow for the markets and regulators to exploit the full potential of the Lamfalussy process.[41]

The 2005 post-FSAP strategy is illustrative of the benign macroeconomic environment in which banks and financial institutions made steady profits. Its objective was to manage the ever more integrated marketplace, focusing on the concrete application of rules and implicitly assuming an overall stability. Although some problems in the financial markets were becoming apparent, no alarm signal was triggered, nor was any ambitious project put on the table.

10 Regulatory reactions prompted by the crisis

The financial crisis that erupted in August 2007, sharpened in the second half of 2008 and is still ongoing at the time of writing, changed financial markets dramatically and turned regulatory projects upside down. The causes of the crisis are complex, multiple and still in the process of being uncovered. Yet it can be said with certainty that regulatory, supervisory and crisis management failures played an important role. Prudential aspects were at the core of such failure, as prevention and warning is what most obviously failed.

The crisis demonstrates that the emerging dense regulatory framework had inbuilt important flaws. Such flaws existed globally and were not mitigated in Europe. The flaws were essentially of a structural nature and caused the inertia of specific regulatory approaches, without sufficiently stimulating regulatory adjustments. Excessive policy focus on refining specific and time-consuming aspects of the regulatory framework resulted in

40 Commission 2005c: 10. Such an evolutionary approach foresaw that supervisory arrangements needed to be improved through reinforced cooperation and exchange of information, clarification and optimisation of home–host responsibilities, exploring the delegation of tasks and responsibilities between supervisors, taking practical steps for improving efficiency of supervision, achieving more consistent and timely cooperation and developing a real pan-EU supervisory culture.

41 In Annex III to the 2005 White Paper, containing the feedback on the consultation to the Green Paper, the Commission states:

> it is far too early to discuss new systems and the creation of new institutions going beyond the existing structures. Such an approach would not realistically correspond to the current and foreseeable stages of market integration and entails the risk of supervision remote from practice.
>
> (Commission 2005c: 15)

overlooking a series of interlinked developments that proved fatal. This refers to specific substantial aspects of prudential regulation, such as the major focus on capital requirements and their calculation methods, and to the detriment of adequate risk-management methodologies, supervision, proper corporate governance and reliable rating providers. It refers also to the scope of regulation, which mainly concentrated on well-known financial products and financial intermediaries, and led to neglecting emerging instruments (complex structured finance products, derivatives, etc.) and new actors or the substantial transformation of traditional intermediaries. Finally, from the perspective of the EU's integration project, it refers to the excessive focus on efficiency and competition aspects, to the detriment of stability concerns. This is not to say that the immense regulatory efforts undertaken especially in the decade preceding the crisis were worthless, but to maintain that they were not sufficient to prevent a widespread crisis in the banking system.

Within the EU, the regulatory response to the crisis was remarkable and regulatory production attained an unprecedented pace, from both the perspective of the quantity produced and that of the time needed for proposing and even passing legislative projects. The most astonishing examples are the quick revision of the Directive on Deposit Guarantee Schemes (Directive 2009/14/EC) and the Regulation on Credit Rating Agencies.[42] This was especially motivated by the severity of the situation and was possible because of major political willingness to act.[43] It also proves that the European decision-making framework is solid and quick enough to react to regulatory demands (the same cannot be said about supervisory or crisis management demands).

The Commission also came up with an action plan, published in March 2009, which targets restoring and maintaining a stable and reliable financial system (Commission 2009d). Besides the ambitious project of reforming the supervisory framework, which is specified in the Commission's European financial supervision package from 27 May 2009, followed by the concrete legislative proposals issued in September 2009, and based on an initial design by the de Larosière High Level Group, the Commission put forward a rather intrusive and dense plan for fixing and filling the gaps in regulation. This plan is substantially correlated with important and unprecedented international regulatory efforts that receive input from the Group of Twenty (G20) and are managed by the reinforced Financial Stability Board, and allows the EU to affirm itself in the international arena.

The Capital Requirements Directive thus again moves to the top of legislators' agenda. A regular review of the CRD, initiated in early 2008

42 The regulation was finally adopted in September 2009: Council Regulation 1060/2009.

43 The speed of reaction by policy-makers was also largely fuelled by the fact that 2009 was an election year for the European Parliament, as well as the year for the appointment of the new Commission.

and dealing with the planned amendments to the large exposures regime and the introduction of a common definition of hybrid capital instruments, was used as an opportunity to insert first regulatory provisions in reaction to the crisis (addressing mainly the problems related to the originate-and-distribute business model). The first review of the CRD (CRD2) was adopted in September 2009 (Direcive 2009/111/EC). At the time of the adoption of this first revision to the CRD there were already further proposed amendments in the pipeline, aiming to improve the quality and quantity of prudential capital for trading book activities and complex securitisation activities, and proposing new rules on liquidity risk, dynamic provisioning, excessive leverage, own funds and disclosure requirements, as well as remuneration policies and the sanctioning regime. Also, the Commission announced forthcoming proposals on tools for early intervention accompanied by proposals for new arrangements for crisis management and resolution (a Commission Communication was issued for public consultation in October 2009 – Commission 2009j). It also intends to run a rolling programme of actions to establish a far more consistent set of supervisory rules, leading to a common rulebook. In addition, the Commission has published legislative proposals establishing regulatory and supervisory standards for hedge funds, private equity and other systemically important market players, and has announced appropriate initiatives to increase transparency and ensure financial stability with regard to derivatives and other complex structured products.

This new regulatory project builds on and reinforces the existing regulatory framework of prudential rules by adding new layers, without actually questioning the framework as such. The momentum is used at maximum to push forward measures for repairing the main shortcomings in the regulatory framework. Yet there is a sense of short-termism in such a course of action and a lack of an overall view on the impact of the multiple regulatory changes. At first sight, it seems that the emphasis on risk-based measures, which has characterised regulation since the FSAP, has been abandoned in the crisis-driven regulatory proposals. Non-risk-based measures are pushed forward, especially under the *leitmotiv* of procyclicality – broadly understood as the fact that certain regulatory provisions tend to be excessively correlated with the economic cycle and therefore are unable to reach their objective. This development may impinge on the character and foundation of the prudential framework if the overall direction of reforms is not clearly ascertained. In our view, it is particularly important that European policy-makers don't act impulsively, but according to a coherent project with clearly defined long-, medium- and short-term objectives. Fundamental questions should not be avoided in the quest for reconstructing the credibility and functionality of financial markets.

4 The multiple layers of prudential rules

Attempting to understand thoroughly European prudential regulation supposes tackling the broader context in which rules are shaped. So far, we have reviewed the evolution of prudential rules from the perspective of European integration strategies. In addition, European prudential rules are the outcome of regulatory developments specific to the financial services. Two – the work undertaken by the Basel Committee on Banking Supervision and the Lamfalussy framework – hold particular significance, as they substantially dictate the directions to be taken. The first reflects prudential concerns as expressed at the international level, which substantially influence the content of European rules. The second is the outcome of efforts for improving European decision-making in the financial services sector, and is relevant because the regulatory structure determines the characteristics of the rules produced. These two regulatory realities support the view that the evolution of European prudential regulation has its own dynamics reflecting developments and sophistication in financial markets. They highlight the complex structure of EU prudential measures and the hereto linked intricacies. To complete the multi-layered framing of prudential rules, we will briefly touch on their interaction with a range of other categories of norms.

1 The EU and the Basel Committee

International rule-making undertaken by the Basel Committee on Banking Supervision (BCBS, Basel Committee) increasingly influences European prudential regulation. European measures constitute an intermediate layer between the traditional and very diversified national rules, which attempt to cope with the ever increasing financial globalisation, on the one hand, and the international standards adopted by the epistemic bankers' community, lacking direct enforcement powers, on the other hand. Undoubtedly, European prudential regulation implements at regional level what has been decided by the Basel Committee.[1] However,

1 Recital 37 to the CRD explicitly underlines the link between the new framework and the Basel II Accord. So do most of the prudential regulatory proposals presented since 2008.

its mandate allows the EU to adopt measures 'appropriately differentiated where necessary to take account of the specificities of the EU context' (Commission 2003e: 22). Several questions arise. What are the legal effects of transforming the Basel-produced regulation into a piece of binding European law? What is the acceptable margin of discretion of the EU in implementing the Basel regulations? What role does the EU play in the Basel Committee? How is the EU represented in the groups to which the Basel Committee is accountable, i.e. the G10/G20, FSF/FSB? To what extent is prudential policy decided at European level?

The relationship between the EU and the Basel Committee is a fascinating topic requiring a thorough examination that exceeds the ambit of the current work. Nevertheless, the strong influence exerted by the international 'bankers' club' on European prudential regulation does require some explanation. A short inquiry into several aspects of this rather obscure interaction will set the background for the analysis of both normative and institutional aspects of prudential banking regulation and supervision in the EU. First, we will briefly deal with the legal nature of the Basel Committee and the legal force of its measures. Further, we will try to identify the role played by the EU in the works of the Basel Committee, especially from the perspective of EU/EC external relations law.

1.1 The specific features of the Basel Committee and its work

There is a vast literature on the international financial architecture underlining the role played by the Basel Committee. Nevertheless, the Committee, set up in 1974 pursuant to a serious banking crisis,[2] remains quite an obscure institution, whose organisation and working modalities stay largely unpublicised and radiate a pronounced 'club effect'. Hosted by the Bank of International Settlements (BIS), the Basel Committee is composed of senior officials from central banks and supervisory authorities and reports to a joint committee of central bank governors and (non-central bank) heads of supervisory authorities from its member countries. The Basel Committee is distinct from the entities mentioned. Its extended composition is remarkable and goes beyond the hermetic character of the 'central bankers' club'. This could be interpreted as highlighting an intrinsic propensity of the Basel Committee towards cooperation and networking. As to geographical representation, the membership of the Basel Committee was initially limited to the most developed countries represented in the

2 The Basel Committee was established as the Committee on Banking Regulations and Supervisory Practices at the end of 1974 in the aftermath of serious disturbances in international currency and banking markets (notably the failure of Bankhaus Herstatt in West Germany). The first meeting took place in February 1975 and meetings have been held regularly three or four times a year since. For a historical perspective on the Basel Committee, see Lee 1998–9: 16; Norton 1995: 176.

Group of Ten (G10).[3] It was extended to 27 Members[4] in June 2009 to include representatives from the Group of Twenty (G20),[5] plus Hong Kong SAR and Singapore.

After years of operating far from the spotlight, in the past decade the Basel Committee has set up an informal framework which allows involvement of stakeholders and interested parties (through ample consultation and quantitative impact assessment exercises) as well as constant collaboration with authorities from non-Member States. Nevertheless, with regard to the effective mechanisms of decision-making within the Basel Committee, still very little is known. The club character endows it with valuable discretion, the key for its efficiency and flexibility. Its informal and opaque character and the selectiveness of its membership until 2009 have raised important questions about its accountability and legitimacy. Fair representation problems (Giovanoli 2000b: 30) and accusations of 'regulatory imperialism' (Barr and Miller 2006: 20) become acute when considering the implementation of its regulatory output (e.g. the Basel Accords) worldwide, in more than 100 countries. The intense efforts towards more participative and transparent decision-making, as well as the recent opening up to new members, do not completely eradicate such concerns. Deliberative processes are essentially an informal way of balancing legitimacy and effectiveness in the Committee's work, and their effectiveness depends very much on the capacity of individual countries to make use of them, hence the importance of the interaction between the domestic and international arenas. Our focus will be mostly on the dimension involving the EU.

The Basel Committee could be generally subsumed to the so-called category of 'soft organisations', a class that emerged in response to the inadequacy of formal traditional international organisations to handle trans-boundary problems that require international cooperation (Klabbers 2001). It is effectively applying 'soft power' and adopting 'soft law' instruments, concepts not precisely defined in legal theory but conceived for overcoming the shortcomings of formal politics. It constitutes a catalyst for the continuous interaction between the various levels of policy-making. Like the sponsoring organisations (G10 and G20), which themselves 'defy

3 G10 is an informal group of industrialised countries established in 1962.

4 Pursuant to the 2009 expansion, the Basel Committee has the following Members: Argentina, Australia, Belgium, Brazil, Canada, China, France, Germany, Hong Kong SAR, India, Indonesia, Italy, Japan, Korea, Luxembourg, Mexico, the Netherlands, Russia, Saudi Arabia, Singapore, South Africa, Spain, Sweden, Switzerland, Turkey, the United Kingdom and the United States. The Basel Committee's governing body will likewise be expanded to include central bank governors and heads of supervision from these new member organisations; see BCBS 2009b.

5 The G20 is an informal group created in 1999 to bring together the leaders of industrialised countries and developing economies to enable the discussion of key issues for the global economy.

any attempt at definition and classification' (Klabbers 2002: 12) in terms of the law of international organisations, the Basel Committee appears to be a loose organisation lacking any formal standing. The legal ambivalence of its institutional status seems to be inherent to its design and to its nature as what is termed, in socio-political parlance, an 'epistemic community'[6] with competences in the area of banking stability. Legal scholarship has not yet established clear-cut theories about the legal position of such actors and their status under international public law. Epistemic communities may be seen as one of the authoritative expert actors taking part in 'cooperative networks'[7] that heterarchically link organisations established at different levels and that cannot be constrained into any formal institutional structure. Another concept that might describe the organisational peculiarity of the Basel Committee is that of 'transnational regulatory networks', characterised as being 'composed of experts and representatives of national regulatory bodies, who come to agreement among themselves, guided or supported by European bodies' (Eberlein and Grande 2005: 100).

The Committee presents itself as not possessing any formal supranational *supervisory* authority and states that its conclusions are not and never were intended to have legal force. Nevertheless, despite the effects of such a declaration under traditional international public law, its acknowledged influence actually makes the Basel Committee a 'de facto international organisation' (Klabbers 2001: 407; Schermers and Blokker 1995: 30)

The de facto authority of the Basel Committee is linked to its regulatory output, which has steadily grown over time. A series of influential documents adopted by the Basel Committee since the mid-1970s have largely shaped the content of national and European prudential rules: the Basel Concordat (BCBS 1975), the first Basel Accord (BCBS 1988), the Core Principles for Effective Banking Supervision (BCBS 1997) and their subsequent amendments. These were largely principle-oriented documents, which have paved the way to the adoption, in June 2004, of the prominent detailed Basel II framework (BCBS 2004–5). This document, as subsequently amended in April 2005, was transposed in EU law through the CRD and will be further discussed in a later chapter. In response to

6 An epistemic community has been defined as a knowledge-based group of experts and specialists who share common beliefs about the cause-and-effect relationships in the world and political values concerning the ends to which policies should be addressed (Haas 1990; King 2005).

7 According to Ladeur 1997: 46, the network concept

> must not be reduced to a bare notion of regular cooperation. Rather, it is the process of cooperation itself which furnishes solutions to complex problems via joint problem definition and the drafting of a possible decision, which is then subject to ongoing evaluation on the basis of 'new' knowledge (that is new technology, new management forms, the definition of new social risks and so forth).

the crisis, the Basel Committee has issued a package of measures and is preparing further proposals to address revealed shortcomings of the Basel II framework and to provide a more robust supervisory and regulatory framework for the banking sector.[8]

As to the legal value of its rules, we have already mentioned that the Basel Committee had made it clear that its conclusions are without legal force. Consequently, Basel standards may not amount to a treaty agreement and cannot be subject to the Vienna Convention of 1969 on the Law of Treaties. According to the Committee's wording, its Basel II Accord 'formulates broad supervisory standards and guidelines and recommends statements of best practice in the expectation that individual authorities will implement them through detailed arrangements – statutory or otherwise – which are best suited to their own national systems'. The introduction to the 250-page Basel II Accord explicitly states that it was intended for national rule-making and approval processes.

Basel regulations have often been labelled 'soft law' (Lee 1998–9; Ho 2002), a jolly-joker concept held to designate something beyond the realm of law. The 'soft' status was praised initially as a positive vehicle capable of overcoming deadlocks and bringing about consensus in situations that require flexible decision-making, especially within an international context. Nevertheless, in international law theory 'soft law' has remained a quite 'mushy' concept lacking a comprehensive account of its effects and limits, which seem to be largely context-dependent. Hence, there is a certain distrust on the part of international lawyers whenever they are confronted with soft legal forms (Klabbers 2002: 338, 341). At the same time, lawyers need to recognise that this 'soft' approach has proven particularly effective, given that the Basel I Accord was implemented in more than 110 countries. Large-scale compliance with the Basel Committee's rules implicitly attaches legal effects to them.

The Basel II Accord and its endorsement by the G10/G20 countries does not merely constitute a declaration of shared values and interests; we have to deal with a detailed elaborated set of standards and rules, the outcome of long negotiations and consultation processes, which biases the future action of the involved parties. The commitment of the signatories goes beyond mere implementation and includes endeavouring to spread the new rules to non-signature countries. In this context, it appears that

8 In 2008–9, the Basel Committee published guidelines, standards or consultative documents on the following issues: better coverage of banks' risk exposures, including for trading book, securitisation and derivative activities; more and higher quality capital to back these exposures; countercyclical provisioning and capital buffers that can be built up in good times and drawn down in times of stress; the introduction of a non-risk-based measure to supplement Basel II and help contain leverage in the banking system; higher liquidity buffers; stronger risk management and governance standards; more regulatory focus on system-wide or 'macro-prudential' supervision; and greater transparency about the risk in banks' portfolios; compensation principles; proposals to strengthen global capital and liquidity regulations; stress testing; cross-border resolution. For concrete proposals, see www.bis.org/list/bcbs/index.htm.

the binding political effect of the Basel regulations is not substantially different from the binding legal force of any formal treaty agreement.

Since the negotiations of the Basel II framework, a substantial interaction between the international and the national/regional levels has been installed, with balanced input from both directions. This has led commentators to assert that 'one ought to treat administrative mechanisms at the transnational and national levels as part of an integrated whole' (Barr and Miller 2006: 23). In addition, although there are no formal enforcement mechanisms, in practice powerful international financial organisations efficiently enforce Basel rules worldwide. The International Monetary Fund and the World Bank, through their conditionality policies accompanying lending decisions, explicitly impose adherence to the Basel standards.[9] Consequently, we may infer that Basel standards have evolved into de facto binding rules.

Without inquiring as to whether Basel standards have gradually evolved into a set of 'binding principles of customary international law' (Alexander 2002b), our interest is to point to a certain legalisation process they are undergoing – which is not only acknowledged through de facto compliance but is also becoming increasingly institutionalised. Similarly, it is not our aim to outline the consequences of such a legalisation process or assess its political legitimacy. These are complex issues requiring an accurate inquiry into international public law and an in-depth analysis of the role assumed by the major international financial institutions in promoting and compelling compliance with Basel standards.

What we are interested in is highlighting the fact that, in our view, much of the substance of European banking legislation lies with the Basel Committee. Internationally agreed standards actually represent the first phase of the EU banking regulatory process (Smits 2005: 208). The 'soft law' form and the discretion left to the 'official' or 'formal' regulators, be they national, regional or international actors when implementing Basel standards, should not obscure the importance of this supranational level. It will also continue to influence the interpretation of existing standards and the further development of new prudential rules, as is already apparent for regulatory responses to the crisis. Concentrating exclusively on prudential policy-making at the EU level, without at least pointing to the way the EU has the opportunity to participate and influence the development of the Basel standards, would mean ignoring one of the core aspects of prudential regulation. It would be misleading to think that European prudential norms are a genuine output of European decision-making, as it would also be misleading to think that European legislators merely rubber-stamp

9 Compliance with Basel standards is monitored within the framework of the country reports on Financial System Stability Assessment, conducted under the umbrella of the joint initiative of the IMF and the World Bank – the Financial Sector Assessment Program; see IMF (2005) *Financial Sector Assessment Program*; see also Barr and Miller 2006: 41–5.

rules produced by the Basel Committee. The two rule-making processes have become so intermingled that it would be mistaken to tackle them in isolation. Also, in the context of the increased legalisation of the Basel Accords and the ever sharper discussions about the creation of a new framework for international financial regulation, it is important to delineate the stance of the European institutions and their eventual future role.

1.2 The participation of the EU/EC in the Basel Committee

In the 1990s, the reciprocity provisions in the Second Banking Directive triggered a debate on the international position of the European Community (EC). A more prominent role of the European Community within international economic policy-making was claimed – especially in key areas, such as liberalisation of financial services, where the Community had accumulated rich experience (Christophersen 1991b: 21). Such a debate has been central in defining the position of the European institutions in the negotiations leading to the creation of the World Trade Organisation (WTO), as well as in determining their role within the latter. The enactment of the new capital requirements framework based on Basel II and especially its ongoing review in response to the crisis constitute an ideal opportunity for initiating a debate for clarifying the relationship between the European Community/European Union[10] and the Basel Committee. This could contribute to establishing a framework that offers more legal certainty and overcomes mere ad hoc participation of the European institutions in such informal organisations. It could set a clear outline in EU external relations guiding the interactions with 'soft' international organisations.

Irrespective of debates about the legal force of the Basel Committee's regulatory output, it is a fact that the EU transforms it into hard EU law via specific EU legal instruments, mainly directives. Thus, the preamble to the CRD simply and explicitly states that the directive forms 'an equivalent to the provisions of the Basel framework agreement' (recital 37 CRD). The text of the CRD did indeed use the structural skeleton, given by the Codified Banking Directive, to insert extensive substantial provisions agreed in Basel, often using the same wording. Yet no other indication exists in the text on the intimate link with the Basel II framework.

The interest of the EU and of individual countries in adopting globally valid prudential norms is justified mainly by systemic risk concerns – especially in globally interconnected financial markets – and by competitive concerns – where a level playing-field is needed for ensuring access to foreign markets. Furthermore, there is strong interest in international

10 Until the coming into force of the Lisbon Treaty the EC was competent in matters related to the work of the Basel Committee. Now this is an EU competence. For considerations of simplification we will refer generally to the EU.

coordination of supervision, in view of both exchanging information on developments in foreign jurisdictions and precluding 'strategic games by multinational firms and races to the bottom on forbearance' (Barr and Miller 2006: 21).

The main counterargument against global prudential standards also represents the main criticisms brought against international harmonisation as a whole, and refers to the negative effects of inhibiting regulatory competition. The argument goes that harmonisation hampers competition between regulators and, thereby, lowers incentives for regulatory innovation and flexibility. The imposition of global standards creates a level playing-field among jurisdictions, which reduces regulators' fear of flow towards lower-burden jurisdictions. However, it also encourages regulatory inertia to the detriment of developing efficient regulation (Macey 2000: 147, 2003: 1353). With regard to prudential rules, it is implicit that no jurisdiction will attract or retain business on the basis of low quality standards, thus the risk of a race to the bottom is considered rather slight. Yet the risk of promoting inefficient or ineffective regulation is relatively high, as demonstrated by the 2007–9 crisis. Global regulation may have inhibiting effects on regulatory innovation, crucial for dynamic financial markets where actors constantly look for ways to evade regulatory burdens. These aspects should be given consideration when analysing the relationship between the EU and the Basel Committee.

The EU/EC is not a member in the Basel Committee, nor is it a signatory of the Basel Accords. Only nine EU Member States, all from the EU15, and of which seven belong to the Eurozone, enjoy such status. Up to June 2009 this represented about 69 per cent of overall membership of the Basel Committee, and now about 33.3 per cent. However, the European Union is directly represented in the Basel Committee through its own institutions: the European Commission and the European Central Bank, both enjoying formal observer status. The two European bodies also participate in the various task forces and working groups established by the Basel Committee.[11] This clearly underlines the active role of the European institutions in the elaboration of the Basel standards. Furthermore, the Commission often acts as an intermediary, filtering and aggregating input and information for the whole EU area, and also for acceding countries prior to their becoming EU Members. In addition, the representatives of EU countries participating in the Basel Committee (central banks and supervisory authorities) are also members of the Committee of

11 So far, it seems that the Commission and the European Central Bank (ECB) have the same formal status within the Basel Committee (as observers). Nevertheless, while the ECB, given its specific mandate and independent status, acts on its own account, the situation is different for the Commission, which has the monopoly of initiative as regards European prudential regulation, performs on behalf of all the Member States and seems to have taken the lead in reaching a common EU position.

European Banking Supervisors (CEBS), which prepares much of the technical regulatory work for banking in the EU. Also, the Commission participates in the Financial Stability Board (FSB), the revamped former Financial Stability Forum (FSF), which has taken the lead role in preparing the regulatory agenda at global level.

The Basel Committee owes its reputation as an efficient decision-making body partly to its closed membership policy. Until 2009, it was in only a few situations that the informal group opened up the floor to new participants. From the perspective of such selectiveness, the observer status of the European Commission and of the ECB can be seen as an important achievement. Nevertheless, the concrete modalities of participation remained quite obscure and our presupposition regarding the Commission's leading role is based more on intuition than on formal proofs. The legitimacy of the presence of European institutions is entirely justified from the perspective of EU law that ascribes competences in this area to the supranational level. The fact that there has never been formal recognition of the full participation of the European institutions in the Basel Committee processes might be attributed to the inherent structural ambiguity of such 'soft' organisations and the secrecy surrounding their internal operations and deliberations.

It is obvious that there is a lot of interference and concomitance of agendas between the Basel Committee and EU regulatory bodies. The work on the Basel II framework, as well as ongoing work on trading book capital requirements, complex securitisations, stress testing, liquidity risk, procyclicality, leverage ratio, etc., involves parallel efforts by the Basel Committee and the European Commission. This leaves room for mutual influences and is illustrative of the existence of what legal scholarship calls 'multi-level and overlapping cooperative networks' (Ladeur 1997: 34). Such networks are characterised by diverse relationships at different levels (heterarchical relations) that are difficult to formally integrate in coherent institutional structures. Nevertheless, the substantive correlation of the regulatory outputs, especially when one (the European level) purports to give effect to the other (the Basel level), leads to the suspicion that such networked policy-making, even if taking place outside the traditional conceptual scheme of general international law, does not exclusively occur on an ad hoc basis.

The traditional EU/EC external relations approach does not help much in deciphering the position of the EU vis-à-vis the Basel Committee. We are not in the presence of EU participation within a classic international organisation, nor are we confronted with the conclusion of a formal international agreement. So far, the Basel Committee has generally been kept out of public and doctrinal debates on the intricate division of competences between the EU and its Member States at international level, as well as on the cooperation of the latter within international organisations.

Without entering into an in-depth analysis, we intuitively suggest that the Basel regulations could be assimilated to partial mixed agreements.[12] Thereby we keep in mind the fact that mixity constitutes a harshly criticised legal reality because of its intricate complex nature (Rosas 1998; Eeckhout 2004). Also, the 'soft law' nature of the Basel framework deprives it of the possibility of formal enforcement and hence automatically sets aside most of the legal consequences attached to mixity in EC external relations (e.g. the liability issues).

Still, the theoretical comparison to mixity might prove helpful in order to identify the various concrete aspects of EU and Member States' participation in the Basel Committee. So far, the unitary position of the EU within the Basel Committee has not been publicly challenged, nor were there general complaints regarding legitimacy concerns on the part of the EU Members not participating in the Basel Committee. Yet important divergences in the Council when discussing EU draft legislation transposing Basel regulations are indicative of the fragility of the EU's position in the international arena. Calls for a stronger European representation in financial standard setting also highlight the need to speak with one voice and to coordinate beforehand so as to achieve precise European negotiating positions (Commission 2005c, 2009d).

Mixed agreements are a widespread technique, the outcome of the practice of joint participation of the EU and its Member States in international agreements. Joint participation does not refer only to the conclusion of the agreement but also to its negotiation, representation, implementation, responsibility, etc. The reasons for mixity relate generally to the shared competences in a specific area (as would also be the case of banking supervision) and/or the formal participation in international fora. It is often the case that the EC/EU will not be a signatory itself, given the fact that its status frequently depends on the political willingness of non-EU participant States and on the nature of the international framework harbouring the negotiations. Also, there is the specific category of 'partial mixity' (Eeckhout 2004: 223), referring to international agreements where alongside the EC/EU only some of the Member States participate, whereas the non-participating Member States are also bound by the concluded agreements. In our opinion, the Basel regulations, whose formal signatures are only those States participating in the G10/G20, can be assimilated to a partial mixed agreement. This is because the European institutions have played a central role during the elaboration and negotiation, and because EU law imposes the outcome of the Basel regulatory process on all EU Member States. The European Court of Justice has made clear that even if an agreement is not strictly speaking a mixed agreement because of the impossibility of the EC/EU

12 On mixed agreements see Björklund 2001; Timmermans 2000: 239–47; Hyett 2000: 248–75.

to become a party to it, the international agreement will be treated as a mixed agreement if part of the matters covered by it fall within the competence of the EU.[13]

The transformation of the Basel regulation into hard law through Community measures, binding for all Member States, requires some procedural guarantees for the non-G10/G20 EU Member States so as to ensure that they can be given a meaningful role in influencing the outcome of the international negotiations. Furthermore, these safeguards are important when considering the frequent criticism directed at the Basel Committee for lack of accountability and political legitimacy (Alexander 2002b). Such guarantees are imperative irrespective of the internal decision-making processes within the Basel Committee, which has been characterised as having 'antidemocratic qualities' like centralisation, opacity, remoteness from popular or representative politics, elitism and lack of accountability (Rubenfeld 2003: 22, 34, 36).

The major interest of assimilating the Basel Accord to a partial mixed agreement is the application of the principles of close cooperation and unity of EU representation in external relations as the values guiding the coordination of the participating Member States and European institutions. These would be the only guarantees which would ensure the representation of the interests of non-participating Member States. The principle of close cooperation requires the Community institutions and the Member States to take all the measures necessary for the coordination of both the process of negotiation and conclusion, and of the fulfilment of the obligations entered into. In practice, such coordination takes place through mutual information on the respective positions, through the endeavour to reach a common position and establish a unitary line of action. Frequently, such cooperation is pinned down in informal arrangements between the Commission and the Council, establishing the concrete modalities of a unitary representation.

The undisclosed proceedings in the Basel Committee negotiations do not allow us to evaluate the positions of the various European actors (institutions and Member States) in that process, nor has there been any arrangement describing the concrete cooperation modes publicised. Nevertheless, this does not seem to be an issue in public debates and the impression is that the Commission has taken the lead, despite the absence of any formal powers vested in it. Seen from the outside, it seems that there is a common Community front, ensuring the unity of representation and standing for the interests of all Member States. Yet the

13 ECJ, Opinion 2/91 (Re ILO Convention 170) [1993] ECR I-1061, para. 37. In this case, cooperation between the Community and the Member States is all the more necessary in view of the fact that the former cannot, as international law stands at present, itself conclude an ILO Convention and must do so through the medium of Member States. We recall that, unlike the soft nature of the Basel Accord, the ILO Convention is a 'hard' international Treaty.

Commission's calls for unitary representation, as expressed in the 2005 White Paper on Financial Services Policy, and divergences apparent in the Council when discussing the same topic, indicate that European representation is not always straightforward. In this context, at least a general commitment to prior coordination should be made explicit, even if no clear streamlined cooperation procedures can be devised or disclosed beforehand, so as to give legal certainty regarding the unitary representation within the Basel Committee of a European position, reflecting the concerns of all Member States. The recent activism of the EU on global level in view of promoting a quick recovery and its efforts to promote the reform of the international financial regulatory and supervisory framework highlight the EU's willingness to use the momentum for fostering its international position (Commission 2009d: 17–19). Speaking with one strong voice in the international arena presupposes clear internal arrangements for achieving agreement. Yet, disappointingly, so far there is no firm commitment to promote more transparent arrangements for EU representation in the Basel Committee.

To conclude, we argue strongly that the external dimension of European prudential regulation cannot be ignored, as rules adopted in the Basel Committee are effectively integrated in EU norms. Therefore, we consider that more transparency is needed as to the internal arrangements underpinning the EU's effective participation in the decision-making process of the Basel Committee. The time is ripe for legal writing to face this problem and enter the 'process of "catching up" with existing practice' (Cremona 1999: 152). In our view, for legal certainty reasons it is important to clarify the exact modalities of coordination. Especially, given that European prudential regulation is largely centralised, in accordance with the doctrines of parallel competences and implied powers, the European institutions should also have the corresponding powers to act in external relations.

Furthermore, clarification of EU representation within the Basel Committee and more broadly in the G20 would ensure more efficiency and also increased legitimacy of decision-making. Also, the explanation of the position of the European Union vis-à-vis the Basel Committee would contribute to the debates about a future international financial architecture and to discussions on legal effects attached to 'soft' legal instruments. Only if competences are unequivocally delineated and cooperation mechanisms firmly established can the EU be perceived as a powerful and credible actor within the international arena.

2 The Lamfalussy framework

The second development that largely influences the production of European prudential rules is the new four-level regulatory framework for financial services in the EU. In the following we will present only the general background for the introduction of this so-called 'Lamfalussy framework', with a view of identifying the way it influences the design of prudential rules. Further considerations, particularly with regard to the institutional set-up, will be made at a later stage in the institutional analysis.

As occurred in the mid-1980s with the internal market project and the procedural changes introduced by the SEA, impetus for action in the late 1990s was underpinned not only by legislative planning and strict deadlines, but also by some procedural reforms aiming to facilitate the timely implementation of the entire project. Thus, the FSAP was accompanied by measures improving and speeding up the rule-making process. It was considered to be slow, unable to respond to changing market conditions and inclined to produce ambiguous texts. The adoption of directives took on average two to three years, followed by further one to two years for their implementation – a long interval that did not allow regulation to keep pace with rapidly evolving financial markets (Lastra 2003: 61). Furthermore, the legislative output often consisted of hybrid provisions mixing broad principles with detailed technical issues, oscillating between ambiguity and over-prescriptiveness. Moreover, the command-and-control regulation associated with traditional banking activities was not suited for modern dynamic financial activities, which rely more on market reactions and implicitly require more interaction between the various parties involved.

The FSAP explicitly required that 'the EU should be endowed with a legislative apparatus capable of responding to new regulatory challenges'. As a consequence, on 17 July 2000 the Ecofin Council set up the Committee of Wise Men under the chairmanship of Alexandre Lamfalussy, which was entrusted with elaborating proposals for reforming the law-making process concerning securities markets regulation in Europe. The mandate required the Wise Men to identify the imperfections in the existing legislative process and to make recommendations aimed at speeding it up and making it more flexible, and thus able to respond to market developments. It was beyond the scope of the mandate to identify what should be regulated, or to look at specific issues such as international implications or prudential considerations. The Wise Men Report, published on 15 February 2001, was officially endorsed on 23 March 2001 by the Stockholm European Council. Several misgivings on the part of the European Parliament delayed the final approval of the Lamfalussy report and triggered the adoption of the European Parliament's resolution of 5 February 2002 (EP 2002b), which imposed a number of safeguards and finally launched the reform.

Following the initial success of the new regulatory framework in the securities sector, on 8 October 2002 the Ecofin Council endorsed a report by the Economic and Financial Committee providing for the extension of the Lamfalussy framework to all financial sectors, while recognising sectoral specificities. The Parliament's support for the extended Lamfalussy approach was given through the Van den Burg Resolution of November 2002. On 6 November 2003, the Commission issued a package of seven measures, composed of a draft directive and six decisions, extending the committee structure and the regulatory procedures used since 2002 for the securities sector to banking, insurance, occupational pensions and collective investment schemes (UCITS).[14]

The Lamfalussy approach has a 'procedural' character outlining an organisational setting, which draws on the institutional arrangement known as comitology and is based on article 202 EC Treaty. The report constructs a four-level legislative process, commonly referred to as the 'Lamfalussy framework/process'. At Level 1, legislation containing framework principles should be adopted in accordance with the co-decision procedure foreseen by article 251 EC Treaty. Such legislation should also provide for powers to be delegated to the Commission in order to define implementing measures. The comitology procedure steps in at Level 2, where the Commission elaborates technical implementing measures. The finalisation of the Commission's technical implementing measures is dependent on the approval by the relevant regulatory committee – the Level 2 committee (the European Securities Committee (ESC), the European Banking Committee (EBC) and the European Insurance Committee (EIC)), which acts as a regulatory committee in accordance with the Council Comitology Decision 1999/468/EC. The Commission's word at Levels 1 and 2 is underpinned by the advice of the respective committee of supervisors – the Level 3 committee (Committee of Securities Regulators (CESR), Committee of European Banking Supervisors (CEBS) and Committee of European Insurance and Occupational Pensions Supervisors (CEIOPS)). The preparation of such advice entails consultation with market participants, end-users and consumers. Level 3 emphasises the need for cooperation of national regulators so as to ensure consistent day-to-day implementation of legislation. At this level, the committee composed of supervisors works on joint interpretation, so as to ensure consistent implementation and application of EU law, carries out peer reviews, compares regulatory practice and elaborates recommendations, guidelines and common standards (in areas not covered by EU legislation) with a view to fostering regulatory and supervisory convergence. Level 4 emphasises enhanced enforcement measures and requires the Commission to check Member States' compliance with EU legislation and

14 While the decisions setting up the new regulatory committees for banking and insurance, and those amending the already established European Securities Committee and Committee of European Securities Regulators to include UCITS, were suspended until the adoption of the proposal for a directive containing technical adjustments, the decisions establishing the committees of supervisors for banking and insurance came into effect immediately. The Committee of European Banking Supervisors (CEBS) was established from 1 January 2004 and the Committee of European Insurance and Occupational Pensions Supervisors (CEIOPS) took effect from 24 November 2003.

to take legal action in case of inconsistent or delayed implementation. We will go into more detail on the various implications of such design when discussing the institutional framework for prudential regulation. For the time being we confine ourselves to developing some ideas related to the sensitive balance that needs to be drawn between the political Level 1 and the technical Level 2 measures. This may help us to better understand the nature of financial regulation in Europe.

2.1 Essential versus non-essential implementing measures

The essential measures at Level 1 are embodied in legislative acts (directives or regulations) and consist of basic political choices expressed as broad but sufficiently precise framework norms and principles. According to the Wise Men report:

> the framework principles are the core political principles, the essential elements of each proposal. They reflect the key political choices to be taken by the European Parliament and the Council of Ministers on a proposal by the European Commission. Level 1 principles should clearly specify the nature and the extent of technical implementing measures that should be taken at the second level and the limits within which the resulting provisions can be adapted and updated at that level without requiring a change of framework legislation.
>
> (Committee of Wise Men 2001: 21)

Level 1 measures were characterised as rules of 'high political importance, and by extension, structural and significant' (Avgerinos 2002: 274). They are conceived from the very beginning as stable rules that should not vary in the medium term, and therefore have high significance and authoritative legal character. Such an understanding may also be inferred from the ECJ's case-law, which had already stressed in 1971 the difficulty of including all policy details in regulations adopted by the Council, stating that it was sufficient that such a legislative act only addressed 'the basic elements of the matter to be dealt with'.[15] Subsequent jurisprudence confirmed that 'essential rules' consist of 'provisions intended to give concrete shape to the fundamental guidelines of Community policy',[16] which include also the definition of concepts.[17] The Lamfalussy procedure seems to further narrow down the scope of European framework legislation by allowing the Commission to 'clarify' or 'adapt' the definitions of the various concepts used, in order to take account of developments on financial markets and to

15 Case 25/70 *Einfuhr-und Vorratsstelle für Getreide und Futtermittel* v. *Köster* [1971] ECR 1161, para. 6.

16 Case C-240/90 *Germany* v. *Commission* [1992] ECR I-5383, para. 37.

17 Case C-104/97, *Atlanta AG and Others* v. *Commission and Council* [1999] ECR I-6983.

ensure the uniform application of the Level 1 measures.[18] Essential measures aim at setting general policy criteria that constitute the foundation for the continuously evolving regulatory framework. Rigid and mandatory definitions, that once were required in order to impose a common language, seem no longer to correspond to dynamic markets that favour flexible rules – and thus, regulatory rules to the detriment of legislative rules.

While essential framework measures consist of stable rules that have to respond to the dynamics of the markets, implementing measures apparently have flexibility as their main characteristic, as they allow for faster and easier amendment. Their nature and scope have to be predetermined by the Council and the European Parliament on the basis of a Commission proposal, and subsequently made the object of the comitology procedure. In order to identify and examine the general characteristics, nature and role of delegated implementing measures, Avgerinos observes that various hints can be found in the case-law. Thus, the European Court of Justice had quite early on recognised in *Köster* that the legal basis test was not enough for distinguishing implementing measures and had to be accompanied by a more substantive test. Inevitably, such a substantive test concentrated on the compatibility between the implementing measures and the 'basic elements' laid down in the essential rules,[19] whereby all implementing powers had to be seen in the light of the objectives and scope of the basic rules.[20] In order to ensure such compatibility, legislation should comprehensively stipulate the essential elements of conferred powers, in accordance with 'sufficiently precise criteria and limits to enable it to be applied to the specific case and, therefore, to enable its exercise to be reviewed by the Court' (Avgerinos 2002: 276). Such specified limits,[21] if regarded as exhaustive, preclude the establishment of supplementary rights or duties within the implementing measures.[22] At the same time, implementing measures should not be defined rigidly and exhaustively and should allow the Commission significant discretion in deciding how to act, sometimes with urgency, to market developments. Also, it should be considered that not all non-essential measures pertain to the realm of legislation, as many are made the object of Level 3 acts.

However, despite theoretical attempts in the literature to discern the dividing line between essential and implementing measures, in practice

18 Avgerinos (2002) notes such a change with regard to the proposals for the Market Abuse Directive, for the Conglomerates Directive.

19 Case 46/86 *Albert Romkes* v. *Officier van Justitie for the District of Zolle* [1987] ECR 2671, para. 16.

20 Joined Case 6/88 and 7/88 *Spain and France* v. *Commission* [1989] ECR 3639, para. 14.

21 Such specific criteria may include, for instance, the situations in which protective measures may be taken, the criteria for assessing whether such a situation exists, the kind of measures to be adopted and the period of their validity (Case 291/86 *Central-Import Munster GMbH & Co. KG* v. *Hauptzollamt Munster* [1988] ECR 3679, para. 15).

22 Case 264/86 *France* v. *Commission* [1988] ECR 973, paras 15–20.

the distinction is done on a case-by-case basis. This was the approach encouraged by the European Council in its 2001 Resolution, where it held that

> the split between framework principles (level 1) and implementing measures (level 2) should be determined on a case-by-case basis in a clear and transparent way … The Commission is invited, when it presents its proposals, to give indications as to what kind of implementing measure is foreseen.
>
> (European Council 2001)

So far, with regard to banking regulation, experience with Level 2 measures is still limited.[23] The Inter-Institutional Monitoring Group (IIMG), set up for observing the functioning of the Lamfalussy framework, has from the beginning expressed concerns about excessive legislative detail at both Level 1 and 2, and the need to confine Level 1 measures to framework principles (IIMG 2003a, 2003b, 2004). It also recommended that more frequent use should be made of Level 2 measures, which have to be kept as lean as possible and should provide unambiguous rules so as to ensure consistent interpretation. The Final Report by the IIMG, issued in October 2007, confirmed that the distinction between basic principles and implementing measures remained an important open issue and was mainly linked to the level of detail in legislation. While the report restated its recommendation to avoid technical rules in Level 1 measures, it also admitted that many apparently technical rules are inevitably of high political importance or sensitivity. Hence it decisively discarded a one-size-fits all approach and called for pragmatism and flexibility to ensure efficiency (IIMG 2007). A firm commitment by the Commission that Level 2 measures adhere strictly to Level 1 principles, supplementing existing procedural safeguards, would probably cast off some of the superfluous detail at Level 1. Yet, as long as the fear persists that additional underlying principles at Level 2 will be dissimulated under technical implementing norms, it is likely that the distinction between essential and non-essential measures will remain blurred.

Despite the absence of clear criteria that ascribe substantive issues straightforwardly to one of the first two levels, there is a general sense of achieving a more efficient and systematic legislation, as well as a swifter legislative procedure (IIMG 2003b: 13). At this point, it is important to acknowledge the distinction and to understand the intricacies inherent

23 In relation to the new prudential framework (CRD and recast CAD) to our knowledge only three comitology measures have been adopted: Commission Directive 2007/18/EC concerning the treatment of multilateral development banks; Commission Directive 2009/27/EC amending certain annexes to the recast CAD, and Commission Directive 2009/83/EC amending certain annexes to the CRD. The latter, prior to adoption, had to be resubmitted to the Commission following criticism from the European Parliament.

to its functioning in order to assess the degree of detail that Community legislation covers. This is important for measuring the extent to which it shapes Member States' regulatory systems and for acknowledging the new scope of the European regulatory strategy, which seems to move away from minimum harmonisation. The aspects tackled in this subsection are relevant for understanding the link between the various levels of rules and the corresponding decision-making bodies.

3 The multi-layered character of prudential regulation

Any attempt at systematising the legal sources behind prudential rules results in a multidimensional puzzle, where reassembling the pieces is by no means straightforward. The complexity stemming from the multiplicity of actors and the variety of instruments renders prudential regulation almost inaccessible to laypeople. The norms applicable at national level to credit institutions hide intricate decision-making and multiple underlying rationales, while they also reflect specific features of the respective banking market. Increased internationalisation of financial regulation and greater influence of international actors, accompanying globalisation of capital markets, resulted in supranational regulation forming the core of national legislation, while local peculiarities have a rather ancillary status.

Such realities have to be kept in mind when identifying the sources of European prudential regulation. The latter is located at the crossroads between international norms contained in soft-law instruments and national legislation immediately affecting the regulated institutions. At the same time, it is also concerned with the realities of the European financial services market.

As already highlighted, endeavours for adopting common standards at European level had a genuine impulse in the quest of establishing the single market. Nevertheless, concrete achievements have been always paralleled by international action (especially from the Basel Committee), which allegedly has a more modest scope in terms of both objectives pursued and the legal force of norms. While active participation of EU individual actors definitely ensures that international norms also entail a European dimension, there are some concerns that the international standard-setting process can be used in the limited interest of those who effectively participate in the negotiations. This is particularly problematic given the opacity of decision-making in the Basel Committee, uncertainty as to the process of reaching a representative EU position and doubts as to leadership in the EU delegation. From the perspective of self-interest theories of regulation, this increased influence of international regulation might also be seen as a way of circumventing difficulties in achieving a common position at the European level. Thus, international commitments taken in the framework of the Basel Committee may be used to bypass cumbersome decision-making in the Council and the European Parliament, given their reluctance to reverse complex international agreements. In this context, excessive concerns for ensuring the global level playing-field should be more cautiously expressed and should not pre-empt the European legislator from democratically evaluating substantial policy trade-offs and controversial issues behind the apparent technocratic expert rules adopted at international level.

Furthermore, European prudential directives have to be implemented at the national level, which is an occasion for national regulators to add further substantive aspects. Consequently, European legislation should also envisage bringing about convergence and harmonisation of national prudential regulation. The European legislator has to lay down the limits of national discretion so as to ensure that the internal market in financial services is not affected by the disparities resulting from national implementation. Convergence in the transposition and implementation of European norms was one of the important reasons for the establishment of the four-level Lamfalussy procedure, which introduces additional layers into the hierarchy of sources and which consists of both hard and soft-law measures.

Apart from these vertical layers of prudential regulation, there is also a complex horizontal dimension. First, prudential banking regulation is located throughout various directives. Despite the welcome codification that brought some coherence into the body of EU prudential norms, the multiplicity of legal instruments persists, as do the difficulties in creating a single clear and comprehensive code of prudential regulation – a so-called rulebook.

Further intricate horizontal layers are linked to the well-rooted universal bank model, and the blurring of frontiers between the various financial sectors. Institutions operating in financial markets spread their business beyond the sector for which they were granted authorisation, and engage in activities entailing different kinds of risks. Thereby, credit institutions may become subject to additional requirements such as sector-specific prudential norms[24] or prudential regulation applying to complex financial structures. The latter case is of specific importance, as Directive 2002/87/EC on financial conglomerates is a Community legal instrument addressing loopholes in sectoral legislation. The Conglomerates Directive sets specific solvency requirements, concentration of risks rules and principles aimed at ensuring appropriate risk-management and internal control systems within the conglomerate that prevail over sectoral requirements.[25]

24 Such requirements might stem from the regulations applicable to investment services, insurance or reinsurance business, UCITS and pension funds.

25 With regard to solvency rules and internal risk management systems, the Conglomerates Directive prohibits the use of the same capital more than once as a buffer against risk in different entities in the same conglomerate (the so-called 'multiple gearing of capital') and intends to prevent 'downstreaming' by parent undertakings, consisting of the issue of debt and the subsequent use of the proceeds as equity for their regulated subsidiaries (what is known as 'excessive leveraging').

We may identify a composite picture of legislative instruments at the European level, where core prudential rules are still laid down in sectoral instruments, being traditionally linked to requirements for market access in those specific sectors. Increased market liberalisation and financial innovation, allowing financial institutions to expand their activities beyond their traditional sectors, have resulted in the adoption of functional regulation that makes prudential treatment dependent not on the type of institution but on the type of services provided. CAD was the first example of functional regulation in the EU applicable to both credit institutions and investment services; it was followed by other functional norms centred on the idea of primarily regulating markets and financial instruments (e.g. the MiFID and its implementing directives, the Market Abuse Directive, the Prospectus Directive and the UCITS Directive). These all comprise or make reference to prudential aspects and often contain cross-references that highlight the tendency of sectoral regulation to be increasingly interdependent and head towards what may be called functional financial regulation.

4 Coordination of conflicting prudential norms

European prudential regulation consists of a plurality of norms adopted at different layers and enshrined in different instruments that are to be used cumulatively, and not alternatively. Such a plurality is reinforced by the coexistence of sectoral/institutional and functional approaches to regulation. Also, the continuous extension and growing complexity of prudential concerns accompanying the expansion of financial activities results in greater interaction between prudential norms and other categories of rules. The issue arises as to how the various legislative pieces prescribing prudential rules should be related to each other, as well as prudential with non-prudential legislation when they become conflictual. The hierarchy between layers is generally clear, except for the indicated difficulties in distinguishing between essential and implementing measures. The most severe coordination problems relate to prudential norms pertaining to the same layer.

While the CRD occupies de facto a central position for prudential banking regulation, its application might interfere in several instances with other prudential rules, especially with the recast CAD. Potential problems may arise because of largely overlapping subject matter, such as the rules for the calculation of capital requirements and for prudential supervision covered by both the CRD and recast CAD. For instance, the recast CAD explicitly states in its first article, defining the scope of the directive, that a 'Member State may impose additional or more stringent requirements on those investment firms and credit institutions it has authorised', thus setting EU minimum harmonisation as one of the defining features of the directive. The CRD, apart from certain individual norms that indicate the possibility of Member States to adopt more stringent rules (e.g. some items of own funds, large exposures), has carefully avoided a general provision implying that minimum harmonisation is perceived as a leading principle. On the contrary, there are indications that the CRD aims towards maximum harmonisation. Such different approaches might create inconsistencies and conflicts, given the numerous references in the recast CAD to the CRD and the provisions in the CAD that provide for the application of various articles in the CRD *mutatis mutandis* to investment firms. Another example of possible conflicts of horizontal norms results from the possibility under the current rules of allocating certain exposures to both the banking book (CRD) and the trading book (recast CAD).

Also, the MiFID rules focusing on the prevention of conflicts of interests and the organisational requirements attached to it may interfere with prudential requirements on internal control mechanisms in the CRD, as may also the provisions regarding the competent authorities (article 13 MiFID). There is no provision in the two directives to give eventual prevalence of prudential norms over conflict-of-interest rules. Another source of potential conflicts of norms is linked to the increased prudential character of non-prudential rules and the growing reliance of prudential rules on other fields (corporate governance, accounting, auditing and consumer protection).

Currently, no formal hierarchy may be identified with clear structures that would enhance predictability, nor would this probably be desirable given the evolutionary nature of financial regulation. It is hardly imaginable that the solution to such conflicts would be the adoption of a provision formally consecrating a certain hierarchical relationship or the generic priority of prudential rules with regard to any conflicting norm. Nevertheless, a principles-based prioritisation might prove useful for settling situations of conflicting norms and for guaranteeing that the application of norms remains within the scope of the fundamental principles agreed. The lack of coordination among these rules constitutes a problem of quality of legislation that substantially impinges on legal certainty.

5 The interaction of prudential regulation with other categories of norms

Notwithstanding the autonomous character of prudential regulation, its efficacy and efficiency is highly dependent on compliance with other categories of norms, which eventually might be included under a very broad understanding of safety-and-soundness regulation. We have already discussed in the introductory section the interplay between prudential regulation and protective regulation (safety-net arrangements such as deposit guarantee schemes and lender of last resort). We underlined the difficulties even in clearly distinguishing between these two types of rules and admitted that the distinction might be artificial. Further important complements to prudential regulation are the norms pertaining to the fields of corporate law, accounting, auditing, consumer protection and competition law.[26] They all operate in parallel with prudential standards, and are helpful in controlling the financial health of the participants in the banking market. They also play an equally important role with regard to exit policies (e.g. insolvency procedures) and *ex post* measures applicable in the case of banking crises (e.g. lender of last resort). It is not our purpose here to provide an accurate description of these rules; we will only give an overview of their interference with prudential regulation. This is relevant for understanding the complexity of the context in which banking supervisors operate and the variety of policy instruments aimed at achieving 'safety and soundness' objectives.

5.1 Prudential regulation and corporate law

Credit institutions are corporations which can take a variety of structural and organisational forms[27] and are, as a rule, subject to the principles of general corporate law. Some corporate aspects have a special impact on the banking business, such as: the rules concerning management and internal control mechanisms; the role of banks' boards in balancing the diverging interests of shareholders and other stakeholders (e.g. creditors, depositors); various aspects of ownership (e.g. large versus concentrated ownership, representation of minority shareholders); the importance of the corporate structure for identifying the head office and determining the competent authorities, issues related to the reorganisation and liquidation of credit institutions, etc. The incentives for bank managers and owners stemming from such rules may interfere with the incentives originated in prudential rules. Grasping the complexity of the relationship between such provisions and prudential norms would require an in-depth legal analysis of private and business law topics related to companies, contracts and corporate governance. This would go beyond the frame of the present analysis. Instead, we will refer briefly to those aspects of corporate law that are perceived as a 'precondition for the successful operation of financial supervision' (Mayes *et al.* 2001: 91): corporate governance, understood broadly as the rules and mechanisms by which companies are directed and controlled.[28]

26 Another category of norms which is extremely relevant for prudential regulation is insolvency law. This will be mentioned later, in the institutional analysis, as part of the interaction between prudential supervision and crisis management.

27 Credit institutions may be State-owned or private, wholly owned or part of a larger group, cooperative or mutual institutions, savings banks or joint stock companies. The legal form of incorporation is a matter of national legislation and reflects the large diversity stemming from national company law.

28 For discussions on the concept of corporate governance, see Mayes *et al.* 2001: 93–8 and Lannoo 1999: 269–94.

The issue of banking corporate governance as a factor impinging upon systemic stability received increased attention only in the late 1990s (BCBS 1999c; OECD 1999, 2004). In the EU, corporate governance came to the forefront through efforts undertaken for the creation of a single market (Lannoo 1995), particularly the work done for promoting the Societas Europaea (the European Company).[29] Thus, within the broader FSAP framework, the Commission has issued a Communication on Company Law and Corporate Governance including an Action Plan that comprised prioritised legislative and non-legislative initiatives. Also, the emerging paradigm shift in prudential policy related to the Basel II internal risk-based approach, which recognises the importance of banks' risk-management processes and internal control mechanisms, has invigorated considerations of corporate governance for banking. Further impetus came during the financial crisis, with debates on remuneration schemes and executive pay, and hereto linked incentives for risk-taking, becoming most topical. Broader topics, such as those focusing on the role of shareholders and the board of directors in controlling management and on ways of improving their capacity for understanding and influencing the risk appetite of their bank, are also increasingly considered.

Corporate law and prudential regulation are intrinsically linked, as obviously resulting from the authorisation requirements of credit institutions, as well as from supervisors' powers to control and intervene in the arrangements between shareholders and management that would negatively impact on the financial health of a bank. Also, regulatory requests for boosting capital levels can directly impact on the ownership structure of a bank. Corporate law often has the role of complementing prudential principles, set in a concise form in the CRD, for instance with regard to the form of authorisation[30] or the structure of the management board.[31] Also, prudential restrictions on shareholders and those on qualifying

29 See Council Regulation 2157/2001; see also the Nordea restructuring case discussed by Dermine 2005; Wymeersch 2005.

30 The CRD sets out in art. 6 the substantive requirement of obtaining an authorisation before the banking activity is commenced. It leaves Member States to determine the form and the precise conditions, provided these are in conformity with the other requirements of the CRD. As a consequence of this procedural freedom, some Member States (e.g. Italy and the UK) have maintained a two-tier system, whereby they request two authorisations: one for the establishment of the legal person in accordance with corporate law and a subsequent authorisation for the carrying on of the business of banking.

31 As the structure of the corporate boards varies greatly across the Member States and strong corporate traditions will most likely impede the adoption of a specific model at EU level, the CRD only concisely sets the precise 'four-eyes principle' (e.g. there should be at least two persons who direct a bank) and a general requirement that these persons be of sufficiently good repute and have sufficient experience to perform such duties. As a result, European prudential regulation allows Member States to determine the exact corporate framework under which the two persons will 'effectively direct the business of the credit institution'. In Europe there are a multitude of models: one-tier boards, two-tier boards and in-between forms.

holdings in a credit institution have a strong corporate law component (Harm 2002). Such examples demonstrate the intensive interaction between the two categories of norms and their common aim of ensuring stable and sound institutions. Moreover, article 22 CRD explicitly determines good corporate governance arrangements as a prerequisite for the authorisation of a credit institution. Thereby, good corporate governance is recognised as a key element of the prudential regulatory framework. The technical criteria determining arrangements, processes and mechanisms of robust governance, laid down in Annex V to the CRD, will derogate, as *lex specialis*, from any contrary arrangement provided by general corporate law.

Recent research has highlighted the specificity of the financial sector and claims that the governance models applicable to banking should consider the institutional dynamics of the specific sector. From this perspective it is held that banking regulation is a substitute for corporate governance (Adams and Mehran 2003: 124). However, from a European perspective, this would be too radical a view, especially in the light of some vague or generic concepts used in the CRD (Alexander 2004: 33). We consider that prudential regulation acts as *ius speciale* in relation to the general norms stemming from corporate law, and thus prevails if there is any collision between the two categories. Also, in several instances prudential rules contain general principles that explicitly or implicitly refer to corporate law for their implementation.

In light of the crisis, increased attention has been given to remuneration policies and compensation packages.[32] It is held that inadequate remuneration contracts of management promoted inappropriate incentives for short-termism, to the detriment of the overall financial health of banks. Therefore, attempts are now being made, through regulation,[33] to mitigate those wrong incentives that allowed for excessive risks and to ensure that all levels of management act in the long-term interest of a bank. Thus, for financial stability purposes, bank supervisors seem to be becoming ever more influential in the appointment of a bank's management, as well as in assessing the suitability of compensation policies.

It follows that the corporate governance arrangements of banks have moved to the very core of banking supervisors' concerns. In this context, it becomes imperative that the interaction between the two sets of norms is tackled in a more systematic way, so as to clarify the exact scope and role attributed to each of them, as well as their interaction.

32 The Commission had already issued a recommendation on directors' pay in 2004; however, it was only partially observed by Member States. Commission Recommendation 2004/913/EC.

33 The European Commission in April 2009 issued two recommendations on remuneration issues in financial services (2009/384/EC and 2009/385/EC) and in July 2009 issued proposals for amending the CRD with regard to remuneration policies (CRD 3).

5.2 Prudential norms and accounting rules

Prudential rules are intrinsically linked to accounting principles, which provide the framework for presenting the financial situation of a bank (the bank's accounts, the various positions in the balance sheet) in accordance with predefined criteria. Prudential supervision in the EU cannot be carried out in the absence of common accounting rules that ensure comparability. Therefore, calculation of own funds and their adequacy with regard to the risks incurred by credit institutions is carried out in accordance with European or international accounting standards. The CRD stipulates that accounting techniques should apply in accordance with three legislative instruments that prescribe specific rules on annual accounts and consolidated accounts of banks and financial institutions (Council Directive 86/635/EEC), the accounting treatment applicable to branches (Council Directive 89/117/EEC) and the application of international accounting standards (i.e. the International Accounting Standards (IAS) and International Financial Reporting Standards (IFRS)) to listed banks and financial firms (Regulation (EC) No. 1606/2002).

The importance of accounting rules for prudential regulation results from the fact that accounting concepts and categories are used for calculating or mitigating capital requirements. An illustrative example is that of the concept of 'goodwill', which was at the centre of a dispute in the US: *United States* v. *Winstar Corporation*.[34] The case concerned the enforceability of contracts between the government and some regulated banks, by which the latter had been encouraged to acquire insolvent thrifts in exchange for the official promise of favourable accounting treatment for meeting their own regulatory capital requirements. Such treatment implied that the supervisory goodwill[35] attached to the merger transactions could be counted in consideration of regulatory capital requirements. Nevertheless, as such a tool (devised by the regulator to induce healthy banks to acquire insolvent institutions) was going against the very purpose of capital requirements, it was subsequently prohibited by the Congress. The effect was that the acquired thrifts were liquidated for failure to meet the new capital requirements. The Supreme Court had found the government liable for breach of its contractual obligations to the acquiring institutions, while underlining the illegality of the promise to consider regulatory goodwill for capital adequacy purposes. This case illustrates the importance of accounting rules for capital adequacy – the need to ensure that the sophisticated capital measurement models do not rely on ambiguous accounting concepts that might undermine the very purpose of capital requirements.

34 518 US 839 (1996); see Macey 2003: 300.

35 Goodwill refers to the amount by which the price paid for a firm, including any liabilities assumed, exceeds the fair value of the firm's identifiable assets.

An accounting concept particularly highlighted during the crisis is the so-called fair value or mark-to-market accounting,[36] which requires that banks' balance sheets reflect the current market value of assets to the detriment of their original historical costs. It is considered as one of the culprits for the severity of the financial crisis. It is held that fair value accounting substantially contributed to the systemic liquidity problems and the reduced resilience of the system. The main reason is that it excessively encouraged short-termism, as it did not distinguish between short-term-oriented risk-traders and risk-absorbers, which because of their long-term funding liquidity have a better capacity for market and liquidity risk (Persaud 2008). Furthermore, fair value accounting is accused of having aggravated the crisis and contributed to increased financial instability as it triggered sudden substantial writedowns and panic sales and thus widened the losses of banks and decreased the value of capital. All these concerns, as well as guidance on how to use fair value in times of crisis, are now considered by accounting regulators worldwide, while banking regulators are closely involved in the debate. Many of the envisaged changes to banking regulation (e.g. the introduction of countercyclical capital buffers and dynamic provisioning) are intrinsically linked to the parallel achievement of the reform of accounting rules (e.g. on the treatment of impaired assets, provisioning, etc.).

5.3 Prudential regulation and auditing

Closely linked to corporate governance and accounting rules, auditing has the objective of verifying banks' compliance with accounting practices and accounting standards. As such, the statutory audit function is a major line of defence against fraudulent financial reporting and contributes substantially to ensuring financial health. Prudential regulation, which purports to limit risk-taking by credit institutions, often relies on reporting by auditors. These provide evidence as to the financial health of the audited firm. For this purpose, the CRD stipulates that Member States should establish a duty for auditors of a credit institution (or of an undertaking which has close links with a credit institution) to report promptly to banking supervisors whenever, during the performance of their duties, they become aware of facts which are liable to have a serious effect on the financial situation or the administrative and accounting organisation of a credit institution (recital 24 and article 53 CRD). The increased importance of auditors' work for prudential regulatory purposes can also be inferred from the placing of the article laying down reporting duties for auditors towards banking supervisors under a new separate section in the CRD, within the chapter on the principles of prudential supervision.[37]

36 For a critical review of the concept of fair value, see King 2008.

37 Section 3 – Duty of persons responsible for the legal control of annual and consolidated accounts, in Chapter 1 (Principles of Prudential Supervision) of Title V (Principles and Technical Instruments for Prudential Supervision and Disclosure) of the CRD.

Recent corporate scandals in the US and Europe (Enron, Worldcom, Cirio, Parmalat), where complex company and financial structures have been used in order to obscure fraudulent business practices over long periods, resulted in urgent calls for a reinforced role of statutory audit.[38] These scandals hugely impacted on investors' confidence in the capacity of public authorities to limit large-scale frauds. The public at large does not differentiate between the various competent authorities, and thus public mistrust regarding the statutory audit function spilled over to banking supervisors. This demonstrates the delicate interdependence between various financial regulators. Therefore, it is essential to coordinate reforms in both fields, as well as to enhance regular cooperation between authorities competent in the field of audit and those acting in banking supervision.

5.4 Prudential norms and consumer protection law

The separation of prudential rules from consumer protection is extremely difficult to map out, as both categories of norms have their roots anchored in the issue of securing confidence in the market. Their intricate relationship is a consequence of the fact that financial stability and consumer protection constitute the very objectives of all financial market regulation.[39] The interaction of the two categories is particularly relevant with regard to the consequences that classification within one or another category might trigger with respect to the competent authorities. *Grosso modo*, it is held that prudential rules pertain to the realm of the home country, whereas conduct of business rules and other consumer protection measures that could be qualified as 'general good' are the competence of the host country.

The literature distinguishes between prudential rules, focusing on the financial health of individual institutions, and transactional rules, addressing the relationship between individual firms and their clients, with a focus on consumer protection (Avgerinos 2003: 20). Prudential rules deal with the analysis of the balance sheet, the various categories of risk incurred and other indicators of prudential soundness. Transactional rules have as their object rules of conduct, disclosure, integrity, honesty, fair business practice, marketing of financial services, etc. Nevertheless, such a distinction may seem purely theoretical, without straightforward consequences for practical arrangements, and thus

38 As a consequence, European legislators adopted Directive 2006/43/EC, amended by Directive 2008/30/EC.

39 As already highlighted in Chapter 2, consumer protection rules and prudential regulation constitute two categories of banking regulation which, although pursuing the same objectives (protection of depositors and financial stability), focus on these objectives with different intensity. For an analysis of the roles of consumer protection in financial services, see Coleman 2000; Alpa 2004.

indicative of the fact that prudential rules and consumer protection measures often overlap.

Special attention should be given to the various provisions in the CRD, which directly refer to the protection of savers/depositors. Thus, measures to coordinate credit institutions aim at protecting savings (recital 5 of the preamble); equivalent financial requirements are necessary for ensuring similar safeguards for savers and fair conditions of competition (recital 9); reporting duties for auditors are foreseen both for strengthening the prudential supervision of credit institutions and for the protection of clients of credit institutions (recital 27); consolidated supervision aims, in particular, at protecting the interests of the depositors and at ensuring the stability of the financial system (recital 57). Hence, all prudential rules (including capital requirements and prudential restrictions) entail protective effects for consumers of banking services. Broadly speaking, it could be maintained that all rules promoting financial stability or competition in the banking sector indirectly protect the interests of depositors.

Such a broad view of consumer protection has been so far rejected by the ECJ, which in the banking field has underlined the distinction between consumer protection and banking regulation. The ECJ differentiates consumer protection by reference to its objective of ensuring the protection of savers, which is an aspect of general good justifying derogations from Community banking regulation.[40] The case law reflects the general approach towards consumer protection regulation, which limits the analysis to the interaction between the consumer and the financial institution (in terms of types of transaction, quantity and repetitiveness).[41] Yet, for the purposes of identifying the eventual rights of depositors resulting from European law, we would argue for a broader approach and the recognition of a consumer protection dimension in prudential rules.

It is interesting to note that the ongoing reforms of the European financial regulatory and supervisory framework do not tackle straightforward consumer protection issues. This is in contrast with the US plans for regulatory reform that even envisage the creation of a Consumer Financial Protection Agency.

5.5 Prudential norms and competition law

The intersections between competition law and banking regulation are multiple and intricate. However, there are two aspects of competition law that are of the utmost importance for prudential regulation – namely,

40 Case C-366/97 *Criminal Proceedings Against Romanelli* [1999] ECR I-855 and Case 222/95 *Société Civile Immobilière Parodi* v. *Banque H. Albert de Barry et Cie* [1997] ECR I-3899, para. 22.

41 This is also the approach preferred by the Commission; see the work of the European Consumer Law Group, Commission 2001b.

rules on mergers and acquisitions and State aid rules. Both are complex topics that may each constitute the subject of extensive separate research. Here, we will sketch only the most acute aspects of their interplay with prudential issues.

Several provisions in the CRD deal with the situation when a natural or legal person has taken a decision to acquire or increase a qualifying holding. As the CRD does not contain either detailed criteria for the prudential assessment of the proposed acquisition or a procedure for their application, the European legislator has adopted Directive 2007/44/EC to fill in this gap. The latter directive amends the CRD and introduces identical procedural rules and criteria aiming to provide the necessary legal certainty, clarity and predictability with regard to the prudential assessment process, as well as to the result thereof (Kerjean 2008). In a nutshell, the 2007 directive sets harmonised conditions for the notification of a holding in a financial institution to supervisors by proposed acquirers. It also establishes a procedure and timeframe for the prudential assessment of the proposed acquisition and specifies criteria of a strictly prudential nature for the assessment process.[42]

The control of concentrations also constitutes the object of competition law. The EC Merger Regulation 139/2004 lays down the conditions, procedures and criteria to be applied with a view to making sure that significant structural changes do not result in distorting competition in the internal market. The Merger Regulation applies also to credit institutions. A concentration is deemed to exist in the case of

> an acquisition, by one or more persons already controlling at least one undertaking, or by one or more undertakings, whether by purchase of securities or assets, by contract or by any other means, of direct or indirect control of the whole or parts of one or more other undertakings.
>
> (article 4(1)b) Merger Regulation)

Consequently, there is the possibility that an acquisition will be scrutinised under both prudential rules and competition law. Yet reconciling eventual contradictory outcomes of the two inquiries is by no means unequivocal.

The second competition law aspect, particularly relevant for prudential regulation and of major importance during the crisis, is related to State aid measures pursuant to article 87 EC Treaty. Rescue operations for banks all had to be cleared by the Commission from a 'State aid' perspective. This happened on the basis of a wide interpretation of article 87(3)

42 In December 2008, CEBS, CESR and CEIOPS issued Joint Guidelines for the prudential assessment of acquisitions and increases in holdings in the financial sector required by Directive 2007/44/EC.

(b) EC Treaty, which allows for State aid if it is granted 'to remedy a serious disturbance in the economy of a Member State', the temporary nature of these measures being an important criterion.[43] The Commission enjoys wide discretion when issuing decisions declaring State aid compatible with the internal market, subject to control by the ECJ. In order to provide more guidance and ensure discipline in the process of government assistance to banks, the Commission has recently issued three communications through which it aims to establish a more transparent framework for the application of the State aid rules (2008 Banking Communication; 2009 Recapitalisation Communication; 2009 Impaired Assets Communication).

This is an important area where much of the detail carries considerable weight and touches upon sensitive political aspects. Prudential thresholds could play an important role in assessing instances of State aid. Equally, State aid decisions will substantially affect the prudential supervision of individual institutions. These aspects are definitely worth more detailed inquiry, going beyond the scope of the present work.[44]

This outline of the interaction of prudential norms with corporate law, accounting, auditing and consumer protection rules, as well as with some aspects of competition law, aims to highlight the various aspects that should be observed when analysing prudential norms and their application. It also implicitly stresses the new qualitative dimension inherent in prudential supervision, which finds benchmarks in corporate, accounting and audit standards and entails a reinforced consideration of the objective of consumer protection.

43 In the interval October 2008–March 2009 the Commission adopted more than 50 State aid decisions in the context of the financial crisis. They referred to guarantee schemes, five major recapitalisation schemes, five framework schemes comprising a combination of these measures and a substantial number of ad hoc measures concerning certain banks; see State Aid Scoreboard – Spring 2009 Update, special edition (Commission 2009g).

44 On details: Lastra 2006: 120–2 and 310.

5 Substantive aspects of prudential regulation

Any attempt to assess the European dimension of prudential regulation, especially in view of acknowledging its influence over national regulatory regimes, would be vain without understanding the substantive facets of such regulation. Broadly speaking, current European prudential legislation addresses the following aspects: authorisation requirements; capital adequacy requirements for different categories of risks; large exposures; risk-management procedures and internal control mechanisms; and aspects related to the supervisory review process and market discipline. The weight given to these prudential instruments is by no means balanced. Traditionally, capital adequacy has received overwhelming attention. Large exposures are regulated at the European level as supplementary requirements, while the perceived scarcity and generality of normative indications on risk management and internal controls have left the latter with a rather residual character. This situation has changed to some extent, albeit not radically, with the adoption of the CRD and the recast CAD, which took a more risk-sensitive approach towards financial stability, emphasising internal risk management, supervision and market discipline. Capital adequacy, as the primary focus and quantitatively dominating regulatory tool of prudential regulation, deserves some separate preliminary remarks.

Capital requirements undoubtedly constitute the central pillar of European prudential norms as explicitly recognised in recital 34 CRD. This is because capital – 'own funds' in EU law parlance – fulfils the dual function of absorbing losses, which are not matched by a sufficient volume of profits, and of serving as an important yardstick for supervisors' assessment of banks' financial health. In order to boost such a key role of capital within dynamic financial markets, prudential norms providing for capital requirements have evolved from prescriptive rules (requiring mere compliance) to complex multi-layered risk-sensitive regulatory regimes adaptable to the specific needs of individual institutions. The scope of European prudential regulation expanded to cover rapidly evolving financial activities. Yet, because of limited resources, public regulators can keep pace with such developments only in close cooperation with the industry. Consequently, the modern prudential approach had to be construed as a mixed approach combining various public and private instruments. It seems that the capital adequacy framework mirrors, ever more closely, a complete regulatory regime, where standard setting, monitoring and enforcement need to occur on a continuous basis and imply the distribution of regulatory and supervisory functions to various actors. Yet lessons from the crisis indicate substantial shortcomings in the current framework, which might question its complexity and its aspirations towards completeness.

The European framework for bank capital was initially inspired by the 1988 Basel Accord, which set out the components of capital, a formula for measuring the risk weight to be assigned to certain assets, the treatment of off-balance-sheet items for the purpose of the measurement of capital adequacy and the minimum 8 per cent solvency ratio. This approach was transposed into the EU through the adoption of the Own Funds and Solvency Ratio Directives. Further work of the Basel Committee on market risks has been enshrined in the Capital Adequacy Directive.

Although simplicity was initially indispensable for facilitating the drawing up of common prudential rules at international level, as well as for achieving the minimum harmonisation of the banking regulatory frameworks of EU Member States, in time such an approach was considered inadequate for addressing actual risks faced by credit institutions. The criticisms referred, among others, to the crude classification of credit risk (Hirte and Heinrich 2002: 462), the use of rigid rules and inaccurate formulas, and the categorical assessment of asset risk irrespective of the situation of the counterparty concerned. Such shortcomings in capital regulation were seen as the very reason for imprudent behaviour on the part of banks, something they were actually designed to prevent.[1] Also, another limitation of Basel I was the emphasis on credit risk and market risk, whereby elements decisive for the stability of the financial intermediary (like its competitive position, its organisational structure, etc.), which are indeed difficult to define *erga omnes* and hardly measurable according to abstract categories, were ignored.

This criticism, endorsed especially by academics and practitioners, does not appear in official Brussels documents which, conversely, constantly and carefully praised the merits of the capital adequacy framework as a

1 See Tarbert 2000: 1802. The author identifies 'seven deadly sins' of the 1988 Accord, which may also be said to affect European prudential norms: (1) the Accord has encouraged banks to engage in 'regulatory arbitrage' causing thereby very imprudent behaviour; (2) the Accord failed to bring up an appropriate acceptable definition of 'regulatory capital'; (3) the 8 per cent capital ratio requirement has little or no grounding; (4) the Accord is construed on the false presumption that equity serves as an inherently better cushion than debt, which is intrinsically a liability; (5) the goal of levelling the playing-field among nations cannot be achieved by a regulatory structure that ignores existing supplementary regulations, customs and market structures; (6) the Accord ignores diversification when calculating the total risk-based assets by which the amount of qualifying capital is divided; (7) the Accord was unable to effectively regulate complex financial instruments and transactions that are becoming more prevalent in banking.

regulatory strategy that has 'contributed significantly to the key objectives of financial stability and consumer protection' (Commission 2003d: 4). Nevertheless, confronted with new realities of financial innovation and the emergence of sophisticated techniques for risk measurement and management, the European regulatory and supervisory frame has been put under pressure for urgent 'updating'. The EU's financial reform agenda in the late 1990s (the FSAP) included the revision of the capital adequacy framework as one of its most significant components, especially in the context of the parallel review of the 1988 Capital Accord by the Basel Committee.

The revised capital framework for credit institutions and investment firms was the last FSAP legislative measure to be adopted. On 14 July 2004 the Commission presented its proposal for two directives recasting the CBD and the CAD, shortly after agreement in Basel was reached.[2] The European Parliament approved, with amendments, the Commission's proposal on 28 September 2005 under the first reading, and the Council agreed on 11 October 2005. The final formal approval was given by the Council on 14 June 2006.[3]

1 The 2006 capital requirements framework for banks and investment firms

The long gestation period of the Basel II Accord and of the CRD, characterised by lengthy and frequent public consultations, allowed the emergence of a vast critical literature on the substantive aspects of the new prudential approach even before it came into force.[4] Further critical aspects came into the spotlight during the crisis, some questioning the viability of the new approach.[5] Lacking the necessary expertise to consider the new regulation on its substantive merits, we will confine ourselves to a general presentation of its structure and core principles, with a view to identifying the scope and characteristics of the new regulatory framework. Thereby we ask whether the CRD is merely updating the old prudential framework to make it more comprehensive and responsive to market developments or if, on the contrary, it brings about a radical change in the prudential regulatory strategy. If this were the case, it might involve important consequences, in terms of the interpretation of prudential rules, from the perspective of EU law. Before attempting any assessment, we will underline two preliminary issues: the prudential philosophy of the Basel II Accord and some preliminary aspects concerning the adoption of the CRD.

2 The agreement in Basel was reached on 11 May 2004 – BCBS 2004.

3 The CRD and recast CAD were published on 30 June 2006 in OJ L177 and entered into force twenty days after their publication.

4 See, among others: Tarbert 2000; Alexander 2003; Persaud 2003; Sappideen 2004.

5 On the assessment of the Basel II approach in light of the crisis, see Ayadi 2008; Benink and Kaufman 2008; Borio 2008; Cannata and Quagliariello 2009.

1.1 The general approach of Basel II/CRD

Basel II, the outcome of an unprecedented mobilisation of industry, central banks, supervisory authorities and academics to express their views and to offer technical support, has been qualified as 'a far more comprehensive framework for regulatory capital and risk management than we have ever known' (BCBS 2004) and entitled 'a *New* Capital Adequacy Framework'. Such features may be inferred immediately from the number and detail of its provisions, but they do not result straightforwardly from the four declared objectives of the new Accord. These objectives are largely similar to the ones set out in Basel I: improving the safety and soundness of the financial system, promoting competitive equality, establishing a more comprehensive approach to addressing risks, and making the requirements suitable for institutions of various levels of complexity and sophistication (BCBS 1999: 6). Such a similarity of objectives may be seen as an indication that Basel II is merely an adaptation of Basel I to market developments (Comana 2002: 143). However, the reaffirmation of the same generic objectives, points to the fact that the changes brought about by Basel II mainly concern the means employed for achieving such undisputable objectives.

In our view, irrespective of the declared or inferred continuity, a substantial departure from the previous Basel I approach results especially from the three-pillar structure underpinning the Basel II framework. Regulatory guidance is no longer limited to capital requirements (Pillar 1 – minimum capital requirements), but is complemented with indications on the supervisory review process (Pillar 2) and regulatory incentives for stimulating market discipline (Pillar 3). The three pillars are considered mutually reinforcing and were envisaged to be implemented concomitantly. Underlining the fact that the implementation of only one or two of the pillars does not deliver an adequate level of soundness; the Basel Committee accepted that partial implementation arrangements were tolerable only as temporary measures within jurisdictions where full implementation was shortly impossible. Thus, the new framework based on the three interdependent pillars may be interpreted as the consecration of a structural shift in the prudential regulatory strategy.

Furthermore, substantial change as compared to Basel II can be inferred from the combination of the traditional quantitative with a more qualitative approach to prudential supervision. Increased risk-sensitivity (resulting from greater diversification of risk categories, regulatory reliance on internal risk-measurement mechanisms and external risk assessments), sustained by the reinforced supervisory review process and the measures encouraging market discipline, acknowledges the progressive move away from the mere control of accounts. The new trend is towards the control of banks' processes and mechanisms for measuring, managing and steering the risks they assume. By adding a strong qualitative dimension, it opens the possibility for more individualised supervision. Rules based capital requirements combined with principles-based supervision allow for a more holistic approach to the financial health of an institution.

From a declaratory perspective, the EU cautiously avoided emphasising the 'revolutionary' character of Basel II. In its consultation documents, the European Commission used language emphasising continuity with the old framework: 'Review of Capital Requirements for Banks and Investment Firms'. Also, the recourse to the recast technique, which allows the insertion of substantive amendments in existing legislation without submitting the entire document for debate, is symptomatic of the cautious attitude of the Commission and its reluctance to radically depart from the earlier approach. However, these formal declarations cannot hide the substantial impact of the effective changes entailed by the Basel II approach. The crisis revealed the huge impact of the Basel II changes affecting capital requirements under Pillar 1 (use of external ratings and internal risk models), which quantitatively occupy the largest part of the CRD. Pillars 2 and 3, concentrated within a few articles in the CRD, were much less in the spotlight, partly because they remained largely unexploited. This reflects an unbalanced implementation of the three pillars that, in our view, contributed to the supervisory failure, but also reflects the important potential they offer for improving banking supervision.

1.2 Some preliminary remarks

The 2006-adopted CRD consists of the main body text including 72 recitals and 160 articles (which contain the principles and central rules) and fourteen annexes (comprising technical detailed norms). The recast CAD adds further 54 articles and eight annexes. With over 250 Official Journal pages (of which about three-quarters represent the annexes), the new capital requirements framework is thus an extremely long and hybrid EU piece of legislation composed of general, special and very technical rules. Despite the fact that political agreement on the extension of the four-level Lamfalussy procedure to banking regulation had been reached in December 2002 and the whole new institutional framework was in place by May 2005,[6] the entire CRD has been decided through the co-decision legislative procedure. The first opportunity to make use of the Lamfalussy framework in the banking sector was missed. This might seem surprising in the light of the fact that the very demand for extending the Lamfalussy procedure to the banking sector was justified by the urgent need for adapting the capital adequacy rules. Thus, it would have appeared logical to adopt

6 The directive establishing the institutional structure for the banking sector came into force in May 2005, with the European Banking Committee assuming its comitology role, whereas the Committee of European Banking Supervisors had already taken up its duties on 1 January 2004.

the articles as Level 1 measures through the co-decision procedure, while leaving the annexes to the comitology procedure under Level 2.

The new European capital requirements framework is underpinned by a series of impact studies and industry feedback. It was subject to EU-wide consultations of all stakeholders, in the framework of the structured dialogue coordinated by the Commission, at European level, and by Member States' supervisory authorities at national level, as well as of the QIS3 exercise launched by the Basel Committee. A 'Consequences Study' by PricewaterhouseCoopers, issued on 8 April 2004, estimated an overall positive outcome of the revised capital requirements for the EU's macro-economy and prudential structures. An additional quantitative impact study (QIS5), conducted by CEBS in the first half of 2006 and published two days after the definitive adoption of the CRD, indicated the most likely decrease on average in capital requirements, especially if positive macro-economic conditions were to persist. However, the utility of these studies needs to be questioned in the light of the insufficient capital cushion of many banks, as revealed by the crisis.

The scope of the EU capital requirements framework is larger than the one of the Basel II Accord that it transposes, as it applies to all banks and investment firms in the EU and not just to internationally active banks. Furthermore, it has also incorporated from the very beginning the rules on the trading book adopted by the Basel Committee in 2005.[7]

The EU capital framework entered into force on 20 July 2006, with a series of transitional arrangements ensuring its smooth introduction. Thus, while most of the provisions applied as of 1 January 2007, the application of the most sensitive aspects, related to the new internal risk-based approach and to the capital requirements for operational risk, was postponed until 1 January 2008. Also, a range of transitory arrangements was designed to remove gradually national discretions allowing for diverging implementation in specific areas.[8] Moreover, the review of specific aspects was prescheduled, with the Commission being obliged to submit reports and 'appropriate proposals' by the end of 2007 (e.g. the large exposures regime), by the end of 2010 (on the overall application of the recast CAD) and by the end of 2011 (on the overall application of the CRD, with specific emphasis on certain articles) (articles 119, 157 CRD, article 51 recast CAD).

Before going into details, let us make some general remarks about the normative quality of the CRD. Calls and efforts for improving the quality

7 In July 2005 the Basel Committee adopted a paper entitled 'The Application of Basel II to Trading Activities and the Treatment of Double Default Effects', which was incorporated into a November 2005 updated version of the Basel II Accord and, subsequently, into the July 2006 comprehensive version of the Basel II Framework.

8 Most of these transitory measures are enumerated in arts 152–54 CRD and arts 43–47 recast CAD. Listed national discretions are to be removed by 2009, 2010, 2011 or 2012.

of European law and for better law-making[9] have been largely ignored in the case of the review of the capital framework: overall clarity and coherence are much undermined in this legislative compilation. The extremely long preambles of the CRD and recast CAD are a melange of the preambles of previous directives and justifications for their amendment that do not clearly reflect the conceptual background. The two preambles contain confusing political statements, repeat substantive provisions in the texts or are not echoed at all in the body of articles. Innumerable references in the articles to provisions in the same directive or in other directives contribute to difficulties in accessing the two legislative texts. Inconsistent terminology and redundant definitions add to the lack of clarity. Also, the long and complex phrases characterising both directives are prone to creating ambiguity and can result in conflicting interpretations.

The new provisions are scattered throughout the two amended directives and inserted within the old titles and chapters, thereby failing to reflect in the structure of the CRD the three pillars backing the Basel review.[10] New sections and subsections have been delineated; nevertheless, they do not manage to clearly differentiate between capital requirements, supervisory review processes and provisions inducing market discipline. To identifying the provisions corresponding to the three pillars it is helpful to look at the working documents of the Commission, and at the initial directive drafts circulated by the Commission for consultation purposes.[11]

The chosen recast technique, despite obvious merits of a pragmatic nature, has the major shortcoming of maintaining the hybrid structure entailed in the 2000 codification of disparate directives and the ever less justifiable separation of the capital requirements enshrined in the CAD. The missed opportunity of bringing the capital framework under a single umbrella results in an intricate, hardly accessible structure and fails to reflect, in an open way, the philosophy behind the whole review exercise.

The autonomy of the recast CAD is questionable for various reasons. First, capital requirements, although calculated separately for each category of risks incurred by a credit institution or an investment firm, are a unitary reference

9 For a detailed analysis of the EU's endeavours towards producing better-quality legislation, see Xanthaki 2001.

10 In keeping with the structure of the CBD, the new CRD is structured under seven titles: (1) Subject matter, scope and definitions; (2) Requirements for access to the taking up and pursuit of the business of credit institutions (3) Provisions concerning the freedom of establishment and the freedom to provide services; (4) Relations with third countries; (5) Principles and technical instruments for prudential supervision and disclosure; (6) Powers of execution; (7) Transitional and final provisions.

11 The draft circulated for consultation had a much clearer structure. It was divided into six titles: the first set out the definitions, general principles and the scope of consolidation, the second title laid down the quantitative capital requirements, the third regulated the supervisory review process, the fourth prescribed disclosure requirements aimed at encouraging market discipline, the fifth set the powers of execution, while the last title contained transitional and final provisions.

concept. Very frequent cross-references demonstrate that the CRD and the recast CAD are intrinsically connected; and especially that the latter cannot be read without the framework provided by the former. Also, the scope and the subject matter of the two directives point to overlaps: both aim to regulate 'prudential supervision', whereby the recast CAD focuses exclusively on capital adequacy in relation to the trading book activities, while the CRD has a broader scope and covers risks associated to the banking book (including market risk) and operational risks. The prudential principles apply, albeit with some variations, to all capital requirements, irrespective of whether they refer to the banking book or the trading book (article 75 CRD). Only by monitoring overall risk-taking can the safety and soundness of institutions be safeguarded and the overall stability of the financial system ensured. This is rendered more difficult if capital requirements for the same type of risk (e.g. market risk) are scattered throughout two legislative instruments. It also contradicts increased calls for an integrated approach for the measurement and management of various types of risks, especially in light of the ever blurred distinction between market and credit risk (BCBS 2009a). Merging into a single document all capital requirements would be a first step towards a more coherent, if not necessarily integrated, regulatory treatment of risks.

Without trying to give an exhaustive presentation, we will attempt to summarise the essentials of the three pillars as transposed in the CRD, and to introduce readers to the most controversial aspects. We will try to grasp the possible impact of the new approach on the interpretation of EU banking legislation. Subsequently, we will discuss the ongoing and envisaged reviews of the CRD and the more general criticism to the Basel II approach brought in the light of the crisis.

2 Definitions and general prudential principles

The CRD starts with an extensive list of definitions of the key concepts underpinning the whole capital framework, which partly replaces, partly adds to the definitional platform already provided by the Codified Banking Directive. The definitions aim to make sure that a common terminology will constitute the solid foundation for uniform and coherent implementation. Although the list is not systematic and by no means exhaustive, and is strongly biased by the object of the directive (mixing general and very specific concepts), it promotes a common understanding of the various concepts and this entails a substantive rapprochement of the national interpretations.[12] Yet many highly pertinent definitions can

12 In relation to the Codified Banking Directive, it was held that

> the definitions of the Community legislator contribute to the construction of a common vocabulary that imposes an articulated list, which provides that there is a *definium* corresponding to any *definiendum*, and which, beyond the usual limits of logical, semantic and structural nature, tends to improve the capacity of the designator to identify as univocally as possible a specific designate.
>
> (our translation)

See Gaggero 2002: 57.

be found only in the relevant sections of the directives or their annexes. This is the case of the concepts of 'exposure' and 'large exposure', for instance, defined in articles 106 and 108, respectively. Also, important definitions of technical terms are contained in the annexes (especially Annex III and IX) of the CRD. Overall, the roughly 100 definitions in the CRD and the recast CAD reinforce harmonisation of prudential regulation at European level and trigger more consistency in its implementation at national level. Yet many fundamental concepts (e.g. own funds) require further guidance in EU law, if capital requirements are indeed to be applied uniformly throughout the EU.

It is interesting to observe that the CRD does not include under the first title a provision spelling out the overarching principles guiding the application of the capital requirements framework. The Commission's preliminary proposal contained such a general provision within the envisaged article 2. It reflected the core principles underpinning the three-pillar structure of the new framework, as well as the correlative general obligations of the competent authorities. Thus, letter (a) of the preliminary version of article 2 contained the requirement of adequate capitalisation entailing two important features: permanence and individualisation. Letter (b) reflected the principle of a sound control environment imposing on banks, as a central 'soundness' criterion, the obligation to devise appropriate risk-management, reporting and adequate capital adequacy assessment processes. Letter (c) set information disclosure (especially on own funds, capital adequacy, risk exposure and assessment) as a principle of the new approach. As regards supervisory review, letters (d) and (e) highlighted the general obligation of review and evaluation, accompanied by intervention, as appropriate. These rules reflected the main values of the new approach. They can all be found explicitly or implicitly in the wording of the final CRD. Nevertheless, their enshrinement in the introductory part would have been welcome, as overarching principles guiding the application of the whole framework.

Another key principle that defines the overall obligations of credit institutions with regard to capital requirements was initially envisaged under article 3 in the preliminary draft and is now enshrined in article 75 of the CRD, under a separate subsection entitled 'Minimum Level of Own Funds'. It indicates the various categories of risk for which a capital cushion should be provided, the minimum amount of this capital and the legal provisions relevant for calculating the capitalisation corresponding to the various risks. The article consecrates the so-called 'building block' approach which has been used since the adoption of the CAD. This consists of devising the appropriate amounts of capital cover corresponding to the aggregated exposures for each category of risks; the overall amount of minimum capital required from an institution is obtained by adding these separately calculated amounts. Article 75 also prescribes the general rule that the own funds of an institution should at all times be more than or equal to the sum of the requirements identified for various risks.

Further, article 136 of the CRD clearly differentiates between the minimum capital requirements under Pillar 1 (article 75) and the capital obligations of individual institutions stemming from the supervisory review pillar, the so-called capital add-ons (article 136). The CRD does not elucidate the relationship between minimum capital and capital add-ons. It does not provide the solution to the longstanding debate as to whether different concepts should be used for designating the two categories of capital: 'internal' or 'economic' capital (to design overall capitalisation needed by individual institutions) and 'regulatory capital' or 'own funds' (corresponding to minimum capital adequacy standards for specific risks; (Commission 2003d: 17).

3 Credit risk – the revised standardised approach

The largest part of the substantive amendments brought by the CRD[13] is dedicated to the regulatory treatment of credit risk, which continues to be the major risk for banks. The mechanism for calculating these minimum requirements remained unchanged in its fundamental structure. Thus, the risk-based capital ratio was maintained at 8 per cent and continues to be calculated by dividing the qualifying capital (the numerator of the ratio, still composed of tier 1 and tier 2 capital) by its risk-weighted assets (the denominator). The novelty consists of the fact that risk weighting is now permitted in accordance with two approaches: the standardised methodology, a revised version of the Basel I rules, and the internal ratings-based (IRB) approach, available in two versions (foundation and advanced). Extensive rules on credit risk mitigation (articles 90–3 and Annex VIII CRD), as well as on the treatment of securitised assets (articles 94–101 and Annex IX CRD) and the treatment of counterparty credit risk of specific transactions (Annex III), apply to both approaches, adjusted where appropriate.[14]

The Standardised Approach (SA), laid down in articles 78–83 and Annex VI CRD, is particularly important as it represents the 'default' mechanism for determining capital requirements. This approach is relatively simple and less risk-sensitive, for which reason it is often qualified as the second best in comparison with the IRB Approach. Under the SA, risk weights continue to be expressed in whole percentages of 0, 20, 50, 100 and 150 per cent, depending on the credit quality of the counterparties, but a more flexible approach is taken so as to avoid a too rigid allocation of exposures to a certain risk weight. Thus, an expanded list of asset

13 The provisions are contained in section 3 of the chapter on technical instruments of prudential supervision, entitled 'Minimum own funds requirements for credit risk'.

14 For more details on these aspects, see Ayadi 2008: 29–36.

classes, into which loans can be placed, is provided so as to reflect underlying risks with greater precision.[15] Furthermore, an innovative provision makes possible the use of external credit ratings for determining credit quality, provided that the issuing institutions are recognised in accordance with the prescribed rules (article 80 CRD). Articles 81–3 and Annex VI lay down the criteria for the recognition of external credit assessment institutions and their ratings and establish the rules for the use of external ratings, with the double aim of ensuring consistency and integrity in the application of such ratings, as well as the impartiality of the rating institutions.[16] Also, the SA made ample progress with regard to credit risk mitigation (articles 90–3 and Annex VIII CRD). Thus, an expended range of credit protection instruments may be taken into account for the purposes of reducing capital requirements and more sophisticated calculation methods can be employed. These are backed by principles that seek to ensure that the effects of credit risk mitigation take into consideration key aspects like certainty and timeliness, liquidity, price availability, creditworthiness, etc.

Although the SA is generally characterised by precise rules, mandatory for those subject to them, it also entails some important national discretions. These allow Member States to exempt specific exposures (i.e. when the counterparty is the parent undertaking or a subsidiary, or there is a relationship involving a qualifying holding, or when the counterparty is a member of the same institutional protection scheme as the lending institution) from the minimum capital requirements, provided that several criteria are fulfilled (article 80 (7) and (8) CRD).

Increasing reliance on ratings for setting prudential standards is the most radical departure within the standardised approach from the previous methods for calculating capital requirements. It has been characterised as a 'breath of fresh air in a system now stale from regulatory imprecision' (Tarbert 2000: 1831). In fact, by allowing such institutions to determine the quality of an asset or counterparty, one of the operations

15 Art. 79 CRD provides that assets or off-balance-sheet items have to be assigned to one of the following classes: claims on central governments and central banks, on regional governments and local authorities, on administrative bodies and non-commercial undertakings, on multilateral development banks, on international organisations, on institutions, on corporates, retail claims, claims secured on real estate property, past due items, items belonging to regulatory high-risk categories, claims of covered bonds, items constituting securitisation positions, short-term claims on institutions and corporate, claims in the form of collective investment undertakings (CIUs), other items.

16 In order to be recognised, an external credit assessment institution should use a methodology that complies with the principles of objectivity, independence, ongoing review, and transparency and disclosure. The credit assessments should observe the following principles: credibility and market acceptance, and transparency and disclosure. The regime in the final Commission proposal applicable to external rating institutions seems to be more concise than the one submitted for consultation in the working document; see also EP 2004 and CESR 2005.

that are central to the determination of capital requirements and that used to be performed in accordance with the categories laid down by law is now delegated to private entities. Such a major change was obviously accompanied by enthusiasm but was also associated with doubts and suspicion from the very beginning. Sceptics have immediately doubted the accountability of such institutions and called for the design of sufficient incentives that could constrain them to consider the full impact of their ratings on the overall financial system (Hirte and Heinrich 2002: 468, referring to Walker 2001: 6; Dhumale 2001: 38). Another problematic aspect is related to conflicts of interest resulting from the possibility of agencies being captured by clients. Further concerns arise with regard to the availability of credit ratings for small and medium-sized enterprises, given that it is inefficient for credit rating agencies to commit resources for the rating of small banks and corporations, especially in continental Europe where no real tradition of ratings exists. Such concerns led the European Parliament to insert in the preamble to the CRD a vague commitment for review, asserting that 'in view of the importance of external ratings in connection with the calculation of capital requirements under this Directive, appropriate future authorisation and supervisory process for rating agencies need to be kept under review' (recital 39 CRD).

The crisis showed that these worries were well founded and that the impact of regulatory reliance on credit ratings had not been sufficiently scrutinised. The sudden and substantial downgrades of many credit ratings impinged substantially on the capital cushion of banks. We will come back to the role of rating agencies later; for now, it is important to note that ratings have been incorporated into the regulatory framework together with incentives for institutions and supervisors to use them when calculating capital requirements.

4 The internal ratings based (IRB) approach for credit risk

The possibility of employing internal risk-measurement models for determining regulatory capital had already emerged at the beginning of the 1990s, when a first proposal for addressing market risks was discussed within the Basel Committee. This was then enshrined in the 1996 amendments to the Basel I Accord, and the 1998 amendment brought to the Capital Adequacy Directive, which allowed for the use of internal value at risk (VaR) models for measuring market risks. As regards credit risk, only the CRD and Basel II introduced this alternative regulatory technique, permitting the calculation of capital requirements in line with the institution's own methodologies for estimating internal capital needs. The underlying principle is that banks usually make use of internal systems to assess the quality of all borrowers in some manner, and that in their capacity of lenders they hold more information on the latter than third parties.

The IRB Approach, laid down in articles 84–9 and Annex VII CRD, provides complex rules for determining capital requirements for banks having sufficiently developed risk-management and measurement mechanisms to qualify for using IRB. It has two options: a simple foundation option, and the more sophisticated advanced option. Three risk parameters are central to the IRB Approach: probability of default (PD), loss given default (LGD), exposure at default (EAD).[17] These parameters are different for wholesale and retail deposits (Scott 2006: 325). Under the foundation option, banks are allowed to estimate the likelihood of default of each borrower over one year; the supervisory authority supplies the remaining input. More sophisticated banks may use the advanced IRB methodologies so as to also supply the LGD and/or EAD, in accordance with their own estimates. Another factor to be observed for determining capital requirements is the maturity of an exposure (M): while the foundation IRB approach uses an average implicit maturity assumption of 2.5 years for all exposures, the advanced variant requires an explicit maturity for each exposure. The directive also prescribes several methodological and disclosure requirements in order to ensure the continuous reliability of banks' internal risk-measurement mechanisms.

The use of internal ratings has been warmly welcomed, in response to complaints deploring the rigidity and inadequacy of the 'one-size-fits-all' methodology used under the Basel I capital regime. Nevertheless, such flexibility based on incentives for active sophisticated risk management on the part of the regulated entities requires considerable resources that may only be committed by large actors. Further, there are data limitations concerning default and credit history, especially with regard to new financial products and the new Member States, which impinge on the accuracy of IRB estimates. The most acute concern about IRB is linked to the fear that bank regulators fail to understand the intricacies of the internal models and risk thereby 'effectively handing the reins of regulation over to the regulated banks themselves' (Tarbert 2000: 1835) without providing for the corresponding accountability.

The IRB approach does not constitute a complete self-regulatory model, where private actors are devising concrete regulatory standards in the shadow of the State. It makes only an initial step in that direction by providing the framework for a relatively open regulatory space, where private actors receive incentives for contributing to the regulatory substance, given their better knowledge of the underpinning conditions. Under the foundation approach, banks may use their own default

17 The PD regards the likelihood of defaulting of borrowers over a one-year period. LGD refers to the proportion of the exposure that will be lost if a default occurs. EAD is defined as the exposure amount that is likely to be outstanding if a default occurs. Closely linked to these three parameters is the remaining maturity of the exposure (M).

experience, whereas the resulting loss ratios and the capital matrix remain the competence of supervisors. Under the advanced IRB approach, more sophisticated banks may use their own default experience as well as their own estimates of resulting losses, after enforcement of collateral. But the capital ratios will still be ultimately determined by the supervisors. Only the denominator of the solvency ratio may be delegated to the regulatees themselves, while supervisors will retain responsibility for determining the minimum amount of own funds to be provided.

The IRB approach provides the legal basis for relating internal credit risk-measurement systems and prudential supervisory tasks more closely. It implicitly underlines the potential value and accuracy of banks' own quantitative and qualitative assessment of individual assets. Such a shift in regulatory strategy can be seen as a step in the direction of the delegation of the entire regulatory capital adequacy process to the regulatees themselves. This can ultimately happen through the regulatory recognition of the so-called credit risk models, which are already used by complex financial institutions in order to determine their actual capital requirements.[18] The IRB, as yet, does not allow for the use of credit risk models; nevertheless, it confers some regulatory value to internal models, which constitutes a substantial change in the prudential approach. It is conditional upon the explicit approval given by regulatory authorities. Thus, as a counterpart to the delegated regulatory responsibility, new forms of supervisory responsibility arise on the part of regulators concerning the authorisation of such models and the evaluation of their qualitative and quantitative reliability.

However, the crisis has shown the regulators' limited capacity to detect the flaws inherent to banks' risk-management models and their almost blind reliance on sophisticated mathematical calculations that were ignoring important aspects of economic reality. Models based on statistics and probability generally neglected extreme scenarios (the so-called tail risks). IRB models can reflect more accurately the position of individual institutions, yet they do so from the perspective of the regulated entities and without necessarily taking into consideration more general developments in financial markets. Internal models as such should not be considered a failure and regulatory input from such models should not be abandoned altogether. While IRB models demonstrated flaws, these flaws can eventually be corrected in the light of the crisis experience and especially in combination with much more severe stress test scenarios.

18 Compared to internal rating models, which evaluate only the creditworthiness of borrowers in accordance with more or less sophisticated methodologies, credit risk models constitute complex processes involving procedures for determining the individual's bank target default risk – estimating the risk of the entire portfolio and activities for a specific time period and allocating sufficient capital to ensure a cushion up to the target default risk; see Tarbert 2000: 1820.

Supervisors should also be more vigilant and accurately scrutinise the assumptions of models from the perspectives of both the risk appetite of individual institutions and macro-prudential developments. If appropriate solutions can be found, the IRB approach will continue to have an important role in determining capital requirements.

5 Market risk and operational risk

The CRD did not bring structural changes to the calculation of the capital cushion for market risks, which substantially continued to be done in accordance with the old provisions of the CAD, largely copied in the recast CAD. Only a few rearrangements were made to ensure compatibility between the old CAD and the new capital requirements or to update some specific aspects related to the trading book in order to reflect developments in the markets and industry practices.[19] A relatively small number of articles, as compared to those dedicated to credit risk, regulate the various aspects that aim to bring market risk requirements in line with the new capital framework. In general terms, these concern eligibility criteria for trading book capital treatment, so as to restrict possible arbitrage between the banking book and the trading book; credit risk mitigation in the trading book; treatment of collective investment undertakings (CIUs) in the trading book; specific risk modelling, etc. The provisions on market risk are further detailed in nine substantially amended annexes, attached to the recast CAD. These amendments do not bring structural changes and the determination of capital requirements for market risks continues to rely on two approaches: internal models for measuring value at risk for larger or more sophisticated banks, and the more general standardised method – the 'building blocks' approach for the rest of the industry.[20] As already mentioned, the difference between market and credit risk is becoming blurred and difficulties in attributing banks' activities to the banking book or the trading book are equally increasing. This is particularly apparent in the intricate net of cross-references between the CRD and the recast CAD.

As opposed to the relatively few changes affecting the market risk treatment, the CRD brought about a revolutionary approach to operational risks. Operational risk was introduced into the risk categories that require a capital buffer, risk-management standards and disclosure (articles 102–5 and Annex X CRD). Operational risk is defined as 'the risk of loss resulting from inadequate or failed internal processes, people and systems or

19 The recast CAD contains the 2005 Basel Committee's recommendations on the Application of Basel II to trading activities. These provisions, especially those concerning the modelling of specific risk, aim to introduce a greater degree of flexibility that should allow models to better capture risks linked to ever more complex activities.

20 For details on the two approaches, see Scott 2006: 342–51.

from external events, including legal risk' (article 4(22) CRD). A separate capital charge is imposed; it is calculated in accordance with one of the three alternative methodologies: the Basic Indicator Approach, the Standardised Approach and the Advanced Measurement Approach. Under the Basic Indicator Approach, which may be used by any bank except for those internationally active and those with significant operational risk exposure, capital corresponding to operational risk is determined as a certain percentage applied to the relevant income indicator, in accordance with the parameters detailed in the annex. The Standardised Approach aims to address operational risks more accurately by dividing banks' activities along business lines to which separate indicators are assigned, so as to reflect the size or volume of the banks' activities in the particular area: a fixed percentage is applied to such indicators. Banks need to qualify for the Standardised Approach by satisfying a set of clearly defined eligibility criteria, which provide for effective risk management and control and appropriate measurement and validation standards. The Advanced Measurement Approach (AMA) is the most risk-sensitive and it requires institutions to develop their own assessment of exposures to operational risk, subjecting them to more stringent risk management standards. The use of this model is conditional upon the explicit approval by the supervisory authority.

In order to respond to the demand for flexibility coming from market participants, the CRD foresees the possibility of combining the different approaches so as to allow institutions to use a mix of different methodologies for different business lines, geographical locations and legal entities. Limits and conditions for such a combination are detailed in the annex, which also pays due attention to the regulatory need of limiting arbitrage and cherry-picking. The underlying optic is to encourage banks to move along the spectrum of available approaches (BCBS 2001).

6 The supervisory review process

The provisions on supervision are spread throughout the text of the CRD. They are not limited to articles 124–43 in Section 1 of Chapter 4 under Title V, entitled 'Supervision', but encompass important provisions laid down among others in articles 17, 22, 75, 123, and 145 CRD.[21]

The supervisory review process (SRP) is an integral and critical part of the new capital framework that is complementary to the quantitative capital requirements and the rules supportive of market discipline (Commission 2003e: 62). The CRD provides for an improved regulatory framework for the prudential supervision of banks, which puts more emphasis

21 Furthermore, the supervisory review pillar has received specific attention in the work of CEBS, which adopted the ample guidance contained in the 2006 Guidelines on the application of the supervisory review process under Pillar 2, as well as in the 2005 Guidelines on supervisory disclosure.

on the control of banks' risk-management processes and not merely on compliance with specific regulatory ratios. Four principles, developed under the Basel II framework, underpin the CRD provisions regarding supervisory review: (1) the obligation for banks to have a process to assess the adequacy of their capital; (2) the need for supervisory review, evaluation and intervention as appropriate; (3) the expectation that banks operate above the minimum capital level with supervisors having the power to require them to hold additional capital; (4) the importance of early supervisory intervention.

The CRD underlines the twin functions to be pursued by the competent authorities: review and enforcement. Review implies the monitoring of compliance with all requirements in the CRD, as well as the evaluation of risks to which banks are or might be exposed (article 124 CRD). The review function is double-edged: the competent authority has to ensure that the capital of an institution is consistent with its overall risk profile and strategy (article 75 CRD), and additionally it has to be satisfied with the internal processes and strategies of the institution (article 123 CRD), its governance arrangements and organisational structure (article 22 CRD). The enforcement function requires supervisory authorities to intervene promptly, through the adoption of appropriate prudential measures where weaknesses or deficiencies are detected (article 136 CRD). The parameters for supervisory review may be found in various specific provisions[22] of the CRD that prescribe basic requirements to be observed by banks when devising internal assessment processes for ensuring capital adequacy, while the core elements enumerated in the directive are developed in more detail in the annexes.

The regulatory strategy enshrined in the CRD aims to leave substantial freedom to banks for developing risk-management and risk-measurement techniques in accordance with their own needs. It avoids creating an abstract model that should accommodate the reality of single banks, but instead offers broad guidance that aims at encouraging and supporting banks' efforts to design individualised analytical tools, capable of enhancing their efficacy and credibility. An important tool is the internal capital adequacy assessment process (ICAAP) – the mechanism for assessing the internal capital needed against the risks of an institution – that is owned by the institution developing it. Such an approach also entails a more complex role for the supervisory authorities, which have to systematically and consistently evaluate individual risk-management systems and internal governance processes, concentrating on concrete substantive aspects and going beyond verification of compliance with an abstractly devised stereotype.

22 For instance, article 84 CRD, which lays down the standards to be considered by competent authorities when granting permission to use the internal ratings-based approach for calculating credit risks. These standards are further detailed in Annex VII to the directive.

Hence, the supervisory review process prescribed in the CRD consists of a complex mechanism relying on the substantial cooperation between supervisory authorities and supervised institutions. The dialogue between supervisors and banks occurs via the so-called supervisory review and evaluation process (SREP), as well as through the regular supervisory monitoring. SREP sets the supervisors' framework for evaluating the ICAAP and the capital adequacy of an institution, as well as for assessing which measures are best for addressing a bank's vulnerabilities. The regular monitoring focuses on the adequacy of banks' risk-evaluation systems, particularly their compliance with the terms and conditions in the CRD for being granted permission to use internal models. In this context the interaction between ICAAP and SREP is at the core of the relationship between supervisors and banks. Guidance on these aspects developed by CEBS is of utmost interest, not only for establishing a level playing-field for supervisors' decisions, but also as an indication for banks as to the approach to be expected from their supervisors.

Through this so-called Pillar 2 supervisory approach, the hardcore of supervision is moving away from the control of compliance with capital standards (known also as 'tick box' approach) towards the continuous review of internal risk-control mechanisms conceived as the yardstick of sound and prudent behaviour. European norms regulating this supervisory process can be broadly divided into two categories: those providing the rules and standards for the assessment of internal risk-control devices of banks and those prescribing the tasks and powers of supervisory authorities. Such developments are indicative of the fact that the European supervisory strategy is experiencing substantial changes, moving away from mere compliance checks towards a more dynamic process-oriented approach. In this context, prudential rules no longer only consist of the classic command-and-control prescriptions, but, instead, emphasise the crucial role of the dialogue between the competent authorities and the regulated banks. Hence, with respect to supervision, the CRD incorporates an important amount of incentive-based rules, as well as some provisions that come close to contract regulation.

The principle of 'sound and prudent management' had already appeared in the Second Banking Directive, as a criterion for assessing the quality of shareholders having a qualified holding in a credit institution (article 11(5) SBD). While initially it had a marginal role as compared to the importance attributed to quantitative capital requirements, gradually this principle developed into one of the core aspects of prudential supervision. The content of the principle is not explicitly defined in current European legislation. Sound and prudent management should be interpreted as a generic concept, impossible to capture in an exhaustive list of characteristics. It is often interpreted by reference to actions that go against 'sound and prudent' behaviour, e.g. the pursuit of interests extraneous to the majority of shareholders, forms of organised delinquency, etc. On the contrary, the existence of a suitable internal organisation with clearly defined procedures, competences and responsibilities properly reflecting the dimension and the degree of sophistication of a bank, and the use of efficient internal or external controls, accompanied by a complete and reliable informative framework, are indicative of a sound environment. Prudence is usually understood as avoiding assuming risks that go beyond a bank's control ability or capacities to absorb losses. Consequently, it entails a qualitative assessment (with regard to organisational arrangements) and a quantitative assessment (the proportionality between assumed risks and available own funds) (Comana 2002: 133). It is a dynamic principle, whose interpretation should take account of the developments of management practices, technological progress, theoretical knowledge, etc.

Before the adoption of the CRD, in the absence of straightforward criteria for a sound and prudent management system, banks were expected to devise management techniques and algorithms primarily according to criteria of reasonableness. This left room for flexibility, but also for vagueness, and resulted in reluctance in applying this principle as a yardstick for assessing required supervisory action. Lacking codified instruments for applying the sound and prudent management principle, supervisory authorities enjoyed a considerable margin of discretion when assessing individual institutions. Such discretion has been feared at the European level, as a factor distorting competition within financial markets and potentially creating regulatory arbitrage.

The CBD contained only one generic provision imposing 'that every credit institution have sound administrative and accounting procedures and adequate internal control mechanisms' (article 17 CBD). Left for the national competent authorities to define in more detailed and precise terms, such a broadly conceived requisite was a convenient choice of regulatory technique in a context where national supervisory practices were largely dependent upon knowledge of local practices and supervised institutions, and when convergence of supervisory practices was not yet perceived as a priority by European decision-makers.

However, with ever growing cross-border banking structures that increasingly centralised risk-management policies at group level, supervisory convergence and enhanced supervisory cooperation became a priority at European level and a stated objective. The CRD inevitably had to set a common platform ensuring minimal harmonisation of the supervisory review process. The old article 17 was thus replaced by the new article 22, foreseeing that:

> Home Member State competent authorities shall require that every credit institution have robust governance arrangements, which include a clear organisational structure with well defined, transparent and consistent lines of responsibility, effective processes to identify,

manage, monitor and report the risks it is or might be exposed to, and adequate internal control mechanisms, including sound administrative and accounting procedures.

Article 22 sets out supervisors' expectations in relation to the internal governance of the supervised institutions. Several technical criteria for the governance structure and organisational arrangements, processes and mechanisms required are set in Annex V of the CRD. Supplementary detailed guidance on these aspects has also been developed by CEBS in its 2006 Guidelines on the Application of the Supervisory Review Process under Pillar 2, as well as in its Internal Governance Compilation (CEBS 2009d).

Another key provision of the supervisory review pillar is contained in article 124 CRD, which introduces a clear obligation for the competent authorities to review and assess whether the internal processes implemented by credit institutions, and the own funds held by the latter, are capable of ensuring sound management and coverage of risks. Substantial guidance for such an assessment is included in Annex XI, and also in the articles of the directive dealing with the different approaches to risk management. Although the competent authorities have the freedom to establish the frequency and intensity of their review, in accordance with the systemic importance, nature, scale and complexity of the activities of a credit institution, the CRD establishes with precision that the review and evaluation should be updated at least on an annual basis.

With the enhanced focus on the supervisory process, in the CRD there is a rebalancing between quantitative and qualitative prudential requirements. While the small number of articles dealing with the supervisory review process might still point to the complementarity of the second pillar with respect to the overwhelming minimum capital provisions, this observation may be misleading. The incentives provided under the first pillar, for making use of internal models as an alternative to standardised approaches to risk measurement, make capital requirements ever more interwoven with qualitative supervisory examination of banks' overall risk-management process. The importance given to the supervisory approval of internal models in the provisions regulating capital requirements, combined with the specific requirements on the supervisory review process, unequivocally consecrate the shift occurring in the regulatory and supervisory strategy from control of results to the control of processes. This means that not only the focus of control changes (from comparing various elements in the balance sheet to assessing complex processes), but also the dynamic aspects of supervision are more strongly emphasised along the static elements. Such a change in the regulatory paradigm also entails a substantive change in the role of competent authorities, to which new complex responsibilities are attached.

The expanded control function of the competent authorities would be vain if it were not underpinned by effective competences, allowing supervisors to require and enforce prudential measures. Under the previous framework, Member States were left complete discretion as to defining the powers to be exercised by the competent authorities. Within the new framework, which entrusts competent authorities with a new role, such a laissez-faire approach would have been inappropriate. The supervisory review pillar, departing from the traditional approach, sets out, although in apparently general terms, the minimum powers required for the carrying out of the evaluation process and lays down the obligation of early supervisory intervention. Thus, European law does not merely prescribe generically a duty of supervision, but also establishes the requisites of the monitoring and enforcement functions of competent authorities.

Thus, article 136 creates a direct obligation for national competent authorities to take the necessary actions or steps at an early stage, in case a credit institution does not meet the requirements of the directive. It also enumerates the minimum categories of measures to be applied in case supervisory intervention is needed. These measures include (without being limited to): obliging the credit institution to hold own funds in excess of the minimum level; reinforcing the arrangements and strategies implemented to comply with requirements of robust governance arrangements and internal risk-assessment processes; requiring credit institutions to apply a specific provisioning policy or treatment of assets in terms of own funds requirements; restricting or limiting the business, operations or network of credit institutions; and reducing the risk inherent in activities, products and systems of credit institutions. Article 136 is addressed directly to competent authorities, not to Member States, thus appearing to ascribe directly, irrespective of further implementation, the enumerated powers and the correlative obligation to use them when the provisions in the directive are infringed.

These provisions reflect the delicate issue of finding the right balance between harmonisation and scope for discretion when setting a common European regulatory and supervisory framework. An ever clearer distinction emerges in EU law that discerns between supervisory discretion, characterising competent authorities' decisions on individual institutions, and national discretion, which leaves Member States the ability to draw up the framework within which the competent authorities will take individual decisions. From the perspective of such a distinction it can be observed that the CRD reinforces supervisory discretion, while restraining Member States in their choice of the implementing framework.

A significant consequence triggered by the reinforced position of the competent authorities results from article 144 of the CRD, which imposes disclosure requirements on the competent authorities as a complement to the enhanced competences for taking action. It requests that the following are made public: the texts of the laws, regulations, administrative rules and general guidance adopted in the field of prudential regulation; the manner of exercise of the options and discretions allowed by European legislation; the general criteria and methodologies used for review and evaluation; and the aggregate statistical data on key aspects of the implementation of the prudential framework. Disclosure requirements echo two principles of the EU legal order – transparency and accountability – and aim to ensure minimal conditions against abusive practices (Commission 2003e). Accountability-enhancing measures at European level may be interpreted as building a common ground for a harmonised responsibility regime for supervisory authorities.

Last but not least, we would like to recall that the provisions on supervisory review in the CRD need to be corroborated with the criteria laid down in the Market in Financial Instruments Directive, which prescribes a consistent framework regulating essential features and powers of the competent authorities[23] that can serve as a model for more convergence in the field of prudential banking supervision. Also, the detailed organisational requirements set out in article 13 of the MiFID are compulsory criteria of evaluation and review for all competent authorities that authorise a credit institution to carry out investment activities.[24]

7 Market discipline

Recourse to market discipline as a regulatory tool has been constantly advocated since the intermingling of financial sectors, which rendered banks less immune to market pressures. The inclusion in the CRD of a separate chapter on market discipline,[25] thus consecrating the three-pillar structure devised by the Basel Committee, seeks to create, at the European level, the first comprehensive approach to disclosure requirements imposed to credit institutions. The underlying assumption is that timely and reliable information will enable market participants to evaluate more precisely the financial performance of banks. It is considered that a solid regulatory framework supporting the market's function of analysing and verifying the conduct of individual banks will induce increased market

23 The articles on the designation of competent authorities, the cooperation between authorities in the same Member State, the powers to be made available to competent authorities, administrative sanctions, right of appeal, extra-judicial mechanisms for investors' complaints, cooperation in supervisory activities, on-the-spot verifications or in investigations apply also to credit institutions; see Directive 2004/39/EC, especially arts 48–53, 57, 61, and 62.

24 As laid down in the 18th indent of the preamble to MiFID, credit institutions authorised under the CRD do not need another authorisation under the MiFID in order to provide investment services or perform investment activities. Nevertheless, in case a credit institution decides to engage in such activities, the competent authorities are obliged, before granting authorisation, to verify whether the respective credit institution complies with the relevant provisions of MiFID. Art. 2 MiFID lists the provisions that should apply to credit institutions authorised under the CRD, when providing one or more investment services and/or performing investment activities.

25 Chapter 5, 'Disclosure by Credit Institutions' under Title V includes arts 145–9.

discipline. Concomitantly, disclosure requirements are considered as a strong incentive for the regulated entities to carry out their activities in a safe, sound and efficient manner, as well as to maintain a level of capital adequate to their business and organisation. Undoubtedly, market discipline has the potential of reinforcing prudential regulation and of assisting supervisors to promote safety and soundness, especially in the context of the supervisory review process.

Disclosure requirements are addressed directly to credit institutions, thereby reducing Member States' discretion. Credit institutions, on the one hand, have to publicly disclose the set of information listed under the annex, subject to the derogations allowed for in article 146 and, on the other hand, must adopt a formal policy to comply with the disclosure requirements and have internal policies to assess the appropriateness of their disclosures. These policies have to refer to the procedures for validation and the frequency of their publication. Article 147 sets the frequency of disclosures at a minimum of one year, but requires that regulated entities determine in accordance with the criteria provided in Annex XII whether a higher frequency is necessary. Supplementary disclosure requirements are imposed on the entities intending to receive recognition from the competent authorities in relation to IRB approaches, credit risk mitigation and asset securitisation. Article 149 CRD requires that supervisory authorities be endowed with specific powers in relation to banks' disclosures.

Recognising that disclosure requirements need to take due account of confidentiality concerns and of the necessity to avoid excessive costs to the regulatees, the CRD also allows for certain derogations to the disclosure requirements. Thus, article 146 aims to ensure proportionality in the application of the disclosure requirements, by permitting some entities not to disclose information that would not be material[26] or items that would include proprietary or confidential information.[27] Also, the burden of costs could be minimised by allowing intermediaries to choose for themselves the medium and location of disclosures, in accordance with some criteria on concentration and traceability of disclosures (article 148 CRD).

Although it has been strongly argued in favour of a more market-based regime for financial regulation (Mayes *et al.* 2001), the new capital framework takes a cautious approach, acknowledging implicitly the as yet ambigu-

26 In accordance with Annex XII, 'an information is to be regarded as material in disclosures if its omission or misstatement could change or influence the economic assessment or decision of a user relying on that information'.

27 In accordance with Annex XII, information is to be regarded as proprietary to an entity if sharing that information with the public would undermine its competitive position, whereas information is to be regarded as confidential whenever there are obligations to customers or other counterparty relationships binding an entity to confidentiality.

ous role of enhanced disclosure requirements. It has been observed that, while emphasis on market discipline is consistent with ongoing trends in securities regulation currently focusing to a large extent on the achievement of an informationally efficient market, it does not necessarily entail the same effects for banking regulation, given its specific nature (Hirte and Heinrich 2002: 471). Thus, disclosure is constrained not only by banks' obligations with regard to confidential and proprietary information, but also by the very mechanisms within the banking market. On the one hand, the publication of negative information can trigger excessive market responses resulting in potential massive withdrawals of deposits: one of the very rationales behind prudential regulation. On the other hand, wholesale banking markets are held to be very efficient and capable of reacting by absorbing negative information before its dissemination by the institution concerned (Hadjiemmanuil 1996a: 103, 106). The crisis starting in 2007 was preceded by herding behaviour of market participants, which prevented market discipline from efficiently accomplishing its prudential function. Consequently, the effectiveness of the third pillar of Basel II may be largely questioned.

Given the afore-mentioned considerations we cannot say that the new capital regime marks a radical shift towards a market-based regulatory strategy, as the content of the articles on disclosure is relatively moderate. Nevertheless, it represents a foundation on which it can be further built. The efforts of CEBS to create common reporting standards (COREP and FINREP), as well as industry initiatives[28] to increase transparency have further developed this incipient market-based prudential platform.

8 The home–host issue

The relationship between home and host country authorities lies at the very core of the supervision of cross-border banking and, therefore, at the centre of EU banking rules. The CRD continued from the previous regulatory framework the principles defining the distribution of competences between home and host countries. Thus the home-country control principle is seen as the guiding principle that indicates that cross-border banking activities undertaken via the provision of cross-border services or the establishment of foreign branches have to comply with the legislation in the country where their parent has received authorisation and are subject to its supervisory jurisdiction. Instead, host countries remain in principle responsible for the

28 See, for instance, the Good Practice Guidelines on CRD Pillar 3 disclosures for securitisation, issued jointly by the European Banking Federation, the London Investment Banking Association, the European Savings Banks Group and the European Association of Public Banks, December 2008.

regulation and supervision of subsidiaries,[29] as well as of specific aspects related to the activities of all banks operating on their territory (e.g. liquidity rules, conduct of business). Traditionally, consolidated supervision and coordination between supervisory authorities (especially via Memoranda of Understanding) are the main tools for handling cross-border situations. The CRD foresees specific criteria for determining the consolidating supervisor, which in most cases is the home supervisor of the parent credit institution, but can also be a different authority.

The CRD has introduced additional provisions foreseeing new tasks for supervisors in view of coping with situations stemming from the new regulatory framework. Article 129 CRD is particularly important in this respect. It underlines the coordination role of the consolidated supervisor with regard to the gathering and dissemination of relevant or essential information, and its leading position in planning and coordinating supervisory activities in going concern and emergency situations. Furthermore, the second paragraph provides concrete ways of dealing with permissions for using internal models (the IRB and AMA approaches) in the case of subsidiaries of EU parent credit institutions. In such cases, it is foreseen that applications for permission should be submitted to the competent authority responsible for consolidated supervision, which should work together with all concerned supervisory authorities and in full consultation in order to decide whether to grant the permission and to determine the conditions to which such permission should be subject. A joint and fully reasoned decision on these aspects should be reached within six months. If no joint decision can be reached, it is for the consolidated supervisor to take his or her own reasoned decision, stating the views and reservations of the other supervisors, and to provide it to the applicant. Joint decisions, as well as the decisions taken by the consolidated supervisors, have to be recognised as determinative and applied by the supervisors in the Member States concerned.

The CRD thus clarifies that the decision on the use of internal models under Pillar 1 at group level is the competence of the consolidated supervisor. However, it falls short of spelling out the division of competences between home and host countries under the Supervisory Review Pillar. Thus, the CRD left unclear how articles 123 and 124 on the ICAAP and SREP apply at group level and who will ultimately take decisions falling under Pillar 2. This is particularly problematic in view of the fact that cross-border banking groups or financial holding companies usually manage these aspects in a centralised way. Hence, it will be very difficult to decide on the adequacy of the processes of individual subsidiaries and

29 According to article 131, competent authorities responsible for authorising the subsidiary of a foreign bank, may delegate, on the basis of a bilateral agreement, their responsibility for supervision of the subsidiary to the competent authority that authorised and supervises the parent undertaking of the subsidiary. In this case the latter will assume responsibility for the supervision of the subsidiary in accordance with the CRD. The Commission needs to be informed of such arrangements.

especially on the application of specific capital add-ons pursuant to article 136(2) CRD.

Reaching agreement on home–host aspects of supervision is one of the most challenging outstanding issues with regard to banking supervision in the EU. The distribution of competences is still a controversial aspect of the European framework that is largely responsible for the fragmentation in EU banking supervision. The home–host aspects are also intimately linked to the issue of burden-sharing, i.e. the bearing of the fiscal responsibility in case of the failure of an institution. The solutions considered have to take account of the need to properly address the concerns of all Member States involved (e.g. specific market structures, economic cycles), and also of efficiency aspects (e.g. avoiding duplication). Reliable communication and information-sharing between competent authorities is essential, but so is also effective decision-making on issues of common interest. The first review of the CRD (CRD 2), addressing also the supervisory arrangements in the CRD, has opted for the establishment of supervisory colleges for all cross-border banks, as a tool for dealing with cross-border aspects and for the imposition of a generic European mandate on all supervisory authorities, obliging them to consider the effects of their decisions on all other Member States. Still, under the CRD (CRD 2) solution, in case of the failure to reach a joint decision on Pillar 2 issues, responsibility will be split among the concerned authorities. We will come back to the home–host problems when dealing with the institutional arrangements for supervision, as it is a particularly important element in the discussions on the future EU supervisory architecture.

9 The review of the CRD

Despite the fact that its provisions came fully into force only recently (1 January 2008) and that many aspects of the CRD are still applied on a transitional basis, the CRD is currently under substantial review. This is partly as a result of the review clauses that were enshrined in the text adopted in 2006, but mainly a consequence of inadequacies in the regulatory framework revealed by the crisis. First review measures (CRD 2) were adopted by the EU legislator in September 2009. Further amendments are also currently under intensive discussion, in parallel with discussions taking place in the Basel Committee and the Financial Stability Board[30] and will probably constitute the object of subsequent reviews of the CRD.

The first review of the CRD was informally initiated in 2007 and was

30 The Financial Stability Board (FSB) was established in April 2009 to give a stronger institutional foundation to the expanded Financial Stability Forum. The FSB has a strengthened mandate to address global financial stability issues and, thus, is intended to ensure better effectiveness as a mechanism for national authorities, standard-setting bodies and international financial institutions to address global vulnerabilities and put in place strong regulatory, supervisory and other necessary policies. For a detailed description of the new tasks and composition of the FSB, see BIS press release 14/2009 from 2 April 2009.

followed by a first formal Commission proposal in April 2008, supplemented in June and finalised in the October 2008 proposal for amending the CRD and recast CAD. After intensive negotiations, a compromise version was reached between the Commission, the Council and the European Parliament, which was adopted by the latter under the first reading procedure in May 2009, confirmed by the Council in September and published in November 2009 (Directive 2009/111/EC). CRD 2 was initiated in order to update aspects of the Codified Banking Directive that had not been discussed when the CRD was adopted. Three issues were initially central to the first review: the large exposures regime, the definition of hybrid capital instruments, and the supervisory arrangements. The discussions were largely influenced by the first lessons drawn from the crisis, which led not only to substantial changes as regards the Commission's proposals on the three mentioned topics, but also to the addition of further important amendments related to securitisation and liquidity aspects.

Reflecting the emerging criticism of the risk-based approach in Basel II, CRD 2 takes a more restrictive and prescriptive prudential approach, imposing a series of limits, interdictions and obligations on banks in the quest of reducing excessive risk-taking permitted under the CRD. Important aspects of the amendments concern the elimination of the favourable treatment of inter-bank lending under the large exposures regime; the obligation of credit institutions to undertake thorough due diligence with regard to investments in securitisations; and the imposition on the originators, sponsors or original lenders of securitisations of the obligation to retain on an ongoing basis at least 5 per cent of material net economic interest in the securitisation (the retention requirement). Furthermore, new rules will complete the CRD setting more restrictive EU-wide criteria for assessing whether 'hybrid' capital, i.e. capital including both equity and debt, is eligible to be counted as part of a bank's overall own funds. As regards the supervisory arrangements, CRD 2 imposes the mandatory use of colleges of supervisors for cross-border banks, but has abandoned proposals on a reinforced role of the consolidated supervisor with regard to Pillar 2 aspects, an issue that is currently being discussed under the broader revision of the supervisory framework.

CRD 2 contains some prompt regulatory responses to the crisis and demonstrates that decision-making in Europe can be effectively accelerated in case of need. However, although it involved public consultations at almost all stages, the first review of the CRD did not necessarily respect the better regulation principles. Not only were the consultation periods shortened, but there were no clear explanations for the substantial changes proposed, nor was the feedback from stakeholders seriously discussed. The disparate lengthy changes with potential high impact do not seem to be underpinned by a clear vision as to the way forward. Only occasionally backed by parallel proposals at international level, the provisions in CRD 2 seem to be an improvised patchwork and do not reflect more structural questions on the most appropriate prudential approach for EU regulation. Proper impact assessments are missing and bizarre review clauses request the assessment of the adopted norms even before they come into force (for instance, the revised article 156 in CRD 2 requests the Commission to report by December 2009 on the expected impact of the proposed securitisation provisions, and to make appropriate proposals). A long list of further issues to be inserted in the CRD basically sets up the regulatory agenda for the next years on banking regulation.

Thus important amendments are already in the pipeline. On 13 July 2009, the Commission published a second legislative proposal for amending the CRD (CRD 3). It concerns the treatment of the controversial complex securitisations, a more severe regime for the trading book, specific disclosure requirements for resecuritisations, more restrictive and transparent remuneration policies and a more effective sanctioning regime. These issues address shortcomings in the current regulatory framework, and are also discussed at international level and backed by proposals and consultations of the Basel Committee. A further set of proposals for amendments to the CRD, especially covering identified gaps in the European regulatory framework, is expected to be issued in the first half of 2010 following a public consultation launched by the Commission on 24 July 2009 (CRD 4). These amendments are expected to address the following controversial issues: procyclicality and the introduction of countercyclical buffers and of dynamic provisioning to be built in good times and used in downturns so as to mitigate the oscillations of business cycles; the removal of national discretions and options from the CRD. Most likely, CRD 4 will substantially address the problems of own funds, proposing common criteria for their definition. CRD 4 will thus further contribute to establishing an extensive and reinforced European prudential regulatory framework. This will be complemented by proposals on the introduction of supplementary measures to the risk-based requirements in view of constraining the building up of leverage in the banking system (the leverage ratio); liquidity risk rules (most probably introducing some liquidity buffers, a net stable funding ratio and contingency plans); and stress testing. Furthermore, it is planned to reassemble technical standards into a comprehensive European prudential rulebook for credit institutions.

Thus, the CRD is becoming a particularly dense normative framework covering extensively prudential aspects and leaving ever less room for manoeuvre at national level. The new substantial prudential provisions will also entail new competences for the competent authorities and further emphasise home–host issues.

Regulatory measures drawing lessons from the crisis and purporting to amend the CRD do not so far seem to change its structure, nor to substantially question the underlying general approach. They mainly address gaps, tighten over-lenient regulatory treatment, reinforce the so far largely unexploited potentialities of Pillar 2 and rebalance an allegedly excessively risk-based approach. The EU regulatory reactions take place in parallel to debates and consultations on the same topics in the Basel Committee, eventually leading to what is referred to as 'Basel III'.

6 The principles characterising the European prudential regulatory regime

We have seen that the emergence of European prudential rules adhered to several regulatory patterns supporting European integration. The standard way of depicting prudential policy, as reflected in European legislation, is by reference to the three principles launched in the 1985 White Paper on the Internal Market: minimum harmonisation, mutual recognition and home-country control. Yet, in light of the latest normative developments, we consider that these regulatory principles have a limited capacity in describing the actual evolution of European prudential rules. We suggest that only a critical account of these principles may help in delineating the characteristics of the prudential regulatory strategy.

1 Harmonisation of prudential banking regulation

We have observed that the normative framework already provided, before the adoption of the CRD, a consistent body of prudential norms at European level. With the extension of the Lamfalussy process to all financial sectors, the required additional implementation measures were *a priori* subjected to the four-level procedure, a powerful tool for the proliferation of prudential regulation at the EU level (Wymeersch 2005: 1009). The purpose of this section is to identify the degree of harmonisation characterising the European normative framework for banking supervision.[1] Our main thesis is dual. First, the CRD results in extensive harmonisation of prudential rule and policy-making, an evolution which would call for the minimum harmonisation paradigm to be definitively abandoned. Second, a closer look at the scope of harmonisation reveals that recent reforms have put in place at EU level a regulatory regime, capable of providing constant regulatory input. This shifts the balance within the shared competences between the EU and Member States to the former.

1 The practical importance of establishing the de facto degree of harmonisation, characterising prudential rules, is related to the weight attributed to the regulatory strategy by the ECJ and national courts when assessing the content of the prudential norms in the European directives. This aspect will be touched upon in Part IV.

1.1 The harmonisation paradigm – from minimum towards maximum harmonisation

As we have seen, the first prudential measures contributing to the achievement of the common banking market were adopted in the pursuit of an ideal normative uniformity across the Member States. Such a model of 'total harmonisation' proved to be unsuccessful[2] and was abandoned very early, especially in light of the new pragmatic approach to the creation of the internal market promoted in the mid-1980s. In the context of steady expansion of Community powers under the *leitmotiv* of the 'internal market', but also of increased recourse to regulatory competition as a tool for convergence, the concept of 'minimum harmonisation' made its way into the language of banking regulation. Minimum common standards were necessary for laying the foundation of a common market; the Community was setting the floor (minimum threshold), while the Member States were permitted to maintain or even introduce more stringent regulatory standards, provided that such standards were compatible with the Treaty and justified by specified objectives protecting the 'general good'. It was argued that 'minimum harmonisation is the legal expression of fundamental tensions in the Community's wider economic and political evolution' (Dougan 2000: 856). Indeed, minimum European prudential standards reflected the reluctance of Member States to give up regulatory competences in sensitive areas, while shedding light on the indispensable need for creating a common language and thresholds that would foster mutual confidence among the various regulatory systems.

The intricate multi-layered decision-making process in the EU adds complexity to the meaning of 'minimum harmonisation'. It was rightly underlined that:

> the complex boundaries of the Community's diverse policy mandate as manifested in the Treaty text and adjudicated over by the Court mean that the opportunities for and character of minimum harmonisation are to some degree innately difficult to describe with any great precision.
>
> (Dougan 2000: 885)

'Minimum harmonisation' should be understood as a descriptive concept defining a certain degree of convergence between Member States' laws. It designates the minimum rule-base for politically acceptable mutual recognition of national regulatory systems. Substantially, in accordance with the specific needs of individual fields, this may imply lower or higher regulatory thresholds, contained in concise or extensive norms.

2 'Producing roughly ten directives a year, the chosen method was time-consuming and costly and failed to dent, let alone reduce, barriers to trade', Lannoo and Levin 2004: 2; see also Pelkmans 1987: 249.

It was clear from the very beginning that prudential standards could not be 'minimalist', understood as the lowest common denominator. Capital requirements and prudential instruments have been conceived at the EU level as obligatory and detailed rules, fit for ensuring financial safety and soundness in the common market. Therefore prudential rules had to prescribe high quality standards. Member States' leeway to go beyond the high standards set at Community level is limited.

The CRD permits Member States to adopt more stringent rules in a limited number of situations listed in recital 15. There is no generic clause stipulating a general right of Member States to adopt more stringent standards, nor a recital in the preamble in this sense. The CRD emphasises that EU legislation should deal with the 'essential harmonisation' (recital 7 CRD). This is contrary to the recast CAD that broadly provides that a Member State may impose additional or more stringent requirements on the investment firms and credit institutions that it has authorised. This should not be confused with Member States' discretion to make several choices within the prescribed prudential framework or to add regulatory substance to the extent necessary for adapting norms to local conditions. Often European prudential rules may be seen as a menu or set of norms allowing the choice from several alternatives. The frequency of such menu European norms has risen, along with the multitude of approaches offered by the new capital framework.

Analysed individually, the different areas covered by prudential rules reflect different degrees of harmonisation: total harmonisation, partial harmonisation and minimum harmonisation. Total harmonisation does not allow for derogation in the pre-empted area, except for safeguard measures or to the extent permitted by EU law itself (Van Gerven 2004a: 508). Partial harmonisation is understood as regulating only some aspects of the subject matter, while minimum harmonisation puts emphasis on the possibility for Member States to impose stricter rules.

Whether there is minimum or maximum harmonisation depends also on the angle from which one looks at prudential aspects: regulation or supervision; specific prudential instruments (e.g. capital requirements, large exposures, supervisory tools) or the whole prudential framework. A broad assessment of the normative framework would indicate that approximation of laws (alias harmonisation) has largely been achieved at the European level with regard to capital requirements, while supervision has only been harmonised in some essential aspects. At the same time, when looking at the details of the CRD, one might identify three categories of norms: fully harmonised prudential rules for which no regulatory additions – the so-called 'gold plating' – are permitted; harmonised rules that allow expressly for differentiated treatment; and minimally harmonised norms. Altogether it may be said that norms related to Pillar 1 tend to be characterised by maximum harmonisation, whereas Pillar 2 provisions that rely on specific assessments do not lend themselves to maximum harmonisation.

European prudential regulation was initially conceived as a free movement device, centred on the idea of removing entrance barriers to domestic markets. Such a market-construction-driven harmonisation concentrated on eliminating the most obstructive differences in national legislations. Consequently, the harmonised regime focused on some substantial aspects (e.g. authorisation, initial capital requirements, ongoing capital-adequacy requirements, operational prudential rules and firm-ownership controls), whereas procedural and institutional aspects were considered ancillary and coordinated through the home-country control and mutual recognition principles.

In the late 1990s, once the effects of the internal banking market directives (SBD and complementary directives) had become apparent, attention shifted from free movement in a strict sense to the consequences of free movement and the operation of the common marketplace. Taking account of the transformations and dynamics of ever-global financial markets, European legislation had to go beyond harmonising the hard core of rules indispensable for opening up markets, towards a more active involvement in the regulation of the market so as to address new aspects brought about by integration. The Lamfalussy process facilitated a more interventionist European approach to prudential matters by establishing a framework capable of the sustained creation of common standards and principles and fostering the dialogue between national authorities. Thereby, the scope of what is considered essential for prudential purposes is unquestionably widening.

The current normative framework underpinned by the Lamfalussy procedure may be seen as entailing a 'presumption of maximum harmonisation' (Moloney 2003: 813). The Lamfalussy process has set the premise for a radical shift towards a system in which there is substantive convergence (if not identity) between the prudential requirements in the Member States. Such a framework provides the possibility of introducing the highest prudential standards at European level, by increasingly removing the capacity of Member States to regulate this field. The quest for maximum harmonisation can be inferred also from the current regulatory reactions that address shortcomings identified during the crisis. A regulatory mechanism is now in place at EU level that can flexibly change or add to the prudential substance of European norms.

First responses to the regulatory shortcomings uncovered by the crisis confirm this view. The regulatory efforts for addressing loopholes in the prudential framework are concentrated at European and international level. Solutions to controversial regulatory issues, such as the originate and distribute model, the prudential treatment of complex securitisations, liquidity risk, excessive reliance on ratings, the issues of leverage and procyclicality, are all discussed authoritatively at the supranational level and are backed by Member States' call for a common regulatory approach.

1.2 The scope of European prudential harmonisation

As observed, European prudential rules are biased by two developments: new European integration strategies reinforcing the single market and extensive international reforms aiming at refining the capital framework so as to respond to the new complex financial structures, instruments and risks.

With regard to integration strategies, the reforms initiated in the late 1990s covered both policies and decision-making mechanisms. As to the financial market policy trends, we have observed that the focus has shifted from exclusively pursuing the establishment of a common marketplace, consolidating the created market and managing its inherent risks. This revised policy orientation targets loopholes that have the potential of adversely affecting the cohesion and coherence of the integrated marketplace. In this context, the role of the EU becomes more intrusive, as input has to occur on a constant basis in order to be able to respond to rapid developments. European regulation cannot limit itself to providing minimum harmonised rules that constitute an abstract benchmark in relation to which supervision is exercised. Instead, EU prudential regulation becomes a continuous process that assumes a strategic role for disciplining the common market. This entails new developments for the exercise of both normative and administrative EU powers.

EU regulation cannot be easily inserted into debates about the traditional distinction between legislative and executive functions, given that in the EU such powers are not clearly allocated and there is no obvious hierarchy of norms.[3] Such a divide becomes ever more blurred in light of Europe's emergence as a 'regulatory State', which invades ever more fields opened up by technological development and innovative market instruments. It became almost impossible for EU prudential regulation to manage effectively, at the initial 'legislative' phase, all the general and essential aspects regarding the safety and soundness of banks. Being essentially concerned with risks, important aspects of prudential policy have to focus on individualising the precise nature of risks, their probability of occurring, and the most adequate measures to be taken, etc. Initially, Community legislation was limited to minimal common prescriptive rules that were providing broad categories of risks and their prudential treatment. However, with increased integration in the banking sector, as an ongoing process, the cohesion of the internal banking market and the stability of the whole financial system require a larger European platform capable of ensuring greater convergence of national prudential regulatory frameworks and supervisory practices. Thus, the intervention of the EU legislator is expanding now beyond legislation representing minimum harmonisation into the realm of designing more streamlined regulatory and supervisory structures.

3 For a general analysis of the role of regulation from the perspective of Community normative and executive powers, see Bassan 2003.

As observed in legal literature, it seems that 'the FSAP/Lamfalussy model and, in particular, the use of Level 2 rules, is increasingly producing rules which seem to regulate, rather than construct the single capital market, and so intervene more intensively in Member States' regimes' (Moloney 2003: 817). The same can be said about the Level 3 prudential measures aimed at contributing to greater day-to-day cooperation and consistent implementation and enforcement; and therefore constitute key factors in ensuring convergence of the national regulatory requirements. Although the distinction between 'rules that regulate' and 'rules that construct' the market may be perceived as artificial, it has the potential to reflect the change in the focus of banking regulators. Their emphasis no longer falls exclusively on the basic underpinnings of the common banking market, e.g. ensuring the exercise of Treaty freedoms and eliminating legal barriers. It extends to new phenomena, brought about by evolutions in the marketplace, and consequently promotes convergence of concrete prudential practices.

Minimum harmonisation disappears from the vocabulary accompanying the new regulatory strategy. Instead, the Lamfalussy model explicitly provides for the adoption, at EU level, of framework legislation, implementing measures and non-legislative standards and guidelines. Thus it establishes a regulatory system flexible enough so as to permit timely adjustments and further harmonisation of prudential rules. Such an approach is indicative of an independent regulatory system, a coherent framework regulating the new risk environment resulting from the integrated market. It institutes the presumption that the output of such framework consists of high-level standards of protection forming a detailed body of harmonised rules.

The extended scope of European prudential harmonisation inevitably raises concerns related to the accountability of the use of the new regulatory competences. Therefore, the new regulatory process was made subject to the broader measures for guaranteeing transparency, clarity and scrutiny of EU actions as devised in the 2001 White Paper on European Governance and the Better Regulation Agenda. These promote better governance and better rule-making through enhanced cooperation between EU institutions and increased participation of all stakeholders through regular consultations. Also, they require the balancing of the costs and benefits of removing barriers and fragmentation via European regulation and impose accurate impact assessments before their final adoption.

Consequently, the transformation of the financial regulatory framework follows the patterns designed by the more general reforms that aim at improving governance within the European Union and by the special strategy of the FSAP directed towards getting the most out of an integrated European financial services market. The outcome is a complex regulatory framework, which distributes decision-making to various bodies and outlines a more participatory regulatory frame.

The European regulatory arrangements appear even more complex when considering the second dimension of current reforms: the substantive changes in prudential strategies. Thus, the current trends within one of the most relevant components of prudential regulation – the capital framework – require a more sophisticated regulatory approach. The setting of capital requirements moves from formal categories towards more risk-sensitive devices that allow for more flexibility. More receptive to the complexity of financial instruments, actors and risks, the new capital requirements concentrate on processes, not just outcomes, and thus prescriptive rules are increasingly combined with incentive-based norms. The latter allow for the scope of European regulation to expand so as to encompass new prudential aspects – especially related to supervision. Broadly, it may be observed that prudential rule-making is increasingly concerned with implementation aspects, whereas supervision involves ever more prudential standard-setting. Regulation and supervision are becoming ever more interwoven and this implies that European harmonisation extends to supervision.

In summary, the scope of European prudential harmonisation is determined by external factors such as developments in European governance in general and broader EU integration strategies, as well as internal evolutions of prudential policies, like the refinement of capital requirements. Both factors favour increased European intervention supposing a comprehensive European regulatory framework for prudential policy. Such a regulatory framework does not merely consist of a common platform of prescriptive rules, but entails a mechanism that allows for the adjustment and complementing of such rules in accordance with the dynamics of the financial markets.

1.3 European prudential regulation between the public–private domains

The emergence of a European regulatory regime should not overshadow a specific dimension of the new prudential strategy: the increasing contribution of private parties in devising prudential standards, which goes beyond mere participation in consultation processes that underpin the adoption of regulation. Prudential standards are not only enshrined in norms of public law, but are also developed by banks and financial institutions themselves, within their efforts to set up appropriate risk-management processes and benchmarks, or by specific actors, such as credit rating agencies. While avoiding an excursus into the debate on the public–private divide it is important to note that the CRD attributes an important, increased weight to regulatory input provided by the regulated entities themselves and thereby attaches to the European prudential framework a ‘private’ dimension.

The European prudential normative framework used to be exclusively concerned with public regulation. However, the CRD opens the door to 'privatising' prudential rules to a certain extent. Public authorities lack sufficient resources and expertise to address comprehensively, on the basis of prescriptive categories, the ever more complex financial realities that banks are facing when pursuing their activities. Instead, the regulated entities themselves, as well as specialised information firms (rating agencies), are considered more knowledgeable concerning new developments and needs related to innovative financial products. As such, they are held capable, if properly incentivised, of contributing effectively to the achievement of regulatory objectives. Thence, the State takes a step back into the shadows and relies increasingly on regulatory input from private parties. The regulatory incorporation of credit ratings and internal models for the determination of capital requirements is illustrative of this development. Thus, European law induces private actors in the financial markets to act so as to identify (from within their own priorities) the public interest. The State continuous to be predominant, as the failure of providing regulatory input by private parties triggers the application of public regulation that falls short of paying due attention to the peculiarities of each regulated entity (the 'default' standardised approach). An important consequence of the privatisation of prudential norms is the increased number of provisions aimed at reinforcing the supervisory powers of public authorities to counterbalance the 'delegated' standard-setting.[4]

Based on the principle of flexibility, imperative for contemporary economic regulation, the new capital framework offers various alternatives for privatising regulation, differing by the amount of regulatory components that may be transferred from the public regulator to market participants. This is not sufficient to allow us to infer the privatisation of prudential regulation. The classic command-and-control approach of capital requirements, with the public regulators setting and enforcing the standards, continues to be the main approach (the standardised approach), from which only those regulated entities that fulfil the criteria set by the public regulator may depart, and then only to the extent permitted by the regulator. Nevertheless, we cannot ignore that a certain 'disaggregation'[5] of what prudential regulation entails in functional and procedural terms is more than obvious, in light of the incentive-based norms providing for internal risk-measurement models. The entire philosophy has undergone a significant change and there is much greater focus on the risks incurred by individual firms and their internal capacity to properly conduct risk management.

First lessons from the crisis indicate that private parties consistently made use of the possibility of contributing substantially to devising prudential standards. Yet the events also proved that supervisors were relying

4 We will come back to these aspects when discussing the position of the different actors within the institutional arrangements for regulation and supervision.

5 The term is used by Julia Black to describe recent regulatory trends in UK financial services regulation; see Black 2003.

too much on this private regulatory input, without adequately scrutinising its quality. The accuracy of both credit ratings and internal risk-measurement models is now severely questioned. This regulatory capture of supervisors via ratings and internal models, corroborated with the major focus of supervisors on micro-prudential aspects of banking supervision, can be considered one of the main causes of supervisory failure. This should not be seen as discrediting private regulatory input altogether, which indeed adds to the flexibility and risk sensitiveness of the prudential framework. However, it is imperative that effective safeguards be put in place, capable of preventing excessive or uncontrolled reliance by regulators on such input. The absorption of private standards into prudential regulation should be set on a new basis and firmer criteria, while supervisors should be sufficiently equipped with resources to accurately assess the viability of private regulatory input. This should be done also from the perspective of the mandatory consideration of both micro- and macro-prudential aspects.

Last but not least, it should be noted that self-regulation by industry could bring added value in areas that are not subject to extensive and detailed regulation. As suggested in a 2004 Commission report, boundaries between public and private regulation could be drawn up in accordance with criteria such as the intensity of public policy objectives or the extent of conflicts of interest between market participants and public policy objectives (Commission 2004b). The report indicated that self-regulation might be a powerful tool for promoting the importance of the third pillar of the new capital framework: market discipline.[6] In addition, self-regulation can be a useful instrument that ensures the smooth interaction between prudential rules and consumer protection measures, or corporate governance regulation.

1.4 Prudential regulation between EU and Member States' competence

In light of the afore-mentioned observations, we will now consider how the regulatory space is divided between the European and the Member States levels from the perspective of the discourse on the division of competences. Here, we will focus on the so-called vertical distribution[7] of competences related to prudential regulation. This concerns the relationship

6 An important example in this sense are the Good Practice Guidelines on CRD Pillar 3 disclosures for securitisation (the so-called Transparency Industry Initiative), adopted in December 2008 by the European Banking Federation, the London Investment Banking Association, the European Savings Banks Group and the European Association of Public Banks. These self-regulatory measures aim to achieve sound, consistent and appropriately detailed implementation of Pillar 3 securitisation disclosure requirements in all EU Member States.

7 For a wide-ranging theoretical framework of the issue of distribution of competences between the EU and its Member States, see von Bogdandy and Bast 2002; Davies 2003; Michel 2003; Lenaerts and Gerard 2004; Dougan 2008.

between Member States and the European Union, as opposed to the horizontal competences analysis with its two components: the division of powers between the various institutions within the EU and the distribution of powers between Member States. We will attempt to grasp the relevant implications of doctrinal debates for prudential regulation, both as a means of better understanding current state-of-the-art and potential developments, and as an analytical tool helping to explain the concrete distribution of roles between Member States and the EU.

The starting point is obviously the legal basis, or the so-called 'enabling clause',[8] as the source of the EU's power to adopt normative provisions in the field of prudential supervision. In the case of European prudential legislation this is article 47(2) EC Treaty on the right of establishment.[9] Thus, prudential regulation and supervision is subsumed to the debates on the broader category of internal market regulation. Henceforth, prudential regulation, as most of the internal market matters, qualifies as a non-exclusive Community competence.[10] This character is definitively confirmed by the reference in the preambles to the CRD and recast CAD to the subsidiarity principle, which is not applicable in cases of exclusive competence (recital 8 CRD and recital 5 recast CAD).

The Lisbon Treaty[11] adopted in December 2007 introduced in the EC Treaty, which was renamed the Treaty on the Functioning of the European

8 For a definition of the concept, see Von Bogdandy and Bast 2002: 229, 234. The authors highlight the importance of differentiating between enabling norms, which are competence norms that confer the power to act through abstract titles, and standard-establishing norms, which delimit the exercise of power by specifically providing formal, procedural and material conditions for the proper exercise of the particular competence and the general scheme relating to the proper exercise of power. In practice, most enabling norms do not simply constitute the source of power but provide also some substantive standards for its exercise.

9 Under the Treaty of Lisbon, the first two paragraphs in art. 47 EC Treaty were merged into a single paragraph, namely art. 53(1) TFEU.

10 There are also some diverging opinions that claim that internal market issues are an exclusive Community competence. For instance, it was argued that since manifestly only the Community can take measures to harmonise European conditions or ensure cross-border movement, competences related to internal market issues should be exclusive; Toth 1994, referred to by Davies 2003: 689. From such a perspective, Member States' action would have only a completive role, filling in gaps left by Community law, but without being based on a proper national competence. Also, the Commission has taken the view that an area falls within the exclusive competence of the Communities if the Treaties impose an obligation to act on the Community because it is regarded as having sole responsibility for the performance of a particular task. It identified, among others, removal of barriers to the free movement of goods, persons, services and capital, and maintained that exclusive competences will expand as integration progresses; see Commission 1992.

11 On 2 October 2009 Ireland held a second referendum, the result of which returned in favour of the Lisbon Treaty. As a consequence the remaining countries (Poland and the Czech Republic) also ratified the Lisbon Treaty, which entered into force on December 2009.

Union (TFEU), a new Title I on the categories and areas of Union competence. The proposed article 2 TFEU lists the Union's powers under three categories: exclusive competences, shared competences and areas of supporting action. Proposed article 4 TFEU would definitively and explicitly consecrate internal market powers as shared competences. Under shared competences, Member States may act to the extent that the Union has not exercised its competence or has decided to cease exercising its competence.

The TFEU addresses EU competences in a rather conservative way and does not clarify the precise nature and boundaries of the functionally defined competences – issues that are at the very root of the discontent of EU sceptics and of fears of erosion of national powers. Given the specific evolutionary, integration-biased features of the EU, it is probably neither feasible nor desirable to establish a detailed catalogue listing alternatively material tasks corresponding to each competence attributed to the Union. Neither is curbing the process of European centralisation an end in itself, especially in an integrated market necessitating public regulation at Union-wide level. Instead, what is necessary is a higher level of predictability of the division of competences between the EU and the Member States and more reliable mechanisms for the control of Union-exercised competences. This does not entail a substantive characterisation of functions in view of facilitating the objective allocation of specific legislative or administrative competences to either the Union or the Member States, but instead the encouragement of a more participatory approach. The Lisbon Treaty aims to achieve this by strengthening the subsidiarity principle in two ways: giving an enhanced role to national parliaments and enforcing its consistent application, subject to control mechanisms. Although such a control is mainly political, it cannot be excluded that it could be eventually interpreted as rendering subsidiarity a ground for judicial review.[12]

The debates on improving the division of powers between Member States and the EU in connection with the work on the European Constitution and the Lisbon Treaty[13] have demonstrated the manifold approaches and the difficulties of establishing a common typology of competences. Various ways in which EU institutions share powers with the Member States were identified in accordance with EU practice and case-law. These categories may be pertinent for the analysis of prudential regulation, as they highlight the importance of identifying the scope of the respective shared competences

12 See the Protocol No. 1 on the role of national parliaments and Protocol No. 2 on the application of the principles of subsidiarity and proportionality attached to the Consolidated versions of the Treaty on the European Union and the Treaty on the Functioning of the European Union (as proposed by the Lisbon Treaty), as well as art. 5 of the TEU (consolidated after Lisbon).

13 The Convention on the Future of Europe has prepared the European Constitution signed in 2004, which was rejected through the French and Dutch referendums. After a period of reflection, negotiations restarted in 2007 that led to the signing of the Lisbon Treaty in December 2007.

and the way they refer to each other. The distinction between so-called concurrent powers and parallel (or shared) powers (Von Bogdandy and Bast 2002: 241) might be particularly relevant. The TFEU's use of the term 'shared' competences comes close to what the literature refers to as 'concurrent' powers (Louis 2008).

In the case of concurrent powers, Member States are allowed to regulate a particular field as long as the Union has not exercised its regulatory power. Given the Union's right to exhaustively regulate that area, the possibility of national competences is limited by the density of European secondary law (i.e. the pre-emption doctrine). Hence, EU competences are considered as having a 'dynamic' nature as determined by the constantly changing edge of shared competences due to the enactment of further legislation. The EU's competence for internal market harmonisation is considered the typical example of concurrent powers, as it is consistent with national regulatory competences or even requires them in case of approximation of laws. Although the EU may limit itself to enacting minimum or essential legislation, the mere possibility of enacting exhaustive regulation on the basis of concurrent competences creates legal certainty. It also allows freedom in the choice of the more appropriate strategy (e.g. total harmonisation, minimum harmonisation and mutual recognition). Drawbacks relate to the risk that, given the slowness of the EU legislator in adapting or abolishing outdated norms, concurrent competences may impede Member States from enacting necessary national legislation in fields already regulated by the EU. With regard to European financial regulation, such deficiency has been addressed through the implementation of the Lamfalussy process, which allows for quicker amendment procedures with a view to keeping abreast of market developments.

Parallel powers, in legal scholarship also called cumulative-concurrent competences, let EU and Member States' competences coexist, whereby the exercise of power by the former does not prohibit the latter from acting autonomously in the same field. Parallel competences are supposed to strengthen each other. Member States may continue to adopt policy measures according to their respective internal order, whereas the Union complements the activities of Member States pursuing the achievement of common objectives (e.g. cross-sectoral, cross-border issues).[14]

14 Scholarship identifies research, technological development and industrial policy as some examples of parallel competences. Under the changes proposed in the Lisbon Treaty, the areas of research, technological development, space, development cooperation and humanitarian aid are considered shared competences (art. 4 TFEU paras 3 and 4), with the explicit specification that the exercise of EU competences in these fields does not prevent Member States from exercising their own. Such specification is not made in the case of the principal areas subject to shared competences listed under para. 2 and including the internal market. Industry, on the contrary, is listed, according to the proposals of the Lisbon Treaty, under the supporting competences enumerated in art. 6 TFEU, in view of supporting, coordinating or supplementing actions of Member States.

In the area of prudential regulation, the EU disposes of the typical internal market-related powers, characterised as shared/concurrent competence. Harmonisation of prudential regulation is a continuing process whereby the European legislator, relying also on the institutionalised comitology framework and the European supervisory committees, has shown a propensity towards exhaustive regulation. The CRD and its subsequent reviews further move the dividing line of shared competences by increasing the scope of EU intervention and implicitly reducing the freedom of Member States to regulate. Such a development was predictable and will continue, as explicitly provided in the recent CRD amendment (e.g. further EU legislation is expected with regard to the trading book, complex securitisations, liquidity risk, remuneration issues, sanctions, procyclicality, leverage ratio, etc.) and the declared commitments to establish a common rulebook (Commission 2009d). The quest for achieving uniform prudential rules is also reflected in the abandoning of minimum harmonisation as a guiding principle of European banking law. National legislative discretion is continuously curtailed and the scope of the principle of mutual recognition implicitly reduced. Although we cannot ignore the tendency towards overwhelming centralisation of prudential legislation, be it through binding or non-binding norms, there is still a long way before this will develop to such an extent as to pre-empt completely national legislations.

As opposed to prudential regulation, supervision used to be left almost entirely to the Member States, with the European directives confined to the provision of broad coordination and conflict-of-law rules. Such a pattern could be qualified under the parallel competences, whereby the exercise of EU powers does not trigger concomitant restraint of the competences of Member States. Parallel powers are mutually reinforcing, and it is only in case of contradiction that the primacy of European law may render national provisions inapplicable. Yet the new supervisory pillar of CRD/Basel II and the subsequent more intrusive EU approach resulted in the adoption, at EU level, of substantial provisions on supervision, aiming to influence the conduct of supervision by national authorities. These supervisory hints, corroborated with the forthcoming reforms of the EU supervision framework, suggest a stronger involvement of the EU also at the supervisory level. This may be interpreted as indicating that, currently, banking supervision is more likely to fall under the shared/concurrent powers.

The categories suggested for the analysis are simplified and basic and we do not claim that prudential regulatory powers fit easily and categorically into the outlined frame. The exact scope of particular shared competences depends mainly on the analysis of the individual provisions that support such competences. However, the above analytical exercise may be helpful for a better understanding of the distribution of powers and the legal consequences they trigger.

2 The home-country control principle

As already highlighted, the European banking market is underpinned, apart from harmonisation efforts, by two regulatory principles developed pursuant to the ECJ's *Cassis de Dijon* case-law and generalised through the 1985 White Paper on the Internal Market: mutual recognition and home-country control. The home-country control principle has been seen as 'a major conduit for the natural development of variation in regulatory practice, since it defines the powers and the limits of national jurisdictions in the European Union' (Thomadakis 2003: 76). In the following, when referring to the home-country control principle, we will, unless specifying otherwise, use it in the widest sense so as to encompass both facets – namely, attribution of competences and mutual recognition of such competences.

Reforms of the prudential regulatory framework have been constantly accompanied by criticism of the home-country control principle, as applied pursuant to the banking directives (Lomnicka 2000: 330). We maintain that, from its very introduction, the home-country control principle only constituted a descriptive regulatory instrument indicating the predominant home-country's responsibilities for prudential supervision. It was not capable of bringing about regulatory convergence by itself. Nor was it conceived as an exclusive, absolute rule, but was subject to various limitations from the very beginning. This is mainly justified by the fact that the European prudential framework does not contain sufficient safeguards for ensuring the proper consideration of the potential impact of national supervisory decisions on other Member States concerned. Home-country control as prescribed by the European directives is thus only imperfect.

In the following we inquire into the scope of the home-country control principle in the area of prudential supervision, with special reference to the competences pertaining to the host countries.

2.1 The scope of the home-country control principle

The introduction of the principle of home-country control into European banking law has to be understood within the context of the paradigm change accompanying the efforts for achieving the internal market. The home-country control principle is the key for the distribution of competences between Member States with regard to banking activities entailing a cross-border element. Home-country control indicates that it is for the Member State, in which a bank has its head office, to authorise its access to the banking market, as well as to continuously supervise the authorised entity (including in a different Member State). An authorisation to take up banking activities is considered tantamount to a 'European passport' for banking, as it allows the authorised institution to pursue banking activities in other Member States (either by cross-border provision of services, or by way of establishing branches) under the supervision of its home country. Mutual recognition is inherent to home-country control, and ensures, in principle, the *ex ante* recognition of the authorisation and of home-country supervisory competences by all the other Member States, potential host countries.

The overwhelming underlying objective of the home-country control principle when introduced was that of creating a common banking market that provides the various participants with the opportunity to enjoy the Treaty freedoms, and particularly the freedom to provide services and the freedom of establishment. The regulatory strategy employed is subordinated to this primary objective and, consequently, has to be sufficiently flexible to accommodate new ways of achieving Treaty freedoms or providing other public goods. This was clearly stated by the European Court of Justice in its deposit guarantee case,[15] where it acknowledged that the principle is not provided in the Treaty itself. This brings about two consequences: first, it was not laid down in order to systematically subordinate all other rules in the sphere of banking; and, second, the legislature could depart from it provided it did not infringe legitimate expectations. Hence, the principle should be attributed only a relative value; its primacy, although presumed, can be put aside if justified.

Home-country control operates as a choice of jurisdiction rule attributing the primary role to the Member State where a company has its head office. Such supervision by only one Member State, the home State, was devised for avoiding credit institutions being subject to a double regulatory burden, and thereby for reducing 'restrictions' or 'barriers' to the Treaty freedoms applicable to credit institutions in a common market.

The practical operation of the principle, as laid down in the directives, was from the very beginning much more limited than the regulatory ideals behind it. This results directly from the narrow definition of the 'host country' that comprises only the Member State in which a bank has a branch or in which it provides services and excludes Member States where a foreign bank establishes a subsidiary (article 4(8) CRD). Moreover, from the very beginning it was not designed to exclude host State supervisory competences, but instead to act as a *prima facie* key for allocating competences. As long as the harmonisation was restricted to the minimum absolutely indispensable for launching the internal market programme, there were still many instances where host countries could intervene. The first banking directives merely reflected a European regulatory strategy based on imperfect mutual recognition and imperfect home-country control. At that time, it was sufficient to have a simple rule providing the distribution of powers between the home and the host regulators. As long as cross-border banking occurred in traditional forms, such a choice of jurisdiction rule provided enough legal certainty and corresponded to the

15 C-233/94 *Germany* v. *European Parliament and Council* ECR 1997 page I-02405.

institutional supervisory set-up. However, ever more extensive and detailed prudential aspects covered by European legislation and increased instances of cross-border banking in the EU involving complex structures have gradually revealed the limits of imperfect home-country control and moved the focus on to cooperation and coordination. Especially in the light of the crisis, home-country control is increasingly questioned and new solutions are considered for ensuring effective supervision in the EU.

2.2 Host-country competences provided in EU legislation

Before assessing the home-country control principle, we will look at the allocation of competences in the banking directives. The home State was given general competence with regard to access to the taking up of banking business on its territory and the ongoing supervision (including supervision on a consolidated basis when so provided by EU law). However, the home country's powers extend cross-border only to branches or provisions of services, and do not cover subsidiaries. Moreover, home-country supervision is explicitly limited by provisions giving responsibility to the authorities of the host Member State and those relating to supervision on a consolidated basis (article 40 CRD). Furthermore, there are implicit limitations stemming from the possibility of the host country to elaborate its powers on general good grounds (Avgerinos 2003: 50–82, 102–42).

It is now relevant to examine the competences retained by the host Member State in order to find out to what extent they may downgrade the principle of home-country control. We shall analyse such competences as they result from the CRD, which did not modify the allocation of powers established in previous banking directives. The provisions in the CRD should be analysed in consideration of the overall message of the directive, as well as of the broader Lamfalussy framework. Furthermore, home–host arrangements were one of the main topics of the first review of the CRD (CRD 2) and lie at the core of debates on the future architecture for financial supervision in the EU.

Within the CRD, we may identify two sets of supervisory competences for the host Member State. One category is explicitly foreseen as an exception to the principle of home-country control under the chapter regulating the principles guiding prudential supervision. The other category concerns powers that the host Member State's competent authorities may exercise in relation to the application of the Treaty freedoms. The former are explicit residual powers laid down in the directive, whereas the latter are enforcement powers supporting the substantial explicit and implicit residual host State's powers. In the following, we will briefly describe the relevant provisions, in order to grasp the extent of the host State's competences in the field of prudential supervision.

Under the so-called residual competences of the host Member State there is first the shared responsibility, in cooperation with the authorities of the home Member State and pending further harmonisation, for the supervision of the liquidity of branches of credit institutions (article 41(1) CRD). Thus, host countries can impose on branches from other Member States the same liquidity requirements as applied to domestic banks and may also use the adequate supervisory tools in relation to their liquidity supervision. Second, there is the complete responsibility for the measures resulting from the implementation of host State's monetary policy, without prejudice to the measures required for the reinforcement of the European Monetary System (article 41(2) CRD). In addition, pursuant to provisions in the MiFID, the host country retains responsibility for conduct of business and market transparency rules (Art. 32(7) MiFID). Moreover, the host Member State's competent authorities retain supervisory competences with regard to the prevention of money laundering and terrorism financing (article 3(2) (f) Directive 2005/60/EC). Such residual competences cannot be discriminatory or restrictive on grounds that the credit institution had been authorised in a different Member State (article 3(3) Directive 2005/60/EC).

Often, the relevance of these explicit residual competences (especially liquidity and monetary policy) was underestimated, on the grounds that they constituted the objective of cooperation between Member States, especially in the light of the establishment of the European Monetary Union. Yet in 2006 the CRD in article 41 CRD steadily reaffirmed the host State's powers, continued to make reference to the envisaged future harmonisation of liquidity risks, and recalled host countries' 'complete responsibility' for their monetary policies within the limits of the EMU. The prospect of achieving harmonisation in matters of liquidity supervision still belongs to the realm of future measures. Neither the FSAP nor the post-FSAP strategies have presented it as a priority, and it is only in the light of the crisis and the ascertained importance of liquidity risk management for the soundness of financial institutions, including for branches of foreign banks, that liquidity supervision has moved up the agenda of policy-makers and regulators. Thus, in October 2008 CEBS issued high-level principles for banks and supervisors on liquidity risk management, and the CRD has been amended to slightly reinforce the broad criteria on liquidity laid down in Annexes V and IX. Still, as for now, there is no European framework for liquidity regulation and supervision, and endeavours to harmonise rules in this field still have a long way to go.[16] With regard to monetary policies, with the advent of enlargement, the scenario for a single unitary monetary policy in the EU has been further postponed and more Member States

16 The regulatory framework for liquidity risk largely varies across countries. Ongoing discussions reflect the lack of common concepts and common understanding, and so far efforts have been mainly employed in defining an initial common conceptual framework; see CEBS' Guidelines on Liquidity Buffers, published on 9 December 2009 and the Basel Committee public consultation of 17 December 2009 on an international framework for liquidity risk measurement, standards and monitoring.

continue to retain their powers in this field. Consequently, the residual host Member State competences (provided in article 41 CRD) can by no means be neglected or understated when considering the allocation of supervisory powers. Also, despite enhanced provisions on consolidated supervision and the role of the consolidated supervisor, host States' competences regarding subsidiaries remain an important limitation to the home-country control principle under the CRD.

Host Member States also enjoy a range of supplementary competences explicitly referred to in the CRD. The powers of the competent authorities of the host Member State in the context of the freedom of establishment and freedom to provide services are described in Title III of the CRD (articles 25–8) and are controversial as regards their precise meaning and legal consequences. One of the most contentious issues is related to the notification procedure: according to articles 25 and 28 CRD, the host State shall be given notice and receive various pieces of information from the home Member State. This should occur within a certain timeframe, running from the notification of the home Member State by the credit institution interested in doing cross-border business (three months in case of the exercise of the freedom of establishment – article 25(3) – and one month for the freedom to provide services – article 28(2)). Although the abolition of the notification procedure was fervently argued, on the grounds that in practical terms it detracts from the Treaty freedoms and involves numerous interpretative doubts (e.g. the concept of branch, the mandatory character of the notification, etc.) (Lomnicka 2000: 325), the provisions regulating the latter have been preserved in the draft directive without any substantial change. The notification procedure is particularly important because it provides the possibility for the host State to communicate to the credit institution intending to open a branch within its territory the conditions under which, in the interests of the general good, those activities must be carried on in the host Member State (article 26(1) CRD). In case of the exercise of the freedom to provide services, this is not explicitly provided.

Further competences of the host Member State are enumerated in articles 29–37 under Section 5 of Title III of the CRD entitled 'Powers of the Competent Authorities of the Host Member State', which took over article 21 of the SBD. Unfortunately, dividing the content did not bring about more clarity and perpetrated the ambiguity related to the scope and extent of such powers of the host State. It might be inferred that a certain ambiguity is intentionally maintained in order to allow the smooth interference of jurisdictions, especially in the context of the strong emphasis on supervisory cooperation.

Among the host State's powers, enumerated in section 5, there is the power to impose reporting requirements, for statistical purposes, to foreign credit institutions having branches within their territories. As underlined in 29(2) CRD, host Member States may impose the same reporting requirements as in the case of domestic banks, especially when discharging their 'residual' responsibilities concerning liquidity supervision and monetary policy. Such parallel reporting to the host country may be particularly cumbersome for banks, as reporting requirements differ substantially across Member States in terms of formats, frequency and reporting dates.[17]

Article 30 CRD sets the framework for the enforcement of the host Member State's powers. It allows the host State, after following a prescribed procedure, to take the appropriate measures for punishing and preventing activities that are contrary to the host State's rules adopted pursuant to the powers recognised to it by the directive. Also, in accordance with article 33 CRD, the host Member State may take precautionary measures before following the procedure in article 30, when these are necessary for protecting the interests of depositors, investors and others to whom services are provided. Furthermore, article 31 introduces a clear difference between the powers of host States, related to statistical purposes and to the enforcement of their rights provided in the CRD, and 'the power of host Member States to take appropriate measures to prevent or to punish irregularities committed within their territories which are contrary to the legal rules they have adopted in the interests of the general good'. Another differentiation is implicit in article 37 CRD, from which it may be inferred that the host Member State's competences related to the regulation of the form and content of advertising of financial products in the interests of the general good constitute a different category of host State powers. Any preventive or punishing measures taken pursuant to articles 30 or 31 must be properly justified, communicated to the credit institution and subject to the right of appeal to the courts of that Member State whose authorities adopted it.[18]

To sum up, there are three categories of competences pertaining to the host Member State. First, there are the residual competences, which may be explicit (monetary policy, liquidity) or implicit (subsidiaries). Second, there are the complementary competences, such as those with regard to statistics, the notification procedure, enforcement powers. Last but not least, there is the category related to the power of adopting measures in the interests of the general good.

2.3 The general good clause and prudential regulation

It is not our intention to provide a comprehensive overview of the general good concept as applied in financial services.[19] Our ambition is limited to

17 CRD 2 has introduced a new subparagraph under article 74 (2) CRD requesting Member States to apply uniform reporting requirements on the calculation of capital requirements by the end of 2012. In this sense, CEBS is entrusted with the task of elaborating uniform reporting formats by the end of 2011.

18 Art. 32 CRD.

19 On the general good in financial services, see Katz 1992; Usher 1994: 38–9; Tison 1997; Björkland 1998; Avgerinos 2003: 119–23.

understanding its bearing on the home country control principle and on the concept of free movement as developed by the ECJ.[20] It has been argued that minimum harmonisation is supposed to achieve the codification of what, in the absence of harmonisation, would fall under the general good exception (Tison 2002: 350). For prudential issues, this would imply that, given the substantial harmonisation achieved by the banking directives in the areas of market access and prudential supervision, the general good clause may not possibly be invoked in these fields (Tison 2002: 364). Conversely, it may still be invoked in the domains pertaining to residual competences of the host Member States – like rules on market behaviour, the national private law regulation of financial products, liquidity supervision, etc.

In our view, denying or mitigating the relevance of the general good clause with regard to prudential supervision is too simplifying and ignores the complexity of the provisions of the CRD, as well as the evolving nature of prudential supervision. Considering that European harmonisation, as achieved through the CRD, aims at creating a common regulatory platform for a dynamic, evolving supervisory process, largely based on both quantitative and qualitative standards, we argue that the general good concept is capable of playing an important role. Here, we do not intend to overstate eventual recourse to the general good clause, but are principally interested in determining the way it may circumscribe the home-country control principle. General good is a key strategic instrument that has the potential of inclining the balance either in favour of home-country control (if its use is restricted) or in favour of cooperation between supervisory authorities (if recourse to it is less prohibitive). Moreover, it should also be considered that a too rigid allocation of competences to the home country could undermine the effectiveness of supervision and impair the emerging market discipline dimension of the supervisory strategy.

In light of the residual host States' competences, we may say that a broad understanding of general good in the banking field would include safeguards linked to monetary policy or liquidity supervision. In these situations the host State may interfere with home States' supervisory competences, without any need for justification. Measures taken by the host country pursuant to its residual competences are subject to the procedure laid down in article 30 CRD. This enforcement procedure is quite lax and provides neither deadlines nor criteria for determining the adequacy or appropriateness of the measures to be taken. It basically consists of a generic information duty towards the home State's authorities, and a generic requirement to observe a reasonable grace period before taking

20 See ECJ, 26.02.1991, C-154/89 Commission v. France (*French tourists case*) ECR 1991, I-659; ECJ, 27.07.1991, C-76/90 *Saeger* ECR 1991, I-4239; ECJ, 7.05.91, C-340/89 *Vlassopoulou*, ECR 1991, I-2357; ECJ, 3.02.93, C-148/91 *Veronika* ECR 1993, I-487; ECJ, 30.11.95, C-55/94 *Gebhard*, ECR 1995, I-4165.

action. As to the actions to be taken, the host Member State has substantial discretion for determining the appropriate measures to prevent or to punish irregularities and, if necessary, can even stop the credit institution from undertaking further transactions on its territory.

The general good clause in the narrow sense refers to the scope of article 26 CRD. According to the latter, the competent authorities of the host Member State have to communicate to the foreign bank intending to open a branch on its territory, the conditions under which, in the interest of the general good, those activities shall be carried on in the host Member State. Such powers of the host States to act in the interest of the general good are, according to article 31, not affected by the provisions in article 30. Consequently, they will be enforced in accordance with the common EU law conditions applicable to the general good as an exception to the Treaty freedoms. Indeed, it is commonly accepted in legal literature that, in the absence of a definition of general good in the banking directive, the concept has to be understood in light of the ECJ's case-law on the justification of restrictions to free movement and on the conditions attached to the use of the general good exception (Van Gerven 1990: 57; Dassesse *et al.* 1994: 43; Sousi-Roubi 1995: 145; Tison 2002: 322).

The extent to which host countries may expand their powers to the detriment of the home country by virtue of the general good has to be regarded as an exception to the fundamental Treaty freedoms and to the European banking passport, and must therefore be interpreted strictly. Definitely, the enforcement of general good powers will be more difficult as enforcement of the residual powers of the host country under article 30 CRD. From the ECJ's case-law, it may be inferred that general good is an evolutionary, open-ended concept whose applicability needs to be verified on a case-by-case basis and in accordance with the material scope of the specific Treaty freedom it might restrict. In order to be qualified as adopted in the interest of the general good, a national measure has to comply with the following generic conditions, as established by the ECJ: (1) justification by a general good motive (e.g. the ground invoked should be a legitimate aim of general interest); (2) absence of harmonisation; (3) absence of discrimination on grounds of nationality; (4) absence of duplication of home State rules; (5) objective necessity (adequacy and proportionality) (Tison 2002: 342).

As a reaction to concerns in connection with the ambiguous general good references in the SBD, the Commission in 1997 elaborated an interpretative communication intending to explain the scope of the general good concept (Commission 1997). Yet the 1997 Communication has been widely criticised, especially for its inability to define and clarify the meaning of the general good exception in the area of banking services. Although deprived of legal force, the Communication provides some authoritative guidance. While the Commission did not manage to spell out descriptive criteria that would allow the identification of general good situations, it has succeeded in specifying the conditions under which a Member State can invoke this exception, as developed in the ECJ's jurisprudence.

As observed, 'the lesser the supervisory rules are harmonised, the greater the power of the host State to impose its rules under the general good' (Avgerinos 2003: 123). Also, the greater the power of the host State, the weaker the role of the home-country control in the prudential regulatory framework. The scope and degree of harmonisation may vary widely, especially in dynamic areas where competences are shared between the EU and the Member States. Under these circumstances, 'absence of harmonisation', the second ECJ-demanded condition, is by no means straightforward. We should keep in mind that prudential supervision will still be subject to harmonisation efforts, and convergence of the national regulatory frameworks is one of the stated objectives in this area. As long as there is scope for further harmonisation, there is definitely scope for national measures to be adopted in the general good interest.

Tison enumerates five general good motives that have been so far accepted by the ECJ in the area of financial services: consumer protection; fairness of commercial transactions; the integrity of the financial system; the coherence of the fiscal system; the effectiveness of fiscal supervision. It is not our objective to analyse all of them and their generic capacity to create restrictions to the free movement of banking services. Our more limited aim is to find out how they interfere with the principle of home-country supervision, as laid down in the directive. From this perspective, we observe that action of the host Member State on the grounds of consumer protection can be justified under article 33 CRD, without any need of circumvention via the general good exception.[21] The second motive, the fairness of commercial transactions, is also partially considered in article 37 CRD, which also indicates its link with the general good concept. Hence, advertising by credit institutions has to conform to the host State's rules adopted in the interest of the general good (article 37 MiFID). Furthermore, consumer protection aspects, transparency and fair trading are already largely harmonised in the EU through the MiFID and its implementing directives.

The two motives concerning taxation have received only limited acceptance from the ECJ, because of the various cooperation forms between Member States in the field of taxation and traditional reluctance to

21 Indeed, art. 33 CRD allows the host State to take '*any* precautionary measures necessary to protect the interests of depositors, investors and others to whom services are provided' even before following the procedure provided in art. 30. As a safeguard against misuse of this clause, a Commission control is installed, which, after due consultation with the competent authorities of the other Member States, may request the host Member State to amend or even abolish such measures.

address straightforward tax harmonisation in the EU. Yet, in the light of the crisis, fiscal arguments may become ever more pertinent in justifying host State measures pursuing the general good, especially with regard to foreign branches. Under the current arrangements for burden-sharing, the failure of a cross-border institution may impinge largely on the host country's fiscal resources.[22] This is primarily because of the host country's competences as a lender of last resort, intimately linked to its powers with regard to liquidity supervision, as well as the host country's power to bail out, both of which ultimately rely on taxpayers' money. Second, it is because of the fragmentation of deposit coverage in case of failure, illustrated through the lack of efficient cooperation between deposit guarantee schemes and the topping-up arrangements requested by the Deposit Guarantee Directive that often subject a foreign branch to two different schemes.[23] Deposit coverage could also involve the use of public money if the guarantee schemes are not sufficiently funded. Taking these aspects into consideration, we may envisage the 'need to preserve the coherence of the fiscal system' as a plausible rationale justifying host State action in the interest of the general good.

Furthermore, another pertinent general good justification appears to be prudential supervisory policy itself, performed in view of maintaining financial stability and, implicitly, the integrity of the financial system. Indeed, we have to take account of both dimensions of prudential supervision: the micro-dimension connected to the soundness of individual institutions and the macro-level, which relates to the particular functions of the financial intermediaries in the overall economic process. These two dimensions are intrinsically connected and only their joint consideration is capable of addressing the vulnerability of financial markets and bringing about the enhanced confidence of consumers. The home-country control principle ascribes the supervisory competence to the home State, which, due to its strong links to the parent undertaking, is considered the most capable of assessing the solidity of a branch – even when acting outside the host State territory. The situation might, however, be the opposite when examined from the perspective of the macro-level, which is primarily concerned with financial stability, including the containment of contagion effects and bank runs. Such systemic aspects will probably be more familiar to the host State's competent authorities that are closer to the market realities in which a foreign branch will operate. Equally, it has been underlined that countercyclical

22 This was the case of the failure of the Icelandic banks Kaupthing and Landsbanki in 2008, especially with regard to the businesses they had in the UK, Luxembourg and Belgium.

23 At the end of May 2009 the European Commission launched a public consultation on the review of the Directive on Deposit Guarantee Schemes, in which it addresses the above-mentioned aspects and makes proposals on how to deal with them.

measures, as currently discussed in the process of the CRD review, would be better applied by the host countries even to foreign branches, which are those that will best know the asset price cycles and the pace of credit expansion on their territory (Brunnermeier *et al.* 2009). Furthermore, there is no evidence that the home country would be better placed to decide on supervisory measures pursuant to Pillar 2; on the contrary, the envisaged dialogue between supervisors and the supervised entities might benefit substantially from the proximity between the two. Consequently, it is justified that there is a possibility for the host State to take measures in case of threat to the integrity of its banking market, where foreign branches may have systemic relevance. Such intervention normally occurs by way of cooperation between the Member States' competent authorities. Notwithstanding this, the host country may need to intervene on a more spontaneous basis and thus disregard apparently exclusive home State supervision. This is particularly the case in times of crisis and when coordination mechanisms are deficient and lack firm decision-making processes. The general good exception will be the most appropriate vehicle justifying host State measures, as it is duly equipped with guarantees ensuring that legitimate expectations will be properly protected from discretionary powers.

In our opinion, the existence and the maintenance of the provisions on general good in the CRD demonstrate that, from the very beginning, the home-country control principle did not possess an absolute value. The general good clause is, however, an exception and therefore it can be applied only under strict conditions. The explicit stipulation of residual host country competences is not intended to suppress any effect of the general good exception in the area of prudential supervision, but instead to subtract enforcement of residual competences from the more restrictive conditions applicable to host State powers justified under the general good clause. While residual host State competences will only be checked against the conditions laid down in the CRD, any host country measure justified under the general good will be scrutinised from the perspective of restricting Treaty freedoms and under the more severe conditions attached to general good exceptions, as developed by the ECJ.

2.4 Assessing the home-country control principle

We have seen that prudential supervision is a complex process, which has been largely harmonised through the banking directives but which, through the dynamic character of financial innovation, technological progress and globalisation, continuously unravels new aspects susceptible to regulation. The new regulatory strategy in the area of financial markets acknowledges this evolving character of financial regulation and creates a mechanism for bringing about convergence between the national regulatory responses to new challenges in financial markets.

The CRD and recast CAD attempt to harmonise all the essential aspects of the taking up and pursuit of the business of credit institutions. As a consequence, the mere fact that a Member State has stricter rules than those prescribed by EU law will, in principle, not allow it to impose more severe rules on banks from other Member States when carrying out activities on the basis of the European passport. Nor can the host Member State question, or control by means of the general good exception,[24] the authorisation conditions for granting the passport laid down in the home country's legislation. Mutual recognition of authorisations is one of the key elements of the common banking market and will be very difficult to challenge on the grounds of general good. However, the general good clause has the potential to restrict home-country competences with regard to supervision.

Prudential supervision often owes its effectiveness to convention and practices, as well as to a range of subtle persuasion tools. Prudential supervision is no longer based on mere compliance with home-country regulation, but increasingly focuses on the assessment of the soundness of banks' risk-management systems and internal controls. Internal risk-measurement techniques and control processes are linked to the risks specific to the market where the bank operates. From this perspective, the home-country competent authorities might not have access to all relevant information for producing an accurate risk assessment and choosing the most appropriate actions in response to the assessment.

The home-country control, seen as a procedural norm that allocates competence for supervision, should itself be subject to evaluation from the perspective of its capacity to guarantee that the objective of safety and soundness will be met. It might be that it does not pass such a test, in which case the intervention of the host Member State is justified under the general good clause. In this context, the host State is allowed 'to prepare for the supervision' of foreign branches intending to operate on its territory and, if necessary, to indicate the conditions under which, in the interest of the general good, the business must be carried out in the Member State.

A certain devaluation of the home-country control principle also comes from the Deposit Guarantee Schemes Directive 94/19/EC, which has adopted a modified version of the principle reflecting ongoing disparities between the home and host country schemes. The directive, as it stands now, sets minimum standards and stipulates the obligation of the home Member State to provide depositor compensation in case of failure of the credit institutions it has authorised, including for foreign branches. This allocation of competences is restricted by the so-called supplementary

24 Member States may complain at the ECJ that another Member State did not fulfil its obligations (e.g. did not implement the standards set in the CRD), in accordance with article 227 EC Treaty, or it may ask the Commission to take action, on the basis of article 226 EC Treaty; see Commission 1997: 14.

guarantee,[25] which requires the topping-up of the coverage offered by the home State's deposit guarantee scheme. Thus, whenever the host State's compensation scheme is more generous than that of the home country, the host State should ensure that non-host State regulated firms have the possibility of supplementing their home coverage. Such responsibility sharing has determined the ECJ to ascertain that the principle of home-country supervision had not been laid down in the banking directives in order to systematically subordinate all legislation in the sphere of banking, and may be departed from if it does not infringe legitimate expectations.[26] The ECJ's ruling reflects the change of focus in the European prudential framework, from delimitation of jurisdictions through home country and mutual recognition to enhanced procedures for co-operation and information exchange, in the quest of effectiveness and stability.

The Commission's 1997 Interpretative Communication, as well as legal scholarship, has criticised the notification procedure as constituting a restriction to the free movement of services and the freedom of establishment, and advocated its elimination. The Commission even declared that it 'could, in due course, envisage proposing the abolition of the procedure altogether', at least in the context of the freedom to provide services (Commission 1997; Lomnicka 2000). Despite this, the CRD has maintained unaltered the provisions instituting the notification procedure (articles 25(1) and 28(1) CRD). This could be interpreted as confirming the understanding of the nature of the notification procedure, not as a procedural condition affecting the validity of operations carried out by means of the Treaty freedoms, but as a tool for the indispensable exchange of information between supervisory authorities. Its preservation may also be linked to the possibility given to the host Member State, within the notification procedure, to inform the credit institution intending to set up a branch in its territory of the conditions to be fulfilled in the interest of the general good. Such a possibility does not constitute an obligation for the host country, nor does failure to notify general good conditions result in the non-applicability of the relevant rules. Moreover, the communication of the general good conditions by the host State is only foreseen in the framework of the notification procedure concerning the establishment of branches, and not in the case of the freedom to provide cross-border services. Yet the general good exception can be invoked by the host State irrespective of the mode used by a bank for undertaking cross-border

25 Until 31 December 1999, the Deposit Guarantee Schemes Directive entailed a temporary arrangement, limiting the principle of home-country control through the so-called 'export prohibition'. The export prohibition restricted compensation due to a consumer of a bank operating in a host State to the maximum foreseen by the host State's compensation scheme, impeding firms operating cross-border to take advantage of more generous schemes in their home country.

26 Case 233/94, *Germany* v. *European Parliament and Council* [1997] ECR I-2405 para. 64.

activities, and owing to its extreme and overwhelming character it cannot be made conditional upon prior notification. The very possibility of invoking the general good, formalised in legislation, should trigger awareness of the host Member State's capacity to intervene, which hangs over the home-country control principle.

The European passport is and will remain the central pillar of the European banking market, and implicitly mutual recognition and home-country supervision will remain guiding principles in European banking law. There are, nonetheless, elements that indicate that the division of responsibilities between national supervisory authorities cannot merely rely on the home-country control principle and the complementary cooperative arrangements as they now stand. The possibility that host countries seek to exert additional powers over foreign banks beyond those explicitly given to them was, from the very beginning, in the contemplation of the European legislator, and the references to the general good have been maintained in the CRD. Theoretically, the residual powers left to the host countries and the restricted but still possible recourse to the general good exception are both capable of justifying derogations from the home-country control principle. Furthermore, existing fragmentation of national financial markets and the associated information asymmetries, as well as the current decentralisation of crisis management and crisis resolution, demonstrate that exclusive reliance on home-country control is not viable. This is even more the case if we consider the predominant position held by banks operating under the European passport in the new Member States. The complexity of prudential issues in increasingly integrated financial markets cannot be addressed by means of simple delimitation of competences, but instead requires increased focus on continuous interaction between the competent authorities in the Member States concerned.

Home-country control remains a guiding principle and is likely to be strengthened through growing harmonisation. The CRD, the Lamfalussy regulatory framework and the future participation of more Member States in the monetary union are all factors that will contribute to increased market integration and an extended platform of common rules and practices. More European rules and ongoing convergence of supervisory practices will strengthen reciprocal confidence and implicitly reduce the scope for host States' intervention. Yet, as observed, there are some material limits to home-country control derived from the limited capacity of home countries to address all cross-border prudential aspects. Hence, the importance of the home-country control principle should by no means be overstated.

The home-country control principle has two facets: in the first place, it serves as a means for achieving the Treaty freedoms in the banking sector (by mandating mutual recognition of authorisations) and, complementarily, it constitutes a procedural rule that devises supervisory jurisdiction (the home State supervision). While the former aspect is solid and almost unalterable, the latter facet is questioned, more and more, by the peculiar dynamics of financial markets. The former contributes to the achievement of a liberalised framework of financial regulation that emphasises free market access, whereas the latter would be a means for achieving financial stability within truly integrated financial markets. Market integration requires more than mere liberalisation; it needs adequate supervision. Proper supervision of financial markets is more complex and demanding than simple mutual recognition of home-country regulation. We have acknowledged the transformation of the supervisory activity into a complex regulatory process that relies on continuous rule-making, information-gathering, quantitative and, especially, qualitative assessments. Moreover, we have underlined the two equally important and inextricably linked dimensions of supervision: micro-prudential aspects focusing on individual institutions and macro-prudential aspects emphasising overall financial stability in the market. Such transformation requires that the home-country control, as a criterion for attributing supervisory competences, is not rigidly perceived and applied. The 1985 White Paper strategy tended to ascribe to the home-country control principle an absolute role, with the objective of forcing the integration of deeply traditionalist supervisory cultures. The new regulatory approach cannot but ascribe to it a more contextual role, capable of reconciling the allocation of supervisory competences with the necessity of an effective and realistic assessment of the soundness of institutions and of the system as a whole.

The dismantling of remaining barriers to market integration will be mainly an issue of substantially improving the quality and intensity of co-operation between home- and host-competent authorities. The home-country control principle continues to be a useful but rather descriptive tool, indicating that supervisory jurisdiction remains primarily with the home Member State, especially as regards authorisation.

It is also important to underline that European legislation has consistently highlighted the importance of supervisory cooperation as a complement to home-country control. Especially, the underlying idea behind complex procedural rules on consolidated supervision is that of coordination among supervisory authorities, along with due observance of the primacy of the home supervisors. Also, Directive 2002/87/EC on conglomerates emphasises closer cooperation and information-sharing among supervisory authorities and the importance of the 'coordinator supervisor' in contributing to achieving prudential supervision beyond the sectors. This evolution of the regulatory framework confirms that while the country of origin facet maintained its pivotal position in the regulatory philosophy, the procedural allocation of supervisory jurisdiction to the home country was necessarily accompanied by cooperative strategies, hence the perceived erosion of the home-country control principle.

The real challenge is that of creating a framework for regulatory coordination capable of addressing prudential concerns in a consistent and efficient manner throughout the single market. The Lamfalussy framework constitutes merely an initial step that established a platform for facilitating cooperation and coordination between the competent national supervisory authorities. As highlighted in the 2005 White Paper on Financial Services Policy, there is a need for clarifying and optimising the distribution of roles and responsibilities between home and host supervisors. Interestingly, the White Paper did not refer to the 'home country control' principle; instead, it qualified 'the home–host principle, underpinned by mutual recognition and consolidated supervision', as being at the core of the EU supervisory system (Directive 2002/87/EC). This provision can be interpreted as emphasising the principle of cooperation and coordination to the detriment of the principle of home-country control.

Under the first review of the CRD, the European decision-makers have inserted two amendments that further mitigate the effects of the home-country control principle. Thus, CRD 2 adds a new paragraph to article 40, which attributes, to all Member States' competent authorities, a European mandate. Such mandate requires them to duly consider the potential impact of their decisions on the stability of the financial system in all other Member States concerned. The provision[27] is spelled out in vague terms and is not enforceable; it merely declares the importance of overall EU financial stability and the responsibility of national supervisors in achieving it. However, it implicitly acknowledges diverging interests between home and host supervisors and the need for taking a holistic approach in supervision. Furthermore, CRD 2 introduces the mandatory establishment of colleges of supervisors for cross-border banking groups,[28] in view of a more effective coordination of supervisory activities. The establishment of colleges does not change the responsibilities between home and host States, but reinforces their interaction by providing a framework for stronger cooperation that should help them reach agreement on key supervisory tasks. The legislative consecration of supervisory colleges is indicative of the limited capacity of the home country's authorities to provide effective supervision and the need to add host State expertise. These changes reflect the pivotal role of regulatory coordination and cooperation, as well as the shift in the European normative framework from regulating mere distribution of competences to focusing on the supranational mechanisms fostering the interaction of national regulators. Forthcoming reforms of the supervisory architecture will inevitably impinge on the role of the home-country control principle. Various instruments to be discussed in subsequent chapters, such

27 According to art. 40 para. 3 CRD 2:

> the competent authorities in one Member State shall, in the exercise of their general duties, duly consider the potential impact of their decisions on the stability of the financial system in all other Member States concerned and, in particular, in emergency situations, based on the information available at the relevant time.

28 See art. 131a introduced by CRD2.

as delegation of supervisory authority, leadership in supervision, and the establishment of a European authority, will define the future contours of home-country control.

Since the SBD, prudential regulation has been characterised in light of the regulatory principles underpinning the internal market strategy: minimum harmonisation and home-country control. Yet the capacity of these regulatory principles to define the prudential regime in Europe was limited from the very beginning and became even more so as a result of substantial and ongoing reforms.

We consider that even the first prudential directives did not reflect a minimalist approach, and that what in the 1985 White Paper was considered 'essential harmonisation', necessary for the achievement of the internal market, in the banking sector included from the very beginning a comprehensive set of prudential rules. Recent reforms (Basel II/CRD and the Lamfalussy framework) facilitate the expansion of European normative intervention so as to cover both framework prudential legislation and implementing measures consisting of extensive and detailed prudential issues. Therefore, we may characterise the new framework as a complex regulatory regime comprehensively addressing 'safety and soundness' aspects arising in the common banking market and not merely intended to eliminate regulatory barriers. Such a development institutes a presumption of maximum harmonisation with regard to prudential regulation and indicates increased centralisation of prudential competences with the EU.

Home-country control continues to have its merits as a choice of jurisdiction rule and could eventually be further reinforced by extensive harmonisation. Still, home-country control has been, since its introduction, only an imperfect regulatory strategy as the host State could limit its scope, either by way of exercising its residual competences or by making use of the general good safeguard. Although such possibilities of intervention will diminish in an enlarged monetary union and in the context of centralised detailed and almost all-encompassing prudential regulation, we maintain that a too rigid allocation of competences to the home country is not necessarily appropriate in view of attaining the objective of overall financial stability in the EU. We argue that, for the sake of financial stability, emphasis should be placed on more streamlined and reassuring cooperative and coordination arrangements between the various supervisory jurisdictions, rather than on exclusive attribution of supervisory competences.

Part III

Institutional aspects of prudential regulation and supervision

7 The institutional framework – general aspects

1 Setting the context

We have acknowledged the changing nature of prudential rules and supervisory processes and the impressive activism in international and European rule-making reflecting the dynamics of financial actors and markets, coupled with new risk patterns. In parallel to these developments, European policy-makers have also set up new institutional arrangements (the Lamfalussy framework) intended for delivering rules in a more flexible way so as to respond to market developments, while at the same time addressing calls for transparency and legal certainty. The establishment of the Lamfalussy framework had an experimental character; the monitoring and review clauses laid down in the establishing document itself are indicative of the process of 'learning by doing with goodwill and trust' (IIMG 2004). Since its establishment, various shortcomings of the Lamfalussy approach have been highlighted, and even strongly deplored in light of the first lessons drawn from the crisis. This encourages institutional reform in financial regulation and supervision to continue at EU level.

Several main drivers triggered the reform of the institutional framework in the late 1990s. First, the traditional Community method failed to address rapid developments in the market effectively and a more flexible and reactive mechanism, backed by sufficient expertise, was needed. Second, minimum harmonisation and home-country control had reached their limits without sufficiently addressing financial stability concerns in the common market. Hence, more Community intervention was needed to ensure consistent application of the ever more comprehensive common regulatory framework, and stronger European coordination among the wide array of national financial regulators and supervisors became imperative. Lastly, the European framework's role as a transmission belt between the international and the national levels – the EU is not only a guarantor of harmonious implementation of the Basel framework in all Member States with due observation of the Treaty freedoms, but is also responsible for the fair representation of all Member States in the restrictive circle of the Basel Committee. All these aspects should also be considered against the broader context of governance concerns in the EU, as mirrored in the debates surrounding the European Constitution and the Lisbon Treaty. Additional institutional reforms prompted by the crisis are justified, on the regulation side, mainly by the failure of the current structures to deliver an authoritative European rulebook capable of ensuring the level playing-field in the application of EU prudential norms and to address particularly controversial implementing aspects. With regard to supervision, institutional changes are required because of the inadequacy of existing arrangements, which lack both a macro-prudential mechanism for identifying and warning against emerging systemic risks and an effective mechanism for common supervisory action in the case of cross-border institutions.

The development of EU law has been constantly accompanied by questions as to the balanced accommodation of commonality and diversity. Inherent to this are also ambiguities with regard to the institutional distribution of competences, and frequently there is recourse to dispersed bodies for avoiding excessive centralisation of power, whereby a range of formal and informal discussion and decision-making platforms are established that bring together all institutional stakeholders. This network[1] approach to regulation has emerged in response to shortcomings resulting from confronting the two main theoretical trends on the allocation of regulatory authority within the EU: Europeanisation versus nationalisation.[2] According to the network approach, the dilemma (i.e. the regulatory gap) resulting from the functional pressure of delegating regulatory tasks to the European level and the bulk of formal powers vested in national institutions may be partly addressed by new types of informal institutions: transnational regulatory networks that may 'offer a back road to the informal Europeanisation of public regulation' (Eberlein and Grande 2005: 91). The egress of such new political theoretical accounts reflects the ongoing quest for understanding the allocation of regulatory powers within the EU and the absence, as yet, of a dominant theory. Complementarily, they illustrate the shift from a narrow analysis focusing on formal institutions and static allocation of powers towards a dynamic, evolutionary perspective that emphasises formal and informal coordination

1 On the use of the network concept with regard to EU policy-making, see Börzel 1997: 16.

2 For an account of the two theories and of the network approach, see Eberlein and Grande 2005. In short, the Europeanisation thesis, sustained especially by Majone (1996), argues that a transition from the 'positive state' to the 'regulatory state' has occurred in Europe. This resulted in the transfer of regulatory powers to the supranational levels; as a consequence, regulatory tasks are primarily to be handled by European institutions. On the contrary, the nationalisation thesis locates the regulatory tasks primarily with the nation-state, arguing that measures of market regulation (positive integration) require explicit political legitimacy, which is lacking at the European level in that it can confine its intervention only to measures aimed at market opening (negative integration) – this approach is defended by Scharpf 1999.

and exchange of information between the various actors performing within the European multi-level system of policy-making. The ambiguities, related to the underlying paradigm for institutional change and the continuous oscillation between the regulatory and parliamentary model, prompt a hybrid analysis of institutions from both perspectives: functional analysis – as a premise of the regulatory model – and democratic legitimacy – as the assumption underpinning the parliamentary paradigm.

Until the crisis, there was no convincing argument either for or against radical reform of the financial architecture. Instead, there was a rather general acceptance of the fact that the changes brought about by the Lamfalussy framework constitute a transitory phase. More centralisation with regard to banking supervision, eventually resulting in the establishment of a European banking or financial regulator/supervisor, was an implicit long-term objective, ideally to be pursued in a fully integrated market.

Undeniably, we have witnessed growing involvement of the EU in banking regulation. This has been mainly justified by functional concerns related to the need for reconciling market integration with a number of complex externalities. Initially, the EU intervention was confined to the creation of the legal framework required for creating the internal market, conceived in terms of removal of regulatory hurdles and minimum common rules able to ensure sufficient trust as necessary for ensuring the Treaty freedoms. The regulatory instruments used were directives adopted pursuant to the ordinary EU legislative procedure. Nevertheless, such initial harmonisation, although particularly useful in laying the foundations of the European banking market, did not manage to contribute decisively to integration, nor was it able to provide efficient solutions for new challenges arising from the internal market. The process of adopting or updating common rules constantly underwent the risk of being overruled by market developments and attracted strong criticism on the grounds that slowness and rigidity of European law-making were compromising the efficiency of European rules. Furthermore, the sophistication and new process-oriented nature of prudential supervision, corroborated with the rise of cross-border banking, called for more common guidance and guarantees for a level playing-field in the cross-border application of EU prudential standards. In parallel, systemic stability was increasingly acknowledged as essential for financial markets and, hence, justified European intervention not only at the regulatory but also at the supervisory level.

All these concerns have been considered in the Wise Men report that led to the practical establishment of the four-level Lamfalussy framework. This new regulatory framework makes initial steps in the direction of a comprehensive regulatory regime – considerably enhancing a common approach to the application of prudential rules and sowing the seeds for better European supervisory coordination. Such an evolution implicitly sets the ground for further potential centralisation at European level of both regulatory and supervisory responsibilities.

This discourse, already accompanying the regulatory reforms related to the Basel II transposition in the EU and the implementation of the Lamfalussy framework in all financial sectors, has been strongly revived pursuant to the crisis. Regulatory and supervisory failures are increasingly ascertained among the main contributing factors to the crisis.[3] On the regulatory side, blame has been attributed not only to substantial gaps in prudential rules, but also to too much leeway in implementation and insufficiently authoritative guidance as regards their application. On the supervisory side, deficient coordination and decision-making mechanisms with regard to cross-border situations have been deplored. Also, the mismatch resulting from exclusively decentralised supervisory arrangements in increasingly interlinked financial markets has favoured one-sided supervision of individual institutions and unacceptably ignored macro-developments and growing systemic risks. The costs of these failures were particularly high. This led to an unprecedented political willingness to reform the European supervisory arrangements in the quest for more effectiveness of prudential rules and better prevention, and also in establishing a robust framework capable of detecting risks and efficiently acting upon them, as well as reliable arrangements for cross-border crisis management and resolution. Concrete measures addressing these concerns are currently discussed by EU policy-makers, on the basis of the so-called de Larosière report issued in February 2009 and the follow-up Commission Communication of 27 May 2009 (Commission 2009h) and legislative proposals from September 2009.

These concerns relating to the vertical division of competences between European and national levels are paralleled by discussions on the horizontal distribution of powers. The horizontal aspects entail questions as to the organisation and distribution of tasks at the European and at the national level, respectively. At European level a plethora of bodies is involved in regulation and supervision; at national level, ever more communalities are prompted by EU developments.

Lastly, institutional reforms in the area of banking regulation and supervision have to be considered against the more contextual background of governance-related concerns and constitutional reforms in the European Union.[4] The quest for enhancing accountability and legitimacy in the EU implicitly impinges upon the design of the institutional arrangements for financial market regulation. The reform of the latter has to respond not only to specific financial market challenges (as identified in the FSAP, Lamfalussy), but also to more general institutional trends in the EU.

Before analysing the current European institutional framework and its further reforms, we will highlight some aspects that we consider relevant

3 In this sense see de Larosière report (Commission 2009c), the Turner Review (2009), etc.

4 These aspects are addressed in the White Paper on European Governance, the works of the European Convention entrusted with drafting of the Constitutional Treaty, the Lisbon Treaty.

for the evolution of the EU financial architecture. At this point, it is also appropriate to warn that in the coming chapters we will only examine the European influence on the national institutional supervisory frameworks, without entering into the comparative analysis of the latter. Also, we aim to concentrate on the legal issues, albeit prudential concerns constitute an enmeshment of economics, politics and law.

2 Preliminary remarks concerning the European regulatory framework

It is commonly accepted that institutional arrangements influence the behaviour and expectations of economic agents (Lucas 1976). They are implicitly impinging on the effectiveness of the rules they produce and determine their acceptability, as they are intimately linked to legitimacy and accountability concerns (Alexander 2002a). In this context it is legitimate to question whether traditional EU decision-making is adequate for devising rules that respond to the organic regulatory needs elicited by developing financial market trends. Such scepticism resulted in calls for the establishment of specialised regulatory bodies with the necessary expertise, which, however, do not fit neatly into the existing system of institutional checks and balances in the EU.

The initial regulatory approach focused on the elimination of free movement barriers and implied the elaboration of clear principles and firm, albeit minimum prudential standards, as well as the overriding prohibition of applying or introducing national regulatory obstacles to credit institutions authorised in other Member States. As long as the predominant paradigm was the one drawn by the functionalist logic of market integration, the usual decision-making process within the EU was perceived as adequate. Europe intervened only at the legislative level, leaving it for the national systems to implement and concretise European rules. The issue was to determine the legitimate scope of European intervention by reference to Member States' powers. In time, changes in financial markets and in European governance have challenged the status quo and triggered, apart from increased harmonisation, the emergence of a distinct European regulatory system. In the area of prudential regulation, the European dimension was slowly creeping from the legislative level into the executive domain by means of a learning-by-doing strategy.

The Lamfalussy framework was created pursuant to calls for rendering the legislative process for financial markets more responsive and flexible. It did so by institutionalising the substantive differentiation between legislative rule-making and executive rule-making. The former is subject to the ordinary EU law-making procedure, while the latter has been assigned to an enhanced comitology procedure (Level 2 measures) and to an informal interpretation and guidance mechanism (Level 3 measures). The Lamfalussy regulatory structure reinforced concerns related to the scope of EU legislative authority in the field of prudential regulation and fears linked to eventual infringements of EU constitutional principles, in the light of possible institutional 'imbalances' triggered by the new framework. In order to mitigate such risks inherent to the learning-by-doing approach, the new framework has been supplemented by a series of safeguards, some declaratory (e.g. the commitments undertaken by the Commission vis-à-vis the other institutions) and some procedural (e.g. the 'sunset' clause, the 'call-back' clause). These all reflect real preoccupations with the viability of the regulatory framework and its compatibility with the overall EU infrastructure. Further upgrades of this regulatory framework in the context of crisis-triggered debates on the reform of the European financial architecture will have to thoroughly consider such institutional concerns.

Before engaging in the description of the regulatory framework for banking, we would like to emphasise the genuine nature of the EU framework as a multi-level system, characterised by the hybrid intermingling of federalist and intergovernmental elements. Blurred hierarchies in the fields that do not exclusively fall under the jurisdiction of the EU have brought about reliance on 'a plethora of policy networks and on cooperative problem solving' (Joerges 2005: 71). This also reflects the growing complexity of specific economic areas necessitating regulation. Complexity has been depicted in regulatory theory as 'disaggregation' of what regulation entails in functional terms: actors, their regulatory capacity, their regulatory functions, and interrelations between them (Black 2003). The variety of actors and the compound distribution of competences have as a consequence the dispersal of regulatory authority, not only vertically, between the European and national levels or between regulators and regulated entities, but also horizontally. Dispersed interests and powers inevitably result in interdependences and continuous negotiations of positions and relationships within the regulatory space. The only way of managing such a fragmented regulatory space is by promoting and reinforcing clear coordination rules between the actors concerned. The imperative of coordination goes beyond vertical and horizontal competence distribution and has been said to be a feature of the so-called 'diagonal constellations' (Joerges 2005: 78). Diagonal constellations capture a structural characteristic of the European multi-level system where neither the European level nor the national level is able to address a specific issue entirely.[5]

5 The author further argues that

> Europe is no federation, but more than a regime. It is a heterarchically structured multi-level system. It must organise its political action in networks. Since the powers and resources for political action are located at various and relatively autonomous levels in the EU, the coping with functionally interwoven problem-constellations will depend on the communication between the various actors who are relatively autonomous in their various domains, but at the same time mutually dependent.
>
> (Joerges 2005: 81)

2.1 The evolutionary approach towards institutional change

The 'story' of the report drawn up by the Committee of Wise Men and the subsequent saga of its endorsement by the European political players has been either presented as a tale of success or portrayed in sceptical terms, as a project devoid of viability.[6] The extension of the four-level structured regulatory process to all financial sectors (including banking) proved that the Lamfalussy framework passed its first feasibility test. This section will discuss the background for the extension of the four-level regulatory approach.

In the late 1990s, in parallel with the substantive measures envisaged by the FSAP, the Council acknowledged the need to reform the regulatory infrastructure of financial services and to streamline the legislative process. In this context it had mandated the Committee of Wise Men under the leadership of Baron Alexandre Lamfalussy to draw up proposals; the tasks of the Committee were restricted to the securities regulatory framework. The terms of reference given by the European Union's Economic and Finance Ministers to the Wise Men on 17 July 2000 explicitly excluded prudential supervision from the mandate (Council 2000: 3).

In the meantime, the issue of prudential supervision was tackled within the parallel work on crisis prevention and management in integrated financial markets, as reflected in the 2001 report on financial crisis management, drafted by an ad hoc group of the Economic and Financial Committee chaired by Henk Brouwer. This so-called Brouwer II report (EFC 2001), although concerned mainly with issues related to crisis situations, also emphasised the importance of the preventive aspects. Its recommendations highlighted the need to improve the institutional arrangements with regard to both crisis prevention and crisis management at the EU level. Although a first Brouwer report, issued in 2000, had argued in favour of the institutional status quo and called only for some practical adjustments (EFC 2000), under the pressure of the FSAP deadlines, as well as in view of initial experience with the Lamfalussy framework, the second Brouwer report took a different stance. It suggested that institutional arrangements had to be seen from the perspective of market evolution and integration, and thus a constant monitoring was necessary in order to assess their adequacy. Institutional reform in banking, although not explicitly called for, was implicitly envisaged as a long-term objective.

It was at the informal Ecofin meeting in Oviedo, on 13 April 2002, that the Council decided to continue institutional reforms to ensure that the EU has appropriate structures in place in all financial sectors. Subsequently, on 7 May 2002 the Ecofin Council adopted the formal mandate for the Economic and Financial Committee (EFC), which was further completed at the Ecofin meeting of 12 July 2002. The EFC was entrusted

6 See, for instance, Lannoo and Levin 2004; Sousi 2004; Ferran 2004.

with the task of elaborating, with the Commission's support, the new regulatory approach for all financial sectors based on the four-level Lamfalussy framework for securities. The Council endorsed the final EFC report (EFC 2002), at its meeting on 3 December 2002, and invited the Commission to extend the committee structure applied in the securities sector to banking, insurance, and UCITS.

In response to the Council's call and with the support of the European Parliament,[7] the Commission issued, on 6 November 2003, a package of seven measures to improve regulation and supervision of banking, insurance and investment funds.[8] The decisions creating the Level 3 committees (the committees of supervisors) came into force immediately: the Committee of European Banking Supervisors (CEBS) was in place as of 1 January 2004, while the Committee of European Insurance and Occupational Pensions Supervisors (CEIOPS) had already been established, on 24 November 2003. The other four decisions establishing the new regulatory Level 2 committees and respectively adapting the already existing securities committees so as to include UCITS were suspended until the adoption of legislative amendments necessary for avoiding duplication. The relevant directive was adopted on 9 March 2005, after its first reading in the Parliament (Directive 2005/1/EC).

The justification of the extension of the Lamfalussy framework has been widely accepted in terms of the need for more homogenous regulatory structures across financial sectors within an increasingly integrated market, as well as of the requirement of more reactive and flexible institutional set-ups capable of improving the slow, rigid and ambiguous rule-making. Nevertheless, the urgency of such an extension was intensively questioned, especially by the European Parliament, and in particular against the background of the political debates surrounding the general comitology issue. Arguments related to insufficient experience with the four-level approach in the securities field and recurrent concerns associated to institutional imbalances managed to postpone political agreement on the establishment of the new regulatory committees. It took eleven months for the

7 In its Resolution from 21 November 2002 – the Van Burg Resolution – the European Parliament endorsed its own initiative report on prudential supervision in the European Union and welcomed the institutionalisation of a regular dialogue between supervisors at European level, through the creation of CESR, and expressed hopes that its extension to the other financial sectors would indeed lead to more coherent implementation and enforcement of prudential legislation within the EU.

8 The package issued by the Commission contained: a proposal for a directive replacing any references to existing committees in current financial legislation; two Commission decisions setting up the Level 2 committees, the European Banking Committee and the European Insurance and Occupational Pensions Committee; two Commission decisions amending the securities Level 2 and Level 3 committees so as to include UCITS; two Commission decisions establishing the Level 3 committees, the Committee of European Banking Supervisors and Committee of European Insurance and the Occupational Pensions Supervisors.

Commission to come forward with the package called for by the Council at the beginning of December 2002. The delay was explained in terms of the complexity of the matter and particular challenges stemming from 'painstaking efforts ... to graft the new committees onto the existing structures without creating any legal or organisational uncertainty' (Commission 2003f). Sixteen more months had to pass before the final political agreement on the new regulatory structure was transformed into a binding legal document, through the adoption of Directive 2005/1/EC on 9 March 2005. Such a decision was accelerated by the imminent deadline for the adoption of the FSAP legislative measures (particularly the review of the capital requirements framework), but also by the emerging post-FSAP strategy with its emphasis on implementation and enforcement. The new committees had to be in place in order to ensure efficient and timely adoption of the Level 2 measures and to be able to consistently coordinate implementation at Level 3. The preliminary experiences with the Committee of European Banking Supervisors (CEBS), which had initiated consultations and the preparation of advice since 2004, were also an incentive for politicians to advance with the regulatory reform.

Although the extension of the Lamfalussy procedure to banking did not constitute a radical change from a structural perspective since European banking regulation had traditionally relied on the advice of more or less formally established committees, it is remarkable that within an interval of two years the idea of institutional change had become widely accepted. The institutionalisation of recourse to committees under a new mode and the expressed willingness to proceed to further reforms, if the established formalised monitoring process were to reveal such a necessity, demonstrate that policy-makers had recognised the institutional device as being essential for adopting effective prudential measures. The political willingness to declare the existing system as ill-suited for a truly integrated single EU financial market was particularly significant in a field where EU law already provided the legal basis for further institutional reform.[9]

The extension of the Lamfalussy institutional design to banking acknowledged that the achieved stage of integration in the financial markets required new regulatory and cooperative arrangements in relation to banking activities, with more focus on consistent and rigorous implementation of EU banking law. As in the case of securities, the new committee structure in banking had to be closely scrutinised by the Inter-Institutional Monitoring Group, from the perspective of its efficient implementation and of the detection of possible bottlenecks.[10] It was also subject

9 We refer to the possibility of transferring prudential tasks to the ECB, which will be analysed subsequently.

10 The Inter-Institutional Monitoring Group, re-established in July 2005 to cover the extended Lamfalussy process, issued two interim reports in March 2006 and January 2007 and its final report and recommendations on 15 October 2007.

to full and open review. The 'learning by doing' approach reflects a genuine willingness to identify the institutional set-up best suited to the degree of market integration. The likelihood of institutional changes with regard to supervision was already underlined in the preamble to Directive 2005/1/EC, which explicitly provides that the extension of the Lamfalussy procedure should not impinge upon possible future decisions regarding the organisation of supervision at European level (Recital 13 Directive 2005/1/EC).

Long-lasting institutional immobilism and complacency with the status quo were beginning to be questioned and prepared the ground for further reforms, which are now being accelerated as a consequence of serious shortcomings revealed by the crisis. Two measures have been already adopted in order to immediately reinforce the position and work of the Level 3 committees in EU decision-making. Thus, following the publication in November 2007 of a Commission Communication on the review of the Lamfalussy process in view of strengthening supervisory convergence (Commission 2007), in May 2008 the Commission put forward concrete proposals for changing the decisions governing the Level 3 committees and for proposing adequate financing mechanisms. In January 2009, the Commission adopted the three revised decisions[11] establishing the Level 3 committees and proposed a financing framework programme that was adopted by the Parliament in May 2009.

The revised decisions do not radically change the framework for the Level 3 committees, but mainly formalise already established practices used by them. The 2009 decisions set out to homogenise the Committees' mandates by clarifying their functions and competences, and to enhance their operational framework until further reforms. The Committees' role as 'independent advisory groups' of the Commission has been streamlined.[12] The decisions make it clear that the Committees do not have any regulatory powers at EU level and the measures adopted by them remain non-binding. The working processes of the Committees were improved by the introduction of qualified majority voting when consensus cannot be reached. A 'comply or explain' procedure was introduced, requiring

11 Commission Decision 2009/77/EC for CESR; Commission Decision 2009/78/EC for CEBS; Commission Decision 2009/79/EC for CEIOPS.

12 A non-exhaustive list of tasks has been enshrined in the Decisions to strengthen the Committees' contribution for enhancing supervisory cooperation and fostering convergence of supervisory practices and approaches. The decisions insist particularly on the Level 3 Committees' role concerning: mediation between supervisory authorities; delivery of opinions to supervisory authorities; promotion of effective bilateral and multilateral exchanges of information between supervisors; facilitation of the delegation of tasks between supervisors; contribution to the efficient and consistent functioning of colleges; contribution to developing high quality and common supervisory reporting standards; review of the practical application of the non-binding guidelines, recommendations and standards.

national supervisors that do not follow the measures adopted by the Committees to present reasons for this choice. As regards the financing proposals, a three-year Community framework programme is envisaged for providing direct funding from the Community budget to the three EU Committees of Supervisors and to key international and European bodies involved in the standard-setting process for financial reporting and auditing.

All these recent measures have a transitional character and recognise the overall inadequacy of the current institutional arrangements. The financing programme explicitly foresees that the three Level 3 committees will be replaced by other beneficiaries selected by the Commission. This reflects the parallel discussions on a new supervisory architecture in the EU, based on proposals made in the de Larosière report that we will discuss in later chapters. The kick-off regarding the institutional reform was slow; only exceptional circumstances managed to enliven debates on how to address long-ascertained shortcomings. Reluctance is still high and no perfect solution exists, yet the crisis momentum managed to mobilise political willingness in an unprecedented way. Hence, further concrete substantial changes to the institutional framework are highly likely to be operated in the near future.

2.2 Institutional balance – the constant concern

Arrangements in the field of financial regulation have to be reconciled with the broader EU institutional framework and constitutional principles. It has been argued that the Lamfalussy framework not only reflects a regulatory development in the financial sector, but also

> represents a continuing trend in EC economic regulation whereby inter-governmental negotiations and bargaining produce an institutional and policy-making process that respects EU constitutional principles, yet proves adaptable and flexible enough to address the specific economic challenges posed by increasing liberalisation and deregulation in financial markets.
>
> (Alexander 2002a: 7)

As it affects decision-making in a particularly influential policy area, it is no wonder that the political acceptability of the Lamfalussy project was intimately linked to the structuring of the interaction between the main policy actors at EU level and the due observance of the distribution of power within the EU. Consequently, at the core of political debates were preoccupations related to the control modalities over the Commission and the position of the European Parliament with respect to the Council, from the perspective of the Parliament's striving for an equal position as legislature. So far, the issue of balancing the powers between the

Commission, the Council and the Parliament has been seen especially from the standpoint of increased European legislative intrusion in banking regulation and supervision. These concerns about the institutional balance will inevitably also be mirrored in all debates on further institutional reform, to which we will refer later. They are also very likely to creep into discussions about the institutional reform with regard to supervision.

The institutional reform in the late 1990s was called for by structural changes in the regulated domain. Obviously, European rule-making has to reflect the complexity of the regulated field and take account of the multi-level framework for its implementation. As we have observed, the transformation of the prudential approach into a dynamic risk-sensitive prudential process has brought about the need for more EU regulatory intervention in order to ensure a common platform.

As in every national legal system, European legislation with a high degree of generality needs to be backed by interpretative ancillary norms in order to acquire sufficient legal clarity and certainty in view of its implementation. Given the high technicality and detail involved by such executive rule-making, this task often requires delegation of authority to bodies with more expertise in the field than the legislator. Within the EU legal framework, it was article 202 EC Treaty, which provided the possibility of such delegation of powers under the comitology procedure, with due observance of the institutional balance between the various EU actors. The reform of financial regulatory arrangements in the EU is inextricably linked to the wider debates on the comitology procedure. Such debates focus particularly on the possibility of controlling the Commission when exercising delegated powers and on the role to be played by the European Parliament. An evolutionary approach to these issues is reflected in the new 1999 Comitology Decision (Council Decision 1999/468/EC), its 2006 amendment (through Council Decision 2006/512/EC) and the relevant provisions in the Lisbon Treaty (article 14 TEU – consolidated version and articles 290–1 TFEU).

Every institutional reform within the EU is carefully scrutinised from the perspective of the principle of institutional balance, in its two modes: legal and political.[13] Inevitably, this was also the fate of the Lamfalussy framework, when it was initially adopted and subsequently extended. The primary fears were expressed in relation to the absence of precise criteria as to the differentiation between legislative framework measures and

13 From a legal perspective, the institutional balance refers to the formal constitutional allocation of competences between the various European institutions, whereas the political approach to institutional balance emphasises the real, substantive mode in which power is exercised by institutions, by looking at the conventions and practices existing among the various actors. For an analysis of the principle of institutional balance, see Jacqué 2004 and de Búrca 1999.

implementing measures, each of which involved different actors in the decision-making process. This implied conflicts between the EU legislators and the *sui generis* EU executive and the plethora of bodies supporting their decisions. Dispersed decision-making authority and the related ambiguity of institutional arrangements mirror the difficulties of substantially differentiating between legislative and executive powers. We have already referred to the problems related to the substantive aspects of this division in our normative analysis.

For now, we will try to identify the specific institutional framework applicable to each level of the Lamfalussy approach and how the new structure might impinge upon the relationships between the various institutions. We should keep in mind two aspects. First, implementation of EU banking legislation involves increasingly detailed rule-making, in addition to the actual application and enforcement. Such supplementary regulatory action is distributed across various layers in the framework of a multi-level governance system. The institutional balance analysis grasps only the interactions at the European level; nevertheless, if one considers the composition and the working procedures of European bodies, the real distribution of powers is inevitably influenced by interactions at the other levels (national authorities, regulatees). Second, changes in specific legislative procedures may reflect political bargaining engaged in the broader context of European governance (e.g. the case of comitology in the EU), without being necessarily related to the substance of the policy concerned. This aspect should be borne in mind, especially when exploring the attitude of the European Parliament and its reluctance to support the establishment of regulatory committees without guarantees for due observance of its long-contended co-legislature status.

2.3 The four-level approach in brief

In this subsection we will briefly outline the essence of the four-level Lamfalussy regulatory structure and how it has been envisaged as working in the banking sector.[14]

The first level represents the normal legislative process, whereby the Council and the Parliament adopt EU framework legislation in accordance with the co-decision procedure and on the basis of proposals drawn

14 The background documents for understanding the extension of the Lamfalussy structure to banking are quite dispersed. The final report of the EFC on financial regulation, supervision and stability (Brussels, 9 October 2002) and the minutes of the Ecofin Council meeting from 3 December have to be read in conjunction with the Wise Men report applicable in the securities field (Final Report of the Committee of Wise Men on the Regulation of European Securities Markets, Brussels, 15.02.2001). The legislative underpinning is also spread throughout several Commission decisions and a directive.

up by the Commission. To prepare the draft legislation, the Commission may request advice from the Level 3 Committee of European Banking Supervisors (CEBS). At this stage, the Level 2 committee constituted of high-level representatives of the Member States (e.g. the European Banking Committee (EBC)) is involved in an advisory capacity to the Commission. The Economic and Finance Committee (EFC) has explicitly recommended in its report on the extension of the Lamfalussy framework that the EBC be consulted on policy issues, especially but without being limited to the kinds of measures that the Commission proposes at Level 1 (EFC 2002: 10). In such an advisory capacity the EBC may interact with the policy committees established by the Council: the Financial Services Committee (FSC)[15] and the EFC.

At this level, formal allocation of legislative powers between the major EU institutions has remained unchanged. However, the Lamfalussy approach brought some procedural amendments for enhancing the legislative process. Thus, it required making use of earlier and more systematic consultation mechanisms with all stakeholders so as to achieve adoption of Level 1 measures after the first reading in the Parliament (the so-called 'fast-track' procedure). Furthermore, the Lamfalussy approach recommended making more extensive recourse to regulations, as compared to directives – a requirement that is difficult to reconcile with the traditional use of directives in EU banking.

It is thanks to the innovations at Level 2 that the Lamfalussy process has often been praised as an enhanced comitology procedure. The second level is designed for the adoption of the technical implementing measures, i.e. those norms that need to be adopted at European level in execution of the framework principles contained in a European legislative measure. The organisation of Level 2 is inspired by and relies on the provisions of article 202 of the EC Treaty and of the Council Comitology Decision. The adoption of Level 2 implementing measures has to be explicitly delegated under specified conditions laid down in Level 1 legislation. Accordingly, the CRD dedicates Title VI, entitled 'Powers of Execution', to circumscribing the scope of implementing measures to be adopted by the Commission (article 150) and indicating the regulatory committee procedure prescribed by the Council Comitology Decision to be followed (article 151).[16] In this context, we note that the EBC will rely on two different legal bases when performing entrusted activities: the

15 The Financial Services Committee is the successor of the Financial Services Policy Group (FSPG), reconfigured and entrusted with a policy-shaping role, so as to fill the gap between the political and technical regulatory levels.

16 Thus, according to article 151 CRD, the Commission shall be assisted by the EBC, in accordance with the comitology procedure laid down in article 5 of Decision 1999/468/EC applied in compliance with article 7(3) and article 8 thereof. The period referred to in the comitology decision should be three months.

establishing Commission Decision whenever it acts in its advisory capacity for the development of Level 1 legislation, and the Council's comitology decision, corroborated to the relevant provisions in the banking directive, whenever it assists the Commission in adopting implementing measures at Level 2.

At the second level, both of the new committees have the occasion to assist the Commission in determining how to implement the Level 1 measures. According to the extended Lamfalussy framework the Commission will, within the scope of implementing powers conferred by Level 1 measures, ask CEBS to give technical advice within a certain timeframe and pursuant to extensive consultation of market participants and users. Taking account of CEBS advice and without prejudice to its right of initiative, the Commission will draw up a proposal and present it to the EBC (meeting as a Level 2 committee). The EBC will vote upon the proposal according to its decision-making rules. The follow-up to the EBC's vote depends on whether the EBC does or does not endorse the measures envisaged by the Commission.

Until the 2006 amendments to the Comitology Decision, the EBC was subject to the regulatory procedure, which broadly concerns comitology measures of general scope designed to apply essential provisions of basic instruments, as well as measures designed to adapt or update certain non-essential provisions of a basic instrument (recital 7 and article 5 of the amended Comitology Decision). Under the regulatory procedure, where the EBC agreed with the proposal, the Commission could decide to enact it. In the scenario where the EBC voted against the Commission's proposal or did not offer an opinion, the draft measures could still be adopted according to a prescribed procedure that gives a dominant role to the Council. The Parliament had limited powers; it had to be constantly kept informed, so that it could review the conformity of Level 2 proposals with their legal basis and request the Commission to re-examine the draft proposal if the latter were considered *ultra vires* (i.e. exceeding implementing powers). It is especially in relation to these aspects that institutional balance concerns have emerged, and that a network of substantive and procedural guarantees was established by means of more or less formal instruments so as to support the equilibrium between the two legislative powers in controlling the Commission.

In response to continuous discontent from the Parliament, in 2006 a more complex comitology procedure was introduced, the so-called regulatory procedure with scrutiny (recital 7a and article 5a of the amended Comitology Decision). This procedure aims to balance the comitology-related powers of the two arms of the EU legislator when comitology proposals concern the implementation of legislative acts that have been adopted under co-decision. The new procedure governs the adoption of comitology measures

> of general scope which seek to amend non-essential elements of a basic instrument adopted in accordance with the procedure referred to in Article 251 of the Treaty, *inter alia* by deleting some of those elements or by supplementing the instrument by the addition of new non-essential elements.
>
> (Recital 7a of the amended Comitology Decision)

The CRD, adopted under the co-decision legislative provision, was amended in 2008 (through Directive 2008/24/EC) to ascertain that the Commission's powers of execution under Title VI would also be subject to the new regulatory procedure with scrutiny. Under this new comitology procedure, a complex mechanism is established which enables both the Council and the Parliament to scrutinise comitology measures before they are adopted. Scrutiny occurs irrespective of whether the EBC agrees with the Commission's proposal, albeit in different forms. The Parliament is given scrutiny powers equivalent to those of the Council, and may ultimately block the adoption of the respective comitology measure, thus forcing the Commission to propose either a new comitology measure or a new legislative act subject to co-decision.

Under the Lisbon Treaty, article 202 EC was repealed and it is envisaged that the existing system of comitology will be substituted with two procedures corresponding to the two categories of non-legislative acts allowed under the new TFEU. Article 290 TFEU consecrates 'delegated acts', adopted pursuant to the explicit delegation of powers, to adopt 'non-legislative acts of general application to supplement or amend certain non-essential elements' of the delegating legislative act. The objectives, content, scope and duration of the delegation of powers should be specified. Further conditions imposed on the delegation may lead the Parliament or the Council to revoke the delegation and/or cause the delegated act to enter into force only when the Parliament or the Council does not make any objection within a specified period. The second category of non-legislative measures is provided for in article 291 TFEU and concerns 'implementing acts'. Thus, 'where uniform conditions for implementing legally binding Union acts are needed', the Commission and, in certain situations, the Council shall be given implementing powers. The rules and general principles concerning the Member States' control mechanisms of the Commission's exercise of implementing powers will have to be laid down in advance in regulations adopted by the Parliament and the Council according to the ordinary legislative procedure. At first sight, it appears that delegated acts will cover the current comitology measures falling under the regulatory procedure with scrutiny, while the implementing measures refer to those comitology measures that are currently subject to the advisory, management and regulatory procedures laid down in the Comitology Decision. Yet much remains to be clarified as regards concrete ways of transposing the two new concepts into practice, and a substitute for the current framework Comitology Decision needs to be adopted (Best 2008: 7–12).

The first two Lamfalussy levels represent, at the same time, an improvement to existing decision-making practices of European institutions with regard to banking regulation and a specific application of the comitology framework to the banking area. However, the most important innovation brought about by the Lamfalussy framework is the third level, where only informal cooperative fora have existed previously. Under Level 3, a mechanism is institutionalised, the role of which is to improve the common interpretation and uniform implementation of EU law and promote its consistent enforcement. It is also at this level that advantages may be taken from the synergies between banking supervision and central banking.

The absolute protagonist is the Committee of European Banking Supervisors (CEBS) with its triple role that, in our opinion, retains a key position in harmonising rules on prudential banking regulation and supervision in the EU. In the pursuit of its prescribed objective of improving the consistency of the transposition and day-to-day implementation of Level 1 and Level 2 measures, CEBS enjoys a variety of 'soft' powers. Apart from the technical advice it can give on request or on its own initiative at Level 2, CEBS' powers extend, at Level 3, to competences related to convergence of regulatory and supervisory practices, cooperation, coordination, and information exchange. CEBS is an independent advisory group and, as such, has no direct subordination to any EU institution. Notwithstanding this, its activities evolve within an intricate network that relates it to all the major institutional players and demonstrates once again the complexity and hybrid nature of EU policy-making. We will come back to a detailed analysis of CEBS in the next chapters; here we only want to point to the fact that Level 3 has the potential to constitute the tool for further Europeanisation of banking supervision; its creation laid the foundation for institutional reform in the direction of establishing an independent regulatory agency.

The fourth level does not bring much that is new, as most of the recommendations made in the Wise Men report were not formalised in subsequent legislative measures. Level 4 underlines the need for strengthened enforcement of Community rules, with the major responsibility vested in the Commission and informal incentives encouraging all stakeholders (including market participants) to file complaints. The Commission, in its role as 'guardian of the Treaty', has to take the lead in ensuring compliance with EU obligations; nevertheless, it cannot bear sole responsibility. The Parliament also has information duties and is considered better placed for observing the transposition of EU law at national level, and thus more likely to know of eventual breaches of EU law in the Member States.

3 Supervisory arrangements – two underlying dilemmas

Prudential regulation has been extensively centralised at European level, a development also mirrored in the institutional arrangements that were adjusted over time in order to better respond to centralised regulatory needs. Conversely, it is commonly acknowledged that supervision has remained national and that little has been achieved to bridge the disparate institutional arrangements (Wymeersch 2005: 994). Two major issues can be seen as being at the root of stopping initiatives towards centralising supervisory arrangements: the equivocal relationship between integration and financial stability and the contentious aspect of burden-sharing.

It is generally admitted that the necessity of some European arrangements for supervision ultimately depends on the intensity of cross-border spill-over effects or externalities within the European Union (Schoenmaker and Oosterloo 2005: 2). Yet the relationship between financial integration and financial stability has not been conclusively established. Two characteristics of integrated markets with opposite effects on financial stability have long precluded straightforward conclusions. Integration is linked to both greater financing opportunities and risk diversification and, at the same time, easier transmission of shocks across interlinked institutions (Commission 2009a). The difficulties might also be linked to the dynamic character of the concept of 'financial stability' that primarily highlights the capacity of resilience of a financial system, 'a continuum, changeable over time and consistent with multiple combinations of finance's constituent elements' (Schinasi 2006: 77).

The second major impediment to the establishment of some centralised supervisory arrangements at European level is linked to the fact that there are no adequate burden-sharing arrangements at European level capable of equitably distributing responsibilities and costs between the Member States in case of a crisis. The current EU arrangements for dealing with crisis situations affecting cross-border banking groups leave the responsibility for resolution with the national authorities responsible for the individual entities that constitute part of a group. Existing principles for stimulating coordination between national authorities in case of cross-border crisis are lax and laid down in instruments with uncertain status (e.g. Memoranda of Understanding). Hence, in case of bank failures the fiscal costs implied by depositor compensation, nationalisation, emergency lending, State guarantees, government support to creditors of distressed banks, etc., are ultimately borne by individual Member States, which therefore also strive to retain their controlling powers over financial institutions. Consequently, the supervisory function is intimately linked to crisis management and resolution, lender-of-last-resort and deposit insurance responsibilities. As long as the latter are exclusively or predominantly national responsibilities, any attempt to reinforce supervisory arrangements at European level is doomed to encounter fierce opposition.

The dual nature of the relationship between integration and financial stability was acknowledged explicitly in the Wise Men report launching the Lamfalussy framework.[17] Yet it was not considered sufficient to prevent further institutional improvements in the EU. Therefore, going beyond their mandate, the Wise Men thought it necessary to send out a warning and call for supervisory action at EU level:

> However, given the growing interlinkages between all segments of the securities markets and the full range of financial intermediaries, the Committee believes that there is an urgent need to strengthen cooperation at the European level between financial market regulators and the institutions in charge of micro and macro prudential supervision.
>
> (Committee of Wise Men 2001: 20)

More recently, Baron Lamfalussy re-endorsed the above warning and maintained that in the light of the crisis he would have added another major call for action concerning the controversial issue of establishing crisis-management and crisis-resolution arrangements at European level:

> I would say that the general welfare effects of increased efficiency could be reduced, or even wiped out, if we were unable or unwilling to put in place solid defenses against the possibility that unavoidable (and up to a point useful) crisis manifestations turn into a full blown systemic crisis ... Since the management and even more the resolution of such a crisis amount to a monumental task, no effort should be spared to enhance our systemic crisis prevention capability.
>
> (Lamfalussy 2009)

In consideration of the recent crisis experiences, there is growing political willingness to address supervisory concerns under a European framework, thereby going beyond uncertainties as regards the link between integration and stability. EU solutions for preventing inefficient handling of cross-border institutions are imperative and should be found irrespective of whether they address straightforward or circumvent the delicate and politically sensitive issue of burden-sharing.

17

> While the Committee strongly believes that large, deep, liquid and innovative financial markets will result in substantial efficiency gains and will therefore bring individual benefits to European citizens, it also believes that greater efficiency does not necessarily go hand in hand with enhanced stability. Increasing integration ... entails more interconnection between financial intermediaries on across-border basis, increasing their exposure to common shocks.
>
> (Committee of Wise Men 2001: 20)

8 The European institutional framework for prudential banking regulation

In this chapter we will focus on the analysis of the various actors involved in the European regulatory process. We start by examining the interactions between the main European institutions in the process of adopting legislative measures. We will then deal with the plethora of committees, which have acquired an increasingly important position. Furthermore, we will focus on the participation of the ECB in devising prudential rules, and will briefly highlight the position of private parties in the regulatory process.

1 Interaction between Commission, Council and Parliament

The Lamfalussy framework entails specific legislative procedures that involve the Commission, the Council and the European Parliament to different degrees. The core of banking regulation consists of the framework directives that are adopted by Council and Parliament under the regular co-decision legislative procedure, following a proposal from the Commission. Level 2 implementing measures rely on the comitology procedure, which – as already indicated – has for a long time provoked tensions between the three institutions, particularly with regard to the balance of powers between the Parliament and the Council when controlling the Commission's exercise of comitology powers.

The problem resided in the fact that primary and secondary EU law on comitology (article 202 EC Treaty and the Council's Comitology Decision) did not reflect the institutional position of the Parliament as a co-legislator and inclined the balance of power in favour of the Council. As a consequence, the Parliament was reluctant to support an extensive use of the comitology procedure.[1] In anticipation of an agreement over this controversial issue, the implementation of the Lamfalussy framework had to improvise through a set of political and legal arrangements

1 On comitology, see Joerges and Vos 1999; Andenas and Türk 2000; Lenaerts and Verhoeven 2000.

intended for establishing a viable, although precarious, institutional equilibrium.[2]

The compromise that finally allowed the Lamfalussy framework to be activated in the banking sector was enshrined in the Commission's decisions creating the new committees and the accompanying directive. This gave the Parliament the opportunity to enhance its position and use the occasion for further recalibrating the relationship between the two branches of the EU legislative authority. Indeed, in 2006 the Parliament managed to formally reinforce its position with regard to comitology, as reflected in the amendments brought to the 1999 Comitology Decision (through Council Decision 2006/512/EC). By introducing an additional regulatory procedure with scrutiny, the Council's Comitology Decision now guarantees that the Parliament is placed on an equal footing in supervising the exercise by the Commission of implementing powers entrusted through legislative acts adopted under co-decision. The CRD, which is the sectoral legislation conferring comitology powers on the Commission, was accordingly amended through Directive 2008/24/EC to ensure that such implementing measures based on the CRD are subject to the new regulatory procedure with scrutiny.

The reliance on the comitology framework for adopting EU banking regulation was not new, although it had been only very rarely employed.[3] The general legal basis for comitology was provided by article 202 third indent EC Treaty,[4] which foresees that except for specific cases when it may choose to reserve implementing tasks for itself, the Council will confer on the Commission the powers for the implementation of the rules that it has laid down. By doing this, the Council can impose conditions on the Commission's implementing action. The Treaty article does not give any further indications of the concrete exercise of the Commission's implementing powers but explicitly requires that this be consistent with a pre-established set of rules and principles laid down in advance by the Council, after having obtained the opinion of the Parliament. These rules materialised in the Comitology Decision of the Council,[5] which traces the legal framework

2 The Stockholm European Council Resolution of 23 March 2001 on more effective securities market regulation in the EU has been completed with the solemn declaration by Commission President Prodi of 4 February 2002 and the letter from Commissioner Bolkenstein to the European Parliament of 2 October 2001, as well as the European Parliament resolution of 5 February 2002 on the implementation of financial services legislation.

3 The Commission observed in its explanatory memorandum to Directive 2005/1/EC that the BAC has only acted as a 'comitology' committee on four occasions since it had been granted comitology powers in 1989 through the Solvency Ratio Directive.

4 The article was introduced in the Treaty through the Single European Act in order to reflect practices already used *praeter legem* in the 1960s.

5 The first Comitology Decision of the Council dates from 1987 (Council Decision 87/373); it was entirely replaced by the Council decision of 1999; for an accurate analysis of the latter, see Lenaerts and Verhoeven 2000.

applicable to the Commission when exercising implementing powers, and lays down the position of the Council and the Parliament in that connection. The Comitology Decision introduces several procedures to be followed by the Commission when adopting implementing measures, and criteria for the choice of the applicable procedure. The 1999 version of the Comitology Decision foresaw only a limited role for the Parliament in the framework of the regulatory procedure. Thus, the Parliament had a right to be informed (article 7), and also the right to issue a resolution on *ultra vires* grounds whenever it considers that implementing measures exceed the implementing powers conferred to the Commission through article 8. This had no binding consequences for the Commission or the Council. Conversely, the Council's wider powers entailed the right to take direct action by assuming to itself responsibility for the implementing measures. The 2006 amendments to the Comitology Decision substantially improved the position of the European Parliament, which has been placed on an equal footing with the Council in relation to Commission measures falling under the new regulatory procedure with scrutiny.

Several instruments have been put in place to sustain the institutional equilibrium in the context of the four-level regulatory approach. Their primary aim is to contain the Commission's action within the boundaries of the executive function, with due democratic control. Furthermore, such safeguards attempt to ensure parity between the two legislative branches, in view of achieving a proper degree of democratic accountability.

There are two categories of institutional safeguards: substantive and procedural. These are enshrined in legal and political instruments so as to provide sufficient certainty. There is, first and foremost, the substantive guarantee implicit in the requirement that legislative Level 1 measures explicitly delegate implementing powers. Such a provision allows the Parliament and the Council to oppose the delegation of implementing powers to the Commission or to narrow down substantially the scope of implementing powers. It also allows for politically sensitive rules, although technical in nature, to be adopted from the outset through the legislative procedure. Unfortunately, in practice this substantive limit has been regularly used in the banking sector, where the Commission has employed its comitology powers on only a few occasions since the adoption of the CRD; abuse of it results in very dense and detailed Level 1 legislation.

A second substantive warranty of inter-institutional balance results from the requirement that Level 2 measures do not modify the essential provisions of the legislative norms they set out to implement. This principle has been replicated in article 150 (3) CRD, but deleted during the 2008 amendments to the CRD (article 1(1) (c) Directive 2008/24/EC). At the suggestion of the Parliament, the principle has been nailed down as positive law into the directive implementing the Lamfalussy structure in the banking sector (article 12 Directive 2005/1/EC). Finally, another substantive safeguard consists of the general principles prescribed for guiding work at Level 2. These were initially enshrined in the Market Abuse Directive, and have been transposed correspondingly into the preamble to Directive 2005/1/EC (recital 19). These principles have been ascribed a rather symbolic value and commentators have expressed substantial doubts as to their capacity to form the basis for a successful legal challenge against implementing measures (Ferran 2004: 73). Nevertheless, despite their broadness and the absence of any hierarchy, they do reflect certain basic criteria that cannot be ignored by the Commission.

At the procedural level, there are several mechanisms for controlling the exercise of implementing powers by the Commission. One of the most relevant was the 'full and open review' clause of the committee arrangements by the end of 2007 at the latest (article 9 of Directive 2005/1/EC), which is also indicative of the experimental character of the four-level approach. Furthermore, the CRD imposed through article 150(4) a 'sunset' clause that limited the duration of the delegation of implementing powers to the Commission until 1 April 2008. Thereby, the Parliament and the Council were given the possibility of broadly reviewing the application of the respective implementing powers, and – if satisfied – renewing the relevant provisions. Following the amendment of the Comitology Decision, in March 2008 the CRD was also amended and the Parliament agreed to the deletion of the time restrictions concerning implementing powers enshrined in article 150(4) CRD. Moreover, the 2008 amendment introduced a new general review clause, this time requiring the Commission to review the provisions concerning its implementing powers by 31 December 2010 and thereafter at least every three years, and to report to the Parliament and Council on the functioning of those powers. This also allows the Commission to make legislative proposals in view of extending the scope of its implementing powers under the CRD.

The information rights and intervention possibilities of the Council and the Parliament are specified in the Comitology Decision and in Directive 2005/1/EC. It is made clear that the Parliament should enjoy a period of at least three months (from the first transmission) when it is allowed to examine the draft comitology measures and to present its opinion.[6] Within this period, the Parliament, like the Council, may oppose the proposed measures on grounds that the Commission exceeded its implementing powers, or that the Commission's draft measure is not compatible with the aim or content of the basic instrument, or does not respect the principles of subsidiarity and

6 Recital 18 of the preamble to Directive 2005/1/EC and art. 5a of the amended Comitology Decision. The three-month period applies to the case when the EBC agrees with the Commission's proposals. In case the EBC disagrees or does not issue an opinion within the prescribed time, a slightly different procedure is applied, which allows the EP four months to issue an opinion on the Commission's proposed implementing measures. In cases of high complexity, the above-mentioned periods may be extended by an additional month. They may be also curtailed for efficiency reasons. If for imperative grounds of urgency the timelines cannot be applied, a special procedure will apply.

proportionality. In case of opposition by the Parliament or the Council, the Commission cannot adopt the measure and may choose either to propose an amended comitology measure or to submit a legislative proposal.

The delicate issue of the institutional (im)balance between the Parliament and the Council had been settled, since the insertion of the new regulatory procedure under scrutiny in the Comitology Decision and the subsequent amendment of the CRD. Yet the relevance of the comitology saga in the adoption and application of the Lamfalussy framework is particularly illustrative of the powerful political and constitutional interests involved in any change to decision-making processes within the EU. The Lisbon Treaty does not reproduce article 202 EC, but introduces instead provisions allowing the Commission to adopt delegated acts (article 290 TFEU) and implementing acts (article 291 TFEU), underpinned by different procedures. So far, there are no clear criteria for the differentiation between the two categories. This is very likely to reopen the discussions about the institutional balance between the Commission, the Council and the European Parliament. The power games, underpinning the design of the three institutions' competences to control, participate, intervene or review the activities of an eventual European Banking Authority vested with regulatory powers, will most probably substantially influence the outcome of the reform project.

2 The committees

The focus on the institutional balance reflects a legalistic–constitutional approach emphasising formal competences and procedures set out in the Treaty, but does not necessarily reflect the core of the institutional innovations introduced through the Lamfalussy framework. One of the genuine contributions of the four-level approach consists of its emphasis on the effective decision-making process in the area of financial regulation. Thus, the Lamfalussy process manages to partially rationalise and render more transparent the influence of actors and practices that developed behind the facade of the Treaty institutions. The whole debate about the institutional balance constitutes an end in itself, reflecting the Parliament's endeavours to overcome its 'outsider' status with regard to comitology. Notwithstanding this, it says little about actual rule-making and the functional motivation behind the refinement of the financial institutional architecture.

The Wise Men acknowledged that financial regulation had to respond quickly to rapid market developments and thus was in need of an institutional framework that would simultaneously provide guarantees for accountability, legitimacy and legal certainty, and quick and flexible solutions addressing continuously emerging challenges. Hence, there was a need to ensure that binding legal acts of a legislative and administrative (implementing) nature are the outcome of balanced decision-making, and show deference to the formal and political powers of Community institutions. At the same time, increased need of expertise in this highly technical field resulted in the call for a more structured involvement of specialists at all stages of decision-making. Additionally, given that financial supervision is evolving into a complex process requiring continuous rule-making, incentives had to be devised at EU level to stimulate regulatory convergence. Consequently, the institutional architecture also had to incorporate these aspects and foresee institutional solutions adequate for providing both professional expertise to the political actors and a forum for stimulating regulatory and supervisory convergence.

It is increasingly frequently argued that the institutional design should depend on the extent of integration (Alexander 2002a: 8; Schoenmaker and Oosterloo 2005: 2). At the time of the adoption of the Lamfalussy process, the degree of integration in financial markets was not considered sufficient to be translated into a revolutionary revision of the regulatory framework; hence, the Wise Men project was quite moderate in character. To a large extent, it attempted to bring existing practices under the umbrella of the more formalised and familiar comitology procedure, adapted to the exigencies specific to the various financial sectors. Yet it also succeeded in creating a structure that manages to provide the institutional frame for launching a permanent channel of communication between national experts and the ultimate decision-makers (the Council, the Parliament and the Commission), as well as ensuring a regular and guided dialogue between supervisors in different Member States. Such an evolution, in our view, indicates the path towards institutional centralisation understood as the first step towards the creation of a European regulator. In addition, the activist coordination through the committee structure most definitely is a sign of Europeanisation[7] of banking regulation and supervision.

2.1 Multiplicity and variety

One of the reasons for change invoked in the Wise Men report was the variety of public bodies at EU level dealing with financial market regulation and supervision, which perpetrated fragmentation and confusion.[8] The Lamfalussy procedure aimed at bringing some order to the various committees acting under the auspices of the Commission; nevertheless, it left almost untouched the plethora of bodies serving the other EU institutions. Before reviewing the two banking committees instituted through the Lamfalussy framework, we will reconstruct concisely the institutional puzzle – populated by a vast range of committees supporting the activities of the 'formal' political actors. Thereby, we bear in mind that 'committees are in any event an inevitable feature of modern, regulatory government, originated in the

7 In this context 'Europeanisation' denotes the increased influence and use of intervention modes (through hard- and soft-law instruments) in sectors and areas that have belonged traditionally to the realm of the Member States in the context of shared competences.

8 The authors of the report argued that there were about 40 public bodies acting in the securities sector; see p. 18.

need for "joined-up government"' (Harlow 2002: 32) and this is plainly reflected at all stages of European decision-making. Banking regulation – a highly technical sector – does not represent an exception; the decisions of each political actor are underpinned by the work undertaken by an array of committees. In the following, we will endeavour to provide a picture of these backstage actors and their influence in the decision-making process.

Council's committees

The Council, when acting in the area of financial markets, is configured as the Economic and Financial Affairs Council (Ecofin). It is one of the oldest configurations and brings together the Economic and Finance Ministers of the Member States. On issues related to financial markets Ecofin acts by qualified majority and in co-decision with the Parliament. Its work is supported by several working parties and committees, some of which have significant influential potential. The work of all in-house services and advisers of the Council is filtered by the overarching Committee of Permanent Representatives (COREPER) before being passed to the ministerial level. COREPER has, at least theoretically, a pivotal role in the decision-making process, recognised also formally in the EC Treaty (article 240 TFEU, ex 207 EC). This results from its capacity to provide a constant forum for dialogue among the national Permanent Representatives and between the latter and their respective national governments.[9] Acting far from the spotlight, COREPER is the platform where many of the compromises between divergent national positions are reached. The concrete work and substantive influence of this powerful committee remains largely confidential. Therefore, it has been frequently criticised as a politically unaccountable decision-maker (Harlow 2002: 35) and has triggered calls for transparency in Council decision-making. It is important to note that COREPER has a key role not only in the bargaining process but also in providing support for the preparation of implementing measures at national level and facilitating inter-institutional cooperation.

Much more important for matters dealing with financial regulation is another body provided for in the EC Treaty (ex article 114 EC, now 134 TFEU): the Economic and Financial Committee (EFC).[10] The EFC is not

9 Real decisions are rarely taken by COREPER itself, as it actually relies on the work of subordinate committees. Thus there is COREPER I, consisting of the Deputy Permanent Representative and dealing with technical matters, including the single market, and COREPER II, composed of the Permanent Representatives themselves, which handles the political questions.

10 The EFC is the successor of the Monetary Committee that was originally the only committee directly created by the EEC Treaty. Requested by the Maastricht Treaty for supporting work on the third stage of Economic and Monetary Union, the EFC was set up through Council Decision 98/743/EC, as amended by Council Decision 2003/476/EC. Under the Lisbon Treaty, the EFC's legal basis is art. 134 TFEU.

formally a Council committee,[11] and its secretariat is located with the Commission. However, we have opted to list it here because of the Council's Treaty-based competence to adopt detailed rules regarding the functioning of the EFC. Entrusted with the regular review of the economic and financial situation of the Member States and with the preparation of the work of the Council, particularly with regard to the multilateral surveillance and excessive deficit procedures, the EFC may act either on request of both the Council and the Commission or on its own initiative. Meeting since 2003 in two configurations,[12] the EFC assembles 'experts possessing outstanding competence in the economic and financial field' coming from national administrations, national central banks, the Commission and the ECB (articles 1 and 2 Council Decision 98/743/EC). The EFC, propelled by the Ecofin, has begun to exert an increasingly strong influence, with regard to financial stability issues. It is often de facto responsible for the development of legislation (without prejudice to COREPER's formal tasks) and takes the lead with regard to policy advice on designing financial regulatory and supervisory structures and policy choices concerning financial market integration (e.g. see EFC 2002). The EFC is constantly monitoring all developments related to financial stability issues and reports regularly to Ecofin members, for whom it constitutes the primary source of advice on economic and financial matters.

Another prominent link in the chain of bodies giving support to the Council's work in financial markets is the Financial Services Committee (FSC), the reconfigured Financial Services Policy Group (FSPG).[13] The FSC was conceived outside of the legislative process, as an adviser on financial 'policy-shaping' to the Council, entrusted with the task of devising cross-sectoral strategies and responsible for identifying short-, medium- and long-term issues, as well as assessing progress and implementation. Without interfering with existing institutional prerogatives, and keeping the Parliament constantly informed about its activities, the FSC is subordinated directly to the EFC, from which it takes instructions and to which it reports in order to prepare advice to the Council. The FSC comprises high-level representatives of the Member States' financial ministries and the Commission. The ECB, the Chairs of the Level 3 committees, the

11 Defining the EFC as a Council committee would have made the participation of NCB representatives problematic – see Louis 2009: 117.

12 According to art. 4 EFC Statute, the two configurations of the EFC are: either with the members selected from the administrations, the national central banks, the Commission and the ECB; or with the members from administrations, the Commission and the ECB.

13 The FSPG was established in November 1998 at the initiative of the Commission in order to give advice on the priorities outlined in the FSAP. The FSPG was composed of representatives of the Ministries of Finance and the ECB and chaired by Commissioner Monti. On 12 July 2002, the Ecofin decided to reconfigure the FSPG under Member State chairmanship. Initially, it was suggested that it be renamed the Financial Policy Committee to underline its policy-shaping role; the final option was nevertheless for 'Financial Services Committee', which reflects the double task of political advice and oversight on financial market issues.

Council Secretariat and the EFC Secretariat have observer status. The FSC has a strong contribution via the EFC to the discussions within the Ecofin on prudential regulation and financial stability issues, especially as concerns cross-sectoral structural issues, vulnerabilities in the EU financial system and the build-up and functioning of networks of supervisors.[14]

European Parliament committees

The European Parliament also relies on the work of internal committees, which are substantially involved in the financial regulatory process. The prominent role is detained by the Committee on Economic and Monetary Affairs (ECON) which, apart from making concrete amendments to the Commission's legislative proposals on prudential and supervisory issues, has also taken an active stance for defending the Parliament's position within the institutional equilibrium. ECON is responsible for regulation and supervision of financial services, institutions and markets and is in charge of the preparation of reports and parliamentary resolutions on draft legislation regarding financial markets. ECON's contribution is complemented by the work of the Committee on Legal Affairs (JURI) and the Committee on Constitutional Affairs. Moreover, ECON benefits from the steady input of market participants and academics, sometimes formalised under specific structures. Thus, in May 2002 ECON established an Advisory Panel of Financial Services Experts (APFSE), composed of ten independent recognised professionals in financial markets (six market practitioners and four university professors) with advisory tasks to ECON, whose work is not public.[15] Pursuant to the June 2009 EP elections, a special Committee on the Financial, Economic and Social Crisis (CRIS) was established, which is expected to make policy recommendations without however carrying out legislative powers.

Commission committees

The Commission is surrounded by a host of bodies involved in financial regulation. Apart from its directorates general, of which two, DG Internal Market (MARKT)[16] and DG for Economic and Financial Affairs (ECFIN),

14 See, for instance, the May 2004 Report from the EU Financial Services Committee on Financial Integration (FSC 4156/04); see also the agendas for the FSC's meetings in the Public Register of Council's Documents.

15 IIMG 2003b. Yet to our knowledge there is no explicit reference to the APFSE during the 2004–9 mandate of the EP, although ECON has benefited from substantial advice, studies and hearings of financial market experts; see a list of expert studies requested by ECON online at www.europarl.europa.eu/activities/committees/studiesCom/searchPerform.do.

16 DG Internal Market holds general responsibilities for making the single market work and is therefore entrusted with specific tasks regarding various sectors, including financial services. It is the organisational unit of the Commission participating in the Basel Committee, the Financial Stability Board, the Banking Supervision Committee of the ECB and the Joint Forum of Financial Conglomerates.

take the lead in the area of financial markets – not without friction – and apart from the Level 2 and Level 3 committees involved in devising implementing measures, the Commission is also assisted by other actors. Thus, for instance, the DG MARKT in 2003 set up specialist groups to take stock of the FSAP and to closely assess the state of integration of European financial markets. More recently, it established the Capital Requirements Directive Transposition Group to deal closely with technical aspects of the CRD and recast CAD, and especially to provide all stakeholders with responses on specific aspects in EU banking legislation. Besides, DG ECFIN had already set up the Giovannini Group in 1996, composed of financial market participants advising the Commission on financial market issues, with a focus on identifying concrete inefficiencies in EU financial markets and proposing practical solutions. To our knowledge, the Giovannini Group has so far not acted on prudential issues, but such a possibility cannot be excluded from the outset.

Furthermore, the Commission often decides to establish ad hoc bodies in view of preparing advice on specific topics. This was the case when in October 2008 it set up a High Level Group chaired by Jacques de Larosière to give advice on the future of European financial regulation and supervision. The Group's recommendations now constitute the backbone for the concrete proposals of institutional reforms for European supervision, under intensive discussion by European policy-makers at the time of writing.

Other bodies

Finally, we should mention the bodies with an autonomous status that exert different influence on the European regulatory process for financial markets. Among these, there is the European Economic and Social Committee, a self-standing body established by the EC Treaty, which has to be consulted on any draft legislative measure on financial services. The formal advisory position of the European Economic and Social Committee is not backed by any binding force attached to its opinions and consequently its real power in the domain of financial markets is restrained.

Much more influence was exercised by the Inter-Institutional Monitoring Group (IIMG), set up in July 2002 by the Commission, the Council and the Parliament. The IIMG, composed of independent experts, has published three authoritative reports on the implementation of the Lamfalussy framework in the securities sector. In July 2005, the IIMG was re-established with an extended mandate to cover the implementation of the 'Lamfalussy process' in the banking and insurance sectors. The re-established IIMG issued further three reports that highlighted the feasibility of the Lamfalussy approach and made recommendations for its improvement.

The multiplicity of bodies demonstrates that the production of decisional knowledge requested for regulating financial markets is highly complex and entails overlapping structures that do not necessarily compete with each other, but endeavour to provide complementary views so as to ensure a final qualitative outcome. In the following, we will individually analyse the Lamfalussy committees – namely the European Banking Committee and the Committee of European Banking Supervisors. First, we will briefly describe their predecessor, the Banking Advisory Committee.

2.2 The Banking Advisory Committee

The new bodies established within the Lamfalussy framework did not arise out of a vacuum but succeeded the experienced Banking Advisory Committee (BAC).[17]

The BAC was a prominent influential body which contributed substantially to the drawing up of European banking legislation.[18] Set up by the First Banking Directive, BAC was entrusted with a set of specific monitoring tasks (articles 58, 59 CBD). It also pursued broader tasks aimed at ensuring the correct implementation of EC directives, assisting the Commission in drawing up new proposals for European banking legislation and supporting the Commission in its exercise of implementing powers. While its role in contributing to correct implementation was detailed through the specific tasks and tools for cooperation laid down in legislation (article 59 CBD), the other two tasks were less formalised. BAC's advisory role with regard to draft legislation was not subject to a formalised procedure.

BAC's composition and modes of operation were public and laid down in the rules of procedure, but its activities, including the documents produced, were largely confidential. Over the years, BAC also acquired a comitology role,[19] being required to assist the Commission in its exercise of implementing powers. This involved issuing supplementary technical details and even modifying some aspects of secondary EC law so as to keep pace with financial market developments. The possibility of having recourse to BAC in its comitology mode was a compromise between a Commission eager to have more autonomy in adopting implementing measures in the banking field and a Council keen on maintaining its influence on the decision-making process. It was a delicate settlement that subsequently resulted in reluctance to actually make use of BAC in its regulatory mode and contributed to the proliferation of BAC in its advisory function.

17 For a detailed analysis of the Banking Advisory Committee, see Godano 2004.

18 In the BAC report for the years 1991–4, the Chairman of the Committee referred to 'co-management' of European banking legislation between the Commission and the Banking Advisory Committee.

19 The Second Banking Directive, Solvency Directive and Large Exposures Directive all contained provisions attributing comitology tasks to BAC.

BAC was a formally established body, but its influence pertained more to its informal qualities and non-transparent interventions. It had a crucial role, before the adoption of the SBD, as in the context of the preparations related to the single market it constituted the platform where the main issues and strategies related to banking regulation and supervisory controls were discussed. BAC also constituted the catalyst for interaction and coordination between the national supervisory authorities and had an important voice in the conclusion of bilateral Memoranda of Understanding (Godano 2004: 766). The influential position of BAC stemmed not only from its expertise, but also from the fact that it constantly favoured personal contact and mutual trust. It is still to be determined whether the institutionalisation of the new banking committees and the proceduralisation of the advice to be given by them do, in fact, impinge on the efficacy of such advice.

2.3 The European Banking Committee (EBC)

The two Lamfalussy committees established in the banking sector have taken on the tasks previously entrusted to BAC. The main successor of BAC is the EBC, but some of its tasks were also ascribed to CEBS. The establishment of the EBC (together with the other Level 2 committees) was the most problematic, as it had to duly observe the smooth transfer of competences already foreseen in EU legislation and receive the support of Council and Parliament in the midst of comitology-related disputes.

Agreement on the establishment of the EBC as a substitute to BAC was finally reached on 9 March 2005, when the directive on the establishment of a new organisational structure for financial services committees was adopted. The entry into force of the directive also put an end to the suspensive effect attached to the Commission's decision of November 2003 regarding the advisory capacity of the EBC (Commission Decision 2004/10/EC). As a consequence, the EBC finally became a reality with a double advisory and regulatory function.

Accordingly, the dual role of the EBC is exercised under two different legal bases: the Commission decision, whenever it carries out advisory functions, and the Council's Comitology Decision corroborated with the provisions in secondary EU law, when it acts as a regulatory committee in relation to the Commission's exercise of implementing powers. As opposed to BAC, the central role of the EBC should be its regulatory task leading to the adoption of Level 2 measures. Nevertheless, this should not undermine the complex advisory function in respect to which the EBC may draw substantive benefits from the experience of its predecessor. The EBC's advisory role covers guidance to the Commission on legislative instruments to be adopted as Level 1 measures; counselling the Commission on Level 2 mandates and on calls for advice to CEBS; and more broadly giving advice on any policy issues related to banking activities whenever the Commission so requests. The pivotal position of the EBC stems mainly from its expected role in enhancing harmonisation of technical rules, but also from its capacity to give Member States the possibility of having a say on the Commission's legislative agenda in the banking field and the concrete distribution of roles between the various levels and actors involved in rule-making.

The EBC has a more restrained composition than its predecessor (article 3 Commission Decision 2004/10/EC). Thus, while Member States could appoint up to three high-level representatives to the BAC so as to facilitate involvement of all relevant authorities (central banks, ministries of finance, supervisory authorities), the EBC permits the appointment of only one high-level representative per Member State, backed by one technical expert. The EFC report on the extension of the Lamfalussy procedure suggested that the national representative should be nominated by the relevant ministry, according to national models, arguing that accountability lies ultimately with ministries. The restrained membership of the EBC gives the impression of a more compact composition that would facilitate more consistent and efficient action. At the same time, it implicitly stimulates *ex ante* cooperation between the various authorities responsible at national level. Moreover, the chairmanship of the EBC was given to the Commission, irrespective of the advisory or regulatory mode in which it is acting. This might be interpreted as enhancing the Commission's position as compared to BAC, which was chaired by a representative of the Member States whenever it acted in an advisory capacity. Furthermore, a representative of CEBS and one of the ECB have formal observer status at all EBC meetings. EBC also enjoys discretion as to the possibility of inviting, as observers, the chairpersons of other relevant bodies (the Groupe de Contact, the Banking Supervision Committee, or any new committee that might be established in the future).

The rules of procedure of the EBC have not been made public, although initially this was explicitly requested in article 151(3) CRD. The provision was unfortunately deleted on the occasion of the 2008 amendments to the CRD with a view to aligning it with the revised Comitology Decision. As a consequence, the concrete working modalities of the EBC remain opaque, as does its agenda. For 2006 an EBC Activity Report was issued, as well as a tentative work programme for 2007–9. Yet, despite the complex events since 2007 that triggered a range of regulatory initiatives in the banking field, no update of the work programme was published. The scarce information about the EBC's effective contribution may be extracted only from the newsletters it publishes every four months. It appears that the EBC is abreast of all the important Commission files in the area of banking regulation and supervision, yet its precise contribution cannot be inferred.

Since its establishment in 2005, the EBC agreed to four Commission proposals under the comitology procedure. The first two were adopted in

2006 and concerned the amendment or removal of certain credit institutions from the scope of the Codified Banking Directive and respectively from the CRD and the amendment of the list of multilateral development banks in the annex to the CRD (Commission Directive 2007/18/EC). After the amendment in 2006 of the Comitology Decision and until the amendment of the CRD to reflect the new comitology arrangements, the EBC did not act in its regulatory capacity. This was taken up again in the framework of the first review of the CRD, and in December 2008 the EBC agreed on two further comitology measures, one with amendments to the CRD (Commission Directive 2009/83/EC), the other to the recast CAD (Commission Directive 2009/27/EC).

The EBC is an important factor in the inter-institutional play between the Commission and the Council. Especially from the perspective of its predominantly ministerial membership, it is an important tool for accommodating Member States' views within the Commission's preparatory and implementing work. Although not amounting to a mini-Council, given its organisational stance, the EBC can become a forum for smoothening and accelerating the legislative process and a catalyst between Council's and Commission's views with regard to banking regulation.[20] The Commission chairmanship of the EBC might be seen, however, as a sign of reinforcement of the Commission's implementing powers.

Because of the opacity of the EBC's activities, it is not easy to weigh its role in the final regulatory outcomes. However, the deliberate choice of not promoting transparency and predictability of its actions may be justified by effectiveness considerations and the fact that BAC's efficiency has been attributed to its informal and sometimes ambiguous interventions. The EBC's limited experience in a regulatory mode is also, to a large extent, the consequence of comitology-related institutional quarrels and the associated reluctance to delegate powers to the Commission. A more extensive use of EBC's comitology role would have been an opportunity to deliver framework legislation from much of its technical encumbrance.

2.4 The Committee of European Banking Supervisors (CEBS)

While the EBC is in essence a reconfigured BAC, the outstanding institutional innovation brought about by the extended Lamfalussy framework is the Level 3 committee CEBS. Its importance stems from its fourfold

20 Similar to the European Securities Committee, the EBC

> provides a mechanism for the resolution of minor political skirmishes without invoking the full panoply of level 1 and it has at least the potential to operate more flexibly and quickly than might be possible within the formalities of the Council.
>
> (Ferran 2004: 109)

function as a technical adviser of the Commission, a catalyst for regulatory and supervisory convergence, a platform for cooperation and information exchange between supervisors, and a monitoring and assessment device for developments in the banking sector. This complex role has enabled CEBS to eventually become the real centre of European rule-making in the banking field.

Unlike CESR, which succeeded the Forum of European Securities Commissions (FESCO), CEBS does not have a predecessor; it inherited only some competences previously exercised by BAC. Also, it does not replace but instead supplements and 'integrates' activities previously exercised by the Groupe de Contact. Although set up in accordance with the model offered by its securities counterpart, it has a series of specificities related to its composition, specific focus and activities.

The basic documents regulating the organisation and functioning of CEBS are the Commission Decision 2009/78/EC establishing CEBS and the CEBS Charter.[21] According to these documents, CEBS is composed of high-level representatives designated by each Member State and the ECB. Each Member State will appoint one voting senior representative from the national competent supervisory authority in the banking sector and one non-voting member, representing the national central bank (NCB) when this is not the competent authority for banking supervision, or otherwise a second representative from the NCB. The ECB will also designate a high-level representative to the Committee, who will be a non-voting member (article 1.1 CEBS Charter). The European Commission and the Chairs of the Banking Supervision Committee of the ESCB (the BSC) and of the Groupe de Contact will have observer status that allows them to participate in the meetings and debates of the Committee, but not in the decision-making process (article 1.4 CEBS Charter). Equally, the competent banking supervisory authorities from non-EU countries of the European Economic Area, as well as from acceding countries that have signed an Accession Treaty, will enjoy observer status. Moreover, CEBS is open to any additional observers whenever a common interest to work together is present and may invite external experts each time this is relevant to its work (article 1.2 and 1.6 CEBS Charter). Furthermore, CEBS keeps close operational links with the EBC and requires its members to make all appropriate national arrangements so as to ensure that the EBC's members (usually representatives of the finance ministries) are informed about CEBS' work and that CEBS' members are in the position of speaking for all competent national authorities. This participatory framework has been designed in order to benefit from synergies in the banking sector, particularly between banking supervisory authorities and central banking.

21 The CEBS Charter became effective on 29 January 2004. It was revised in 2008 with effect from 10 July 2008.

The constitutive documents denote openness towards participation of national and European authorities in the work of CEBS and a thorough concern for allowing the Commission active involvement in all debates, except those on confidential matters. These participatory possibilities should not impinge on CEBS' character as 'an independent advisory group on banking supervision in the Community' (article 1 Commission Decision 2009/78/EC). The charter does not reaffirm CEBS' independence, which only indirectly transpires from the Committee's organisational and working arrangements, voting rights, the appointment of the Committee's Chair and the general commitment to act in conformity with the Commission decision establishing CEBS. The independent status of CEBS is counterbalanced by arrangements for ensuring its accountability and clarifying its institutional links. According to article 6 of CEBS' Charter, CEBS is obliged to submit an annual report to the Commission, which will be also forwarded to the Council and the European Parliament. The Chair of the Committee has also to report periodically to the Parliament, and/or when requested to the Council, and to maintain close links to the EBC. Financially, CEBS has so far relied mainly on contributions from its members.[22] Yet, as its resources proved insufficient compared to the tasks it is expected to perform, the CEBS Charter was amended to allow CEBS to receive external contributions or financing for specific projects, notably from the European institutions. On 6 May 2009, the EP adopted a Commission proposal for a Community programme providing direct funding from the Community budget to the three EU Committees of Supervisors.

A distinctive feature of CEBS is the transparency attached to its activities resulting from intense interaction with all stakeholders. Thus, the constitutive decision obliges CEBS to undertake extensive consultation at an early stage in an open and transparent manner with market participants, consumers and end-users. Moreover, when dealing with issues regarding both credit institutions and investment firms, it requires CEBS to consult all authorities competent for supervision of investment firms that are not already represented in CEBS. The Charter further specifies the modalities of the *ex ante* and *ex post* consultation processes, which are further detailed in a Public Statement of Consultation Practices.[23] Last but not least, transparency is reinforced through the establishment of a

22 The individual annual contribution is calculated on the basis of the number of votes in the Council; for those countries not represented in the Council it is agreed on a proportional basis.

23 The first public statement of 11 March 2005 was replaced by a revised Public Statement of Consultation Practices on 8 August 2008. The Public Statement provides detailed information on who is consulted, areas of consultation, modes of consultation, timing of consultation, standard timelines for advice on Level 2 issues, standard timelines for work on Level 3 issues, follow-up to consultations and amendments to standard consultation procedures.

Consultative Panel of representatives of market participants and end-users to assist in the performance of CEBS' functions and to ensure that the consultation process functions effectively. Hence, CEBS is one of the key actors responsible for collecting the input of private parties to the regulatory process in the banking field.

The real potential of CEBS may be inferred from the statutory role attributed to it, and the priority areas it chooses to pursue through its work programme. According to articles 2–5 of the constitutive Commission decision, CEBS has been attributed a fourfold role: (1) to advise the Commission (either at the latter's request or on its own initiative) in particular in the preparation of draft implementing measures in the field of banking activities or financial conglomerates; (2) to contribute to the common and uniform implementation and consistent application of EU legislation by issuing non-binding guidelines, recommendations and standards; (3) to enhance cooperation between national banking supervisors and foster convergence of supervisory practices and approaches throughout the EU;[24] and (4) to monitor and assess developments in the banking sector and inform the relevant authorities about potential or imminent problems.[25] During its first five years of existence, CEBS has acted mainly in pursuance of the first two functions listed, which reflect its mandate with regard to regulatory issues.

The CRD introduces a multi-layered complex framework, and its implementation in EU countries does not merely consist of the transposition of the EU norms into the national legal and regulatory systems. The CRD unleashes a regulatory machine whose task is to bring about convergence and harmonisation beyond the legislative level, namely at the implementing executive/administrative level in the Member States. Thus, the complex approaches to the calculation of capital requirements, the emphasis on appropriate internal risk-management systems, disclosure requirements and the institutionalised dialogue between supervisors and the regulated entities offer numerous occasions for CEBS to provide expert advice or guidance on the implementation of the EU directive and the exercise of supervisory powers by the national authorities. In this setting, it is obvious that in its first years, coinciding with the period surrounding the adoption of the CRD, CEBS focused mainly on the further details needed for the implementation of the CRD.

The necessity of devising details outside the legislative framework, within the limits of legality, lies at the core of national administrative

24 The 2009 decision establishing CEBS made the role of CEBS with respect to supervisory cooperation and convergence more explicit, by enumerating a series of tasks attributed to it to this effect. We will come back to these when analysing the role of CEBS with regard to supervision.

25 This is a new role attributed to CEBS only in 2009, to which we will come back when dealing with supervisory arrangements.

systems. These have also constituted the main channel for the implementation of Community law, in the absence of a European administrative infrastructure capable of coping with such a complex task. Ideally, there should be in the EU a consistent and unitary European administrative law framework entailing a codification of administrative procedures applicable in all Member States (Harlow 1999). At the current stage of European construction, this is not yet the case. There are, rather, informal mechanisms capable of determining convergence of national practices in specific sectors without being too intrusive. Such mechanisms are being now somehow institutionalised, especially where national interests and deep-rooted traditions risk causing important discrepancies.

In the area of financial markets, the application of legislation is particularly important because of the specific dynamics of the sector implying continuous innovation and rapid obsolescence of standards. Hence, legislative framework principles can be sustained as long as they have a high degree of generality. General rules need to be further detailed at the stage of implementation, according to the specific developments in the sector. The Lamfalussy mechanism already provides a more flexible Level 2 phase, allowing for implementing legislative measures to be adopted and changed more easily within the comitology procedure. Nevertheless, even legislative implementing rules need further elaboration in order to be concretely applied.

This stage gives the greatest potential for divergent interpretations and different policy outcomes, and thereby risks reversing the efforts undertaken at the legislative level for creating an integrated European financial market. The European legislator, conscious that 'rule making is carried out more by regulatory than legislative action',[26] has empowered CEBS to contribute through soft mechanisms to the harmonisation of areas that so far have been exclusively regulated by Member States. CEBS, composed of representatives of the competent national authorities who are ultimately entrusted with the application of European rules, is well placed to comparatively assess the divergent implementation trends at national level. Therefore, it appears to be a viable and legitimised institutionalised framework for the transfer of some executive power at the supra-national level. At the same time, CEBS' obligation to undertake wide and transparent consultation processes, as well as impact assessments, constitutes a guarantee that its work does not reflect unilateral views or isolated inputs, but that, instead, takes account of the broader picture and the interests of all stakeholders.

The 'soft' nature of CEBS' regulatory competence has been made explicit in the 2009 Commission decision that replaced the initial 2003 constitutive decision of CEBS. Article 3 underlines the non-binding nature

26 Lenaerts and Verhoeven 2000: 660, citing Koopmans 1970.

of the guidelines, recommendations and standards[27] issued by CEBS when delivering its functions. Before such amendment, CEBS' soft character could be deduced from the absence of coercive instruments attached to its powers. Moreover, the CEBS Charter clarified that the guidelines, recommendations and standards have to be introduced by the Committee's members in their regulatory/supervisory practices on a voluntary basis (article 4.3 CEBS Charter). Article 5.6 CEBS Charter explicitly provides that 'Level 3 measures (e.g. guidelines, recommendations and standards) taken either by consensus or by qualified majority are not legally binding'. Although CEBS instruments are soft-law instruments deprived of coercive force, they are essential for the consistent implementation of binding European directives. CEBS itself holds that its guidelines and standards

> are not legal instruments, but they clearly sit within the legal framework created by the Directives, and by common consent of the members they carry a good deal of weight. They should be seen as a reference point for all supervisory authorities.
>
> (CEBS 2005c)

This soft nature should not be underestimated, especially when seen through the lenses of the specific features of the bankers' community – probably one of the last examples of 'trust societies'.[28] In a field, where moral suasion and personal commitments are important instruments for unfolding common projects, the establishment of an institutionalised framework, even deprived of 'hard' powers, entails a de facto authority that could bring about compliance similar to binding mechanisms. CEBS' non-binding instruments, more than common soft-law measures, have an inherent

27 According to CEBS:

> guidelines are further specification of EU legislation, especially where such legislation provides for minimum harmonisation, covering the substance as well as processes. Guidelines will be addressed to supervised institutions and supervisory authorities. They may also be addressed to national legislators in so far as some authorities have the power or need to incorporate them in national legislation.

Further:

> standards are related to a legislative provision which per se is directly applicable, but whose application requires particular guidance for any other reason, or they are not directly related to Community legislation. Standards cover the substance as well as processes and can be addressed to supervised institutions as well as to supervisory authorities. For example, they may be used to explain to industry practitioners what supervisors will expect from them. They may also be addressed to national legislators in so far as some authorities have the power or need to incorporate them in national legislation.

28 Harlow (referring to Chalmers 1998) noted 'a move from "trust" societies, in which elite groups are both trusted and trust each other, to an impersonal or bureaucratic society, in which obligations are imposed on individuals by external authorities' (Harlow 1999: 279).

capacity to produce convergence of national regulatory and supervisory practices through the specific relationship between the various actors in the banking sector and particularly the longstanding tradition of 'smooth' non-conflictual cooperation between banking supervisors and regulators.

In support of an authoritative CEBS, we may invoke not only the large consultative processes underpinning and legitimising its decision-making, but also its working procedures. First of all there are the voting requirements that commit CEBS to strive for consensus between its members as a general rule when fulfilling the tasks entrusted to it, apart from when giving advice to the Commission. According to article 5.6 CEBS Charter, if consensus cannot be achieved, it is also possible to make decisions by qualified majority, with each representative of the Member States having the same voting rights as in the Council. In such cases, the Committee is obliged to identify and elaborate the opinion of the individual members, and to keep records of them.

Unsurprisingly, given their non-binding nature, CEBS is deprived of formal powers to assure the application of its Level 3 measures. In the case of non-compliant Members, it may merely indicate the inadequacy of the situation and 'invite that Member to endeavour to adapt accordingly its legal or regulatory framework and report on progress, if possible'. This weak statutory power is, to a certain extent, counterbalanced by the peer review mechanism established by CEBS in order to monitor effective compliance with the Level 3 measures. Thus CEBS established an independent and transparent Review Panel, endowed with a clear and objective methodology[29] and a mandate to conduct reviews on the implementation of supervisory provisions laid down in both EU legislation and Level 3 measures, in view of encouraging their timely and consistent day-to-day application and enhancing supervisory convergence.

Furthermore, enforcement of CEBS soft measures is ensured through what has become known as the 'comply or explain' mechanism, introduced through the revised charter. This procedure, which requires that, in case of non-compliance with Level 3 measures, CEBS Members publicly 'state their reasons in full, clarifying in detail the legal, political or technical impediment', impinges on the meaning of the concept of 'legal bindingness'. The same article consecrating non-bindingness enumerates, albeit in vague and broad terms, the cases when non-binding Level 3 measures may be ignored, with due explanation from the non-compliant CEBS Members. Article 5.6 refers to (a) the incompatibility of a Level 3 measure with their national law or lack of competence due to legal impediments;

29 The Protocol and Methodology of the Review Panel were built on CESR's experience, and were published on 15 October 2007. The Protocol sets out the principles of peer review, the role of the Review Panel, the purpose of its work, its tools and working procedures. The methodology sets out guidance and procedures for the completion of both self-assessments and review by peers, the reporting and publication requirements, and the procedures for self-assessments and review updating.

or (b) the case of a Level 3 measure for which they expect vital political or technical impediments to exist; or (c) the situation where the objectives of the measure are met through other means, or where the measures would be disproportionate in the context of the local market. This may be interpreted also *per a contrario*, in the sense that whenever a CEBS Member cannot demonstrate that one of the listed situations is met, the measure will have to be applied. Thus, at least for CEBS Members, Level 3 measures appear to have a semi-binding nature. This can be justified not only in the light of the established peer review mechanism, but also considering that CEBS Members have actually taken part in the adoption of the concerned measures and that, in principle, *pacta sunt servanda*. An analogy with the estoppel concept in international public law might come to mind.

Overall, it appears that the legal effects of CEBS guidelines and standards are not entirely clear and the provisions in the CEBS Charter reflect delicate political compromises. The interpretation of the 'comply or explain' mechanism leads to the following conclusions: (1) CEBS instruments are not legal acts that may be enforced by CEBS through formal control mechanisms; (2) they are not deprived of all legal force, but have to be applied if no plausible explanation falling within predetermined situations can be invoked. Moreover, given the public nature of Level 3 measures and the underpinning consultations with various stakeholders, the latter might request compliance with unanimously agreed guidelines and standards, on the basis of legitimate expectations and legal certainty. This private enforcement of Level 3 measures is not completely unrealistic, given that CEBS itself declared that 'market discipline will play a major role in ensuring their effective application' (CEBS 2005c: 14).

Another key aspect of CEBS' position, which also generates legitimising capital, concerns its special relationship with the Groupe de Contact (GdC), which since its establishment in 1972 has acquired a strong reputation and acceptance as a supranational forum. Such a relationship is not limited to the observer status given to the GdC's Chair, but extends also to the explicit commitment that CEBS 'will rely predominantly on the GdC, which will be its main expert group and which will report to it' (article 5.4 CEBS Charter). Additionally, CEBS will rely on the work of permanent or temporary expert groups that it may establish, with a flexible composition and a clear mandate.

Given that Level 3 measures on the one hand aim to specify further the binding rules laid down at Level 1 and Level 2 and on the other hand touch upon issues that are not addressed (yet) in EU law, CEBS' formally non-binding regulation may have the de facto effect of the 'soft' transferral of regulatory competences to the European level. Such a phenomenon has been acknowledged frequently and was classified in European governance literature as an example of 'competence creep' (Scott and Trubek 2002: 7). The peculiar mechanism enshrined in the CEBS Charter and its establishing decision is intended to contain the consequences of competence creep within the limits of the existing legal framework. Yet such legal artifice seems to have attained its limits and carries the risk of entailing contradictions (e.g. the semi-binding nature of Level 3 measures) that might further limit the legitimacy and efficacy of regulatory efforts towards convergence. Forthcoming reforms of the EU financial architecture should address the issue directly, given the imperative for uniform application of EU law. Level 3 measures should be explicitly declared binding if so needed. Furthermore, precise criteria should be laid down defining the situations when derogation from binding regulatory measures is necessary and the conditions under which this should be permitted. In parallel, the institutional and legal status of CEBS should also be reinforced, so as to guarantee legitimacy, accountability and liability in relation to its actions.

3 The European Central Bank's involvement in prudential regulation

The European regulatory process in the banking field is accompanied by the constant involvement of the ECB through two main channels: the participation of the ECB in the relevant European institutions and policy fora and the mandatory consultation of the ECB pursuant to its formal advisory functions on draft EU and national legislation in its fields of competence. Although it appears a marginal player in devising banking regulation and is detached from the debates on the institutional balance between the more prominent political actors, the ECB's continuous contribution to the regulatory process is essential for various reasons. The main rationale is the objective necessity to ensure compatibility of banking regulation with monetary policy, and to give expression to the competences assigned to the ECB with regard to prudential supervision and financial stability.

The ECB's concrete involvement in the legislative/regulatory process is based on primary EU legislation, which in case of non-observance might trigger consequences for the regulatory outcome. The participation of the ECB in the regulatory process is a consequence of the joint reading of its statutory tasks related to prudential supervision and financial stability and its advisory function.

It is worth mentioning at this point that the ECB is assisted in the performance of its article supervision-related functions by the Banking Supervision Committee (BSC), one of the ESCB committees established for assisting the decision-making bodies of the ECB.[30] The BSC's main tasks relate to prudential supervision; nevertheless, it also has an ancillary contribution to ECB's regulatory powers in this area, particularly as regards to the devise of policy strategies to be reflected in ECB opinions.[31]

30 See art. 9 of the ECB's Rules of Procedure – Decision ECB/2004/2 and art. 8 of the Rules of Procedure of the Governing Council of the ECB – Decision ECB/2004/12.

31 It was held that the ESCB committees 'play *grosso modo* a role similar to that of the COREPER and its groups in preparing decisions for the EU Council' (Louis 2004: 588).

3.1 ECB's advisory functions

It is not our aim to provide a detailed analysis of the legal framework applicable to the general consultative function of the ECB in its fields of competence,[32] but instead to highlight the aspects that define the ECB's advisory contribution to the European regulatory process in the field of prudential regulation. Our inquiry will be particularly oriented towards the clarification of the incidence of the multiple legal basis of the ECB's consultative function regarding prudential regulation, the determination of the scope *ratione materiae* of such advisory competence and, last but not least, the identification of the legal consequences in case of non-observance of the consultative function of the ECB.

The ECB's general consultative function on draft EU acts and national draft legislation has as its legal basis article 127(4) TFEU (ex 105(4) EC Treaty) and article 4 ESCB Statute, which require that the ECB be consulted 'in its fields of competence'. The plural term used and the absence of further specification indicate that all ECB tasks, irrespective of whether they are basic or not, are included in the scope of its advisory role. Hence, the provision may be interpreted as also referring to issues related to prudential supervision of credit institutions and financial stability, which, although not being basic tasks of the ESCB, fall under the category of other ESCB tasks provided in article 127(5) TFEU (ex article 105(5) EC Treaty).[33] Thus the Treaty wording may be seen as sufficiently broad to facilitate ECB advice whenever an EU act is somehow impinging on financial stability issues (understood in a wide sense) and to compel the European institutions to consult the ECB every time prudential regulation is at stake.

Conversely, the consultative role of the ECB with regard to national draft legislation appears more restricted, as it is circumscribed by the limits and conditions set out by the Council pursuant to article 127(4), second indent TFEU (ex 105(4) EC Treaty). These explicitly refer to 'rules applicable to financial institutions insofar as they materially influence the stability of financial institutions and markets'. Such a specification – the material influence condition – can be interpreted as a filter for avoiding double consultation of the ECB on national legislation implementing EU measures that have already been the object of ECB advice. Altogether, the corroboration of paragraphs (4) and (5) of article 127 TFEU (ex 105 EC

32 On in-depth legal analysis of the ECB's advisory tasks, we recommend Smits 1997; Arda 2004.

33 With regard to the duality of ESCB–ECB, we recall that in accordance with article 9.2 of the ESCB Statute it is for the ECB to ensure that the tasks conferred upon the ESCB under article 127(2), (3) and (5) TFEU (ex 105 EC) are implemented either through the ECB's own activities or through the NCB's. Also article 129 TFEU (ex 107 EC Treaty) indicates that the ECB and the ESCB are not separate entities but are structurally and functionally interwoven. Consequently, it has no relevance that the advisory function refers to ECB's tasks, whereas prudential supervision has been assigned to the ESCB.

Treaty) and articles 3 and 4 of the ESCB Statute seem *prima facie* to provide sufficient legal basis for the contribution of the ECB's technical expertise to the design and definition of financial rules and supervisory requirements, including prudential aspects.

Nevertheless, there is another special advisory function of the ECB laid down in article 25.1 ESCB Statute, which seems to question the scope of the general consultative powers mentioned above. According to article 25.1:

> the ECB may offer advice to and be consulted by the Council, the Commission and the competent authorities of the Member States on the scope and implementation of Union legislation relating to the prudential supervision of credit institutions and to the stability of the financial system.

It might appear that article 25.1 constitutes *lex specialis* governing consultation of the ECB in the field of prudential supervision, and thereby excluding the application of the general provision on advisory powers within the specified field. Although at first sight attractive, such an interpretation would suppose that the special provision has the features of the general provision – along with some supplementary specification. That is not the case for article 25.1, which seems to have a different although related scope. First, we observe that it regulates non-mandatory ECB consultation, as compared to the mandatory advisory role of the ECB imposed by article 4 of the ESCB Statute. Also, the general advisory task is intended to insert the ECB – as an independent actor – into the EU and national law-making procedures, so as to ensure consistency of legislation with the policies unfolded by the ECB according to its statutory competences. On the contrary, the scope of ECB's advice in accordance with article 25.1 is not limited to its statutory tasks and does not aim to align EU or national legislation to ECB tasks, but gives the ECB the possibility of providing expert advice on broader matters of prudential banking supervision and financial stability that go beyond reviewing an existing or envisaged text in terms of compatibility with its own tasks. For instance, it could allow the ECB to issue warnings and recommendations related to macro-developments. It constitutes an opportunity for using synergies between central banking and supervision. Such an interpretation may also explain why it was possible for the general advisory function not to be applicable to the United Kingdom, whereas the specific provision in article 25.1 applies to all Member States, even those with a derogation.

Another specificity of article 25.1 needs to be underlined – namely, its incidence only in case of 'Union legislation', and not the broader 'Union acts', as is the case of ECB's general advisory functions under article 127(4) TFEU (ex 105(4) EC). While Union legislation was not specifically defined under the EC Treaty, the Lisbon Treaty differentiates between legislative and non-legislative acts in articles 288–91 TFEU. A narrow understanding of 'Union legislation' might exclude the latter and thus leave delegated acts (article 290 TFEU) and implementing acts (article 291 TFEU) – the vehicles for Level 2 measures and eventually of binding technical standards – outside the scope of ECB's consultative role under article 25.1 ESCB Statute. Also, it would exclude ECB's advice on non-binding regulatory measures adopted by the Level 3 committees. Consequently, on the basis of article 25.1, ECB would seem to have only a specific competence to express its views on implementation aspects of prudential regulation within the process of adoption of Level 1 framework legislation. Under this narrow interpretation of 'Union legislation', it would seem that the specific advisory function on EU legislation under article 25.1 is more restricted than the general advisory role. Article 25.1 proves useful only when a specific act would not fall under the broad interpretation of the ECB's role with regard to prudential supervision and financial stability, and thus would not be covered by the general advisory function.

Furthermore, article 25.1 has a supplementary role with regard to national legislation. It may be seen as a substitutive solution when mandatory consultation is explicitly barred, as is the case of draft national legislation, whose exclusive purpose is the transposition of EU directives into the law of Member States (article 1(2) of the Council Decision 98/415/EC). This would indicate a specific and autonomous task of the ECB, aimed at promoting synergies between central banking expertise and supervisory functions, and thus underpinning ECB's policy-making role in this area.

Consequently, we may assert that the two legal bases for ECB's advice are not mutually exclusive, but rather complement each other by providing two consultative modes of a different nature. In practice, it may be observed that the ECB chooses article 127(4) TFEU (ex 105(4) EC) as the legal basis for its opinions on EU or national legislation regarding financial stability. To our knowledge, there is no ECB advice that explicitly refers to article 25.1 as its legal basis. The probability that the ECB will be denied the mandatory advisory capacity in the area of banking prudential supervision and financial stability is merely theoretical, as all political institutions involved in financial regulation are eager to preserve good relations with the ECB and to give more legitimacy to EU acts by having the expert support of the ECB. Preference for the general advisory role for the ECB should nevertheless not overshadow the consultative role under article 25.1, which allows the ECB to play a proactive role in the reform of prudential regulation and supervision, including persuading the Commission to put forward initiatives relating to financial stability.

As to the consequences of the ECB's advisory functions, the ECB's opinion is not binding, whether issued at the initiative of the ECB or at the request of an EU institution or national authority, and irrespective of whether adopted under article 127(5) TFEU (ex 105(4) EC Treaty) or under article 25.1 ESCB Statute. Nevertheless, while the advisory function under article 25.1 is a purely voluntary one and might generate, at most, dissatisfaction with passive attitudes, failure to consult the ECB under the general advisory function will impinge upon the legality of the adopted acts. The consequences of the failure to consult have to be distinguished in the case of Union acts, where the ECB has become an integral part of the EU legislative process through primary law, and in the case of national legislation, which involves infringement of secondary EU law (the Council decision). Such consequences have also to be seen in light of the OLAF judgment, where the ECJ held that consultation on EU acts:

> is intended ... essentially to ensure that the legislature adopts the act only when the body has been heard, which by virtue of the specific functions that it exercises in the Community framework in the area concerned and by virtue of the high degree of expertise that it enjoys, is particularly well placed to play a useful role in the legislative process envisaged.[34]

On the consequences of non-compliance with the ECB consultation requirement there is an elaborate legal literature (Smits 1997; Arda 2004; Zilioli and Selmayr 2006). Here, we confine ourselves to mentioning some generic aspects. Failure to consult the ECB on EU acts may be challenged by the ECB, in protecting its prerogatives, on the basis of article 263 third paragraph TFEU (ex 230(3) EC Treaty) and on the grounds that it constitutes the infringement of an essential procedural requirement. This challenge might eventually lead the ECJ to invalidate the respective act. Although the interpretation of the attribute 'essential' is capable of unleashing debates about the substantive and procedural importance of ECB's advice with regard to financial stability issues, we think that any discussion in that sense is purely theoretical. Considering the above-quoted passage from the OLAF judgment, ECB's procedural consultative rights are crucial for the protection of all its statutory prerogatives. Prudential supervision and financial stability do not constitute an exception and in the light of the crisis need reinforced attention. The fact that the operational powers of the ECB/ESCB regarding this statutory task are not clearly delineated does not raise doubts as to the fact that the ECB is bound to play a certain role in this area and that its expertise is particularly useful to the regulatory/legislative process. Hence, it does not seem plausible to deny the 'essential' character of the requirement to consult the ECB on issues concerning banking supervision and financial stability.

As regards failure to consult the ECB on national draft legislation, enforcement could be obtained in accordance with articles 258 and 259

34 Judgment in Case C-11/00 *Commission* v. *ECB* (OLAF case), para. 110. The ECJ did not directly address the issue of failure to comply with the ECB consultation requirement, as the area covered by the OLAF Regulation did not fall under the ECB's specific tasks.

TFEU,[35] via the Commission or the Member States, whereby infringement of the Council Decision 98/415/EC on the consultation of the European Central Bank by national authorities regarding draft legislative provisions would amount to a Member State's 'failure to fulfil an obligation under the EC Treaty'.[36] Still, according to article 260 TFEU (ex 228 EC Treaty), the ECJ is limited to finding whether the Member State has failed to consult and to request it to take the necessary measures. It is left to national legal systems to determine the consequences and remedies to be attached to the breach of such substantive procedural requirement. Thus, only a case-by-case approach analysing the relevant legislative and regulatory framework can indicate the consequences of the failure to consult the ECB on national legislation.[37]

3.2 Participation of the ECB in regulatory bodies

ECB's involvement in the regulatory process occurs also through its participation in the relevant European bodies. We have already observed that the ECB takes part in the work of both international and European regulatory bodies, where it is granted, as a rule, observer status[38] without voting or veto rights. Such participation represents a formal recognition of the role of the ECB in the area of financial stability/banking supervision. Participatory rights are crucial, especially when the output of the work of the regulatory bodies takes the form of soft law (the case of the Basel Committee, or the regulatory measures adopted by CEBS).

The ECB has given its support to the implementation of the Lamfalussy framework in the financial services sector.[39] Thereby, it has accepted the position assigned to it within the four-level mechanisms, which involves it in the work of the committees constituted at both Level 2 and Level 3. Thus, the ECB was given observer status within the European Banking Committee (EBC) and non-voting membership status in CEBS. There was, from the very beginning, a major interest in closely associating the ECB

35 Under the EC Treaty these were arts 226 and 227 TFEU.

36 The ECB cannot directly challenge the legality of national measures, except when responsibility could be attributed to the national central bank (NCB). Only in such cases could the ECB initiate infringement proceedings, on the basis of art. 271(d) TFEU (ex 237(d) EC Treaty) and art. 35.6 ESCB Statute, against the NCB for the failure to fulfil an obligation under the Statute.

37 It has been held that the efficiency of ECB's advisory function with regard to national legislation is largely dependent on the prior dialogue between the national authorities and the ECB, particularly as regards the interpretation of the scope of the Council decision; see Kerjean 2005: 6.

38 The exception is CEBS, where the ECB is considered a non-voting member.

39 See ECB's Opinion of 20 February 2004 on a new financial services committee organisational structure; ECB's contribution to the review of the application of the Lamfalussy framework to EU securities market legislation of 17 February 2005; Eurosystem's contribution to the review of the Lamfalussy framework of 30 November 2007.

and all national central banks without direct supervisory functions in the banking sector to the work of CEBS, so as to benefit from the synergies between banking supervision and central banking.

The issue arises as to how its observer status in the EBC and its non-voting CEBS-Member position impinge upon its consultative function. When participating in the debates of the EBC and of CEBS, the ECB is getting involved in the preparatory works leading to the Commission proposal of Level 1 legislation, and to the adoption by the Commission of Level 2 measures. The involvement at an early stage of the ECB in the drafting of EU acts might raise the question of whether it replaces the formal consultation requirement pursuant to article 127(4) TFEU (ex 105(4) EC Treaty). We maintain that the two participatory modes of the ECB in the regulatory process are and remain distinct, with neither being capable of substituting the other, as each pursues different objectives.

In the framework of Level 1 measures, the advisory competence of the ECB has the function of providing an expert input with regard to draft measures at the late stage of the legislative process, during the phase of consultation with other relevant institutions (e.g. the Committee of the Regions, the Economic and Social Committee). According to the legislative procedure, such advice is usually requested by the Council. It enforces the ECB's independent position in the institutional architecture. On the contrary, ECB's participation in the preparatory work allows it to become more deeply involved at an early stage, so as to ensure timely building of a coherent approach acceptable to all policy-makers. Moreover, participation in the EBC and the CEBS occurs through specific directorates or committees that are merely empowered to contribute to the policy discussions on financial stability or banking supervision, whereas the opinion delivered pursuant to article 127(4) TFEU (ex 105(4) EC) is adopted by the Governing Council, according to the ECB's decision-making procedure, and constitutes the official position assumed by the ECB.

In relation to Level 2 legislation (i.e. implementing measures adopted by the Commission), the ECB has constantly asserted its right to be consulted pursuant to article 127(4) TFEU (ex 105(4) EC). It is, however, less clear – when compared to the normal legislative process – at which stage such consultation may intervene. The observer status of the ECB within the EBC appears to provide a suitable occasion for the assertion of the ECB's opinion. Nevertheless, limiting the advice of the ECB to the ambit of the EBC risks diverting from the role of the ECB's general consultative function, aimed at contributing its expertise to all actors implied in the decision-making process. A solution would be that the ECB's advice be requested by the Commission on the draft comitology proposal, before it is sent to the EBC.

In light of the above remarks we claim that the involvement of the ECB in the Lamfalussy committees cannot justify, for either Level 1 legislation or Level 2 measures, the departure from the mandatory requirement to consult the ECB on draft EU acts falling within its fields of competence.

3.3 A latent autonomous regulatory function for the ECB

Last but not least, we have to take into consideration that the ECB has been attributed its own regulatory powers, which enables it to fulfil its mandate autonomously.[40] Thus, according to article 132(1) TFEU (ex 110(1) EC Treaty) and article 34.1 ESCB Statute, the ECB may adopt legal acts (ECB regulations and ECB decisions) that are binding in their entirety and are directly applicable to their addressees. Furthermore, the ECB may adopt guidelines of general applicability in the performance of its tasks (article 12.1 ESCB Statute), as well as guidelines and instructions for the NCBs (article 14.3 ESCB Statute). The regulatory powers of the ECB are, nevertheless, not to be seen as a *carte blanche* allowing for the unlimited exercise of powers in its fields of competence. Instead, they are circumscribed by the very provisions that confer them to the ECB, as well as by other basic principles of EU law. Particularly, the adoption of binding legal acts by the ECB is conditioned by the requirement of necessity (ECB regulations need to be necessary for the implementation of defined tasks, and ECB decisions have to be necessary for carrying out the tasks entrusted to the ESCB under the Treaty). This implies that the ECB, when pursuing its regulatory function, has also to observe the principles of proportionality and of subsidiarity (article 5(3) consolidated TEU, ex 5 EC Treaty).

Furthermore, the adoption of ECB regulations is confined to the cases enumerated in the first indent of article 132(1) TFEU (ex 110(1) EC Treaty)[41] and is possible only to the extent necessary to implement the tasks described therein. The ESCB's role regarding prudential supervision and financial stability issues, laid down in article 3.3, is not listed. Nevertheless, this does not definitively remove ECB regulations from the instruments to which the ECB may make recourse in order to contribute to prudential regulation, as article 132(1) TFEU (ex 110(1) EC Treaty) mentions the so-called 'enabling clause' in article 25.2 of the Statute.[42] This clause envisages the possibility that the ECB performs 'specific tasks concerning policies relating to the prudential supervision of credit institutions and other financial institutions with the exception of insurance undertakings'. Such specific tasks can be attributed to it through a Council decision pursuant to article 127(6) TFEU (ex 105(6) EC), which prescribes a fast-track adoption procedure. The explicitly attributed tasks could eventually endow the ECB with the power to issue legal acts in the field of prudential supervision. This would constitute a

40 For details on the ECB's regulatory powers, see Louis 1998, 2004; Zilioli and Selmayr 2001; Malatesta 2003.

41 Article 132(1) TFEU (ex 110(1) EC Treaty) refers to 'the tasks defined in art. 3.1 first indent, arts 19.1, 22 and 25.2 of the Statute of the ESCB and in cases which shall be laid down in the acts of the Council referred to in art. 129(4) ex 107(6)'.

42 The enabling clause in art. 25.2 ESCB Statute allows the ECB to eventually perform specific tasks concerning policies relating to the prudential supervision of credit institutions and other financial institutions with the exception of insurance undertakings.

specification of the generic role of the ESCB foreseen in article 127(5) TFEU (ex 105(5) EC Treaty). Tasks conferred pursuant to the enabling clause may be shared or supportive of national supervisory competences or even exclusive ECB competences, preventing national authorities from undertaking activities conflicting with ECB's powers.

Thus, the ECB's regulatory powers for prudential banking supervision could be deemed as being already enshrined in article 132(1) TFEU (ex 110(1) EC), first indent EC Treaty and article 34.1 ESCB Statute. It is only the exercise of such powers that is still conditioned by the adoption of the Council Decision referred to in article 25.2, which should define such ECB tasks and clarify their precise scope. What is needed is that the ECB be formally entrusted with precise responsibilities according to a simplified legislative procedure, which has some important limits nevertheless. First, it could be enacted only with respect to competences related to the prudential supervision of banks and financial institutions, and not in the wider context of financial stability. Furthermore, the procedure prescribed by article 127(6) TFEU (ex 105(6) EC Treaty) requires unanimous agreement in the Council, which should act on a proposal from the Commission after consulting the ECB and the European Parliament.[43] The unanimity requirement renders the transfer of specific tasks to the ECB particularly difficult, as it requires the agreement of all Member States, including those not participating in EMU (because of an opt-out or a derogation), which may be even less inclined to reinforce the position of the independent ECB. Another limit stems from the fact that the regulatory jurisdiction of the ECB in the area of prudential supervision would be confined to the Member States having adopted the single currency. This can be inferred from article 43.1 of the ESCB Statute, which provides that article 34 cannot confer rights or impose any obligations on the Member States with a derogation.[44] Accordingly, the transformation of the ECB into a body competent for adopting prudential regulation at the EU-wide level would still require a Treaty amendment through the normal procedure.

There is also the possibility for the ECB to exercise regulatory powers by adopting decisions that are necessary for carrying out its tasks, including those conferred through article 127(5) TFEU (ex 105(5) ESCB Statute). The decision is an ECB legal act binding, in its entirety, upon those to whom it is addressed. Decisions may also be collective acts intended for a plurality of addressees. Hence, it might be envisaged that ECB decisions (like ECB regulations in case of article 25.2) be addressed to national authorities entrusted with supervisory powers, but also to banks and financial institutions. ECB decisions, like ECB regulations, are also

43 Under art. 105(6) EC Treaty the procedure required the assent requirement of the Parliament. Under the Lisbon Treaty the assent requirement was replaced by a simple consultation requirement.

44 Also, the general task assigned to the ESCB with regard to financial stability is not applicable to non-participating Member States.

constrained by jurisdictional limitations, i.e. they are applicable only to the Member States that have adopted the euro.

Last but not least, one of the favourite legal instruments of the ECB is the guideline, which is adopted in the performance of the ECB's tasks. The ECB's Rules of Procedure explicitly list ECB guidelines immediately after regulations, as one of the ECB's legal instruments (Art. 17.2 Decision ECB/1999/7 concerning the Rules of Procedure of the Executive Board). De facto, guidelines are of general application and are compulsory. As consistently mentioned in the preambles to the ECB guidelines 'in accordance with Articles 12.1 and 14.3 of the Statute, ECB guidelines form an integral part of EU law'. Yet they are not backed by a formalised detailed framework. Thus, they eventually may be seen as ECB legal instruments transcending the specific limits constraining the scope and application of ECB regulations and decisions. Hence, guidelines may appear as a vehicle suitable for the exercise of ECB's regulatory tasks with regard to prudential supervision.

So far, the ECB has not exercised its regulatory powers in the areas of prudential supervision and financial stability, but demonstrated a preference for opinions in order to make public its views in these fields. However, *de lege lata*, the ECB might be envisaged as also exercising regulatory functions when carrying out the ESCB's task of 'contributing to the smooth conduct of policies pursued by the competent authorities of the Member States participating in the EMU relating to the prudential supervision of credit institutions and the stability of the financial system' (article 127(5) TFEU, ex 105(5) EC Treaty). Recourse to the enabling clause conferring specific tasks upon the ECB in the field of prudential banking supervision would open up the possibility that the ECB directly adopts applicable and entirely binding regulations or decisions. Nevertheless, the mentioned ECB prudential regulations and decisions would have effect only in the Member States of the EMU, whereas transferral of European-wide regulatory competences to the ECB would require a Treaty amendment.

Altogether, we could interpret the broad and ambiguous wording of the Treaty provisions conferring prudential tasks to the ESCB as also entailing a regulatory component. This can be exercised either through binding legal instruments with limited effects (regulations, decisions or guidelines) or by means of soft-law devices (e.g. opinions, recommendations, atypical decisions). The latter could be issued at the initiative of the ECB pursuant to the general advisory tasks provided by article 4 ESCB Statute, as well as in the exercise of the specific advisory powers enshrined in article 25.1 of the Statute.

4 The role of private parties in the regulatory process

The account of the participants to the regulatory process leading to European prudential regulation would be incomplete without reference to the devices that allow input from private parties. These consist primarily of consultation mechanisms accompanied by an enhanced emphasis on transparency from the part of the public actors involved in the regulatory process. Such mechanisms mirror the more general trends in European governance that promote better involvement of all stakeholders in the decision-making process, as well as the establishment of platforms for information, feedback and debate so as to achieve a 'reinforced culture of consultation and dialogue' (Commission 1999: 16). The Lamfalussy framework has further reinforced this trend by requiring the Level 3 committees to ensure the private sector's early and institutionalised involvement in the regulatory process (Committee of Wise Men 2001: 48). Thus, according to article 12 of the decision establishing CEBS, the latter shall, before transmitting its opinion to the Commission, at an early stage extensively consult (in an open and transparent manner) with market participants, consumers and end-users. CEBS is accordingly one of the main contact points between private stakeholders and public regulators, and in pursuing its role it has adopted the Public Statement of Consultation Practices. Furthermore, as already indicated, CEBS has established a Consultative Panel of representatives of market participants and end-users to assist in the performance of CEBS' functions and to ensure that the consultation process functions effectively. The role of the Panel is laid down in an own charter. The Panel acts also as a 'sounding board' for CEBS in strategic issues. Composed of a limited number of independent high-profile professionals committed to the objectives of the European Union and appointed on a personal basis, the Panel is intended to deliver expert advice, not to represent sectoral or national interests.

The role of public consultation mechanisms is twofold: on the one hand they contribute to the improvement of the quality of financial regulation, while on the other hand they are deemed to enhance the legitimacy and accountability of the regulatory process (Ferran 2004: 92). Yet such consultation mechanisms involve costly resources and high expertise, which makes us doubt their legitimacy- and accountability-enhancing potential. In practice they only manage to involve industry representatives effectively in the decision-making process, while consumers and end-users do not have the necessary resources to provide their input. This notwithstanding, consultative processes have undeniable merits in enhancing openness and transparency and thus in providing a better understanding of the regulatory outcome to all stakeholders. They also incontestably contribute to an organic development of regulation which takes market trends into account.

Another aspect of private party involvement in the regulatory process is through self-regulation by industry. The boundaries between self-regulation[45] and public (statutory) regulation become ever more blurred, particularly in the financial sector, which has a long tradition of

45 Self-regulation is understood here not as pure self-regulation, but as regulation by private parties with some public label attached. On the concept of self-regulation, see Cafaggi 2001, 2005.

self-regulation. Such enmeshment of public and private domains is due to the dynamics of the financial sector, which triggered the need for creating genuine mechanisms to enable the regulatory recognition of private standards. This is particularly the case in the area of prudential supervision, where the change in the nature of the supervisory approach and the rapid pace of financial innovation required regulators to be constantly on guard, supposing a close collaboration with market players. We will discuss these aspects in more detail, with a specific focus on the private actors involved, in the next chapter.

Last but not least, self-regulation could also be seen as a particularly useful tool for achieving convergence when implementing EU legislation. This potential of private rule-making was explicitly recognised in various policy documents.[46] Thus it could be envisaged that, through self-regulation, the industry explicitly endorses the non-binding rules elaborated by CEBS or proposes its own standards (e.g. the 2008 industry initiative on Pillar 3 disclosure requirements for securitisation). Also, industry could take the initiative and fill in the regulatory gaps not covered by the work of European or international regulatory bodies.

46 For instance, the Commission's Expert Group on Banking recommended recourse to self-regulation, considering that it could bring added value in areas that are not already subject to extensive and detailed regulation; Commission 2004b: 11.

9 The European institutional framework for prudential banking supervision

Prudential supervision is complementary and indispensable to the effectiveness of prudential regulation. Nevertheless, it is much more than mere monitoring and enforcement of compliance with prudential rules.[1] In the pursuit of the general objectives of protecting depositors and maintaining financial market stability, supervision endeavours to induce credit institutions to behave prudently. It is an intrinsically complex task, whose fulfilment requires the institutions entrusted with it to consider a broad range of qualitative and quantitative information by reference to clear objectives targeting individual institutions and broader market developments, so as to produce accurate risk assessments and choose the appropriate actions. Undeniably, supervision involves a large amount of discretion linked to a traditional preference in the banking sector to rely more on subtle (soft) tools of persuasion (e.g. moral suasion) than on formal law.

The driving forces behind the design of institutional supervisory structures are prominently political and depend largely on the national legal systems. Consequently, very diverse institutional structures for banking supervision have been developed at the national level. In the abstract, there is no evidence that a particular supervisory structure is preferable to another, nor are the advantages of the different institutional models very clear-cut (Schoenmaker and Goodhart 1993; Marotta 2003).

European legislation broadly refers to the 'competent authorities' that are defined in article 4 point 4 CRD as 'the national authorities, which are empowered, by law or regulation, to supervise credit institutions'. Such a broad definition merely requires that Member States specifically designate an authority as the banking supervisor, and leaves it up to the national legal system to choose the form, powers and procedures applicable to this authority. The current analysis will not enter into a comparative study of the various institutional models – a fascinating burgeoning topic – but focuses on the European dimension that, in our view, can be increasingly perceived in the design of national supervisory structures.

1 It has been held that 'Regulation can be seen as reinforcing supervision, and supervision can be seen as correcting for the failures of regulation' (Ward 2002: 14).

Furthermore, we note that the home-country control principle – the foundation of the organisation of banking supervision on a European scale – is accompanied (from the very first banking directives and increasingly so since the CRD and the Lamfalussy framework) by the long-marginalised supervisory cooperation principle. Empirical evidences from financial crises and normative proposals highlight that supervisory cooperation is becoming central to efforts for maintaining financial stability in an integrated market. Hence, we will review the role and responsibilities of the various European structures implicated in coordinating banking supervision and indicate the instruments developed for sustaining cooperation between the various responsible authorities. Lastly, in view of the fact that banking supervision is a multi-layered activity, we will also examine the part played by private parties pursuant to several provisions in the CRD.

1 National supervisory authorities

Despite largely centralised regulatory arrangements in the EU, it is undisputed that the main actors responsible for prudential supervision are the national competent authorities. These authorities are established by Member States' laws in forms that are considered to better fit national political interests. European law does not require a particular institutional structure; hence, there is a great diversity of supervisors across Member States: separate agencies for each financial sector, separate functional agencies (micro-prudential, macro-prudential, conduct-of-business), combined supervisors (banking and securities, banking and insurance, securities and insurance) and single financial supervisory authorities (within the central bank or outside the central bank).

During the past decade many countries have undergone reforms aiming at restructuring their financial supervision framework, with an apparent trend towards the creation of integrated supervisory authorities. The outcome of such restructuring has been broadly characterised as incorporating three features: a broader consolidation of supervisory structures leading to a decrease in the number of supervisory authorities; a consistent involvement of central banks in banking supervision; and reinforced formalised cooperation arrangements (EBC 2003b). Without entering into the comparative analysis of the various organisational developments in the Member States,[2] we confine ourselves to observing that no common model has emerged and that the variety of institutional structures still remains broad.

The issue arises as to what extent such diversity is sustainable in a financial market which has the ambition of becoming increasingly integrated.

2 For an analysis of the national institutional structures for prudential supervision and the recent trends, we refer to Louis 1995; Llewellyn 1999c; Mwenda and Fleming 2001: 12–13; ECB 2003b; Nieto and Peñalosa 2004.

Banking integration is partly conditioned by the supervisory framework, and, conversely, the institutional design and scope of banking supervision in Europe has to take account of the advancing degree of market integration.[3] While institutional uniformity would not be desirable, not even in the case of a completed common market, the current degree of integration and the growing share of cross-border banking activities would justify the harmonisation of some features of national competent authorities. Considering this, we find that some provisions in the CRD can be interpreted as impinging upon the power of Member States to define the legal and procedural framework applicable to national competent authorities. Thereby, a European component is becoming ever more visible in national supervisory structures. Its acknowledgement is essential for understanding the supervisory developments in Europe, as forthcoming institutional reforms may be built on it to ensure continuity.

Before identifying the extent to which current European legislation influences certain features of national authorities, let us briefly point to the reasons for European intervention in supervision. Domestic prudential policies are increasingly penetrated by fairly detailed and articulated European regulation. The post-FSAP emphasis on effective implementation and enforcement of European legislation as well as on convergence of supervisory practices (Commission 2005a; Lannoo and Casey 2005) highlights concerns as to the effective consistent application of EU legislation in the Member States. Moreover, the reinforced role for the supervisory authorities under the CRD (the supervisory review pillar) and the sophistication of the supervisory approach will require that even more common rules be produced during the process of supervision and application of EU laws. Member States should have administrative infrastructures in place that, on the one hand, provide sufficient support for rendering enforcement of the new supervisory approach credible and, on the other hand, ensure that no reversion is possible to protectionist national supervisory policies entailing further fragmentation. This is a difficult task in the area of banking supervision, where the competent authorities need considerable space for discretion when making judgements in accordance with quantitative and qualitative prudential rules and standards. As the diversity of institutional supervisory structures prompts fears of distorted implementation of EU prudential norms, the European legislature has envisaged certain safeguards to guarantee the convergence of supervisory approaches, and hence some powers and procedures should be common to all national competent authorities. Such provisions constitute minimum harmonisation of the supervisory infrastructure and contribute to creating a basic level playing-field among the different supervisory authorities.

3 See Alexander 2002a: 7; he argues that the degree of integration is one of the main criteria to be considered when envisaging the centralisation of supervisory functions at European level.

Furthermore, the need to define some common institutional and organisational conditions is entailed by the Lamfalussy regulatory framework, whose third level relies overwhelmingly on the substantial participation of national supervisory authorities. Although no specific prerequisites are explicitly required from the competent authorities which are CEBS Members, we are of the opinion that the important role ascribed to CEBS, if it is to function effectively, will gradually and implicitly contribute to the convergence of the powers entrusted to national banking supervisors. Legal certainty, with regard to the third level of the Lamfalussy process, can only be ensured by endowing the supervisors of Member States with equivalent degrees of authority (in their respective jurisdictions) to implement measures agreed in the ambit of CEBS. The necessity of equivalent legal powers of national authorities, sufficiently similar but not necessarily identical, has also been highlighted by the IIMG in its reviews of the Lamfalussy framework (IIMG 2003b: 33).

1.1 Member States' autonomy

In front of the alleged increased European dimension of supervision, the issue arises as to whether EU law constraints on national supervisory authorities would infringe an alleged claim to 'organisational autonomy' of the Member States. The diversity in national banking supervisory structures of Member States can be attributed to the freedom of Member States to organise their own administrative infrastructure, which entails two components: institutional and procedural autonomy.[4] The issue is part of a broader discourse, developed by European administrative lawyers in connection with the enforcement of European law by national authorities.

Given the limited resources of the EU institutions, it is primarily the task of Member States to implement European policies. When fulfilling such a task, Member States enjoy structural autonomy of organisation and procedure that has been explicitly acknowledged on various occasions.[5] Member States' autonomy has been defined as being not a 'synonym for sovereignty, but the basis for the national legal orders' ability to define and produce legal norms the Union does not provide and which comply with the purposes of the administrative system of which EU policies form part' (Kadelbach 2002: 170). Thus, in principle, EU law does not interfere

4 Institutional autonomy allows Member States to choose the organisational model they deem most appropriate, whereas procedural autonomy refers to the procedural rules employed.

5 For instance, at the European Council of Edinburgh in 1992 it was asserted that the Member States should be left as much independence as is compatible with the object and purpose of the Treaties and the safeguarding of Community policies and that the institutional structure and the administrative law of the Member States were to be respected.

with the internal organisation of the Member States, but instead takes value from the plurality and diversity of legal cultures and institutional set-ups. Nevertheless, it has been observed that as integration intensified, various European policies required Member States to establish a particular organisational structure for their implementation.[6] Such intrusions into the organisational autonomy of the Member States are motivated either by a specific necessity for containing disparities during the implementation of EU law by Member States, or by the fact that European law provides for a choice of law rule attributing the final decision on a certain matter to one Member State and thereby waiving other Member States' jurisdiction.

In the case of the banking directives, the limitation of national organisational autonomy can be justified by the existence of the home-country control principle, which gives cross-border supervisory responsibilities for branches and provision of services to the supervisory authority granting the banking authorisation. This involves operational or decision-making powers of home banking supervisors being exercised beyond their national jurisdictions, while the supervisory responsibility of the host State's authorities is partly waived.

Yet it should be understood that, as long as European law is implemented through the Member States and not by European institutions themselves, the general rule is that Member States will act autonomously in organising the framework for implementation. Interference of European law into that organisational autonomy will be either punctual or indirect. Given the specific nature of prudential supervision, whose implementation goes beyond mere enforcement of European prudential rules by involving a complex process that combines 'autonomous risk-based auditing, management consultancy and credit analysis' (Ward 2002: 10), banking supervisors will have a dual character. On the one hand, they will be the 'competent authorities' implementing the European prudential rules and as such the direct addressees of EU legislation. On the other hand, they will act as supervisory institutions integrated in their respective national administrative hierarchies. In order to avoid conflicts that might arise out of such *dédoublement fonctionnel*, there is a need to protect the 'European' component of supervisory tasks. Therefore, the autonomy of Member States should not be taken in absolute terms, but understood as a presumption that can be restricted if that is in the public interest of the EU. Such public interest is not immutable but develops along with progress in integration – hence the need for accepting a certain, eventually increasing, degree of 'Europeanisation' of supervisory structures.

6 Kadelbach enumerates some of the instances where Community law imposed a specific organisational set-up on the Member States: administration of Community funds, the provisions on public enterprises, etc.

1.2 The Europeanisation of national banking supervisory structures

There are three ways, in our view, by which European law restricts the autonomy of Member States in devising their national supervisory infrastructures. The first is directly provided by the banking directives, while the other two are more implicit.

The banking directives preceding the CRD already contained several provisions directly influencing the powers of national supervisory authorities. The purpose of those directives was mainly to harmonise minimum prudential standards necessary for opening up national markets. This entailed also setting several generic powers for competent authorities (e.g. on-the-spot verification of branches established in another Member State, power of sanction). The relevant provisions were addressed to the Member States, which were obliged to accommodate such powers in their supervisory structures.

Contrary to its predecessors, the CRD goes beyond the promotion of the Treaty freedoms in the field of banking, and aims to refine and streamline the prudential framework by introducing in the Member States the new process-oriented supervisory approach. The CRD aims especially to ensure that the complex capital requirements under Pillar 1 of the Basel II Accord are applied in the same way in all Member States so as to avoid distortions or the creation of new obstacles to the free movement. Also, it seeks to transpose into European law the second pillar of Basel II – the supervisory review process, which, while highlighting the crucial role of national competent authorities, also constrains their operation. Chapter 4, Section 1 (articles 124–43) CRD allocates new powers to the competent authorities[7] and introduces procedural aspects in relation to such powers.[8] Contrary to its predecessors, the CRD refers directly to the competent authorities and only exceptionally to the Member States as addressees. This aspect may be interpreted in the sense that the relevant competences are conferred directly by the directive to the national supervisory authorities, which should exercise them even in the absence of national implementing legislation.

A second, indirect stance of Europeanisation of competent authorities comes from Directive 2004/39/EC on Markets in Financial Instruments (MiFID), whose scope also extends to credit institutions authorised under the CRD when providing one or more investment services and/or performing investment activities. MiFID contains detailed provisions on the designation, powers and redress procedures of national competent authorities (Title

7 See art. 124 CRD, which refers to Annex XI as the technical criterion against which to measure the competent authorities' powers to review the arrangements, strategies, processes and mechanisms implemented by banks and to evaluate risks to which banks are exposed. Also, art. 136 CRD enumerates the minimum measures that should be available to the competent authorities in case a bank does not meet the requirements set out in the directive.

8 Art. 124 refers to the frequency and intensity of the review by competent authorities. Art. 131 requests written coordination and cooperation arrangements between the consolidated supervisor and other competent authorities.

IV, articles 48–63). Article 50 MiFID includes the general request that competent authorities shall be given all supervisory and investigatory powers necessary for exercising their functions within the limits of their national legal framework, and a comprehensive list of the minimum aspects included in such powers. The list comprises a series of precise procedural rights, most of which are not mirrored in the CRD. Furthermore, article 48 MiFID imposes some common features to all competent authorities. The provision also affects banking supervisors who might be appointed, at the discretion of the Member States, as the competent authority for the supervisory tasks requested in the MiFID; in this case the appointed supervisor should possess the requested characteristics. According to article 48, the competent authorities should be 'public authorities', a requirement that apparently excludes national regulators established under private law from supervisory tasks under the MiFID. Nevertheless, the label 'public' does not have a unitary meaning in all Member States and should be broadly interpreted, so as to include also regulators formally established under national private law but entrusted with a public function. Further characteristics of the competent authorities result from the conditions attached to the delegation of tasks in article 48(2) MiFID: effective capacity and resources and organisational arrangements capable of avoiding conflicts of interest.

To sum up, we observe that, although Member States undeniably enjoy substantial autonomy as regards the national institutional setting for prudential banking supervision, there is also an identifiable European dimension. Such European interference has to date a low profile and pertains to the minimum harmonisation approach that primarily aims to build confidence (among supervisors) as to the equivalent conduct of supervision in all Member States. With intensified integration, more harmonisation of national supervisory frameworks will be called for. It is increasingly often advocated for eliminating the diversity in the national regulatory architectures and proceeding to the harmonisation of the basic features and powers of supervisors.[9]

In March 2009, CEBS published a comprehensive study prepared by its Review Panel assessing the commonalities and divergences of supervisory objectives and powers in the EU Member States (CEBS 2009a). As regards the fundamental prudential objectives of supervisors, CEBS observed that, despite differences in wording, there is de facto a very high degree of commonality. Also, the powers of supervisors related to licensing, information-gathering, inspections and rule-making appear to be largely convergent.

9 See Thomadakis 2003. According to Abrams and Taylor (2000: 213), the regulatory institutional structures should have the following prerequisites: defined objectives as to the goals of prudential regulation as well as to transparency; independence and accountability; appropriate resources and their efficient use; effective powers to enforce norms; overall comprehensiveness as to actual and future regulation; efficacy of regulation with respect to the structure of the financial industry.

This is the merit of extensive European legislative harmonisation of prudential aspects. However, it is important to note that common powers do not necessarily imply common practices, which apparently still diverge substantially. CEBS also investigated intervention powers of national authorities, covering tools ranging from corrective supervisory measures for restoring compliance and soundness to interventions on ailing banks and resolution procedures. The report concluded that, overall, supervisors appear to be well equipped with enforcement powers in going concern situations; however, there are substantial differences as regards the range of intervention measures available once problems are ascertained. Considerable differences were observed as regards the powers available for dealing with ailing institutions, as well as the conditions under which measures can be taken.[10] Furthermore, the CEBS study indicates significant fragmentation of supervisory powers to adopt extreme measures; while the majority of supervisors play at least some role in insolvency proceedings, the concrete powers differ largely, depending on whether reorganisation or winding-up is considered. As regards sanctioning powers, despite the absence of a common legal definition of 'sanctions', substantial differences could be ascertained as regards the amounts of pecuniary sanctions, the frequency of meetings of the sanctioning body, and the publication of sanctions. Overall, the CEBS report points to some important differences among the powers of national authorities responsible for supervision, yet it also emphasises a certain degree of commonalities, which are capable of laying the ground for a common supervisory culture. The harmonised European regulatory framework seems to be an efficient catalyst for developing such commonalities.

The third mode of limiting Member States' autonomy impacts in designing national institutional arrangements relates to the ESCB framework applicable to national central banks.

1.3 National central banks and prudential banking supervision

Traditionally, banking supervision has been the task of national central banks (NCBs) or executed in close cooperation with them. Nevertheless, since the propagation of integrated financial supervisory authorities in the early 1990s, a certain erosion of the role of NCBs in banking supervision has been observed (Lannoo 2002: 2). Still, the current supervisory arrangements continue to provide for extensive involvement of NCBs in the prudential supervision of the banking sector, albeit in different forms and to a varying extent (ECB 2003b: 2). These two depictions of the role of central banks

10 These include notably the powers of supervisors towards the persons who effectively direct the business (i.e. suspending or replacing directors and managers, appointing an administrator), and the related conditions and processes vary widely. Even more fragmentation was ascertained with regard to supervisory powers vis-à-vis banks' shareholders.

reflect current strategies devised for accommodating traditional supervisory arrangements to new dynamic and global financial realities. On the one hand, challenges in highly dynamic financial markets have resulted, in several instances, in depriving NCBs of primary competences for prudential supervision – the micro-supervisory tasks. On the other hand, the global and European dimension of financial markets has brought about increased cooperation and coordination, which has slightly boosted the macro-prudential role of NCBs through their role in liquidity provision and their macro-economic expertise. According to the ECB, there are three forms of involvement of NCBs in supervision that are not mutually exclusive: the carrying out of specific supervisory tasks, participation in supervisory boards and/or management committees of supervisory agencies and sharing of resources with the supervisory agency.

Central banks are generally entrusted with a broad role of maintaining financial stability. Financial stability was characterised as an evolving, broad and discretionary concept, usually referring to the 'safety and soundness of the financial system and to the stability of the payment and settlement system' (Lastra 2006: 92–3). Financial stability competences are situated at the crossroads between monetary policy and supervision (Padoa-Schioppa 2004a) and entail mainly what we would call the macro-prudential dimension of supervision. Although NCBs' competences regarding financial stability are only vaguely defined in national systems, they constitute the main rationale for associating NCBs to micro-prudential supervision, especially in view of the NCBs' role as a lender of last resort for troubled institutions. The ECB's explicit role with regard to financial stability in the integrated market pursuant to article 127(5) TFEU (ex 105(5) EC Treaty) is a trigger for improved cooperation and communication between NCBs, as well as for a better definition of their macro-prudential tasks. It justifies the ECB's position requiring an active role of national central banks in banking supervision. Such an active role is also underpinned by article 14.4 ESCB Statute, which allows NCBs to perform non-ESCB functions.

ECB's position on the role of NCBs in banking supervision

In response to the wave of reorganisations of national financial supervisory structures launched in the 1990s, the ECB has on several occasions made public its views on the role of central banks in prudential supervision.[11] The central message is that 'there are valid reasons, also in relation to the

11 ECB (2001) *The Role of the Central Banks in Prudential Supervision*, and ECB press release of 22 March 2001; ECB Opinion CON/2001/10 of 25 May 2001 on the Austrian *Finanzmarktaufsichtgesetz*, para. 4; also ECB Opinion CON/2001/35 on the German *Gesetz über die integrierte Finanzdienstleistungsaufsicht*, ECB Opinions CON/2002/13 and CON/2003/19 on the Belgian royal decree on prudential supervision of the financial sector and financial services; ECB Opinion CON/2004/16 on the Italian law on the protection of savings; ECB Opinion CON/2005/24 on the Czech law on the integration of financial market supervisors.

effects of the introduction of the euro, arguing in favour of maintaining a strong involvement of central banks in prudential supervision' (ECB 2001: 2). The main arguments relate to systemic risk, which is traditionally controlled by NCBs, and to synergies resulting from NCBs' dual position, as part of the ESCB and, at the same time, as national institutions. To dispel fears as to possible conflicts of interest and concentration of power, the ECB invokes the institutional separation between monetary policy competences that were taken away from NCBs and supervisory functions, which were not transferred from NCBs to the ECB. The latter may be performed in accordance with article 14.4 ESCB Statute, on the responsibility and liability of NCBs and shall not be regarded as being part of the functions of the ESCB. Hence, the ECB considers that from the point of view of the Eurosystem, the NCBs should be ascribed broad supervisory competences of both a macro- and a micro-prudential nature. In support for entrusting NCBs with some supervisory tasks, the ECB relies also on the enabling clause in article 127(6) TFEU (ex 105(6) EC Treaty).

Nevertheless, the ECB also admitted that in some national institutional frameworks the separation model may be preferable, provided that the central bank will be still largely involved in effective supervision. Such involvement could take place through common decision-making bodies, the common use of experts and resources, and effective mechanisms for cooperation and information exchange.

The ECB's position on the role of NCBs in banking supervision does not have a binding character, hence it could not be enforced if Member States departed from it by completely isolating their NCB from prudential supervisory functions. Nor does it set a formal standard for assessing the effectiveness of cooperative arrangements between a separate supervisory authority and the NCB. It only institutes a general obligation for NCBs to urge for acquiring supervisory rights during the debates on supervisory reform occurring at national level. Furthermore, the ECB's position has important political weight, hard for national legislators to neglect.

The legal regime applicable to NCBs' supervisory functions

This section aims at identifying the scope of article 14.4 ESCB Statute,[12] which constitutes the legal basis allowing NCBs to carry out functions different from those they have to perform within the ESCB. These so-called non-ESCB functions include also prudential supervision. We consider article 14.4 to be particularly important for understanding the compatibility between the supervisory tasks of the NCBs and their functions as parts of the ESCB, as well as the resulting interactions.

The provision under discussion is inserted in article 14 of the Statute, which defines the place of NCBs within the organisational scheme of the

12 The Lisbon Treaty has not amended article 14.4 ESCB Statute.

ESCB. It acknowledges the two dimensions of the ESCB system (i.e. national and European) and their interaction. In this context, article 14.3 ESCB Statute sets the stage by foreseeing that NCBs are an integral part of the ESCB and shall act in accordance with the guidelines and instructions of the ECB. Other functions exercised by an NCB outside the ESCB framework are therefore exceptions to the rule.

Discussions about the admissibility for NCBs to maintain residual autonomous functions, either outside the ESCB or as part of it, emerged when drafting the ESCB Statute in the context of discussions on the role of NCBs as a channel for executing monetary policy. On the basis of the principle of subsidiarity and because of the need to avoid the creation of a super central bank performing an omnipotent role (especially with regard to supervision), it was considered that NCBs could continue to perform in parallel, on their own account, other tasks and functions, as long as these do not interfere with ESCB-related functions.[13] The provisions allowing for such non-ESCB tasks had to be conceived in a sufficiently flexible way to consider the evolutionary nature of the integration process, which may lead over time to centralisation of additional functions.[14]

Article 14.4 consecrates what legal scholarship analyses under the heading *'dédoublement fonctionnel'* (Zilioli and Selmayr 2001: 76; Scelle 1956: 324). This doctrine describes a functional approach, allowing a single entity (e.g. a NCB) to perform multiple functions within different institutional frameworks (e.g. the ESCB and the national framework). It can be found explicitly in article 14.4, which states that non-ESCB functions 'shall not be regarded as being part of the functions of the ESCB' and they should be performed on the responsibility and liability of the NCBs (contrary to the ESCB-related tasks which are attributed to the ECB). Yet such *dédoublement* does not necessarily entail equivalence between the functions. Indeed, the prevalence of ESCB-related functions may be inferred from the right of the Governing Council to decide that a non-ESCB competence of a NCB interferes with system-related tasks.

So far, there is no evidence of a decision taken by the Governing Council on the basis of article 14.4 or an ECB opinion evaluating non-ESCB functions of NCBs in terms of their compatibility with the objectives and tasks of the ESCB. The practice of the ECB is to insert in its opinions a safeguard clause, requiring that the assessed national legislation does

13 Initial versions of art. 14.4 referred separately to (1) the continuation of performance of tasks other than those described by the Statute and Treaty, and (2) the taking up of new non-ESCB tasks subject to prior approval.

14 See letter by Gunter D. Baer of 25.09.1990 to the members of the Group of Legal Experts, whereby he recalled the fundamental principles underpinning the system. Along the indivisibility of monetary policy and centralised decision-making power and execution of monetary policy operations either by the ECB or the NCBs, it was explicitly underlined that there should be sufficient flexibility so as to allow adaptation to new evolutions.

not impede the proper performance by the NCB of its ESCB-related tasks.[15] Article 14.4 was considered by the ECB's Governing Council in the context of discussions on emergency liquidity assistance (ELA).[16] Although a large majority explicitly supported the view that ELA operations carried out by NCBs fall under article 14.4, the Governing Council carefully avoided referring to it as the formal legal basis. Nevertheless, it laid down a set of principles for ELA that broadly reflect the content of the Statute provision.[17]

The scope of article 14.4 and NCBs' possibilities to act outside the system-related tasks are limited, both in substantive and procedural terms (Zilioli and Selmayr 2001: 79). Substantive limitations arise from the encompassing character of the ESCB's functions laid out in the Statute, which only leaves limited room for purely national activities for NCBs. There is a presumption that the majority of functions entrusted to the NCBs are subsumed to the objectives and tasks of the ESCB, since monetary policy is at the core of central banking. Therefore, only NCB tasks ancillary to monetary policy functions will be susceptible of qualifying as non-ESCB functions – the most prominent fields are prudential supervision and emergency liquidity assistance.[18] Article 14.4 does not contain any criteria for distinguishing between ESCB and non-ESCB functions. This is particularly relevant in light of the vague definition of the ESCB/ECB role with regard to prudential supervision and financial stability and the possible transfer of supplementary tasks pursuant to the enabling clause.

15 For instance, the ECB has delivered two opinions on draft legislation reforming financial supervision in the Netherlands, which transfers to De Nederlandsche Bank new non-ESCB tasks in the field of prudential supervision of the insurance sector – CON/2003/23 and CON/2004/21. None of these opinions contain reference to art. 14.4, but only the aforementioned safeguard clauses.

16 ECB 1999. Since the financial crisis the ECB issued several opinions on national legislation concerning ELA; they all avoid any reference to art. 14.4: ECB Opinion CON/2008/44; ECB Opinion CON/2008/46.

17 The Governing Council agreed in 1999 on the following principles for the ELA: not only responsibility but also the risk of losses should be borne at national level; ECB should be kept informed of all ELA operations; ELA operations in excess of a 'relatively high threshold' should be subject to prior consultation with the ECB; the Executive Board should refer to the Governing Council cases where the size of the problem may have an impact on the Eurosystem's monetary policy; the Governing Council has the authority to reject implementation of the proposed ELA by means of a two-thirds majority; retention of a high degree of flexibility; review of the principles. The 2008 Opinions added another principle, namely that 'the same degree of independence is granted to the NCB as regards the provision of emergency liquidity assistance as with respect to the performance of its ESCB-related tasks'.

18 Other NCB tasks falling under art. 14.4 are statistical tasks on behalf of the national governments; centralising functions concerning balance of payments, credits, etc.; minting; conclusion of international agreements binding the Member States; representation of the State through participation in international fora, such as the OECD, IMF, etc.

Procedural limitations as to the performance of non-ESCB tasks by NCBs result from the right of the Governing Council of the ECB to bring to an end functions undertaken by NCBs, other than those specified in the Statute, when it considers that they interfere with the objectives and tasks of the ESCB. A majority of two-thirds of the votes cast is needed to acknowledge such interference and consequently prohibit the performance of the respective non-ESCB function by the NCB. Article 14.4 allows the Governing Council to take such a decision on its own initiative, whenever it considers this necessary. It may do so either with regard to functions that are already exercised by the NCBs or with regard to new functions envisaged for the latter. Such flexibility is needed, given that non-ESCB functions might develop over time and become contrary to the Statute, for instance through increased influence from other public bodies that gradually impinges also upon central bank independence. The Governing Council should not be biased by previously adopted positions on specific non-ESCB functions; nevertheless, serious reasons should be given in case of departure from earlier opinions.

The absence of an explicit provision requiring prior approval in case of the attribution of new tasks to a NCB (as envisaged during the preparatory work to the Statute) is justified by the consultative role of the ECB. In accordance with article 127(4) TFEU (ex 105(4) EC Treaty), article 4 ESCB Statute and Council Decision 98/415/EC, the ECB must be consulted on any draft legislative provision within the ECB's fields of competence, the enacting national authority being requested to await the ECB's opinion and to take into consideration even a belated opinion, as long as the act at issue was not finally adopted.

It has been maintained that article 14.4 contains an implicit duty of consultation that would take national legislation setting out to entrust the NCB with new non-ESCB functions outside the scope of the general consultation requirements laid down in article 127(4) TFEU (ex 105(4) EC) (Arda 2004). Such an approach disregards article 2 of Decision 98/415/EC, which explicitly requires that national legislation affecting NCBs be subject to consultation by the ECB, without distinguishing between ESCB and non-ESCB functions. We do not see any justification for taking out of the scope of the consultation obligation, legislation on non-ESCB functions, *ubi lex non distinguit, nec nos distinguere debemus.* It is also important not to limit the ECB's possibility of opposing the attribution of non-ESCB functions to an NCB by conditioning the Governing Council's assessment on a formal special consultation request.

It is indisputable that a decision taken by the Governing Council based on article 14.4 will put an end to the performance of the respective non-ESCB task by the NCB. There is, nevertheless, no indication as to the precise mechanisms that would ensure the implementation of such a decision. It was held that this could take the form of a decision addressed to the concerned NCB, binding in its entirety upon the NCB (Louis 1998: 58).

However, we do not see any restrictions as to the alternative use of decisions without addressee, guidelines or instructions, prohibiting all NCBs from undertaking specific activities or prescribing for all NCBs the conditions or criteria for the exercise of specific non-ESCB functions.[19]

Article 14.4 clarifies which is the legal regime applicable to non-ESCB functions performed by NCBs. These functions are performed on the responsibility and liability of national central banks in their capacity as national authorities.[20] To the extent the NCBs act under such retained competences and adopt acts outside the ESCB system, they are subject to national liability rules and competition rules. Also, they remain subject to monitoring of compliance with the Statute and the Treaty, especially with regard to their potential of impinging upon independence requirements, as well as monetary financing prohibitions.[21] Moreover, the impact of non-ESCB tasks on the finances of the NCB should be carefully scrutinised.

Non-ESCB functions, entrusted to NCBs, might be subject to a higher degree of political influence from other public authorities. This may have repercussions upon NCBs' independence and implicitly on their acceptability. Thus, article 14.4 can be seen as a means of redress against indirect influences capable of impinging upon central bank independence and interfering with the objectives and tasks of the ESCB.

A final remark on article 14.4 concerns the position of Member States outside the Eurozone. It is interesting to note that article 14.4 is not listed (in article 43 of the Statute) among the provisions that do not apply to Member States outside the Eurosystem, hence it applies to Member States with a derogation. Nevertheless, the two Member States with a special status have different arrangements: the UK has explicitly negotiated the non-applicability of article 14 of the Statute,[22] while Denmark is assimilated to a State with a derogation and has obtained a limited exemption from article 14 of the Statute (Protocol No. 22 on Denmark). At the same time, the Governing Council, if confronted with a decision on the non-ESCB tasks of an NCB outside the Eurosystem, will have to pay due account to the provisions in article 42.2 consolidated ESCB Statute (ex 43.2 ESCB Statute) foreseeing that Member States with a derogation retain their powers in the field of monetary policy according to national law. Also, article 14.3 does not apply to countries with a derogation. Consequently, the scope for 'interference' with ESCB tasks and objectives will be substantially limited.

19 Nevertheless, instruments with general bearing should be used carefully, as in this field individual circumstances are usually particularly relevant.

20 It may be inferred *a contrario* from art. 14.4 that responsibility and liability for ESCB-related tasks performed by the NCBs is borne by the ECB/ESCB.

21 It is particularly important to avoid the prohibition of monetary financing being circumvented by entrusting a non-ESCB task to the NCB and not to a separate public authority.

22 Art. 8 of the Protocol on certain provisions relating to the United Kingdom of Great Britain and Northern Ireland, annexed to the Treaty establishing the European Community.

2 The meta-level of supervision

Banking supervision in an integrated market, if exclusively exercised through national competent authorities, is prone to ignore risks that transcend national markets. There is a strong argument that the objective of financial stability, by reason of scale and effects of prudential actions in an integrated market, cannot be sufficiently achieved by Member States. Hence, with due observance of the subsidiarity principle, some action at the EU level is required. Under the current framework such EU action takes two forms. One is the adoption of prudential regulation through European legislative instruments, subsequently implemented according to the decentralised administration of EU law by national supervisors. The other is the coordination and cooperation between national competent authorities, which to be effective throughout the European banking market cannot merely rely on bilateral arrangements, but need to be underpinned by European cooperation networks. It is this latter facet that we call 'the meta-level of supervision',[23] because it is a cooperative platform located on the continuum in between decentralisation and centralisation of supervisory tasks at the European level. Supervisory cooperation is complementary to the principle of home-country supervision and its intensity has evolved proportionally to the degree of market integration. We might identify also a third mode of EU participation in banking supervision that is latent in the current framework: the possibility of centralising some supervisory functions with the ECB pursuant to article 127(6) TFEU (ex 105(6) EC Treaty) and article 25.2 ESCB Statute. However, as this has not been the case so far, we will deal with it in the next chapter.

In the following, we will review the European organisational structures in place that foster cooperation among national competent authorities and provide a platform for cross-border supervisory cooperation. These are the Committee of European Banking Supervisors, the Group de Contact and the European Central Bank with its Banking Supervision Committee. Finally, we will look at the basic vehicles of cooperation: Memoranda of Understanding, leadership in supervisory coordination, colleges of supervisors and supervisory delegation.

2.1 The role of CEBS in banking supervision

In the previous chapter we explained in detail the origins and characteristics of CEBS, the Level 3 committee set-up pursuant to the extension of the Lamfalussy framework to the banking sector. We underlined the role that CEBS is expected to play with regard to regulation in its double capacity, as an adviser of the Commission and a forum for regulatory convergence using soft-law techniques. Also, we have pointed to its statutory role with

23 The expression was introduced by Aglietta *et al.* 1998.

respect to convergence of supervisory practices, cooperation and information exchange, as well as to its recently attributed task of identifying and assessing developments in the banking sector and informing about potential or imminent problems. By referring to what has already been said, it is apparent that CEBS' work provides a typical example of the complexity of the supervisory function. Banking supervision presupposes a comprehensive regulatory regime entailing complex phases of standard-setting, monitoring and enforcement. CEBS' implication in supervision so far has been mainly concerned with standard-setting (article 4.3 CEBS Charter) (the regulatory aspect of supervision) and monitoring (articles 4.3 and 4.5 CEBS Charter), the latter being ancillary to the former. CEBS' standard-setting and monitoring powers consider – apart from guiding the implementation of EU law – the promotion of a common approach to supervision across Europe. This means convergence of the practical application of rules and legislation, and of supervisory objectives and techniques.

The recent amendments to the CEBS Charter and the new Commission decision establishing CEBS have reinforced its tasks with regard to supervision. It has been made much clearer that one of the main objectives of CEBS' activities consists of stimulating supervisory convergence, which is of utmost importance for the 'common and uniform' application of EU legislation. This is not limited to the standard-setting function but requires CEBS to review and assess the degree of convergence in the effective implementation of given supervisory provisions and practices in real time and to identify and address the remaining obstacles (article 4.2 Decision 2009/78/EC). Moreover, CEBS is expected to develop new practical convergence tools to promote common supervisory approaches (article 4.3 Decision 2009/78/EC) and to foster a common supervisory culture among its members (article 4.8 CEBS Charter). Furthermore, CEBS is required to contribute to the development of common supervisory practices not only in the banking field but also on a cross-sectoral basis, in close cooperation with the other Level 3 committees (article 6 Commission Decision 2009/78/EC).

The revised constitutive documents of CEBS explicitly enumerate a set of concrete tools to be used by CEBS for enhancing cooperation between its members and fostering convergence of supervisory practices and approaches. Article 4 Decision 2009/78/EC requires CEBS to at least: mediate among supervisory authorities; provide opinions to supervisory authorities; promote effective bilateral and multilateral exchange of information; facilitate delegation of tasks; contribute to the efficient and consistent functioning of colleges of supervisors; develop common supervisory reporting standards; review the practical application of its guidelines, recommendations and standards (article 4.1 letters (a)–(g) Decision 2009/78/EC). The closer specification of the competences underpinning CEBS functions can be interpreted as reinforcing CEBS position and authority and legitimising its endeavours.

An outstanding new provision enshrined in the two constitutive documents endows CEBS with competences in relation to macro-prudential supervision (article 5 Decision 2009/78/EC and revised article 4.5 CEBS Charter). In this capacity CEBS will have to assess, from a supervisory perspective, the developments, risks and vulnerabilities in the EU banking sector that could affect the stability of EU markets. It will have to inform the other Level 3 committees, finance ministries and NCBs about potential or imminent problems and report to the Commission and the Council. Moreover, CEBS 'shall have in place procedures enabling the supervisory authorities to react promptly' and, where appropriate, it 'shall facilitate a joint assessment amongst supervisors' of the threats to the stability of the EU financial system (article 3 Commission Decision 2009/78/EC). The attribution of such tasks is an immediate reaction to the financial crisis and the unfortunate acknowledgment that the EU did not have in place any structured mechanism for monitoring and identifying interactions between complex developments in the ever more integrated financial markets, and for accordingly taking action. New institutional settings for dealing with macro-prudential supervision are currently discussed on the basis of the de Larosière report, yet the new Decision establishing CEBS anticipated and provisionally filled in a gap in EU competences. This new task conferred to CEBS is particularly complex and will require, in order to be duly performed, important resources that CEBS currently does not have. Also, because of its soft powers, the requirement to establish procedures that would enable supervisors' prompt reaction is merely declaratory. Yet the provision should be highlighted as an important step in the EU's evolutionary approach towards supervision.

CEBS does not have enforcement powers. This is understandable, as long as CEBS, from the perspective of its legal form, constitutes just a 'network' (IIMG 2004: 28) of national competent authorities, deprived of legal personality as such. Only national supervisors that enjoy legal competences and are held accountable may engage in legal enforcement of the common European supervisory approach. CEBS is a forum for discussion and consent-building on standards and rules; it only enjoys soft powers. During quiet and prosperous times, this situation was not necessarily considered a deterrent factor to achieving compliance with CEBS' regulation, given that prudential supervision traditionally relied on suasion rather than on formal enforcement. Yet in troubled times this soft approach appears to be insufficient and a stronger stance is needed to maintain control and to block divergent national tendencies. Also, it raises questions related to legal certainty with respect to the consistent implementation of agreed supervisory practices.

Furthermore CEBS has a key role with regard to information exchange on supervisory issues (articles 4.4 and 4.6 CEBS Charter). The numerous meetings and common work allow national supervisory authorities to have regular contacts and exchange information on a formal and informal basis. A remarkable capacity of CEBS is also the statutory capacity to organise, in exceptional circumstances and at the explicit request of an individual member, restricted sessions in order to discuss strictly confidential micro-prudential matters (article 4.6 CEBS Charter). The potential of this provision, enshrined already in the first constitutive documents, increases in light of the new role of CEBS with regard to the activities of colleges of supervisors. It could allow CEBS to exert a stronger coordinating role among the members concerned.

Yet merely developing a functional networking mechanisms and providing an operational platform in view of facilitating the exchange of information is only partly a success. Efficient supervision would require that all relevant and useful information be imparted under strict confidentiality rules. However, CEBS does not have the power to request national supervisors to provide specific information, nor do there exist any sanctioning or enforcement mechanisms capable of deterring national authorities from concealing relevant information from fellow supervisors. This is a shortcoming that needs to be addressed in the forthcoming reforms.

2.2 The Groupe de Contact

The Groupe de Contact (GdC) is the oldest banking supervisory forum in Europe; it was set up in 1972 by the banking supervisors of the EEC and EFTA Member States on a cooperative basis. The GdC deals with micro-prudential cooperation, including information-sharing both on general policy matters and on individual cases, and carries out comparative studies on policies and techniques of supervision. It also assembles, as required by EU directives, various EEA-wide statistical data, including those on solvency, profitability and liquidity. Established as an informal group, it brings together one representative from each banking supervisory authority in the EEA countries. The Committee allows also for the participation of an official from the Commission as adviser on legal issues, but no attendance is permitted in discussions referring either to individual cases or to sensitive supervisory arrangements.

The existence of the GdC was formally acknowledged in the preambles of the first banking directives (recitals 23 and 66 Codified Banking Directive). The CRD deleted both references and inserted instead references to CEBS in recital 22 of the preamble. The GdC has also been integrated into the Lamfalussy framework. According to article 5.4 of its Charter, CEBS will predominantly rely on the GdC, which will be its main expert group[24] and which will report to it. Also, CEBS has endorsed the Charter of the GdC and its work programme.

As the work of the GdC is largely confidential because of the particular sensitivity of most aspects it deals with, the formalisation under the aegis of CEBS may be interpreted as rendering its existence somehow more transparent and accountable. This integration of the GdC's

24 Until the amendment of the CEBS Charter in 2008, the GdC was referred to as the main working group of CEBS. The new wording, designating it as an expert group, points to its autonomy vis-à-vis CEBS.

activities into CEBS' work needs to be linked to the specific task entrusted to CEBS with regard to individual micro-prudential matters (the above-mentioned article 4.6 second phrase of the CEBS Charter). We could also see it as a way for ensuring smooth transferral to CEBS of supervisory competences related to individual cases. Such a micro-prudential function considerably reinforces the role of CEBS in the European supervisory infrastructure.

2.3 The Banking Supervision Committee

As already mentioned, the Treaty (article 127(5) TFEU, ex 105(5) EC) and the ESCB Statute (article 3.3) ascribe to the ESCB a role regarding prudential supervision of banks and financial stability. The phrasing of this non-basic task – 'the ESCB shall contribute to the smooth conduct of prudential policies pursued by the competent authorities' – has unleashed a complex debate about the scope of ECB's involvement in prudential supervision (Cloos *et al.* 1994: 255; Smits 1997: 338). The delineation of the scope of the ESCB intervention is further complicated by the enabling clause in article 127(6) TFEU (ex 105(6) EC Treaty) and article 25.2 ESCB Statute that foresees a fast-track procedure for the conferral to the ECB of specific tasks concerning supervisory policies with regard to credit institutions and other financial institutions with the exception of insurance undertakings.

We have already touched on some dimensions of this debate when dealing with the ECB's involvement in regulation, but left out of the discussion the ECB's role with regard to supervision. At this point we will not enter into speculative interpretations of the language used in the Treaty, but maintain that the imprecise wording of the Treaty should receive a 'bold' interpretation,[25] in the sense that the ECB is entrusted with a co-ordinating role in the area of prudential supervision and financial stability. Such an interpretation is confirmed by the proactive role taken by the ECB with regard to financial stability matters, and the explicit indication of the Banking Supervision Committee as responsible for performing the role of macro-prudential and structural monitoring of the EU financial system (ECB 2000b: 49; ECB 2004: 81).

The Banking Supervision Committee (BSC) was established in October 1998 within the framework of the European System of Central Banks.[26] It took over the functions performed since 1994 by the Banking Supervisory

25 See Smits 1995: 45. The author contrasts two lines of interpretation: a modest interpretation restricting the ECB's involvement to the explicit consultation function and, on the other hand, a bold interpretation, implying some coordinative role for the ECB.

26 The BSC has been established by the Governing Council of the ECB under art. 9 ECB Rules of Procedure, the legal basis for all twelve ESCB committees. The ESCB committees have the task of assisting the work of the ECB's decision-making bodies by providing expertise in their fields of competence and facilitating the decision-making process and implementation of decisions.

Sub-Committee of the European Monetary Institute, which in its turn was preceded by the Banking Supervisory Group, created in 1990 by the Committee of Governors. The BSC is composed of high-level representatives of the ECB, the NCBs and the Member States' supervisory authorities. The BSC has a dual mandate, which was reviewed in 2004. First, acting as an ESCB committee, it assists the ESCB in its supervision and financial stability-related tasks. In this capacity, the BSC examines issues of macro-prudential nature, reviews developments in the banking and financial systems and fosters the emergence of common stances on the challenges of an increasingly integrated system (Scheller 2004: 113). The BSC examines structural developments or incidents in the EU banking systems of systemic or major relevance and their implications for the conduct of prudential supervision. It also analyses the impact of regulatory and supervisory requirements on financial stability. Furthermore, in this capacity, the BSC assists the ECB in preparing its advice on draft EU and national banking legislation.

Second, the BSC functions as a forum for the exchange of views and information among EU banking supervisors and central banks, thereby fostering cooperation beyond the interests of the Eurosystem. In this capacity, it serves as a channel for bilateral flows of information between the ESCB and other supervisory authorities. There appear to be large overlaps between the role of the BSC as a forum for information exchange and CEBS' function as an operational network for exchange of supervisory information. The composition is largely the same with probably a more influential role given to central banks in the framework of the BSC and to supervisors under the auspices of CEBS. The BSC, underpinned by the complex ESCB framework, can be seen as having more formal powers in constraining its members to deliver relevant information. However, the doubling of supporting structures for the exchange of information is indicative of a dispersal of authority in gathering information, which is detrimental to the imperative of having consistent, reliable and complete information in an integrated market.

Additionally, the BSC is given a specific role to play along with the ECB in the Lamfalussy committees. Also, as part of its mandate the BSC, particularly through its High Level Working Group on Crisis Management, prepared the European arrangements of institutional cooperation between the competent authorities (the so-called Memoranda of Understanding). Two members of CEBS are also represented in this working group. In the pursuit of its tasks, the BSC has organised crisis simulation exercises for highlighting bottlenecks and identifying further work areas for improving supervisory cooperation between competent authorities.

It appears that the BSC represents the main vehicle for the exercise by the ESCB of its role with regard to prudential supervision and financial stability. The BSC is closely involved in the cooperative arrangements between relevant national authorities agreed at the European level and keeps close links with CEBS. Furthermore, in close collaboration with the national competent authorities and as a complement to the national views on financial stability, the BSC works on developing a comprehensive framework for the regular analysis of structural developments and potential vulnerabilities in the EU banking sector (ECB 2003b, 2005c, 2008b). From this perspective, it may be said that the provision in article 127(5) TFEU (ex 105(5) EC Treaty) requires the ESCB to engage into macro-prudential surveillance so as to provide, in close collaboration with the national competent authorities, a European-wide perspective on financial stability in the banking sector.

Yet the effectiveness of this provision is largely undermined by the absence of a mechanism that would constrain a follow-up to the macro-prudential analysis undertaken by the BSC. There is no explicit requirement for the BSC to issue policy recommendations pursuant to its findings, nor are decision-makers within the EU obliged to take action to address the eventual problems identified by the BSC. Therefore, despite warnings stemming from the BSC's assessments and analysis undertaken by various ECB departments, and despite unsatisfactory results of the crisis simulation exercise organised in the wake of the financial crisis, no measures were taken. This situation is regrettable, especially in the light of ECB's competence as a lender of last resort and the effective substantial liquidity assistance provided since summer 2007. We see here a strong argument for making the role of the ECB more precise pursuant to article 127(5) TFEU (ex 105(5) EC Treaty) with regard to macro-prudential aspects.

2.4 The instruments underpinning the meta-level of supervision

Cooperation between national competent authorities is at the core of what we have called the meta-level of supervision. It is explicitly required, by the European directives, both in cases when competences are shared between home or host countries (e.g. liquidity issues) and in situations where there is a clear attribution of supervisory responsibilities entailing a cross-border element. Apart from various forms of information exchange, four instruments have been given particular attention at EU level in view of fostering supervisory cooperation: Memoranda of Understanding (MoUs), leadership in supervisory coordination, colleges of supervisors and supervisory delegation.

Memoranda of Understanding

The Memorandum of Understanding (MoU) is an agreement between supervisory authorities which provides the concrete framework for their cooperation. Developed as a bilateral arrangement (used either for cross-border supervision or for the supervision of financial institutions subject to the control of several sectoral regulators), MoUs multiplied after the adoption of the Second Banking Directive in order to make effective the cooperation between home and host country authorities. Bilateral MoUs provide the practical framework for communication between supervisors, by establishing regular information exchange, and by defining procedures, tools and reciprocal commitments related to the supervisory process (Padoa-Schioppa 2004a: 87). Bilateral MoUs are, from a practical point of view, essential for the efficient supervision of cross-border banking activities.

Traditionally, MoUs were agreed especially with a view to putting in place some arrangements for supervisory cooperation in cases of crisis. An increasingly integrated financial market, which also entails a broader scope for cross-border contagion and thus growing potential for systemic risk, calls, among others, for concerted action at the European level in crisis situations. This rationale underpinned the agreement of multilateral MoUs signed under the auspices of the BSC.

The first European MoU was signed in March 2003 by EU banking supervisors and central banks (ECB 2003a). In focusing on crisis management, the 2003 MoU set out specific principles and procedures for the identification of the authorities responsible for crisis management in the EU, the required flows of information between banking supervisors and central banks, and the practical conditions for sharing information at the supranational level. In May 2005, another MoU was adopted to complement the cooperative framework (ECB 2005b). It built on the existing EU and national legislation and arrangements and also associated the EU finance ministries to the supervisory cooperation. Furthermore, it promoted the role of the Lamfalussy committees as facilitators of processes of exchange of information, views and assessments, along with the central role of the supervisor. The 2005 MoU also required the development of national and EU contingency plans for the management of crisis situations, along with stress testing and simulation exercises, but unlike the 2003 MoU it did not deal with processes for detecting emerging crises or for activating specific supervisory and central banking tools.

In June 2008, a third EU-wide Memorandum of Understanding was agreed (ECB 2008a). Its signatories include all national financial supervisory authorities, finance ministries and other relevant ministries according to national competences, national central banks and the ECB. Underlining the major danger entailed by systemic risks, the 2008 MoU establishes concrete EU arrangements for financial stability to be used as of the end of 2008. The MoU provides details on ways to strengthen crisis preparedness in normal times, together with crisis alert and information exchange, establishes cross-border cooperation mechanisms – the so-called Cross-Border Stability Groups (CBSG) – and provides concrete procedures for the cooperation between the Parties to the MoU in financial crisis situations. At the same time, the MoU gives guidance as to the development of other possible Voluntary Specific Cooperation Agreements (VSCA), regarding particularly colleges of supervisors and the establishment of mediation panels. The 2008

MoU is the first published European MoU and provides important information on what can be expected from public authorities responsible for maintaining financial stability. Yet its language is largely inconsistent with EU legislation (e.g. the definitions of home and host countries, of financial groups, etc.) and appears to be inadequate in the light of the crisis and the ongoing debates on the reform of EU financial supervision. At the time of writing, it can be reasonably expected that the 2008 MoU will be largely overtaken by envisaged reforms in EU financial supervision, early intervention and crisis management and resolution mechanisms (Commission 2009j).

MoUs are important tools of prudential supervision. Although they mainly refer to crisis situations, they constitute arrangements devised *ex ante* and largely aim at preventing the development and propagation of crises. This dimension of MoUs is straightforward in the 2008 European MoU, which underlines the importance of timely assessing potential systemic risks and therefore the imperative of establishing a common analytical framework to enhance communication and facilitate agreement on joint assessment (point 5 ECB 2008a). MoUs constitute a code of conduct regulating interaction among supervisors, codifying the various procedures and channels for cooperation and creating a mechanism for managing conflicts. Their incidence is not only punctual or conditioned by the release of a potential financial crisis, but it also extends to regular cooperation and preventive information exchange and risk analysis.

MoUs are not necessarily public documents because of the confidential information they deal with. The publication of the 2008 European MoU occurred in the context of increased public awareness of the need for effective crisis management arrangements, yet it explicitly provides that it 'does not create any legal commitment for any of the parties to intervene in favour of anyone affected by a financial crisis' (point 7 ECB 2008a). MoUs' legal nature is controversial. Some authors assert that they are deprived of legal force (Lannoo 2002: 6). In our view, however, MoUs can be seen as binding upon the parties that agreed to them, according to the principle *pacta sunt servanda*. Furthermore, we consider that theoretically they are also likely to create rights in favour of third parties (e.g. banks, depositors), in view of preventing inactivity of competent authorities, or forestalling measures contrary to the provisions of the MoU that might be damaging for third parties. The mere existence of practical and operational arrangements between national competent authorities as regards cross-border situations creates a legitimate expectation that the authorities will take action if necessary. Such legitimate expectations result also from article 131 CRD, which explicitly requires that the authorities responsible for consolidated supervision have in place written cooperation and coordination arrangements.

It is obvious that a network of bilateral MoUs is too cumbersome and is hardly reliable in system-wide crises. The adoption of EU-wide multilateral MoUs is therefore welcomed. Nevertheless, their efficiency might be undermined if there is no clear understanding as to the hierarchical position between the various levels of practical arrangements. Although MoUs are *sui generis* acts, ultimately signed by the national authorities outside the EU legal framework, they actually implement EU law requiring coordination and thus may be seen as part of the panoply of mechanisms supporting the multi-layered administration of EU law. From this perspective, and given the large centralisation of prudential regulation, the EU MoUs could be seen as being hierarchically superior to bilateral MoUs and, thus, as having precedence over contrary provisions laid down in individual arrangements.

Yet there is still a lot of uncertainty surrounding the operation of MoUs, and no straightforward distribution of competences and efficient mechanisms for common problem-solving are therein enshrined. Their blurred status and 'soft' nature even under international public law impinges on their effectiveness. The crisis highlighted the imperative necessity of establishing streamlined crisis management arrangements. In the context of the reform of the EU financial supervision architecture, this might involve an institutionalisation and formalisation of mechanisms for the prevention, management and resolution of crises within the EU legal framework. If this were to happen, we can imagine MoUs as a tool for the concrete application and individualisation of principles and framework mechanisms provided in EU law. Bindingness and legal rights and duties will then stem directly from European legislation, to which EU-wide and individual MoUs will have to conform.

Leadership in supervisory coordination

In order to seize all the benefits of cooperation among supervisory authorities, there is a strong call for coordination. Such coordination cannot merely limit itself to policy coordination inside the various cooperative fora or networks but needs a concrete coordinator at the practical/operational level. This understanding is inherent to the very concept of consolidated supervision, and the criteria for designating the consolidating supervisor. Yet, given the limits of the home-country control principle already discussed and the importance of coordination between home and host countries supervisory responsibilities, coordination aspects have to go beyond mere designation of the responsible authority for consolidated supervision. The problem was already addressed after the BCCI crises, when the banking directives were amended so as to include reinforced provisions on consolidated supervision. Further progress with regard to supervisory coordination has been achieved through the Directive 2002/87/EC regulating the supervision of conglomerates, which promotes the concept of coordinator supervisor. Nevertheless, this approach has been considered insufficient and only a substitute for effective consolidated supervision. It is designated as the 'solo plus' solution (Aglietta *et al.* 1998: 13), as supervision remains organised on an individual – 'solo' – basis but is supplemented by some qualitative and quantitative assessments at group level.

During the negotiations of the CRD the so-called lead supervisor was pushed forward by part of the industry in response to the criticism to consolidated supervision. The lead supervisor would be chosen according to the specific composition of the group and is not necessarily the banking supervisor. The concept was defined by the European Financial Services Round Table in a study published in 2004, and was subsequently elaborated (EFR 2004, 2005; Schoenmaker and Oosterloo 2006). These documents provide that the lead supervisor of each cross-border financial institution in the EU should be the competent authority clearly empowered to take the driver's seat for all aspects of prudential supervision, including those related to the consolidated level and those referring to branches or subsidiaries. The lead supervisor should be supported by a college of supervisors composed of the supervisory authorities of the Member States concerned. The college would provide host States with the possibility to contribute their knowledge of the local markets and to express their own concerns. Yet such colleges would have mainly advisory functions and would not be able to delay decisions of the lead supervisor.

The CRD contains several detailed provisions on consolidated supervision, most of which aim at filling gaps regarding the scope of consolidation and the designation of the competent supervisory authority in case of groups. The CRD also envisages some enhanced responsibilities for the 'consolidating supervisor' (article 125–35 CRD) who would act more clearly as a coordinator. The consolidating supervisor would have the ultimate responsibility to decide on the validation of banks' applications for the use of internal models on a group-wide basis in case of disagreement between the supervisors of the group's parent institution and those competent for subsidiaries. The 2009 review of the CRD (CRD 2) only slightly improved the position of the consolidating supervisor with regard to Pillar 2 (supervisory review) but fell short of attributing him or her Pillar 2 supervisory powers at group level (article 129 (3) CRD 2). The consolidating supervisor as currently provided in European legislation does not amount to what is defined as lead supervisor. CRD 2 actually moved away from the lead supervisor concept by institutionalising the colleges of supervisors without reinforcing leadership (article 131a CRD 2). One-sided leadership in supervision is now broadly discarded, as it is generally admitted that multiple interests and varied realities need to be considered in the context of cross-border supervision, which go beyond the capacities of single national competent authorities. Yet this does not mean that no strong coordination is needed. Appropriate arrangements should be urgently devised and should aim at ensuring objectivity and a holistic approach that guarantees firm action.

Colleges of supervisors

In the past years, regulators and policy-makers have expressed their preference for colleges of supervisors as vehicles for supervisory cooperation. Colleges have the capacity to offer a permanent structure for each cross-border group, thereby reassembling all relevant competent authorities in view of information exchange, cooperation and coordination on common issues. The main purpose of colleges is to foster joint decision-making on matters concerning a cross-border institution. Ever more centralised risk-management process within cross-border institutions need to be addressed through a joint approach, taking into consideration all national realities and supervisory interests concerned. Colleges would thus provide a framework where all interested supervisory authorities can contribute their views and participate in decision-making on aspects that regard the group as a whole.

The effectiveness of colleges in the common market depends much on the formal arrangements that underpin such colleges. Particularly relevant are the distribution of roles between the authorities participating in the college (the controversial home–host issues), the determination of effective joint decision-making procedures, the establishment of objective mediation modalities in case of disagreements, the clear indication of the legal and practical consequences of joint decisions, and the safeguards for the countries whose opinions are overruled in the joint decision-making process.

The 2009 review of the CRD introduced the mandatory establishment of colleges of supervisors for cross-border groups, without however changing the responsibilities of competent authorities or extending their decision-making powers (article 131a CRD 2). It is for the consolidating supervisor to establish colleges of supervisors. The arrangements for the organisation and functioning of the colleges should be laid down in written form. The consolidating supervisor chairs the meetings and decides about the competent authorities that may participate in specific activities or meetings of the college, after considering the relevance of the planned joint supervisory activity, especially in terms of the potential impact on the stability of the financial system in the Member States concerned (article 131a paragraph 2 CRD 2).

Under new article 131a CRD colleges are entrusted with the following tasks: exchange of information; reaching agreement on voluntary entrustment of tasks and voluntary delegation of responsibilities where appropriate; determining supervisory examination programmes based on a risk assessment of the group under Pillar 2; increasing the efficiency of supervision by removing unnecessary duplication of supervisory requirements; consistently applying prudential requirements across all entities within a banking group. In order to maintain a level playing-field between the activities of colleges across the EU, CEBS is asked to monitor their functioning and to issue guidance for their organisation and operation (e.g. CEBS 2009c).

Under CRD 2, colleges are merely an instrument for strengthened cooperation and facilitation of supervision in cross-border situations. This solution is seen only as temporary and is qualified in the preamble to CRD 2 as 'a phase in a development towards further regulatory convergence and supervisory integration'. The preamble also indicates that, in case of conflicts between the supervisors participating in a college, there should in future be 'neutral and independent advice, mediation and conflict resolving mechanisms at Community level' (recital 8A CRD 2). If underpinned by appropriate joint decision-making mechanisms, colleges will be valuable practical tools for supervisory cooperation that will most likely also find their place in the future supervisory architecture.

Delegation

Another instrument underpinning cooperation and coordination between competent supervisory authorities is the voluntary delegation of tasks and responsibilities. The voluntary character is of the essence of delegation and implies that all supervisory authorities concerned explicitly agree to it. Mandatory delegation in banking supervision would amount, in our view, to a 'conflict of jurisdictions' rule, e.g. the combination between mutual recognition and home-country control, which entails different characteristics[27] Delegation can be based on legislation or on an agreement between supervisory authorities. The CRD explicitly foresees delegation in two instances.

Article 141 CRD allows for the delegation, in specific cases, of the verification of information concerning an institution situated in another Member State to the competent authority in that country, who can either carry it out or allow the delegating authority to carry it out or, alternatively, allow it to be performed by an auditor or expert. This is a case of delegation of tasks, implying that the delegating authority entrusts the competent authority from another Member State (the delegatee) with carrying out, on its behalf, specific pieces of supervisory work (2006 Francq report). The delegatee has to report back on the performance of the delegated tasks to the delegating authority, which retains ultimate responsibility. In a 2008 document, CEBS has identified further areas where in practice delegation of tasks takes place on the basis of the CRD – namely, on-site examinations, model validation and liquidity concession models (CEBS 2008).

A second explicit rule on delegation is contained in article 131 CRD. According to this provision, the competent authorities responsible for authorising a foreign subsidiary may, 'by bilateral agreement, delegate their responsibility for supervision to the competent authorities which

27 On a detailed discussion about the differences and similarities between the concepts of delegation, outsourcing and mutual recognition, see Wymeersch 2006.

authorised and supervise the parent undertaking so that they assume responsibility for supervising the subsidiary'. This is a case of delegation of responsibility or authority, when the delegating authority transfers to the delegatee the power to make decisions. The delegatee assumes, on the basis of a bilateral agreement, full responsibility on behalf of the delegating authority and is accordingly liable. For this reason, the delegation of authority in cross-border situations is more problematic than the delegation of tasks, as it entails – because of the different national legal and administrative systems – some uncertainties related to the legal basis, applicable legal regime, legal consequences, differences in procedures and practices, diversity of supervisory powers and enforcement instruments, etc. The delegation of responsibilities is an instrument capable of changing the default distribution of competences between home and host countries.

The 2009 amendments brought to the constitutive decisions of the Level 3 committees entrust them explicitly with the role to 'facilitate delegation of tasks between supervisory authorities, in particular by identifying tasks which can be delegated and by promoting best practices' (article 4.1 (d) Decision 2009/78/EC). However, the provisions do not mention any role for the committees with regard to the delegation of responsibilities. This is consistent with the current policy approach that does not allow CEBS to interfere with the allocation of rights and competences of the competent authorities.

In response to calls from the Ecofin Council and the European Commission for developing a framework for delegation with regard to supervision in the financial sector, the three Level 3 committees published, on 2 June 2009, key principles for the delegation of tasks (CEBS, CESR and CEIOPS 2009b) and a paper on the delegation of responsibilities (CEBS, CESR and CEIOPS 2009a). In the Committees' views, delegation of tasks can take several forms: (a) multilateral or bilateral agreements or a combination of multilateral and bilateral MoUs; (b) sectoral or cross-sectoral; (c) from the home to the host competent authority or vice versa; (d) on a case-by-case basis or through a general approach; (e) joint and coordinated supervision or pure delegation. The delegation of responsibilities may take place in (a) a simple form involving a single determination; (b) through ongoing supervision as a follow-up either of a single initial decision (e.g. 'fit and proper' test) or more complex decisions (e.g. approval of the IRB models), or (c) through ongoing supervision of an entire entity (e.g. pursuant to article 131 CRD all group-related powers, including supervision of subsidiaries, can be delegated to the consolidating supervisor).

In order to facilitate the delegation of tasks and create a common EU ground, the Level 3 committees propose to use the same wording across EU sectoral legislation, which should clearly lay down the possibility of delegation and the conditions for such delegation. It is also recommended that further areas for delegation of tasks be explored. The delegation of responsibilities is also explicitly recognised as useful on grounds that it would allow for the flexible allocation of competences to the supervisor, who is considered best placed to deal with a specific supervisory issue. Furthermore, it would permit a better and more optimal use of technical expertise and encourage economies of scale or scope in supervision. Yet in order to make cross-border delegation of supervisory responsibilities operational, various important legal and practical issues need to be addressed. The Level 3 committees suggest the establishment of an EU legal framework for delegation to be transposed in national law and supplemented by voluntary agreements among individual supervisory authorities. The EU framework should regulate the most important general aspects, such as the applicable law vis-à-vis third parties, the general criteria for the designation of courts, the liability standard applicable to supervisory authorities, the sanctioning regime, etc. Instead, it will be for the voluntary agreements to specify the scope of delegation, the conditions, the reporting rules and other detailed aspects. This is an ambitious project that proposes extensive harmonisation in areas that pertain to national civil and administrative law. In our view, if supervisory cooperation is to benefit in the short and medium term not only from delegation of tasks but also from delegation of responsibilities, it would be more realistic to think first of creating simple incentives in sectoral legislation for recourse to bilateral delegation of responsibilities and to undertake increased efforts towards achieving a common supervisory culture.

3 Private parties' involvement in supervision

Last but not least, the review of the European supervisory framework cannot ignore the role of private actors in supervision. This is particularly important in the context of the new, more risk-sensitive supervisory approach and of the emphasis on market discipline in the CRD. The role of private parties can be explained by the fact that the regulatory capacity of competent authorities is bounded, and thus likely to be improved by input from various market participants who have a comparative advantage in terms of practical expertise. Reliance on private parties in prudential supervision has also been seen as a typical example of the information revolution provoking decentralisation of power (Ortino 2004: 727). Such involvement may be qualified as shared standard-setting (Freeman 1999), when part of the standard-setting tasks is formally delegated to a private party. There are various instances of shared standard-setting in the CRD: the internal ratings-based approach, the recourse to external credit assessment, the reliance on value-at-risk models for calculating market risk, the use of internal advanced risk-measurement approaches for determining operational risk, and the credit institutions' internal capital adequacy assessment process. Such input from private parties constitutes a form of concrete standard-setting occurring during the supervisory process, when general prudential rules are applied for the concrete calculation of capital requirements. Hence, it may be said that the validation of banks' capacity to use internal models and the recognition of the eligibility of credit-rating agencies amount to the delegation of the afore-mentioned supervisory tasks to these private parties.

Moreover, the increased promotion of market discipline reveals a different dimension of the enrolment of private actors in the supervision of banks through pressures they are expected to exert in view of discouraging excessive risk-taking. Although, as discussed, the precise role of market discipline as a complement to public supervision is not clear-cut, especially in light of tendencies of herding in financial markets, it is implicit that market mechanisms suppose, alongside disclosure incentives in regulation, the existence of organisations that produce and spread market opinion. The CRD regulates aspects of disclosure of information only in the context of the norms implementing the third pillar of the new Basel Accord, but does not regulate the market players capable of forming and diffusing market opinion, i.e. rating agencies, external auditors and financial analysts.

In the following, we will not insist on the institutions exerting market discipline, as we consider that, so far, there is no straightforward European dimension as to the exercise of their functions with regard to prudential supervision. Thereby, we do not deny their paramount importance as a major line of defence against excessive risk-taking and would like to point also to the fact that they attract increased focus of European law-makers.[28]

3.1 Banks' internal models

As already mentioned, there are various instances in the new prudential approach, which allow banks to play an active part in the process of supervision. Such instances constitute a genuine delegation of supervisory tools to the credit institutions themselves. Their use puts default public standards aside. Regulatory reliance on internal models of risk measurement is intrinsically linked to the capacity of banks to assess accurately the risks associated to their different activities. This supposes that credit institutions have in place sound and effective strategies and processes for both devising quality risk-assessments and ensuring sound organisation and management of the identified risks: internal control mechanisms.

To ensure the quality of such private input, the legislator has regulated minimum conditions in advance. Banks envisaging using their own risk-measurement models have to receive explicit permission from the competent authority certifying, upon a thorough check-up according to predetermined detailed criteria, their suitability for using internal models

28 For instance: Directive 2006/43/EC improving the framework applicable to auditors, the 2009 Regulation of Credit Rating Agencies, CEBS' work on the role of auditors in validating the information disclosed in relation to Pillar 3.

(article 84 and Annex VII Part 4 of the CRD). Unless these conditions are complied with on an ongoing basis or properly adjusted to changes in circumstances, supervisors have to reconsider the eligibility of individual banks for using internal models or take punitive measures such as imposing capital add-ons.

Supervisory approval for the use of internal models is a complex process with many facets, which seeks to make sure that banks allowed to determine their own capital cushion are reliable. It is based on a steady dialogue between the regulator and the regulated entity, which aims at warranting that all prudential requirements are correctly understood and transposed into the internal models. Supervisory approval is part of a more complex assessment and implementation process that endeavours to ensure that the parameters agreed between the bank and the supervisor in order to qualify for the use of internal models will be observed on a continuous ongoing basis. In this context, enforcement is essential and the supervisor is endowed with instruments for action. The minimum requirements laid down in the CRD are an essential safeguard against regulatory capture of the supervisory authorities during the dialogue with banks.

The validation of internal models and the constant monitoring by supervisors of banks using internal models come close to what, in regulatory theory, has been qualified as contract regulation. Seeing the relationship between supervisors and banks in terms of a contract might help to clarify the different responsibilities and accountability mechanisms.

3.2 External credit ratings

The other category of private parties involved in the supervisory process on the basis of the provisions in the CRD are the rating agencies or, in the language of the CRD, the external credit assessment institutions (ECAIs). Thus, external credit assessments may be used to determine the risk weight of an exposure for the calculation of capital requirements under the conditions of ECAI providing it has been recognised as eligible for those purposes by the competent authority. ECAIs have to be recognised in accordance with articles 81–3 and Annex VI CRD, which prescribe criteria for the recognition of external credit assessment institutions and their ratings and the rules for the use of such ratings. These norms have the dual aim of ensuring consistency and integrity for the application of such ratings, as well as the impartiality of the rating institutions (Katzengruber 2003; EP 2004; CESR 2005). Also, CEBS has undertaken work on detailing the framework applicable to ECAIs (CEBS 2006).

The recognition process of ECAIs for eligibility in view of regulatory reliance is more problematic than the validation of internal models of banks. When the CRD was adopted, there was major concern in Europe to ensure that formal ECAI recognition for capital requirements purposes did not amount to a form of government regulation or licensing of rating agencies, which at that time existed in the US but not in the EU. Yet some safeguards were needed to underpin the public policy choice to ascribe regulatory force to private credit ratings and thereby delegate regulatory power to the rating agencies. The result was the establishment of some broad principle-based criteria for the recognition of ECAIs, much less detailed than in the case of the regulatory recognition of internal models. The recognition of ECAIs pursuant to the CRD also does not imply a constant dialogue between the banking supervisors and the eligible ECAIs, but only an initial evaluation, which may be subsequently recognised by competent authorities in other Member States without any supplementary determination process.

In 2006, there was intense public debate on the creation of a European framework for credit rating agencies (CRAs), which ended up with the EU institutions stepping back from any regulatory initiatives in this sense in favour of self-regulation by the credit rating industry.[29] Yet the policy was completely reversed in 2008, when it became clear in the light of the crisis that both regulators and market participants relied excessively on private ratings provided by ECAIs, which proved not to be accurate in many cases characterised by sudden substantial downgrades. In an extremely short period, a complex regulatory proposal on credit rating agencies was put forward by the Commission and a Regulation was adopted in April 2009.[30] The Regulation will subject credit rating agencies in the EU to a common regulatory approach to enhance the integrity, transparency, responsibility, good governance and reliability of credit rating activities, in view of improving the quality of credit ratings issued in the EU. CRAs will be expected to comply with some strict standards and will be subject to registration and ongoing supervision by public authorities. Also, the CRA Regulation provides incentives for the users of credit ratings in the EU to exercise their own due diligence and assess the trustworthiness of specific credit rating agencies or ratings. Under current reforms, it is also proposed that CESR or a European Securities and Markets Authority (ESMA) be in charge of the registration and supervision of credit rating agencies in the EU. The conceivable consequences of this stricter approach to credit rating agencies are a reduction over time of the use of ECAIs' ratings in banking regulation and eventually a more fundamental review of the CRA model (de Larosière report 2009).

29 European Commission, Communication setting out the Commission's approach to credit rating agencies, 9 January 2006. This approach follows CESR's opinion on sustaining the opposition of the ratings industry to more European harmonisation and supplementary rules; see also Buck 2005.

30 Regulation (EC) 1060/2009.

10 The way forward

The institutional frameworks for EU prudential banking regulation and supervision have undergone important restructuring following persistent calls for further EU action since the mid-1990s. Two factors, in particular, accelerated institutional innovation: the imminence of the agreement on the Basel II Accord entailing a new process-oriented supervisory approach to be implemented in the EU and the implementation of the Lamfalussy regulatory framework. The institutional change that occurred was pragmatic in character. It concentrated on immediate necessities (e.g. the need for some coordination in the implementation of the new complex capital requirements framework) and avoided open public debates about the most suitable institutional set-up in an increasingly integrated market.

The outcome was a polished European framework for the largely centralised regulation, combined with an enhanced European platform for supervisory cooperation and coordination on issues of common concern to supplement the decentralised supervision. Behind this synthetic presentation, there lies an intricate network of committees endowed with a series of hard and soft competences. The new institutional star is undoubtedly CEBS with its soft regulatory powers. It has taken over a large range of regulatory tasks and elaborated an ambitious working programme. At the same time, it has engaged in close cooperation with the other Level 3 committees (CESR, CEIOPS) and the BSC and integrated the GdC into its framework – the only body at European level that has dealt for more than thirty years with micro-prudential supervisory aspects of individual institutions.

Despite the ever growing degree of integration, the common banking market is far from being complete. The many instances of fragmentation especially in retail banking were consistently highlighted as justifying the decentralisation of prudential supervision in the EU and the reluctance to transfer any substantial tasks to the supra-national level. Still, with cross-border banking activities growing and ever more common infrastructures in place (e.g. payments system, clearing and settlements system), systemic risk concerns and increased contagion fears were acknowledged and fuelled enhanced cooperation arrangements. There was a common understanding that the discrepancy between centralised prudential regulation and decentralised supervision was not entirely satisfactory and that, with time, the emergence of a common supervisory culture and the growing trust between national competent authorities would trigger some centralisation of supervision. The pragmatic approach underpinning the establishment of the Lamfalussy committees entailed an evolutionary understanding of the regulatory framework and was conceived in view of preparing the ground for further institutional changes (Committee of Wise Men 2001: 41).

Indeed, in the White Paper on Financial Services Policy 2005–10, the Commission confirmed that an evolutionary approach to supervision is needed and set out the first measures to be taken for improving the supervisory environment. In the underlying consultative Green Paper, the Commission explained that such an evolutionary approach involves three steps. First, the various stakeholders had to agree on overall policy objectives of supervision. Second, the current framework should be exploited to the maximum (especially all possibilities of cooperation under the Lamfalussy framework), gaps should be identified and existing tools developed. Lastly, the Commission declared that it considered, as a last resort, the possibility of creating new supervisory structures in the long run.[1]

This moderate evolutionary approach was completely shattered by the financial crisis, which revealed that the existing supervisory arrangements were not fit for adequately addressing the high degree of interconnection in the markets. This triggered immediately unprecedented political commitment to revise the European institutional framework for supervision in view of making it more respondent to the needs of the integrated marketplace. It became obvious that Europe lacked first of all a prudential mechanism compelling the monitoring of overall developments in the EU financial markets and signalling timely and authoritatively the emerging risks and the relevant preventive policy actions required. Furthermore, there was also no obligation for policy-makers to take action once they became aware of such risks. Also, the arrangements for supervisory cooperation proved to be inefficient because, on the one hand, no specific and clear crisis management principles exist at EU level and, on the other hand, the delicate balance between home and host country competences established in European law proved unable to counteract national protectionist tendencies. It became also clear that information exchange was selective and insufficient and that the degree of trust between national competent authorities was ultimately unsatisfactory, despite their intensive gathering in multiple fora.

1 According to Annex I to the Green Paper:

> new structures should only be developed if all possibilities for cooperation under the current framework have been exhausted and if there is compelling evidence that, once fully implemented and developed, this framework cannot fulfil its financial stability and integration objectives or meet the requirements of European legislation.
> (Commission 2005a)

To address the deficiencies in EU's financial architecture, the European Commission established in October 2008 a group of high-profile experts under the leadership of Jacques de Larosière to give advice on the future of European financial regulation and supervision. The approach suggested in the de Larosière report was broadly followed by the Commission, which issued its first concrete proposals in May 2009. These were endorsed by the Ecofin Council and the European Council in June 2009. At the time of writing, the details of the new EU framework for supervision still need to be determined. Some of them will request tough negotiations, yet there appears to be a firm political commitment to have a new institutional architecture in place by 2010–11.

In the following sections, we will first point to some general aspects to be considered when devising the institutional reform of supervision. Subsequently, we will broadly review the possible reform scenarios and the related difficulties. Finally, we will briefly assess the concrete proposals put forward by the Commission in May 2009.

1 Constraints for devising the supervisory arrangements in the EU

1.1 Conferral, subsidiarity and proportionality

Debates about the readjustment of the supervisory architecture in Europe entail the consideration of the allocation of responsibilities with regard to supervision between the EU and the Member States. The first legitimate question would be whether prudential supervision falls within the competences conferred to the EU through primary law. According to article 5(2) consolidated TEU (ex 5 paragraph 1 EC Treaty), the EU 'shall act within the limits of the powers conferred upon it by the Treaty and the objectives assigned to it therein'. The only provisions in primary law dealing with prudential supervision are the articles consecrating the role of the ESCB with regard to prudential supervision and permitting eventually the transfer of supervisory tasks to the ECB. All the rules on supervision are contained in secondary legislation based on the Treaty provisions related to the internal market. The corroborated interpretation of these legal provisions suggests that prudential supervision falls within the broader internal market competences and thus constitutes a shared responsibility. Its exclusive exercise so far by the Member States does not mean that, if necessary and with due respect to the principles of subsidiarity and proportionality, the EU is deterred from assuming supervisory competences.

Once it is ascertained that banking supervision constitutes an EU competence, its use is subject to the limits posed by the principles of subsidiarity and proportionality. According to the subsidiarity principle, the EU shall take action:

> only if and in so far as the objectives of the proposed action cannot be sufficiently achieved by the Member States either at central level or at regional and local level, but can rather, by reason of the scale or effects of the proposed action, be better achieved at Union level.
>
> (article 5 paragraph 3 consolidated TEU)[2]

Thus, any transferral of prudential responsibilities should pass the two tests introduced by the subsidiarity principle – namely, the absolute necessity of EU action for the sufficient performance of the relevant task and the added value of that action. Consequently, the subsidiarity principle should permit EU action only when the objective can be better attained than it would be at national level and only through means proportional to the objective pursued.[3]

When applying these tests the underlying objectives have to be considered. As regards the pursuit of macro-prudential objectives, there is a straightforward case for the allocation of responsibilities at European level. The EU would be better placed because of its supranational focus and jurisdiction that endow it with a better capacity to identify and address cross-border spill-over effects giving rise to negative externalities (i.e. systemic risk), as opposed to the limited jurisdictions of Member States. From the point of view of micro-prudential objectives, the case for a supervisory role for EU institutions is less obvious. Strong arguments, related to the need for proximity between the supervisor and the supervised entities and for an intimate knowledge of the markets and economic cycles affecting the jurisdictions where banks operate, would indicate that the safety and soundness of individual institutions can be better ensured at national level. This is further reinforced by Member States' financial responsibility in case of failures. From this perspective, the EU could eventually bring an added value if it were to have specific supervisory competences with regard to pan-European banks and thus create efficiency gains.[4] The direct supervision at EU level of pan-European institutions, has obvious benefits for such banks that would profit from a single point of contact for supervisory aspects. It would imply the creation of a two-tier system, which would eventually unlevel the current playing-field between local, regional and cross-border institutions who ultimately compete in the same markets. However, a stronger argument in favour of EU micro-prudential competences derives from the problems related to the cooperation between home and host countries (e.g. disagreements on prudential treatment at cross-border group level) and protection-

2 Under the Lisbon Treaty art. 5 TEU consolidated version provides explicitly that the use of Union competences is governed by the principles of subsidiarity and proportionality.

3 See Conclusions of the Edinburgh meeting of the European Council, 11–12 December 1992, general part, Annex 1 and the Protocol on the application of the principles of subsidiarity and proportionality annexed to the EC Treaty by the Amsterdam Treaty.

4 On economies of scale allowing for efficiency gains as justifying the performance of tasks at a higher level, see Christophersen 1991a: 67.

ist tendencies of national supervisors (the creation of national champions). The neutral settling of conflicting national interests, the establishment of a firm coordination framework at EU level and the efficient prevention of new market integration barriers would all be tools for better attaining certain micro-prudential supervisory objectives, compared to the national level.

Thus, not only systemic risk, but also specific micro-prudential aspects related to the supervision of individual cross-border institutions indicate that in several instances the EU could be better placed than Member States to attain supervisory objectives. Consequently, the subsidiarity principle might prove helpful in determining the degree of centralisation or decentralisation of macro- and micro-supervisory tasks in an integrated market. However, it says little about the most appropriate institutional framework at European level.

The proportionality principle provides for a supplementary test imposing limits to the form and extent of EU actions in terms of their suitability to achieve the envisaged objective (article 5(4) consolidated TEU, ex 5 (3) EC Treaty). The requirement of proportionate action also means that the centralisation of specific supervisory functions does not imply the exercise at EU level of all supervisory functions (Lastra 2006: 308).

1.2 EU checks and balances

The design of the new institutional framework for banking supervision in the EU is substantially influenced by the constraints stemming from the need to safeguard the balance of powers between EU institutions. We have seen the difficulties accompanying the establishment of the Lamfalussy framework and the struggles to ensure that the two legislative arms have equivalent powers when controlling the exercise of implementing powers. The reform of banking supervision, eventually implying the creation of a new EU body is likely to invigorate such arguments and set them into the context of the broader governance debates on the limits of delegation of powers to European agencies.

If supervision requires the setting up of a body entrusted with legal personality, such body, irrespective of its precise name, is very likely to fall under what in EU terminology is called European agency.[5] European agencies are independent decentralised EU bodies established by means of secondary law and endowed with legal personality.[6] There are a variety of agencies within the EU, which lack a common framework[7] and display

5 Under the Lisbon Treaty, agencies are explicitly mentioned along with institutions, bodies and offices; see, for instance, arts 15 and 16 TFEU.

6 The EU legal personality allows an entity to enjoy the largest legal capacity granted in the Member States to legal persons established under their jurisdiction.

7 A common EU framework exists only for executive agencies (Council Regulation (EC) 58/2003). Several attempts to define a similar framework for European regulatory agencies (Commission 2002b, 2005e) were abandoned in 2008 because of various misunderstandings. In 2008, the Commission tried to relaunch the debate through a new Communication (Commission 2008d), so far not concluded.

heterogeneous governance features. Delegation of powers to these entities entails several accountability and legitimacy questions.

The Treaties were silent about the delegation of powers, except for article 202 EC Treaty that constituted the legal basis for the delegation of implementing powers to the Commission. The article also allowed the Council to reserve the right, in specific cases, to directly exercise implementing powers. Under the Lisbon Treaty article 290 TFEU introduces the possibility of delegation of powers to the Commission to amend and supplement non-essential elements of EU legislation, while article 291 TFEU foresees the conferral of implementing powers to the Commission for the uniform application of binding EU acts. In specific cases the Council may itself exercise implementing powers (article 291(2) TFEU) Consequently, several scenarios may be envisaged in the case of a new EU entity for banking supervision: (1) the Commission may delegate its own implementing powers to a separate entity; (2) the Council may decide to retain implementing powers and eventually delegate them to the Member States; (3) powers are delegated directly by secondary legislation adopted through co-decision to a new autonomous body.

The first situation would be constrained by the limits imposed through the *Meroni* doctrine developed by the ECJ.[8] According to this doctrine, delegation of powers is allowed for only if a number of preconditions are fulfilled: (1) delegation must be express and cannot be presumed; (2) delegation can only relate to powers which the Commission itself possesses; (3) delegation must relate to the preparation and performance of executive and implementing acts alone; (4) discretionary powers may not be transferred; (5) the Commission must retain oversight over the delegated competence and will be held responsible for the manner in which it is performed; (6) delegation must not disturb the 'balance of powers' among EU institutions. These restrictions to the delegation of powers to agencies were confirmed in subsequent case-law,[9] and are broadly reflected in the various Commission documents on European agencies issued since the White Paper on European Governance (Commission 2001a, 2002b, 2005e, 2008d).

The *Meroni* doctrine, which developed into a tool for restricting delegation within the EU and an argument against the creation of regulatory agencies, despite the severe criticism it has encountered (Lenaerts 1993; Majone and Everson 2001; Yataganas 2001), remains for the time being 'good law'. Consequently, it appears that 'a delegation of wide discretionary powers is

8 Case 9–56 *Meroni & Co., Industrie Metallurgiche, SpA* v. *High Authority of the European Coal and Steel Community*, judgment of the Court of 13 June 1958.

9 Case 18/62 *Barge* v. *High Authority* [1962] ECR 565 and Case 30/65 *Macchiorlati Dalmas* v. *High Authority* [1966] ECR 50. More recently it was explicitly referred to in Cases C-154–155/04, *The Queen, on the application of Alliance for Natural Health and Nutri-link Ltd* v. *Secretary of State for Health* [2005] ECR I-6541, Case C-301/02 P, *Tralli* v. *ECB* [2005] ECR I-4071.

clearly unlawful under present primary law and that the creation of regulatory agencies which typically would dispose of such powers, is violating the principle of institutional balance and is therefore not permissible' (Griller and Orator 2007: 15). The *Meroni* doctrine would imply, first, that an agency entrusted with implementation may not have the power to make policy choices and, second, that it does not have the power to apply already made policy choices in a discretionary way. These aspects are particularly important for the delegation of competences related to supervision.

As regards the retention of implementing powers by the Council itself, a relatively recent ECJ judgment has clarified the conditions under which the Council may retain such powers for itself and eventually delegate them directly to the Member States.[10] Thus, it is only in specific cases and with detailed explanation of the grounds for such a decision that the Council may reserve the right to exercise implementing powers. The ECJ held that the specificity requirement is fulfilled if the area covered is of a specific nature, which might be induced, for instance, from specific derogations to the legislative procedure. Furthermore, the area has to be 'clearly circumscribed'. This condition would be definitely satisfied if there were an exhaustive list of implementing provisions, but the Court appears also to take a lenient approach, accepting merely that the retained competences do not cover all aspects of a given field (Randazzo 2005). Moreover, the temporal limitation of retained powers (e.g. the delegating measure is backed by a review clause following a transition period) indicates the specificity of a situation.

In the context of the supervisory reform, it may be envisaged that the Council would want to retain specific controversial implementation aspects, in view of either exercising them itself or leaving these aspects to the Member States for implementation. The ECJ noted that transferring competences at EU level 'did not, of itself, result in the Member States being immediately stripped' of the powers they have been entitled to exercise in the fields at issue.[11] The Council could thus allow the Member States to deal with the most delicate and politically sensitive issues, such as those affecting their fiscal responsibilities.

Finally, there is the situation when the legislator (either the Council or the Council and the Parliament) entrusts powers directly to an agency, and not to the Commission. The limits of such delegation of powers to an agency were set by the ECJ in the *Romano* case.[12] Legal scholars have differentiated between this situation of direct delegation to an agency and that of the sub-delegation by the Commission, thereby trying to mitigate the restrictions of the *Meroni* doctrine on delegation of powers to European agencies. Thus, it is proposed that in case of direct delegation

10 Case C-257/01, *Commission* v. *Council* [2005] ECR I-345.

11 Case C-257/01, para. 69.

12 Case 98/80 *Giuseppe Romano* v. *Institut national d'assurance maladie-invalidite* [1981] ECR 1241.

through the legislator, the strict limits of *Meroni* be loosened without giving up their legal fundaments. The need for limiting agencies' powers within the framework set by the legislator needs to be balanced against the need for flexibility in the operation of agencies (Griller and Orator 2007: 9, 18).

This would imply that it is not forbidden from the outset to give agencies discretionary powers, provided that the legislator has established sufficient safeguards (through the policy choices underpinning the delegation, through participation in decision-making of the agency, through call-back powers, etc.). Also, the Commission's prerogatives in implementing EU law cannot be undermined and the administration via such an agency should be an exception, justifiable through specific circumstances. The measures adopted by such an agency should be subject to legal review and there should be mechanisms for holding such agencies accountable to the Parliament and the Council (through regular reports, hearings, etc.). The governance structure of the new EU body is of utmost importance for its legitimacy and accountability, in light of the EU system of institutional checks and balances.

1.3 The broader unfinished puzzle

In the EU, one of the major reasons for the exercise of banking supervision at national level is linked to the fact that crisis management and crisis resolution and the hereto linked fiscal burden pertain to Member States' jurisdictions. There is an intimate link between prevention and crisis management and it can be in practice very difficult to distinguish when preventive action – consisting of early interventions on banks that show a deterioration of their financial situation – ends and crisis management starts. Furthermore, crisis management, irrespective of which authority takes the lead for it, relies to a large extent on supervisory information.

In the EU the responsibility for crisis management lies at national level. This is completely understandable for crises affecting individual institutions or geographically limited within a country, yet it raises problems with regard to cross-border crises. As already mentioned, at EU level three MoUs have been adopted laying down principles and practical arrangements guiding the cooperation of national authorities in such situations. In the light of the current crisis and of the unfortunate experience with cross-border institutions such as Fortis, Dexia or the Icelandic banks, these MoUs appear to be largely ineffective and crisis management is ultimately split and done at national level with little cooperation. A mechanism for joint decision-making in cross-border crisis management is absent, and, moreover, there is not even a framework for ensuring the consistent coordination of national responses. This is particularly problematic considering the differences in the legal systems, especially in insolvency and company law, which for instance may limit the possibility of transferring assets within a group or rank creditors in different ways. This may lead to dramatic misallocations of resources and liquidities within a cross-border group that are ultimately detrimental to all entities of the group.

Devising a consistent and reliable framework for crisis management will be a big challenge for the EU. It should provide certainty as to the endowment of all competent authorities within the EU with equivalent intervention instruments and powers. It should also set up effective coordination arrangements in cross-border situations. Eventually, a special body should be entrusted with handling cross-border banking crises in the EU.[13] If supervisory functions are to be exercised effectively at EU level, then it is imperative that a streamlined framework for cross-border crisis management is also adopted in the EU.

For such arrangements to be effective, probably the most difficult issue to be addressed concerns the allocation of financial responsibility in case of cross-border banking failures – the so-called burden-sharing. Financial support in case of a crisis is not limited to liquidity assistance through the lender-of-last-resort operations but entails also injections of capital into ailing institutions or several implicit government guarantees pursuant to the 'too-big-to fail' dictum. This implies the involvement of public (taxpayers') money and relies on the intervention of the fiscal authority, apart from central banks' LOLR operations. However, while the ECB has the competence to provide emergency liquidity assistance, there is no fiscal authority in the EU. Consequently, the costs of bailing out and other forms of public support for troubled institutions will be completely borne by the Member States through their Treasuries or ministries of finance. The European MoUs have devised only two broad principles for the sharing of the fiscal burden between Member States in cross-border situations: the equity principle and the accountability principle (de Larosière report, Commission 2009c: 35). The former sets as a quantitative yardstick the economic impact of the crisis in a specific Member State; the latter indicates the allocation of home–host supervisory powers as a guiding rule.

The reform of the supervisory arrangements cannot be disconnected from the debates on burden-sharing. The attribution of centralised powers at EU level will have to consider also the consequences of failures in the exercise of such powers. If fiscal consequences are to be exclusively borne by national authorities without clear, *ex ante* defined and equitable criteria for burden-sharing, it is likely that every Member State will also try to impose its own views with regard to supervision. It was rightly pointed out that the allocation of costs should be done under the motto 'he who pays the piper calls the tune' (Goodhart 2004). One solution would be the establishment of an EU mechanism for financing cross-border crisis-resolution efforts. However, this appears to be too idealistic in the current context, given that fiscal federalism in the EU is a highly sensitive topic,

13 See, for instance, the proposal for the creation of a European Standing Committee for Crisis Management (Lastra 2006: 311–17).

almost taboo among policy-makers. Another way out would be to establish preventively detailed burden-sharing criteria and a framework to ensure that they will be consistently applied in cross-border crisis situations.[14] Tackling these issues at EU level may require either a Treaty change or measures based on article 352 TFEU (ex 308 EC Treaty), which allows for the definition of new powers at EU level, necessary for the operation of the common market. In October 2009, the Commission issued for consultation a Communication on an EU framework for cross-border crisis management in the banking sector, which discusses several possible arrangements. It is expected that the Commission will follow up with some concrete proposals in 2010.

2 Institutional scenarios for future European banking supervision

The EU supervisory framework developed in accordance with an evolutionary approach along the continuum between complete decentralisation and centralisation of supervisory functions. The fundamental question of the reform of the European supervisory framework relates to identifying with clarity which supervisory functions can be effectively performed at EU level and thus would require more centralisation. The issue of determining the most suitable European set-up that should perform such functions, as well as the most appropriate instruments to be used, is addressed only at a second stage.

Thus, the assumption that the reform should prompt some enhanced European dimension to prudential supervision does not indicate anything about where supervisory competences should be allocated. In the literature there are two contrasting views on the future European framework for financial supervision, one emphasising the need for decentralisation and improved coordination, and the other promoting centralisation at European level (Lastra 2003: 54). Accurate studies[15] indicate various possible institutional models for banking supervision in the EU that could be ascribed to these two approaches. It is not our purpose to evaluate these models; we will simply indicate the main stances of the discussions without entering into details and without pretending to exhaust all the possible alternatives. It is important to keep in mind that a pragmatic approach is most likely to prevail, and hence, 'we must avoid becoming trapped in a sterile debate of what is better: supranational institutions or improved cooperation. There

14 The de Larosière report suggests the following criteria for burden-sharing to be considered: the deposits of the institution; the assets (either in terms of accounting values, market values or risk-weighted values) of the institution; the revenue flows of the institution; the share of payment system flows of the institution; the division of supervisory responsibility, account being taken of the fact that the party responsible for supervisory work, analysis and decision will be also responsible for an appropriately larger share of the costs.

15 We refer among others to: Di Giorgio and Di Noia 2000; Goodhart 2000; Vives 2000; see also Briault 1999, 2002; Taylor 1995; Lannoo 2002; Lastra 2003; Marotta 2003; Gulde and Wolf 2004; European Financial Services Round Table 2005.

might be a need for supranational institutions in some areas, but not in others' (Lamfalussy 2000). Such a pragmatic approach underpins the concrete proposals for supervisory reform put forward by the European Commission, which we will discuss in the last section of this chapter.

2.1 Decentralisation-based scenarios

The current European supervisory framework is characterised by 'decentralisation, cooperation and segmentation (by specialist financial institutions conducting distinct financial activities: banking, securities and insurance)' (Lastra 2003: 50). This is mainly justified by the fact that supervision is deeply rooted in domestic institutional, economic and political contexts. Moreover, supervision relies on the detailed knowledge of markets and actors, which assumes the proximity of the supervisors authorities to the supervised entities. Supervision also supposes continuity, hence the importance of domestic supervisory practices. These are particularly pertinent arguments that make a strong case for preserving the supervisory function at national level. The proponents of decentralisation-based scenarios for future EU supervisory arrangements underline that an eventual centralisation of supervisory functions at EU level would be deprived of all these essential characteristics. Under decentralised scenarios, the role of national supervisors is seen as crucial, and the EU's capacity to improve coordination between national supervisors is largely discarded.

Reform is envisaged as building on existing domestic structures, by improving the distribution of competences between national supervisors. From this perspective, the emphasis is on the reinforcement of the role of the consolidating supervisor with regard to the whole group, and the establishment of sufficient safeguards to ensure that the views of all supervisors concerned are duly taken into account. The reinforcement of the consolidated supervisor is seen especially in terms of extending prudential competences to cover the subsidiaries of the parent credit institutions it has authorised. Colleges of supervisors would offer a framework for all supervisors concerned to express their views on specific issues regarding a particular institution. Colleges would have mainly an advisory function, with the final decision being taken by the consolidated supervisor. The various existing EU networking platforms for supervisors (CEBS, BSC, GdG) are considered suitable for building up mutual trust and supervisory convergence, but not for dealing with individual cases.

The typical example of a decentralisation-based scenario for the EU financial architecture is the lead supervisor model (EFR 2004, 2005; ELEC 2005). It builds on the concepts of consolidating supervisor and coordinator supervisor, which have been strengthened under the CRD and the directive on financial conglomerates. Still, these improvements were considered 'only a first step towards a lead supervisor regime' (EFR 2005: 6), 'a half-way solution which can lead to inconsistencies in implementation' (EFR 2005: 24).

The model of the lead supervisor proposed by the EFR is based on the core idea that the home-country authorities should supervise all EU-wide operations of an authorised bank, irrespective of whether they are conducted through branches or subsidiaries. The lead supervisor would be the single point of contact for all prudential issues, would coordinate reporting duties, would validate internal group-wide models and approve capital and liquidity allocation, coordinate licensing procedures, approve cross-border setting up of central functions, and decide upon and coordinate on-site inspections. The lead supervisor would be supported by a 'college of supervisors' reassembling representatives of the host supervisors. The college would be entrusted with advisory tasks, contributing to a better understanding of local market conditions in the host countries, and a catalyst role for information-sharing (EFR 2005: 24). In case of crisis, the college of supervisors will change in character and become, under the leadership of the lead supervisor, a management team for all involved supervisory authorities.

It was observed that such an institutional design would consist of a national mandate allowing domestic supervisors to retain their competences, accompanied by some form of cooperation (Oosterloo and Schoenmaker 2004: 40). This model, although superior to the current home-country control paradigm, from a market efficiency perspective, is considered to be deficient from a financial stability point of view, notably in terms of its capacity to induce the lead supervisor to consider cross-border externalities (Oosterloo and Schoenmaker 2004: 41). It is suggested that such shortcomings could be overcome by endowing the lead supervisor with not a national but a European mandate that would 'ensure that the interests of all depositors/countries are taken into account'. The lead supervisor with a European mandate would operate in a more institutionalised framework, composed of national supervisors working in tandem with a centralised body.[16] Day-to-day supervision would be conducted at national level, but key supervisory decisions and policy design on cross-border aspects would be done jointly. We observe that, although building on the 'decentralised' element of the lead supervisor concept, the model put forth by Schoenmaker and Oosterloo would have an important centralised dimension as it requires the attribution of cross-border competences to a domestic authority, together with the institutionalisation of cooperation.

16

> In some form of European system of financial supervisors, national supervisors could work together with a decision-making body or agency at the centre. Within the system, the supervisor in the country where the bank is headquartered can then act as consolidated or lead supervisor. Accordingly, for financial stability purposes, the home country authorities (supervisor and central bank) within the European system of financial supervisors and the European System of Central Banks (ESCB) can act within their respective systems.
>
> (Oosterloo and Schoenmaker 2004: 39)

Furthermore, the lead supervisor concept was also criticised for its reliance on the home-country control principle for the appointment of the lead supervisor. Particularly, with regard to complex corporate structures and the expansion of cross-border financial activities, it was questioned whether the home supervisor (i.e. the authority in the country where the parent company had been incorporated) is the authority best suited for conducting consolidated supervision (ELEC 2005: 3). First, it was underlined that the home country might not be the one where the major weight of operations is conducted, or where risk management of the group is centralised. There is the risk of leaving some local supervisors without significant functions, in countries where foreign banks occupy large parts of the domestic market. This would call for the lead supervisor to be appointed in accordance with more substantive criteria (e.g. comparing the size of the balance sheets of the various entities operating in different Member States). Moreover, the decentralised lead supervisor model ignores the interaction with the substantial 'residual' competences of the host countries, such as those regarding liquidity risk management. Also, it disregards the issue of burden-sharing.

All these remarks underline the fact that, if they do not merely aim to pursue efficiency objectives but also contribute to the maintenance of financial stability, decentralisation-based scenarios for supervision in an integrated market have to be backed by some form of reinforced supervisory cooperation coordinated at the European level. The individual delegation of tasks and responsibilities among national supervisory authorities is still a rarity, given that the degree of trust among supervisors and of convergence between supervisory practices is still at an incipient level. Legislation cannot impose such delegation of powers between supervisors, unless it also provides sufficient safeguards for all concerned authorities and a strong coordination of information-sharing and decision-making in common concern situations.

2.2 Centralisation-based scenarios

As opposed to decentralisation-based scenarios with their emphasis on the strengthening and clarification of national authorities' leadership in the supervision of cross-border institutions, centralisation-based scenarios focus either on the institutionalisation of the cooperation of domestic supervisors in cross-border situations or on the transfer of direct supervisory tasks at EU level. In this context, various settings could be envisaged that may be considered either as evolutionary (i.e. foresee a gradual evolution of the current coordinative set-up towards a European agency) or revolutionary (i.e. comprise radically new proposals).

The options are set on a continuum ranging from enhanced supervisory cooperation and coordination, somehow institutionalised at EU level, to the creation of a European institution entrusted with supervisory tasks. The choice of the model will depend on the functions to be performed at EU level (e.g. coordination, mediation, authorisation, direct supervision, crisis management, crisis resolution) and a defined domain of application (e.g. different sectors/EU financial markets, prudential aspects/conduct of business). The institutional framework for a future centralised supervisory function might already be in place (e.g. ECB, CEBS) or can be created from the scratch. The supervisory architecture might be organised along the lines of regulatory functions (licensing, supervision, enforcement and crisis management), business sectors (banking, securities, insurance, cross-sector), business categories (wholesale or retail) or objectives (prudential considerations, investor protection, competition). Hence, various institutional models may be considered for the European supervisory design: an ESCB-type supervisory system; supervisory networks led by a central authority; a single integrated umbrella supervisor; multiple sectoral authorities (by institution or activity); twin peaks models (by objective); combined supervisory authority for two financial sectors but excluding the third (banking and securities, securities and insurance, banking and insurance); a single authority entrusted with specific tasks (lender of last resort, prudential supervision of pan-European financial institutions, European market surveillance body).[17]

The possible institutional modalities for a future EU supervisory architecture are, in theory, innumerate and all subject to the constraints described at the beginning of this chapter. Depending on the allocation of supervisory functions at EU level, centralisation might fit into the current limits of EU law or might require a Treaty change (e.g. in case it would affect the allocation of fiscal responsibilities implied in banking supervision). Even with the current unprecedented political willingness to reform EU supervision, there is no support yet for such far-reaching reforms that would suppose a Treaty change and it is more plausible to expect an evolutionary scenario outstretching the interpretation of the current legal provisions.

Another aspect to be considered when devising centralised scenarios for supervision relates to the latter's impact on national models for supervision. Institutionalising supervisory coordination would also entail levelling the playing-field between the powers and competences of all domestic authorities involved. Also, it requires the adaptation of national legal frameworks so as to allow for the smooth exercise of cross-border supervisory functions (ELEC 2005: 30).

Broadly speaking, centralisation of supervisory functions can take two forms: one emphasising coordination through some European body placed at the node of the network of national supervisors, and another focusing on the attribution of specific supervisory tasks directly to a EU body. The essential feature of both typologies is that each would request the setting up of a new institution at the European level with the legal and political hurdles implied.

17 Wymeersch 2007.

The first typology would be mainly based on the interaction between national competent authorities acting as a network of supervisors when dealing with cross-border situations or issues of common interest. Such a network would be coordinated from the EU level by a specifically established body whose powers may range from mere operational coordination to mediation and decision-making in case of disagreement between the network members. The European body will not replace or take over the supervisory functions of national competent authorities, but would instead build on them, providing added value through enhanced coordination.

One possible way forward under this typology is the establishment of an ESCB-type European System of Financial Supervisors (ESFS) entailing a central European authority for policy-making, which would operate in a decentralised way through national supervisory authorities.[18] The central supervisory authority would solve all conflicts between national regulators. It would, on the basis of collegial decision-making, determine the consolidating supervisor and define clearly his or her mandate, thus limiting the possibility of domestic supervisors to take supplementary measures by invoking the general good. It might also play a role in, and thereby create more legal certainty with regard to, crisis management. Scepticism related to this model concerns the possible stifling of constructive regulatory competition, and the risk of overregulation and lack of accountability (European Financial Services Round Table 2005: 42).

A similar model was put forth by Di Giorgio and Di Noia who conceived a European System of Financial Regulators (ESFR) encompassing a European Financial Supervision Authority at the centre. This authority would be entrusted with competences for micro-economic stability and would participate within the ESFR in the definition of general strategies and principles of financial regulation, along with two other centralised authorities: the ECB, responsible for systemic stability, and the European Authority for Market Transparency, competent for market, investor protection and disclosure requirements.

The new EU bodies involved in supervision could be established from scratch or built on the existing coordinative structures under the Lamfalussy framework.[19] Given the positive experience already accumulated with the Level 3 committees, it appears that this is a valid solution, which could also simplify much of the preparations of the reform. Such a possible evolution was already suggested in 2004 during the first assessments of the functioning of the new Lamfalussy committees.[20] It could be also envisaged that

18 See Schoenmaker and Oosterloo 2006: 16–17. The authors develop the ESFS as a way to legitimise the model of the lead supervisor with a European mandate they propose.

19 In theory, the European Commission could also directly take over the coordination of national supervisors. Yet, given the need for expertise and the high workload of the Commission, it is most likely that such tasks would be further delegated to an Authority.

20 See the 2004 Himalaya Report of CESR envisaging a vertical scheme of supervisory competences that would eventually lead to a single supervisor for the European securities sector.

several EU bodies be established with different functions, whereby micro-prudential supervisory functions could be performed by upgraded Level 3 committees, whereas macro-prudential functions could be entrusted to a completely new body at EU level, that would coordinate input from the network of national authorities.

Under the second centralisation typology, supervisory functions would be directly entrusted to an EU body. The emphasis is not on the coordination of national competent authorities but on independent supranational decision-making. Thus an EU body could be explicitly entrusted, among others, with issuing early warnings on risks identified from macro-developments; with specific tasks for crisis management; with the enforcement of common prudential rules against national authorities; or with direct supervisory tasks (authorisation, validation of models, monitoring and intervention) for cross-border institutions.

The latter is the most extreme centralisation-driven scenario and would imply the transfer of supervisory powers from the national to the EU level with regard to certain institutions. Such a model envisages the creation of a separate, mandatory regime for institutions operating in multiple jurisdictions within the EU and having obvious systemic implications (European Financial Services Round Table 2005: 41). It would introduce a two-tier system consisting of a European supervisory structure for pan-European institutions, parallel to the national supervisory structures that will continue to govern institutions operating only in their home countries. Apart from the political and legal intricacies related to such transfer of powers, this proposal is criticised from the point of view of the distortion of the principle of competitive neutrality, as it introduces different supervisory regimes for institutions that compete with each other in the same local markets. Furthermore, although it might display some advantages from an efficiency perspective (e.g. with the cross-border institutions being subject to a unified regime and a single supervisor), there is no evidence whatsoever that the model could also improve financial stability. A distant supranational supervisor does not deeply know the features of all markets in which cross-border institutions operate, nor does it have full information on the broader economic context underpinning those markets. Also, it would be hard to justify altogether eliminating the possibilities of intervention of domestic authorities in the interests of the general good.

2.3 Centralisation within the ECB – the enabling clause

EU primary law contains one explicit legal basis envisaging the possible centralisation of supervisory functions within the ECB. This may be an attractive solution as it offers an already functioning network of European and national central banks, endowed with powerful instruments.

There are some valid arguments that have been invoked in support of attributing formal tasks to the ECB in the area of prudential supervision.

First, there is the advantage of providing the ECB with first-hand information for exercising its 'unquestionable macro-prudential duties in the case of an impending systemic crisis' (Lamfalussy 2004: 20). Also, synergies and information-sharing would be particularly useful for the performance of ECB tasks related to the smooth functioning of payments systems. Furthermore, it would benefit from the ECB's cooperation experience with national supervisors in the framework of the BSC. Also, such a scenario could provide clarity and guarantees as regards the institutional balance within the EU. Last but not least, if substantial powers involving a new allocation of responsibilities were to be transferred at EU level (e.g. competences for crisis resolution), entrusting them to the ECB would have the advantage of avoiding Treaty changes, due to the enabling clause in article 127(6) TFEU (ex 105(6) EC Treaty).

However, there is also some heavy criticism against this solution. Apart from the fears of too much power concentration, such a solution would entail further limits. It would apparently be a more comfortable institutional solution for the Eurosystem but not for the EU as a whole, given the ECB's limited jurisdiction with regard to Member States with a derogation. Another concern of utmost importance refers to the risk that entrusting the ECB with supervisory tasks might dilute its mandate with regard to monetary policy. The debate on the suitability of institutional separation between banking supervisors and the monetary authority is intrinsic to the institutional design of banking supervision. There are no conclusive arguments[21] either in favour of separation or for unifying both functions under the same roof. On the contrary, it is constantly highlighted that the choice depends very much on the underlying legal and economic system, on the reputation and degree of independence of the central bank. With regard to attributing some supervisory role to the ECB, it is also particularly important to clarify the arrangements for crisis management at European level. Thus, ECB's supervisory competences will need to be correlated with the ECB's role as a lender of last resort[22] and with the overall European policy on deposit insurance schemes. Eventually entrusting the ECB with micro-prudential tasks would call for its substantial involvement in crisis management and resolution, which is largely a political issue that risks exposing ECB's independence to political pressures and interference.

21 The arguments favouring unification relate to the possible synergies between the monetary policy and financial stability functions, the better management of systemic risk, the functioning of payments system, the reputation benefits stemming from central bank independence and the related decrease in risk of regulatory capture. Arguments in favour of separation emphasise the potential conflicts between monetary policy and financial stability, the fears of a too powerful independent institution, the need for unified financial supervision due to the blurring of frontiers between the traditional financial sectors. On these debates, see Schoenmaker and Goodhart 1993; Goodhart 2000.

22 See the policy of the ECB on the Emergency Liquidity Assistance (ELA), ECB 1999: 98; Teixeira and Schinasi 2006.

We have already referred to the so-called enabling clause enshrined in article 105(6) EC Treaty that provided for a special fast-track procedure to decide the allocation of prudential tasks to the ECB. According to this procedure, the Ecofin Council may, by unanimity, confer on the ECB specific tasks in the area of prudential supervision, upon a formal proposal from the Commission and after consulting the ECB and receiving the assent of the European Parliament. This procedure has been characterised as a 'rather swift although weighty legislative action' (Smits 1997: 357).

The provision has been transposed with minor changes in the Lisbon Treaty. According to article 127(6) TFEU, the Council may confer, through a regulation, specific tasks upon the ECB concerning policies relating to the prudential supervision of credit institutions and other financial institutions, with the exception of insurance undertakings. Article 127(6) TFEU, like article 105(6) EC Treaty, applies also to the Member States with a derogation. Consequently, the non-participating Member States are called upon to vote for the transferral of supervisory powers to the ECB. Nevertheless, contrary to the procedure foreseen by article 105(6) that required more vigilant involvement of the Parliament through the assent procedure,[23] under the new TFEU provision the transfer of prudential competences can be achieved through unanimity in the Council, upon mere consultation of the ECB and the European Parliament. This change in the procedure may be interpreted as facilitating an eventual transfer of prudential competences to the ECB.

The scope of the enabling clause is very broad and the expression 'specific tasks concerning policies relating to prudential supervision' can be all-encompassing. A broad interpretation of the word 'tasks' is not limited to executive functions and operational tasks related to prudential supervision but can also be extended to cover the formulation, interpretation or implementation of policies. It may be used for macro- and micro-prudential aspects. In both cases, it allows the transfer to the ECB of competences covering all or only certain aspects of prudential supervision. By contrast, a narrow interpretation of the enabling clause could rely on the fact that the legislator did not use more generic words such as 'functions', 'competences' or 'powers'. From this perspective, the specific reference to 'tasks' can be understood as merely referring to the transfer of specific pieces of supervisory work, but not of large policy-making powers with regard to supervision. In our view, given the inconsistent terminology throughout EU primary legislation, there are no pertinent reasons compelling us to interpret the enabling provision too narrowly.

There is an important limit to the scope of supervisory competences transferable to the ECB by means of article 127(6) TFEU (ex 105(6) EC) – namely the explicit exclusion of insurance undertakings. Hence, the

23 Compared to mere consultation, assent by the European Parliament entails a right to veto.

ECB cannot become, by enactment of the enabling clause, the European umbrella supervisor for all financial sectors. This would require a Treaty amendment, according to the regular procedure.

The enabling clause is not a special flexibility provision, but a special Treaty review clause. Recourse to it has been envisaged as a simplified procedure for Treaty amendment. The use of it would amount to a change of primary EU law, compulsory for all Member States, hence the unanimity requirement. Centralisation of supervisory tasks, through the enabling clause, would add a further task to the Eurosystem. The effects would be irreversible and would impinge upon all Member States. The transfer of competences to the ECB would become part of the *acquis*. Unanimity would be required because, from the moment the enabling clause is enacted, full participation in EMU will also entail full submission to the ECB's prudential supervisory powers. Thus, convergence criteria in the process of preparation for the adoption of the euro might need to be assessed also from the perspective of prudential supervision issues. Yet a major limit remains: the acts of the ECB adopted in the area of prudential supervision would still be applicable only to the 'ins', as, according to article 42.2 consolidated ESCB Statute, acts of the ECB do not apply to Member States with a derogation.

2.4 Enhanced cooperation

The mechanism of enhanced cooperation was introduced by the Treaty of Amsterdam, amended by the Treaty of Nice, and received renewed attention in the Lisbon Treaty. The relevant provisions on enhanced cooperation were scattered throughout the Treaty on the European Union (Title VII, Provisions on closer cooperation, articles 43–5) and the EC Treaty (article 11–11a). Under the Lisbon Treaty they continue to be divided between Title IV TEU (article 20) and Title II TFEU (articles 326–34 TFEU).

Enhanced cooperation was conceived as a mechanism allowing for a faster development in specific areas, with full respect of EU law and with the aim to gradually involve all Member States. Enhanced cooperation allows groups of Member States, under certain circumstances, to 'borrow the EU institutional system to achieve objectives and to undertake tasks defined by the Treaties, which could not be achieved or undertaken by applying the normal institutional rules governing that particular objective/ task' (Shaw 2003: 281).

From the relevant articles, the following features of enhanced cooperation may be induced: (1) it remains within the framework of the Union's non-exclusive competences; (2) it aims at furthering the objectives of the Union, protecting its interests and reinforcing its integration process; (3) it shall be open at any time to all Member States; (4) it is a last-resort measure, taken in case that the Council has established that the objectives of such cooperation cannot be attained within a reasonable period by the Union as a whole; (5) it shall involve at least one third of the Member States or, under the Lisbon Treaty, at least nine; (6) it has to comply with the Treaties and the law of the Union; (7) it shall not undermine the internal market or economic, social and territorial cohesion; (8) it shall not constitute a barrier to or discrimination in trade among Member States and not distort competition among them; (9) it shall respect the competences, rights and obligations of the non-participating Member States. On their turn, the latter shall not impede the implementation of enhanced cooperation by the participating Member States. Furthermore, the Council and the Commission have to ensure the consistency of the activities undertaken in the context of enhanced cooperation and their consistency with the policies of the Union.

The authorisation to proceed with enhanced cooperation requires a decision of the Council, acting on a proposal from the Commission and after obtaining the consent of the European Parliament. The Council decision shall be taken by unanimity of the votes of the representatives of the Member States participating in enhanced cooperation, whereas all members of the Council may participate in the deliberations. Interestingly, the involvement of the Parliament would be stronger in case of enhanced cooperation (the consent procedure confers to the Parliament powers of delay and power of rejection), as compared to the bare requirement of consultation in case of the enabling clause allowing the transfer of specific supervisory tasks to the ECB under the Lisbon Treaty.

As for the scope of enhanced cooperation, we note that it is circumscribed by the institutional framework and the exercise of non-exclusive competences provided in the Treaties. Thus, Member States could not, by means of enhanced cooperation, adopt acts or conduct actions that they could not adopt or conduct within the framework of the Treaties. Moreover, the institutional framework of enhanced cooperation is identical to the one established for the Union as a whole. Also, the instruments for action and the decision-making procedures laid down in the Treaties apply in principle in the same way.

So far, there have been no instances when the provisions on enhanced cooperation were applied. The new wording in the Lisbon Treaty may be interpreted as encouraging recourse to this flexibility clause, through procedural changes aimed at facilitating its activation. In principle, progress on integration may be achieved through enhanced cooperation in any field, except for exclusive Union competences. The shared competences with regard to the internal market could be considered as a suitable context for the enactment of the enhanced cooperation mechanism, as long as they contribute to more market integration and do not result in more fragmentation.

It is worth noting that enhanced cooperation can take place only within the institutional framework set by the Treaty, which also includes the ECB.

Although the framework for the single currency was characterised as 'a form of enhanced cooperation organised directly in the Treaty',[24] the general provisions on enhanced cooperation do not per se exclude the ECB as a potential institutional support for enhanced cooperation.

With regard to banking supervision, enhanced cooperation may be used when no agreement can be reached among all Member States on whether or how to reform the supervisory architecture in the EU. This may occur in the context of two broad scenarios: centralisation of supervisory tasks within the ESCB or centralisation of supervisory tasks into some other framework, existing or newly created. Under the first scenario, it will constitute an alternative to the enabling clause in case no unanimity can be achieved for its activation. In the second scenario, it will provide an alternative solution to the impossibility of achieving the qualified majority necessary under article 114 TFEU (ex 95 EC Treaty) for adopting measures for the achievement of the internal market, or the unanimity required by article 352 TFEU (ex 308 EC Treaty) for taking actions necessary for achieving EU objectives that prove to be necessary for the operation of the common market and for which no necessary powers have been provided in the Treaty.[25]

In our view, the permissive language of the enhanced cooperation provisions, as well as the very objective of such flexibility clause to facilitate further integration where it is hard to achieve agreement according to ordinary procedures, is a solid argument for considering it as a potential instrument for achieving progress on supervisory matters in Europe. Moreover, during the preparatory work for the European Constitution and the Treaty of Lisbon it was underlined that enhanced cooperation was conceived from the beginning as a substitute for unanimity. Also, it has been held that the mechanism of enhanced cooperation may prove useful for extending certain flexibility systems pre-established in the Treaty.[26]

It is the very purpose of enhanced cooperation to allow for a group of Member States to advance in integration, by using the existing institutional framework, in those cases where action by all Member States is difficult to agree on. In the enlarged Union enhanced cooperation provides a solution for potential deadlocks capable of blocking the dynamics of the integration process and impinging upon the evolving nature of the European project.

Enhanced cooperation would not imply a change in the Treaty and allows for a more moderate form of centralisation, without irreversible implications for the non-participating Member States. The acts adopted in the framework of enhanced cooperation only bind participating Member

24 The European Convention (2003) Cover note CONV 723/03.

25 Case-law and doctrine have constantly attributed a wide interpretation to art. 308 (ex art. 235) EC Treaty. The 'wide reading, in which all the institutions partook, meant that it would become virtually impossible to find an activity, which could not be brought within the objectives of the Treaty' (Weiler 1991: 2245).

26 See European Convention (2003) Cover note CONV 723/03: 10.

States and do not constitute part of the *acquis* to be accepted by candidate States. The costs resulting from the implementation of enhanced cooperation, other than administrative costs entailed for the institutions, are in principle borne by the participating Member States only.

Consequently, we may see in the enhanced cooperation procedure a safety mechanism that could allow some Member States to progress on supervisory matters, in case no agreement can be reached at EU-wide level.

3 The 2009 proposals for reforming the EU supervisory architecture

The imperative of policy action for improving EU financial supervision in response to the crisis constrained policy-makers not only to adopt immediate measures correcting the existing framework,[27] but also to contemplate a broader overhaul of the supervisory architecture. Consequently, in October 2008, the European Commission mandated a High Level Expert Group, under the chairmanship of Jacques de Larosière, to make concrete proposals for strengthening European financial supervisory arrangements.

The report of this group (called the de Larosière report) was issued on 25 February 2009 and took an allegedly pragmatic approach. The de Larosière report makes separate recommendations for macro- and micro-prudential supervision in the EU. The Commission broadly endorsed the de Larosière approach in a Communication of 4 March 2009 (Commission 2009d) and published concrete proposals on a future EU financial supervisory architecture on 27 May 2009 (the Commission's May Communication, Commission 2009h). The broad lines of the Commission's Communication were approved by the Ecofin Council on 9 June 2009 and by the European Council at the summit of 18–19 June 2009. Concrete legislative proposals building on the May proposals were published in September and October 2009 with a view to establishing the new architecture during 2010–11. At the beginning of 2010 the package of six legislative proposals put forward by the Commission is debated in the EU Parliament, whilst the Council had already reached agreement on a general approach on the package in December 2009.

The proposals are to be welcomed for at least finally facing the supervisory issue and its shortcomings in the EU. The crisis has revealed unequivocally that the current arrangements were incapable of preventing, managing and resolving supervisory problems in the EU. Although there are no easy or straightforward solutions, the proposals put forward by the Commission and the political support backing them are guarantees for

27 Immediate measures for improving the current set-up were adopted in the framework of the review of the CRD (e.g. imposition of colleges for cross-border groups, better arrangements for information exchange) and the review of the Lamfalussy framework (the tasks of the Level 3 committees were systemised, quality majority voting permitted, and the comply-or-explain mechanism introduced).

moving away from the deficient *status quo*. Whether the concrete proposals are indeed an improvement compared to the current situation will depend much on the final details. These details are discussed at the time of writing on the basis of the Commission's supervisory reform package of September 2009. This consists of four regulations upgrading the three Level 3 committees into authorities and establishing a new macro-prudential body, and one Council decision clarifying the role of the ECB. Furthermore, a draft directive containing comprehensive proposals for amendments to sectoral legislation specifies much of the details related to the new functions of European supervisory authorities and circumscribes their scope.

The idea underpinning the reform is that of creating, through various building blocks, 'an integrated EU supervisory structure necessary to promote timely and consistent policy responses among the Member States and, thus, preventing diverging approaches and, subsequently, improving the functioning of the internal market' (Commission 2009h: 8). This reflects an evolutionary approach to the current set-up. Revolutionary proposals have so far not been put on the table, yet they might still be forthcoming and concern especially crisis-management and crisis-resolution arrangements, as well as the conferral of direct supervisory powers to the new micro-prudential authorities. Given that the concrete legislative proposals were published after the completion of this manuscript and the final legislative outcome is largely uncertain, it was not possible to integrate here detailed references to the draft legislation submitted by the Commission in September–October 2009. In the following, we will briefly present and discuss the ways forward as proposed by the Commission in its May Communication.

3.1 Macro-prudential supervisory arrangements

We have seen that in the context of general economic growth and apparent financial stability, macro-prudential concerns were until the crisis rather marginal among the interests of EU policy-makers. However, the macro imbalances accumulated in the financial system, as a consequence of the various disregarded developments, appear to be at the very root of the financial crisis. In response to this, policy-makers explicitly recognised the importance of preventively identifying the emerging risks in the system and issuing accordingly early warnings and recommendations, on which follow-up should be compelling.

For this purpose, the Commission proposes to create a European Systemic Risk Board (ESRB), as a new independent body with responsibilities for safeguarding financial stability and conducting macro-prudential supervision at European level.[28] More concretely, the ESRB will have to

28 Commission 2009h: 5. The conclusions of the Ecofin and of the European Council use for the macro-prudential body the denomination 'European Systemic Risk Board' (ESRB). Initially the Commission called it 'European Systemic Risk Council' (ESRC).

collect and analyse financial stability-relevant information on macro-economic developments and developments in the financial system; assess potential threats for financial stability coming from such developments; identify and prioritise risks; issue risk warnings; give recommendations on the measures to be taken where necessary; monitor follow-up and liaise with international counterparts.

It is explicitly stated that the ESRB will not have legal personality and will have no legally binding powers. Also, the ESRB will have no direct crisis-management responsibilities. Yet the ESRB is expected to exert a major influence on the addressees of its warnings and recommendations, which may be of a general nature or of individual concern for certain Member States, may be public or confidential, and will have to contain specified timelines. Consequently, the follow-up policy response is ensured through an 'act or explain mechanism', channelled through the Ecofin Council and/or the new European supervisory authorities.

The composition of the ESRB is dominated by central banks (NCBs and ECB), which will also appoint the chairperson,[29] and includes also the chair-persons of the European micro-prudential supervisory bodies and a member of the Commission. Representatives of the national supervisory authorities and the Chairperson of the EFC have observer status. The ESRB will be politically accountable to the Council and the Parliament through regular reporting. The activities of the ESRB will be managed by a small steering committee preparing its meetings and an advisory technical committee contributing detailed technical analysis. The analytical, administrative and logistic support will be provided by the ECB. The envisaged legal basis for the Regulation establishing the ESRB is article 114 TFEU (ex 95 EC Treaty) requiring the normal co-decision procedure. The possibility of conferring on the ECB responsibilities concerning tasks in respect to the ESRB on the basis of article 127(6) TFEU (ex 105(6) EC Treaty) is also explicitly acknowledged. Most probably, a separate decision based on article 127(6) TFEU (ex 105(6) EC) will clarify the relationship between the ECB and the ESRB.

The idea of the ESRB is definitely to be welcomed. The mere acknowledgement of the macro-prudential function and the envisaged enumeration of the concrete tasks that it involves in secondary EU law already constitute a progress compared to the vague formulation of the current roles of the BSC and CEBS in this regard. Yet we observe that the legal status of the ESRB does not reflect the declared importance of the macro-prudential function. Being deprived of legal personality according to the May Communication, the ESRB merely appears as another supervisory

29 The initial proposal was to have the President of the ECB automatically as the ESRC president. However, as this raised concerns for the Member States that were not in the Eurosystem, it was agreed at the European Council that the ESRC Chairperson be elected by the General Council of the ECB, which reassembles the governors of all national central banks in the EU.

platform with vague lines of responsibility involving in an equivocal way a plurality of other EU bodies. The institutional affiliation of the ESRB is not unambiguous; although its membership would indicate close links with the ECB, the ESRB is not part of the ESCB and thus the ECB cannot take responsibility for its actions. Nor is the role of the Ecofin and the European micro-prudential supervisory bodies clear. More worryingly, the arrangements for the follow-up to the early warnings and recommendations are so far summarised by a vague indication of the 'act or explain' mechanism, without being at all clear who would have the obligation to act and to whom explanations are owed in case of non-action. Nor is it clear what the consequences would be if no explanation (or no plausible explanation) is provided in case of non-action. Being deprived of legal personality and authority, the ESRB can simply monitor the follow-up but not enforce its recommendations. The follow-up to macro-prudential analysis is crucial for the effectiveness of the new mechanism. It is what would differentiate it from the current arrangements. Yet it appears that there is still great political reluctance in this respect.

Because the ESRB's early warnings and recommendations are not capable of producing binding legal effects and the ESRB is deprived of legal personality, the ESRB's measures cannot be directly challenged before the ECJ on the basis of article 263 TFEU (ex 230 EC Treaty). Yet they are not completely deprived of legal effects. Given that the refusal to take follow-up policy actions has to be justified, it is indirectly, through the follow-up measures, that the ESRB's warnings and recommendations could be eventually legally challenged. This may be induced from the *Artegodan* case,[30] where it was held that although the scientific opinion of the Medicines Agency EMEA was not binding on the Commission, it was not completely deprived of legal effects insofar as the Commission had to give reasons when departing from it. Consequently the Court of First Instance held that assessing the lawfulness of the Commission decision would imply first reviewing the formal legality of the scientific opinion and, second, reviewing the exercise by the Commission of its discretion when adopting the final measure (Griller and Orator 2007: 17).

In our opinion, the proposals on the macro-prudential architecture put forward so far are largely blurred and tend to weaken the position of the ESRB in the intended European integrated supervisory framework. This is regrettable, as the macro-prudential task is extremely important for the stability of an integrated market. The distribution of responsibilities with regard to the follow-up policy actions is equivocal, as are also the arrangements for judicial, financial and administrative accountability of the ESRB. Also, its explicit designation as an independent body is not reflected in the proposed governance arrangements. Such an ambiguous status risks

30 Cases T-74, 76, 83–5, 132, 137 and 141/00, *Artegodan GmbH* v. *Commission* [2002] ECR II-4945, paras 197–9.

undermining the desired authority of early warnings and recommendations. More legal certainty would have been achieved through a solution either relying on the establishment of a separate agency entrusted with the macro-prudential function or on the reinforcement and clarification of the macro-prudential function of the ESCB, with a more streamlined mandate for the BSC. The constructive ambiguity affecting the lines of responsibility in the current proposal of the Commission does not benefit the reform project. It is hoped that forthcoming legislation will address many of these uncertainties.

3.2 Micro-prudential supervisory arrangements

As regards micro-prudential supervision, European policy-makers envisage streamlining and reinforcing the current sectoral arrangements in the EU. The Commission's May Communication proposes the establishment of an 'operational European network with shared and mutually reinforcing responsibilities' (Commission 2009h: 8) – the European System of Financial Supervisors (ESFS). The ESFS will rely on three new European Supervisory Authorities (ESAs): the European Banking Authority (EBA), the European Insurance and Occupational Pensions Authority (EIOPA) and the European Securities and Markets Authority (ESMA). These will replace the current Level 3 committees. National supervisors will continue to perform the day-to-day supervision of financial institutions and cooperate through supervisory colleges in cross-border situations. Ecofin and the European Council in their June meetings gave guarantees that the decisions taken by ESAs would in no way affect the fiscal responsibilities of Member States.

The new Authorities will all be endowed with legal personality and will have, apart from the missions of the current Level 3 committees, increased responsibilities supported by defined legal powers and greater authority. Any decision by ESAs should be subject to review by the EU courts. It is envisaged that the new Authorities will have a Board of Supervisors composed of high-level representatives from the national supervisory authorities and a Management Board that would assure the operational issues. A Steering Committee would coordinate the actions between the three new Authorities and the Commission. Political accountability would be ensured by regular reporting to the Council, the Parliament and the Commission. The legal basis chosen is article 114 TFEU (ex 95 EC Treaty), which allows for the adoption of measures for the approximation of legislation for the establishment and functioning of the internal market via the normal co-decision procedure, renamed the ordinary legislative procedure under the Lisbon Treaty.

The Commission's May Communication broadly enumerates the functions of ESAs, and announces that precise details will be specified in sectoral legislation. The envisaged roles and responsibilities of the new ESAs are underpinned by a series of objectives and instruments. Thus, ESAs are responsible for devising a single set of harmonised rules through the adoption of: (a) binding technical standards in specific areas defined in EU law, which should 'apply within a fixed period of time, provided the Commission endorses by non-opposition' (Commission 2009h); and (b) interpretative guidelines and recommendations to be applied by national authorities when adopting individual decisions. A second function entrusted to ESAs is that of ensuring consistent application of EU rules. Therefore, ESAs should be endowed with means for: (a) facilitating the dialogue, in case of disagreement between supervisors, and assisting national supervisors in reaching a joint agreement; (b) providing, as a last resort, dispute settlement between national supervisors in case of failure of conciliation, including adopting a decision; (c) issuing recommendations for action that would constrain national supervisory authorities to comply with EU law, to be followed up by a Commission decision in case of persistent breach; (d) adopting decisions directly applicable to financial institutions in relation to prudential requirements in order to overcome inaction of national supervisors in implementing EU law or in case there is need for urgent action. A third function of ESAs consists of ensuring a common supervisory culture and consistent supervisory practices via common training programmes, participation in colleges and delegation of tasks and responsibilities among national supervisors. Fourth, ESAs will be endowed with full supervisory powers for pan-European credit rating agencies and will be involved in the prudential assessment of European mergers and acquisitions. Furthermore, ESAs have to play a role in crisis situations by facilitating cooperation and exchange of information between supervisors, verifying the reliability of information and acting as a mediator. At the same time, they would have the power to adopt some emergency decisions in case of specific crisis situations (e.g. short-selling); the scope of such emergency procedures should be defined in EU law. Moreover, ESAs will be key players in the collection of micro-prudential information through aggregation of data from national authorities, establishment of a central European database and transmission of information to colleges of supervisors. Last, but not least, ESAs will be international actors: interacting with international organisations and third countries, especially on technical issues; assisting the Commission when preparing equivalence decisions of third-country supervisory regimes.

The new micro-prudential design, while building on the current structures, seems largely to address the shortcomings of the current supervisory arrangements. It does not strip national authorities of their current competences but mainly fills gaps at the supranational level, by establishing the necessary authority for dealing with disagreements concerning cross-border institutions. ESAs are envisaged not only to have an authoritative mediation role between national authorities during a phase of conciliation, but may also constitute a genuine dispute settlement mechanism resulting in binding decisions to be imposed on all concerned parties, in case of failure to reach a joint agreement. This is a very significant step forward compared to the current arrangements. It does not change the distribution of powers between Member States, but ensures that a decision is taken regarding the cross-border institution as a whole. The mere possibility of such dispute settlement will constrain competent authorities to strive harder for a joint decision. The enhanced enforcement powers and ESAs' competence to adopt directly applicable decisions in case of inaction or delay of action by the national supervisors in emergency situations are particularly important and highlight the extensive competences envisaged for the new Authorities. They reflect ESAs' capacity to adopt binding prudential standards.

While these extensive powers are indeed needed at EU level and would also pass the subsidiarity test, the question arises as to their legitimacy, particularly in light of their largely discretionary character. As we have seen, the institutional balance between the European actors and the strict respect of the principle of conferred powers are of utmost importance when setting up new bodies in the EU. ESAs would definitely fall under the category of European agencies and thereby would be subject to the limits applicable to the delegation of powers to such agencies.

ESAs would be established directly by the legislator on the basis of the Treaty provision that allows for the adoption of measures for the establishment and functioning of the internal market. Article 114 TFEU (ex 95 EC Treaty) permits broad EU action in the interest of the internal market, which may also include, in particularly sensitive fields (such as financial supervision), the establishment of a separate expert body shielded from direct political influences. Such a body, whose activity would not be limited to executive tasks, but would involve broader regulatory and policy-making functions, should enjoy sufficient discretionary powers allowing it to authoritatively deal with specific situations. Hence, it should not be subject to the restrictive limits implied by the sub-delegation of concrete implementing tasks, but to the broader limits of direct delegation via EU legislation adopted by the Parliament and the Council. This interpretation would circumvent the *Meroni* doctrine and apply the more lenient approach to the delegation issue, as developed on the basis of the *Romano*-type of situation. The independence of ESAs with respect to national authorities and European institutions is of particular relevance in this context. This is also recognised in the May Communication, yet not fully reflected in the concrete proposals, where it is suggested that the Commission participate in the Management board of the ESAs.

More problematic than the discretionary character of ESAs' powers is their capacity to adopt binding general rules. Even in *Romano*, the ECJ made it clear that the institutional balance demanded that the power to adopt acts having the force of law cannot simply be entrusted to a body created by the Council and the Parliament.[31] To overcome this restraint, the May Communi-

31 Case 98/80, para. 20.

cation envisages the application of several limits to the adoption of binding technical standards. Thus the specific areas and criteria for these binding standards will be clearly circumscribed by EU legislation, they will have to apply within a fixed period of time and assume endorsement by the Commission, which is entitled to oppose them. From this perspective there seem to be substantive, temporal and jurisdictional safeguards in place that legitimise ESAs' powers to adopt binding rules. However, we note the ingenious legal mechanism whereby the Commission would endorse such binding standards by non-opposition and question its feasibility. Will this take the form of a *carte blanche* given *ex ante* by the Commission to ESAs or will it involve an *ex post* rubber-stamp by the Commission of the standards that need to be declared as binding? Bindingness must be made explicit and cannot be inferred. There also needs to be legal certainty as to the legal status and the entry into force of these binding standards.

We note also that the Commission's proposal might trigger some mutations within the four-level Lamfalussy framework. The Commission would gain preponderance by controlling all three regulatory levels: it would be in charge of preparing the legislative proposal (Level 1), of adopting comitology measures (Level 2) and of endorsing binding standards devised by ESAs (Level 3). On the contrary, the involvement of the legislator, especially of the Parliament, would decrease, being completely absent at Level 3, despite the fact that all provisions have identical legal effects. This is understandable given that the Parliament cannot engage in detailed and technical rule-making. Yet this should be counterbalanced by solid accountability mechanisms and sufficient guarantees, to prevent policy choices, hidden in technical measures, from being imposed through binding decisions taken by ESAs without any role for the legislator.[32]

Another problematic aspect concerns the foreseen role for ESAs to substitute national supervisors by taking directly applicable decisions in order to overcome inaction or delayed action for implementing EU prudential rules. This amounts to a direct enforcement of the respective prudential rules and does not even require an endorsement by the Commission (as the proposal stands now). It risks creating legal uncertainty in the context where the Commission is the only EU body responsible for the enforcement of EU law in the Member States and where the ECJ is exclusively competent to ascertain a breach of EU law by a member State. It would definitely change the way the Level 4 of the Lamfalussy process functions and would, in our view, be at the limits of the legality of EU law. The precise device of such a function will have to be carefully designed.

32 For instance, CEBS measures often cover aspects that are not touched in the CRD. This is, for instance, the case of CEBS 2009 high-level principles on remuneration policies, which are now proposed for incorporation in the CRD. It would be problematic if such principles were given binding force, without passing the scrutiny of the EU legislator.

Altogether, the proposals of the Commission appear to be a decisive step forward on the evolutionary path towards an integrated supervisory structure in the EU. While the devise of micro-prudential supervisory arrangements seems to address most of the current shortcomings firmly, the proposals for a macro-prudential structure are much more modest. Criticism could be made of the equivocal channels of interaction between the macro-prudential device and European and national institutions. Also, it is not clear what the future of the Lamfalussy framework will be, given the substantial proposals for changes affecting Level 3 and Level 4. Also, with the disappearance of the comitology procedure after the entry into force of the Lisbon Treaty and the introduction of delegated and implementing acts, new rules will have to be designed for integrating the current Level 2 and Level 3 measures into the new categories. Furthermore, apart from indicative Communication (Commission 2009j), no proposal has been made to tackle the delicate issues of early intervention, crisis-management and crisis-resolution, which is intimately linked to the supervisory reform. Despite the role envisaged for ESAs on ensuring a coordinated response in crisis situations, their authority is limited given the safeguards related to Member States' fiscal policies. These would impede ESAs, for instance, in promoting the development of concrete detailed burden-sharing arrangements or decisively take the lead in case of ailing or failing cross-border institutions. Yet a comprehensive, maybe even revolutionary, EU framework for crisis management and resolution, including guarantee schemes and burden-sharing, is still to be provided in response to the ever growing number of calls in this respect.

Part IV

The European dimension of supervisory liability

11 The issue of supervisory liability

1 Actuality

The normative and institutional frameworks concerning prudential regulation and supervision have been substantially transformed in the EU during the past decade. In parallel with further reforms they undergo, their effectiveness comes ever more to the forefront. In this context, the issue of the liability of supervisory authorities appears as particularly concrete and realistic. Here, we will explain why, in our view, the prudential approach devised in the CRD and the envisaged reforms of the EU supervisory architecture impinge also upon the issue of supervisory liability.

1.1 Juridification and formalisation

We have observed in Part II that the supervisory approach is more process-oriented and relies increasingly on the interaction of various stakeholders. Prudential norms are becoming more detailed and complex and supervisory action is getting ever more complex, entailing new facets. In an integrated financial market the new approach inevitably needs to be backed by efforts for ensuring the level playing-field between the national prudential frameworks. Henceforth, the European component becomes ever more intrusive and a European regulatory apparatus was put in place with a view to creating convergence between national regulatory and supervisory practices. As a consequence, prudential norms are increasingly formalised, detailed standards and guidelines are explicitly spelled out and procedures supporting the interaction between stakeholders are established. This juridification occurs at the European level, from which it is then propagated to the national legal systems.

The CRD, incorporating the supervisory review pillar, defines supervisory objectives and priorities in more detail, imposes coordination and also prescribes various measures to be taken by the banking supervisors in case of defective compliance by a credit institution with prudential rules. These aspects will be even more strengthened through the reforms in response to the crisis.

Furthermore, the Lamfalussy framework reinforces juridification by providing the means for adopting common non-legislative measures, indispensable for the application of the binding provisions contained in the directives and regulations adopted through co-decision or comitology. Although these Level 3 measures do not have the potential per se to create any rights, their purpose is to explain the content of the legislative provisions, facilitate their implementation and thereby contribute to the ascertainability of the content of prudential norms. The Level 3 measures are the product of joint interpretation of legislation by all national supervisory authorities and therefore create the legitimate expectation that the supervisors have committed themselves to observe them, despite the declared non-binding character of such norms. Soft law might not be immediately enforceable, but 'non-binding' does not mean being deprived altogether of legal effects. Moreover, juridification would be straightforward if, as currently proposed, the supervisory reforms would allow the upgraded Level 3 committees (the future European Supervisory Authorities) to adopt binding prudential standards.

Against this background, the issue appears of whether the CRD has a more far-reaching impact than its predecessors on national supervisory systems, so as to also somehow impinge on national tort law aspects related to supervisory liability. National legal systems have proved to be very divergent on this issue and national solutions are ranging from absolute supervisory immunity to proportionate liability. The issue arises as to whether such divergence in the judicial protection does not risk undermining the effectiveness of EU law. European prudential norms in the CRD and recast CAD are characterised by more quantity and detail. The implementation of the Basel II Accord in the EU has resulted in more formalised regulation, subsequently subject to further details within the Lamfalussy framework. The concern for the uniform and coherent application of these rules would also justify a common approach as to the judicial remedies attached to breaches of EU law by supervisory authorities. In this sense, the foreseen reforms endowing ESAs with the power to adopt measures in case of breaches by national supervisors or to substitute national supervisors in emergency situations are remarkable.

In this context it needs to be asked whether the new harmonised European norms contain sufficient details to allow ascertaining the existence of rights in favour of depositors, based on EU law. If that is the case, then it would be indispensable for the uniform enforcement of such rights to rely on a common approach with regard to national remedial law. The CRD contains no explicit reference to the supervisory liability issue; this should nevertheless not exclude considerations as to whether the new prudential normative framework is capable of bringing about a 'communautarisation'/ 'Europeanisation' of national remedial law in this field. When analysing this hypothesis, one also needs to consider that, as a reverse, the emergence of a common supervisory liability approach in the tort law systems of Member States would subsequently spill over and affect the liability regime of European institutions eventually entrusted with functions related to banking supervision. Conversely, providing for explicit liability of the European Supervisory Authorities – as envisaged in the Commissions proposals for reform – will inevitably impinge on the liability regime of national supervisors.

By no means does increased juridification automatically entail harmonisation of judicial protection, nor are we entitled to infer that more rules and more details in EU law are inevitably intended to confer rights upon individuals against national supervisors. At this point, we would like only to underline that substantial and extensive changes have occurred in European prudential legislation, which, in our view, suffice for reopening an inquiry into the issue of supervisory liability. The complex discourse of EU law-created rights and remedies with regard to the liability of supervisory authorities in the EU has been limited so far to the provisions of the first banking directives (FBD, SBD, CAD and complementary directives). These reflected the minimum harmonisation approach. As argued earlier, we consider that current European legislation in this field cannot be brought down to a minimalist approach, but the harmonisation of essential aspects expands beyond minimum thresholds to cover large substantive parts of prudential legislation. At this point, we do not infer that this tendency towards maximum harmonisation necessarily results in the attribution of rights to depositors, but we only submit that such a hypothesis cannot be excluded *a priori*. The far-reaching transformation of European prudential regulation calls for a thorough analysis of the new legal provisions and hence reopens the apparently recently settled debate on supervisory liability.

1.2 Focusing on enforcement

Intensive regulation at EU level has been accompanied by a stronger emphasis on implementation. There is a series of official documents underlining the importance of application and enforcement for the implementation process (Council 1992a, 1995; Commission 1993, 2002c). These identify better enforcement of EU law as a tool for improving efficiency of the internal market and for strengthening the credibility of the Union and its institutions (Commission 2001a: 5). While prime responsibility for the application of EU law belongs to the national administrations and the national courts, the Commission has also been assigned a central role in taking infringement actions.

As regards financial regulation, the enforcement discourse emerges particularly in the context of: the Lamfalussy framework, the post-FSAP strategy and the proposals for enhancing enforcement under the ongoing debates on the supervisory reform. The Lamfalussy structure is conceptually oriented towards achieving better compliance with EU law: Level 3 aims at facilitating the application of EU legal norms at national level, through the guidance provided by CEBS. Concern for effective implementation is at the core of Level 4 of the Lamfalussy framework: compliance is essential and legal action is required in case of breaches of EU law. The forth level is intended to reinforce the Commission's position in taking action against infringements and concomitantly underlines the importance of the commitment of all Member States and their respective institutions to consistently apply EU law. National courts are major actors in acknowledging and sanctioning, at national level, non-observance of the directives.

Furthermore, enforcement is central to the post-FSAP strategy. The White Paper on Financial Services Policy 2005–10, envisaged to limit legislative initiatives to targeted measures aiming at consolidating legislation, and requested regulators to focus on the transposition and enforcement of the existing measures. Supervisory authorities were seen as having a central role in consistently applying EU financial regulation, and were called on to fully assume their responsibilities stemming from EU law (Commission 2005c).

Last but not least, under the proposals for a new EU financial supervision architecture put forward by the Commission in its May 2009 Communication, the new European Supervisory Authorities (ESAs) should have an enhanced role as regards the enforcement of EU prudential rules against national supervisory authorities (Commission 2009h: 10). Thus it is envisaged that a mechanism will be put in place whereby ESAs, on their own initiative or at the request of another supervisory authority or the Commission, would investigate whether a certain national supervisor is manifestly disregarding EU legislation. If that is the case, ESAs will adopt a recommendation for action addressed to the respective authority, with which the latter will have to comply within a certain period. If the breach of EU law persists, ESAs will inform the Commission, which will act to enforce the law. Furthermore, in specific cases, ESAs will be allowed to take directly applicable measures, binding upon national authorities and financial institutions in response to inaction by domestic supervisors.

Enforcement is used in these instances in a generic sense, encompassing various phases ranging from transposition into the national legislation to the actual application in its various modalities. European rules may be implemented either by national or European authorities' implementing measures, or directly by market actors, through recourse to national courts under the direct effect doctrine (Snyder 1993: 25). Judicial review of administrative action has the potential of modifying and sanctioning behaviour of administrative authorities, rendering litigation an effective enforcement mechanism.

Given the limited resources of the Commission, its enforcement function merely focuses on the transposition of EU law into national legislation and only to a limited extent on the actual implementation of EU norms, as a consequence of complaints received from individuals. Hence, in case of concrete application of EU law, there is 'an apparent preference of Court and Commission for an army of "citizen enforcers", active both in complaining to the Commission and in enforcing EC law in national courts' (Harlow 2002: 73). In the context of banking supervision, the instrument at hand is State liability for breach of EU law. Also, according to the ECJ, where a directive imposes on a Member State an obligation to pursue a particular course of conduct, this obligation is strengthened if individuals are able to rely on the directive before their national courts and if the latter were not prevented from taking an element of EU law into consideration.[1] Hence, an important aspect of implementation regards the possibility of private parties to enforce EU law provisions in national jurisdictions (Louis and Ronse 2005: 321).

Enforcement needs to take account of several peculiar aspects of prudential banking regulation. As opposed to European securities regulation, which is largely directed towards ensuring transparency and availability of information (see provisions on market abuse, prospectus, transparency, disclosures, etc.), banking regulation focuses mainly on the conditions for the taking up of banking activities, on capital requirements and internal risk-management mechanisms. Disclosure of information by credit institutions has only recently been required by European law (articles 145–9 CRD). These provisions will nevertheless have only a limited impact on dissipating banks' opaqueness, as most of banks' disclosures are intended for supervisory authorities, who may even authorise credit institutions not to make them public. Also, such disclosures are not understandable to simple depositors. Under such circumstances, depositors, unlike securities investors, have much less information about the financial situation of their bank and will rely to a greater extent on the guarantees and signals from the supervisory authorities.

Banking directives, unlike securities directives, focus on the relationship between credit institutions and supervisory authorities and less on the relationship between banks and their depositors. This does not *a priori* exclude that third parties (depositors) derive rights and interests from the regulated interaction between supervisors and banks. Rights may be derived from explicit duties imposed by EU law. Hence, enforcement actions by depositors and investors are likely to be directed not only against the credit institutions that have abused depositors' trust, but also against supervisory authorities that acted against depositors' expectations by falling short of their duty to supervise appropriately. It is up to the national courts to find out whether, in specific cases, EU law is susceptible to creating rights or legitimate expectations, and correspondingly allow proportionate remedies.

1.3 The depositor as a consumer

There are strong links between prudential banking supervision and consumer protection. The European prudential directives include among

1 ECJ Case 41/74 *Van Duyn* v. *Home Office* [1974] ECR 1337, para. 12.

their declared objectives the protection of depositors. This may be not only inferred from the substantive provisions of the banking directives and the overall philosophy underpinning supervisory rules, but is also explicitly referred to in the preamble of the CRD. In spite of terminological inconsistencies in European legislation (savers, clients, depositors), it is evident that European prudential rules are designed, among others, to protect those who entrust their money to credit institutions for deposit purposes.[2] At the same time, it is beyond doubt that a broad interpretation of the 'consumer' concept includes the depositor. Hence, the protection of depositors should also benefit from increasing interest and evolution in the field of consumer protection.

The literature on securities markets regulation has openly addressed the issue of investor protection and acknowledged the need for going beyond mere regulation of access to markets, by moving towards more substantive rules protecting the investor, in his quality as a financial consumer (Moloney 2003). In the banking field, such an approach would claim enhanced protection of depositors. This is particularly justified if we consider that current bank accounts and deposits constitute by far the most popular financial savings instruments used by EU citizens.[3] Furthermore, depositor protection was explicitly listed among the overall objectives of the Commission's financial services policy for 2005–10 (besides the adequate and effective levels of prudential control, financial stability and a fostered internal market for financial services and capital). Also, in response to the crisis, many of the policy measures discussed aim to re-establish consumers' confidence in financial markets, implicitly recognising the importance of an informed and proactive consumer (Commission 2009d).

The relationship between the depositor and the banking regulator has to be seen from the perspective of information asymmetries as one of the rationales justifying the very existence of prudential regulation. Much more than the financial investor in securities markets, banking depositors lack the resources and information for assessing the quality of the depository institution to which they lend their savings. Hence, the relation of the

2 Recital 5 in the Preamble of the CRD refers to the protection of savings. Further, recital 9 provides that equivalent financial requirements are needed to 'ensure similar safeguards for savers'. Recital 27 justifies the imposition of reporting obligations to the auditors of a credit institution for the purpose of strengthening the prudential supervision of credit institutions and the protection of clients of credit institutions. Recital 57 of the Preambles states that 'supervision of credit institutions on a consolidated basis aims at, in particular, protecting the interests of the depositors of credit institutions and at the stability of the financial system'.

3 According to Eurobarometer, *Public Opinion in Europe: Financial Services Report*, January 2004, 80 per cent of the EU15 population had a current account with a payment card and a chequebook, and 44 per cent had a deposit account that paid interest but had no payment card or chequebook. From another perspective, around 84 per cent did not hold stocks/shares, 85 per cent had never had collective investments and more than 90 per cent did not personally own bonds.

depositor with the bank is highly fiduciary, and should be sustained by supervisory mechanisms capable of inducing and maintaining depositors' confidence in the soundness and safety of their bank. In such a context, it has been observed that 'consumer expectations may not only apply to the relation between bank and consumer, but also to that between bank, consumer and the State, particularly the regulator' (Cartwright 2004: 2).

Hence, it is undeniable that banking regulators are entrusted with some responsibilities with regard to the protection of the depositors of banks and their savings. Such responsibilities, although not clearly defined, influence the perception of depositors' rights in the context of European directives. Also, the depositor, inspired by the increasingly influential consumer concept, will become ever more proactive. Such depositors' emancipation entails a higher probability that depositors will claim compensation for defective supervision infringing their rights. It has been held that, given increased awareness, it is increasingly likely that 'financial consumers will use court action as a natural way to seek redress by finding in the State or the supervisory authorities a "deep pocket" to compensate for their losses' (Tison 2005: 640).

1.4 Refined distribution of responsibility for supervision

The single market legislation addresses the question of responsibility for supervision, but not that of supervisory liability (Smits and Luberti 1999: 369). The provisions of the CRD, together with the implementing Level 2 measures and the guidelines and standards delivered by CEBS at Level 3, provide much detail about how supervisory tasks are to be exercised. The prescription of substantive supervisory rules in EU law is also accompanied by a more refined distribution of roles to the different jurisdictions and their cooperation. The CRD corroborated to the directive on financial conglomerates improves the framework for supervision on a consolidated basis and supervisory coordination through colleges of supervisors. Moreover, the forthcoming reform of the EU financial supervision architecture envisages conferring some supervisory responsibilities to the foreseen European Supervisory Authorities (i.e. final decision-making in case of disagreement between national supervisors, direct decisions in case of inaction or breach of law by national supervisors).

Under the previous legal framework (the Codified Banking Directive), the organisation of supervision was almost entirely left to the national legal systems. The procedural and institutional set-up for banking supervision constituted the exclusive competence of Member States; hence, the issue of supervisory liability was also seen as a matter exclusively for national law. Various attempts[4] to base claims of supervisory liability on EU

4 These cases will be presented later in this part of the book: the *Three Rivers* affair, the *Peter Paul* case.

law have failed, as the banking directives considered, coming under the sign of minimum harmonisation, were found too imprecise and as such incapable of precluding national rules prescribing supervisory immunity. Instead, the CRD and the current reforms substantially affect not only the content of prudential rules but also the institutional framework in which they operate. They reflect a tendency towards maximum harmonisation and increased European intervention in supervisory issues.

The refinement of the distribution of responsibilities for supervision in cross-border situations (e.g. validation of Pillar 1 capital requirements by the consolidated supervisor) and the explicit mechanisms for supervisory cooperation and coordination (e.g. colleges of supervisors, the European mandate for national competent authorities) raise questions about the responsibility incumbent upon the actors involved. The distribution of roles between the home and host authorities requires a level playing-field in the national approaches to supervisory liability. The question arises as to whether the current European regulatory and institutional framework contains elements that could induce a common approach among Member States in the area of supervisory liability. Furthermore, it should be inquired whether the proposed European Banking Authority, endowed with powers to adopt binding decisions and authoritative dispute settlement, can be established without a clear, uniform position on supervisory liability. These are arguments that would justify reopening the debate on supervisory liability in the light of the new regulatory framework.

1.5 The **Peter Paul** *affair – not yet the end of the debate*

In October 2004, the ECJ issued its judgment in the *Peter Paul* case.[5] This was the first time the ECJ had the occasion to rule on the issue of whether the European prudential rules laid down in the various EU directives impinge upon the national regimes on supervisory liability. EU law had also previously been relied on by applicants claiming compensation for damages resulting from defective banking supervision in the UK courts. However, the EU provisions discussed (in the UK courts only the provisions of the First Banking Directive have been invoked) were considered clear enough to avoid the request for a preliminary ruling on the issue to the ECJ. In the *Peter Paul* judgment, pursuant to a very synthetic and succinct reasoning, the ECJ concluded that the European banking directives 'do not preclude national legislation to the effect that the functions of the national banking supervisory authorities be conducted only in the public interest, which precludes individuals from claiming compensation for damages resulting from defective supervision'.[6] In short, European law was considered incapable of imposing liability for defective banking supervision.

5 Case C-222/02, judgment of the ECJ from 12 October 2004, ECR I-09425.
6 Case C-222/02, para. 47.

The ECJ judgment in the *Peter Paul* case was welcomed as putting an end to a lengthy academic debate on the issue of supervisory liability, and it was assumed that the decision of the ECJ would constitute the yardstick for any future claims (Binder 2004: 475). Such a view is partially acceptable, to the extent that the ECJ's judgment, although susceptible to criticism, ascertained the limited capacity of the Second Banking Directive to create rights for depositors. Nevertheless, ascribing to the ECJ's judgment a general principle value, and thereby accepting that depositor protection is only an ancillary objective of prudential regulation, is not as easily acceptable. Nor is the assertion that depositors' interests are exclusively dealt with by the Deposit Guarantee Directive to be accepted without scepticism.

In our view, the ECJ's *Peter Paul* decision is only contextual. The substantive transformation of the prudential approach through the CRD (with the enhanced role for supervisory authorities under the supervisory review pillar), as well as the move towards more extensive harmonisation and the emerging European dimension of national supervisory structures, call for a different approach. Already open to criticism, the judgment cannot be held rigidly as the definitive dictum on supervisory liability in the EU. On the contrary, given the dynamics of the European integration process and especially the rapid legislative and institutional changes underpinning the single market of financial services, we cannot *a priori* exclude that recent and ongoing regulatory developments will reopen the issue of supervisory liability. The ECJ's judgment should be thoroughly reviewed in light of regulatory changes coming from the CRD and its subsequent amendments, from the Lamfalussy regulatory framework and its updates, and from the forthcoming overhaul of the financial supervisory architecture. From this perspective, the ECJ's judgment could be considered useful for providing a series of criteria against which the new framework may be assessed, in terms of its ability to impinge upon national supervisory liability regimes.

Taken together, the above-mentioned aspects bring back to fore the issue of supervisory liability and may render the ECJ's position in the *Peter Paul* judgment precarious in the long run. According to the ECJ's judgment, under the previous banking directives there was no common approach, but only diverging national liability regimes applicable to supervisors. Also, it was ascertained that the Codified Banking Directive (CBD) did not confer rights on depositors to be enforced against the competent authorities in case of poor supervision. With the CRD and its amendments, these aspects are, in our opinion, called back into question. In this context, the prudential provisions in the CRD need to be assessed in detail, from the perspective of their ability to create rights that would impinge upon supervisory liability.

The invasive European element in prudential regulation and supervision, as well as the institutional reforms planned in response to the crisis, call for a reassessment of the liability issue in the light of the new developments, so as to confer more legal certainty. A clarification of the issue of supervisory liability would be particularly beneficial for any further refinement of supervisory responsibilities, as well as for the potential centralisation of some supervisory tasks at European level. Furthermore, the focus on uniform implementation and enforcement of the prudential rules based on a common European rulebook might also demand levelling the playing-field between the various remedies available according to the national legal systems for infringement of EU law.

2 Supervisory liability – what is at stake?

Before analysing whether the CRD ascribes a European dimension to the liability issue, we will attempt to circumscribe the concept of supervisory liability. Thereby we purport to identify the situations that might give rise to liability issues and try to differentiate supervisory liability from other instances effectively resulting in depositor compensation. Also, we will attempt to highlight the main aspects characterising supervisory duties as well as the various facets of imposing liability on supervisory authorities.

2.1 Instances of supervisory liability

Legal literature generally identifies two broad categories of supervisory liability related to the nature of the potential plaintiffs: third parties (depositors, investors, various creditors of a financial institution) and the regulated institutions that are subject to supervision (Tison 2005: 641). Depositors will generally sue supervisory authorities, in order to retrieve loss incurred pursuant to the bankruptcy of a credit institution. They reproach the supervisor for either passivity or inadequate action.[7] On the contrary, the regulated institutions may accuse the banking supervisor of overreaction and misuse of law, and will try to obtain recompense for damage caused through unjustified supervisory requirements.[8] These liability threats, coming from two opposite directions, reflect the delicate equilibrium that the supervisory authority is supposed to establish. They also justify the specific enforcement strategies to which banking supervisors make recourse for applying banking regulation.

7 Tison holds that one of the most plausible accusations against the supervisor is failure to take adequate measures such as replacing bank managers or temporarily prohibiting business, although he had or ought to have had knowledge of serious dysfunctions (e.g. fraud) or financial difficulties of the supervised bank. He considers that allegations of failure to follow and monitor closely a financially distressed bank through periodical verifications or through *ex post* assessment of adopted prudential measures is 'less pronounced' (Tison 2005: 641–2).

8 More or less easily quantifiable losses may result from prohibitions imposed by the supervisor with regard to undertaking various activities, withdrawal of authorisation and disclosure of information that affects the reputation of the credit institution and diminishes depositor confidence.

All liability claims against banking supervisors need to be considered with due regard to the special methods of banking supervision. Traditionally, banking supervision has been characterised by moral suasion strategies based on persuasion and continuous dialogue, assuming trust relationships between the regulator and the regulated entities. Cooperative supervisory practices are essential as the regulator needs to rely on the industry practitioners to provide him or her with knowledge on best practices. The emphasis of banking supervisors is on compliance strategies based on cooperation rather than on deterrence tactics based on punishment.[9] This is furthermore supported by the regulatory framework that moves away from command-and-control towards incentive-based and contract regulation.

Hence, banking supervisory authorities usually enjoy wide discretion as to the most appropriate ways of ensuring conformity with standards. Discretion is related to two aspects: (1) choosing from a wide range of more or less formalised remedial or retributive measures, and (2) recognising a heterogeneous regulatory environment where supervisory measures depend largely on the various regulatory interests and objectives related to the specific regulated firm. In such an informal non-legalistic approach, accusations against supervisors, based either on over-stringent measures (coming from regulated banks) or on over-accommodative solutions towards banks in distress (coming from depositors), are particularly difficult to prove. Largely unfettered supervisory discretion provides a powerful shield for supervisory authorities from liability claims, especially in countries where there is no general principle of liability applicable to public authorities or where the legislation lays down express immunity.

The CBD merely harmonised the technical instruments of prudential supervision and only laid down carefully, in rather non-compelling terms, a general principle on the sanctioning power of the supervisory authorities (articles 14 and 32 CBD) and the correlative right to apply to courts against decisions taken in respect of credit institutions (article 33 CBD). Thus the CBD established an explicit means of redress against supervisory action only for the regulated institutions. The CBD did not explicitly limit to banks the right of access to courts, but left it up to the Member States to determine the sphere of subjects having legal standing against supervisory authorities. Nevertheless, while the case for banks, especially in view of the sanctioning powers of supervisors, can be easily supported, nothing in the European norms seemed to encourage depositors, creditors or other third parties to apply to courts against supervisory measures.

Consequently, we observe that the previous regulatory framework – the CBD – required expressly judicial protection only for one of the two categories of supervisory liability, that towards regulated entities. EU law

9 For a cogent analysis of the enforcement strategies used by banking authorities, see Singh 2002: 4.

merely provided the general principle, without spelling out the concrete remedies to be applied by courts in case of breach of prudential norms. Nevertheless, once a general principle of judicial review applied, all other principles developed by the ECJ with regard to remedies, such as equivalence and effectiveness, were implicit. No such mandatory judicial protection could have been inferred from the CBD with regard to depositors. This may be explained by the fact that the CBD gave only a little guidance on how supervision should be conducted. The CRD brings some changes in this respect and as such may open up the possibility for depositors to rely on EU law.

Supervisory liability is commonly used in the context of micro-prudential supervision. However, in principle it could also refer to macro-prudential functions, provided that damages and a breach of a duty of care can be shown. Macro-prudential responsibility is dispersed among various bodies, each of which could eventually be held liable.

2.2 Various layers of implementation of European prudential norms

Establishing Member States' liability with regard to prudential supervision by reference to EU law needs to take account of the various layers of implementation of European prudential norms. The first layer consists of the transposition of the European directives (adopted at Level 1 and Level 2 in accordance with the Lamfalussy process) into the national legal systems. Failure of a Member State to transpose, at all or correctly, a directive into national law will always give rise to Member States' liability, irrespective of whether the provision is of direct applicability. This aspect comes under the general duty of Member States to apply EU law, which imposes on national legislators and governments to create the normative framework defining the substantive and procedural aspects required by European directives. Yet it may also occur that national supervisory authorities are directly in charge of such transposition. In such cases, national supervisory authorities may be held responsible for breach of European law. Furthermore, national authorities are obliged to consider EU law, even if the Member States did not take implementing measures within the prescribed deadline.

A second layer of the implementation process of European prudential rules consists of the non-legislative regulatory cushion, which aims at refining such rules while accommodating European law to national specificities and preferences. It is at this stage that implementation guidelines and standards are elaborated, which increasingly find a common denominator in the Level 3 measures devised by the national supervisory authorities within the framework of CEBS. This layer plainly involves the supervisory authorities, which bear responsibility for the lawfulness of adopted regulation and its consistency with superior norms. A European dimension is inherent to such responsibility and the eventually implied liability, given the increased harmonisation of administrative Level 3 rules and the requirement of conformity with EU law.

The actual implementation and concrete enforcement of EU prudential norms constitutes only the third layer. Most depositors' claims for compensation correspond to alleged grievances arising from concrete application of supervisory measures. Under the previous regulatory framework, this layer consisting of operative supervision was almost completely left to the Member States' discretion. EU law did not require either specific powers or any precise line of action when applying the common prudential standards. The CRD as amended changes the picture and brings about more convergence of supervisory practices within the Member States. Currently, the obligations of supervisory authorities are increasingly codified in the European directives and further developed in detailed rulebooks drawn under the auspices of CEBS. Moreover, ongoing reforms of the EU normative and institutional frameworks will bring additional indications about supervisory powers and their exercise. The question arises as to how much diversity can be tolerated with regard to national approaches to supervisory liability in an increasingly harmonised and legalistic supervisory framework.

2.3 Responsibility in case of banking failure

There are some issues that have to be clearly understood before inquiring into the possible liability of supervisory authorities. First and foremost, it should be always kept in mind that the primary responsibility, in the case of banking failure, stays with the credit institution itself and its stakeholders. The bank (shareholders and management) will be held liable for a bank's failure and obliged to provide redress for damages caused to its creditors. Depositors may always resort to the insolvency procedures and request compensation, on the basis of either contract law or tort law. Also, other actors providing immediate compensation to depositors (deposit guarantee funds, insurance companies) will, by subrogating themselves to the depositors, become creditors of the insolvent bank. However, the liability of banks' shareholders is limited to the subscribed capital, which may not suffice for covering all losses. Hence, depositors and bank creditors will have incentives for turning to other responsible parties – particularly the supervisory authorities – to recuperate losses.

It has been argued that imposition of supervisory liability 'would undermine the fundamental normative principle of self-responsibility, which is implicit in the enjoyment of economic freedom' (Hadjiemmanuil 1996b: 384). Against such arguments, scholars have underlined that banks' own responsibility is not mitigated through prudential supervision, seeing this as 'merely a specific external monitoring device regarding the financial solidity and integrity of financial institutions, which basically does not modify the allocation of risks in the case of banking failure' (Tison 2003: 5). The perceived risk of mitigating banks' own responsibility comes from the moral hazard related to supervisory liability – i.e. banks' incentive to take on higher risks, knowing that profits may be high while losses are limited. Indeed, from such a perspective liability distribution might seem blurred. However, from a legal perspective, the two instances of liability (that of the bank and that of the supervisor) are clearly separated and underpinned by specific legal bases. Prudential supervision is an additional controlling mechanism to the bank's own risk management; while supervisory liability is supplementary to the bank's own liability.

Furthermore, it has to be understood that the purpose of banking supervision is not to impede banks from failing. Retreat of individual nonperforming actors from the market is a natural fact in a functioning market economy and should not, per se, pose particular threats to financial stability. The purpose of micro-prudential supervision is to monitor the financial health of individual institutions and the effectiveness of their risk-management arrangements and to take the necessary supervisory measures so as to induce more prudent behaviour or eventually ensure the orderly exit of insolvent institutions. As already observed, supervisory action is not necessarily legalistic and supposes drawing a delicate balance between the various interests at stake. The threat of supervisory liability may constrain the supervisory authority's choice of the most effective supervisory action.

The liability of the supervisor may be at stake only when the failure of a bank is caused, at least partially, by the failure of the supervisor to detect distress and act accordingly. Usually, the causality link is not straightforward, nor are there any objective criteria for determining the contribution of supervisory action to the worsening of a bank's solvency. The burden of proof belongs to the plaintiffs, who will find it difficult to obtain redress by merely invoking the subjective liability of the supervisor.

However, there is a dimension of prudential supervision that might ascribe to the competent authority a degree of objective liability – namely, the perceived public good dimension of supervision. Depositors see in the public regulator a guarantor of the financial stability and therefore rely heavily on his public statements concerning particular institutions. In the context of information asymmetries, macro- and micro-prudential concerns become substantially interwoven, and depositors will expect the supervisor to also defend their interests when adopting supervisory measures. The expectations that the supervisor creates vis-à-vis banking depositors, seen from the perspective of the principle of legal certainty, may justify the depositors' recourse to supervisory liability for obtaining compensatory damages.

Last but not least, the depositor him- or herself is also a risk bearer. Thus, 'in circumstances of financial failure, regulation does not attempt to eliminate all risk to the consumer – *caveat emptor* does apply' (Singh 2004: 198). The *caveat emptor* maxim presumes that the depositor is aware of the risks assumed while depositing money with a bank. Such personal responsibility of the consumer should not be overemphasised for the purpose of shielding the banking supervisor from possible liability, but rather should be balanced against the need to support depositors' confidence and ensure that they will not lose their savings. Also, the risks of depositors should be understood in the light of their bounded capacity of assessing the financial safety of a bank. It has been frequently underlined that 'unsophisticated depositors are in no position to be vigilant' (Cranston 1995: 79) and 'even where up-to-date information is available, the average bank customer would be unlikely to be able to make sufficient sense of it to perform the type of calculation necessary to evaluate the risk potential of the institution' (Cartwright and Campbell 2003: 15). Considerations of fairness and equity require that it should be ensured that the depositor does not ultimately bear most of the risks in case of banking failure, especially when defective or negligent supervisory action has contributed to the final losses.

Consequently, the supervisory liability does not constitute a substitute for the liability of banks' shareholders, nor does it exonerate the financial consumer of assuming his or her own risks and diligence. Still, the supervisor has clear public duties and a precise role in keeping the balance between the various actors in the financial markets in order to maintain financial stability. Supervisory liability is triggered by the improper conduct of such duties and may give rise to legal remedies. It is a means for inducing supervisory authorities to act diligently. The supervisor can be held liable only for his or her own actions or inactions. There is no solidarity duty between the supervisory authority and the failing bank – as the supervisor is no guarantor of the banks' solvency, but instead is a controller who is concerned with keeping on the market only viable institutions.

2.4 Supervisory liability versus rescue operations and deposit insurance

Understanding supervisory liability also supposes its differentiation from other mechanisms effectively providing for compensation – namely, deposit insurance and rescue operations. The common denominator of the three concepts consists of the eventual possibility to provide compensation in the case of bank failures. Nevertheless, the rationale for and the objective of compensation are different in each case. So also are the mechanisms and institutions they employ. While rescue operations and deposit insurance come into action *ex post*, when a crisis situation is imminent, either as an emergency or as a compensatory device (Padoa-Schioppa 1999), supervisory liability concerns *ex ante* situations. However, even in the case of supervisory liability, damages will be identifiable only *ex post* and after the incidence of the other safety mechanisms. Although there seems to be no conceptual confusion between the three strategies, in practice the demarcation might be somewhat blurred, because of some overlaps or too vague a delineation of the supervisory tasks and objectives.

With regard to rescue operations, confusion arises because of the implication of the banking supervisor in crisis management and against the background of a very subtle borderline between prudential early intervention and crisis management. Difficulties relate to detecting the moment of the outburst and, especially, to identifying the causes of an individual bank failure or general banking crisis. As long as the origins of failure may be attributed not to external factors but instead to uncontrolled excessive risk-taking and insufficient capital cushions, there is a case for examining the way the supervisory authority has exercised its role, and supervisory liability comes to the forefront. This is even more the case in a legalistic context which triggers prompt supervisory corrective action or 'structured early intervention and resolution' (Benston and Kaufman 1988). Given the lack of transparency of emergency strategies, the so-called constructive ambiguity related to rescue operations, it is difficult to understand when preventive supervisory action stops and crisis risk management starts. This situation is particularly acute when the authority taking the leading role in crisis management is the supervisory institution.

The depositor will be barely capable of distinguishing between these phases, and will have expectations that, whenever his bank is not rescued, he might retrieve losses by other means (supervisory liability). It is important to make the depositor understand that prudential supervision by no means entails an obligation of saving or keeping a bank functioning and that prudential authorities enjoy discretion as to forbearance before they take more radical corrective supervisory measures. It should be considered that, although supervisory action and rescue operations both take place under the umbrella of financial stability, the reasons and objectives for prudential supervision (protecting depositors and controlling the solvency of institutions) differ from those behind rescue operations (impeding individual bank failures from disrupting the financial system). Hence, liability for supervisory failure cannot constitute a substitute for rescue operations.

The interaction between prudential supervision and deposit insurance is multifaceted and reflects the various tensions stemming from moral hazard[10] that dilutes market discipline, and also the synergies coming from deposit guarantee schemes' interest in keeping banks out of insolvency. The issue arises as to whether mandatory deposit guarantee is compatible with further compensation based on supervisory liability. This is particularly the case in EU law, where it has been argued that the directive regulating deposit guarantee schemes constitutes an exhaustive set of special

10 We recall that moral hazard has two facets. One regards the behaviour of depositors, who, if fully covered by deposit protection schemes in case of banking failures, are considered as losing incentives to ascertain the riskiness of their bank. The other concerns the behaviour of the bank management who, conscious of the fact that savers will be bailed out, might be encouraged to engage in excessive risk-taking.

rules for all cases of unavailability of deposits, which would exclude compensation as a remedy to supervisory failure.[11] Also, it has been argued that the Deposit Guarantee Directive is the only piece of European legislation that provides specific and limited rights for depositors of banks (Proctor 2005: 111).

In our view, there cannot be such limitation either at European or at national level, particularly when the deposit guarantee covers only up to a limited amount of losses.[12] The aim of such limited deposit protection is to ensure the immediate partial recuperation of deposits entrusted to the failing bank. The reasons behind this pertain more to social solidarity than to civil law principles, and have as their aim to allow depositors to access a reasonable amount of their savings, without undergoing the cumbersome and lengthy insolvency proceedings for recuperating them. Deposit guarantee schemes are not set up for protecting supervisory authorities from pressure arising from potential liability claims. Their mere existence cannot be interpreted as excluding supervisory liability. Deposit guarantee makes available an automatic compensation irrespective of the causes of a banking failure and without requiring particular efforts from the depositor. Supervisory liability resulting in compensation presupposes that the banking failure can be, at least partially, ascribed to the supervisory authority, to be demonstrated by the depositor. Consequently, the existence of limited coverage deposit guarantee is compatible with supervisory liability and may be cumulated with compensatory remedies.

Furthermore, even limited coverage deposit protection schemes often partially incorporate the responsibility of depositors, by means of the so-called co-insurance. Co-insurance requires depositors to bear a part of any losses resulting from the failure of a bank, making them co-responsible (Cartwright and Campbell 2003: 15). This is, in our view, a further argument for not excluding the complementarity between deposit insurance and supervisory liability.

In the EU, Member States were free to establish their own coverage of deposit guarantee schemes, provided that it was at least 20,000 euros (Directive 94/19/EC). This led to a large diversity in coverage. One of the

11 Conclusion of A.G. Stix-Hackl, 25 November 2003, Case C-222/02, published in *ZIP* 50/2003, p. 2288.

12 According to Cartwright and Campbell (2003: 10), there are five types of deposit protection schemes. At one extreme there is the 100 per cent State guarantee, encountered mainly in poorly capitalised banking systems or States undergoing financial crises. Second, there is the explicit system with limited coverage, whereby the amount of coverage may vary greatly. A third category consists of the implicit guarantee, where there is no formal arrangement but a strong expectation that deposits will be protected. Fourth, there may be ambiguity as to the extent of coverage and last, deposit protection may consist in the priority given to depositors in insolvency proceedings (e.g. Australia). At the other extreme there are situations where no deposit protection is offered at all, but strong incentives are created for reliance on disclosure and market discipline.

first measures to be adopted in response to the crisis was to increase the minimum coverage to 50,000 euros and eventually to 100,000 euros, in order to maintain depositor confidence (Directive 2009/14/EC). In the impact assessment accompanying the legislative proposal, the Commission estimated that under the new coverage about 80 per cent of eligible deposits would be covered. Consequently, only 20 per cent of deposit holders may have an interest in invoking supervisory liability. In addition, deposit guarantee schemes, subrogating themselves into depositors' rights, may also be interested in invoking supervisory liability.

2.5 Supervisory discretion and judicial control

Undeniably, the position of supervisory authorities entrusted with upholding the balance among a variety of sometimes divergent interests requires them to be endowed with a large margin of discretion and freedom of action. From this perspective, it has often been said that judicial control, and the threat of liability over banking supervisors, would be detrimental to the effective exercise of their discretionary regulatory powers. Some authors have firmly argued that banking regulators must approach their supervisory functions uninhibited by the threat of liability and, at the same time, show independence and confidence in carrying them out (Hadjiemmanuil 1996b: 339).

We agree that such concerns are legitimate and, given the competing interests the banking supervisor is supposed to consider, we maintain that he or she should not be subject to undue pressures, but should instead enjoy considerable leeway to implement prudential regulation. Nevertheless, it cannot be ignored that the banking supervisor may also be prone to capture by the regulated entities (who, as opposed to the depositors, have facilitated access to the regulatory process). Moreover, regulators themselves face perverse incentives in their own interest (as do bank managers and bank owners as a consequence of moral hazard) or, like any administrative authority, they may neglect or abuse their function. Unfettered discretion might exacerbate such perverse incentives, which for bank supervisors most often take the form of excessive forbearance[13] that may increase the losses incurred by depositors.

One way to reconcile the tensions between supervisory discretion and legal certainty required by the protection of depositors is that of the juridification and institutionalisation of both the interaction between supervisors and supervised institutions (the supervisory review process) and of early intervention instruments available to the supervisor in case of distressed banks that deviate from prudential standards. This system of mainly capital-based corrective actions prescribes various intervention

13 Forbearance is defined as failure to take timely and appropriate action to reduce the risk an unhealthy institution poses (Macey *et al.* 2001: 311).

tools and thus sets some parameters for the exercise of supervisory discretionary powers. It would be illusory (and also undesirable) to think that such provisions may completely remove abuse of discretion and provide absolute legal certainty. It is, however, unquestionable that they manage to provide a framework against which the lawfulness of supervisory action may be checked. The regulation of early intervention mechanisms creates legitimate expectations for depositors who will wait for supervisory authorities to act to force banks to re-establish prudential parameters and thereby avoid or minimise losses. Depositors will thus expect the supervisor to choose from among the various intervention instruments at his or her disposal so as to bring about the restoration of the capital cushion and the improvement of the bank's internal risk-management mechanisms. Only as an extreme solution will the depositors envisage the supervisor withdrawing the authorisation or otherwise initiating the closure of the bank. Therefore, the argument that a more lenient approach adopted by the supervisor is justified in terms of the intention of restructuring institutions rather than outright closure (Binder 2004: 476) does not per se run counter to the expectations of depositors, who will also prefer that banks be kept running viably. The problematic issue is how to ensure that no abuse of discretion takes place within such a lenient approach, which might result in further risks to the depositors. A plausible solution for controlling discretion, especially in an ever more formalised context, consists of assuring judicial review of supervisory action.

The threat of judicial review is no miraculous recipe against misuse of discretionary powers, but an instrument for controlling whether supervision has been exercised within the parameters set by legislation and in conformity with underlying policy objectives. Thereby, it creates incentives for supervisors to fulfil their functions diligently. Moreover, the role of courts is also to ascertain whether general principles (e.g. good faith in discharging a public duty) have been duly observed during the exercise of discretionary powers. Concepts like reasonableness and proportionality, whose scope is to a large extent contextual, will help the courts when ascertaining whether the supervisory authority has exercised its discretionary powers within the limits of its authority. In pursuing this review task, it is generally recognised that it is not the function of the court to substitute its own decision for that of the authority enjoying discretionary powers, but only to set the limits on the exercise of discretion (Delamy 2001: 55). Nevertheless, in practice it may be more difficult to distinguish between the merits and legality of a supervisory measure; hence courts are somehow reluctant to intervene firmly in situations that involve discretion and special expertise. Courts exercise even more caution when matters falling within economic policy-making are at issue. Notwithstanding these difficulties, it must be admitted that judicial review is one of the ways whereby the weakest party (depositors) can defend their interests and contain the exercise of discretionary powers by supervisory authorities.

It is worth noting that the issue of discretion has constantly received attention from the ECJ, particularly when discussing matters falling under either institutional liability or State liability.[14] Also, the ECJ has pointed to the distinction between discretion as a matter of EU law, implying that EU legal provisions determine its existence and scope, and, on the other hand, discretion conferred by national law.[15]

2.6 Statutory immunity of the banking supervisor

Another element to be taken into account when considering supervisory liability is the immunity that might be conferred on the banking supervisory authority. Thereby we refer to the immunity from civil law liability expressly granted by law or statute, not to the implicit immunity resulting from other legal considerations incident in the ambit of regulatory activities. Indeed, Member States' legislations contain provisions awarding total or partial immunity to their banking supervisory authorities (Tison 2005: 645).

There are multiple policy considerations supporting the immunity from liability of the banking supervisors. In the context of considering the liability of the Bank of England, it was maintained that supervisory liability would undermine the fundamental normative principle of self-responsibility incumbent upon the banks themselves (Hadjiemmanuil 1996b: 384). Furthermore, supervisory liability would distort the balance between regulatory gains and losses, particularly from the perspective of depositors who would be capable of claiming and recovering damages for the loss of a benefit, which would have been free of charge had the supervisor performed his or her duties properly. Complementarily, it is often argued that if supervisors were constrained to pay compensation to depositors of a failed bank, the ultimate bearers of the costs would be the taxpayers (Proctor 2005: 110).

In addition, the threat of liability for discretionary regulatory decisions is considered to distort the decision-making process by inducing inhibition and a defensive position in the supervisory authority – the 'inhibition argument' (Rossi 2003: 669). This argument reflects a broader pattern in recent economic regulation that considers that the emergence of liability in damages would be detrimental to the effective exercise of the regulatory functions (Hadjiemmanuil 1996b: 339; Arora 1988: 450). Also, it has been considered that such liability, if based on a duty of care to the depositors, would conflict with the general duties of the supervisory authority to reconcile various interests for the benefit of the financial markets as a whole (Proctor 2005: 110). Furthermore, there is the so-called 'floodgates'

14 On a detailed analysis, see Hilson 2005.

15 See ECJ judgment from 4 July 2000, Case C-424/97, *Haim*, Rec I-5123: 38.

argument calling for the protection of regulators in order to stop them becoming 'defendants of last resort when all other defendants are bankrupt or defunct' (Rossi 2003: 670). Also, there is the influential argument of the scarcity of resources of the supervisory authority referring to the high costs entailed in defending actions and compensation due to successful claimants. Lastly, liability claims are considered to inevitably put into question the efficiency and credibility of the whole banking system (Andenas and Fairgrieve 2000a: 360).

Obviously, the supervisory authorities themselves primarily favour supervisory immunity. This is openly expressed in the Basel Committee's Core Principles for Effective Banking Supervision, which explicitly refer to the need for 'legal protection for supervisors' (BCBS 1997: Principle 1). According to the explanatory memorandum, such requirement includes 'protection (normally in law) from personal and institutional liability for supervisory actions taken in good faith in the course of performing supervisory duties'. Such a principle, nevertheless, is not legally enforceable and merely reflects self-interest in promoting supervisory liability as a common standard (Tison 2005: 644).

It should be observed that supervisory immunity is not a unitary concept, but merely a generic term designating exemption from liability of supervisory authorities under certain circumstances. The precise content of the 'legal protection' offered by it may vary not only with respect to the wording of the provisions explicitly conferring it,[16] but also in relation to constitutional and fundamental rights considerations, as well as to the general tort law system applicable to a determinate situation. Without entering into details, we shall only mention that immunity will always have to be balanced against aspects such as access to courts or fundamental rights of depositors (Proctor 2005: 84). Immunity may be generic or cover specific supervisory actions; it may impinge differently on macro- and micro-prudential functions. The subjective element also plays an important role in determining the scope of actions covered by supervisory immunity. Thus, immunity may cover actions resulting from negligence, gross negligence, intention, good or bad faith. While it is more common that immunity covers instances of negligence and even gross negligence, it is less likely that it will serve as a shield against measures taken in bad faith.[17]

16 On the interpretation of the specific language of the statutory immunity, see the interesting analysis by Proctor 2005: 103–7, in relation to the Privy Council's decision in *Gulf Insurance Limited* v. *The Central Bank of Trinidad and Tobago* (Privy Council Appeal no. 78 of 2002). In that case the language was considered to restrict immunity only to those activities that were in performance or in connection with the performance of the functions of the bank, but not those purporting to be in performance but being actually beyond the powers conferred.

17 Tison finds that, out of the eleven countries surveyed, two national legislations (German – section 6 III Kreditwesengesetz – and Polish – art. 133(4) Banking Act of August 1997) conferred supervisory immunity also in cases of bad faith.

2.7 Public expectations

In the previous section we enumerated some of the most influential policy arguments invoked in favour of granting immunity to the banking supervisor. Here, we will give an overview of the arguments usually invoked to the contrary or at least for containing immunity so as to be compatible with other policy interests, particularly depositor protection. This set of arguments is firmly anchored in the expectations the public at large has with regard to the role that supervisors should play, at least from the more narrow perspective of depositor protection.

The main policy argument in favour of at least some supervisory liability considers liability as a means of protection against undue or arbitrary damage incurred pursuant to inappropriate administrative action (Hadjiemmanuil 1996b: 384). It is considered that the more ample resources of the public authorities allow for absorbing unjust losses provoked to exposed individuals who are the weaker party. A second line of argumentation relies on the educational and disciplinary function of liability, according to which the threat of liability induces public servants to perform with due care and observance of their duties (Harlow 1982: 160).

Furthermore, in the context in which the role and accountability, including potential liability for secondary actors (e.g. auditors, accounting firms, lawyers, underwriters), is brought to the forefront, the responsibility of the public regulator has to be assessed partially from the same perspective. Thus, in the context of the Enron scandal, US courts have considered, at the suggestion of the Securities and Exchange Commission, that secondary actors can be held liable if, acting alongside or with others, they create misrepresentations (on which the investor-plaintiffs relied) and if they have knowledge of such misrepresentation.[18] We argue that the responsibility of the supervisory authority should also be judged in terms of its ability to contribute to creating misrepresentations on which depositors rely. Fairness arguments would discard double standards and request that supervisors' activities also be assessed from the same angle as in the case of other actors and proportionally to their effective contribution to a certain state of affairs.

General principles of good administration and judicial protection obviously also militate for the supervisory authorities to assume liability for their own faults. Supervisors, like other administrative authorities, are also bound by the commonly accepted principles of administrative law, legality, subsidiarity, proportionality and non-discrimination (Giovanoli 2000a: 111). It has been maintained that 'it would not be in accordance with basic principles of law if it were possible to fully exonerate a supervisory authority, regardless of the gravity of the mistakes that had been made or

18 *In re Enron Corpn Securities Derivative & ERISA Litigation*, MDL-1446, SD Tex 20 December 2002. For a comment of the ruling, see Hanks and Nardini 2003: 245–6.

the consequences thereof' (Smits and Luberti 1999: 377). Nevertheless, legitimate expectations of the citizens, as deriving from these principles, should be valued through the filter of the peculiarity of the banking business and the special and complex character of supervisory tasks.

Public expectations constitute an important counterweight to the considerable discretion conferred upon supervisors, whose actions are by design intended to serve the public interest in general (Fortsakis 2005: 208). They are necessary for safeguarding the observance of lawful interests and individual rights, particularly those covered by the declared supervisory objective of depositor protection. In this sense, it has been often recognised that the supervisory authority must be accountable in some way, even if the degree of accountability may largely depend on the specific national and statutory contexts (Hüpkes *et al.* 2005: 26).

2.8 The quest for common normative boundaries for supervisory liability

There are wide disparities across domestic rules on supervisory liability. As has been observed, 'national courts are wary of chilling legitimate administrative activities by unduly intrusive judicial oversight and the balance between accountability and efficiency has been struck in different ways across the European Community' (Craufurd Smith 1999: 302).

At present, there is no dominant opinion as to the issue of supervisory liability; literature contains approaches that range from supporting total immunity of banking supervisors to encouraging the imposition of generous liability on the supervisor. In between these extremes, so far, there is no clearly contoured middle way, but only the firm conviction that an equilibrium should be found between the self-interest of the depositors and the objectives and interests of the public authority.[19] Furthermore, deposit insurance schemes constitute only a limited compensatory tool, which does not necessarily establish the balance between the various actors.

The frameworks in the various Member States reflect this large diversity which triggers uneven situations. The issue of supervisory liability will ultimately always be a matter of national law, to be determined by national courts in concrete situations and in the context of national tort law.[20] The question arises as to the need to have, within the common banking market, common underlying policy considerations for the treatment of supervisors. The search for a dominant argumentation has pushed legal research in the direction of comparative analysis of the solutions given within national jurisdictions. In the area of supervisory liability of banking authorities, there are

19 'Statutory immunity needs to be balanced against legitimate claims for compensation for the loss that ensues from financial insolvency'; Singh 2004: 199.

20 Mental requirements, tests for determining the causal link, as well as the scope of damages to be covered, are largely differing among the various jurisdictions.

several rigorous comparative law studies[21] that weigh the competing considerations and the various aspects of balancing public and private interests that have emerged in different jurisdictions. These studies underline the most important issues raised at national level, and thus may contribute to indicating the common denominator capable of inducing a European standard in the area of supervisory liability. Only by taking into consideration concrete policy concerns could a normative benchmark for supervisory liability emerge. Furthermore, the comparative perspective helps with interpreting EU law in a unitary way, as it highlights the differences in national systems and indicates the extent to which EU law might intervene for containing divergent enforcement.

All comparative studies analysing national case-law and legal frameworks indicate that supervisory authorities are subject to differing liability rules. The consequence is that, within the European common market, depositors and banks will receive differentiated treatment, which might constitute a further barrier to cross-border banking activities. It is no wonder that depositors who have suffered loss from the failure of a bank in a Member State will be inclined to look for support and legal certainty in European law. Also, divergences and inequalities might be mitigated if the foundations of supervisory liability were to be looked at with a stronger emphasis on EU prudential rules. In the following chapters, without entering into a comparative analysis, we will focus on the possibilities of EU law to influence national choices with regard to the liability of banking supervisors. While aware that uniformity cannot be achieved, nor is it desirable, we acknowledge the capacity of EU law to influence national administrative and tort law so as to keep diversity within the boundaries of what is deemed in the interests of a single market.

21 See Smits and Luberti 1999; Andenas and Fairgrieve 2000a, 2002; Rossi 2003; Tison 2005.

12 The current state of supervisory liability under European law

In order to identify how the European legal framework can influence supervisory liability, we will first sketch the framework under which European law has imposed State liability in damages, in the context of remedies for breach of EU law. This serves to avoid misunderstandings or confusions with other instances where Member States have been held liable according to EU law. Then, we will analyse some of the most important conditions requested by EU law for imposing liability. Furthermore, we will give an overview of national jurisprudence that has addressed EU law in the context of supervisory liability. Finally, we will give a critical appraisal of the ECJ's latest jurisprudence on this issue.

1 The scope of Member States' liability for breaches of EU law

The application of EU law within the Member States has been ensured through the gradual development by the ECJ of a policy on remedies for breach of EU law. Unlike the case of non-contractual liability, which was always explicitly provided for by the Treaty (ex-article 288(2) EC Treaty and now 340 TFEU), there is no provision foreseeing the liability for damages caused through infringement of EU law by Member States. Given this absence, it was initially considered that remedies were a matter of national laws, governed by national substantial and procedural rules and subject only to the dual requirement of equivalence (non-discrimination) and minimum protection (practical impossibility).[1] In a second phase, the limitations linked to this approach, which was leading to non-uniform application of EU law, in parallel with the expansion of the doctrine of direct effect, have brought about a stronger emphasis on the duty of

1 Illustrative for this view are Case 33/74 *Rewe-Zentralfinanz eG and Rewe-Zentral AG* v. *Landwirtschaftskammer für das Saarland* [1976] ECR 1989, 1997; Case 45/76, *Comet BV* v. *Produkthap voor Siergewassen* [1976] ECR 2043, Case 158/80, *Rewe-Handelsgesellschaft Nord mbH* v. *Hauptzollamt Kiel* [1981] ECR 1805. For a more detailed analysis, see Craig and de Búrca 2003: 213; Louis and Ronse 2005: 301–32.

national courts to provide full and effective protection of EU rights. This development resulted in the early 1990s in a more interventionist approach of the ECJ as regards national remedies and culminated in the recognition in *Francovich*[2] of the right to reparation for breach of EU law. The period of judicial activism, when the Court established the general principles applicable to State liability for infringement of EU law, was followed, in the late 1990s, by a phase of selective deference to national rules of procedure (Tridimas 2000), when national courts were left with discretion in determining whether national rules of procedure provide a sufficient level of protection for the EU rights at issue.

It is not the purpose of this chapter to engage in a thorough analysis of the principle of State liability for breaches of EU law. Our endeavour confines itself to identifying the extent to which State liability may be relied upon for modelling supervisory liability within the national legal orders. Before analysing the three EU law conditions for liability (existence of an EU rule intended to confer rights on individuals, a sufficiently serious breach of that EU rule, and a direct causal link between the breach and the damage suffered by the individual), it is important to first understand the scope of the principle and some of the policy considerations behind it.

The general wording of the ruling in *Francovich* has, from the very beginning, indicated the universality of the right to reparation. According to the ECJ's judgment, liability is incident 'where a Member State fails to fulfil its obligations under the third paragraph of article 189 [renumerated 249 EC, now 288 TFEU] of the Treaty to take all the measures necessary to achieve the result prescribed by a directive'.[3] The Court confirmed in *Brasserie du Pêcheur*[4] that the principle of State liability inherent to the Treaty applies to every case where a Member State breaches EU law. Nevertheless, the conditions for liability or their application depend on the type of breach that is at stake[5] and on the seriousness of the breach. Thus, while failure to implement a directive constitutes per se a serious breach[6] – a *sine qua non* condition of liability – in cases of inadequate implementation, the ECJ takes a more lenient approach and considers further factors for establishing infringement of EU law. Correct implementation is a

2 Joined Cases C-6/90 and 9/90, *Francovich and Bonifaci* v. *Italy* [1991]ECR I-5357; at para. 37 the ECJ established that it was 'a general principle of Community law that the Member States are obliged to pay compensation for harm caused to individuals by breaches of Community law for which they can be held responsible'.

3 *Francovich* para. 39.

4 Joined Cases C-46/93 and C-48/93 *Brasserie du Pêcheur and the Queen* v. *Secretary of State for Transport ex parte Factortame* [1996] ECR I-1029.

5 *Francovich*, para. 38; *Brasserie du Pêcheur and Factortame*, para. 38; Case C-5/94, *The Queen* v. *Ministry of Agriculture, Fisheries and Food, ex parte Hedley Lomas (Ireland) Ltd* [1996] ECR I-02553 para. 24.

6 Joined Cases C-178, 179, 188–90/94 *Dillenkofer and others* v. *Germany* [1996] ECR I-4845, paras 27–8.

much more complex matter than transposition, and it presupposes the assessment of three aspects: the content of the measures, their nature and their effective application and enforcement in practice (Prechal 2005: 31).

It follows that liability for damages arises for the following breaches of EU law: non-transposition of the directive, incorrect or incomplete transposition of the directive, and failure to apply and enforce in practice the directive. This typology should not be taken rigidly, as the Court is very willing to consider each situation from the angle of its own complexity.[7] It is generally perceived that the case-law on non-implementation is the most consolidated, whereas the case law on incorrect or incomplete transposition[8] is more nuanced and is still under construction. Furthermore, the ECJ's case-law on State liability for breach by the administration is relatively new and is just beginning to clarify some important points.[9]

In the context of supervisory liability, it will be important to identify, in each case, to what extent the breach of EU law by supervisory authorities can be attributed to the inadequate transposition of the European directives or to the inadequate application or enforcement, despite correct normative implementation in national legislation. Also, given the detailed content of the European prudential directives, it will be necessary to take into consideration the fact that, even in the absence, or in the case of incomplete transposition, of the directives into national legislation, supervisory authorities may directly apply the EU prudential provisions. This is particularly the case in the context of the close and direct implication of national authorities in the European regulatory process (through their participation in the Lamfalussy committees and involvement at all four levels), as well as of the envisaged common European rulebook. Hypothetically, State liability in the context of prudential supervision may take two forms: (1) failure of a Member State to transpose European norms resulting in depriving supervisory authorities of necessary powers or imposing on them obligations contrary to EU law (non-transposition or incorrect transposition), or (2) failure of supervisory authorities to exercise supervision in accordance with correctly transposed EU provisions (non-application and enforcement in practice).

7 For instance, if the Member State has failed to transpose the directive, it may be that national administration still proceeds to implementation by way of directly applying the directive's provisions or by interpreting national law in light of the provisions of the directive. In such a case, the ECJ will not consider the failure to transpose as a serious breach per se, but will assess whether inadequate application by the administration amounts to a serious breach; see Case C-319/96 *Brinkmann Tabakfabriken GmbH* v. *Skatteministeriet* [1998] ECR I-5255.

8 Representative of the incorrect/incomplete implementation is the following line of cases: C-392/93 *British Telecom* [1996] ECR I-1631, Joined Cases C-283/94, C-291/94 and C-292/94 *Denkavit* [1996] ECR I-5063 and C-140/97 *Rechberger* [1999] ECR I-3499.

9 Case C-5/94 *The Queen* v. *Ministry of Agriculture, Fisheries and Food ex parte Hedley Lomas (Ireland) Ltd* [1996] ECR I-2553; Case C-319/96 *Brinkmann Tabakfabriken GmbH* v. *Skatteministeriet* [1998] ECR I-5255; Case C-424/97 Haim II [2000] ECR I-5123.

For the sake of State liability for breach of EU law, the term 'State' receives a wide interpretation, so as to achieve the intended objectives.[10] In accordance with the constant case-law of the ECJ, it has now become commonplace for Member States to be held liable, irrespective of which organ of the State is responsible for the breach, be it the legislator, the administration or the judiciary.[11] It has been observed that:

> the Court is willing to apply a broad-brush approach which covers the whole panoply of bodies which exercise public authority in one way or another, through which the State pursues its policies, whether in its regulatory capacity or in its interventionist capacity or where the State operates as a market participant.
>
> (Prechal 2005: 60)

Within such wide interpretation of the concept of State, two concrete issues call for attention. One relates to the identification of the actual addressees of a directive. It might already be identifiable from the provisions of the directive whether the State, generically, or a specific body infringes EU law. Thus, in the context of EU banking legislation, it is often the case that specific provisions are addressed directly to the competent authorities, although the directive generically has the Member States as an addressee. Consequently, supervisory authorities may be held directly responsible for breaches of EU law.

The second issue concerns the question of which authority is the bearer of the obligation to provide reparation, which is particularly relevant in relation to independent public bodies enjoying budgetary autonomy. The ECJ's answer underlines the necessity for individuals to recover loss or damage caused to them by non-compliance with EU law. The ECJ asserted that a Member State cannot escape liability by pleading the distribution of powers and responsibilities as between the bodies which exist within the national legal order or by claiming that the public authority responsible for the breach of EU law is deprived of the necessary power, knowledge, means or resources.[12] The Court also made clear that EU law does not preclude a public law body from being liable to make reparation in addition to the State itself.[13] The issue of whether the State itself or a specific authority is liable ultimately depends on national law and the degree of discretion left to the authority (Tridimas 2002: 165). All these considerations have an important bearing on supervisory liability, as they clarify first that the limited resources of banking supervisors cannot be invoked as

10 See Opinion of AG Van Gerven in Case C-188/89 Foster [1990] ECRI-3313, para. 11.

11 State liability for breaches of Community law by the judiciary is the most recent; see Case C-224/01 *Köbler*, judgment of 30 September 2003 [2003] ECR I-10239.

12 Case C-424/97, *Haim II*, para. 28.

13 Ibid., para. 32.

such for restricting the responsibility of supervisory authorities. State liability is predominantly concerned with identifying the breach of EU law irrespective of the body to be held responsible at national level. Consequently, difficulties stemming from national law concerning the distribution of competences and of financial resources cannot be invoked in order to circumvent the Member State's liability for breach of EU law.

As already mentioned, the ECJ's case-law on State liability has entered into a third phase, characterised by the fact that the general conditions of liability have been firmly stated and sufficiently refined so as to allow national courts to apply them and adapt national remedies without further intrusion from the EU. This tendency to leave more matters to national courts, known also as 'selective deference', has been qualified from the point of view of judicial policy as a 'tactical relaxation' of liability (Tridimas 2002: 152). Furthermore, this relaxation reflects fears of transforming liability into a 'safety net' or a 'panacea for various problems in the area of judicial protection' (Prechal 2005: 301). Such fears are amplified by the acknowledgement of the fact that EU law, evolving from a source for invoking rights within national procedures into the source for creating new remedies in national law, may open up the gate for an *actio popularis* (Eilmansberger 2004: 1232). Thus, concerns for mitigating State liability have lately brought about, by way of refinement, a tightening of the conditions attached to it.[14] This cautious approach of the ECJ when considering national remedies should nevertheless not be overestimated, as the attitude of the ECJ depends largely on the specific context and is not necessarily predictable.

2 The conditions for Member States' liability – the centrality of rights

The principle of State liability for breach of EU law has been construed as an illustration of the principle *ubi ius, ibi remedium* (where there is a right, there is also a remedy). Despite such constitutive association between rights and remedies under EU law, the concept of right and the criteria for identifying rights in EU legislation are not unequivocal. In the following, we will quickly review some of the problematic aspects that might also have relevance for establishing whether the banking directives entail rights upon which individuals may base their claims against supervisory authorities.

The interdependence between rights and remedies is generally recognised in every legal system (Van Gerven 2000; Eilmansberger 2004). Furthermore, it has been observed that, while in national legal orders it does not really matter which one of the two is dominant, in the EU context,

14 Illustrative of this approach are the following cases: C-208/90 *Emmott* [1991] ECR 4269; C-338/91 *Steenhorst-Neerings* v. *Bestuur van de Bedrijfsverening voor Detailhandel, Ambachten en Huisvrouwen* [1993] ECR I-5475, C-188/95 *Fantask and Others* v. *Industriministeriet* [1997] ECR I-6783.

given the necessity of enforcing EU rights through national remedies, it is crucial to establish whether rights or remedies detain the commanding position.[15] Given the particular character of the EU legal order, and especially fundamental principles such as supremacy and *effet utile*, the answer seems obvious: rights defined at supranational level will take the lead and shape remedies at national level. For this to take place, it is imperative that EU rights are given sufficient substance in EU legislation, in a way capable of directing national remedial law so as to safeguard their essence. Otherwise, vaguely defined EU rights will be prone to receive their contours through national remedial law (Eilmansberger 2004: 1223).

'Rights' are the central concept for establishing State liability for breach of EU law, as it results from the consolidated case-law of the ECJ: the EU provision 'must be intended to confer rights on individuals'.[16] This notwithstanding, the ECJ never engaged in defining with precision what a right is,[17] nor did it firmly establish the criteria for identifying rights conferred to individuals under EU law. This unfortunate situation leads to particular difficulties, above all in the case of directives and in the context of the multi-layered process of their implementation. Undoubtedly, directives like any normative act are intended to create a 'whole conglomerate of rights and obligations between Community institutions and Member States, Member States *inter se*, Member States and individuals, and individuals amongst themselves' (Prechal 2005: 95).

Nevertheless, the rights and obligations provided in directives, although latent since the very enactment of the directive, receive their complete substance only once implemented in national legal orders. Thus, directives constitute, in principle, an indirect source of rights, and only exceptionally, where provisions apply by virtue of direct effect, an immediate source of individual rights. Furthermore, their legal protection depends on national procedures and remedies, so that it is not possible to secure EU rights in a uniform manner throughout the Member States (Van Gerven 2000: 521). In this context, it is important to note that, although preliminary questions referred to the ECJ are usually formulated in terms of whether an EU provision creates rights, the Court's response will ultimately be reclassified in accordance with national legal concepts (e.g. subjective right, individual interest, etc.). Consequently, what counts is identifying the legal position that an individual might derive from EU law,

15 In principle, the opposite rule, *ubi remedium, ibi ius*, might be equally valid; see Eilmansberger 2004: 1237.

16 *Brasserie du Pêcheur* paras 51, 74.

17 The legal literature consistently refers to the tentative definition given by Van Gerven (2000: 502): 'the concept of rights refers … to a legal position which a person recognised as such by the law … may have and which in its normal state can be enforced by that person against (some or all) others before a court of law by means of one or more remedies.'

irrespective of the classification of that position under national law. In this sense, the 'creation of rights' requirement should be understood broadly (Louis and Ronse 2005: 321).

For an EU right to be safeguarded and entail compensation for individuals in case of its infringement, despite such national divergences, it is imperative that it be identifiable as to its constitutive substantial elements. As in the case of any *iuris vinculum*, this supposes that the legal norm establishes a specific obligation to do something or abstain from doing something incumbent upon an identifiable subject (the bearer of the obligation or duty) towards the person to be regarded as the holder of the right. It has been held that a clear and unequivocal obligation actually constitutes a concrete claim and makes the necessary remedy for the protection of the corresponding right immediately apparent (Eilmansberger 2004: 1238).

The ECJ does not consistently apply precise criteria for determining the circumstances when EU provisions prescribe with sufficient clarity legal duties creating legal rights. While in cases of directly effective norms the existence of obligations may be more easily established, the majority of the provisions enshrined in directives will not be as clear and precise as to permit immediate identification of indirectly conferred rights (i.e. rights resulting from EU norms that do not have direct effect). In an endeavour to contain such significant legal ambiguity, the doctrine has identified (from existing case-law) a series of parameters to be checked. These suppose a complex inquiry into the terms, objectives and purposes of the directive, the determination of the parties to the legal relationship in the concrete case, the detection of an individual interest to be protected by the norm and, equally relevant, the ascertainability of the EU right at issue with regard to both its content and the availability of judicial protection (Prechal 2005: 111). These parameters have to be checked not only against individual provisions but also by reference to the directive as a whole, in accordance with the well-established practice of systemic interpretation.

Only once the existence of the EU right in principle is established will it be possible to assess whether a Member State has infringed that right and might therefore be held liable. For this, it is necessary and sufficient that two further conditions are fulfilled: seriousness of breach of the EU provision conferring the right and the direct causal link between the damage suffered by the injured party and the breach of EU law. The guidelines for determining the seriousness of breach have been laid down in the so-called first-generation cases on State liability (Tridimas 2002). Thus, in accordance with the ECJ's judgment in *Brasserie du Pêcheur*, the seriousness of breach depends on the clarity and precision of the rule breached, the scope of discretion left to national authorities, whether infringement and damage caused was intentional or involuntary, whether any error of law was excusable or inexcusable, whether the position taken by an EU institution may have contributed towards the omission, and whether the respective Member State has adopted or retained national measures or practices contrary to EU law (paragraphs 56–7). The condition of causation has been refined only in the second generation of cases on State liability, which made clear that it is for the national courts to establish whether the causal link exists, but this has to be determined in the first place by reference to EU law (Tridimas 2002: 158).

Only if the three conditions are fulfilled is the right to reparation of the injured party established under EU law, and national rules on liability governing the action for damages should ensure that damage caused through breach of EU law is made good. In this context, national remedies 'must not be less favourable than those relating to similar domestic claims and must not be such as in practice to make it impossible or excessively difficult to obtain reparation' (*Brasserie du Pêcheur*, paragraph 67). More recent ECJ case-law appears to go beyond such minimal protection and to require that national restrictions do not impede adequate protection of the EU right infringed.[18] The core of the requirement of adequate protection consists of imposing such national remedial rules as to ensure that individuals can obtain sufficient protection in national courts for the rights they derive from EU law. This operation entails a pondering act aiming at striking the right balance between the national interests as reflected in national remedial law and the EU interests requiring the safeguard of the specific right. This balancing act is highly complex and should duly consider basic conceptions prevailing in the Member States, as well as the guarantee of the substance of the EU rules at issue. It was also held that national judges should also consider 'whether the relief granted under a particular national legal system does not put the complainant at too large a competitive disadvantage as compared with complainants looking for similar relief in other Member States' (Van Gerven 2000: 534).

3 The issue of direct effect

Acknowledging the differences between direct effect and State liability for breach of EU law is necessary because of the frequent confusion between the creation of individual rights requirement for State liability and the establishment of direct effect, whereas the two concepts do not coincide

18 Van Gerven 2000: 531. The author argues strongly in favour of the application of the adequacy test ('not preventing the remedy from being sufficiently adequate') rather than the minimum effectiveness test ('not rending the remedy virtually impossible or excessively difficult'). Cases such as C-312/93 *Peterbroeck* [1995] ECR I-4599 and C-430 and 431/93 *Van Schijndel* [1995] ECR I-4705 are illustrative of the willingness of the ECJ to proceed to a more nuanced balancing of the national and EU interests at stake and moving away from merely checking whether a national rule precluded entirely or almost entirely the enforcement of an EU right.

(Louis and Ronse 2005: 319). To start with, we recall that the doctrine of direct effect as developed by the ECJ refers to the immediate enforceability (applicability) of EU law provisions in national courts by individual applicants. Construed initially in relation to Treaty provisions,[19] the doctrine of direct effect has been carefully extended to directives in an effort by the ECJ to ensure their effectiveness.[20] Consequently, in order to ensure legal certainty and the protection of legitimate expectations of individuals, the ECJ held that direct effect of a directive could be pleaded by an individual against the State which had failed to implement it. As regards the conditions to be fulfilled for direct effect of directive provisions, it seems that the ECJ is satisfied if the provisions are unconditional and sufficiently precise, without further requiring the absence of discretion or the absence of the necessity of further implementing measures. It has now been consistent case-law that:

> wherever the provisions of a directive appear, as far as their subject matter is concerned, to be unconditional and sufficiently precise, those provisions may ... be relied upon as against any national provision, which is incompatible with the directive or in so far as the provisions define rights which individuals are able to assert against the state.[21]

Thus, direct effect is a matter of invocability of EU law for the purpose of protecting individual rights or interests in national courts. Direct effect cannot be equated with the existence of individual rights, nor is the intention to grant rights a condition for the direct effect of a provision. The confusion between creation of rights and direct effect has emerged and is perpetrated by the language used by the ECJ, which often refers to 'creating rights' or similar expressions for determining direct effect. It should nevertheless be recalled that direct effect of a legal norm is much broader than the reference to the creation of rights and duties, in the sense that a directly effective provision of EU law may be relied upon for several purposes, even if it does not create rights (Prechal 2005: 101). Although often directly effective provisions also create individual rights, it should be understood that EU law may confer rights upon individuals without being directly effective. Direct effect is a way of protecting rights stemming from an EU provision, along with other legal institutions aiming at

19 Introduced in the famous *Van Gend en Loos* case, C 26/62, *NV Algemene Transporten Expeditie Onderneming van Gend en Loos* v. *Nederlandse Administratie der Belastingen* [1963] ECR 1 and subsequently developed by the ECJ, the conditions for direct effect were that a EU law provision should be clear, unconditional, should not allow for discretion and should not need further implementing measures.

20 The seminal case applying the doctrine of direct effect to directives is Case 41/74 *Van Duyn* v. *Home Office* [1974] ECR 1337, para. 12.

21 Case 8/81 *Becker* v. *Finanzamt Münster Innenstadt* [1982] ECR 53, para 25; see also Case C-221/88 *Busseni* [1990] ECR I-495, para. 22.

such protection (e.g. consistent interpretation, State liability for breach of EU law).

Furthermore, attributing direct effect to an EU norm does not say anything about the consequences in case of its infringement. The right to damages is subsequent to the infringement of an EU right, not to the quality ascribed to the norm creating the right. Direct effect is intended to provide primary protection through direct enforcement of the right, and its invocation is aimed especially at securing compliance with the specific right. It is not particularly helpful for clarifying the issue of secondary protection through compensatory remedies.

Also, the conditions for direct effect should not be equated with those attached to the creation of rights requirement, as they pursue different purposes. The latter supposes an inquiry into the content of a norm, whereas the former assesses the quality ascribed to a norm (Prechal 2005: 96). Furthermore, requiring precision and unconditionality for purposes of direct effect does not coincide with the State liability requirement that 'the result prescribed by the directive must entail the grant of rights to individuals, and that the content of those rights must be identifiable on the basis of the directive' (Andenas 2000: 407). Although it is more immediate that a provision having direct effect also creates rights, for the purposes of establishing State liability the courts should leave aside the matter of invocability and concentrate only on the ascertainability of the EU right and the correlative duty, as well as on the respective holders.

This distinction has particular relevance in the case of supervisory liability based on EU law. This comes from the fact that supervisory liability concerns secondary remedies and is essentially about the consequences arising from infringement of EU law. In this context, it does not make any difference that compliance may have been requested by way of direct applicability of EU rules before national courts. An inquiry into direct effect would be of no relevance and might distract the court from providing adequate protection.

4 The EU law issue before national courts

Under this section we will not exhaustively tackle the question of the liability of banking regulators before national courts, which would require complex comparative analysis of the various tort law regimes applicable to national authorities. The assumption is that there is a wide diversity of national approaches, not only in terms of the modalities through which liability may be engaged but also in terms of the very principle allowing that a banking regulator be held liable towards individuals. We will focus only on the way that EU law has been used in national proceedings, which is particularly instructive for understanding existent jurisprudence as well as indicative of possible future developments. This is chiefly important in the context of banking legislation, which has been often amended or complemented pursuant to uncomfortable court decisions that were responding to open questions by relying on general law principles.[22]

At first glance, we can observe that, although liability of bank supervisors has constituted an issue before various national jurisdictions and at different times,[23] plaintiffs have relied on EU law for obtaining damages only seldom – two instances are well known: the UK *Three Rivers* saga[24] and the German *Peter Paul* affair.[25] The *Three Rivers* case has been brought up by depositors suffering loss pursuant to the failure of the Bank of Credit and Commerce International (BCCI), who claimed damages by invoking the liability of the Bank of England for its negligent supervision on the basis of the First Banking Directive. The *Peter Paul* case was the consequence of the failure of the Bank für Vermögensanlagen und Handel AG in Düsseldorf (BVH), which was perceived by depositors as resulting from defective supervision by the Federal Banking Supervisory Authority (Bundesaufsichtsamt für Kreditwesen). Such defective supervision constituted, in their view, a breach of the provisions of the Deposit Guarantee Directive and of the various banking directives in force. Both cases involved national legislation, which provided explicitly for the immunity of the banking supervisory authority: in the UK for every situation which did not involve bad faith; in Germany, in principle, so as to bar any claim by individual depositors. While the British courts dealt with the EU law issue at length and finally decided

22 This is the case of the introduction of specific immunity provisions for the banking supervisors in Germany after the Herrstatt scandal. Also, at the European level, the secrecy provisions in the First Banking Directive were extensively amended as a consequence of the interpretation given by the Supreme Court of the Netherlands (Hoge Raad, 14 April 1984, Nederlandse Jurisprudentie 1986, 822).

23 To give some examples: in France – *Cour Administrative d'Appel de Paris*, 30 March 1999, *El Shikh*, AJDA, 1999, 951; *Conseil d'Etat*, 30 November 2001, *Kechichian*, AJDA 2002, 136; in Germany – *Wetterstein*, BGH Z 74, *Herstatt*, BGHZ 75; in Austria – *Oberster Gerichtshof* (1 Ob 103/02g), unreported, 11 June 2002, *Landesgericht* (Vienna) (31 Cg 18/96 m), 2 July 2001; in the Netherlands – *Gemeente Hillegom et al.* v. *De Nederlandsche Bank NV*; in Italy – *Banco de Calvi* case, Court of Appeal of Genoa, 15 January 1958, Banca Borsa e Titoli di Credito, 1958, II: 52, *Banca Bertolli* case, Tribunal of Rome 30 April 1963, Banca Borsa e Titoli di Credito, 1964, II: 106; *Banca Privata Italiana* case, Tribunal of Rome 27 April 1977, Banca Borsa e Titoli di Credito, 1978; *Banco Ambrosiano* case, Corte di Cassazione 29 March 1989, n. 1531, Banca Borsa e Titoli di Credito, 1990, II: 425, case of *Cassa di Risparmio di Prato*, Tribunal of Prato 13 January 1990, Banca Borsa e Titoli di Credito, 1991, II: 63, Court of Appeal of Florence 20 May 1991, Banca Borsa e Titoli di Credito, 1991, II.

24 Court of Appeal, *Three Rivers District Council and Others* v. *Bank of England* [2000] 2 WLR 15; House of Lords, *Three Rivers District Council and others* v. *Governor and Company of the Bank of England* [2000] 2 WLR 1220.

25 LG Bonn, 16 April 1999, (1999) *ZIP*, 959; (2000/5) *Entscheidungen im Wirtschaftsrecht*, 233; OLG Köln, 11 January 2001 (2001) NJW, 2724; BGH, 16 May 2002, (2002) NJW, 2464.

on the basis of the *acte clair* doctrine, the German courts referred the issue to the ECJ for a preliminary ruling.

Here, we will focus on the ruling in the *Three Rivers* case, the first judicial analysis of the issue of supervisory liability from the perspective of the EU directives. English courts have undertaken a complex analysis which reflects the way in which EU law may be employed within national jurisdictions and which, to a large extent, has influenced the way the *problématique* was posed subsequently in the legal doctrine and in other courts. In *Three Rivers*, the plaintiffs filed a claim for breach of EU law mainly in order to circumvent the stricter requirements attached to the tort of misfeasance in public office, which was based on very restrictive mental elements.[26] The final judgment of the House of Lords on the cause of action based on EU law was contained in the speech by Lord Hope of Craighead, who confirmed the ruling given by the majority of judges in the Court of Appeal, despite the dissenting opinion of Lord Justice Auld.

The reasoning centred on the issue of whether the Bank of England was capable of being liable to the appellants in damages for violations of the First Banking Directive (FBD). From the very beginning, the House of Lords engaged in delineating the criteria to be fulfilled for claiming damages against the State for non-implementation or mis-implementation of a directive. It distinguished between two routes available – direct effect and State liability – and reviewed the conditions for each one. Without choosing or discarding either of the two routes, the Court merely asserted the equivalence of the conditions[27] and relied for its analysis on the two critical questions formulated by LJ Auld: whether the FBD entails the grant of rights to individual depositors and potential depositors; and whether the content of those rights is identifiable on the basis of the provisions of the directive.

To answer these questions, the Court proceeded with an inquiry into the legislative basis and the purpose of the FBD. Article 57(2) – subsequently 47(2) EC Treaty and now 53 TFEU, in the old wording – required unanimity in the Council for measures concerned with the protection of savings. The Court held that the explicit reference to the protection of savings was not sufficient for identifying depositor protection among the purposes of that Treaty article, but was merely mentioned for establishing specific voting requirements. Consequently, the Court found that no assistance could be drawn from the legal basis. With regard to the purpose of the FBD, it acknowledged that it seemed undisputed by the parties that protection of depositors was an important underlying purpose of the

26 For a detailed review of the whole *Three Rivers* saga, see Hadjiemmanuil 1997; Andenas 2000: 379; *Euredia* Editorial Board 2000: 307.

27 'The conditions which the appellants must satisfy in order to establish right to damages against the Bank under each route are so closely analogous that they can be taken to be, at this stage of the case, the same'; [2000] 2 WLR 1220.

directive. Nevertheless, after examining the ECJ's case-law,[28] Lord Hope of Craighead left the issue open and concluded that 'whether FBD granted rights should be answered by examining the recitals and articles of the directive itself without any pre-conception as to the purpose'.[29]

The House of Lords asserted that within the triangular relationship of competent authorities–credit institutions–depositors, the directive definitely conferred rights upon the credit institutions affected by it, but it had to be established through a detailed analysis of the text whether it also conferred rights to third parties (depositors and potential depositors). It also found, in the light of the case-law of the ECJ, that the absence of an indication of the individuals who were granted rights by a directive was irrelevant. Moreover, the question of whether provisions in a directive create rights and obligations for individuals was seen as contextual, depending in each case 'on the subject matter of the Directive, on the context and on the nature and purpose of the provisions which are at issue'.[30]

Contrary to the opinion of LJ Auld, who inferred from article 6 of the FBD (mandating observation ratios) an immediate duty of a technical nature imposing on regulators an obligation to 'ensure savings are protected', the House of Lords considered that it did not impose any duty of supervision. It only set a duty to formulate structural ratios that would make it possible for national authorities, pending subsequent coordination, to cooperate with each other in the setting of standards or coefficients to ensure sound management of credit institutions. The House of Lords concluded that the provision could not contain any minimum standards to be observed by supervisors, but only the duty to cooperate between competent authorities so as to achieve harmonisation of prudential standards at a later stage.

Equally, the assertion of LJ Auld that article 7 imposed a duty to supervise was struck down by the speech of Lord Hope of Craighead, on the grounds that the article only entailed a duty to cooperate in order to assist the competent authorities in the performance of their supervisory functions under national law with regard to banks operating outside their home country. Consequently, it was considered that:

28 In particular the House of Lords considered two cases where the ECJ dealt with the FBD. The first is the *Parodi* case, C-222/95 [1997] ECR I-3899, where the ECJ held that the FBD was no more than a first step towards mutual recognition and Member States were entitled to apply their own consumer protection measures in the banking sector, pending the entry into force of the measures in the Second Banking Directive. The second case is *Criminal Proceedings against Romanelli* (Case C-366/97) [1999] All ER (EC) where the ECJ asserted, in para. 12, that it was clear from the FBD and the SBD that the protection of savings constituted one of the objectives of the measures taken to coordinate credit institutions.

29 [2000] 2 WLR 1220, speech by Lord Hope of Craighead.

30 Ibid.

> none of the provisions in articles 6 and 7 of the Directive of 1977 define any categories of individuals on whom rights were being conferred, nor do they state in obligatory terms that the credit institutions 'shall be subject to appropriate supervision' by the competent authorities. Even if such an obligation in general terms could be said to be implied, the absence of even the slightest amount of detail as to the system of supervision required by Community law, which was to be adopted and enforced by the national courts would make it impossible to say that, as a matter of Community law, the obligation to supervise was unconditional and sufficiently precise to satisfy the Becker-type liability test.[31]

With regard to article 8, which enumerates the situations for the withdrawal of authorisation, the dissenting judge in the Court of Appeal considered that it should be read as imposing a duty on competent authorities to withdraw authorisation in the situations where the bank does not fulfil the conditions under which authorisation was granted. Also, authorisation may be withdrawn when a bank no longer possesses sufficient own funds or can no longer be relied on to fulfil its obligations towards creditors, and, in particular, where it no longer provides security for the assets entrusted to it.[32] The House of Lords, underlining the permissive language employed in the article, refused to see in the text anything entailing the granting of rights to individuals which would allow them to insist on the withdrawal of authorisation in those circumstances. It further highlighted that the key for understanding the purpose and effect of the directive was to perceive it as an initial step in the process of harmonisation of provisions for the regulation of credit institutions acting within the EU. Consequently, the effect of the provisions of the directive should be confined to what was intended to be achieved by the directive.

The conclusion of the dissenting judge in the Court of Appeal, holding that the FBD imposed clearly defined obligations on Member States and on their regulatory bodies and that, in doing so, it gave rise to corresponding EU law rights for depositors to enforce those obligations by an action for damages, was dismissed.[33] Instead, the conclusion of the House of Lords coincided with the views of Clarke J., as expressed in the appeal proceedings:

31 Ibid.

32 [2000] 2 ELR 15, 114G. In justifying such a view, LJ Auld explained:

> It is inconceivable that the directive should be read so as to require banking regulators to insist on certain minimum requirements of authorisation and to supervise to ensure continued satisfaction of them, yet leave them with a discretion, unspecified as to the criteria, to permit continuance of trading without check or condition when those requirements are no longer met.

33 [2000] 2 WLR 15, 102H–103A.

> the Directive was not intended to require the imposition of a duty to supervise upon the supervisory authority because, whatever the underlying purpose of the system of supervision, the immediate purpose of the Directive ... was a first step towards the harmonisation of the systems in the member states, which was assumed to and no doubt did exist. Its purpose was not to lay down the duty to supervise or radically to alter the existing systems ... it was not ... to confer rights upon either savers or other creditors.[34]

Several remarks can be made with regard to the decision of the House of Lords. The most important stems from the critical argument used by the UK courts: the fact that the FBD was merely an initial step towards the harmonisation of the regulation on the taking up and pursuit of banking activities in the single market. Such an argumentation not only points to the relativity of the conclusions, circumscribed by the text of the FBD and its position as the first brick on the foundation of a common banking market, but it especially underlines the dynamic feature of European banking regulation, with the implicit assumption that it will evolve into more detailed and complete rules.[35] It has been argued that, in the light of subsequent regulation providing for a more comprehensive regime, 'the House of Lords judgement has opened up for a wide liability of banking supervisors and other regulators based on Community law. The judgment will not discourage litigation' (Andenas 2000: 406).

The legal reasoning of the House of Lords was subordinated to the overwhelming argument that the EU law provisions at issue were merely incipient European banking norms and the concern that such norms do not impinge upon the content and quality of subsequent provisions. In this context, the House of Lords, although admitting that protection of depositors was a legitimate aim underpinning the FBD and recognising that the directive provided for a duty of cooperation between competent authorities for the purpose of supervision, refused to accept an EU duty to supervise and the correlative right of depositors. By doing this, the House of Lords refused to enter into a deeper analysis of the substantial content of supervisory duties, falling short of inquiring into the very substance of the duty of cooperation and the content of the protection of depositors required by the first legislative steps towards a common banking market.

A noticeable aspect of the decision of the House of Lords is the equation between the conditions for direct effect and those for State liability. We have already highlighted the different purposes of the two concepts and the diverse nature of the requirements of precision and unconditionality

34 [2000] 2 WLR 1220, speech by Lord Hope of Craighead citing the opinion expressed by Clarke J. – [1996] 3 All ER 558, 616.

35 At the time the House of Lords delivered its judgment, the banking directives subsequent to the FBD were plainly in force, and discussions on Basel II had already started.

under the direct effect doctrine as compared to those for assessing whether an EU provision is intended to confer rights upon individuals. Legal literature has criticised the *Three Rivers* judgment for being illustrative of the danger of not making the appropriate distinction between the two concepts (Prechal 2005: 126). Two major negative consequences are attached to this reasoning of the House of Lords. First, the House of Lords introduced this confusing language between rights and direct effect into the field of banking directives, a misunderstanding that was perpetrated subsequently.[36] Second, it has been observed that following the *Three Rivers* litigation, the requirement of granting rights to individuals has become in the UK courts 'materially different from what is required according to the authoritative case law of the European Court' (Andenas and Fairgrieve 2002: 769).

Another interesting aspect of the judgment of the House of Lords was the recourse to the *acte clair* doctrine, which avoided the need to make a reference to the ECJ for a preliminary ruling on the question as to the granting of rights to individuals by the FBD.[37] Despite the fact that the interpretation by the House of Lords was not necessarily straightforward, it seemed that it had no doubts as to its capacity to assess the content of the FBD. It has been held that reliance on the *acte clair* doctrine in a controversial field (such as supervisory liability) was unsustainable and deprived the ECJ of the possibility of taking a clear position for the sake of legal certainty within the EU. The attitude of the House of Lords may also be attributed to the more general context: the evolution of EU banking law and the UK developments of tort law at the time of the judgment. Thus, the FBD was considered *acte clair* from the perspective of subsequent EU legislation which, given its complexity, could have justified qualification of the FBD merely as a first step in the process of dismantling barriers between national banking markets.

Furthermore, the *Three Rivers* case should be placed within the context of national developments of tort law on governmental liability. It has been argued that the rulings in the *Three Rivers* saga are 'illustrative of a gradual liberalising of the conditions for State liability that has been a feature of recent cases on the tort of negligence' (Andenas and Fairgrieve 2002: 778). Thus it can be considered also that the House of Lords intended to base tort law developments of governmental liability exclusively on domestic law considerations, without pressure from EU law elements. Altogether, the *Three Rivers* case has to be discarded for the purpose of interpretation of current and future EU banking directives. It is nevertheless an interesting example of how national courts might employ the *acte clair* doctrine for preserving the reach of national law and resist Europeanisation in the area of supervisory liability.

36 See Opinion of AG Stix-Hackl of 25 November 2003 in the *Peter Paul* case.

37 See *Euredia* Editorial board 2000: 307; see also Case 283/81 *Srl CILFIT and Lanificio di Gavardo Spa* v. *Ministry of Health* [1982] ECR 3415. On the *acte clair* doctrine, see Craig and de Búrca 1999a: 420–27.

5 The *Peter Paul* affair

The ECJ was given the opportunity to express its views on the banking directives a couple of years after the judgment handed down by the House of Lords, in the context of the reference for a preliminary ruling by the German Supreme Court.[38] The background to the case is given by the failure of BVH, against which bankruptcy proceedings were started on 1 December 1997 (Roeges 2003; Binder 2004; Tison 2005). After having received authorisation to start a banking business from the Bundesaufsichtsamt in 1987, BVH had unsuccessfully applied, up to 1992, for admission to the deposit guarantee fund of the Bundesverband Deutscher Banken e.V. The authorisation had been granted under the conditions that BVH would become a member of the deposit guarantee fund and that, so far as this was not the case, customers of the bank should be informed about the lack of such guarantees. Notwithstanding the refusal of the deposit guarantee fund, the bank continued to accept deposits from the public, a situation that was tolerated by the banking supervisor despite two on-site inspections undertaken between 1991 and 1995. It was not until August 1997 that the banking supervisory authority intervened, first by imposing a special moratorium on BVH, which effectively closed the bank and froze its assets, and then by revoking the authorisation and opening up the proceedings for insolvent liquidation.

Peter Paul and others were customers of BVH who had made deposits with the bank of between 66,976 and 131,455 DM in the interval between June 1993 and February 1995. After the failure of the bank, they introduced an action against the German State for compensation in respect of the losses of their deposits, thereby relying on the fact that Directive 94/19/EC on deposit guarantee schemes had not been transposed promptly within German law[39] and the fact that the supervisory authority had failed to take supervisory measures against BVH in due time. The first-instance court – the Landgericht Bonn – acknowledged the belated transposition of the Deposit Guarantee Schemes Directive. In the light of the ECJ's jurisprudence on the liability of Member States for breach of EU law, it considered that the plaintiffs had a right to reparation corresponding to the compensation they would have been guaranteed if BVH had been a member of a deposit guarantee scheme, in accordance with directive 94/19/EC: i.e. the equivalent of 20,000 euros, plus interest. With regard to the loss of depositors exceeding that amount, the Landgericht, like the appeal court, Oberlandesgericht Köln, rejected the claims on the ground that the German banking

38 Reference of the Bundesgerichtshof for a preliminary ruling of 16 May 2002 (202) NJW, 2464.

39 Directive 94/19/EC should have been transposed into national legislation by 1 July 1995. Owing to belated transposition, the implementing German legislation had come into force only on 1 August 1998.

legislation[40] subjected the Bundesaufsichtsamt to a specific administrative liability regime stemming from the requirement that it should exercise the functions assigned to it only in the public interest.[41]

Within the procedure of appeal on a point of law (*Revision*) before the Bundesgerichtshof the plaintiffs requested the payment of damages for breach of various EU banking directives. They alleged that the banking directives contained obligations as to the proper exercise of prudential supervision over credit institutions, which were infringed by the supervisory authority. The Bundesgerichtshof, contrary to its UK counterpart, suspended the procedure and referred various questions to the ECJ on the interpretation of the banking directives.

The following sets of questions were posed to the ECJ. (1) Did the Deposit Guarantee Directive also confer (apart from the right to compensation up to the amount specified) the more far-reaching right to require that the competent authorities avail themselves of the measures mentioned in article 3(2) to (5) and, if necessary, revoke authorisation? Additionally, it was asked whether such a right would also include the right to claim compensation for damage resulting from misconduct of the competent authorities beyond the amount specified. (2) Did the directives harmonising the law on the prudential supervision of banks,[42] individually or combined, contain rights to the effect that the competent authorities of Member States must take prudential supervisory measures, with which they are charged by those directives, in the interest of savers and investors and must incur liability for any misconduct? Alternatively, it was asked whether the directive on deposit guarantee schemes contained an exhaustive set of special provisions for all cases of unavailability of deposits. (3) In the case that it was found that one of the directives conferred on savers the right to require the competent authorities to avail themselves of prudential supervisory measures in their interest, it was further inquired as to whether such a right would have direct effect so that national rules which preclude such right must be disregarded. Also, it was

40 Art. 6 para. 4 of Law on Credit Institutions (Gesetz über das Kreditwesen; KWG). Pursuant to the reform of the supervision regime in Germany, the KWG was replaced by the Gesetz über die Bundesanstalt für Finanzdienstleistungsaufsicht (Law on the Federal Institution for the Supervision of Financial Services) as of 22 April 2002, which substituted the BaFin to the Bundesaufsichtsamt für Kreditwesen. The new law reproduces the old provision requiring exercise of functions only in the public interest in art. 4 para. 4.

41 Thereby the court rejected liability on the grounds of domestic law. It considered that liability could be incurred under art. 839(1) of the German Civil Code in conjunction with art. 34 of the German Constitution only in the event of a breach of 'official duty ... as against a third party'. The fact that the Bundesaufsichtstamt exercised its duties only in the public interest precluded that a duty may exist in any case as against the injured depositors.

42 The following provisions were listed: FBD – art. 6(1), recitals 4 and 12; SBD – arts. 3, 4 to 7, 10–17, recital 11; Directive 89/299/EEC – art. 2–7; Directive 95/26/EC – recital 15. Further assistance for the interpretation of the above-mentioned directives was sought from Directive 92/30/EEC – recital 11; Directive 93/6/EEC – recital 8; Directive 93/22/EEC – recitals 2, 5, 29, 32, 41 and 42.

asked whether a Member State failing to respect that right when transposing the directive incurs liability only in accordance with the principles governing claims for damages against the State under EU law. Last, the ECJ was asked whether failure to recognise a right to have prudential supervisory measures taken does amount to a sufficiently serious breach of EU law.

The reference by the German Supreme Court was perceived as being particularly relevant for the development of European banking law (Proctor 2005: 73). The circumstances that five Member States intervened in the proceedings before the ECJ and that the judgment has been delivered in full Court[43] are considered illustrative of the importance of the issue (Tison 2005: 664). All submissions by the Member States were contrary to founding Member State supervisory liability on the banking directives. This was also the opinion adopted by the European Commission and the Advocate General Stix-Hackl.[44]

The ECJ reformulated the questions submitted to it in terms of whether the invoked directive provisions were precluding a national rule to the effect that the functions of the banking supervisors are to be fulfilled only in the public interest, which under national law precludes individuals from claiming compensation for damage resulting from defective supervision on the part of that authority. It then considered the deposit guarantee scheme directive and found that it did not entail an obligation for the Member States to adopt supervisory measures when a credit institution failed to join a guarantee scheme. According to the Court, the provisions in article 3(2) to (5) Deposit Guarantee Directive were circumscribed to the introduction and proper functioning of the deposit guarantee scheme in accordance with Directive 94/19/EC and their purpose was only to guarantee to depositors that the credit institution to which they entrust their savings belongs to a deposit guarantee scheme. Relying also on recital 24 of the preamble, the ECJ asserted that State liability pursuant to the Deposit Guarantee Directive is limited to ensuring compensation under the conditions prescribed therein and ends once prescribed compensation is paid.

The Court proceeded by examining the various banking directives and acknowledged their combination into the Codified Banking Directive 2000/12/EC (the CBD), as well as the common legal basis in article 47(2) EC Treaty. The ECJ inferred from the preamble to the SBD (reproduced also in the CBD) that the approach adopted by the EU legislator for harmonising rules aimed at the creation of the internal banking market was that of essential harmonisation, mutual recognition and home-country control (paragraph 37). It also accepted that several recitals in the preambles referred to the protection of depositors as an underlying purpose of harmonisation and that the directives imposed a number of supervisory

43 Case 222/02, *Peter Paul*, judgment of 12 October 2004.

44 For a thorough analysis of the AG's Opinion delivered on 25 November 2003, see Binder 2004.

obligations on the competent authorities vis-à-vis credit institutions (paragraphs 38, 39). It considered nevertheless that this was not sufficient for conferring rights on depositors in the event of the unavailability of their deposits as a result of defective supervision.

The main arguments supporting the ECJ's conclusions were the following. None of the invoked directives contained an express rule granting such rights to depositors (paragraph 41). Furthermore, the legal basis in article 47(2) confined harmonisation efforts to what was essential, necessary and sufficient to secure mutual recognition, the single banking passport and home-country control. The Court retained that 'the coordination of the national rules on the liability of national authorities in respect of depositors in the event of defective supervision does not appear to be necessary to secure the results described' (paragraph 43). The ECJ also noted that the immunity of banking supervisors towards individuals is accepted in several other Member States (apart from Germany) and is based on considerations related to the complexity of banking supervision stemming from the obligation of the competent authorities to protect a plurality of interests. Last, the ECJ underlined that the Deposit Guarantee Schemes Directive also provides minimum protection in the case where the unavailability of deposits is the result of defective supervision. On those grounds, the ECJ concluded that none of the invoked banking directives was intended to confer rights on individuals, hence it was not necessary to analyse the remaining questions. Given that the requirement of conferring rights was not fulfilled, the Court concluded that there was no liability on the part of the State on the basis of EU law.[45]

6 A critical appraisal of the *Peter Paul* judgment

The judgment of the ECJ in the *Peter Paul* affair affirms authoritatively that EU law, as provided in the CRD, cannot impinge upon the national regimes of supervisory liability. It confirms the reluctance of the ECJ to interfere with complex economic realities as well as its recent deference policy, which encourages increased reliance on national courts. The judgment is dominated by judicial policy considerations that are not necessarily supported by legal analysis, but were definitely welcomed by the national governments and supervisory authorities. Legal literature has expressed some criticism, particularly as to the fact that the judgment departs from and narrows down the scope of previous case-law on State liability and relies on flawed arguments to deny supervisory liability on the basis of EU law (Tison 2005: 667).

The reformulation by the ECJ of the questions referred for preliminary ruling seems to reflect, from the very start, the unwillingness of the Court to

45 The German Supreme Court took over the analysis of the ECJ as to the issue of supervisory liability based on breach of EU law and upheld the regulatory immunity regime, after discarding allegations of non-constitutionality without referring them to the German Constitutional Court; see the judgment of 20 January 2005, BGH, 20 Jan 2005, III ZR 48/0.

make a straightforward assessment whether certain provisions of the enumerated directives were imposing specific supervisory obligations on the national authorities and entailed a correlative right of depositors to require the competent authorities to exercise such duties. Instead, the ECJ related the question as to the conferral of rights through the banking directives to the issue of national legislation precluding enforcement by individuals in national courts. Such an approach reiterates the problem of the equivocal language of the ECJ as regards direct effect and the creation of rights. This neglects the fact that State liability is a complex matter, of which conferral of rights is only the first requirement to be fulfilled. It has been observed that the Court's confusion results from the interpretation of the condition of 'conferring rights' as 'conferring legally enforceable rights' (Tridimas 2002: 328; Tison 2005: 668). This reformulation results in subsuming the inquiry for identifying the eventual conferral of rights to the conditions attached to an EU provision for setting aside national rules that do not allow enforcement. Such a restrictive approach to the conferral of rights, which neglects the importance of determining the content of a provision, departs from previous case-law on State liability. In our view, the ECJ should have concentrated only on the conferral of rights requirement without associating it to national law provisions. The latter should have been assessed in the context of the requirement of a sufficiently serious breach.

Legal doctrine has identified two approaches to the 'conferring rights' requirement in the field of banking supervision (Tison 2005: 668). The narrow approach requires proof of the existence of a right to require from the banking supervisor that certain measures be taken in respect of a supervised entity, whereas the so-called flexible approach is content with the mere demonstration that the banking directives aim at protecting the 'interests' of depositors. Tison argues that the Court has chosen the narrow approach, while the preferable one would have been the flexible one, as suggested by the case-law on Community liability under article 340 TFEU (ex 288 EC Treaty) and by the general principles common to the laws of the Member States. In our opinion, the ECJ did not really try to find out whether the directives conferred any rights or interests on depositors, as it did not proceed to a detailed analysis of the terms and language of the various provisions, nor did it try to ascertain the content of those provisions. The mere assertion that none of the provisions of the directives contained express rules conferring rights is disappointing, as it is not backed by solid arguments. This reluctance of the Court to scrutinise the specific provisions is surprising in the context in which the *Three Rivers* case had already undertaken a careful assessment of the content of the various provisions contained in the FBD.

The ECJ, like the House of Lords,[46] gave decisive weight to the place of the directives within the whole legal framework applicable to credit institutions

46 The House of Lords nevertheless relied on the regulatory context only after having reviewed all incident provisions of the FBD. That was not the case with the ECJ, which in the *Peter Paul* judgment avoided a detailed analysis of the invoked provisions of the banking directive.

operating in the internal market. It emphasised the principles of essential harmonisation, mutual recognition and home-country control and inferred from that the limited purpose of the banking directives. Thereby, it particularly invoked the legal basis in article 47(2) EC Treaty, which it interpreted very restrictively and from the point of view of the internal market strategy devised in the 1985 White Paper. The arguments used by the ECJ are not straightforward, particularly when looked at from the perspective of its previous judgment in the deposit guarantee case, where the Court underlined that article 47(2) constituted the generic legal basis for abolishing obstacles to the right of establishment and the freedom to provide services.[47] There was nothing in article 47(2) that could restrict the EU legislator to proceed only to minimum harmonisation (which would, in principle, exclude the conferral of rights to individuals), nor could such limitation stem from principles that are laid down, not in the Treaty, but in the Commission's White Paper on the Internal Market. Furthermore, the Court ignored the fact that the creation of the single banking market is a gradual process, and that consequently the 'essential, necessary and sufficient harmonisation requirement' should be viewed from an evolutionary perspective.

Furthermore, in our view, the assertion by the ECJ that the coordination of national rules on the liability of national authorities in respect of depositors cannot be seen as necessary for the purposes of article 47(2) is subject to criticism. We consider that the ECJ fails to differentiate between substantive harmonisation aiming at the creation of the conditions necessary for the achievement of a single market, and procedural rules ensuring enforcement of those substantive rules. The EU's legislative competences are restricted to the areas enumerated in the Treaty, which do not include national tort law. The Europeanisation of tort law regimes, to date, comes as an indirect consequence of the harmonisation in the substantive areas of the single market and is due to the necessity of ensuring uniform implementation and hence substantial, equivalent, although not necessarily identical, enforcement of EU law within the Member States. Consequently the only concern of the Court should have been whether national procedural autonomy, as expressed by the supervisory liability regimes, was undermining the effects of EU provisions. That should have been assessed within the seriousness of breach requirement, in case the Court would have found objectively that the banking directives were intended to confer rights.

Another part of the ECJ's judgment which is prone to criticism is the argument that several Member States have introduced supervisory immunity because of the complexity of banking supervision and the plurality of interests to be safeguarded. First, the Court does not make a thorough examination of the regimes of supervisory liability in all Member States so as to be eventually entitled to induce some general common principles.

47 Case C-233/94, *Germany* v. *European Parliament and Council*, judgment of 13 May 1997 [1997] ECR I-02405.

Furthermore, the ECJ ignores the fact that supervisory immunity may have different degrees of intensity and it is rather exceptional that it be absolute, as in the case of Germany. The immunity argument should be considered after having established whether directives conferred any rights to depositors, and the degree of fault covered by a particular immunity regime should be seen in terms of seriousness of breach. Moreover, it is obvious that the judgment is biased by the awareness of the complexity of the field and of the various interests at stake and reluctance to address it. Nevertheless, for these arguments to be acceptable, the Court should have made a comprehensive analysis of the various aspects of prudential supervision and should have acknowledged the various trends and regulatory approaches in this domain.

Last but not least, the statement by the ECJ that the Deposit Guarantee Directive was providing depositor protection irrespective of the cause of the unavailability of deposits, although accurate, does not, in our view, say anything about compensation beyond the minimum prescribed by that directive. By making such an unchallengeable observation, the ECJ avoided answering the explicit question referred by the German Supreme Court as to whether the directive on deposit guarantee schemes contains an 'exhaustive' set of special provisions for all cases of unavailability of deposits. The ECJ did not stimulate the debate on deposit guarantee schemes and fell short of explaining their role in the banking regulatory framework. Also, recognising that the Deposit Guarantee Directive provides exhaustive compensation rules would have been in conflict with previous case-law on compensation. This jurisprudence considered national measures imposing an upper limit on the level of compensation to be inconsistent with EU law, because such measures 'limit the amount of compensation *a priori* to a level which is not necessarily consistent with ... adequate reparation'.[48]

It has been rightly noted that the *Peter Paul* judgment, delivered in full court, cannot be regarded as a mere *incident de parcours* (Tison 2005: 669). It will definitely constitute the yardstick against which supervisory liability will be checked. It tolerates national supervisory immunity regimes, but does not purport to restrain more liberal liability regimes. Given the weakness of the underpinning legal arguments, it is likely that the judgment does not stand up to the far-reaching reforms that took place in the area of prudential supervision. Consequently, if confronted with the supervisory liability issue in the future, the ECJ will be constrained to pay more attention to the effectiveness of EU rules and to go beyond a merely superficial approach to the issue of supervisory liability.

48 ECJ, Marshall II, C-271/91, *Marshall* v. *Southampton and South West Area Health Authority* (no. 2) [1993] ECR I-4367, para. 30.

13 Future European scenarios for supervisory liability

This chapter is concerned with the analysis of the impact that the new regulatory and institutional framework might have on the issue of supervisory liability. It will first analyse the possible change in the ECJ's approach if it were faced with interpreting a liability claim by reference to the CRD. Second, it will provide some broad and *prima facie* remarks on the possible treatment of supervisory liability in the context of the envisaged reforms of the EU supervisory architecture.

1 Supervisory liability under the CRD

Under this section, we will attempt to analyse the issue of supervisory liability in the context of the CRD. We recall, for this purpose, our previous review of the extensive amendments brought about by the CRD at both substantial and institutional level. Based on the Basel II Accord, the substantive changes are reflected in a consistent body of detailed rules promoting a process-oriented approach to prudential supervision. Furthermore, the Lamfalussy regulatory process allows for flexible adjustments of the European prudential framework.

We will try to interpret the three conditions of Member State liability for breach of EU law in light of the new prudential framework. First, we will endeavour to find out whether the CRD entails some rights for depositors. In our view, finding that the new framework entails rights for depositors is crucial for its effectiveness and would offer a way of involving in the regulatory process the marginalised depositors. The conferring rights requirement is, practically, the only one that might be assessed *in abstracto* on the basis of an analysis of the content of European prudential norms. On the contrary, the requirements of a serious breach of EU law, as well as of causality, will always depend on the concrete circumstances. In our view, the incidence of liability for breach of EU prudential rules will in practice depend on these two latter conditions. We will make an effort to outline some specific aspects, which may be considered in the context of banking supervision.

1.1 Does the CRD confer rights to depositors?

We have observed that the ECJ and the House of Lords have placed particular emphasis on the regulatory context applicable to prudential supervision. Therefore, we will start with an inquiry into the background of the new prudential rules. We will then proceed by analysing the various provisions – trying to identify from the terms and language used (as well as from their purpose), whether the parties to the *iuris vinculum* and the content of norms are sufficiently identifiable. Last, we will address the issue of protection of individual interests.

The regulatory context

The CRD has been presented in depth in the previous parts of this book. At this stage, we will only recall and underline some of the aspects that we consider helpful for identifying any rights for depositors therein. We recall also that the House of Lords refused to recognise any rights in the FBD on the grounds that it merely constituted an initial step in the harmonisation process, whereas the ECJ discarded the rights issue in the context of the SBD and CBD, invoking the minimalist approach characterising harmonisation of only essential aspects necessary for the mutual recognition and home-country control.

The CRD as it currently stands, after the amendments agreed on in May 2009, is most likely to undergo further substantive changes in response to the crisis. These reflect, as indicated in the previous parts of this book, efforts to fill in the gaps and repair the shortcomings in the current prudential framework, as well as the reform of the EU supervisory architecture that will require extensive adjustments of the relevant sectoral legislation. Notwithstanding this, the current version of the CRD is definitely the illustration of an advanced legislative stage in the harmonisation process, corresponding to a substantive impulse given to the integration of national banking markets. The CRD was part of an extensive EU programme (the FSAP) whose very purpose was to harmonise remaining national regulatory obstacles to the single market in financial services. By transposing into EU law the Basel II Accord, the new European prudential rules design a comprehensive regulatory framework for capital requirements and risk management, which goes beyond minimum standards. It reflects the necessity to include, under what is considered essential and necessary for the creation of the single banking market, a set of detailed rules covering not only extensive capital rules but also supervisory review and disclosure requirements supporting market discipline. Also, according to the preamble to the CRD, 'the smooth operation of the internal banking market requires not only legal rules but also close and regular cooperation and *significantly enhanced convergence of regulatory and supervisory practices* among the competent authorities of the Member States' (recital

19, italics added). Hence, EU harmonisation is extending to cover all core aspects of prudential supervision. The refined and complex capital rules in the CRD are, as discussed in previous chapters, an illustration of maximal harmonisation of prudential requirements. The mere claim that EU competences are limited to the harmonisation of what is essential for the internal market does not say anything about the content of harmonised essential rules. The scope of essential harmonisation in the area of the single banking market is constantly evolving towards a comprehensive approximation of prudential rules. The consistent highlighting of the need to achieve convergence between still divergent supervisory practices further reinforces this view. The further envisaged amendments to the CRD and especially the regulators' commitment to devise a European rulebook also support the idea that the EU prudential regulation is becoming an extensive coherent unitary framework.

What is remarkably significant, in the new approach to prudential supervision, is the emphasis on the supervisory review process, in addition to risk-based capital requirements. This is a critical part of the new prudential framework that highlights the increased importance attached to continuous control and a substantive dialogue between supervisory authorities and regulated banks. Particularly important for the purpose of supervisory liability is to acknowledge the dual tasks that the CRD imposes upon competent authorities. First, supervisors have to ensure that the capital position of individual credit institutions is consistent over time with the overall risk profile and strategy. Second, they have to review continuously internal risk-management processes, mechanisms and strategies and intervene promptly through the adoption of prudential measures whenever weaknesses or deficiencies are detected. This is reflected in the four principles underpinning the Basel II Accord and the CRD: (1) the requirement that banks have internal processes for assessing the adequacy of their capital; (2) the centrality of supervisory review, evaluation and intervention as appropriate; (3) the expectation that banks operate above the minimum capital level and supervisors' power to require them to hold additional capital; (4) the importance of early supervisory intervention.

Consequently, the CRD consists of a consistent body of norms entailing a wide range of substantive and procedural rules to be applied in the Member States in the field of prudential supervision. There is nothing that could be interpreted as a minimalist approach towards prudential regulation. Furthermore, supervision lies at the very core of the new prudential philosophy, ascribing to the banking supervisory authority a central role by means of the supervisory review pillar. Moreover, prompt supervisory intervention is one of the very principles guiding the activity of competent authorities. In this context, we maintain that the whole new regulatory context and the very concept behind the reforms of prudential rules, will not allow the ECJ to avoid a detailed legal analysis of the CRD provisions, as it did in the *Peter Paul* judgment.

The provisions of the directive

Having established that the supervisory process, as such, constitutes one of the subject matters of the CRD, it is essential to examine more closely the terms and language of the specific provisions referring to supervision. In this context, we recall that the House of Lords has examined the articles of the FBD without finding them capable of imposing a duty to supervise that would go beyond the obligation of cooperation between supervisory authorities. In the *Peter Paul* affair, the ECJ satisfied itself with a preliminary analysis of some of the provisions of the Deposit Guarantee Directive and a general assessment of the other banking directives, without scrutinising any particular provision.

As observed in our normative analysis, the provisions on supervisory review, transposing the second pillar of Basel II, are spread throughout the CRD and should be considered by reference to each other. We maintain that especially the following articles, introduced in 2006, should be given particular attention when assessing the obligations of supervisory authorities under the CRD and the eventually correlated rights: article 22 on the control by the competent authorities of banks' governance arrangements; article 124 on the supervisory review process; article 128 on the requirement for coordination arrangements in case of multiple national supervisors for banks and financial firms; article 131 on the obligation of written coordination and cooperation arrangements; and article 136 corroborated to article 17 on the measures available to competent authorities in case of breach of the CRD provisions. These provisions should be read together with the annexes to the CRD (especially V and XI), the detailed norms on consolidated supervision and the coordination mechanisms introduced by the CRD for cross-border institutions (e.g. the competences of the consolidated supervisor and of colleges of supervisors in articles 129–34 CRD). In addition, these provisions should be correlated with the obligation imposed on Member States by article 54 CRD to endow their respective competent authorities with sanctioning powers against credit institutions and those who effectively control the business of credit institutions, which breach prudential rules. The CRD highlights that such sanctions should aim specifically at 'ending the observed breaches or the cause of such breaches'. We note also that reinforcing the sanctioning regime is one of the issues on the policy agenda for the forthcoming reviews of the CRD.

In our view, the terms of the above-mentioned provisions are unequivocal, in the sense that the CRD imposes on the national competent authorities a duty of supervision. This consists of three main elements: continuous monitoring of banks' capital adequacy, internal arrangements and processes; consistent review and evaluation of the risks to which they are exposed; and timely intervention whenever a bank does not meet prudential requirements. Additionally, there is also a duty of cooperation. The scope of the first two elements of the duty to supervise is provided in the directive itself. The frequency and intensity of the review is to be determined by the competent supervisors proportionately, on a case-by-case basis, in accordance with the peculiarities of the bank and its position within the system, supervisory updates being mandatory at least once a year (article 124 (2) and (4) CRD). Furthermore, the CRD explicitly imposes on competent authorities a duty to intervene and take appropriate measures, at an early stage whenever, pursuant to their review and evaluation, it results that a credit institution does not meet the requirements set in the directive. Article 136 enumerates, without placing them in a hierarchical order, the various measures that should be at the disposal of competent authorities. The measures enumerated in article 136 may be very far-reaching and constraining for banks: imposing capital add-ons in excess of the minimum capital requirements; requiring the reinforcement of governance arrangements or internal risk-management process and mechanisms; requiring the application of specific provisioning policies or treatment of assets; restricting or limiting the business, operations or networks of credit institutions; and requiring the reduction of the risk inherent in the bank's activities, products and systems. The terms of that article do not exclude that other supervisory measures be taken (apart from those enumerated), particularly the measure of withdrawing the authorisation, provided for by article 17 CRD. The provision is clear as to the mandatory nature of the duty of supervisory authorities to take at least one of the supervisory measures expressly foreseen by EU law, every time a credit institution infringes the provisions of the directive.

Once it has been established that the CRD contains provisions that couch in unambiguous terms the duty of supervision, including the explicit obligation to take supervisory measures, it should also be checked as to whether the content of this duty is ascertainable enough so as to result into a concrete claim. In this sense, we observe that the cited provisions are all addressed directly to the competent authorities; accordingly, the duty to supervise is incumbent upon the banking supervisor irrespective of the transposition of the CRD into national law. Also, a range of further articles in the CRD – laying down the parameters for the exercise of prudential supervision and particularly those concerning the calculation of capital requirements and the adequacy of internal control mechanisms – are directly addressed to the competent authorities. Consequently, the discretion left to the Member States for implementing the directive does not impinge upon the very existence of the duty of supervision.

An important issue is to test whether the content of the duty to supervise is sufficiently delineated, so as to identify the concrete obligations to which supervisory authorities are subject. We have already pointed out that the general duty of supervision has, resulting particularly from articles 124 and 136 of the CRD, three interdependent components. These include monitoring, review and evaluation, and intervention. In our view, these three phases of the supervisory process are unequivocally mandatory for national banking supervisors under the CRD. Supervisors falling short of monitoring, reviewing or at all assessing the financial soundness of an institution can be considered in breach of the duty of supervision prescribed by EU law. Also, the absence of any intervention by the supervisor, when, pursuant to the review and assessment effectuated, it is obvious that a credit institution does not meet the requirements of the directive, constitutes an infringement of the supervisory duty. Furthermore, if the update of the supervisory review and assessment has not taken place with the frequency and intensity established beforehand in accordance with the profile of the supervisory institution, or at least on an annual basis, we may infer a breach of article 124(4) CRD. The above-mentioned are nonetheless extreme situations of supervisory inaction that reflect outrageous failure of the supervisory authority to exercise its duties. In these situations, it would be sufficient to demonstrate that the CRD prescribes a firm duty of supervision. Under the proposals for reforming the supervisory architecture, it is envisaged that the ESAs will have the power to overcome such inaction by adopting themselves directly applicable measures to implement EU norms.

The question of the ascertainability of the content of the duty of supervision is more delicate in situations of misconduct of supervision. The most likely situations of supervisory liability claims will be based on allegations of inadequate supervisory review, assessment or intervention. For considering whether the banking supervisor has infringed EU law, it is necessary that EU law contains the yardstick for assessing the adequacy of the various phases of the supervisory process. In this respect, we primarily note that, in accordance with paragraph 2 of article 124 CRD, the scope of the review and evaluation is provided by the requirements of the directive – including the numerous annexes – which contain detailed and precise technical rules. We recall that the new prudential rules are subject to the four-level Lamfalussy process, which permits comprehensive explanations of the principles laid down in framework legislation adopted by Parliament and Council through regulation produced at executive level by the Commission with the help of specialised committees composed of national experts. Thus, under Level 2, the Commission shall adopt, by way of comitology or through delegated and implementing acts, amendments so as to clarify and adapt to market evolutions various technical aspects of the directive, explicitly listed under the first paragraph of article 150 CRD. Furthermore, under the second paragraph of article 150 CRD, the Commission is competent to take additional implementing measures through the comitology procedure for a series of specified articles. In addition, there is the third level, where CEBS adopts non-legislative guidelines, standards and interpretative recommendations intended to improve the consistency of day-to-day transposition and implementation of Level 1 and Level 2 legislation. Under planned reforms, it is proposed that certain technical standards adopted at Level 3 become binding, and hence enforceable.

The work of CEBS is particularly illustrative of the concern to have sufficiently clear prudential rules at the European level and to ensure their consistent implementation in national systems. CEBS has therefore elaborated a compendium of guidelines, the *Electronic Guidebook*, that gives credit institutions and supervisory authorities guidance on how to approach their obligations under the CRD.[1] It is especially the CEBS guidelines on the supervisory review process,[2] and particularly those of its application under Pillar 2, that elaborate on the content of articles 22, 123, 124 and 136 of the CRD. They provide an in-depth understanding of the provisions in the CRD, by means of setting parameters and criteria capable of inducing convergence of supervisory practices. The CEBS compilation contains extensive guidance on what supervisory authorities should expect from institutions under Pillar 2, particularly as regards the internal capital adequacy assessment process (the so-called ICAAP) and internal governance arrangements (Chapter 2). Moreover, Chapter 3 of the CEBS guidelines on supervisory review under Pillar 2 contains detailed guidance to supervisory authorities as to their role for reviewing and evaluating banks' ICAAP and performing independent assessment of the risk profile of institutions, as well as for taking prudential measures and other supervisory actions. Thus, CEBS devised benchmarks for the supervisory review and evaluation process (known under the acronym SREP) required by article 124. These explain the responsibilities incumbent on supervisors and the tools and sources they should employ during SREP. Furthermore, CEBS elaborated on the risk-assessment system (RAS), which is the supervisors' tool for organising (i.e. planning, prioritising and allocating) the use of supervisory resources, and performing and managing the SREP in a structured and practical way. Also, supervisors' obligations under the supervisory review process were further clarified by CEBS through specific guidelines on the interaction between SREP and ICAAP and the systematic dialogue between the supervisor and the credit institution.

Last but not least, the CEBS guidelines on Pillar 2 prescribe two general prudential principles to be applied by supervisory authorities. The first requires that 'prudential measures – addressing issues identified either through the SREP or as part of ongoing supervision – should be applied

1 CEBS' *Electronic Guidebook* reassembles comprehensively and in a structured way the guidelines and standards adopted by CEBS since its establishment in over 500 pages (CEBS 2009e).

2 Under the title 'Guidelines on the Supervisory Review Process' the *Guidebook* compiles the following distinct sets of guidelines: Guidelines on the Application of the Supervisory Review Process under Pillar 2; Additional technical guidance on the Application of the Supervisory Review Process under the CRD (IRB, Concentration Risk and Stress Testing); Technical aspects of the management of interest rate risk arising from non-trading activities under the supervisory review process; Technical aspects of the management of concentration risk under the supervisory review process; Technical Guidelines on Stress Testing under the Supervisory Review Process; Guidelines on Outsourcing.

promptly' (CEBS 2009e: 354). It is explained that, whenever the supervisor considers that the ICAAP of a bank does not reflect its overall risk profile or does not result in adequate capital for that bank, the competent authority should also identify the range of supervisory measures necessary for correcting the situation. The final decision on the precise measures to be implemented will be taken by the supervisor, after considering the outcome of the dialogue with the bank. It is requested that individual or combined measures will have to reflect the severity and underlying causes of the situation. The imposition of capital add-ons should not be automatic, but specific own funds requirements should be always imposed when there is an imbalance that cannot be remedied within an appropriate timeframe between a bank's business risks, on the one hand, and internal control and risk frameworks, on the other hand. It is nevertheless underlined that a balanced view of all available supervisory measures is essential, as additional capital requirements are not always efficient.[3]

The second principle requires that prudential measures be communicated promptly and in sufficient detail. That means that all factors that led to the risk-assessment conclusions should be explained; the areas of weakness and the timeframe for remedial action should be indicated; supervisors should give reasons for any requested capital adjustment; and indicate what improvements could be made to systems and controls to make them adequate for the risks and activities of the bank.

We recall that, according to the CEBS Charter, guidelines constitute further specification of EU legislation, covering substance as well as processes. Under the current framework these are not legally binding and have to be applied on a voluntary basis by the national authorities. Nevertheless, given that they are not completely deprived of legal effects (being subject to the 'comply or explain' mechanism), we maintain that the 'soft' nature of the guidelines prevents them from being immediately enforced, but does not exempt supervisory authorities from applying them without solid reasons. Furthermore, such 'soft' nature cannot be invoked to support allegations to the effect that such guidelines cannot be considered for the purpose of determining the concrete content of EU legislative provisions. It will be impossible to ignore Level 3 guidelines once this becomes binding, as foreseen by current proposals for reform.

To conclude, bearing in mind the extensive provisions in the CRD, the possibility of adopting additional technical implementing measures at the

3 Thus it is explicitly acknowledged that

> there is no 'scientific' method for determining the amount, and that capital is not a long-run substitute for remedying deficiencies in systems and controls. In practice, the process relies heavily on subjective judgement and peer-group consistency to ensure a level playing field and a defence to challenge by institutions.
>
> (CEBS 2009e: 354)

second Lamfalussy level, and particularly the guidelines in CEBS *Guidebook* at the third regulatory level, we consider that the duty of supervision, laid down especially in articles 124 and 136 CRD, is sufficiently delineated so as to declare its content to be ascertainable. Of course, the supervisory authority, like any administrative decision-maker, enjoys discretion as to the application of concrete measures. However, the CRD manages to trace a framework for supervisory action that constrains the competent authority's behaviour, in accordance with some objective parameters. Hence, the provisions considered, especially when taken together, give sufficient indications as to the substance of the duty to supervise pertaining to the competent banking authorities.

The issue of protection of individual interests

Under the ECJ's jurisprudence, an important component of the conferral of rights requirement for the purpose of establishing State liability consists of the necessity to demonstrate that the legal rules on which the alleged right is based are intended to protect the individual interest and not only the general/public interest.[4] This is particularly important in the case of indirectly conferred rights, which are rights that are correlative to legal duties imposed by EU law, as is the situation of the supervisory duty. Thus, in order to find out whether depositors may invoke a right to adequate supervision, it has to be established that EU law imposed the duty of supervision, if not exclusively at least also for the sake of depositors.

Article 55 CRD provides that Member States should ensure the right to apply to the courts against decisions taken in respect of a credit institution in pursuance of national measures adopted in accordance with the CRD, as well as in the case of the absence of a decision in response to an application for authorisation. The CRD does not give any supplementary indication as to those entitled to apply to courts. Undisputedly this provision warrants the access to courts for banks directly affected by supervisory action or inaction. Yet there is nothing in the text that would exclude depositors from applying to courts against supervisory decisions. In our view, there are several aspects that may justify an individual interest of depositors to challenge supervisors' action in front of courts.

We recall that, in the *Peter Paul* judgment, the ECJ acknowledged that several recitals in the preambles to the banking directives stated in a general manner that one of the objectives of harmonisation was the protection of depositors (paragraph 38). However, the ECJ did not accept this as a decisive factor. This attitude of the ECJ has determined commentators to infer that the judgment suggests the Court's intention to tighten the individual interest requirement, as compared to previous case-law where it

4 On the general issue of protection of individual interests as a parameter for individual rights, see Prechal 2005: 118–24.

sufficed that it was explicitly mentioned that a directive be enacted for protecting some individual interests (Prechal 2005: 122). Nevertheless, as we have previously observed, the reasoning of the ECJ in *Peter Paul* was not necessarily systematic, but reflected mainly policy considerations. For the purpose of our current analysis, it is important to recall first that the Court admitted that harmonisation is also intended for protecting depositors and, second, that it did not relate this objective directly to the specific issue of individual interest.

We consider that the repeated references to the protection of depositors in the preamble of the CRD are particularly important for assessing whether the supervisory duty is intended to protect depositors. The preamble of the CRD does not bring new references to depositor protection when compared to the preamble of the CBD, nor does it include a definition of the depositor as was requested by the House of Lords in the *Three Rivers* judgment. Notwithstanding the absence of new references, we consider that the mentioned recitals are sufficient for establishing that depositor protection, along with financial stability, is one of the main purposes of harmonisation of prudential rules. Information asymmetries and externalities affecting depositors justify that banking supervision is conducted in view of protecting those depositing their money with a supervised institution. Furthermore, we do not deem it necessary to have a definition of the depositor, nor do we find the inconsistent terminology used ('depositors', 'savers', 'clients of credit institutions') confusing, as it is the simple consequence of the construction of the CRD as an upgrade of a compilation of initially distinct pieces of legislation. The category of depositors is, in our view, very broad and easily identifiable on the basis of the transfer of repayable funds, as referred to in the definition of a credit institution (i.e. an undertaking whose business is to receive deposits or other repayable funds from the public and to grant credits for its own account).

Other arguments in favour of the individual interest concern stem from the CRD rules on disclosure, which, according to recital 61 of the preamble, have the purpose of affording adequate levels of transparency for EU citizens. Article 144 imposes on competent authorities the obligation to disclose texts of laws, regulations, administrative rules and general guidance in the field of prudential regulation, the manner they exercise the options and discretions allowed by European legislation, the general criteria and methodologies they use in the review and evaluation referred to in article 124, and the aggregate statistical data on key aspects of the implementation of the prudential framework. Such disclosure requirements are particularly helpful for enhancing the capacity of depositors to understand and observe supervisory developments with respect to their bank. They also give important indications on how the supervisory duties are exercised.

A last important argument that we can invoke in favour of the individual interest condition is the current trend of involving private parties in the regulatory process. Thus, we have observed that the new four-level regulatory framework also contains various mechanisms permitting consultation (from an early stage) on forthcoming regulation with market participants, consumers and end-users. In our view, the very possibility of participating in the elaboration of financial market regulation given to consumers and end-users constitutes proof of the fact that financial market regulation, including prudential regulation, is adopted in the interest of depositors and not merely in the general interest.

In light of the above considerations, we suggest that the CRD should be interpreted as prescribing in a clear and precise way the constitutive substantive elements of the duty of adequate supervision incumbent on the national banking authorities, and as implying that such a duty be exercised in the interest of depositors. Consequently, we maintain that depositors may claim a right to adequate supervision of banks under the CRD.

1.2 The seriousness of breach requirement in the context of supervisory liability

As already mentioned, after having established that an EU law provision confers rights on individuals, in order to determine whether there is State liability, it should be found that the Member State under accusation has seriously breached that provision. In the case of supervisory liability, the courts will have to first establish whether the Member State has somehow breached the duty of adequate supervision imposed by the CRD. Such a breach may be attributed to the supervisory authorities whenever they omit to exercise such duty or when the duty is exercised with disregard of the limits imposed by EU law. Moreover, the breach may be ascribed to the Member States' legislators or governments responsible for the transposition of the directive, particularly if they failed to entrust the banking supervisor with the required powers.

Further consideration of this issue implies an inquiry into the seriousness of the breach of EU law, which is extensively dependent on the degree of discretion left by EU law. The content of the condition of serious breach depends 'on the circumstance that the authority concerned had a *wide dis*cretion or, to the contrary, only a *considerably reduced* discretion *or no discretion* at all' (Van Gerven 2004b: 230). Seriousness is inversely proportional to the degree of discretion left by the provision conferring rights. With regard to the duty to supervise as required by the CRD, we consider that it leaves no discretion as to the obligation incumbent on supervisory authorities to undertake an annual review and evaluation process with respect to each credit institution under their control. Furthermore, it only leaves considerably reduced discretion as to taking prudential measures, when the result of the review and evaluation indicate inconsistencies with the requirements of the directive on capital and internal risk-management processes. The CRD provisions and the recommendations for their interpretation provide extensive guidance as to the various alternative tools for exercising review and undertaking evaluation, and prescribe a range of corrective prudential measures. Still, the CRD leaves broad discretion to supervisory authorities when choosing how to act. A large degree of discretion is absolutely essential for the effectiveness of the activity of banking supervisors, which act in a particularly sensitive area, where rigid rules cannot tackle complex realities.

Consequently, only complete failure to engage in the review and evaluation process can be considered to constitute, per se, a sufficiently serious breach of the supervisory duty. Except for such total supervisory inaction, the exercise of supervisory review and assessment is subject to wide discretionary powers of the banking supervisors. In these situations, alleged breaches of EU law through supervisory activities will have to be considered under the test set by the ECJ in *Brasserie de Pêcheur*, regarding the manifest and grave disregard of the limits of discretion.[5] This test supposes that a range of objective and subjective elements be taken into consideration:

> the clarity and precision of the rule breached, the measure of discretion left by that rule to the national or Community authorities, whether the infringement and the damage caused was intentional or involuntary, whether any error of law was excusable or inexcusable, the fact that the position taken by a Community institution may have contributed towards the omission, and the adoption or retention of national measures or practices contrary to Community law.[6]

Other criteria, taken into consideration by national courts for determining whether there was a sufficiently serious breach, include the complexity of applicable legislation, the *bona fides* of the authority accused of having committed the breach and the fact that legitimate expectations of the claimants were not clear and obvious.[7] Also, guidance from the jurisprudence on the liability of EU institutions might be helpful. Thus, Advocate General Van Gerven proposed (in his opinion to the *Mulder* case) four matters to be taken into account for establishing the seriousness of a breach: the particular importance of the rule infringed; the fact that disregard of that rule affected a limited and clearly defined group; the fact that damage went beyond the bounds of the economic risks inherent in the operator's activities in the sector concerned; and the fact that the rule was infringed without sufficient justification.[8]

5 Joined Case C-46/93 and C-48/93 [1996] ECR I-1029, para. 55.

6 Ibid., para. 56.

7 *R* v. *Ministry of Agriculture Fisheries and Food, ex p Lay and Gage* (1998) COD 387; see Amos 2002: 121.

8 Opinion of AG Van Gerven in *Mulder* v. *Council and Commission* [1992] ECR I-3061.

All these factors should be considered together for determining the 'seriousness' of the breach. Clarity and precision in this context demand that the meaning of the provision is reasonably beyond dispute and does not give rise to divergent interpretations (Prechal 2005: 288). The CRD and its supporting guidance might be considered to be sufficiently detailed so as to bring a surplus of precision in comparison with its predecessors. But whether that is enough will always depend on the concrete situation and the pertinent articles. Furthermore, the CRD provides a more constraining framework for the exercise of discretion by the national supervisors. Also, the degree of discretion left for implementation might be considered in principle more reduced than in the case of the directives aiming only at minimum harmonisation.

No standard of fault can be found in EU banking legislation, and national systems are, as we have observed, very divergent on the degree of fault to be attached to supervisory liability. Nevertheless, the very fact that jurisprudence requires that the subjective position of the competent authority be taken into account indicates that, in any case, at least intentional breach of prudential rules should be considered as pointing to a sufficiently serious breach. Indications of the underlying thoughts of the supervisor might be found in the outcome of SREP, which has to contain the reasons and motivations for the choices made by supervisors with respect to the supervision of each institution.

Also, it is important to note that European prudential legislation does not contain any immunity clause in favour of supervisory authorities, although such a proposal was made during the preparation of the Second Banking Directive by the German government. Policy considerations justifying national supervisory immunity regimes should also be considered at this stage of legal analysis, where the seriousness of breach requirement allows balancing of the various interests at stake. It should be also reminded that national immunity regimes constitute part of national procedural autonomy. This means that, once it is established that depositors have (on the basis of EU law) a right to reparation corresponding to the infringement of the EU duty of adequate supervision, it will become necessary to check whether the national liability rules, including eventual partial or total supervisory immunity, are such as in practice to make it impossible or excessively difficult to obtain reparation. Deconstructing the analysis into these two stages is required by the dual nature of the action in damages for breach of EU law, where EU law imposes the principle of State liability, whereas concrete remedies have to be provided within the framework of domestic legal systems (Craig and de Búrca 1999a: 247).

To conclude, the seriousness of breach requirement cannot be established *in abstracto*, but will have to be considered on a case-by-case basis, in accordance with the concrete circumstances of the situation, the specific incidental provisions, the peculiarities of the national context in which they intervene, and the attitude of the supervisory authority. The CRD, further implementing measures and the guidance provided by CEBS together definitely bring more clarity and precision. Yet they regulate a field where supervisory authorities enjoy under EU law a wide margin of discretion in order to be able to consider the various complex interests that are at stake. National courts, which are primarily in charge of determining the concrete situation, may find, when considering the seriousness of breach condition, the occasion to incline the balance in favour of national liability regimes and to remove the threat of *Francovich* liability from supervisory authorities.

1.3 The direct causal link between breach and damages

The third condition for State liability consists of demonstrating the existence of causality between the breach of EU law and the damages sustained by the injured parties. Being a matter of fact, to be assessed in accordance with the concrete situation, it is in principle an issue to be determined by the national courts. However, causation, like the other conditions of liability, must be determined in the first place by reference to EU law (Tridimas 2002: 158). Also, it has been the case that the ECJ has relied on causation to restrict State liability, considering that de facto direct application by administrative authorities of EU law provisions had breached the causal link between non-transposition of a directive and the damage suffered.[9]

In case of supervisory liability, it is necessary to demonstrate that losses incurred by depositors of a failing bank can be directly attributed to the infringement of the EU supervisory duty by the competent authorities. The responsibility of the supervisor should be judged autonomously, only in respect to the way he has exercised his duties, and without diminishing the responsibilities incumbent on the bank.

The depositors will have to show, on the balance of probabilities, that the losses for which they seek compensation can be attributed to the unlawful conduct of the supervisory authority committing a serious breach of EU law. There is a direct causal link when it can be demonstrated that there would not have been losses or that the amount of losses would have been mitigated if the competent authority had properly exercised its duty of supervision. It will have to be considered that it is not the obligation of the banking supervisor to prevent banking failures, but only to ensure (in the interest of depositors and of financial stability in general) that banks comply with prudential requirements and to intervene promptly when that does not happen. Also, it is important to precisely identify the exact contribution of the supervisors to the losses incurred by depositors so as to allow for proportionate reparation.

9 Case C-319/96, *Brinkmann Tabakfabriken* [1998] ECR I-5255.

The CRD, with its elaborate and detailed content, may be more helpful than previous EU banking legislation for determining the various phases in the supervisory process and implicitly also the precise role of the supervisory authorities at each stage. Furthermore, the dialogue between the supervisor and the credit institution, institutionalised through the CRD, may prove helpful for understanding the application of supervisory rules to the bank in accordance with its peculiarities and concrete position in the financial system. Also, the access to concrete supervisory information has been slightly improved by the CRD rules regarding disclosure. These aspects may all prove useful in finding out with more precision where and when the supervisory action influenced a bank's financial situation in a way that contributed to the ultimate losses affecting depositors. It remains to be seen as to whether these aspects of the new prudential rules will favour the establishment of direct causality in national courts. In any case, national rules of causation will have to provide an effective standard of protection (Tridimas 2002: 158).

2 The liability issue at EU level

Our account of the supervisory liability issue would be incomplete without also tentatively considering the liability issue with respect to supervisory tasks potentially exercised at EU level. We perceive that it is important, when assessing the potential of the CRD to induce liability, to keep in mind the impact it may have not only on determining the liability of national supervisory authorities that disregard prudential norms, but also on establishing the responsibility for supervisory functions attributed to the European level. So far, our examination has been based on the presumption that national regimes on supervisory liability are likely to develop and converge, under the influence of EU law. In addition, we observe that EU law itself is often influenced by the solutions found for specific problems under national law. Justifying national supervisory liability on the basis of EU law is very likely to spill over and frame the terms and conditions of supervisory liability applicable to an entity entrusted with supervisory functions at EU level.

Giving that at the time of writing there are no supervisory tasks exercised directly at EU level, we will only make some tentative and speculative reflections on the liability regime of potential candidates for European supervisory functions. Thus, we will start by reviewing the liability regime applicable to the ECB's tasks related to prudential supervision and in the event of the eventual attribution of specific supervisory tasks. We will continue by exploring whether CEBS might incur liability for its contributions to the supervisory process. Last but not least, we will suggest some possible features of the liability regime applicable to a separate European supervisory authority.

As regards the liability regime of the micro- and macro-prudential bodies envisaged under the Commission's 2009 proposals for reforming EU financial supervision, at the time of writing many details are unclear and policy choices still remain to be made with regard to the concrete institutional setups. This does not presently allow us to extend our analysis to the new bodies. We may only generally presume that the envisaged European Banking Authority will have the status of an independent European supervisory authority, whereas the European Systemic Risk Board will have a status comparable to the current position of CEBS. Furthermore, depending on the concrete final arrangements on macro-prudential supervision, there may also be implications for the ECB in terms of liability.

2.1 The liability regime of the ECB with regard to supervisory tasks

We have seen that the ECB has been entrusted with the peculiar role of contributing to the smooth conduct of prudential policies pursued by the competent authorities, which under the current state of law may bring about only a 'soft' implication of the ECB in prudential supervision. We also observed that the ECB exercises such a role mainly by means of issuing opinions, which are not legally binding. Nevertheless, current legislation provides the possibility for the ECB to also adopt binding decisions for carrying out the ESCB's tasks entrusted by the Treaty and the ESCB Statute, including in the area of prudential supervision. Moreover, it is recalled that article 25.2 of the ESCB Statute contains an enabling clause whose activation would result in the conferral of specific tasks upon the ECB in the field of prudential banking supervision. Such specific tasks could be exercised by means of decisions and also by directly applicable and entirely binding regulations.

According to article 35.1 of the ESCB Statute, both the acts and omissions of the ECB are subject to judicial control by the ECJ, in the cases and under the conditions laid down in the Treaty. Under the current state of law, it is practically impossible to find out whether the ECB has failed to act in the area of prudential supervision, whereas if it were endowed with specific tasks in this field the duties of the ECB would be more apparent and failure to act could be more easily conceived as subject to judicial control by the ECJ.

Under article 263 TFEU (ex article 230 EC Treaty), ECB acts (including in the field of prudential supervision) may be challenged on grounds of lack of competence, infringement of an essential procedural requirement, infringement of the Treaty or of any rule of law relating to its application, or misuse of power, by privileged and non-privileged applicants, in accordance with the conditions established by case-law. ECB recommendations and opinions are explicitly excluded from the ambit of article 263 TFEU. All other acts of the ECB are susceptible to judicial review, whenever they have binding legal effects, irrespective of their form. Such a generous submission of ECB acts to judicial review is counterbalanced by the Court's reticence to assess measures involving economic policy choices. The Court would review such acts only in terms of formal parameters underpinning legality, but not on substantial merits. So far, no cases have involved challenges of ECB measures that formulate or implement monetary policy or other specific tasks of the ECB, but it is foreseeable that on such occasions the Court will uphold large discretionary powers in favour of the ECB so as to reflect its independence. As in the case of the Council, the Court will probably intervene only where the ECB makes a manifest error,[10] abuses its competences or goes beyond its powers of appreciation.[11]

The liability regime applicable to the ECB is laid down in article 35.3 of the ESCB Statute and provides that the ECB is subject to article 340 TFEU (ex 288 EC Treaty). The second sentence of article 35.3 further specifies that national central banks shall be liable according to their respective national laws. In practice, such a distribution of liability may not be as clear-cut, because national central banks will most often act as integral parts of the European System of Central Banks upon the instructions and in accordance with the guidelines of the ECB. In these situations the ECB would be liable for damage caused by its institutions and servants. Consequently, the ECB would be responsible for repairing damage resulting from the indirect implementation of ECB law through the national central banks acting as ECB agents that are subject to the supervision and to the instructions of the Executive Board of the ECB (Zilioli and Selmayr 2001: 129). The ESCB Statute provision referring to national liability regimes may be interpreted as indicating the rules applicable to an NCB, if found in breach of its obligations under the Statute.

Article 35.3 second sentence also applies clearly to those cases where damage is caused through actions of national central banks undertaken when exercising functions other than those specified in the Statute. In accordance with article 14.4 of the ESCB Statute, such functions shall be performed under the responsibility and liability of national central banks and shall not be regarded as being part of the functions of the ESCB. As far as prudential supervision is concerned, currently this is a competence pertaining to the national competent authorities. These are often the national central banks and will be subject to national liability regimes, in accordance with articles 14.4 and 35.3 of the ESCB Statute. This notwithstanding, it may also be possible that the NCBs will act as agents of the system when the ECB has adopted measures either pursuant to its current broad contributory task in the area of supervision, or on the basis of specific tasks attributed to it through the enabling clause. In this situation, liability will intervene in accordance with EU law.

10 Case C-122/94, *Commission* v. *Council* [1996] ECR I-881.

11 Case 138/79, *Roquette Frères* v. *Council* [1980] ECR 3333 and Case 265/87, *Schräder* [1989] ECR 2237; for a detailed analysis, see Endler 1998.

The liability provided in article 340 TFEU (ex 288 EC Treaty) covers both contractual and non-contractual liability of all EU institutions. Eventual supervisory liability of the ECB may occur only under non-contractual liability. According to consolidated case-law, article 340 TFEU (ex 288 EC Treaty) provides a general right to reparation for injured parties having suffered damage causally connected with an unlawful act attributable to an EU institution.[12] Traditionally the conditions attached to such right to reparation were caught under the so-called *Schöppenstedt* formula. This requires that there is a violation of a superior rule of law; that such rule is intended for the protection of the individual; and that the violation is serious.[13] The case-law on article 340 TFEU (ex 288 EC Treaty) was for a long time based on the formal distinction between legislative and administrative acts, whereby lighter conditions were attached to the latter.[14] More recent cases seem to abandon this rather artificial criterion in favour of the view that complex discretionary decision-making, irrespective of whether it is legislative or administrative, should be hindered by the prospect of damages action (Hilson 2005: 682). Particularly in the *Bergaderm* case,[15] the ECJ has accepted that EU administrative decision-making can be as difficult, complex and sensitive as legislative choices and should be governed by the same conditions. It was underlined that, while since *Brasserie* EU institutions' liability has consistently influenced State liability, in *Bergaderm* the ECJ relied for the first time on its jurisprudence on State liability for determining the conditions to be attached to EU institutions' liability (Tridimas 2002: 175). Specifically, *Bergaderm* substitutes the condition of violation of a superior rule of law with the condition developed under ECJ's jurisprudence on State liability requiring that the institution should have infringed 'a rule of law intended to confer rights on individuals' (paragraph 62). This reversed correlation is illustrative of the quest for unifying the conditions of liability, and for providing effective protection of EU law irrespective of whether it has been breached by EU institutions or by Member States.

Taking all of the above into account, we might infer that supervisory tasks of the ECB will be treated with deference by the ECJ and with reluctance to enter into the substance of the case. The ECB will be considered to enjoy wide discretionary powers, supported also by its broad independence. In the event that some specific supervisory tasks will be assigned to the ECB, the ECJ will have more tools for controlling the limits of discretion in the area of prudential supervision; and thus the liability threat may not only be theoretical.

12 See Case 4/96 *Lütticke* v. *Commission* [1971] ECR 325, para. 10; Case T-575/93 *Koelman* v. *Commission* [1996] CR II-1, para. 89.

13 Case 5/71 *Zuckerfabrik Schöppenstedt* v. *Council* [1971] ECR 975.

14 It was considered that in the field of administrative action any infringement of law constitutes illegality, which may give rise to liability; see e.g. Case 145/83 *Adams* v. *Commission* [1985] ECR 3539.

15 Case C-352/98 P, *Laboratoires Pharmaceutiques Bergaderm and Goupil* v. *Commission* [2000] ECR I-5291.

It is important also to keep in mind that the ECJ's approach, with regard to State liability for infringement of prudential rules by national supervisory authorities, is likely to have an important impact on the liability of any EU authority endowed with supervisory competences. Thus, once it is established that EU prudential rules are intended to confer rights on depositors, this will have to be equally considered by the ECB or any other EU body acting in the field of prudential supervision.

To conclude, the law as it stands now cannot realistically trigger supervisory liability on the part of the ECB. The granting of specific supervisory tasks to the ECB would make the possibility of liability more likely, albeit under very strict conditions as it concerns a complex, difficult and particularly sensitive domain where discretionary powers are important.

2.2 Responsibility of CEBS for its contribution to the supervisory process

Under the current state of law, CEBS is an independent advisory group, deprived of legal personality, consisting of a network of national supervisory authorities. CEBS is only endowed with soft powers to assist the Commission in preparing legislative proposals and implementing comitology measures and to adopt Level 3 guidance for ensuring uniform interpretation and application of EU prudential legislation. CEBS does not adopt decisions that are legally enforceable; its guidelines and standards have been explicitly characterised as non-binding. Particularly, as regards concrete supervisory action, CEBS is deprived of any decision-making powers and its role is still minimal. The fact that the Groupe de Contact (with its tasks on micro-prudential cooperation and information-sharing on policy matters and individual cases) constitutes CEBS' main expert group does not bring about any defined supervisory duties in charge of CEBS.

The legal status of CEBS and of its adopted measures protects it from judicial review by the ECJ and related claims of liability. Yet CEBS rules are not totally deprived of legal effects, especially when considering the 'comply or explain' mechanism. Thus, when a Member State accepts voluntary guidelines and standards devised by CEBS and incorporates them into national law, it will not be able to escape liability by invoking that it did not need to assume those obligations in the first place. Eventual liability will arise only as a matter of national law, and not of EU law.

This situation is about to change. Under the May 2009 Communication of the European Commission, it was proposed that CEBS be transformed into a European Banking Authority (EBA) with legal personality and endowed with the power to adopt binding decisions. This will subject EBA's acts to the review of legality by the ECJ, pursuant to article 263 TFEU (ex 230 EC Treaty). The liability regime applicable to the regulatory and supervisory actions of the EBA would be similar to that considered in the context of the attribution of specific supervisory tasks to the ECB. Particular attention will have to be given to the pan-European character of such a supervisory authority and, consequently, the protection of depositors' rights will have to be balanced against the supervisory duties regarding the whole single market and its soundness and stability. The liability regime will also depend on the precise tasks and powers to be entrusted to the EBA. It will also have to consider the specific mechanisms underpinning the bindingness of prudential standards adopted by EBA: their envisaged endorsement by the Commission may be seen as a sort of administrative appeal, and might also dilute EBA's responsibility. Last, the Court, as in the case of the ECB, will most likely not undertake a performance-based review, but will control only whether the rule of law and the limits of discretion are observed (Amtenbrink and Lastra 2008: 131).

The European Systemic Risk Board responsible for macro-prudential supervision, as envisaged in the Commission's Communication, has apparently a formal status similar to the current status of CEBS. It is conceived as an independent body, without legal personality and deprived of legally binding powers. ESRB's early warnings and recommendations are accompanied by an 'act or explain' mechanism similar to the current arrangements for CEBS. Consequently, we may say that, in principle, it is not possible to hold the ESRB liable for damages. Yet the way that the ESRB may interact with the ECB, which most probably will provide its logistic support, as well as the concrete arrangements for ensuring follow-up to ESRB's warnings and recommendations, might necessitate a different approach to its liability regime.

2.3 Some final remarks anticipating the liability of a European supervisory authority

The general liability regime for EU institutions is enshrined in article 340 TFEU (ex 288 EC Treaty). However, article 340 does not say anything about the liability of EU agencies and other bodies, despite the explicit extension of judicial review to their acts. Indeed, under article 263 TFEU, the wording in article 230 EC Treaty has been supplemented with the explicit requirement that the Court shall 'review the legality of acts of bodies, offices or agencies of the Union intended to produce legal effects vis-à-vis third parties'. Silence in primary law about the liability regime applicable to agencies gives room for interpretation and a certain degree of freedom in choosing the liability regime when an agency is created. This choice will have to consider the specificity of the field and the general principles common to the laws of the Member States.

It has been observed that, on the issue of liability of public bodies, there were actually no general principles truly common to the Member States. The principles established by the Court in relation to article 288 EC Treaty have, in fact, been those laid down by the systems of domestic law most protective of individuals suffering damage (Usher 2005: 490). Also, with regard to supervisory liability, hardly any commonality among national systems may be identified. Yet it is doubted that the ECJ would be willing to mirror at EU level the national regimes most protective of depositors. At present, it seems that liability of a European supervisory authority is largely ignored in the ongoing political discussions of the reform of the supervisory architecture, although the Commission's legislative proposals include an explict liability clause that reproduces the standard wording in article 340 TFEU.

Total supervisory immunity[16] is only exceptionally encountered in the Member States and would not be a legitimate choice for a European supervisory authority enjoying binding decision-making powers. Complete immunity would also not be conceivable at EU level, where the ECJ's control extends over all acts of EU bodies intended to produce legal effects. Supervisory immunity attached to a European supervisor would unacceptably interfere with such review and limit the remedies.

We support the view that 'submitting prudential authorities to a liability regime might … be regarded as an element of strength of the financial system, as it will discipline the supervisor' (Tison 2005: 672). This argument would also apply to a European supervisory authority. Recognition in principle, of the possibility of supervisory liability would also contribute to reinforcing public confidence in the safety and soundness of the banking system and legitimise the transfer of some supervisory functions to the EU level.

Broadly, there are the following possibilities when determining the liability regime applicable to a European supervisor: explicit immunity, explicit liability or what could be termed a regime of 'rights-based constructive ambiguity'. We think that the latter solution would be the one that is preferable in such a dynamic sector. Total immunity or full liability, as the two extremes, should be completely excluded as their acceptance would mean that one of the objectives of prudential supervision will be completely dominated by the other (i.e. depositor protection versus financial stability). Also, explicit partial immunity or liability appears to be a too rigid solution that might not fairly cover policy interests. Instead, a regime of constructive ambiguity, based on the premise that depositors can invoke against the European supervisor rights conferred upon them by EU legislation, could in our view eliminate moral hazard for authorities, as well as for market participants. It would also be flexible enough to consider effective imposition of liability in accordance with the concrete situation at stake, depending on the seriousness of the breach and the causality link. Such a liability regime would mirror our proposals on the liability of national supervisors based on EU law, previously discussed. The CRD has, in our view, the potential of bringing about the emergence of common principles on supervisory liability not only among Member States, but also between the European and the national level. Given the spill-over of liability regimes from the national to the European level and vice versa, any discussion of supervisory liability should properly consider both sides of the coin.

16 'Immunity' refers here to protection from claims coming from individual depositors, excluding actions by the supervised entities, which are warranted access to courts by EU law.

Concluding remarks

We have identified a strong European dimension in the current EU prudential framework, which largely pre-empts national legislation and increasingly influences the exercise of supervision. Under these circumstances, and precipitated by the crisis, further reforms are required to ensure that supervisory arrangements can effectively address financial stability concerns of an increasingly integrated EU financial market. Legal aspects will be essential for the legitimacy and effectiveness of any supervisory reforms.

Having separately analysed the different facets of banking regulation and supervision, here we will synthesise them in view of providing a coherent characterisation of the European prudential regime. Therefore, we will leave aside a host of ancillary findings discussed throughout the chapters, which mainly provide specific legal interpretations of detailed aspects, and will concentrate on the general issues. Such general aspects can be subsumed into three headlines: Europeanisation of prudential regulation and supervision, refinement of prudential policy and reassessment of supervisory liability.

1 Europeanisation of prudential regulation and supervision

There is a growing European dimension to prudential banking regulation and supervision. Over the past twenty years, European law has extended to cover ever more prudential aspects, thereby reflecting the changed focus of European policy-makers from merely eliminating national regulatory barriers for cross-border banking to addressing the specific needs of the emerging common banking market. Europeanisation results from the extended scope and the detailed content of EU prudential norms. Furthermore, it is a consequence of the regulatory Level 2 and Level 3 measures adopted in accordance with the Lamfalussy framework. Lastly, it stems from the emerging, increasingly intrusive European dimension of supervision.

Without doubt, prudential regulation is largely centralised at EU level. The CRD, its amendments and its implementing rules, standards and guidelines brought about an increased degree of harmonisation of prudential regulation. The CRD, which transposes the Basel II Accord into European law, constitutes a substantial change when compared to its predecessor.

Largely conceived at international level, the new prudential rules have been adapted to the specific internal marketplace and considerably beefed up EU banking legislation. Moreover, the European character of these rules stems from the fact that they represent hard law and trigger legal effects with respect to both public authorities and regulated entities, as opposed to the 'soft' character of the Basel II Accord. This connection between European and international prudential rules should be acknowledged and appropriate representation mechanisms of the EU in the relevant international fora (e.g. the Basel Committee, the Financial Stability Board) need to be devised.

The CRD represents a 'heavy' piece of legislation covering in depth most of the prudential issues. Not only does it have a more extensive scope than previous EU banking legislation, but it is also backed by the four-level Lamfalussy framework that creates procedures by which the provisions of the directive may be further specified and uniformly implemented, through Level 2 legislation or Level 3 guidelines and standards. Given the increasing amount and detail of European prudential hard and soft rules, the current European banking legislation no longer corresponds to the paradigm launched with the 1985 White Paper on the internal market, i.e. minimum harmonisation. Instead, the essential aspects tackled by harmonised legislative measures tend to cover most prudential facets comprehensively. Even when shortcomings or gaps in the legislative framework are revealed, the EU regulatory mechanism in place allows for relatively rapid normative adjustments, as was the case with the regulatory reactions to the crisis (e.g. the adoption within less than one year of extensive amendments in CRD 2 or the advanced stage of legislative proposals such as the CRD 3 and CRD 4). Although some more prudential issues are still in the pipeline awaiting regulation at European level, the current prudential rules are more likely to be characterised as extensive, a level that gets closer to maximum harmonisation. This endeavour to achieve maximum harmonisation at EU level is apparent also from the declared policy goals of developing a common European rulebook and reducing the national options and discretions.

Such extensive harmonisation refers not only to the increased quantity of norms, but also to the degree of detail stemming from their content. This has an important consequence: it reduces the discretion of Member States in this area, which on only a few occasions are allowed to provide stricter rules. Moreover, European prudential norms cannot be qualified as 'minimalist' or the lowest common denominator. That would be unacceptable, particularly because the European legislator has gone beyond an approach that merely considered European law as a tool for eliminating national regulatory barriers and uses harmonisation as an instrument for addressing the specific needs of the common marketplace. Safeguarding financial stability in the common market cannot be based on standards reflecting the lowest common denominator only.

Europeanisation also results from the fact that the European dimension slides down from the legislative stage into the administrative level. Thus, the EU is increasingly concerned with the uniform application of common prudential norms and their proper enforcement. This is supported by the work of the Committee of European Banking Supervisors (CEBS), which, within its tasks related to Level 3 of the Lamfalussy process, pursues the achievement of regulatory and supervisory convergence in the Member States. Although the guidelines and standards adopted by CEBS are currently qualified as soft law, they undeniably produce de facto legal effects through the institutionalised 'comply or explain' mechanism. To ensure the enforceability of Level 3 measures it is currently envisaged in the context of the reform of EU financial supervision to ascribe binding legal force to some of the technical prudential standards. This should guarantee the level playing-field between national prudential regimes and secure consistent implementation of EU prudential rules.

This dominant European normative component of the prudential regime is inevitably mirrored in the institutional framework. Thus, the institutional set-up for the adoption of prudential regulation is highly centralised at EU level: not only do all European institutions intensively participate in the regulatory process, but also new committees have been established to support the ever-intruding European dimension of regulation. Thus, the European Banking Committee (EBC) facilitates the adoption of legislative implementing measures through the institutionalised comitology procedures, whereas CEBS, although deprived of legal personality, emerges as an ever more influential body, giving advice and pursuing administrative convergence. The advisory role of the ECB is rather discrete with regard to prudential regulation. Yet, thanks to its own regulatory powers, the ECB possesses the necessary instruments for eventually exercising regulatory tasks – albeit limited – in this field, if it were to be explicitly so entrusted in accordance with article 127(6) TFEU (ex 105(6) EC Treaty).

The planned reforms of the EU financial architecture foresee transforming CEBS into a European Banking Authority (EBA), endowed, among others, with binding regulatory powers. Apart from the legal difficulties implied by the delegation of such far-reaching competences to a European agency, sceptics may also question its impact on the institutional balance in the EU. Legal certainty would surely be a welcome development. However, also in light of traditionally informal compliance strategies applicable in the banking sector, extensive binding regulation should not result in imposing a rigid prudential framework. Nor should the institutional safeguards counterbalancing binding decision-making trigger the slow-down of the implementation process.

Supervision was traditionally the competence of Member States. However, a common regulatory framework and an incipient common supervisory culture sustaining ever more integrated financial markets trigger the need for also addressing supervisory aspects at the European level. So far, European law only provides the general framework under which national supervisory authorities operate, along with some instances of cooperation and exchange of information.

No European institutional structure exists currently with regard to supervision, which is conducted by the national competent authorities. Member States enjoy procedural autonomy for choosing the most appropriate institutional model. Nevertheless, this does not mean that the European dimension is completely absent. The CRD gives increased consideration to supervision, and also entails provisions that require Member States to assign to their supervisory authorities certain powers. Moreover, similar to many instances (when in the absence of a European executive institutional set-up European policies are implemented by national administrations), national supervisory authorities may be considered as part of the decentralised European administrative apparatus implementing European prudential norms. They are directly bound by the EU normative framework, which often refers to them explicitly as addressees of norms.

The guiding principle for supervision used to be home country control. Nevertheless, such a principle only imperfectly shows the distribution of competences and serves merely as a *prima facie* conflict of jurisdiction rule. Host countries still have a series of substantial residual competences and important room for action in the interest of protecting the general good. In this context, the current framework for supervision can be characterised by reference to both the principle of home-country control and the principle of supervisory cooperation. This approach is confirmed by the 2009 amendment to the CRD, which requires the mandatory establishment of colleges of supervisors and emphasises joint decision-making without boosting the powers of the home consolidating supervisors. Furthermore, coordination and cooperation received more emphasis in the context of increasingly active supervisory platforms or networks created at EU level (the Groupe de Contact, CEBS, the Banking Supervision Committee) and of more streamlined instruments for coordination (Memoranda of Understanding, coordinating supervisor, supervisory colleges, delegation).

Yet systemic stability concerns in a highly integrated market, as well as the hereto related need for consistent implementation of common prudential rules throughout the EU, provide imperative reasons for improving the European dimension of the supervisory framework. This has been definitely ascertained by the 2007–9 crisis, which revealed serious shortcomings in the cooperation between supervisory authorities in cross-border situations that led to fragmented and costly crisis management.

Furthermore, the crisis brought to the fore the severe consequences of the absence of a streamlined mechanism at EU level, capable of carefully surveying emerging interdependencies and macro-developments in an integrated market and of taking the necessary measures to correct imbalances and prevent systemic crises.

The current institutional framework for supervision is an intermediary solution and reforms are imminent in light of the financial stability concerns revealed during the crisis. In May 2009, the Commission put forward plans for reform that aim to considerably strengthen the European dimension of the supervisory architecture. Envisaged reforms, based on the de Larosière report, plan an integrated financial supervision architecture where national supervisors will maintain primary responsibility for the conduct of day-to-day supervision. In addition, the Level 3 committees transformed into European Supervisory Authorities (ESAs) will be able to authoritatively intervene to overcome deficiencies in cooperation between supervisors, but also to correct implementation at national level that is in breach of EU prudential rules. Furthermore, a new independent European body with soft macro-prudential powers (the European Systemic Risk Board, ESRB) will be established with the aim of identifying systemic vulnerabilities and issuing early warnings and recommendations, upon which policy-makers will be called to act or explain inaction.

The macro-prudential and micro-prudential frameworks proposed by the Commission in 2009, although building on the current arrangements, may be considered an ambitious project, in light of traditional political reluctance to address supervision at EU level. The Commission made important choices in some respects (binding standards, compulsory mediation, binding dispute settlement, enhanced enforcement), while leaving some issues for further development (e.g. the follow-up to early warnings and macro-prudential recommendations, crisis management, the precise role of the ECB with regard to its broad supervisory competences). The proposals take an important step on the path towards the Europeanisation of supervision. They fall short of establishing a European supervisor, but introduce an eventually powerful coordination mechanism that would reinforce the supervision of individual cross-border institutions. It may also open the way for further centralisation of supervisory functions at EU level. The emphasis on the macro-prudential dimension is remarkable. However, so far, the underpinning framework for the ESRB is blurred. In the absence of legal personality and clear lines of responsibility for following up upon early warnings, the ESRB might not make a substantial difference when compared to the current functions of the BSC and CEBS.

Reforming the institutional set-up for supervision in the EU is a complex task that needs to be approached from the perspective of legal constraints related to the Treaty principles of conferral, subsidiarity and proportionality. Furthermore, it needs to be carefully scrutinised in the light of the institutional balance and the limits to the delegation of powers in the EU as developed in the ECJ's jurisprudence (*Meroni*, *Romano*). Also, supervisory reform needs to take a holistic view where competences for supervision are considered together with those for crisis management and with burden-sharing in case of crisis resolution. Much will depend on the forthcoming concrete details. It is not sufficient to centralise and institutionalise enhanced coordination mechanisms but, for a European supervisory architecture to be effective, it is essential for it to be solidly anchored into a legitimate and straightforward framework. Therefore, the focus of policy-makers when devising the new architecture should be particularly on a clear definition of the scope of supervisory functions to be exercised at EU level, the instruments available, the responsibilities of each actor involved and the accountability mechanisms.

Considering the above issues, we assert that prudential regulation has a dominant European character, whereas the European dimension of supervision has only timidly emerged so far, but is very likely to be substantially boosted in the near future.

2 Refinement of prudential policy

Increased harmonisation does not only mean more rules at the European level, but also refers to more detail provided in these rules. Such details reflect a refined prudential approach that has been developed in response to the increased sophistication of financial markets. The new European prudential framework, apart from responding to the concerns related to an integrated European banking market, also echoes the international endeavours for ensuring safety and soundness of banks in the globalised era. It is only through a proper understanding of substantive aspects of prudential policy that one can assess the developments regarding the distribution of supervisory competences in Europe.

As explicitly resulting from the work of the Basel Committee, and implicitly from the CRD, the current prudential approach is based on three pillars: more sophisticated capital requirements, reinforced supervisory review and promoted market discipline. The capital requirements, with their more risk-sensitive standardised approaches, and the internal models-based approaches, covering credit, market and operational risk, occupy a large part of what has been harmonised at European level. Capital requirements are also the main target of regulatory amendments in response to the crisis. Yet such amendments do not seem to question the supervisory approach of Basel II/CRD, but focus on filling in identified gaps or correcting the too lenient treatment of specific financial instruments. Moreover, regulatory reforms appear to highlight the largely unexplored potential of the two other pillars: supervisory review and market discipline. It is hoped that this will result in a more balanced consideration of the three pillars and an increased emphasis by supervisors on their interaction.

One important novelty brought by the CRD consists of the increased involvement of private parties in the regulatory process. Thus, a complex regulatory regime becomes apparent, which encompasses not only public prescriptive regulation (of a command-and-control type) but also instances of co-regulation, where private actors are associated (although in a limited form) to the regulatory process (understood widely as entailing standard-setting, monitoring and enforcement). Such increased involvement of private parties takes two forms. The first corresponds to the very alternative to the standardised capital requirements approach: the internal risk-measurement models for credit, market and operational risk (IRB, VaR, AMA). Although not delegating the entire standard-setting process to the regulated entities themselves (as would happen if the so-called credit risk models were recognised), the prudential approach relying on internal models constitutes a regulatory technique permitting the calculation of capital requirements on the basis of the institution's own methodologies for estimating internal capital needs. The second instance of co-regulation regards the resort to external credit risk assessment provided by recognised rating agencies.

The involvement of private parties in the regulatory process elicits three important remarks. First, prudential standards adopted through co-regulatory techniques are more individualised and correspond to the specific risk profile of the regulated entity. This implies that prudential supervision does not merely reflect compliance with abstract capital standards, but becomes process-oriented, so that it can more closely monitor the evolution of the risk profile of a credit institution. Corporate governance and internal risk-management techniques of the regulated institutions gain increasing importance and become essential parameters in the evaluation of the financial health of an institution. Second, closer association of private parties to the regulatory process entails new tasks for the supervisory authorities – who have to validate such a contribution. Accordingly, the CRD and detailed guidance from CEBS prescribe the benchmarks and processes underpinning the recognition, for regulatory purposes, of internal models and credit rating agencies, as well as the ancillary framework for the dialogue between supervisory authorities and the regulated entities (which resembles to what is designated in the literature as contract regulation). Third, ascribing regulatory value to internal models and private ratings should be accompanied by sufficient guarantees that preclude the capture of the supervisory authority by private parties. Models and ratings can be unreliable, as has been proved during the current crisis; therefore, the regulatory framework should contain safeguards that limit excessive reliance on them.

The above considerations indicate the intricate relationship between capital requirements and the supervisory process, as well as their increased intermingling. Prudential regulation does not merely entail standards and principles, but it also provides the framework for processes and dialogue.

In addition, supervision is not limited to verifying compliance with regulation and taking corrective action, but involves a standard-setting component. These characteristics are inherent to a more risk-sensitive approach that seeks to individualise prudential standards in accordance with the specific risk profile of the regulated institution. Hence, it would be more appropriate to talk about a prudential regulatory or supervisory regime.

Furthermore, it comes as no surprise that the reinforced supervisory review pillar also contains – apart from enhanced supervisory tasks and standards – the general obligation for supervisory authorities to take prompt corrective action. Indeed, enlarged supervisory competences would be vain if not backed by appropriate sanctioning powers. The European normative framework also provides the general framework of 'prompt intervention' powers that might prove an important way of influencing supervisory institutional design in the Member States. In response to the crisis, it is expected that the sanctioning regime will be better specified in the CRD and further common early intervention tools developed at EU level.

Prudential policy relies increasingly on the supervisory process. This also explains why there is an increased European dimension to supervision. European law invades the supervisory domain not only because of the necessity to ensure consistent implementation of extensive European prudential regulation, but also because supervision has become an influential prudential tool, in addition to capital requirements. It is not merely a means for implementing prudential standards, but a self-standing instrument of prudential policy.

Finally, the timidly emerging market discipline pillar of prudential policy has so far only a limited potential as a regulatory tool – but it may prove relevant for various reasons. It definitely contributes to enhanced disclosure, an obligation impinging on credit institutions and supervisory authorities. However, disclosure requirements for banks will have a more limited impact in the case of banking as compared to securities markets, because of confidentiality rules. Disclosure by supervisors might be very important for reasons of public expectations, particularly when considering that prudential rules are meant to correct information asymmetries, apart from systemic risk.

All in all, the new prudential regulatory regime, as reflected in the amended CRD, is characterised by greater complexity, stemming from the increased risk-sensitiveness, the intermingling of regulatory and supervisory techniques and the involvement of various actors in the regulatory process. The prudential approach is increasingly process-oriented and associates to prescriptive norms ever more incentives-based rules. Supervision has become a central pillar of prudential policy, besides capital requirements, which justifies the need to underpin it with an adequate normative and institutional framework. In this context, the European policy-makers can no longer rely on the traditional arguments leading to an exclusively decentralised supervision model; supervisory issues lie at the core of prudential concerns, and also have to be considered from the European perspective.

3 Reassessment of supervisory liability

In light of growing Europeanisation and of the central role of supervisory authorities in the conduct of prudential policy, the issue of supervisory liability should be reassessed. This is imperative in the context of the envisaged reform of EU financial supervision and the authoritative role planned for the EBA (especially as regards binding dispute settlement between national supervisors and direct decision-making powers with the aim of implementing EU norms). The approach adopted by the ECJ in its judgment to the *Peter Paul* affair, holding that European law does not influence the national regimes on supervisory liability, cannot be simply endorsed without being assessed against the provisions of the CRD. Also, given that the liability regime of national authorities for breach of EU law and the liability regime of EU institutions increasingly influence each other, account should be taken of both dimensions of supervisory liability: the national and the European.

There are several reasons explaining why the debate on supervisory liability cannot be considered closed pursuant to the ECJ's judgment. Two are particularly relevant. First, the ECJ was confronted with the assessment of the liability issue against the normative background of the Second Banking Directive and based its decision largely on the fact that such legislation reflected only minimum harmonisation, which did not extend to harmonisation of national liability regimes. Second, the Court did not proceed to a systematic analysis of the content of the provisions of the directive, but merely invoked, without entering any details, the general policy argument that supervision is complex and has to take into account a plurality of contradicting interests.

The new extensive and detailed normative prudential framework and the formalisation in European law of various supervisory aspects are sufficient to reopen the debate. The new framework can no longer be characterised as 'minimum harmonisation', as European law regulates a variety of prudential aspects in detail. Essential harmonisation does not entail providing explicit rules on liability. However the need for some common platform to supervisory liability regimes follows from the necessity to respond in a consistent way, throughout the EU, to claims based on EU law.

Also, given the substantial changes in the CRD (especially with regard to the tasks incumbent on supervisory authorities), one cannot simply accept the assertion that EU law does not create any rights for depositors. This has to be checked with respect to the substance of the new European legislation. We assert that there are some provisions that may be considered sufficiently precise so as to derive from their content concrete obligations for supervisory authorities and correlative rights for depositors.

Furthermore, to be acceptable as an influential argument, the complexity of supervision should be considered in more detail. The complex nature of supervision cannot by itself automatically exclude any liability. The divergent interests to be taken into account by the supervisory authority should be effectively balanced in every concrete situation. The default inclination of the balance in favour of some supervisory immunity should not provide an impenetrable shield in cases of serious misconduct or abuses on the part of supervisory authorities, which bring severe damages to depositors.

The CRD does not provide straightforwardly for a common approach for supervisory liability, nor is it obvious that it contains rights for depositors allowing them to claim proper supervision. Nevertheless, neither can the liability issue be considered as being definitively settled, in the new normative and institutional context. Should the ECJ be confronted in the future with a case based on the new legal regime, it will have to complement the contextual motive analysis (used in the *Peter Paul* judgment) with a thorough legal analysis of the new provisions in the CRD, as specified in Level 2 and Level 3 measures.

Finding depositor rights in the current legislative framework has the potential for strengthening depositors' confidence in the system. It would be merely a first step in the Court's analysis of the supervisory liability issue. The other two imperative conditions for liability are seriousness of breach and causality. The complexity argument may play an important role when considering these two elements. Such a 'rights-based constructive ambiguity' approach to liability would also be preferable from the perspective of attributing supervisory tasks to some European authority.

To conclude, allowing aggrieved depositors to claim adequate supervision in courts may be seen as a component of the prudential regulatory regime, which contributes to ensuring compliance with European prudential norms.

Quidquid agis, prudenter agas, et respice finem ('Whatever you do, do cautiously, and look to the end'). This is equally valid for banks, policy-makers and supervisors.

Bibliography

Abrams, R.K. and Taylor, M.W. (2000) 'Issues in the Unification of Financial Sector Supervision', *IMF Working Paper* 213.

Adams, R. and Mehran, H (2003) 'Is Corporate Governance Different for Bank Holding Companies?' *Federal Reserve Bank of New York Economic Policy Review* 9: 123–41.

Aglietta, M. Scialom, L. and Sessin, T. (1998) 'Prudential Supervision Reform in Europe. Arguments and Proposals', *Research Papers in Banking and Finance of the Institute of European Finance*, 10.

Akerlof, G.A. (1970) 'The Market for "Lemons": Quality Uncertainty and the Market Mechanism', *Quarterly Journal of Economics* 84(3): 488–500.

Alexander, K. (2002a) 'Establishing a European Securities Regulator: Is the European Union an Optimal Economic Area for a Single Securities Regulator?' *Cambridge Endowment for Research in Finance, Working Paper* 7.

—— (2002b) *Presentation of the CERF Research Project on International Financial Regulation*, available at www.cerf.cam.ac.uk (accessed on 26 June 2009).

—— (2003) 'Reforming the Basel Accord', *Journal of International Banking Regulation* 4(4): 298–300.

—— (2004) 'Corporate Governance and Banking Regulation: The Regulator as a Stakeholder', *CERF Working Paper* 17.

Alexander, K., Eatwell, J., Persaud, A.D. and Reoch, R. (2007) *Financial Supervision and Crisis Management in the EU*, European Parliament: Policy Department Economic and Scientific Policy Studies, IP/A/ECON/IC-2007–069.

Alpa, G. (2004) 'The Harmonisation of EC Law of Financial Markets in the Perspective of Consumer Protection', *European Business Law Review* 13(6): 523–40.

Alpa, G. and Capriglione, F. (eds) (2002) *Diritto bancario communitario*, Torino: UTET.

Altunbas, Y. and Molyneux, P. (2001) 'Technical Change in European Banking', in E. Gardener and P. Versluijs (eds) *Bank Strategies and Challenges in the New Europe*, Basingstoke, UK: Palgrave.

Amos, M. (2002) 'Eurotorts and Unicorns: Damages for Breach of Community Law in the United Kingdom', in D. Fairgrieve, M. Andenas and J. Bell (eds) *Tort Liability of Public Authorities in Comparative Perspective*, London: BIICL.

Amtenbrink, F. and Lastra, R.M. (2008) 'Securing Democratic Accountability of Financial Regulatory Agencies – A Theoretical Framework', in R.V. De Mulder (ed.) *Mitigating Risk in the Context of Safety and Security. How Relevant is a Rational Approach?* Rotterdam: Erasmus School of Law and Research School of Safety and Security.

Andenas, M. (2000) 'Liability for Supervisors and Depositors' Rights – BCCI and the Bank of England in the House of Lords', *Euredia* 3: 388–409.

Andenas, M. and Avgerinos, Y. (eds) (2003) *Financial Markets in Europe. Towards a Single Regulator?* The Hague: Kluwer Law International.

Andenas, M. and Fairgrieve, D. (2000a) 'To Supervise or to Compensate? A Comparative Study of State Liability for Negligent Banking Supervision', in M. Andenas and D. Fairgrieve (eds) *Judicial Review in International Perspective, Liber Amicorum in Honour of Lord Slynn of Hadley,* The Hague: Kluwer Law International.

—— (eds) (2000b) *Judicial Review in International Perspective: Liber Amicorum in Honour of Lord Slynn,* The Hague: Kluwer Law International.

—— (2002) 'Misfeasance in Public Office, Governmental Liability and European Influences', *International and Comparative Law Quarterly* 51: 757–80.

Andenas, M. and Hadjiemmanuil, C. (1997) 'Banking Supervision, the Internal Market and European Monetary Union', in M. Andenas, L. Gormley, C. Hadjiemmanuil and I. Harden (eds) *European Economic and Monetary Union: The Institutional Framework,* The Hague: Kluwer Law International.

Andenas, M. and Roth, W.-H. (eds) (2002) *Services and Free Movement in EU Law,* Oxford: Oxford University Press.

Andenas, M. and Türk, A. (eds) (2000) *Delegated Legislation and the Role of Committees in the EC,* The Hague: Kluwer Law International.

Annett, A., Decressin, J. and Stevrev, E. (2005) 'Euro Area Policies: Selected Issues', *IMF Country Report* 05/266.

Annunziata, F. (2004) 'Governance delle banche e conflitti di interessi. Il difficile equilibrio tra disciplina bancaria e dei servizi di investimento', *Analisi Giuridica dell'Economia, Studi e Discussioni sul Diritto dell'Impresa,* 1.

Arda, A. (2004) 'Consulting the European Central Bank. Legal Aspects of the Community and National Authorities' Obligation to Consult the ECB Pursuant to Article 105(4) EC', *Euredia* 1: 111–52.

Arora, A. (1988) 'Banking Act 1987' (Part 1), *Company Lawyer* 9(1): 8–13.

Augustin, D. (1995) 'Credit Risk in European and International Regulations', in G. Ferrarini (ed.) *Prudential Regulation of Banks and Securities Firms,* The Hague: Kluwer Law International.

Avgerinos, Y.V. (2002) 'Essential and Non-essential Measures: Delegation of Powers in EU Securities Regulation', *European Law Journal* 8(2): 269–89.

—— (2003) *Regulating and Supervising Investment Services in the European Union,* London: Palgrave Macmillan.

Ayadi, R., F.C. Musch and M. Nieto (2008) *Basel II Implementation in the Midst of Turbulence,* Brussels: CEPS.

Balling, M (2004) 'Objectives and Theoretical Foundations of the European Commission's 1999 Action Plan Concerning the Framework for Financial Markets', *Journal of International Banking Regulation* 5(3): 256–86.

Baltensperger, E. (1980) 'Alternative Approaches to the Theory of the Banking Firm', *Journal of Monetary Economics* 6: 1–37.

—— (1988) 'Die Regulierung des Bankensektors', *Wirtschaftswissenschaftliches Studium* 17(2): 53–7.

Baltensperger, E. and Dermine, J. (1987) 'Banking Deregulation in Europe', *Economic Policy* 2(4): 63–109.

—— (1990) 'European Banking, Prudential and Regulatory Issues', in J. Dermine (ed.) *European Banking in the 1990s,* Oxford: Blackwell.

Barr, M.S. and Miller, G.P. (2006) 'Global Administrative Law: The View from Basel', *The European Journal of International Law* 17(1): 39–41.

Bassan, F. (2003) 'Regolazione ed equilibrio istituzionale nell'Unione Europea', *Rivista Italiana di Diritto Pubblico Communitario* 5: 973–1036.

Becker, W.-D. (1980) 'Geldpolitische Implikationen des Bankenwettbewerbs, in Wettbewerb und Fortschritt', in W. Hamm and R. Schmidt (eds) *Wettbewerb und Fortschritt: Festschrift zum 65. Geburtstag von Burkhardt Röper*, Baden-Baden: Nomos-Verlagsgesellschaft.

Belaisch, A., Kodres, L., Levy, J. and Ubide, A. (2001) 'Euro-Area Banking at the Crossroads', *IMF Working Paper* WP/01/28.

Bende-Nabende, A. (2002) *Globalisation, FDI, Regional Integration and Sustainable Development: Theory, Evidence and Policy*, Aldershot: Ashgate.

Benink, H. and Kaufman, G. (2008) 'Turmoil Reveals the Inadequacy of Basel II', *Financial Times* (28 February).

Benston, G.J. (1998) 'Regulating Financial Markets: A Critique and Some Proposals', *Hobart Paper* 135, London Institute of Economic Affairs.

—— (2000) 'Is Government Regulation of Banks Necessary?', *Journal of Financial Research* 18(2/3): 185–202.

Benston, G.J. and Kaufman, G.G. (1988) *Risk and Solvency Regulation of Depository Institutions: Past Policies and Current Options, Monograph Series in Finance and Economics* 1, New York: New York University Press.

Benston, G.J. and Smith, C.G. (1976) 'A Transaction Cost Approach to the Theory of Financial Intermediation', *Journal of Finance* 31(2): 215–31.

Berman, G., Herdegen, B. and Lindseth, P. (eds) (2000) *Transatlantic Regulatory Cooperation. Legal Problems and Political Prospects*, Oxford: Oxford University Press.

Bernanke, B.S. (2009) 'Financial Innovation and Consumer Protection', Speech at the Federal Reserve System's Sixth Biennial Community Affairs Research Conference, Washington, DC (17 April).

Best, E. (2008) 'The Lisbon Treaty: A Qualified Advance for EU Decision-making and Governance', *EIPASCOPE* 1: 7–12.

Bhattacharya, S. and Jacklin, C.J. (1988) 'Distinguishing Panics and Information-Based Bank Runs: Welfare and Policy Implications', *Journal of Political Economy* 96(3): 568–92.

Bhattacharya, S. and Thakor, A. (1993) 'Contemporary Banking Theory', *Journal of Financial Intermediation* 3: 2–50.

Bhattacharya, S., Boot, A.W.A. and Thakor, A.V. (1995) 'The Economics of Bank Regulation', *Tinbergen Institute Discussion Paper* 163.

Bieber, R. and Slom, I. (1996) 'Hierarchy of Norms in European Law', *Common Market Law Review* 33: 907–30.

Binder, J.-H. (2004) 'The Advocate-General's Opinion in *Paul and Others* v. *Germany* – Cutting Back State Liability for Regulatory Negligence?' *European Business Law Review* 15: 463–76.

Bini Smaghi, L. and Gros, D. (2000) *Open Issues in European Central Banking*, London: Macmillan.

Björkland, A. (1998) 'The Scope of the General Good Notion in the Second Banking Directive according to Recent Case Law', *European Business Law Review* 9: 227–43.

Björklund, M. (2001) 'Responsibility in the EC for Mixed Agreements – Should Non-member Parties Care?' *Nordic Journal of International Law* 70: 373–401.

Black, J. (2003) 'Enrolling Actors in Regulatory Systems: Examples from UK Financial Services Regulation', *Public Law* (spring): 63–91.

Blyth, T. and Cavalli, E. (2001) 'The Liability of the Financial Services Authority after the *Three Rivers*', *Journal of International Financial Markets* 3(5): 199–204.

Borio, C. (2008) 'The Financial Turmoil of 2007–?: A Preliminary Assessment and Some Policy Considerations', *BIS Working Papers* 251.

Börner, C.J. (2000) 'Allfinanz, neue Bankvertriebswege und Resource-based View', *Mitteilungen und Berichte des Instituts für Bankwirtschaft und Bankrecht an der Universität zu Köln*, 31 Jahrgang/83.

Börzel, T.A. (1997) 'What's So Special about Policy Networks? An Exploration of the Concept and Its Usefulness in Studying European Governance'. *European Integration Online Papers* 1, 16.

Breton, A. and Wintrobe, R. (1982) *The Logic of Bureaucratic Conduct: An Economic Analysis of Competition, Exchange, and Efficiency in Private and Public Organizations.* New York: Cambridge University Press.

Briault, C. (1999) 'The Rationale for a Single National Financial Services Regulator', *FSA Occasional Paper* 2.

—— (2002) 'Revisiting the Rationale for a Single National Financial Services Regulator', *FSA Occasional Paper* 16.

Brunnermeier, M., Crockett, A., Goodhart, C., Persaud, A.D. and Shin, H. (January 2009) 'The Fundamental Principles of Financial Regulation', ICMB, CEPR: Geneva Reports on the World Economy 11, Preliminary Conference Draft.

Buck, T. (2005) 'Commissioner Puts Credit Rating Agencies on Watch', *Financial Times* (5 April).

Burstein, M.L. (1988) *Studies in Banking Theory, Financial History and Vertical Control*, New York: St Martin's Press.

Cafaggi, F. (2001) 'The Crisis of Nation State, Pluralism and Self-Regulation Forms', *Politica del diritto* 4: 543–83.

—— (2005) 'Gouvernance et responsabilité des régulateurs privés', *Revue internationale de droit économique* 2: 111–63.

Canals, J. (1997) *Universal Banking. International Comparisons and Theoretical Perspectives*, Oxford: Clarendon Press.

Cannata, F. and Quagliariello, M. (2009) 'The Role of Basel II in the Subprime Financial Crisis: Guilty or Not Guilty?' *CAREFIN Research Paper* 3.

Cartwright, P. (2004) *Banks, Consumers and Regulation*, Oxford and Portland, OR: Hart Publishing.

Cartwright, P. and Campbell, A. (2003) 'Co-insurance and Moral Hazard: Some Reflections on Deposit Protection in the UK and USA', *Journal of International Banking Regulation* 5(1): 9–20.

Central Banking Publications (1999) *How Countries Supervise their Bank, Insurers and Securities Markets*, London: Central Banking Publications.

Chalmers, D. (1998) *European Union Law. Law and EU Government*, Vol. I, Aldershot: Ashgate.

Chalmers, D. and Szyszczak, E. (1998) *European Union Law*, Vol. II, Aldershot: Ashgate.

Christophersen, H. (1991a) 'Subsidiarity and Economic Monetary Union', in Jacques Delors (ed.) *Subsidiarity: The Challenge of Change*, Maastricht: European Institute of Public Administration.

—— (1991b) 'The Community in the World Political Economy', in F. Laursen (ed.) *Europe 1992: World Partner? The Internal Market and the World Political Economy, EIPA Professional Papers* 6, Maastricht: EIPA.

Clarotti, P. (1982) 'La coordination des législations bancaires', *Revue du Marché Commun* 254: 68.

Cloos, J., Reinesch, G., Vignes, D. and Weyland, J. (1994) *Le Traité de Maastricht – genèse, analyse, commentaries*, Brussels: Bruylant, second edition.

Coleman, R.J. (2000) 'Financial Services and Consumer Policy: The Regulatory Challenge', *Euredia* 3: 307–12.

Comana, M. (2002) 'Organizzazione e procedure di controllo interno', in G. Alpa and F. Capriglione (eds) *Diritto bancario communitario*, Torino: UTET.

Cordero, R. (1990) *The Creation of a European Banking System. A Study of its Legal and Technical Aspects*, New York: Peter Lang.

Craig, P. and de Búrca, G. (1999a) *EU Law. Text, Cases and Materials*, Oxford: Oxford University Press, second edition.

—— (eds) (1999b) *The Evolution of EU Law*, Oxford: Oxford University Press.

—— (2003) *EU Law. Text, Cases and Materials*, Oxford: Oxford University Press, third edition.

Cranston, R. (1995) *The Single Market and the Law of Banking*, London: Lloyds of London Press, second edition.

—— (1997) *Principles of Banking Law*, Oxford: Clarendon Press.

Craufurd Smith, R. (1999) 'Remedies for Breaches of EU Law in National Courts: Legal Variation and Selection', in Craig and de Burca (eds) *The Evolution of EU Law*, Oxford: Oxford University Press.

Cremona, M. (1999) 'External Relations and External Competence: The Emergence of an Integrated Policy', in Craig and de Burca (eds) *The Evolution of EU Law*, Oxford: Oxford University Press.

Dale, R. (1992) *International Banking Deregulation. The Great Banking Experiment*, Chichester: Wiley-Blackwell.

—— (1995) 'The Regulation of Investment Firms in the European Union', in G. Ferrarini (ed.) *Prudential Regulation of Banks and Securities Firms*, The Hague: Kluwer Law International.

Dalhuisen, J. (2001) 'Towards a Single European Capital Market and a Workable System Regulation', paper presented at the British Institute of International and Comparative Law Conference 'Towards a Single EU Financial Regulation', London (26 January).

Dashwood, A. and Hillion, C. (eds) (2000) *The General Law of EC External Relations*, London: Centre for European Legal Studies (Cambridge) and Sweet & Maxwell.

Dassesse, M. and Isaacs, S (1985) *EEC Banking Law*, London: Lloyds of London Press.

Dassesse, M., Isaacs, S. and Penny, G. (1994) *EC Banking Law*, London: Lloyds of London Press, second edition.

Davies, G. (2003) 'The Post-Laeken Division of Competences', *European Law Review* 28: 686–98.

Davis, E.P. (1998) 'Problems of Banking Regulation – an EC Perspective', in C.A.E. Goodhart (ed.) *The Emerging Framework of Financial Regulation*, London: Central Banking Publications.

de Búrca, G. (1999) 'The Institutional Development of the EU: A Constitutional Analysis', in Craig and de Búrca (eds) *The Evolution of EU Law*, Oxford: Oxford University Press.

De Mulder, R.V. (2008) *Mitigating Risk in the Context of Safety and Security. How Relevant is a Rational Approach?* Rotterdam: Erasmus School of Law and Research School of Safety and Security.

De Schutter, O., Lebessis, N. and Paterson, J. (eds) (2001) *Governance in the European Union, Cahiers of the Forward Studies Unit,* Brussels: European Commission.

Delamy, H. (2001) *Judicial Review of the Administrative Action. A Comparative Analysis,* London: Round Hall and Sweet & Maxwell.

Demirgüç-Kunt, A. and Levine, R. (eds) (2001) *Financial Structure and Economic Growth,* Cambridge, MA: MIT Press.

Dermine, J. (1994) 'EC Banking Regulation', in B. Steil (ed.) *International Financial Market Regulation,* Chichester: John Wiley & Sons.

—— (1996) 'European Banking Integration, Ten Years After', *European Financial Management* 2(3): 331–53.

—— (2005) 'European Banking Integration: Don't Put the Cart before the Horse', paper presented at the Conference on Cross-Border Banking, Regulatory Challenges (6–7 October).

Dewatripont, M. and Tirole, J (1994) *The Prudential Regulation of Banks,* Cambridge, MA: MIT Press.

Dhumale, R. (2001) 'Levelling the Playing Field in International Financial Markets: The Basel Accord Revisited', *Journal of Financial Regulations and Compliance* 9(1): 38–41.

Di Giorgio, G. and Di Noia, C. (2000) 'Designing Institutions for Financial Stability: Regulation and Supervision by Objective for the Euro Area', paper presented at the Finance and Consumption Conference 'Financial Supervision of Banks and Specialised Banks in the EU', European University institute (December).

Diamond, D.W. (1984) 'Financial Intermediation and Delegated Monitoring', *Review of Economic Studies* 51(3): 393–414.

Diamond, D. and Dybvig, P. (1983) 'Bank Runs, Deposit Insurance, and Liquidity', *Journal of Political Economy* 91: 401–19.

Dougan, M. (2000) 'Minimum Harmonisation and the Internal Market', *Common Market Law Review* 37: 853–85.

—— (2008) 'The Treaty of Lisbon 2007: Winning Minds, not Hearts', *Common Market Law Review* 45: 617–703.

Duisenberg, W.F. (2000) 'The Future of Banking Supervision in the Integration of Financial Markets', speech held at the Euro Group conference 'Improving Integration of Financial Markets in Europe', Turin (22 May).

Dyzenhaus, D. (ed.) (1999) *Recrafting the Rule of Law: The Limits of Legal Order,* Oxford: Hart Publishing.

Eberlein, B. and Grande, E. (2005) 'Beyond Delegation: Transnational Regulatory Regimes and the EU Regulatory State', *Journal of European Public Policy* 12(1): 89–112.

Economist, The (2009a) *A Glimmer of Hope? The Worst Thing for the World Economy Would Be to Assume the Worst is Over, The Economist* (25 April–1 May): 15–16.

—— (2009b) 'Iceland Hunts the Euro', *The Economist* (22 January); available at www.economist.com/displaystory.cfm?story_id=12972641&CFID=57458384&CF TOKEN=38023891 (accessed 26 June 2009).

Eeckhout, P. (2004) *External Relations of the European Union: Legal and Constitutional Foundations,* Oxford: Oxford University Press.

Eeckhout, P., Tridimas, T. and de Búrca, G (2006) *Yearbook of European Law 25*, Oxford: Oxford University Press.

Eilmansberger, T. (2004) 'The Relationship between Rights and Remedies in EC Law: In Search of the Missing Link', *Common Market Law Review* 41: 1199–246.

Endler, J. (1998) *Europäische Zentralbank und Preisstabilität. Eine juristische und ökonomische Untersuchung der institutionallen Vorkehrungen des Vertrages von Maastricht zur Gewährleistung der Preisstabilität*, Stuttgart: Richard Boorberg Verlag.

Euredia Editorial Board (2000) 'European Banking Law as Applied by the House of Lords: Overshadowing the Acte Clair Doctrine', *Euredia* 3: 305–6.

European Central Bank (2005) *Legal Aspects of the European System of Central Banks: Liber Amicorum Paolo Zamboni Garavelli*, Frankfurt: European Central Bank.

European Financial Services Round Table (EFR) (2004) 'The Lead Supervisor for Cross-border Financial Institutions in the EU' (15 June).

—— (2005) 'On the Lead Supervisor Model and the Future of Financial Supervision in the EU. Follow-up Recommendations of the EFR' (29 June).

European League for Economic Co-operation (ELEC) (2005) 'Financial Supervision in Europe' (October).

European Shadow Financial Regulatory Committee (2009) 'The Financial Crisis and the Future of Financial Regulation', Statement No. 28, London (January 19).

Fairgrieve, D., Andenas, M. and Bell, J. (eds) (2002) *Tort Liability of Public Authorities in Comparative Perspective*, London: BIICL.

Ferran, E. (2004) *Building an EU Securities Market*, Cambridge: Cambridge University Press.

Ferrarini, G. (ed.) (1995) *Prudential Regulation of Banks and Securities Firms*, The Hague: Kluwer Law International.

Fischer, S. (2006) 'Financial Market Liberalisation in Financial Globalisation', Fifth BIS Annual Research Conference (June), *BIS Papers* 32.

Fortsakis, T. (2005) 'Principles Governing Good Administration', *European Public Law*, 11(2): 207–17.

Freeman, J. (1999) 'Private Parties, Public Functions and the New Administrative Law', in D. Dyzenhaus (ed.) *Recrafting the Rule of Law: The Limits of Legal Order*, Oxford: Hart Publishing.

Freixas, X., Parigi, B.M. and Rochet, J.-C. (2003) 'The Lender of Last Resort: A 21st Century Approach' (December, last revised 19 May 2004), ECB *Working Paper* 298.

Frison-Roche, M.-A. (2000) 'La prise en charge par le droit des systèmes à risques', in J. Mestre (ed.) *Le droit face à l'exigence contemporaine de sécurité*, Aix en Provence: Presses Universitaires d'Aix-Marseille–PUAM.

Gaggero, P. (2002) 'Definizioni legislative a margine del Banking Code Europeo', in G. Alpa and F. Capriglione (eds) *Diritto bancario communitario*, Torino: UTET.

Galanopoulou, V.A. (2003) 'The FSA as an Institutional Model for the Emergence of a Single (Unified) European Financial Services Regulator', *European Business Law Review* 14(3): 277–323.

Gardener, E. (ed.) (1986) *UK Banking Supervision. Evolution, Practice and Issues*, London: Allen & Unwin.

Gardener, E. and Versluijs, P. (eds) (2001) *Bank Strategies and Challenges in the New Europe*, Basingstoke (UK): Palgrave Macmillan.

Gastineau, G.L. and Kritzman, M.P. (1999) *Dictionary of Financial Risk Management*, Chichester: John Wiley & Sons, third edition.

Giovanoli, M. (ed.) (1999) *International Bank Insolvencies,* The Hague: Kluwer Law International.

—— (2000a) 'Legal Aspects of Standard Setting', in M. Giovanoli (ed.) *International Monetary Law: Issues for the New Millennium,* Oxford: Oxford University Press.

—— (2000b) 'A New Architecture for the Global Financial Market: Legal Aspects of International Financial Standard Setting', in M. Giovanoli (ed.) *International Monetary Law. Issues for the New Millennium,* Oxford: Oxford University Press.

—— (ed.) (2000c) *International Monetary Law. Issues for the New Millennium,* Oxford: Oxford University Press.

Godano, G. (2004) 'Banking Advisory Committee' (Title VI, Arts 57, 8, 59, 60), *European Business Law Review* 15(4): 763–74.

Goddard, J., Molyneux, P. and Wilson, J. (2001) *European Banking. Efficiency, Technology and Growth,* New York: John Wiley & Sons.

Goldberg, L.S. (2009) 'Understanding Banking Sector Globalization', *IMF Staff Papers* 56: 171–97.

Goodhart, C.A.E. (1996) 'Some Regulatory Concerns', *Schweizerische Zeitschrift für Volkswirtschaft und Statistik* 132(4): 613–36.

—— (ed.) (1998a) *Financial Regulation. Why, How and Where Now?* London: Routledge.

—— (ed.) (1998b) *The Emerging Framework of Financial Regulation,* London: Central Banking Publications.

—— (2000) 'The Organisational Structure of Banking Supervision', paper presented at the Finance and Consumption Conference 'Financial Supervision of Banks and Specialised Banks in the EU', European University Institute (December).

—— (2004) 'Foreword', in T. Padoa-Schiopa, *Regulating Finance: Balancing Freedom and Risk,* Oxford: Oxford University Press.

Gramlich, L. (1995) 'Recht der Bankwirtschaft', in R. Schmidt (ed.) *Öffentliches Wirtschaftsrecht, Teil I,* Berlin: Springer Verlag.

Griller, S. and Orator, A. (2007) 'Meroni Revisited – Empowering European Agencies between Efficiency and Legitimacy', NewGov, New Modes of Governance project, Vienna, Europainstitut.

Gros, D. and Lannoo, K. (2000) *The Euro Capital Market,* Chichester: John Wiley & Sons.

Gulde, A.M. and Wolf, H. (2004) 'Financial Stability Arrangements in Europe: A Review', *Proceedings of OeNB Workshops* 4, Vienna: OeNB.

Gurley, J.G. and Shaw, E.S. (1960) *Money in the Theory of Finance,* Washington, DC: Brookings Institution.

Haas, P.M. (1990) *Saving the Mediterranean: The Politics of International Environmental Cooperation,* New York: Columbia University Press.

Hadjiemmanuil, C. (1996a) 'Financial Reporting and Auditing in the Regulated Sector', *Journal of International Business Law* 3: 103–6.

—— (1996b) *Banking Regulation and the Bank of England,* London: Lloyds of London Press.

—— (1997) 'Civil Liability of Regulatory Authorities after the *Three Rivers* Case', *Public Law* 32: 32–42.

Hanks, S. and Nardini, G.G. (2003) 'Enron Ruling Raises Important Issues Regarding Liability of Secondary Actors', *Butterworths Journal of International Banking and Financial Law* 18(6): 245–6.

Harlow, C. (1982) *Compensation and Government Torts*, London: Sweet & Maxwell.

—— (1999) 'European Administrative Law and the Global Challenge', in P. Craig and G. de Búrca (eds) *The Evolution of EU Law*, Oxford: Oxford University Press.

—— (2002) *Accountability in the European Union*, Oxford: Oxford University Press.

Harm, C. (2002) 'Bank Management between Shareholders and Regulators', *SUERF Studies* 21.

Häuser, F. (1995) 'The Structure of Own Funds', in G. Ferrarini (ed.) *Prudential Regulation of Banks and Securities Firms*, The Hague: Kluwer Law International.

Hayek, F.A. von (1952) *Individualismus und wirtschaftliche Ordnung*, Erlenbach-Zurich: Eugen Rentsch.

Hellmann, T.F., Murdock, K.C. and Stiglitz, J.E. (2000) 'Liberalization, Moral Hazard in Banking and Prudential Regulation: Are Capital Requirements Enough?' *American Economic Review* 90(1): 147–65.

Herring, R.J. and Litan, R.E. (1995) *Financial Regulation in a Global Economy*, Washington, DC: Brookings Institution.

Hilson, C. (2005) 'The Role of Discretion in EC Law on Non-contractual Liability', *Common Market Law Review* 42: 677–95.

Hirte, H. and Heinrich, T. A. (2002) 'Principles and Technical Instruments for Prudential Regulation', in G. Alpa and F. Capriglione (eds) *Diritto bancario communitario*, Torino: UTET.

Ho, D.E. (2002) 'Compliance and International Soft Law: Why Do Countries Implement the Basle Accord?' *Journal of International Economic Law* 5(3): 647–88.

Hoenig, T.M. (1998) 'Financial Modernization: Implications for the Safety Net', *Mercer Law Review* 49(3): 787–92.

Hüpkes, E., Quintyn, M. and Taylor, M.W. (2005) 'The Accountability of Financial Sector Supervisors: Principles and Practice', *IMF Working Paper* 05/51.

Hyett, S. (2000) 'The Duty of Co-operation: A Flexible Concept', in A. Dashwood and C. Hillion (eds) *The General Law of EC External Relations*, London: Centre for European Legal Studies (Cambridge) and Sweet & Maxwell.

Jackson, P.M. (1982) *The Political Economy of Bureaucracy*, Oxford: Philip Allan.

Jacqué, J.-P. (2004) 'The Principle of Institutional Balance', *Common Market Law Review* 41: 383–91.

Jensen, M. C. (1994) 'Self-interest, Altruism, Incentives and Agency Theory', *Journal of Applied Corporate Finance* 7: 40–5.

Joerges, C. (2005) 'Europeanization as Process: Thoughts on the Europeanization of Private Law', *European Public Law* 11(1): 63–84.

Joerges, C. and Dehousse, R. (2002) *Good Governance in Europe's Integrated Markets*, Oxford: Oxford University Press.

Joerges, C. and Vos, E. (eds) (1999) *EU Committees: Social Regulation, Law and Politics*, Oxford: Hart Publishing.

Kadelbach, S. (2002) 'European Administrative Law and the Law of a Europeanised Administration', in C. Joerges and R. Dehousse (eds) *Good Governance in Europe's Integrated Markets*, Oxford: Oxford University Press.

Kane, E.J. (1997) 'Ethical Foundations of Financial Regulation', *Journal of Financial Services Research* 12(1): 51–74.

—— (2007) 'Incentive Conflict in Central-Bank Responses to Sectoral Turmoil in Financial Hub Countries', *NBER Working Paper* 13593.

Kashyap, A.K., Rajan, R. and Stein, J.C. (1999) 'Banks as Liquidity Providers: An

Explanation for the Co-Existence of Lending and Deposit-Taking', *NBER Working Paper* 6962.

Katz, S.E. (1992) 'The Second Banking Directive and the General Good Clause: A Major Exception to the Freedom to Provide Services?', *CEPS Research Report* 9.

Katzengruber, B. (2003) 'Loss Given Default, Ratingagenturen und Basel 2', in Bank-Archiv, *Zeitschrift für das Gesamte Bank-und Börsenwesen,* Vienna: OBA, pp. 747–52.

Kaufman, G.G. (1994) 'Bank Contagion: A Review of the Theory and Evidence', *Journal of Financial Services Research* 8(2): 123–50.

Kerjean, S. (2005) 'L'impact de l'obligation de consultation de la Banque centrale européenne sur les projets de réglementation nationale: l'exemple français', *Banque&Droit* 99: 2–13.

—— (2008) 'Legal Implications of the Prudential Supervisory Assessment of Bank Mergers and Acquisitions under EU Law', *ECB Legal Working Paper* 6.

King, A.M. (2008) 'Be Careful What You Ask For: Is Fair Value Accounting Really Fair?' *International Journal of Disclosure and Governance* 5(4): 301–11.

King, M.R. (2005) 'Epistemic Communities and the Diffusion of Ideas: Central Bank Reform in the United Kingdom', *West European Politics* 28(1): 94–123.

Klabbers, J. (2001) 'Institutional Ambivalence by Design: Soft Organisations in International Law', *Nordic Journal of International Law* 70: 403–21.

—— (2002) *An Introduction to International Institutional Law,* Cambridge: Cambridge University Press.

Knill, C. and Lenschow, A. (2003) 'Modes of Regulation in the Governance of the European Union: Towards a Comprehensive Evaluation'. *European Integration Online Paper* 7.

Koopmans, T. (1970) 'De rol van de wetgever', in *Hondred jaar rechtsleven: de Nederlandse Juristenverenigung 1870–1970,* Zwolle: Tjeenk Willink, pp. 221–35.

Kose, A, Prasad, E., Rogoff, K. and Wei, S.-J. (2009) 'Financial Globalization: A Reappraisal', *IMF Staff Papers* 56: 8–62.

Koskenniemi, M. (ed.) (1998) *International Law Aspects of the European Union,* The Hague: Kluwer Law International.

Kupiec, H. and O'Brien, J. (1997) 'The Pre-Commitment Approach: Using Incentives to Set Market Risk Capital Requirements', *Finance and Economics Discussion Series* 14.

Lacoue-Labarthe, D. (1998) 'The Case for Prudential Regulation in the EU Financial Integration Process', *Quaderno CEIS* 90.

Ladeur, K.-H. (1997) 'Towards a Legal Theory of Supranationality – The Viability of the Network Concept', *European Law Journal* 3(1): 33–54.

Laffont, J.J. and Tirole, J. (1991) 'The Politics of Government Decision-Making. A Theory of Regulatory Capture', *Quarterly Journal of Economics* 106: 1089–127.

Lamfalussy, A. (2000) 'Regulation Under Strain', *Financial Times* (8 February).

—— (2004) 'Central Banks and Financial Stability', the Pierre Werner Lecture, Luxembourg (26 October).

—— (2009) 'The Specificity of the Current Crisis', lecture at the Belgian Financial Forum and the Robert Triffin International Foundation, Brussels (30 April).

Lannoo, K. (1995) 'Corporate Governance in Europe', *CEPS Working Party Report* 12.

—— (1999) 'A European Perspective on Corporate Governance', *Journal of Common Market Studies* 37(2): 269–94.

—— (2001) 'EU Securities Market Regulation: Adapting to the Needs of a Single Capital Market', *CEPS Task Force Report* (March).

—— (2002) 'Supervising the European Financial System', *CEPS Policy Brief* 21.

Lannoo, K. and Casey, J.-P. (2005) 'What's Next on the EU's Finance Agenda?' *Financial Times* (19 February).

Lannoo, K. and Levin, M. (2004) 'Securities Market Regulation in the EU. Everything You Always Wanted to Know about the Lamfalussy Procedure', *CEPS Research Report in Finance and Banking* 33.

Lastra, R.M. (2003) 'The Governance Structure for Financial Regulation and Supervision in Europe', *Columbia Journal of European Law* 10: 49–68.

—— (2006) *Legal Foundations of International Monetary Stability*, New York: Oxford University Press.

Lee, L.L.C. (1998–9) 'The Basle Accords as Soft Law: Strengthening International Banking Supervision', *Virginia Journal of International Law* 39(1): 3–6.

Lenaerts, K. (1993) 'Regulating the Regulatory Process: "Delegation of Powers" in the European Community', *European Law Review* 18(23): 22–49.

Lenaerts, K. and Gerard, D. (2004) 'The Structure of the Union according to the Constitution for Europe: The Emperor is Getting Dressed', *European Law Review* 29: 289–322.

Lenaerts, K. and Verhoeven, A. (2000) 'Towards a Legal Framework for Executive Rule-Making in the EU? The Contribution of the New Comitology Decision', *Common Market Law Review* 37: 645–86.

Litan, R. (1985) 'Evaluating and Controlling the Risks of Financial Product Deregulation', *Yale Journal on Regulation* 3: 1–52.

Litan, R. and Santomero, A. (eds) (1999) *Brookings–Wharton Papers on Financial Services*, Washington, DC: Brookings Institution.

Llewellyn, D.T. (1986) *Regulation and Supervision of Financial Institutions*, London: Chartered Institute of Bankers.

—— (1999a) *The New Economics of Banking*, Amsterdam: Société Universitaire Européenne de Recherches Financiers.

—— (1999b) 'The Economic Rationale for Financial Regulation', *FSA Occasional Papers in Financial Regulation*, April.

—— (1999c) 'The Institutional Structure of Regulatory Agencies', in Central Banking Publications, *How Countries Supervise their Bank, Insurers and Securities Markets*, London: Central Banking Publications.

—— (2001) 'A Regulatory Regime for Financial Stability', *Österreichische Nationalbank Working Paper* 41.

—— (2006) 'Globalisation and Convergence on the Shareholder Value Model in European Banking', *BIS Papers* 32.

Lomnicka, E. (2000) 'The Home Country Control Principle in the Financial Services Directives and the Case Law', *European Business Law Review* 8: 324–36.

Louis, J.-V. (1995) *Banking Supervision in the European Community. Institutional Aspects, Etudes Européennes*, Brussels: Editions de l'Université de Bruxelles.

—— (1998) 'A Legal and Institutional Approach for Building a Monetary Union', *Common Market Law Review* 35: 33–76.

—— (2002) 'Mondialisation et contrôle prudentiel. Centralisation ou décentralisation?' *Revue Internationale de Droit Economique* 2: 529.

—— (2004) 'The Economic and Monetary Union: Law and Institutions', *Common Market Law Review* 41: 575–608.

—— (2008) 'Parallélisme des compétences et compétences explicites', in C. Franck and G. Duchenne (eds) *L'action extérieure de l'Union européenne Rôle global, dimensions matérielles, aspects juridiques, valeurs. Actes de la XIe Chaire AGC – Glaverbel d'études européennes,* Brussels: Bruylant, pp. 255–82.

—— (2009) *L'Union européenne et sa monnaie, Commentaire J. Mégret,* Brussels: Editions de l'Université de Bruxelles, third edition.

Louis, J.-V. and Ronse, T. (2005) *L'ordre juridique de l'Union européenne, Dossier de droit européen no. 13,* Paris: Bruylant.

Lucas, R. (1976) 'Econometric Policy Evaluation: A Critique', *Carnegie-Rochester Conference Series on Public Policy* 1: 19–46.

MacDonald, R. (1988) *Consolidated Supervision of Banks,* Bank of England, *Handbooks in Central Banking* 15.

McCauley, R.N., Ruud, J.S. and Wooldridge, P.D. (2002) 'Globalising International Banking', *BIS Quarterly Review* (March): 41–51.

McCoy, P.A. (2008) 'The Moral Hazard Implications of Deposit Insurance: Theory and Evidence', in International Monetary Fund (ed.), *Current Developments in Monetary and Financial Law,* 5. Washington, DC: International Monetary Fund.

Macey, J.R. (2000) 'The "Demand" for International Regulatory Cooperation: A Public-Choice Perspective', in G.A. Berman, B. Herdegen and P. Lindseth (eds) *Transatlantic Regulatory Cooperation,* Oxford: Oxford University Press.

—— (2003) 'Regulatory Globalization as a Response to Regulatory Competition', *Emory Law Review* 52: 1353.

Macey, J.R., Miller, G.P. and Carnel, R.S. (2001) *Banking Law and Regulation,* New York: Aspen Law & Business, third edition.

McLean, H. (1988) 'Negligent Regulatory Authorities and the Duty of Care', *Oxford Journal of Legal Studies* 8(3): 442–56.

Majone, G. (1996) *Regulating Europe,* London: Routledge.

Majone, G. and Everson, M. (2001) 'Institutional Reform: Independent Agencies, Oversight, Coordination and Procedural Control', in O. De Schutter, N. Lebessis and J. Paterson (eds) *Governance in the European Union, Cahiers of the Forward Studies Unit,* Brussels: European Commission.

Malatesta, A. (2003) *La Banca Centrale Europea. Gli aspetti istituzionali della banca centrale della Comunità europea,* Milano: Giuffrè Editore.

Marotta, G. (2003) 'L'assetto istituzionale della regolamentatzione prudenziale. Uno o più regolatori?', Università di Modena e Reggio Emilia, Dipartimento di Economia Politica, *Materiali di discusisione* 443.

Mayes, D.G, Halme, L. and Liuksila, A. (2001) *Improving Banking Supervision,* Basingstoke (UK): Palgrave Macmillan.

Merusi, F. (2004) 'Authorisation for the Carrying On of the Business of Credit Institutions', *European Business Law Review* 15(3): 381–93.

Metzger, P. (1995) *GATS and the European Union: Free Trade in Banking?* Brussels: European University Press.

Michel, V. (2003) '2004: le défi de la répartition des compétences', *Cahiers de Droit Européen* 1–2: 17–86.

Moloney, N. (2003) 'New Frontiers in EC Capital Markets Law: From Market Construction to Market Regulation', *Common Market Law Review* 40(4): 809–43.

Molyneux, P. and Altunbas, Y. (1997) 'Bank Ownership and Efficiency', *Research Paper* 17, Bangor: University College of North Wales.

Montanaro, E., Scala, C. and Tonveronachi, M. (2001) 'The Unified European Banking Market and the Convergence of National Banking Sectors', in E. Gardener and P. Versluijs (eds) *Bank Strategies and Challenges in the New Europe,* Basingstoke (UK): Palgrave Macmillan.

Moreira de Sousa, S. and Heusel, W. (eds) (2004) *Enforcing Community Law from Francovich to Köbler: Twelve Years of the State Liability Principle,* Köln: Bundesanzeiger.

Morgan, D.P. (1997) 'Judging the Risk of Banks: What Makes Banks Opaque?', *Federal Reserve Bank of New York Mimeograph* (23 July).

Musgrave, R. (1959) *The Theory of Public Finance,* New York: McGraw-Hill.

Mwenda, K.K. and Fleming, A. (2001) 'International Developments in the Organisational Structure of Financial Services Supervision', *Journal of International Banking Law* 12–13: 291.

Myers, S.C. and Rajan, R.G. (1995) 'The Paradox of Liquidity', *NBER Working Paper* 5143.

Nieto, M.J. and Peñalosa, J.M. (2004) 'The European Architecture of Regulation, Supervision and Financial Stability: A Central Bank Perspective', *Journal of International Banking Regulation* 5(3): 228–42.

Norton, J.J. (1995) *Devising International Bank Supervisory Standards,* The Hague: Kluwer Law International.

O'Connor, A. and Santos-Arteaga, F. J. (2008) 'Information and Intertemporal Decision Processes in Banking: The Run on Northern Rock (December 9, 2008)', *International Journal of Applied Decision Sciences* 1(4): 359.

OECD (1990) *Liberalisation of Capital Movements and Financial Services in the OECD,* Paris: OECD.

Ogus, A. (1994) *Regulation. Legal Form and Economic Theory,* Oxford: Clarendon Press.

O'Keeffe, D. and Bavasso, A. (eds) (2000) *Judicial Review in European Union Law: Liber Amicorum in Honour of Lord Slynn of Hadley,* The Hague: Kluwer Law International.

O'Keeffe, D. and Twomey, P.M. (eds) (1994) *Legal issues of the Maastricht Treaty,* London: Chancery.

Oosterloo, S. and Schoenmaker, D. (2004) 'A Lead Supervisor Model for Europe', *The Financial Regulator* 9(3): 34–42.

Ortino, S. (2004) 'International and Cross-Border Co-operation among Banking Supervisors: The Role of the European Central Bank', *European Business Law Review* 15(4): 715–34.

Padoa-Schioppa, T. (1999) 'EMU and Banking Supervision', speech at the London School of Economics (24 February).

—— (2000) 'Is a Euroland Banking System Emerging?' lecture given at Société Universitaire Européenne de Recherches Financières (SUERF), Vienna (29 April).

—— (2002a) 'Securities and Banking: Bridges and Walls', lecture at the London School of Economics, London (21 January).

—— (2002b) 'Competition, Co-operation, Public Action: Three Necessary Drivers for European Financial Integration', speech at the Workshop of the ECB-CFS Research Network on Capital Markets and Financial Integration in Europe, Frankfurt am Main (29 April).

—— (2004a) *Regulating Finance: Balancing Freedom and Risk,* Oxford: Oxford University Press.

—— (2004b) 'The Evolving European Financial Landscape: Integration and Regulation', speech at the Colloquium organised by Groupe Caisse des Dépots/KfW, Berlin (22 March).

Panourgias, L.E. (2006) *Banking Regulation and World Trade Law. GATS, EU and 'Prudential' Institution Building*, Oxford: Hart Publishing.

Paroush, J. (1988) 'The Domino Effect and Supervision of the Banking System', *Journal of Finance* 43: 1207–18.

Pastre, O. (2001) 'Industrie Bancaire: Les espoirs des Davids face aux Goliaths', *Revue d'Economie Financière* 61: 53–62.

Pecchioli, R.M. (1987) *Prudential Supervision in Banking*, Paris: OECD.

Pelkmans, J. (1987) 'The New Approach to Technical Harmonization and Standardization', *Journal of Common Market Studies* 33: 252–3.

Persaud, A. (2000) 'Sending the Herd off the Cliff Edge: The Dangerous Interaction between Modern Risk Management Practices and Investor Behaviour', Institute of International Finance, Washington.

—— (2003) 'The Political Economy of Basel II', *European Business Law Review* 14(3): 219–25.

—— (2008) 'Regulation, Valuation and Systemic Liquidity', paper presented at the Centre for International Governance Innovation Workshop 'Crisis and Response; Whither International Financial Regulation?', 26–27 September.

Plihon, D. (2000) 'Quelle surveillance prudentielle pour l'industrie de services financiers?', *Revue d'économie financière* 60: 17–32.

Posner, R.A. (2009) *A Failure of Capitalism: The Crisis of '08 and the Descent Into Depression*, Cambridge, MA: Harvard University Press.

Postlewaite, A. and Vives, X. (1987) 'Bank Runs as an Equilibrium Phenomenon', *Journal of Political Economy* 95(3): 485–91.

Prechal, S. (2005) *Directives in EC Law*, Oxford: Oxford University Press, second edition.

PricewaterhouseCoopers (2004) *Study on the Financial and Macroeconomic Consequences of the Draft Proposed New Capital Requirements for Banks and Investment Firms in the EU*, MARKT/2003/02/F (8 April).

Proctor, C. (2005) 'Regulatory Liability for Bank Failures. The *Peter Paul* Case', *Euredia* 1: 73–111.

Quintyn, M., Huepkes, E. and Taylor, M. (2005) 'The Accountability of Financial Sector Supervisors: Principles and Practice', *IMF Working Paper* 51.

Randazzo, V. (2005) 'Annotation to Case C-257/01', *Common Market Law Review* 42(6): 155–69.

Reig, C.P (1997) 'States and Markets: Regulatory Competition and the Public Law of Banks', unpublished thesis, European University Institute.

Robinson, W.I. (2004) *A Theory of Global Capitalism: Production, Class, and State in a Transnational World*, Baltimore: Johns Hopkins University Press.

Rochet, J.-C. and Tirole, J. (1996) 'Interbank Lending and Systematic Risk', *Journal of Money, Credit and Banking*, 28(4): 733–62.

Roeges, L. (2003) 'L'affaire *Peter Paul*, une affaire à suivre', *Euredia* 1: 5–9.

Rosas, A. (1998) 'Mixed Union – Mixed Agreements', in Martti Koskenniemi (ed.) *International Law Aspects of the European Union*, The Hague: Kluwer Law International.

Rose, A. K. (2000) 'One Money, One Market: The Effect of Common Currencies on Trade', *Economic Policy* 15(30): 7–46.

Rossi, F. (2003) 'Tort Liability of Financial Regulators. A Comparative Study of Italian and English Law in a European Context', *European Business Law Review* 14(6): 743–71.

Rubenfeld, J. (2003) 'The Two World Orders', *Wilson Quarterly*, autumn: 22–36.

Rubin, L. (1991) 'Beyond Public Choice: Comprehensive Rationality in the Writing and Reading of Statutes', *NYU Law Review* 66(1): 1–64.

Sappideen, R. (2004) 'The Regulation of Credit, Market and Operational Risk Management Under the Basel Accords', *Journal of Business Law* 1: 59–93.

Scelle, G. (1956) 'Le phénomène juridique du dédoublement fonctionnel', in W. Schatzel and H.-J. Schlochauer (eds) *Rechtsfragen der Internationalen Organisationen, Festschrift für Hans Wehberg zu seinem 70 Geburtstag*, Frankfurt am Main: Klostermann.

Scharpf, F.W. (1999) *Governing in Europe. Effective or Democratic?* Oxford: Oxford University Press.

Schatzel, W. and Schlochauer, H.-J. (eds) (1956) *Rechtsfragen der Internationalen Organisationen, Festschrift für Hans Wehberg zu seinem 70 Geburtstag*, Frankfurt am Main: Klostermann.

Scheller, H.K. (2004) *The European Central Bank. History, Role and Functions*, Frankfurt: ECB.

Schermers, H.G. and Blokker, N.M. (1995) *International Institutional Law: Unity Within Diversity*, The Hague: Martinus Nijhoff.

Schilder, A. (2001) 'Banking in the New Economy: A Supervisory Perspective', *BIS Review* 16.

Schinasi, G. (2006) *Safeguarding Financial Stability. Theory and Practice*, Washington, DC: IMF.

Schmidt, R. (ed.) (1995) *Öffentliches Wirtschaftsrecht, Teil I*, Berlin: Springer-Verlag.

Schoenmaker, D. and Goodhart, C. (1993) 'Institutional Separation between Supervisory and Monetary Agencies', *LSE Financial Markets Group, Special Paper* 52.

Schoenmaker, D. and Oosterloo, S. (2005) 'Financial Supervision in an Integrating Europe: Measuring Cross-Border Externalities', *International Finance* 8(1): 1–27.

—— (2006) 'Financial Supervision in Europe: Do We Need a New Architecture?' *ELEC, Cahier Comte Boël* 12.

Schwark, E. (1981) 'Die Liberalisierung der nationalen Banktätigkeit und die Schaffung eines einheitlichen Bankenaufsichtsrechts', in U. Blaurock (ed.) *Das Bankwesen im Gemeinsamen Mark*t, Baden-Baden: Nomos Verlagsgesellschaft.

Scott, H.S. (2006) *International Finance. Transactions, Policy and Regulation*, New York: Foundation Press.

Scott, J. and Trubek, D.M. (2002) 'Mind the Gap: Law and the New Approaches to Governance in the European Union', *European Law Journal* 8(1): 1–18.

Shaw, J. (2003) 'Flexibility in a "Reorganised" and "Simplified" Treaty', *Common Market Law Review* 40.

Shaw, R. (2001) 'The Bank is Dead, Long Live the Bank', in E. Gardener and P.C. Versluijs (eds) *Bank Strategies and Challenges in the New Europe*, Basingstoke (UK): Palgrave Macmillan.

Shull, B. and Hanweck, G.A. (2001) *Bank Mergers in a Deregulated Environment*, Westport, CT: Quorum Books.

Simon, H. (1997 [1982]) 'Models of Bounded Rationality', reprinted in H. Simon, *Simon's Papers on Economics*, Volume 3, Cambridge, MA: MIT Press.

Singh, D. (2002) 'Enforcement Methods and Sanctions in Banking Regulation and Supervision', *International and Comparative Corporate Law Journal* 4(4): 307–44.

—— (2004) 'Accountability at Law of Regulatory Decision', *Journal of International Banking Regulation*, 5(3): 198–200.

Smits, R. (1995) 'The Community and International Contexts', in J.-V. Louis (ed.) *Banking Supervision in the European Community. Institutional Aspects*, Brussels: Editions de l'Université de Bruxelles.

—— (1997) *The European Central Bank. Institutional Aspects*, The Hague: Kluwer Law International.

—— (2005) 'The Role of the ESCB in Banking Supervision', in European Central Bank (ed.) *Legal Aspects of the European System of Central Banks: Liber Amicorum Paolo Zamboni Garavelli*, Frankfurt: European Central Bank, pp. 199–212.

Smits, R. and Luberti, R. (1999) 'Supervisory Liability: An Introduction to Several Legal Systems and a Case Study', in M. Giovanoli (ed.) *International Bank Insolvencies*, The Hague: Kluwer Law International.

Snyder, F. (1993) 'The Effectiveness of European Community Law: Institutions, Processes, Tools and Techniques', *Common Market Law Review* 56: 19–54.

Sousi, B. (2004) 'La Procédure Lamfalussy à l'épreuve de la Directive concernant les marchés d'instruments financiers', *Euredia* 2: 209–21.

Sousi-Roubi, B. (1995) *Droit bancaire européen*, Paris: Dalloz.

Steil, B. (ed.) (1994) *International Financial Market Regulation*, Chichester: John Wiley & Sons.

—— (1998) *Regional Financial Market Integration: Learning from the European Experience*, London: Royal Institute of International Affairs.

Stigler, G.J. (1978) 'The Theory of Economic Regulation', *Bell Journal of Economics and Management Science* 2(1): 3–21.

Stiglitz, J.E. (1972) 'Some Aspects of the Pure Theory of Corporate Finance: Bankruptcies and Takeovers', *Bell Journal of Economics and Management Science* 3: 458–82.

Summer, M. (2002) 'Banking Regulation and Systemic Risk', *Working Paper Österreichische Nationalbank* 57.

Tarbert, H.P. (2000) 'Are International Capital Adequacy Rules Adequate? The Basle Accord and Beyond', *University of Pennsylvania Law Review* 148: 1771–849.

Taylor, M. (1995) '"Twin Peaks": A Regulatory Structure for the New Century', pamphlet, Committee for the Study of Financial Innovation (CSFI), London (December).

Teixeira, P.G. and Schinasi, G.J. (2006) 'The Lender of Last Resort in the European Single Financial Market,' *IMF Working Papers* 127.

Tett, G. (2009) 'Lost through Destructive Creation', *Financial Times* (10 March).

Thomadakis, S.B. (2003) 'Fifteen Regulators for a Single Capital Market: The Project of Regulatory Harmonisation in Europe', in M. Andenas and Y. Avgerinos (eds) *Financial Markets in Europe. Towards a Single Regulator?* The Hague: Kluwer Law International.

Timmermans, C. (2000) 'Organising Joint Participation of EC and Member States', in A. Dashwood and C. Hillion (eds) *The General Law of EC External Relations*, London: Sweet & Maxwell.

Tison, M. (1997) 'What is General Good in EU Financial Services Law?' *Legal Issues of European Integration* 2: 1–48.

—— (2002) 'Unravelling the General Good Exception: The Case of Financial Services', in M. Andenas and W.-H. Roth (eds) *Services and Free Movement in EU Law*, Oxford: Oxford University Press.

—— (2003) 'Challenging the Prudential Supervisor: Liability versus (Regulatory) Immunity', *Financial Law Institute Working Paper* 4.

—— (2005) 'Do Not Attack the Watchdog! Banking Supervisors' Liability after *Peter Paul*', *Common Market Law Review* 42: 639–75.

Toth, A. (1994) 'A Legal Analysis of Subsidiarity', in D. O'Keeffe and P.M. Twomey (eds) *Legal Issues of the Maastricht Treaty*, London: Chancery.

Tridimas, T. (2000) 'Enforcing Community Rights in National Courts: Some Recent Developments', in D. O'Keeffe and A. Bavasso (eds) *Judicial Review in European Union Law, Liber Amicorum in Honour of Lord Slynn of Hadley*, The Hague: Kluwer Law International.

—— (2002) 'Liability for Breach of Community Law: Growing Up and Mellowing Down?', in D. Fairgrieve, M. Andenas and J. Bell (eds) (2002) *Tort Liability of Public Authorities in Comparative Perspective*, London: BIICL.

Truchot, L. (2000) 'Comment on Article 47 EC Treaty', in P. Léger (ed.) *Commentaire article par article des Traités UE et CE*, Bâsle: Hebling & Lichtenhahn.

Turner Review (2009) available at www.fsa.gov.uk/Pages/Library/Corporate/turner/index.shtml.

United Nations (1999) *Globalization with a Human Face*, the Human Development Report, Oxford: United Nations Development Programme and Oxford University Press; available at http://hdr.undp.org/reports/global/1999/en/pdf/hdr_1999_full.pdf.

Usher, J.A. (1994) *The Law of Money and Financial Services in the European Community*, Oxford: Clarendon Press.

—— (2000) *The Law of Money and Financial Services in the EC*, Oxford: Oxford University Press.

—— (2005) 'The Reception of General Principles of Community Law in the United Kingdom', *European Business Law Review* 16(3): 504–7.

Van Gerven, W. (1990) 'The Second Banking Directive and the Case Law of the Court of Justice', *Yearbook of European Law* 10: 57–70.

—— (2000) 'Of Rights, Remedies and Procedures', *Common Market Law Review* 37: 501–36.

—— (2004a) 'Harmonisation of Private Law: Do We Need It?', *Common Market Law Review* 41: 505–32.

—— (2004b) 'The Emergence of a Common European Tort Law: The EU Contribution – One Among Others', in S. Moreira de Sousa and W. Heusel (eds) *Enforcing Community Law from Francovich to Köbler: Twelve Years of the State Liability Principle*, Köln: Bundesanzeiger.

Vander Vennet, R. (1998) 'Convergence and the Growth Pattern of OECD Bank Markets', *Universiteit Gent Working Paper* 46.

Vives, X. (1991) 'Banking Competition and European Integration', in M. Giovannini and C. Mayer (eds) *European Financial Integration*, Cambridge: Cambridge University Press.

—— (2000) 'Banking Supervision in the European Monetary Union', paper presented at the Finance and Consumption Conference 'Financial Supervision of Banks and Specialised Banks in the EU', European University institute (December).

Von Bogdandy, A. and Bast, J. (2002) 'The European Union's Vertical Order of Competences: The Current Law and Proposals for its Reform', *Common Market Law Review* 39: 227–68.

Walker, G. (2001) 'The New Capital Accord', *Financial Regulation International* 4(4).

Wallman, S. (1999) 'Information Technology Revolution and its Impact on Regulation and Regulatory Structure', in R. Litan and A. Santomero (eds) *Brookings-Wharton Papers on Financial Services*, Washington, DC: Brookings Institution.

Ward, J. (2002) 'The Supervisory Approach: A Critique', *Cambridge Endowment for Research in Finance, Working Paper* 2.

Weiler, J. (1991) 'The Transformation of Europe', *Yale Law Journal* 100: 2245–6.

White, L.J. (2002) 'Bank Regulation in the United States: Understanding the Lessons of the 1980s and 1990s', *Japan and the Word Economy* 14: 137–54.

Williamson, O.E. (1975) *Markets and Hierarchies: Analysis and Antitrust Implications*, New York: Free Press.

—— (1985) *The Economic Institutions of Capitalism*, New York: Free Press.

Williamson, S. (1987) 'Recent Developments in Modelling Financial Intermediation', *Quarterly Review, Federal Reserve Bank of Minneapolis* 11 (Summer): 19–29.

World Bank (2000) *Entering the 21st Century'. World Development Report 1999/2000*, Oxford: Oxford University Press.

Wörner, I. (2000), *Europäische Bankenregulierung im Spannungsverhältnis zwischen Regulierungswettbewerb und Harmonisierungsbemühungen*, Baden-Baden: Nomos.

Wymeersch, E (2005) 'The Future of Financial Regulation and Supervision in Europe', *Common Market Law Review* 42: 987–1010.

—— (2006) 'Delegation as an Instrument for Financial Supervision' (12 December), available at http://ssrn.com/abstract=952952.

—— (2007) 'The Structure of Financial Supervision in Europe. About Single, Twin Peaks and Multiple Financial Supervisors', *European Business Organization Law Review* 8(2): 237–306.

Xanthaki, H. (2001) 'The Problem of Quality in EU Legislation: What on Earth is Really Wrong?' *Common Market Law Review* 38: 651–76.

Yataganas, X.A. (2001) 'Delegation of Regulatory Authority in the European Union. The Relevance of the American Model of Independent Agencies', *Jean Monnet Working Paper* 3.

Zilioli, C. and Selmayr, M. (2001) *The Law of the European Central Bank*, Oxford: Hart Publishing.

—— (2006) 'Recent Developments in the Law of the European Central Bank', in P. Eeckhout, T. Tridimas and G. de Búrca (eds) *Yearbook of European Law 25*, Oxford: Oxford University Press, pp. 1–90.

Tables of legislation and documents

Legislation

Treaties and protocols

Treaty establishing the European Community (Nice consolidated version) OJ C 325, 24.12.2002, [EC Treaty].

Single European Act, OJ L 169, 1987 [SEA].

Treaty on European Union (Nice consolidated version) OJ C 325, 24.12.2002 [EU Treaty].

Protocol No. 18 on the Statute of the European System of Central Banks and the European Central Bank [ESCB Statute] OJ C 325, 24.12.2002.

Protocol No. 22 on Denmark OJ C 325, 24.12.2002 (Consolidated version).

Protocol No. 26 on certain provisions relating to Denmark (1992) OJ C 325, 24.12.2002 (Consolidated version).

European Convention, CONV 723/03 from 14 May 2003.

Treaty establishing a Constitution for Europe – FINAL ACT, OJ C 310, 16.12.2004.

Treaty of Lisbon amending the Treaty on European Union and the Treaty establishing the European Community, signed at Lisbon, 13 December 2007, OJ C 306 17.12.2007 [Treaty of Lisbon].

Consolidated versions of the Treaty on European Union and the Treaty on the Functioning of the European Union, OJ C 115 9.05.2008 [TEU consolidated and TFEU].

Consolidated versions of the Treaty on European Union and the Treaty on the Functioning of the European Union – Protocols – Protocol No. 1 on the role of national Parliaments in the European Union OJ C 115 9.05.2008.

Consolidated versions of the Treaty on European Union and the Treaty on the Functioning of the European Union – Protocols – Protocol No. 2 on the application of the principles of subsidiarity and proportionality OJ C 115 9.05.2008.

Regulations

Council Regulation (EC) 3603/93 of 13 December 1993 specifying definitions for the application of the prohibitions referred to in Articles 104 and 104b (1) of the Treaty OJ L 332, 31.12.1993.

Council Regulation (EC) 1103/97 of 17 June 1997 on certain provisions relating to the introduction of the euro OJ L 162, 19.06.1997.

Council Regulation (EC) 2157/2001 of 8 October 2001 on the Statute for a European company (SE), OJ L 294, 10.11.2001.

EP and Council Regulation (EC) 1606/2002 of 19 July 2002 on the application of international accounting standards, OJ L 243, 11.09.2002.

Council Regulation (EC) 58/2003 of 19 December 2002 laying down the statute for executive agencies to be entrusted with certain tasks in the management of Community programmes, OJ L11 16.11.2003.

Commission Regulation (EC) 2273/2003 of 22 December 2003 implementing Directive 2003/6/EC of the European Parliament and of the Council as regards exemptions for buy-back programmes and stabilisation of financial instruments (Text with EEA relevance) OJ L 336, 23.12.2003.

Council Regulation (EC) 139/2004 of 20 January 2004 on the control of concentrations between undertakings OJ L 024, 29.01.2004. [the EC Merger Regulation]

EP and Council Regulation (EC) 1060/2009 of 16 September 2009 on credit rating agencies, OJ L 350, 17.11.2009.

Proposal for an EP and Council Regulation on Community macro prudential oversight of the financial system and establishing a European Systemic Risk Board, Brussels, 23.9.2009, COM (2009) 499 final [ESRB regulation proposal].

Proposal for an EP and Council Regulation establishing a European Banking Authority (EBA), Brussels, 23.9.2009, COM (2009) 501 final [EBA regulation proposal].

Proposal for an EP and Council Regulation establishing a European Insurance and Occupational Pensions Authority (EIOPA), Brussels, 23.9.2009, COM (2009) 502 final [EIOPA regulation proposal].

Proposal for an EP and Council Regulation establishing a European Securities and Markets Authority (ESMA), Brussels, 23.9.2009, COM (2009) 503 final [ESMA regulation proposal].

Directives

Council Directive 72/156/EEC of 21 March 1972 on regulating international capital flows and neutralising their undesirable effects on domestic liquidity, OJ L 091, 18.04.1972.

Council Directive 73/183/EEC on the abolition of restrictions on freedom of establishment and freedom to provide services in respect to self-employed activities of banks and other financial institutions of 28 June 1973, OJ L 194/1, 16.07.1973.

First Council Directive 77/780/EEC of 12 December 1977 on the coordination of laws, regulations and administrative provisions relating to the taking up and pursuit of the business of credit institutions, OJ L 322, 17.12.1977 [First Banking Directive, FBD].

Council Directive 78/660/EEC of 25.07.1978 concerning the annual accounts of certain forms of companies, OJ L222 of 14.08.1978.

Council Directive 83/350/EEC of 13 June 1983 on the supervision of credit institutions on a consolidated basis OJ L 193 of 18.07.1983.

Seventh Council Directive 83/349/EEC of 13 June 1983 based on the Article 54 (3) (g) of the Treaty on consolidated accounts OJ L 193, 18.07.1983.

Council Directive 86/635/EEC of 8 December 1986 on the annual accounts and consolidated accounts of banks and other financial institutions, OJ L372, 31.12.1986.

Council Directive 88/361/EEC of 24 June 1988 for the implementation of article 67 of the Treaty, OJ L 178, 08.07.1988.

Council Directive 89/299/CEE of 17 April 1989 concerning the own funds of credit institutions, OJ L124 of 5.05.1989. [Own Funds Directive]

Second Council Directive 89/646/EEC of 15 December 1989 on the coordination of laws, regulations and administrative provisions relating to the taking up and pursuit of the business of credit institutions, OJ L 386, 30.12.1989 [Second Banking Directive, SBD].

Council Directive 89/647/EEC of 18 December 1989 on a solvency ratio for credit institutions, OJ L 386 of 30.12.1989 [Solvency Ratio Directive].

Council Directive 91/633/EEC of 3 December 1991 implementing Directive 89/299/EEC on the own funds of credit institutions, OJ L 339, 11.12.1991.

Council Directive 92/30/EEC on the supervision of credit institutions on a consolidated basis, OJ L110 29.04.1992 [Directive on consolidated supervision].

Council Directive 92/121/EEC of 21 December 1992 on the monitoring and control of large exposures of credit institutions, OJ L 029, 05.02.1993 [Large Exposures Directive].

Council Directive 93/6/EEC of 15 March 1993 on the capital adequacy of investments firms and credit institutions OJ L 141, 11.06.1993 [Capital Adequacy Directive, CAD].

Council Directive 93/22/EEC of 10 May 1993 on investment services in the securities field OJ L 141, 11.06.1993 [Investment Services Directive].

EP and Council Directive 94/19/EC of 30 May 1994 on deposit-guarantee schemes, OJ L 135, 31.05.1994 [Deposit Guarantee Schemes].

EP and Council Directive 95/26/EC of 29 June 1995 amending Directives 77/780/EEC and 89/646/EEC in the field of credit institutions, Directives 73/239/EEC and 92/49/EEC in the field of non-life insurance, Directives 79/267/EEC and 92/96/EEC in the field of life assurance, Directive 93/22/EEC in the field of investment firms and Directive 85/611/EEC in the field of undertakings for collective investment in transferable securities, with a view to reinforcing prudential supervision, OJ L168, 18.07.1995 [UCITS].

EP and Council Directive 98/31/EC of 22 June 1998 amending Council Directive 93/6/EEC on the capital adequacy of investment firms and credit institutions Official Journal L 204, 21.07.1998.

EP and Council Directive 98/33/EC of 22 June 1998 amending Article 12 of Council Directive 77/780/EEC on the taking up and pursuit of the business of credit institutions, Articles 2, 5, 6, 7, 8 of and Annexes II and III to Council Directive 89/647/EEC on a solvency ratio for credit institutions and Article 2 of and Annex II to Council Directive 93/6/EEC on the capital adequacy of investment firms and credit institutions, OJ L 204, 21.07.1998.

EP and Council Directive 2000/12/EC of 20 March 2000 relating to the taking up and pursuit of the business of credit institutions, OJ L 126, 26.05.2000 [Codified Banking Directive].

EP and Council Directive 2000/28/EC of 18 September 2000 amending Directive 2000/12/EC relating to the taking up and pursuit of the business of credit institutions, OJ L 275, 27.10.2000.

EP and Council Directive 2000/46/EC of 18 September 2000 on the taking-up, pursuit and prudential supervision of the business of electronic money institutions, OJ L275, 27.10.2000.

EP and Council Directive 2001/65/EC of 27.09.2001 amending Directives 78/660/EEC, 83/349/EEC and 86/635/EEC as regards the valuation rules for the annual and consolidated accounts of certain types of companies as well as of banks and other financial institutions, OJ L283, 27.10.2001.

EP and Council Directive 2002/87/EC of 16 December 2002 on the supplementary supervision of credit institutions, insurance undertakings and investment firms in a financial conglomerate and amending Council Directives 73/239/EEC, 79/267/EEC, 92/49/EEC, 92/96/EEC, 93/6/EEC, 93/22/EEC, 98/78/EC and 2000/12/EC Official Journal L 35 of 11.02.2002.

Commission Directive 2003/124/EC of 22 December 2003 implementing Directive 2003/6/EC of the European Parliament and of the Council as regards the definition and public disclosure of inside information and the definition of market manipulation (Text with EEA relevance) OJ L 339, 24.12.2003.

Commission Directive 2003/125/EC of 22 December 2003 implementing Directive 2003/6/EC of the European Parliament and of the Council as regards the fair presentation of investment recommendations and the disclosure of conflicts of interest (Text with EEA relevance) OJ L 339, 24.12.2003.

EP and Council Directive 2003/6/EC of 28 January 2003 on insider dealing and market manipulation (market abuse), OJ L 096, 12.04.2003.

EP and Council Directive 2003/51/EC of 18 June 2003 amending Directives 78/660/EEC, 83/349/EEC, 86/635/EEC and 91/674/EEC on the annual and consolidated accounts of certain types of companies, banks and other financial institutions and insurance undertakings, OJ L178, 17.07.2003.

EP and Council Directive 2004/39/EC of 21 April 2004 on markets in financial instruments amending Council Directives 85/611/EEC and 93/6/EEC and Directive 2000/12/EC of the European Parliament and of the Council and repealing Council Directive 93/22/EEC OJ L 145, 30.04.2004 [MiFID].

EP and Council Directive 2005/1/EC of 9 March 2005 amending Council Directives 73/239/EEC, 85/611/EEC, 91/675/EEC, 92/49/EEC and 93/6/EEC and Directives 94/19/EC, 98/78/EC, 2000/12/EC, 2001/34/EC, 2002/83/EC and 2002/87/EC in order to establish a new organisational structure for financial services committees, OJ L 079, 24.03.2005.

EP and Council Directive 2006/43/EC of 17 May 2006 on statutory audits of annual accounts and consolidated accounts, amending Council. Directives 78/660/EEC and 83/349/EEC and repealing Council Directive 84/253/EEC (Text with EEA relevance) OJ L 157, 9.6.2006.

EP and Council Directive 2006/46/EC of the European Parliament and of the Council of 14 June 2006 amending Council Directives 78/660/EEC on the annual accounts of certain types of companies, 83/349/EEC on consolidated accounts, 86/635/EEC on the annual accounts and consolidated accounts of banks and other financial institutions and 91/674/EEC on the annual accounts and consolidated accounts of insurance undertakings, OJ L 224, 16.8.2006.

EP and Council Directive 2006/48/EC of 14 June 2006 relating to the taking up and pursuit of the business of credit institutions (recast), OJ L 177, 30.06.2006 [Capital Requirements Directive, CRD].

EP and Council Directive 2006/49/EC of 14 June 2006 on the capital adequacy of investment firms and credit institutions (recast) of 14 June 2006, OJ L 177, 30.06.2006 [recast CAD].

Commission Directive 2007/18/EC of 27 March 2007 amending Directive 2006/48/EC of the European Parliament and of the Council as regards the exclusion or inclusion of certain institutions from its scope of application and the treatment of exposures to multilateral development banks, OJ L 87, 28.3.2007.

EP and Council Directive 2007/44/EC of 5 September 2007 amending Council Directive 92/49/EEC and Directives 2002/83/EC, 2004/39/EC, 2005/68/EC and 2006/48/EC as regards procedural rules and evaluation criteria for the prudential assessment of acquisitions and increase of holdings in the financial sector, OJ L 247, 21.9.2007.

EP and Council Directive 2008/24/EC of 11 March 2008 amending Directive 2006/48/EC relating to the taking up and pursuit of the business of credit institutions, as regards the implementing powers conferred on the Commission (Text with EEA relevance), OJ L 81, 20.3.2008.

EP and Council Directive 2009/14/EC of 11 March 2009 amending Directive 94/19/EC on deposit-guarantee schemes as regards the coverage level and the payout delay, OJ L 68, 13.3.2009.

Commission Directive 2009/27/EC amending certain annexes to Directive 2006/49/EC of the European Parliament and of the Council as regards technical provisions concerning risk management, OJ L 94, 8.4.2009.

Commission Directive 2009/83/EC of 27 July 2009 amending certain annexes to Directive 2006/48/EC of the European Parliament and the Council as regards technical provisions concerning risk management, OJ L 196, 28.7.2009.

EP and Council Directive 2009/111/EC of 16 September 2009 amending Directives 2006/48/EC, 2006/49/EC and 2007/64/EC as regards banks affiliated to central institutions, certain own funds items, large exposures, supervisory arrangements and crisis management OJ L 302, 17.11.2009 [CRD 2].

Proposal for a Directive of the European Parliament and of the Council amending Directives 2006/48/EC and 2006/49/EC as regards capital requirements for the trading book and for re-securitisations and the supervisory review of remuneration policies SEC(2009) 974 final SEC(2009) 975 final; 13.07.2009 [CRD 3].

Proposal for EP and Council Directive amending Directives 1998/26/EC, 2002/87/EC, 2003/6/EC, 2003/41/EC, 2003/71/EC, 2004/39/EC, 2004/109/EC, 2005/60/EC, 2006/48/EC, 2006/49/EC, and 2009/65/EC in respect of the powers of the European Banking Authority, the European Insurance and Occupational Pensions Authority and the European Securities and Markets Authority, Brussels, 26.10.2009, COM (2009) 576 final [Omnibus Directive poposal].

Decisions

Council Decision 87/373/EEC of 13 July 1987 laying down the procedures for the exercise of implementing powers conferred on the Commission, OJ L 197, 18.07.1987.

Council Decision 98/415/EC of 29 June 1998 on the Consultation of the European Central Bank by national authorities regarding draft legislative provisions, OJ L 189, 3.7.1998.

Council Decision 98/743/EC of 21 December 1998 on the detailed provisions concerning the composition of the Economic and Financial Committee, OJ L 358, 31.12.1998.

Council Decision 99/8/EC of 31 December 1998 adopting the statutes of the Economic and Financial Committee, OJ L 5 of 09.01.1999, as amended by Council

Decision 2003/476/EC of 18 June 2003 adopting the statutes of the Economic and Financial Committee, OJ L 158, 27.06.2003.

Council Decision 99/468/EC from 28 June 1999 laying down the procedures for the exercise of implementing powers conferred on the Commission, OJ L 184, 17.07.1999 [Comitology Decision].

Commission Decision 2001/527/EC of 6 June 2001 establishing the Committee of European Securities Regulators, OJ L 191, 13.07.2001.

Commission Decision 2001/528/EC of 6 June 2001 establishing the European Securities Committee, OJ L 191, 13.07.2001.

Commission Decision 2004/5/EC of 5 November 2003 establishing the Committee of European Banking Supervisors, OJ L 003, 07.01.2004.

Commission Decision 2004/6/EC of 5 November 2003 establishing the Committee of European Insurance and Occupational Pensions Supervisors, OJ L 003, 07.01.2004.

Commission Decision 2004/9/EC of 5 November 2003 establishing the European Insurance and Occupational Pensions Committee, OJ L 003, 07.01.2004.

Commission Decision 2004/10/EC of 5 November 2003 establishing the European Banking Committee (Text with EEA relevance), OJ L 003, 07.01.2004.

Council Decision 2006/512/EC of 17 July 2006 amending Decision 1999/468/EC laying down the procedures for the exercise of implementing powers conferred on the Commission, OJ L 200, 22.07.2006.

Commission Decision 2009/77/EC of 23 January 2009 establishing the Committee of European Securities Regulators, OJ L 25, 29.1.2009.

Commission Decision 2009/78/EC of 23 January 2009 establishing the Committee of European Banking Supervisors (Text with EEA relevance), OJ L 25, 29.1.2009.

Commission Decision 2009/79/EC of 23 January 2009 establishing the Committee of European Insurance and Occupational Pensions Supervisors, OJ L 25, 29.1.2009.

Proposal for a Council Decision entrusting the European Central Bank with Specific tasks concerning the functioning of the European Systemic Risk Board, Brussels, 23.9.2009, COM (2009) 500 final [ESRB decision proposal].

Opinions of the European Monetary Institute (EMI) and the European Central Bank (ECB)

EMI, Opinion CON/95/04 assessing tasks of the Irish central bank in the field of regulation and prudential supervision of investment firms.

EMI, Opinion CON/95/09 analysing the attribution to the Danish central bank of tasks in the field of securities trading, collection of financial statistics, clearing and payment systems.

EMI, Opinion CON/97/02 on the supervision of investment business firms by the Irish central bank.

EMI, Opinion CON/97/03 on the power of Bank of Greece to regulate and supervise legal persons authorised to buy and sell foreign currency.

ECB, Opinion CON/2001/10 of 25 May 2001 on the Austrian *Finanz marktaufsichtgesetz.*

ECB, Opinions CON/2002/13 and CON/2003/19 on the Belgian royal decree on prudential supervision of the financial sector and financial services.

ECB, Opinion CON/2001/35 on the German *Gesetz über die integrierte Finanzdienstleistungsaufsicht.*

ECB, Opinions CON/2003/23 and CON/2004/21 on draft legislation reforming financial supervision in the Netherlands, which transfers to De Nederlandsche Bank new non-ESCB tasks in the field of prudential supervision of the insurance sector.

ECB, Opinion CON/2004/7 of 20 February at the request of the Council of the European Union on a proposal for a Directive of the European Parliament and of the Council amending Council Directives 73/239/EEC, 85/611/EEC, 91/675/EEC, 93/6/EEC and 94/19/EC and Directives 2000/12/EC, 2002/83/EC and 2002/87/EC of the European Parliament and of the Council, in order to establish a new financial services committee organisational structure, OJ C 58/23 of 6.3.2004.

ECB, Opinion CON/2004/16 on the Italian law on the protection of savings.

ECB, Opinion CON/2005/24 on the Czech law on the integration of financial market supervisors.

ECB Opinion CON/2008/44 of 3 October 2008 at the request of the Irish Minister for Finance on a draft Credit Institutions (Financial Support) Bill 2008.

ECB Opinion CON/2008/46 of 8 October 2008 at the request of the Belgian Ministry of Finance on a preliminary draft law on measures promoting financial stability and in particular establishing a State guarantee for the provision of credit in the context of financial stability

Recommendations

Commission Recommendation 87/62/EEC of 22 December 1986 on monitoring and controlling large exposures of credit institutions, OJ L 033, 04.02.1987.

Commission Recommendation 87/63/EEC on the introduction of deposit guarantee schemes, OJ L 33 of 4.02.1987.

Commission Recommendation of 14 December 2004 fostering an appropriate regime for the remuneration of directors of listed companies (2004/913/EC) OJ L 385/55, 19.12.2004.

Commission Recommendation 2009/384/EC of 30 April 2009 on remuneration policies in the financial services sector, OJ L 120, 15.5.2009

Commission Recommendation 2009/385/EC of 30 April 2009 complementing Recommendations 2004/913/EC and 2005/162/EC as regards the regime for the remuneration of directors of listed companies, OJ L 120, 15.5.2009.

Other official documents

European Union

European Parliament (EP)

EP (1999a) Resolution of 15 March 1999 on the Communication from the Commission on Financial Services: Building a Framework for Action (Rapporteur Ben Fayot), OJ C 279, 1.10.1999.

EP (1999b) Prudential Supervision in the context of EMU, ECON 102 EN REV 1.

EP (2002a) Resolution of 5 February 2002 on the implementation of financial services legislation, OJ C 284 21.11.2002.

EP (2002b) Resolution of 21 November 2002 on prudential supervision rules in the European Union (2002/2061(INI)) [Van den Burg Resolution] OJ C 025, 29.01.2004.

EP (2004) Resolution of 10.02.2004 on the role and methods of rating agencies and the Commission's call to CESR for technical advice on possible measures concerning credit rating agencies (Rapporteur Giorgos Katiforis), OJ C 097E 22.04.2004.

EP (2005) Resolution of 28 September 2005 on the proposal for a Directive of the EP and of the Council recasting Council Directive 2000/12/EC (Rapporteur: Alexander Radwan MEP) OJ C 227, 21.09.2006.

Council of the European Union (Council)

Council (1992a) Resolution of 7 December on making the single market work, OJ C 334.

Council (1992b) Conclusions of 21 December on effective implementation and enforcement of Community legislation in the area of social affairs, OJ C 49.

Council (1995) Resolution of 29 June on the effective uniform application of Community law and on the penalties applicable for breaches of Community law in the internal market, OJ C 188.

Council (2000) Ecofin, Brussels, 17 July, 10491/00, Regulation of European Securities Markets – the Terms of Reference for the Committee of Wise Men.

Council (2002a) Ecofin, informal meeting of Ecofin Ministers in Oviedo, 12–13 April.

Council (2002b) Ecofin Conclusions, 3 December.

Council (2004) FSC Report on Financial Integration 4156/04, May.

Council (2005) 'Council Approves New Capital Adequacy Requirements for Banks and Investment Firms', press release of the Council 13166, 11 October.

Council (2006) FSC Report on Financial Supervision, 17 February [Francq Report].

Council (2009) Ecofin Council Conclusions on Strengthening EU Financial Supervision, Luxembourg, 9 June.

European Council

European Council (1992) Edinburgh, Conference of 11–12 December 1992, Bull EC No. 12.

European Council (1998) Presidency conclusions from Vienna European Council, 11/12 December.

European Council (2001) Stockholm European Council Resolution of 23 March 2001 on more effective securities market regulation in the EU.

European Council (2009) Presidency Conclusions of the Brussels European Council 18/19 June 2009, 11225/09.

European Commission

Commission (1966) Segré Committee, *The Development of a European Capital Market*, November.

Commission (1985) *Completing the Internal Market: White Paper to the Council*, COM(85) 310 final, 28 June.

Commission (1992) *The Principle of Subsidiarity*, SEC(92) 1990, 27 October.

Commission (1993) *Reinforcing the Effectiveness of the Internal Market*. Working Document of the Commission on a Strategic Programme on the Internal Market. COM (93) 256 final, 2 June.

Commission (1997a) Interpretative Communication. *Freedom to Provide Services and the Interest of the General Good in the Second Banking Directive*, Brussels, SEC(97) 1193 final, 20 June.

Commission (1997b) 'Credit Institutions and Banking', *Single Market Review*, 2, 4.

Commission (1998) Communication: *Financial Services: Building a Framework for Action*, COM(98) 625 final, 28 October.

Commission (1999) *Financial Services: Implementing the Framework for Financial Markets: Action Plan*, COM(1999)232 final, 11 May.

Commission (2001a) *European Governance. A White Paper*, COM(2001) 428 final, Brussels 27 July.

Commission (2001b) European Consumer Law Group, *Green Paper on Consumer Protection in the European Union*, 2 October, COM (2001) 531 final.

Commission (2001c) Letter from Mr Bolkestein, Member of the Commission, to Mrs Randzio-Plath, Chair of the Committee on Economic and Monetary Affairs (EMAC), dated 2 October.

Commission (2002a) Speech/02/44 of 05.02.2002 by Mr Romano Prodi 'Implementation of Financial Services Legislation in the Context of the Lamfalussy Report', Intervention by President Romano Prodi to the European Parliament's plenary session, Strasbourg, 5 February.

Commission (2002b) Communication *The Operating Framework for the European Regulatory Agencies*, COM/2002/0718 final, 11 December.

Commission (2002c) Communication *Better Monitoring of the Application of Community Law*, COM (2002) 725 final, 11 December.

Commission (2003a) Communication *Company Law and Corporate Governance* COM(2003) 284 Final, 21 May.

Commission (2003b) Staff Working Paper 'Tracking Financial Integration', SEC(2003) 628, 26 May.

Commission (2003c) *Financial Services, Nine Months Left to Deliver the FSAP*, 3 June.

Commission (2003d) *Review of Capital Requirements for Banks and Investment Firms. Commission Services Third Consultation Paper*. Explanatory Document, 1 July.

Commission (2003e) Explanatory Memorandum, Proposal for a Directive of the European Parliament and of the Council amending Council Directives 73/239/EEC, 85/611/EEC, 91/675/EEC, 93/6/EEC and 94/19/EC and Directives 2000/12/EC, 2002/83/EC and 2002/87/EC of the European Parliament and of the Council, in order to establish a new financial services committee organisational structure, COM/2003/0659 final, 5.11.2003.

Commission (2003f) MEMO/03/220, Commission package of measures to improve regulation and supervision of banking, insurance and investment funds – frequently asked questions, 6 November.

Commission (2003g) Communication from the Commission to the Council and the European Parliament, *Reinforcing the Statutory Audit in the EU*.

Commission (2004a) Press release on the proposal of a directive to combat fraud and malpractice IP/04/340 Brussels, 16 March.

Commission (2004b) Expert Group on Banking, *Financial Services Action Plan: Progress and Prospects* (final report), May.

Commission (2004c) *Financial Services. Turning the Corner. Preparing the Challenge of the Next Phase of European Capital Market Integration,* Tenth Report, Brussels, 2 June.

Commission (2004d) Press release IP/04/899 of 14 July.

Commission (2004e) *Study on the Impact of Specific Requirements (e.g. Operational Risk Charge) on Investment Firms,* July.

Commission (2004f) *First Annual Financial Integration Monitor.*

Commission (2005a) *Green Paper on Financial Services Policy* (2005–10) COM(2005) 177, 3 May.

Commission (2005b) *Financial Services Plan Evaluation* (first part), 7 November.

Commission (2005c) *White Paper on Financial Services Policy 2005–2010,* COM(2005) 629 final, 5 December.

Commission (2005d) Press releases IP05/1002, Brussels, 25 July and IP/05/1184, Brussels, 26 September, on the re-establishment of the Institutional Monitoring Group for financial services.

Commission (2005e) *Draft Interinstitutional Agreement on the Operating Framework for European Regulatory Agencies,* COM/2005/0059 final.

Commission (2006a) Communication *Commission's Approach to Credit Rating Agencies,* 9 January.

Commission (2006b) Communication *A Strategic Review of Better Regulation in the European Union,* COM/2006/0689 final.

Commission (2007) Communication *Review of the Lamfalussy Process. Strengthening Supervisory Convergence,* COM(2007) 727 final, 20 November.

Commission (2008a) *Financial Services Provision and Prevention of Financial Exclusion,* March.

Commission (2008b) Second public consultation paper on possible changes on securitisation to the Capital Requirements Directive (CRD, consisting of Directives 2006/48/EC and 2006/49/EC), June.

Commission (2008c) Communication *The Application of State Aid Rules to Measures taken in Relation to Financial Institutions in the Context of the Current Global Financial Crisis,* OJ C 270, 25 October [Banking Communication].

Commission (2008d) Communication *European Agencies. The Way Forward,* COM/2008/0135 final.

Commission (2009a) *European Financial Integration Report 2008,* SEC(2009) 19 final, 9 January.

Commission (2009b) Communication *The Recapitalisation of Financial Institutions in the Current Financial Crisis: Limitation of Aid to the Minimum Necessary and Safeguards against Undue Distortions of Competition,* OJ C 10, 15 January [Recapitalisation Communication].

Commission (2009c) de Larosière, J., Balcerowicz L., Issing, O., Masera, R., Mc Carthy, C., Nyberg, L., Pérez, J. and Ruding, O., 25 February, *Report by the High Level Group on Financial Supervision in the EU* [de Larosière report].

Commission (2009d) *Communication for the Spring European Council. Driving European Recovery,* COM(2009) 114 final 4 March [March Communication].

Commission (2009e) Communication *The Treatment of Impaired Assets in the Community Banking Sector,* OJ C 72, 26.03.2009 [Impaired Assets Communication].

Commission (2009f) Public consultation on possible changes to the Capital

Requirements Directive (CRD, consisting of Directives 2006/48/EC and 2006/49/EC), April.

Commission (2009g) State Aid Scoreboard – Spring 2009 Update, special edition on State Aid interventions in the current financial and economic crisis, COM(2009) 164, April.

Commission (2009h) *Communication on European Financial Supervision*, COM(2009) 252 final, 27 May [May Communication].

Commission (2009i) Consultation regarding further possible changes to the Capital Requirements Directive [Consultation for CRD 4]

Commission (2009j) Communication: *An EU framework for Cross-Border Crisis Management in the Banking Sector*, 20.10.2009, COM (2009) 561 final.

European Central Bank (ECB)

ECB (1999) *Assistance to Temporarily Illiquid Financial Institutions: A Synthesis* (Emergency Liquidity Assistance, ELA), SEC/GovC/12/99/07, 8 April.

ECB (2000a) *Annual Report 1999*, Frankfurt.

ECB (2000b) *EMU and Banking Supervision, Monthly Bulletin*, April.

ECB (2000c) *ECB Annual Report 1999*, Frankfurt.

ECB (2001) *The Role of the Central Banks in Prudential Supervision*, 22 March.

ECB (2002) *Annual Report 2001*, April.

ECB (2003a) Press release of 10 March, on the adoption of the Memorandum of Understanding on high-level principles of co-operation between the EU banking supervisors and central banks in crises management situations.

ECB (2003b) *Developments in National Supervisory Structures*, June.

ECB (2004) 'Developments in the EU framework for financial regulation, supervision and stability', *Monthly Bulletin*, November.

ECB (2005a) *Review of the Application of the Lamfalussy Framework to EU Securities Markets Legislation*, Contribution to the Commission's public consultation, published on 17 February.

ECB (2005b) Press release of 18 May on the agreement on the Memorandum of Understanding on co-operation between the Banking Supervisors, Central Banks and Finance Ministries of the European Union in financial crises situations.

ECB (2005c) *EU Banking Structures*, October.

ECB (2007) *Review of the Lamfalussy framework*, Eurosystem contribution of 30 November.

ECB (2008a) *Memorandum of Understanding on Co-operation between the Financial Supervisory Authorities, Central Banks and Finance Ministries of the EU on Cross-Border Financial Stability*, 20 June.

ECB (2008b) *EU Banking Structures*, October.

ECB (2008c) *The Incentive Structure of the 'Originate and Distribute' Model*, December.

ECB (2009) *EU Banks Funding Structures and Policies*, May 2009.

Economic and Financial Committee (EFC)

EFC (2000) *Report on Financial Stability (Brouwer I Report)*, EFC/ECFIN/240/00-EN (Final), 8.04.2000.

EFC (2001) *Report on Financial Crisis Management (Brouwer II Report)*, 17 April. EFC/ECFIN/251/01-en. Final.

EFC (2002) *Report on Financial Regulation, Supervision and Stability*, revised to reflect the discussion at the 8 October meeting of the Ecofin Council, Brussels, 9 October.

Committee of European Banking Supervisors (CEBS)

CEBS (2004a) Consultation paper. *Public Consultation Practices*, April.
CEBS (2004b) Consultation Paper. *Application of the Supervisory Review Process under Pillar 2* (CP03 revised), May.
CEBS (2005a) *Public Statement of Consultation Practices.*
CEBS (2005b) *Annual Report 2004*, 24 June.
CEBS (2005c) Consultation Paper, *The Role and Tasks of CEBS* (CP08), 5 July.
CEBS (2006) *Guidelines on the Recognition of External Credit Assessment Institutions*, 20 January.
CEBS (2008) *Work on Delegation*, 3 September.
CEBS (2009a) *Mapping of Supervisory Objectives and Powers, including Early Intervention Measures and Sanctioning Powers*, March.
CEBS (2009b) *Interim Report on Liquidity Buffers and Survival Periods*, 18 March.
CEBS (2009c) *Good Practices on the Functioning of Colleges of Supervisors for Cross-border Banking Groups*, 2 April.
CEBS (2009d) *Liquidity Identity Card*, 22 June.
CEBS (2009e) *Electronic Guidebook.*
CEBS, CESR and CEIOPS (2008) *Joint Guidelines for the Prudential Assessment of Acquisitions and Increases in Holdings in the Financial Sector Required by Directive 2007/44/EC*, December.
CEBS, CESR and CEIOPS (2009a) Delegation Task Force, *Delegation of Responsibilities.*
CESR, CEBS and CEIOPS (2009b) *Key Principles for the Delegation of Tasks between Competent Authorities*, CEBS 2008 193, June 2009.

Committee of European Securities Regulators (CESR)

CESR (2004a) Consultation Paper, *Role of CESR at 'Level 3' under the Lamfalussy Process*, April.
CESR (2004b) Preliminary Progress Report. *Which Supervisory Tools for the EU Securities Markets? An Analytical Paper by CESR* [Himalaya Report], October.
CESR (2005) *Technical Advice on Possible Measures concerning Credit Rating Agencies*, March.

Committee of Wise Men

Committee of Wise Men (2001) *Final Report of the Committee of Wise Men on the Regulation of European Securities Markets*, Brussels, 15 February.

Inter-Institutional Monitoring Group (IIMG)

IIMG (2003a) *First Interim Report Monitoring the New Process for Regulating Securities Markets in Europe (the Lamfalussy Process)*, May.

IIMG (2003b) *Second Interim Report Monitoring the Lamfalussy Process,* 10 December.
IIMG (2004) *Third Report Monitoring the Lamfalussy Process,*17 November.
IIMG (2007) *Final Report Monitoring the Lamfalussy Process,* 15 October.

Other international organisations

Basel Committee on Banking Supervision (BCBS)

BCBS (1975) *Report on the Supervision of Banks' Foreign Establishments (Concordat),* September.
BCBS (1983) *Principles for the Supervision of Banks' Foreign Establishments (Concordat),* May.
BCBS (1988) *International Convergence of Capital Measurement and Capital Standards (First Basel Accord),* July.
BCBS (1997) *Core Principles for Effective Banking Supervision,* September.
BCBS (1999a) *A New Capital Adequacy Framework, Consultative Paper,* BIS, Basel, June.
BCBS (1999b) *Core Principles Methodology.*
BCBS (1999c) *Enhancing Corporate Governance for Banking Organisations,* September.
BCBS (2001) 'The Regulatory Treatment of Operational Risk', *BCBS Working Paper,* September.
BCBS (2004) BIS Press Release 11 May, Consensus achieved on Basel II.
BCBS (2004–5) *Basel II: International Convergence of Capital Measurement and Capital Standards: A Revised Framework,* June 2004, revised in November 2005.
BCBS (2005) *Enhancing Corporate Governance for Banking Organisations,* July.
BCBS (2005) *The Application of Basel II to Trading Activities and the Treatment of Double Default Effects,* July.
BCBS (2009a) 'Findings on the Interaction of Market and Credit Risk', *BCBS Working Paper,* 16.
BCBS (2009b) Press Release, 10 June.

Organisation for Economic Cooperation and Development (OECD)

OECD (1961, 1989) *Code of Liberalisation of Current Invisible Operations,* 1961, updated in 1989.
OECD (1999) Ad hoc Task Force on Corporate Governance, *OECD Principles of Corporate Governance,* Paris.
OECD (2004) *OECD Principles of Corporate Governance.*

International Monetary Fund (IMF)

IMF and the World Bank (2005) *Financial Sector Assessment Programme.*
IMF (2009) *Global Financial Stability Report: Responding to the Financial Crisis and Measuring Systemic Risks,* Washington.

Index